New Perspectives on

MICROSOFT® ACCESS 2002

Comprehensive

JOSEPH J. ADAMSKI
Grand Valley State University

KATHLEEN T. FINNEGAN

COURSE TECHNOLOGY

™

THOMSON LEARNING

Australia • Canada • Mexico • Singapore • Spain • United Kingdom • United States

COURSE TECHNOLOGY

™

THOMSON LEARNING

New Perspectives on Microsoft® Access 2002—Comprehensive

is published by Course Technology.

Managing Editor:
Greg Donald

Technology Product Manager:
Amanda Young

Production Editor:
Daphne Barbas

Senior Editor:
Donna Gridley

Editorial Assistant:
Jessica Engstrom

Composition:
GEX Publishing Services

Senior Product Manager:
Kathy Finnegan

Marketing Manager:
Sean Teare

Text Designer:
Meral Dabcovich

Product Manager:
Melissa Hathaway

Developmental Editor:
Jessica Evans

Cover Designer:
Efrat Reis

Preface

Course Technology is the world leader in information technology education. The New Perspectives Series is an integral part of Course Technology's success. Visit our Web site to see a whole new perspective on teaching and learning solutions.

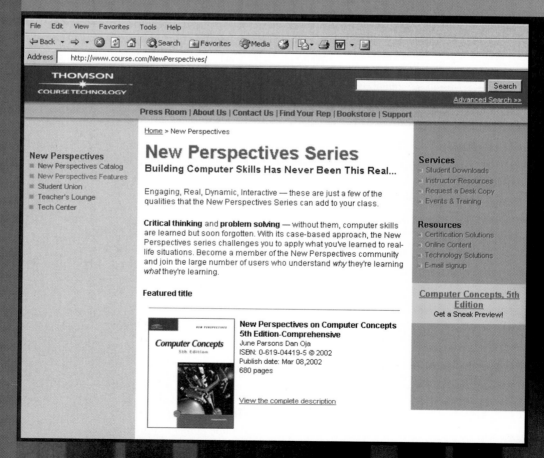

New Perspectives—Building Computer Skills Has Never Been This Real

Why New Perspectives will work for you.

Critical thinking and **problem solving**—without them, computer skills are learned but soon forgotten. With its **case-based** approach, the New Perspectives Series challenges students to apply what they've learned to real-life situations. Become a member of the New Perspectives community and watch your students not only **master** computer skills, but also **retain** and carry this **knowledge** into the world.

New Perspectives catalog
Our online catalog is never out of date! Go to the Catalog link on our Web site to check out our available titles, request a desk copy, download a book preview, or locate online files.

Complete system of offerings
Whether you're looking for a Brief book, an Advanced book, or something in between, we've got you covered. Go to the Catalog link on our Web site to find the level of coverage that's right for you.

Instructor materials
We have all the tools you need—data files, solution files, figure files, a sample syllabus, and ExamView, our powerful testing software package.

How well do your students know Microsoft Office?
Experience the power, ease, and flexibility of SAM XP and TOM. These innovative software tools provide the first truly integrated technology-based training and assessment solution for your applications course. Click the Tech Center link to learn more.

Get certified
If you want to get certified, we have the titles for you. Find out more by clicking the Teacher's Lounge link.

Interested in online learning?
Enhance your course with rich online content for use through MyCourse 2.0, WebCT, and Blackboard. Go to the Teacher's Lounge to find the platform that's right for you.

Your link to the future is at www.course.com/NewPerspectives

What you need to know about this book.

- Student Online Companion takes students to the Web for additional work.

- ExamView testing software gives you the option of generating a printed test, LAN-based test, or test over the Internet.

- New Perspectives Labs provide students with self-paced practice on computer-related topics.

- All cases are NEW to this edition!

- Our clear and concise coverage of database concepts provides students with the solid foundation they need as they progress to creating and working with database objects.

- Students will appreciate the in-depth explanations of creating and modifying forms and reports, including multi-page forms and more advanced reports that reflect real-world situations and go beyond what they can create using Wizards.

- Students will tackle advanced topics, including how to create and use advanced queries to manage and update data, how to create and maintain a switchboard using macros and VBA, and how to manage and secure a database.

- The scenarios in our end-of-tutorial exercises will hold students' interest, and the number of exploratory exercises will challenge students and give them a sense of accomplishment.

- This book is certified at the MOUS Expert level for Access 2002!

CASE	TROUBLE?	SESSION 1.1	QUICK CHECK	RW
Tutorial Case Each tutorial begins with a problem presented in a case that is meaningful to students. The case sets the scene to help students understand what they will do in the tutorial.	**TROUBLE? Paragraphs** These paragraphs anticipate the mistakes or problems that students may have and help them continue with the tutorial.	**Sessions** Each tutorial is divided into sessions designed to be completed in about 45 minutes each. Students should take as much time as they need and take a break between sessions.	**Quick Check Questions** Each session concludes with conceptual Quick Check questions that test students' understanding of what they learned in the session.	**Reference Windows** Reference Windows are succinct summaries of the most important tasks covered in a tutorial. They preview actions students will perform in the steps to follow.

www.course.com/NewPerspectives

APPROVED COURSEWARE

What does this logo mean?

It means this courseware has been approved by the Microsoft® Office User Specialist Program to be among the finest available for learning Microsoft Access 2002. It also means that upon completion of this courseware, you may be prepared to become a Microsoft Office User Specialist.

What is a Microsoft Office User Specialist?

A Microsoft Office User Specialist is an individual who has certified his or her skills in one or more of the Microsoft Office desktop applications of Microsoft Word, Microsoft Excel, Microsoft PowerPoint®, Microsoft Outlook® or Microsoft Access, or in Microsoft Project. The Microsoft Office User Specialist Program typically offers certification exams at the "Core" and "Expert" skill levels.* The Microsoft Office User Specialist Program is the only Microsoft approved program in the world for certifying proficiency in Microsoft Office desktop applications and Microsoft Project. This certification can be a valuable asset in any job search or career advancement.

More Information:

To learn more about becoming a Microsoft Office User Specialist, visit www.mous.net

To purchase a Microsoft Office User Specialist certification exam, visit www.DesktopIQ.com

To learn about other Microsoft Office User Specialist approved courseware from Course Technology, visit www.course.com/NewPerspectives/TeachersLounge/mous.cfm

BRIEF CONTENTS

TABLE OF CONTENTS

Microsoft Office XP — OFF 1

Tutorial 1 — OFF 3

Introducing Microsoft Office XP

Preparing Promotional Materials for Delmar Office Supplies

Microsoft Access 2002

Level I Tutorials — AC 1.01

Tutorial 1 — AC 1.03

Introduction to Microsoft Access 2002

Viewing and Working with a Table Containing Employer Data

Tutorial 2 — AC 2.01

Creating and Maintaining a Database

Creating the Northeast Database, and Creating, Modifying, and Updating the Position Table

Microsoft Access 2002

Level II Tutorials   AC 5.01
Read This Before You Begin   AC 5.02

Tutorial 5   AC 5.03

Enhancing a Table's Design, and Creating Advanced Queries and Custom Forms

Making the Jobs Database Easier to Use

Tutorial 6   AC 6.01

Creating Custom Reports

Creating a Potential Income Report

Tutorial 7   AC 7.01

Integrating Access with the Web and with Other Programs

Creating Web-Enabled and Integrated Information for the Jobs Database

Microsoft Access 2002
Level III Tutorials   AC 8.01
Read This Before You Begin   AC 8.02

Tutorial 8   AC 8.03

Using Query Wizards and Action Queries, and Defining Table Relationships

Enhancing User Interaction with the Overseas Database

Tutorial 9   AC 9.01

Automating Tasks with Macros

Creating a User Interface for the Overseas Database

Tutorial 10   AC 10.01

Using and Writing Visual Basic for Applications Code

Creating VBA Code for the Overseas Database User Interface

Acknowledgments

I would like to thank the following reviewers for their helpful and thorough feedback: Lorraine Bergkvist, College of Notre Dame; Michael Feiler, Merritt College; Eric Johnston, Vatterott College; Donna Occhifinto, County College of Morris; and Rebekah Tidwell, Carson Newman College and Lee University. Many thanks to all the Course Technology staff, especially Greg Donald and Donna Gridley for their leadership and encouragement; Melissa Hathaway and Jessica Engstrom for their tireless support and good humor; Daphne Barbas for her excellent management of the production process; and John Bosco, John Freitas, Marianne Broughey, and Serge Palladino for ensuring the quality and accuracy of this text. Special thanks to Jessica Evans for her exceptional editorial and technical skills in developing this text and her willingness to go the extra mile; and to Joe Adamski for his continued guidance and expertise. This book is dedicated with love to my two terrific sons, Connor and Devon, who always keep me both hopping and grounded at the same time.

Kathleen T. Finnegan

Thank you to all the people who contributed to developing and completing this book, with special thanks to Susan Solomon, who started it all and asked me to join the team nearly ten years ago; Greg Donald for making a smooth transition to the team; the marketing staff for supporting the series over the years; Kathy Finnegan for her many contributions; Jessica Evans for her thoughtfulness, attention to quality, perseverance, friendship, and exceptional skills; and Judy for making it all worthwhile.

Joseph J. Adamski

New Perspectives on

MICROSOFT®

WINDOWS® 2000

PROFESSIONAL

Read This Before You Begin

To the Student

Make Data Disk Program

To complete the Level I tutorials, Review Assignments, and Projects, you need three Data Disks. Your instructor will either provide you with Data Disks or ask you to make your own.

If you are making your own Data Disks you will need three blank, formatted high-density disks and access to the Make Data Disk program. If you want to install the Make Data Disk program to your home computer, you can obtain it from your instructor or from the Web. To download the Make Data Disk program from the Web, go to www.course.com, click Data Disks, and follow the instructions on the screen.

To install the Make Data Disk program, select and click the file you just downloaded from www.course.com, 6548-9.exe. Follow the onscreen instructions to complete the installation. If you have any trouble obtaining or installing the Make Data Disk program, ask your instructor or technical support person for assistance.

Once you have obtained and installed the Make Data Disk program, you can use it to create your Data Disks according to the steps in the tutorials.

Course Labs

The Level I tutorials in this book feature three interactive Course Labs to help you understand Using a Keyboard, Using a Mouse, and Using Files concepts. There are Lab Assignments at the end of Tutorials 1 and 2 that relate to these Labs. To start a Lab, click the **Start** button on the Windows 2000 taskbar, point to **Programs**, point to

Course Labs, point to **New Perspectives Course Labs**, and click the name of the Lab you want to use.

Using Your Own Computer

If you are going to work through this book using your own computer, you need:

- **Computer System** Microsoft Windows 2000 Professional must be installed on a local hard drive or on a network drive. This book is about Windows 2000 Professional—for those who have Windows 2000 Millennium, you might notice some differences.

- **Data Disks** You will not be able to complete the tutorials or exercises in this book using your own computer until you have your Data Disks. See "Make Data Disk Program" above for details on obtaining your Data Disks.

- **Course Labs** See your instructor or technical support person to obtain the Course Lab software for use on your own computer.

Visit Our World Wide Web Site

Additional materials designed especially for you are available on the World Wide Web. Go to http://www.course.com.

To the Instructor

The Make Data Disk Program and Course Labs for this title are available in the Instructor's Resource Kit for this title. Follow the instructions in the Help file on the CD-ROM to install the programs to your network or standalone computer. For information on using the Make Data Disk Program or the Course Labs, see the "To the Student" section above. Students will be switching the default installation settings to Web style in Tutorial 2. You are granted a license to copy the Data Files and Course Labs to any computer or computer network used by students who have purchased this book.

OBJECTIVES

In this tutorial you will:

- Start and shut down Windows 2000

- Identify the objects on the Windows 2000 desktop

- Practice mouse functions

- Run software programs, switch between them, and close them

- Identify and use the controls in a window

- Use Windows 2000 controls such as menus, toolbars, list boxes, scroll bars, option buttons, tabs, and check boxes

- Explore the Windows 2000 Help system

LABS

Using a Keyboard

Using a Mouse

EXPLORING THE BASICS

Investigating the Windows 2000 Operating System

CASE

Your First Day on the Computer

You walk into the computer lab and sit down at a desk. There's a computer in front of you, and you find yourself staring dubiously at the screen. Where to start? As if in answer to your question, your friend Steve Laslow appears.

"You start with the operating system," says Steve. Noticing your puzzled look, Steve explains that the **operating system** is software that helps the computer carry out operating tasks such as displaying information on the computer screen and saving data on your disks. (Software refers to the **programs**, or **applications**, that a computer uses to perform tasks.) Your computer uses the **Microsoft Windows 2000 Professional** operating system—Windows 2000, for short.

Steve explains that much of the software available for Windows 2000 has a standard graphical user interface. This means that once you have learned how to use one Windows program, such as Microsoft Word word-processing software, you are well on your way to under-standing how to use other Windows software. Windows 2000 lets you use more than one program at a time, so you can easily switch between them—between your word-processing software and your appointment book software, for example. Finally, Windows 2000 makes it very easy to access the **Internet**, the worldwide collection of com-puters connected to one another to enable communication. All in all, Windows 2000 makes your computer effective and easy to use.

Steve recommends that you get started right away by starting Microsoft Windows 2000 and practicing some basic skills.

SESSION 1.1

In this session, in addition to learning basic Windows terminology, you will learn how to use a pointing device, how to start and close a program, and how to use more than one program at a time.

Starting Windows 2000

Using a Keyboard

Windows 2000 automatically starts when you turn on the computer. Depending on the way your computer is set up, you might be asked to enter your username and password.

To start Windows 2000:

1. Turn on your computer.

TROUBLE? If you are asked to select an operating system, do not take action. Windows 2000 will start automatically after a designated number of seconds. If it does not, ask your technical support person for help.

TROUBLE? If prompted to do so, type your assigned username and press the Tab key. Then type your password and press the Enter key to continue.

TROUBLE? If this is the first time you have started your computer with Windows 2000, messages might appear on your screen informing you that Windows is setting up components of your computer. If the Getting Started with Windows 2000 box appears, press and hold down the Alt key on your keyboard and then, while you hold down the Alt key, press the F4 key. The box closes.

After a moment, Windows 2000 starts. Windows 2000 has a **graphical user interface** (**GUI,** pronounced "gooey"), which uses **icons,** or pictures of familiar objects, such as file folders and documents, to represent items in your computer such as programs or files. Microsoft Windows 2000 gets its name from the rectangular work areas, called "windows," that appear on your screen as you work (although no windows should be open right now).

The Windows 2000 Desktop

In Windows terminology, the area displayed on your screen when Windows 2000 starts represents a **desktop**—a workspace for projects and the tools needed to manipulate those projects. When you first start a computer, it uses **default** settings, those preset by the operating system. The default desktop, for example, has a plain blue background. However, Microsoft designed Windows 2000 so that you can easily change the appearance of the desktop. You can, for example, add color, patterns, images, and text to the desktop background.

Many institutions design customized desktops for their computers. Figure 1-1 shows the default Windows 2000 desktop and two other examples of desktops, one designed for a business, North Pole Novelties, and one designed for a school, the University of Colorado. Although your desktop might not look exactly like any of the examples in Figure 1-1, you should be able to locate objects on your screen similar to those in Figure 1-1. Look at your screen and locate the objects labeled in Figure 1-1. The objects on your screen might appear larger or smaller than those in Figure 1-1, depending on your monitor's settings.

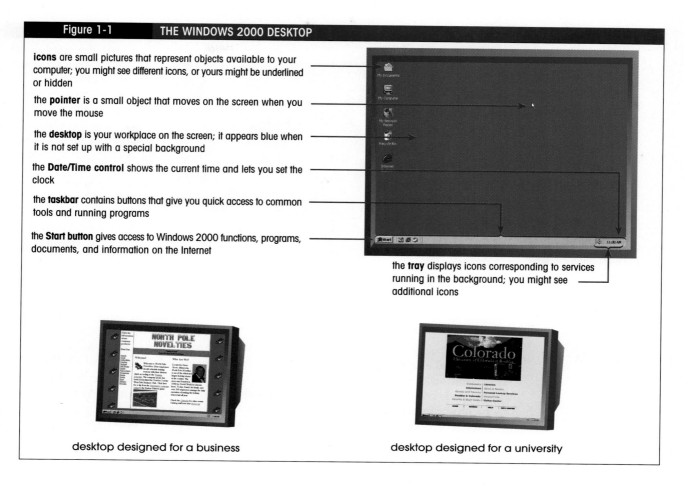

| Figure 1-1 | THE WINDOWS 2000 DESKTOP |

icons are small pictures that represent objects available to your computer; you might see different icons, or yours might be underlined or hidden

the **pointer** is a small object that moves on the screen when you move the mouse

the **desktop** is your workplace on the screen; it appears blue when it is not set up with a special background

the **Date/Time control** shows the current time and lets you set the clock

the **taskbar** contains buttons that give you quick access to common tools and running programs

the **Start button** gives access to Windows 2000 functions, programs, documents, and information on the Internet

the **tray** displays icons corresponding to services running in the background; you might see additional icons

desktop designed for a business

desktop designed for a university

If the screen goes blank or starts to display a moving design, press any key to restore the Windows 2000 desktop.

Using a Pointing Device

Using a Mouse

A **pointing device** helps you interact with objects on the screen. Pointing devices come in many shapes and sizes; some are designed to ensure that your hand won't suffer fatigue while using them. Some are directly attached to your computer via a cable, whereas others function like a TV remote control and allow you to access your computer without being right next to it. Figure 1-2 shows examples of common pointing devices.

The most common pointing device is called a **mouse**, so this book uses that term. If you are using a different pointing device, such as a trackball, substitute that device whenever you see the term "mouse." Because Windows 2000 uses a graphical user interface, you need to know how to use the mouse to manipulate the objects on the screen. In this session you will learn about pointing and clicking. In Session 1.2 you will learn how to use the mouse to drag objects.

You can also interact with objects by using the keyboard; however, the mouse is more convenient for most tasks, so the tutorials in this book assume you are using one.

Figure 1-2   **POINTING DEVICES**

traditional two-button mouse

traditional three-button mouse

to hold the mouse, place your forefinger over the left mouse button and place your thumb on the left side of the mouse

your ring and small fingers should be on the right side of the mouse

newer mouse includes a "wheel" that you can use to move through documents more easily

touch pad pointing devices have no moving parts; you slide your finger to move the pointer and tap to click

trackball pointing devices feature a ball that you roll with your finger

mouse designed especially to prevent hand fatigue

use your arm, not your wrist, to move the mouse

trackballs and touchpads are often embedded into notebook computers

Pointing

You use a pointing device to move the pointer over objects on the desktop. The pointer is usually shaped like an arrow ⌖ , although it can change shape depending on where it is on the screen and on what tasks you are performing. Most computer users place the mouse on a **mouse pad**, a flat piece of rubber that helps the mouse move smoothly. As you move the mouse on the mouse pad, the pointer on the screen moves in a corresponding direction.

You begin most Windows operations by positioning the pointer over a specific part of the screen. This is called **pointing**.

To move the pointer:

1. Position your right index finger over the left mouse button, as shown in Figure 1-2, but don't click yet. Lightly grasp the sides of the mouse with your thumb and little fingers.

   TROUBLE? If you want to use the mouse with your left hand, ask your instructor or technical support person to help you use the Control Panel to swap the functions of the left and right mouse buttons. Be sure to find out how to change back to the right-handed mouse setting, so that you can reset the mouse each time you are finished in the lab.

2. Place the mouse on the mouse pad and then move the mouse. Watch the movement of the pointer.

   TROUBLE? If you run out of room to move your mouse, lift the mouse and place it in the middle of the mouse pad. Notice that the pointer does not move when the mouse is not in contact with the mouse pad.

When you position the mouse pointer over certain objects, such as the objects on the taskbar, a "tip" appears. These "tips" are called **ScreenTips**, and they tell you the purpose or function of an object.

To view ScreenTips:

1. Use the mouse to point to the **Start** button , but don't click it. After a few seconds, you see the tip "Click here to begin," as shown in Figure 1-3.

   TROUBLE? If the Start button and taskbar don't appear, point to the bottom of the screen. They will then appear.

Figure 1-3	VIEWING SCREENTIPS

ScreenTip

pointer

2. Point to the time on the right end of the taskbar. Notice that today's date (or the date to which your computer's time clock is set) appears.

Clicking

Clicking is when you press a mouse button and immediately release it. Clicking sends a signal to your computer that you want to perform an action on the object you click. In Windows 2000 most actions are performed using the left mouse button. If you are told to click an object, click it with the left mouse button, unless instructed otherwise.

When you click the Start button, the Start menu appears. A **menu** is a list of options that you use to complete tasks. The **Start menu** provides you with access to programs, documents, and much more. Try clicking the Start button to open the Start menu.

To open the Start menu:

1. Point to the **Start** button .
2. Click the left mouse button. An arrow ▶ following an option on the Start menu indicates that you can view additional choices by navigating a **submenu**, a menu extending from the main menu. See Figure 1-4.

Figure 1-4	START MENU

an arrow indicates the presence of a submenu

Start menu; yours might show different options

3. Click again to close the Start menu.

Next you'll learn how to select items on a submenu.

Selecting

In Windows 2000, pointing and clicking are often used to **select** an object, in other words, to choose it as the object you want to work with. Windows 2000 shows you which object is selected by highlighting it, usually by changing the object's color, putting a box around it, or making the object appear to be pushed in, as shown in Figure 1-5.

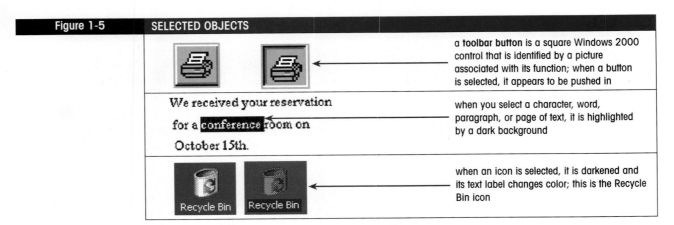

Figure 1-5 SELECTED OBJECTS

a **toolbar button** is a square Windows 2000 control that is identified by a picture associated with its function; when a button is selected, it appears to be pushed in

when you select a character, word, paragraph, or page of text, it is highlighted by a dark background

when an icon is selected, it is darkened and its text label changes color; this is the Recycle Bin icon

In Windows 2000, depending on your computer's settings, some objects are selected when you simply point to them, others when you click them. Practice selecting the Programs option on the Start menu to open the Programs submenu.

To select an option on a menu:

1. Click the **Start** button and notice how it appears to be pushed in, indicating it is selected.

2. Point to (but don't click) the **Programs** option. After a short pause, the Programs submenu opens, and the Programs option is highlighted to indicate it is selected. See Figure 1-6.

Figure 1-6 PROGRAMS SUBMENU

point to option to open submenu; highlighting indicates that option is selected

these options display additional submenus

Programs submenu; yours might show different options

TROUBLE? If a submenu other than the Programs menu opens, you selected the wrong option. Move the mouse so that the pointer points to Programs.

TROUBLE? If the Programs option doesn't appear, your Start menu might have too many options to fit on the screen. If that is the case, a double arrow ❯ appears at the top or bottom of the Start menu. Click first the top and then the bottom arrow to view additional Start menu options until you locate the Programs menu option, and then point to it.

3. Now close the Start menu by clicking 🔲 **Start** again.

You return to the desktop.

Right-Clicking

Pointing devices were originally designed with a single button, so the term "clicking" had only one meaning: you pressed that button. Innovations in technology, however, led to the addition of a second and even a third button (and more recently, options such as a wheel) that expanded the pointing device's capability. More recent software—especially that designed for Windows 2000—takes advantage of the additional buttons, especially the right button. However, the term "clicking" continues to refer to the left button; clicking an object with the *right* button is called **right-clicking**.

In Windows 2000, right-clicking both selects an object and opens its **shortcut menu**, a list of options directly related to the object you right-clicked. You can right-click practically any object—the Start button, a desktop icon, the taskbar, and even the desktop itself—to view options associated with that object. For example, the first desktop shown in Figure 1-7 illustrates what happens when you click the Start button with the left mouse button to open the Start menu. Clicking the Start button with the right button, however, opens the Start button's shortcut menu, as shown in the second desktop.

Figure 1-7	CLICKING WITH THE LEFT AND RIGHT MOUSE BUTTONS

Try using right-clicking to open the shortcut menu for the Start button.

To right-click an object:

1. Position the pointer over the Start button.

2. Right-click the **Start** button . The shortcut menu that opens offers a list of options available to the Start button.

TROUBLE? If you are using a trackball or a mouse with three buttons or a wheel, make sure you click the button on the far right, not the one in the middle.

TROUBLE? If your menu looks slightly different from the one in Figure 1-8, don't worry. Different systems will have different options.

Figure 1-8	START BUTTON SHORTCUT MENU

click the Start button with the right mouse button

shortcut menu

3. Press the **Esc** key to close the shortcut menu.

You again return to the desktop.

Starting **and Closing a Program**

To use a program, such as a word-processing program, you must first start it. With Windows 2000 you usually start a program by clicking the Start button and then you locate and click the program's name in the submenus.

The Reference Window below explains how to start a program. Don't do the steps in the Reference Windows as you go through the tutorials; they are for your later reference.

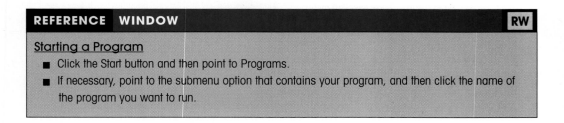

REFERENCE WINDOW   **RW**

<u>Starting a Program</u>
- Click the Start button and then point to Programs.
- If necessary, point to the submenu option that contains your program, and then click the name of the program you want to run.

Windows 2000 includes an easy-to-use word-processing program called WordPad. Suppose you want to start the WordPad program and use it to write a letter or report. You open Windows 2000 programs from the Start menu. Programs are usually located on the Programs submenu or on one of its submenus. To start WordPad, for example, you select the Programs and Accessories submenus.

If you can't locate an item that is supposed to be on a menu, it is most likely temporarily hidden. Windows 2000 menus use a feature called **Personalized Menus** that hides menu options you use infrequently. You can access hidden menu options by pointing to the menu name and then clicking the double arrow ⅀ (sometimes called a "chevron") at the bottom of the menu. You can also access the hidden options by holding the pointer over the menu name.

To start the WordPad program from the Start menu:

1. Click the **Start** button to open the Start menu.

2. Point to **Programs**. The Programs submenu appears.

3. Point to **Accessories**. The Accessories submenu appears. Figure 1-9 shows the open menus.

   TROUBLE? If a different menu opens, you might have moved the mouse diagonally so that a different submenu opened. Move the pointer to the right across the Programs option, and then move it up or down to point to Accessories. Once you're more comfortable moving the mouse, you'll find that you can eliminate this problem by moving the mouse quickly.

   TROUBLE? If WordPad doesn't appear on the Accessories submenu, continue to point to Accessories until WordPad appears.

Figure 1-9 **START MENU**

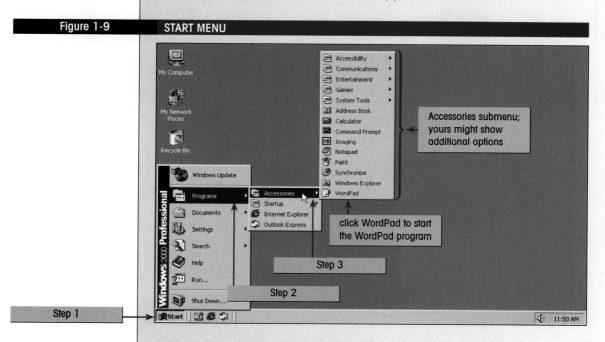

4. Click **WordPad**. The WordPad program opens, as shown in Figure 1-10. If the WordPad window fills the entire screen, don't worry. You will learn how to manipulate windows in Session 1.2.

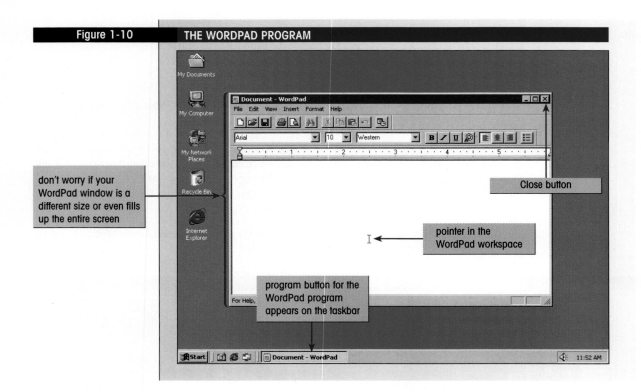

Figure 1-10   THE WORDPAD PROGRAM

don't worry if your WordPad window is a different size or even fills up the entire screen

Close button

pointer in the WordPad workspace

program button for the WordPad program appears on the taskbar

When a program is started, it is said to be **open** or **running**. A **program button** appears on the taskbar for each open program. You click program buttons to switch between open programs. When you are finished using a program, click the Close button ![X].

To exit the WordPad program:

1. Click the **Close** button ![X]. See Figure 1-10. You return to the Windows 2000 desktop.

Running **Multiple Programs**

One of the most useful features of Windows 2000 is its ability to run multiple programs at the same time. This feature, known as **multitasking**, allows you to work on more than one project at a time and to switch quickly between projects. For example, you can start WordPad and leave it running while you then start the Paint program.

To run WordPad and Paint at the same time:

1. Start WordPad again and then click the **Start** button ![Start] again.

2. Point to **Programs** and then point to **Accessories**.

3. Click **Paint**. The Paint program opens, as shown in Figure 1-11. Now two programs are running at the same time.

TROUBLE? If the Paint program fills the entire screen, don't worry. You will learn how to manipulate windows in Session 1.2.

Figure 1-11	THE PAINT PROGRAM

mouse pointer is a pencil when positioned in the drawing area

WordPad window might appear behind the Paint window

WordPad program button is not pushed in, indicating that WordPad is running but is not the active program

Paint program button is pushed in, indicating that Paint is the active program

What happened to WordPad? The WordPad program button is still on the taskbar, so even if you can't see it, WordPad is still running. You can imagine that it is stacked behind the Paint program, as shown in Figure 1-12. Paint is the active program because it is the one with which you are currently working.

Figure 1-12	PROJECTS STACKED ON A DESK

screen is main work area of your desk

another project, such as a letter you're writing, might be hidden under the drawing you are working on

project you are currently working on, a drawing, is on top

Switching Between Programs

The easiest way to switch between programs is to use the buttons on the taskbar.

To switch between WordPad and Paint:

1. Click the button labeled **Document - WordPad** on the taskbar. The Document - WordPad button now looks as if it has been pushed in, to indicate that it is the active program, and WordPad moves to the front.
2. Next, click the button labeled **untitled - Paint** on the taskbar to switch to the Paint program.

The Paint program is again the active program.

Accessing the Desktop from the Quick Launch Toolbar

The Windows 2000 taskbar, as you've seen, displays buttons for programs currently running. It also can contain **toolbars**, sets of buttons that give single-click access to programs or documents that aren't running or open. In its default state, the Windows 2000 taskbar displays the **Quick Launch toolbar**, which gives quick access to Web programs and to the desktop. Your taskbar might contain additional toolbars, or none at all.

When you are running more than one program but you want to return to the desktop, perhaps to use one of the desktop icons such as My Computer, you can do so by using one of the Quick Launch toolbar buttons. Clicking the Show Desktop button ⌐ returns you to the desktop. The open programs are not closed; they are simply made inactive and reduced to buttons on the taskbar.

To return to the desktop:

1. Click the **Show Desktop** button ⌐ on the Quick Launch toolbar. The desktop appears, and both the Paint and WordPad programs are temporarily inactive. See Figure 1-13.

    TROUBLE? If the Quick Launch toolbar doesn't appear on your taskbar, right-click the taskbar, point to Toolbars, and then click Quick Launch and try Step 1 again.

Figure 1-13	ACCESSING THE DESKTOP

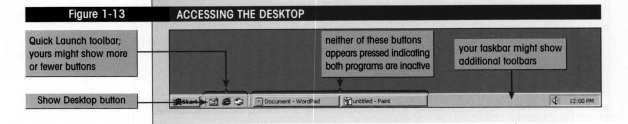

Quick Launch toolbar; yours might show more or fewer buttons

neither of these buttons appears pressed indicating both programs are inactive

your taskbar might show additional toolbars

Show Desktop button

Closing Inactive Programs from the Taskbar

It is good practice to close each program when you are finished using it. Each program uses computer resources, such as memory, so Windows 2000 works more efficiently when only the programs you need are open. You've already seen how to close an open program using the Close button ☒. You can also close a program, whether active or inactive, by using the shortcut menu associated with the program button on the taskbar.

To close WordPad and Paint using the program button shortcut menus:

1. Right-click the **untitled – Paint** button on the taskbar. To right-click something, remember that you click it with the right mouse button. The shortcut menu for that program button opens. See Figure 1-14.

2. Click **Close**. The button labeled "untitled – Paint" disappears from the taskbar, indicating that the Paint program is closed.

3. Right-click the **Document – WordPad** button on the taskbar, and then click **Close**. The WordPad button disappears from the taskbar.

Figure 1-14 PROGRAM BUTTON SHORTCUT MENU

Shutting Down Windows 2000

It is very important to shut down Windows 2000 before you turn off the computer. If you turn off your computer without correctly shutting down, you might lose data and damage your files.

You should typically use the "Shut Down" option when you want to turn off your computer. However, your school might prefer that you select the Log Off option in the Shut Down Windows dialog box. This option logs you out of Windows 2000, leaves the computer turned on, and allows another user to log on without restarting the computer. Check with your instructor or technical support person for the preferred method at your lab.

To shut down Windows 2000:

1. Click the **Start** button ![Start] on the taskbar to display the Start menu.

2. Click the **Shut Down** menu option. A box titled "Shut Down Windows" opens.

   TROUBLE? If you can't see the Shut Down menu option, your Start menu has more options than your screen can display. A double arrow ⮟ appears at the bottom of the Start menu. Click this button until the Shut Down menu option appears, and then click Shut Down.

   TROUBLE? If you are supposed to log off rather than shut down, click the Log Off option instead and follow your school's logoff procedure.

3. Make sure the **Shut Down** option appears in the box shown in Figure 1-15.

   TROUBLE? If "Shut down" does not appear, click the arrow to the right of the box. A list of options appears. Click Shut Down.

Figure 1-15 SHUTTING DOWN

4. Click the **OK** button.

5. Wait until you see a message indicating it is safe to turn off your computer. If your lab staff has requested you to switch off your computer after shutting down, do so now. Otherwise leave the computer running. Some computers turn themselves off automatically.

Session 1.1 QUICK CHECK

1. What is the purpose of the taskbar?

2. The _____ feature of Windows 2000 allows you to run more than one program at a time.

3. The _____ is a list of options that provides you with access to programs, documents, submenus, and more.

4. What should you do if you are trying to move the pointer to the left edge of your screen, but your mouse bumps into the keyboard?

5. Even if you can't see an open program on your desktop, the program might be running. How can you tell if a program is running?

6. Why is it good practice to close each program when you are finished using it?

7. Why should you shut down Windows 2000 before you turn off your computer?

SESSION 1.2

In this session you will learn how to use many of the Windows 2000 controls to manipulate windows and programs. You will also learn how to change the size and shape of a window; how to move a window; and how to use menus, dialog boxes, tabs, buttons, and lists to specify how you want a program to carry out a task.

Anatomy of a Window

When you run a program in Windows 2000, it appears in a window. A **window** is a rectangular area of the screen that contains a program or data. Windows, spelled with an uppercase "W," is the name of the Microsoft operating system. The word "window" with a lowercase "w" refers to one of the rectangular areas on the screen. A window also contains controls for manipulating the window and for using the program. Figure 1-16 describes the controls you are likely to see in most windows.

Figure 1-16	WINDOW CONTROLS
CONTROL	**DESCRIPTION**
Menu bar	Contains the titles of menus, such as File, Edit, and Help
Sizing buttons	Let you enlarge, shrink, or close a window
Status bar	Provides you with messages relevant to the task you are performing
Title bar	Contains the window title and basic window control buttons
Toolbar	Contains buttons that provide you with shortcuts to common menu commands
Window title	Identifies the program and document contained in the window
Workspace	Part of the window you use to enter your work—to enter text, draw pictures, set up calculations, and so on

WordPad is a good example of a typical window, so try starting WordPad and identifying these controls in the WordPad window.

To look at window controls:

1. Make sure Windows 2000 is running and you are at the Windows 2000 desktop.

2. Start WordPad.

    TROUBLE? To start WordPad, click the Start button, point to Programs, point to Accessories, and then click WordPad.

3. On your screen, identify the controls labeled in Figure 1-17. Don't worry if your window fills the entire screen or is a different size. You'll learn to change window size shortly.

Figure 1-17 | WORDPAD WINDOW CONTROLS

Manipulating a Window

There are three buttons located on the right side of the title bar. You are already familiar with the Close button. The Minimize button � hides the window so that only its program button is visible on the taskbar. The other button changes name and function depending on the status of the window (it either maximizes the window or restores it to a predefined size). Figure 1-18 shows how these buttons work.

Minimizing a Window

The Minimize button hides a window so that only the button on the taskbar remains visible. You can use the Minimize button when you want to temporarily hide a window but keep the program running.

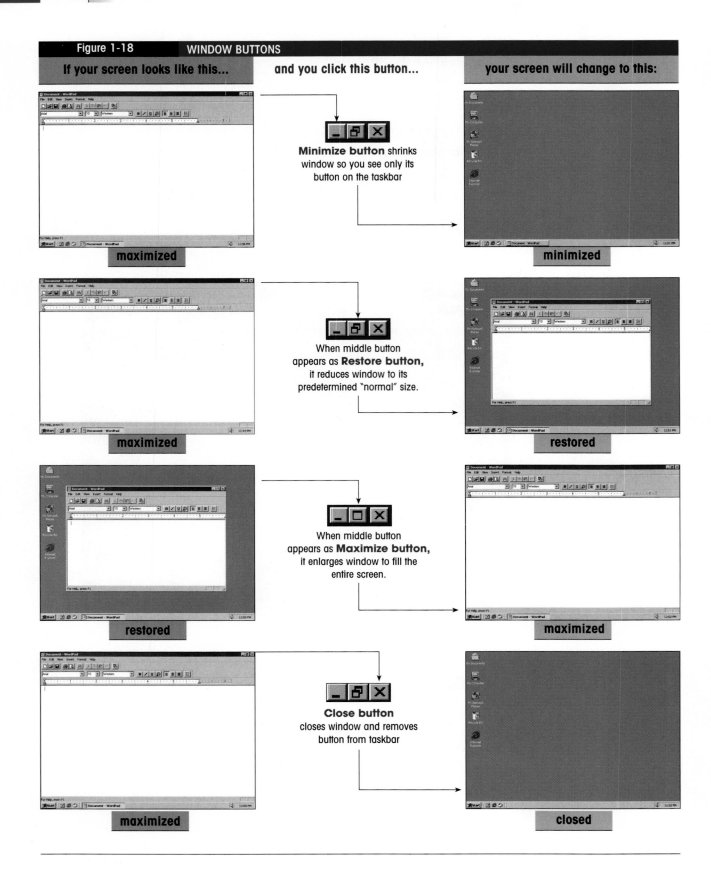

Figure 1-18   WINDOW BUTTONS

If your screen looks like this...   and you click this button...   your screen will change to this:

Minimize button shrinks window so you see only its button on the taskbar

maximized   minimized

When middle button appears as **Restore button,** it reduces window to its predetermined "normal" size.

maximized   restored

When middle button appears as **Maximize button,** it enlarges window to fill the entire screen.

restored   maximized

Close button closes window and removes button from taskbar

maximized   closed

To minimize the WordPad window:

1. Click the **Minimize** button [_]. The WordPad window shrinks so that only the Document - WordPad button on the taskbar is visible.

TROUBLE? If you accidentally clicked the Close button and closed the window, use the Start button to start WordPad again.

Redisplaying a Window

You can redisplay a minimized window by clicking the program's button on the taskbar. When you redisplay a window, it becomes the active window.

To redisplay the WordPad window:

1. Click the **Document - WordPad** button on the taskbar. The WordPad window is restored to its previous size. The Document - WordPad button looks pushed in as a visual clue that WordPad is now the active window.

2. The taskbar button provides another means of switching a window between its minimized and active state: Click the **Document – WordPad** button on the taskbar again to minimize the window.

3. Click the **Document – WordPad** button once more to redisplay the window.

Maximizing a Window

The Maximize button enlarges a window so that it fills the entire screen. You will probably do most of your work using maximized windows because they allow you to see more of your program and data.

To maximize the WordPad window:

1. Click the **Maximize** button [□] on the WordPad title bar.

TROUBLE? If the window is already maximized, it will fill the entire screen, and the Maximize button won't appear. Instead, you'll see the Restore button [⊡]. Skip Step 1.

Restoring a Window

The Restore button [⊡] reduces the window so it is smaller than the entire screen. This is useful if you want to see more than one window at a time. Also, because of its smaller size, you can drag the window to another location on the screen or change its dimensions.

To restore a window:

1. Click the **Restore** button [⊡] on the WordPad title bar. Notice that once a window is restored, [⊡] changes to the Maximize button [□].

Moving a Window

You can use the mouse to move a window to a new position on the screen. When you click an object and hold down the mouse button while moving the mouse, you are said to be **dragging** the object. You can move objects on the screen by dragging them to a new location. If you want to move a window, you drag its title bar. You cannot move a maximized window.

To drag the WordPad window to a new location:

1. Position the mouse pointer on the WordPad window title bar.
2. While you hold down the left mouse button, move the mouse to drag the window. A rectangle representing the window moves as you move the mouse.
3. Position the rectangle anywhere on the screen, then release the left mouse button. The WordPad window appears in the new location.
4. Now drag the WordPad window to the upper-left corner of the screen.

Changing the Size of a Window

You can also use the mouse to change the size of a window. Notice the sizing handle ▨ at the lower-right corner of the window. The **sizing handle** provides a visible control for changing the size of a window.

To change the size of the WordPad window:

1. Position the pointer over the sizing handle ▨. The pointer changes to a diagonal arrow ↖ .
2. While holding down the mouse button, drag the sizing handle down and to the right.
3. Release the mouse button. Now the window is larger.
4. Practice using the sizing handle to make the WordPad window larger or smaller, and then maximize the WordPad window.

You can also drag the window borders left, right, up, or down to change a window's size.

Using **Program Menus**

Most Windows programs use menus to organize the program's menu options. The menu bar is typically located at the top of the program window and shows the titles of menus such as File, Edit, and Help.

Windows menus are relatively standardized—most Windows programs include similar menu options. It's easy to learn new programs, because you can make a pretty good guess about which menu contains the option you want.

Selecting Options from a Menu

When you click any menu title, choices for that menu appear below the menu bar. These choices are referred to as **menu options** or **commands**. To select a menu option, you click it. For example, the File menu is a standard feature in most Windows programs and contains the options typically related to working with a file: creating, opening, saving, and printing a file or document.

To select the Print Preview menu option on the File menu:

1. Click **File** on the WordPad menu bar to display the File menu. See Figure 1-19.

TROUBLE? If you open a menu but decide not to select any of the menu options, you can close the menu by clicking its title again.

Figure 1-19	FILE MENU

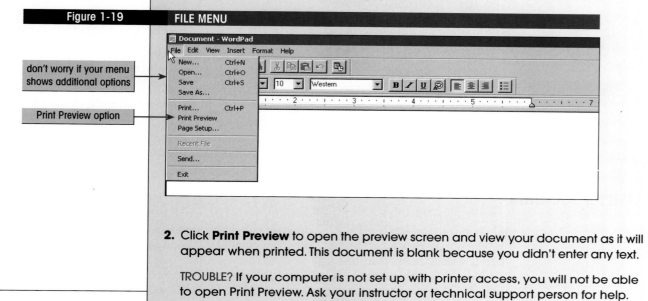

don't worry if your menu shows additional options

Print Preview option

2. Click **Print Preview** to open the preview screen and view your document as it will appear when printed. This document is blank because you didn't enter any text.

TROUBLE? If your computer is not set up with printer access, you will not be able to open Print Preview. Ask your instructor or technical support person for help.

3. After examining the screen, click the button with the text label "Close" to return to your document.

TROUBLE? If you close WordPad by mistake, restart it.

Not all menu options immediately carry out an action—some show submenus or ask you for more information about what you want to do. The menu gives you hints about what to expect when you select an option. These hints are sometimes referred to as **menu conventions**. Figure 1-20 describes the Windows 2000 menu conventions.

Figure 1-20	MENU CONVENTIONS

CONVENTION	DESCRIPTION
Check mark	Indicates a toggle, or "on-off" switch (like a light switch) that is either checked (turned on) or not checked (turned off)
Ellipsis	Three dots that indicate you must make additional selections after you select that option. Options without dots do not require additional choices—they take effect as soon as you click them. If an option is followed by an ellipsis, a dialog box opens that allows you to enter specifications for how you want a task carried out.
Triangular arrow	Indicates the presence of a submenu. When you point at a menu option that has a triangular arrow, a submenu automatically appears.
Grayed-out option	Option that is not available. For example, a graphics program might display the Text Toolbar option in gray if there is no text in the graphic to work with.
Keyboard shortcut	A key or combination of keys that you can press to activate the menu option without actually opening the menu
Double arrow	Indicates that additional menu options are available; click the double arrow to access them

Figure 1-21 shows examples of these menu conventions.

Figure 1-21	EXAMPLES OF MENU CONVENTIONS

check mark

grayed-out option

arrow indicating that submenu will open

ellipsis

keyboard shortcut

submenu

The dialog box opens when you choose an option followed by an ellipsis. A **dialog box** lets you enter specifications for how you want a task carried out.

View
- ✓ Tool Box   Ctrl+T
- ✓ Color Box   Ctrl+L
- ✓ Status Bar
- ✓ Text Toolbar
- Zoom   ▶
- View Bitmap   Ctrl+F

Normal Size   Ctrl+PgUp
Large Size   Ctrl+PgDn
Custom...
Show Grid   Ctrl+
✓ Show Thu...

Custom Zoom
Current zoom: 100%
Zoom to
- ⦿ 100% ◯ 400% ◯ 800%
- ◯ 200% ◯ 600%

OK
Cancel

Using Toolbars

Although you can usually perform all program commands using menus, toolbar buttons provide convenient one-click access to frequently used commands. For most Windows 2000 functions, there is usually more than one way to accomplish a task. To simplify your introduction to Windows 2000 in this tutorial, we will usually show you only one method for performing a task. As you become more accomplished at using Windows 2000, you can explore alternate methods.

In Session 1.1 you learned that Windows 2000 programs include ScreenTips, which indicate the purpose and function of a tool. Now is a good time to explore the WordPad toolbar buttons by looking at their ScreenTips.

To find out a toolbar button's function:

1. Position the pointer over any button on the toolbar, such as the Print Preview button ⬚. After a short pause, the name of the button appears in a box near the button, and a description of the button appears in the status bar just above the Start button. See Figure 1-22.

Figure 1-22	TOOLBAR BUTTON AIDS

toolbar button ScreenTip

toolbar button description also appears in status bar

2. Move the pointer over each button on the toolbar to see its name and purpose.

You select a toolbar button by clicking it.

To select the Print Preview toolbar button:

1. Click the **Print Preview** button [icon]. The Print Preview screen appears. This is the same screen that appeared when you selected Print Preview from the File menu.

2. After examining the screen, click the button with the text label "Close" to return to your document.

Using List Boxes and Scroll Bars

As you might guess from the name, a **list box** displays a list of choices. In WordPad, date and time formats are shown in the Date/Time list box. List box controls usually include arrow buttons, a scroll bar, and a scroll box, as shown in Figure 1-23.

To use the Date/Time list box:

1. Click the **Date/Time** button [icon] to display the Date and Time dialog box. See Figure 1-23.

| Figure 1-23 | LIST BOX |

click up arrow button to move toward top of list

list box shows available date formats

scroll bar appears when list is too long to fit in list box

drag scroll box up or down to view different parts of list

click down arrow button to move toward bottom of list

2. To scroll down the list, click the **down arrow** button [icon]. See Figure 1-23.

3. Find the scroll box on your screen. See Figure 1-23.

4. Drag the **scroll box** to the top of the scroll bar. Notice how the list scrolls back to the beginning.

   TROUBLE? You learned how to drag when you learned to move a window. To drag the scroll box up, point to the scroll box, press and hold down the mouse button, and then move the mouse up.

5. Find a date in the format "July 07, 2002." Click that date format to select it.

6. Click the **OK** button to close the Date and Time dialog box. This inserts the current date in your document.

You can access some list boxes directly from the toolbar. When a list box is on the tool-bar, only the current option appears in the list box. A **list arrow** appears on the right of the box and you can click it to view additional options.

To use the Font Size list box:

1. Click the **Font Size** list arrow, as shown in Figure 1-24.

Figure 1-24	FONT SIZE LIST ARROW

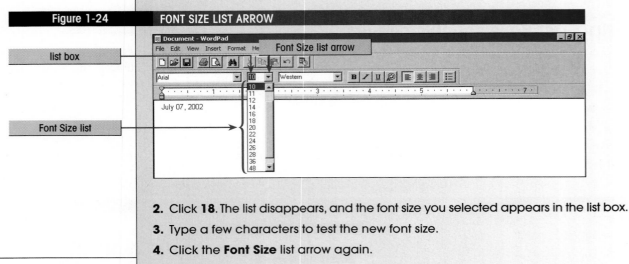

list box

Font Size list

2. Click **18**. The list disappears, and the font size you selected appears in the list box.

3. Type a few characters to test the new font size.

4. Click the **Font Size** list arrow again.

5. Click **12**.

6. Type a few characters to test this type size.

7. Click the **Close** button ☒ to close WordPad.

8. When you see the message "Save changes to Document?" click the **No** button.

Using **Dialog Box Controls**

Recall that when you select a menu option or button followed by an ellipsis, a dialog box opens that allows you to provide more information about how a program should carry out a task. Some dialog boxes group different kinds of information into bordered rectangular areas called **panes**. Within these panes, you will usually find tabs, option buttons, check boxes, and other controls that the program uses to collect information about how you want it to perform a task. Figure 1-25 describes common dialog box controls.

Figure 1-25	DIALOG BOX CONTROLS
CONTROL	**DESCRIPTION**
Tabs	Modeled after the tabs on file folders, tab controls are often used as containers for other Windows 2000 controls such as list boxes, radio buttons, and check boxes. Click the appropriate tabs to view different pages of information or choices.
Option buttons	Also called **radio buttons**, option buttons allow you to select a single option from among one or more options.
Check boxes	Click a check box to select or deselect it; when it is selected, a check mark appears, indicating that the option is turned on; when deselected, the check box is blank and the option is off. When check boxes appear in groups, you can select or deselect as many as you want; they are not mutually exclusive, as option buttons are.
Spin boxes	Allow you to scroll easily through a set of numbers to choose the setting you want
Text boxes	Boxes into which you type additional information

Figure 1-26 displays examples of these controls.

Figure 1-26	EXAMPLES OF DIALOG BOX CONTROLS

click tab to view group of controls whose functions are related

option buttons appear in groups; you click one option button in a group, and a black dot indicates your selection

pane

click check box to turn an option "off" (not checked) or "on" (checked)

click up or down spin arrows to increase or decrease numeric value in spin box

click text box and then type entry

Using Help

Windows 2000 **Help** provides on-screen information about the program you are using. Help for the Windows 2000 operating system is available by clicking the Start button on the taskbar, then selecting Help from the Start menu. If you want Help for a program, such as WordPad, you must first start the program, then click Help on the menu bar.

When you start Help, a Windows Help window opens, which gives you access to help files stored on your computer as well as help information stored on Microsoft's Web site. If you are not connected to the Web, you have access only to the help files stored on your computer.

To start Windows 2000 Help:

1. Click the **Start** button.

2. Click **Help**. The Windows 2000 window opens to the Contents tab. See Figure 1-27.

TROUBLE? If the Contents tab is not in front, click the Contents tab to view the table of contents.

| Figure 1-27 | WINDOWS 2000 HELP |

Contents tab contains table of contents

selected book contents appear in right pane

books contain lists of topics

right pane

Help uses tabs for the four sections of Help: Contents, Index, Search, and Favorites. The **Contents tab** groups Help topics into a series of books. You select a book 📖 by clicking it. The book opens, and a list of related topics appears from which you can choose. Individual topics are designated with the ？ icon. Overview topics are designated with the 📖 icon.

The **Index tab** displays an alphabetical list of all the Help topics from which you can choose. The **Search tab** allows you to search the entire set of Help topics for all topics that contain a word or words you specify. The **Favorites tab** allows you to save your favorite Help topics for quick reference.

Viewing Topics from the Contents Tab

You know that Windows 2000 gives you easy access to the Internet. Suppose you're wondering how to connect to the Internet from your computer. You can use the Contents tab to find more information on a specific topic.

To use the Contents tab:

1. Click the **Internet, E-mail, and Communications** book icon 📖. A list of topics and an overview appear below the book title.

2. Click the **Connect to the Internet** topic icon ？. Information about connecting to the Internet appears in the right pane. See Figure 1-28.

Figure 1-28 — LOCATING INFORMATION ABOUT HOW TO CONNECT TO THE INTERNET

Selecting a Topic from the Index

The Index tab allows you to jump to a Help topic by selecting a topic from an indexed list. For example, you can use the Index tab to learn more about the Internet.

To find a Help topic using the Index tab:

1. Click the **Index** tab. A long list of indexed Help topics appears.

   TROUBLE? If this is the first time you've used Help on your computer, Windows 2000 needs to set up the Index. This takes just a few moments. Wait until you see the list of index entries in the left pane, and then proceed to Step 2.

2. Drag the scroll box down to view additional topics.

3. You can quickly jump to any part of the list by typing the first few characters of a word or phrase in the box above the Index list. Click the box and then type **Internet**.

4. Click the topic **searching the Internet** (you might have to scroll to see it) and then click the **Display** button. When there is just one topic, it appears immediately in the right pane; otherwise, the Topics Found window opens, listing all topics indexed under the entry you're interested in. In this case, there are four choices.

5. Click **Using Internet Explorer** and then click the **Display** button. The information you requested appears in the right pane. See Figure 1-29. Notice in this topic that there are a few underlined words. You can click underlined words to view definitions or additional information.

Figure 1-29	USING THE INDEX TO LOCATE INFORMATION

6. Click **security**. A small box appears that defines the term "security." See Figure 1-30.

Figure 1-30	VIEWING ADDITIONAL INFORMATION

7. Click a blank area of the Windows 2000 window to close the box.

The third tab, the Search tab, works similarly to the Index tab, except that you type a word, and then the Help system searches for topics containing that word. You'll get a chance to experiment with the Search and Favorites tabs in the Review Assignments.

Returning to a Previous Help Topic

You've looked at a few topics now. Suppose you want to return to the one you just saw. The Help window includes a toolbar of buttons that help you navigate the Help system. One of these buttons is the **Back** button, which returns you to topics you've already viewed. Try returning to the help topic on connecting to the Internet.

To return to a Help topic:

1. Click the **Back** button. The Internet topic appears.
2. Click the **Close** button ⊠ to close the Windows 2000 window.
3. Log off or shut down Windows 2000, depending on your lab's requirements.

Now that you know how Windows 2000 Help works, don't forget to use it! Use Help when you need to perform a new task or when you forget how to complete a procedure.

You've finished the tutorial, and as you shut down Windows 2000, Steve Laslow returns from class. You take a moment to tell him all you've learned: you know how to start and close programs and how to use multiple programs at the same time. You have learned how to work with windows and the controls they employ. Finally, you've learned how to get help when you need it. Steve is pleased that you are well on your way to mastering the fundamentals of using the Windows 2000 operating system.

Session 1.2 QUICK CHECK

1. What is the difference between the title bar and a toolbar?

2. Provide the name and purpose of each button:
   a. [_]   b. [□]   c. [🗗]   d. [✕]

3. Describe what is indicated by each of the following menu conventions:
   a. Ellipsis...   b. Grayed-out   c. ▶   d. ✔

4. A(n) _____ consists of a group of buttons, each of which provides one-click access to important program functions.

5. What is the purpose of the scroll bar? What is the purpose of the scroll box?

6. Option buttons allow you to select _____ option(s) at a time.

7. It is a good idea to use _____ when you need to learn how to perform new tasks.

REVIEW ASSIGNMENTS

1. **Running Two Programs and Switching Between Them** In this tutorial you learned how to run more than one program at a time, using WordPad and Paint. You can run other programs at the same time, too. Complete the following steps and write out your answers to questions b through f:
   a. Start the computer. Enter your username and password if prompted to do so.
   b. Click the Start button. How many menu options are on the Start menu?
   c. Run the Calculator program located on the Accessories menu. How many program buttons are now on the taskbar (don't count toolbar buttons or items in the tray)?
   d. Run the Paint program and maximize the Paint window. How many programs are running now?
   e. Switch to Calculator. What are two visual clues that tell you that Calculator is the active program?
   f. Multiply 576 by 1457 using the Calculator accessory. What is the result?
   g. Close Calculator, then close Paint.

Explore ▶ 2. **WordPad Help** In Tutorial 1 you learned how to use Windows 2000 Help. Almost every Windows 2000 program has a Help feature. Many users can learn to use a program just by using Help. To use Help, start the program, then click the Help menu at the top of the screen. Try using WordPad Help:
   a. Start WordPad.
   b. Click Help on the WordPad menu bar, and then click Help Topics.
   c. Using WordPad Help, write out your answers to questions 1 through 4.
      1. How do you create a bulleted list?
      2. How do you set the margins in a document?
      3. How do you undo a mistake?
      4. How do you change the font style of a block of text?
   d. Close WordPad.

Explore

3. **The Search Tab** In addition to the Contents and Index tabs you worked with in this tutorial, Windows 2000 Help also includes a Search tab. Windows 2000 makes it possible to use a microphone to record sound on your computer. You could browse through the Contents tab, although you might not know where to find information about microphones. You could also use the Index tab to search through the indexed entry. Or you could use the Search tab to find all Help topics that mention microphones.

   a. Start Windows 2000 Help and use the Index tab to find information about microphones. How many topics are listed?
   b. Now use the Search tab to find information about microphones. Type "microphone" in the box on the Search tab, and then click the List Topics button.
   c. Write a paragraph comparing the two lists of topics. You don't have to view them all, but indicate which tab seems to yield more information, and why. Close Help.

4. **Getting Started** Windows 2000 includes Getting Started, an online "book" that helps you discover more about your computer and the Windows 2000 operating system. You can use this book to review what you learned in this tutorial and pick up some tips for using Windows 2000. Complete the following steps and write out your answers to questions d–j.

   a. Start Help, click the Contents tab, click Introducing Windows 2000 Professional, and then click Getting Started online book. Read the information and then click Windows 2000 Professional Getting Started.
   b. In the right pane, click New to Windows? Notice the book icons in the upper-right and upper-left corners of the right pane.
   c. Read each screen, and then click the right book icon to proceed through the Help topics. Alternately, you can view specific Getting Started Help topics by clicking them on the Contents tab. To answer the following questions, locate the information on the relevant Help topic. All the information for these questions is located in Chapter 4—"Windows Basics." When you are done, close Help.
   d. If your computer's desktop style uses the single-click option, how do you select a file? How do you open a file?
   e. What features are almost always available on your desktop, regardless of how many windows you have open?
   f. How can you get information about a dialog box or an area of the dialog box?
   g. How does the Getting Started online book define the word "disk"?
   h. If your computer is connected to a network, what Windows 2000 feature can you use to browse network resources?
   i. Why shouldn't you turn off your computer without shutting it down properly?

5. **Favorite Help Topics** You learned in this tutorial that you can save a list of your favorite Help topics on the Favorites tab. Try adding a topic to your list of favorites.

   a. Open a Help topic in the Help system. For this assignment, click the Contents tab, click Personalizing Your Computer, and then click Personalizing your workspace overview.
   b. Click the Favorites tab. The topic you selected appears on the right, and the topic name appears in the lower-left corner.
   c. Click the Add button. The topic appears in the box on the Favorites tab. This provides you an easy way to return to this topic.
   d. Click the Remove button to remove the topic from the Favorites list.

PROJECTS

1. There are many types of pointing devices on the market today. Go to the library and research the types of devices available. Consider what devices are appropriate for these situations: desktop or laptop computers, connected or remote devices, and ergonomic or standard designs (look up the word "ergonomic").

Use up-to-date computer books, trade computer magazines such as *PC Computing* and *PC Magazine*, or the Internet (if you know how) to locate information. Your instructor might suggest specific resources you can use. Write a one-page report describing the types of devices available, the differing needs of users, special features that make pointing devices more useful, price comparisons, and what you would choose if you needed to buy a pointing device.

2. Using the resources available to you, either through your library or the Internet (if you know how), locate information about the release of Windows 2000. Computing trade magazines are an excellent source of information about software. Read several articles about Windows 2000 and then write a one-page essay that discusses the features that are most important to the people who evaluated the software. If you find reviews of the software, mention the features that reviewers had the strongest reaction to, pro or con.

3. Upgrading is the process of placing a more recent version of a product onto your computer. When Windows 2000 first came out, people had to decide whether or not they wanted to upgrade to Windows 2000. Interview several people you know who are well-informed Windows computer users. Ask them whether they are using Windows 2000 or an older version of Windows. If they are using an older version, ask why they have chosen not to upgrade. If they are using Windows 2000, ask them why they chose to upgrade. Ask such questions as:

   a. What features convinced you to upgrade or made you decide to wait?
   b. What role did the price of the upgrade play?
   c. Would you have had (or did you have) to purchase new hardware to make the upgrade? How did this affect your decision?
   d. If you did upgrade, are you happy with that decision? If you didn't, do you intend to upgrade in the near future? Why, or why not?

   Write a single-page essay summarizing what you learned from these interviews.

4. Choose a topic to research using the Windows 2000 online Help system. Look for information on your topic using three tabs: the Contents tab, the Index tab, and the Search tab. Once you've found all the information you can, compare the three methods (Contents, Index, Search) of looking for information. Write a paragraph that discusses which tab proved the most useful. Did you reach the same information topics using all three methods? In a second paragraph, summarize what you learned about your topic. Finally, in a third paragraph, indicate under what circumstances you'd use which tab.

LAB ASSIGNMENTS

Using a Keyboard

Using a Keyboard To become an effective computer user, you must be familiar with your primary input device—the keyboard. See the Read This Before You Begin page for information on installing and starting the lab.

1. The Steps for the Using a Keyboard Lab provide you with a structured introduction to the keyboard layout and the function of special computer keys. Click the Steps button and begin the Steps. As you work through the Steps, answer all of the Quick Check questions that appear. When you complete the Steps, you will see a Summary Report that summarizes your performance on the Quick Checks. Follow the directions on the screen to print the Summary Report.

2. In Explore, start the typing tutor. You can develop your typing skills using the typing tutor in Explore. Take the typing test and print out your results.

3. In Explore, try to improve your typing speed by 10 words per minute. For example, if you currently type 20 words per minute, your goal will be 30 words per minute. Practice each typing lesson until you see a message that indicates that you can proceed to the next lesson.

Create a Practice Record, as shown here, to keep track of how much you practice. When you have reached your goal, print out the results of a typing test to verify your results.

Practice Record
Name:
Section:
Start Date: Start Typing Speed: wpm
End Date: End Typing Speed: wpm
Lesson #:   Date Practiced/Time Practiced

Using a Mouse

Using a Mouse   A mouse is a standard input device on most of today's computers. You need to know how to use a mouse to manipulate graphical user interfaces and to use the rest of the Labs. See the Read This Before You Begin page for information on installing and starting the lab.

1. The Steps for the Using a Mouse Lab show you how to click, double-click, and drag objects using the mouse. Click the Steps button and begin the Steps. As you work through the Steps, answer all of the Quick Check questions that appear. When you complete the Steps, you will see a Summary Report that summarizes your performance on the Quick Checks. Follow the directions on the screen to print the Summary Report.

2. In Explore, create a poster to demonstrate your ability to use a mouse and to control a Windows program. To create a poster for an upcoming sports event, select a graphic, type the caption for the poster, then select a font, font styles, and a border. Print your completed poster.

QUICK CHECK ANSWERS

Session 1.1

1. The taskbar contains buttons that give you access to tools and programs.
2. multitasking
3. Start menu
4. Lift the mouse up and move it to the right.
5. Its button appears on the taskbar.
6. To conserve computer resources such as memory.
7. To ensure you don't lose data and damage your files.

Session 1.2

1. The title bar identifies the window and contains window controls; toolbars contain buttons that provide you with shortcuts to common menu commands.
2. a. Minimize button shrinks window so you see button on taskbar

    b. Maximize button enlarges window to fill entire screen

    c. Restore button reduces window to predetermined size

    d. Close button closes window and removes button from taskbar
3. a. ellipsis indicates a dialog box will open

    b. grayed-out indicates option is not currently available

    c. arrow indicates a submenu will open

    d. check mark indicates a toggle option
4. toolbar
5. Scroll bars appear when the contents of a box or window are too long to fit; you drag the scroll box to view different parts of the contents.
6. one
7. online Help

OBJECTIVES

In this tutorial you will:

- Format a disk

- Enter, select, insert, and delete text

- Create and save a file

- Open, edit, and print a file

- Create and make a copy of your Data Disk

- View the list of files on your disk and change view options

- Move, copy, delete, and rename a file

- Navigate a hierarchy of folders

LABS

Using Files

WORKING WITH FILES

Creating, Saving, and Managing Files

CASE

Distance Education

You recently purchased a computer in order to gain new skills so you can stay competitive in the job market. You hope to use the computer to enroll in a few distance education courses. **Distance education** is formalized learning that typically takes place using a computer and the Internet, replacing normal classroom interaction with modern communications technology. Distance education teachers often make their course material available on the **World Wide Web**, a popular service on the Internet that makes information readily accessible.

Your computer came loaded with Windows 2000. Your friend Shannon suggests that before you enroll in any online courses, you should get more comfortable with your computer and with Windows 2000. Knowing how to save, locate, and organize your files will make your time spent at the computer much more productive. A **file**, often referred to as a **document**, is a collection of data that has a name and is stored in a computer. Once you create a file, you can open it, edit its contents, print it, and save it again—usually using the same program you used to create it.

Shannon suggests that you become familiar with how to perform these tasks in Windows 2000 programs. Then she'll show you how to choose different ways of viewing information on your computer. Finally, you'll spend time learning how to organize your files.

SESSION 2.1

In Session 2.1, you will learn how to format a disk so it can store files. You will create, save, open, and print a file. You will find out how the insertion point differs from the mouse pointer, and you will learn the basic skills for Windows 2000 text entry, such as entering, selecting, inserting, and deleting. For the steps of this tutorial you will need two blank 3½-inch disks.

Formatting a Disk

Before you can save files on a floppy disk, the disk must be formatted. When the computer **formats** a disk, the magnetic particles on the disk surface are arranged so that data can be stored on the disk. Today, many disks are sold preformatted and can be used right out of the box. However, if you purchase an unformatted disk, or if you have an old disk you want to completely erase and reuse, you can format the disk using the Windows 2000 Format command. This command is available through the **My Computer window**, a feature of Windows 2000 that you use to view, organize, and access the programs, files, drives and folders on your computer. You open My Computer by using its icon on the desktop. You'll learn more about the My Computer window later in this tutorial.

The following steps tell you how to format a 3½-inch high-density disk, using drive A. Your instructor will tell you how to revise the instructions given in these steps if the procedure is different for your lab.

Make sure you are using a blank disk (or one that contains data you no longer need) before you perform these steps.

To format a disk:

1. Start Windows 2000, if necessary.

2. Write your name on the label of a 3½-inch disk and insert your disk in drive A. See Figure 2-1.

| Figure 2-1 | INSERTING A DISK INTO A DISK DRIVE |

edge with the notch goes into the drive first

floppy disk drive

edge with the label goes in last

TROUBLE? If your disk does not fit in drive A, put it in drive B and substitute drive B for drive A in all of the steps for the rest of the tutorial.

3. Click the **My Computer** icon on the desktop. The icon is selected. Figure 2-2 shows this icon on your desktop.

TROUBLE? If the My Computer window opens, skip Step 4. Your computer is using different settings, which you'll learn to change in Session 2.2.

4. Press the **Enter** key to open the My Computer window. See Figure 2-2 (don't worry if your window opens maximized).

TROUBLE? If you see a list of items instead of icons like those in Figure 2-2, click View, and then click Large Icons. Don't worry if your toolbars don't exactly match those in Figure 2-2.

TROUBLE? If you see additional information or a graphic image on the left side of the My Computer window, Web view is enabled on your computer. Don't worry. You will learn how to return to the default Windows 2000 settings in Session 2.2.

Figure 2-2	MY COMPUTER WINDOW

My Computer icon; don't worry if yours looks different

3½ Floppy (A:) icon

your window might contain different icons and have a different look

5. Right-click the **3½ Floppy (A:)** icon to open its shortcut menu, and then click **Format**. The Format dialog box opens.

6. Make sure the dialog box settings on your screen match those in Figure 2-3.

Figure 2-3	FORMATTING A FLOPPY DISK

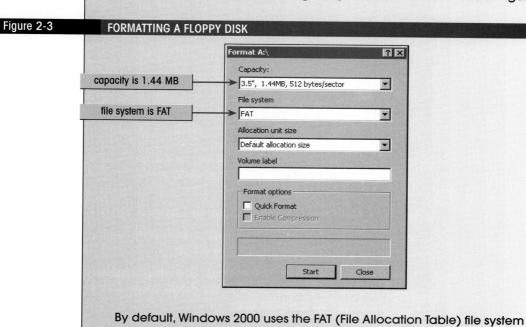

capacity is 1.44 MB

file system is FAT

By default, Windows 2000 uses the FAT (File Allocation Table) file system for floppy disks. A **file system** is the way files are organized on the disk. Windows 2000 supports other file systems such as FAT32 and NTFS, but this is a more advanced topic.

7. Click the **Start** button to start formatting the disk.

8. Click the **OK** button to confirm that you want to format the disk (the actual formatting will take a minute to perform). Click the **OK** button again when the formatting is complete.

9. Click the **Close** button.

10. Click the **Close** button ☒ to close the My Computer window.

Now that you have a formatted disk, you can create a document and save it on your disk. First you need to learn how to enter text into a document.

Working with Text

To accomplish many computing tasks, you need to enter text in documents and text boxes. This involves learning how to move the pointer so the text will appear where you want it, how to insert new text between existing words or sentences, how to select text, and how to delete text. When you type sentences of text, do not press the Enter key when you reach the right margin of the page. Most software contains a feature called **word wrap**, which automatically continues your text on the next line. Therefore, you should press Enter only when you have completed a paragraph.

If you type the wrong character, press the Backspace key to back up and delete the character. You can also use the Delete key. What's the difference between the Backspace and Delete keys? The **Backspace** key deletes the character to the left, while the **Delete** key deletes the character to the right. If you want to delete text that is not next to where you are currently typing, you need to use the mouse to select the text; then you can use either the Delete key or the Backspace key.

Now you will type some text, using WordPad, to practice text entry. When you first start WordPad, notice the flashing vertical bar, called the **insertion point**, in the upper-left corner of the document window. The insertion point indicates where the characters you type will appear.

To type text in WordPad:

1. Start WordPad and locate the insertion point.

   TROUBLE? If the WordPad window does not fill the screen, click the Maximize button ▢.

   TROUBLE? If you can't find the insertion point, click in the WordPad **document window**, the white area below the toolbars and ruler.

2. Type your name, pressing the Shift key at the same time as the appropriate letter to type uppercase letters and using the Spacebar to type spaces, just as on a typewriter.

3. Press the **Enter** key to move the insertion point down to the next line.

4. As you type the following sentences, watch what happens when the insertion point reaches the right edge of the page:

   This is a sample typed in WordPad. See what happens when the insertion point reaches the right edge of the page. Note how the text wraps automatically to the next line.

   TROUBLE? If you make a mistake, delete the incorrect character(s) by pressing the Backspace key on your keyboard. Then type the correct character(s).

TROUBLE? If your text doesn't wrap, your screen might be set up to display more information than the screen used for the figures in this tutorial, or your WordPad program might not be set to use Word Wrap. Click View, click Options, make sure the Rich Text tab is selected, click the Wrap to window option button, and then click the OK button.

The Insertion Point Versus the Pointer

The insertion point is not the same as the mouse pointer. When the mouse pointer is in the text-entry area, it is called the **I-beam pointer** and looks like I. Figure 2-4 explains the difference between the insertion point and the I-beam pointer.

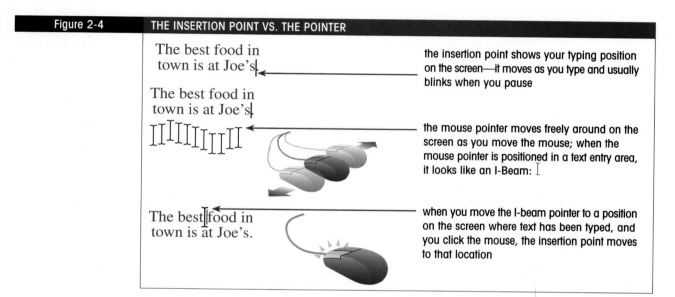

| Figure 2-4 | THE INSERTION POINT VS. THE POINTER |

The best food in town is at Joe's| — the insertion point shows your typing position on the screen—it moves as you type and usually blinks when you pause

The best food in town is at Joe's| — the mouse pointer moves freely around on the screen as you move the mouse; when the mouse pointer is positioned in a text entry area, it looks like an I-Beam: I

The best food in town is at Joe's. — when you move the I-beam pointer to a position on the screen where text has been typed, and you click the mouse, the insertion point moves to that location

When you enter text, the insertion point moves as you type. If you want to enter text in a location other than where the mouse pointer is currently positioned, you move the I-beam pointer to the location where you want to type, and then click. The insertion point jumps to the location you clicked. In most programs, the insertion point blinks, making it easier for you to locate it on a screen filled with text.

To move the insertion point:

1. Check the locations of the insertion point and the I-beam pointer. The insertion point should be at the end of the sentence you typed in the last set of steps. The easiest way to locate the I-beam pointer is to move your mouse gently until you see the pointer. Remember that it will look like ⊷ until you move the pointer into the document window.

2. Use the mouse to move the I-beam pointer just to the left of the word "sample" and then click the mouse button. The insertion point should be just to the left of the "s."

   TROUBLE? If you have trouble clicking just to the left of the "s," try clicking in the word and then using the arrow keys to move the insertion point one character at a time.

3. Move the I-beam pointer to a blank area near the bottom of the workspace and then click. Notice the insertion point does not jump to the location of the I-beam pointer. Instead the insertion point jumps to the end of the last sentence or to the point in the bottom line directly above where you clicked. The insertion point can move only within existing text. It cannot be moved out of the existing text area.

Selecting Text

Many text operations are performed on a **block** of text, which is one or more consecutive characters, words, sentences, or paragraphs. Once you select a block of text, you can delete it, move it, replace it, underline it, and so on. To deselect a block of text, click anywhere outside the selected block.

If you want to delete the phrase "See what happens" in the text you just typed and replace it with the phrase "You can watch word wrap in action," you do not have to delete the first phrase one character at a time. Instead, you can select the entire phrase and then type the replacement phrase.

To select and replace a block of text:

1. Move the I-beam pointer just to the left of the word "See."

2. While holding down the mouse button, drag the I-beam pointer over the text to the end of the word "happens." The phrase "See what happens" should now be highlighted. See Figure 2-5.

TROUBLE? If the space to the right of the word "happens" is also selected, don't worry. Your computer is set up to select spaces in addition to words. After completing Step 4, simply press the Spacebar to type an extra space if required.

Figure 2-5	SELECTING TEXT

position I-beam pointer here

hold left mouse button down while you drag I-beam pointer over text

3. Release the mouse button.

TROUBLE? If the phrase is not highlighted correctly, repeat Steps 1 through 3.

4. Type **You can watch word wrap in action**

The text you typed replaces the highlighted text. Notice that you did not need to delete the selected text before you typed the replacement text.

Inserting a Character

Windows 2000 programs usually operate in **insert mode**—when you type a new character, all characters to the right of the insertion point are pushed over to make room.

Suppose you want to insert the word "page" before the word "typed" in your practice sentences.

> *To insert text:*
>
> **1.** Move the I-beam pointer just before the word "typed" and then click to position the insertion point.
>
> **2.** Type **page**
>
> **3.** Press the **Spacebar**.

Notice how the letters in the first line are pushed to the right to make room for the new characters. When a word gets pushed past the right margin, the word-wrap feature moves it down to the beginning of the next line.

Saving a File

As you type text, it is held temporarily in the computer's memory, which is erased when you turn off the computer. For permanent storage, you need to save your work on a disk. In the computer lab, you will probably save your work on a floppy disk in drive A.

When you save a file, you must give it a name, called a **filename**. Windows 2000 allows you to use up to 255 characters in a filename—this gives you plenty of room to name your file accurately enough so that you'll know the contents of the file by just looking at the filename. You may use spaces and certain punctuation symbols in your filenames. You cannot use the symbols \ / ? : * " < > | in a filename, because Windows uses those for designating the location and type of the file, but other symbols such as & ; - and $ are allowed.

Another thing to consider is whether you might use your files on a computer running older programs. Programs designed for the Windows 3.1 and DOS operating systems (which were created before 1995) require that files be eight characters or less with no spaces. Thus when you save a file with a long filename in Windows 2000, Windows 2000 also creates an eight-character filename that can be used by older programs. The eight-character filename is created from the first six nonspace characters in the long filename, with the addition of a tilde (~) and a number. For example, the filename Car Sales for 1999 would be converted to Carsal~1.

Most filenames have an extension. An **extension** (a set of no more than three characters at the end of a filename, separated from the filename by a period) is used by the operating system to identify and categorize the file. In the filename Car Sales for 1999.doc, for example, the file extension "doc" identifies the file as one created with Microsoft Word. You might also have a file called Car Sales for 1999.xls—"xls" identifies the file as one created with Microsoft Excel, a spreadsheet program. When pronouncing filenames with extensions, say "dot" for the period, so that the file Resume.doc is pronounced "Resume dot doc."

You usually do not need to add extensions to your filenames because the program you use to create the file does this automatically. Also, Windows 2000 keeps track of file extensions, but not all computers are set to display them. The steps in these tutorials refer to files by using the filename without its extension. So if you see the filename Practice Text in the steps, but "Practice Text.doc" appears on your screen, don't worry—these refer to the same file. Also don't worry if you don't use consistent lowercase and uppercase letters when saving files. Usually the operating system doesn't distinguish between them. Be aware, however, that some programs are "case-sensitive"—they check for case in filenames.

Now you can save the WordPad document you typed.

To start saving a document:

1. Click the **Save** button 🖫 on the toolbar. The Save As dialog box opens, as shown in Figure 2-6.

Figure 2-6	SAVING A FILE

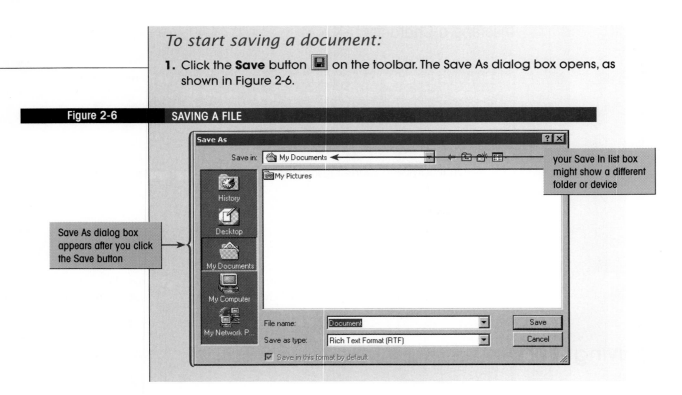

Save As dialog box appears after you click the Save button

your Save In list box might show a different folder or device

You use the Save As dialog box to specify where you want to save your file (on the hard drive or on a floppy disk, in a folder or not, and so on). Before going further with the process of saving a file, let's examine some of the features of the Save As dialog box so that you learn to save your files exactly where you want them.

Specifying the File Location

In the Save As dialog box, Windows 2000 provides the **Places Bar**, a list of important locations on your computer. When you click the different icons in the Places Bar, the contents of those locations will be displayed in the white area of the Save As dialog box. You can then save your document directly to those locations. Figure 2-7 displays the icons in the Places Bar and gives their function.

Figure 2-7	ICONS IN THE PLACES BAR

ICON	DESCRIPTION
History	Displays a list of recently opened files, folders, and objects
Desktop	Displays a list of files, folders, and objects on the Windows 2000 desktop
My Documents	Displays a list of files, folders, and objects in the My Documents folder
My Computer	Displays a list of files, folders, and objects in the My Computer window
My Network P...	Displays a list of computers and folders available on the network

To see this in action, try displaying different locations in the dialog box.

To use the Places Bar:

1. Click the **Desktop** icon in the Places Bar.

2. The Save As dialog box now displays the contents of the Windows 2000 desktop. See Figure 2-8.

Figure 2-8 · USING THE PLACES BAR

click to display the contents of the Windows 2000 desktop

contents of Windows 2000 desktop

3. Click the **My Documents** icon to display the contents of the My Documents folder.

Once you've clicked an icon in the Places Bar, you can open any file displayed in that location, and you can save a file into that location. The Places Bar doesn't have an icon for every location on your computer, however. The **Save in** list box (located at the top of the dialog box) does. Use the Save in list box now to save your document to your floppy disk.

To use the Save in list box:

1. Click the **Save in** list arrow to display a list of drives.

2. Click **3½ Floppy (A:)**.

Now that you've specified where you want to save your file, you can specify a name and type for the file.

Specifying the File Name and Type

After choosing the location for your document, you have to specify the name of the file. You should also specify (or at least check) the file's format. A file's **format** determines what type of information you can place in the document, the document's appearance, and what kind of programs can work with the document. There are five file formats available in WordPad: Word for Windows 6.0, Rich Text Format (RTF), Text, Text for MS-DOS, and Unicode Text. The Word and RTF formats allow you to create documents with text that can use bold-faced or italicized fonts as well as documents containing graphic images and scanned photos. However, only word-processing programs like WordPad or Microsoft Word can work with those files. The three text formats allow only simple text with no graphics or special formatting, but such documents are readable by a wider range of programs. The default format for WordPad documents is RTF, but you can change that, as you'll see shortly.

Continue saving the document, using the name "Practice Text" and the file type Word 6.0.

To finish saving your document:

1. Select the text **Document** in the File name text box and then type **Practice Text** in the File name text box. The new text replaces "Document."

2. Click the **Save as type** list arrow and then click **Word for Windows 6.0** in the list. See Figure 2-9.

Figure 2-9	COMPLETED SAVE AS DIALOG BOX

select the floppy drive for the file's location

save the document in Word 6.0 format

if this check box is selected, future documents will use Word 6.0 format as the default

the file's name

Note that if you want all future documents saved by WordPad to use the Word 6.0 format as the default format rather than RTF, you can select the Save in this format by default check box. If you select it, the next time you save a document in WordPad, this format will be the initial choice, so you won't have to specify it.

3. Click the **Save** button in the lower-right corner of the dialog box.

4. If you are asked whether you are sure that you want to save the document in this format, click the **Yes** button.

Your file is saved on your Data Disk, and the document title, "Practice Text," appears on the WordPad title bar.

Note that after you save the file the document appears a little different. What has changed? By saving the document in Word 6.0 format rather than RTF, you've changed the format of the document slightly. One change is that the text is wrapped differently in Word 6.0 format. A Word 6.0 file will use the right margin and, in this case, limit the length of a single line of text to 6 inches.

What if you try to close WordPad before you save your file? Windows 2000 will display a message—"Save changes to Document?" If you answer "Yes," Windows will display the Save As dialog box so you can give the document a name. If you answer "No," Windows 2000 will close WordPad without saving the document. Any changes you made to the document will be lost, so when you are asked if you want to save a file, answer "Yes," unless you are absolutely sure you don't need to keep the work you just did.

After you save a file, you can work on another document or close WordPad. Since you have already saved your Practice Text document, you'll continue this tutorial by closing WordPad.

To close WordPad:

1. Click the **Close** button ☒ to close the WordPad window.

Opening a File

Suppose you save and close the Practice Text file, then later you want to revise it. To revise a file you must first open it. When you open a file, its contents are copied into the computer's memory. If you revise the file, you need to save the changes before you close the program. If you close a revised file without saving your changes, you will lose them.

There are several methods to open a file. You can select the file from the Documents list (available through the Start menu) if you have opened the file recently, since the Documents list contains the 15 most recently opened documents. This list is very handy to use on your own computer, but in a lab, other student's files quickly replace your own. You can also locate the file in the My Computer window (or in **Windows Explorer**, another file management tool) and then open it. And finally, you can start a program and then use the Open button within that program to locate and open the file. Each method has advantages and disadvantages.

The first two methods for opening the Practice Text file simply require you to select the file from the Documents list or locate and select it from My Computer or Windows Explorer. With these methods the document, not the program, is central to the task; hence, this method is sometimes referred to as **document-centric**. You need only to remember the name of your file—you do not need to remember which program you used to create it.

Opening a File from the My Computer Window

If your file is not in the Documents list, you can open the file by selecting it from the My Computer window. Either way, Windows 2000 uses the file extension (whether it is displayed or not) to determine which program to start so you can manipulate the file. It starts the program, and then automatically opens the file. The advantage of both methods is simplicity. The disadvantage is that Windows 2000 might not start the program you expect. For example, when you select Practice Text, you might expect Windows 2000 to start WordPad because you used WordPad to create it. Depending on the programs installed on your computer system, however, Windows 2000 might start Microsoft Word instead. Usually this is not a problem. Although the program might not be the one you expect, you can still use it to revise your file.

To open the Practice Text file by selecting it from My Computer:

1. Open the **My Computer** window, located on the desktop.

2. Click the **3½ Floppy (A:)** icon in the My Computer window.

   TROUBLE? If the 3½ Floppy (A:) window opens, skip Step 3.

3. Press the **Enter** key. The 3½ Floppy (A:) window opens.

4. Click the **Practice Text** file icon.

   TROUBLE? If the Practice Text document opens, skip Step 5.

5. Press the **Enter** key. Windows 2000 starts a program, and then automatically opens the Practice Text file. You could make revisions to the document at this point, but instead, you'll close all the windows on your desktop so you can try the other method for opening files.

   TROUBLE? If Windows 2000 starts Microsoft Word or another word-processing program instead of WordPad, don't worry. You can use Microsoft Word to revise the Practice Text document.

6. Close all open windows on the desktop.

Opening a File from Within a Program

The third method for opening the Practice Text file requires you to open WordPad, and then use the Open button to select the Practice Text file. The advantage of this method is that you can specify the program you want to use—WordPad, in this case. This method, however, involves more steps than the method you tried previously.

You can take advantage of the Places Bar to reduce the number of steps it takes to open a file from within a program. Recall that one of the icons in the Places Bar is the History icon, which displays a list of recently opened files or objects. One of the most recently opened files was the Practice Text file, so it should appear in the list.

To start WordPad and open the Practice Text file:

1. Start **WordPad** and, if necessary, maximize the WordPad window.
2. Click the **Open** button 📂 on the toolbar.
3. Click **History** in the Places Bar.

The Practice Text file doesn't appear in the list. Why not? Look at the Files of Type list box. The selected entry is "Rich Text Format (*.rtf)". What this means is that the Open dialog box will display only RTF files (as well as drives). This frees you from having to deal with the clutter of unwanted or irrelevant files. The downside is that unless you're aware of how the Open dialog box will filter the list of files, you may mistakenly think that the file you're looking for doesn't exist. You can change how the Open dialog box filters this file list. Try this now by changing the filter to show only Word documents.

To change the types of files displayed:

1. Click the **Files of type** list arrow and then click **Word for Windows (*.doc)**

   The Practice Text file now appears in the list.

2. Click **Practice Text** in the list of files. See Figure 2-10.

Figure 2-10	THE OPEN DIALOG BOX

list only files in Word format

3. Click the **Open** button. The document should once again appear in the WordPad window.

Now that the Practice Text file is open, you can print it.

Printing a File

Windows 2000 provides easy access to your printer or printers. You can choose which printer to use, you can control how the document is printed, and you can control the order in which documents will be printed.

Previewing your Document Before Printing

It is a good idea to use Print Preview before you send your document to the printer. **Print Preview** shows on the screen exactly how your document will appear on paper. You can check your page layout so that you don't waste time and paper printing a document that is not quite the way you want it. Your instructor might supply you with additional instructions for printing in your school's computer lab.

To preview, then print, the Practice Text file:

1. Click the **Print Preview** button on the toolbar.

   TROUBLE? If an error message appears, printing capabilities might not be set up on your computer. Ask your instructor or technical support person for help, or skip this set of steps.

2. Look at your document in the Print Preview window. Before you print the document, you should make sure the font, margins, and other document features look the way you want them to.

   TROUBLE? If you can't read the document text on screen, click the Zoom In button as many times as needed to view the text.

3. Click the **Close** button to close Print Preview and return to the document.

Now that you've verified that the document looks the way you want, you can print it.

Sending the Document to the Printer

There are three ways to send your document to the printer. The first approach is to print the document directly from the Print Preview window by clicking the Print button. Thus once you are satisfied with the document's appearance, you can quickly move to printing it.

Another way is to click the Print button on your program's toolbar. This method will send the document directly to your printer without any further action on your part. It's the quickest and easiest way to print a document, but it does not allow you to change settings such as margins and layout. What if you have access to more than one printer? In that case, Windows 2000 sends the document to the default printer, the printer that has been set up to handle most print jobs.

If you want to select a different printer, or if you want to control how the printer prints your document, you can opt for a third method—selecting the Print command from the File menu. Using this approach, your program will open the Print dialog box, allowing you to choose which printer to use and how that printer will operate. Note that clicking the Print button from within the Print Preview window will also open the Print dialog box so you can verify or change settings.

To open the Print dialog box:

1. Click **File** on the WordPad menu bar and then click **Print**.

2. The Print dialog box opens, as displayed in Figure 2-11. Familiarize yourself with the controls in the Print dialog box.

Figure 2-11	THE PRINT DIALOG BOX

click to view options that control the layout and paper or quality of the print job

list of printers available to you; your list will be different

you can print all or part of a document; to print part, click the Pages option button and then enter the starting and ending pages of the range you want to print

you can print one or more copies, depending on the value in this spin box

3. Make sure your Print dialog box shows the Print range set to "All" and the Number of copies set to "1."

4. Select one of the printers in the list (your instructor may indicate which one you should select) and then click the **Print** button. The document is printed.

5. Close WordPad.

TROUBLE? If you see the message "Save changes to Document?" click the No button.

You've now learned how to create, save, open, and print word-processed files—essential skills for students in distance education courses that rely on word-processed reports transmitted across the Internet. Shannon assures you that the techniques you've just learned apply to most Windows 2000 programs.

Session 2.1 QUICK CHECK

1. A(n) _____ is a collection of data that has a name and is stored on a disk or other storage medium.

2. _____ erases all the data on a disk and arranges the magnetic particles on the disk surface so that the disk can store data.

3. True or False: When you move the mouse pointer over a text entry area, the pointer shape changes to an I-beam.

4. What indicates where each character you type will appear?

5. What does the History icon in the Places Bar display?

6. A file that you saved does not appear in the Open dialog box. Assuming that the file is still in the same location, what could be the reason that the Open dialog box doesn't display it?

7. What are the three ways to print from within a Windows 2000 application? If you want to print multiple copies of your document, which method(s) should you use and why?

SESSION 2.2

In this session, you will learn how to change settings in the My Computer window to control its appearance and the appearance of desktop objects. You will then learn how to use My Computer to manage the files on your disk; view information about the files on your disk; organize the files into folders; and move, delete, copy, and rename files. For this session you will use a second blank 3½-inch disk.

Creating Your Data Disk

Starting with this session, you must create a Data Disk that contains some practice files. You can use the disk you formatted in the previous session.

If you are using your own computer, the NP on Microsoft Windows 2000 menu option will not be available. Before you proceed, you must go to your school's computer lab and find a computer that has the NP on Microsoft Windows 2000 program installed. If you cannot get the files from the lab, ask your instructor or technical support person for help. Once you have made your own Data Disk, you can use it to complete this tutorial on any computer running Windows 2000.

To add the practice files to your Data Disk:

1. Write "Disk 1 - Windows 2000 Tutorial 2 Data Disk" on the label of your formatted disk (the same disk you used to save your Practice Text file).

2. Place the disk in drive A.

3. Click the **Start** button ⊞Start.

4. Point to **Programs**.

5. Point to **NP on Microsoft Windows 2000 – Level I**.

   TROUBLE? If NP on Microsoft Windows 2000 - Level I is not listed, ask your instructor or technical support person for help.

6. Click **Disk 1 (Tutorial 2)**. A message box opens, asking you to place your disk in drive A (which you already did, in Step 2).

7. Click the **OK** button. Wait while the program copies the practice files to your formatted disk. When all the files have been copied, the program closes.

Your Data Disk now contains practice files you'll use throughout the rest of this tutorial.

My Computer

The My Computer icon, as you have seen, represents your computer, with its storage devices, printers, and other objects. The My Computer icon opens into the My Computer window, which contains an icon for each of the storage devices on your computer. My Computer also gives you access to the **Control Panel**, a feature of Windows 2000 that controls the behavior of other devices and programs installed on your computer. Figure 2-12 shows how the My Computer window relates to your computer's hardware.

| Figure 2-12 | RELATIONSHIP BETWEEN COMPUTER AND MY COMPUTER WINDOW |

Each storage device that you have access to has a letter associated with it. The first floppy drive on a computer is usually designated as drive A (if you add a second floppy drive, it is usually designated as drive B), and the first hard drive is usually designated drive C. Additional hard drives will have letters D, E, F and so forth. If you have a CD-ROM drive, it will usually have the next letter in the alphabetic sequence. If you have access to hard drives located on other computers on a network, those drives will sometimes (though not always) have letters associated with them. In the example shown in Figure 2-12, the network drive has the drive letter E.

You can use the My Computer window to organize your files. In this section of the tutorial, you'll use the My Computer window to move and delete files on your Data Disk, which is assumed to be in drive A. If you use your own computer at home or work, you will probably store your files on drive C instead of drive A. In a school lab environment, you can't always save your files to drive C, so you need to carry your files with you on a floppy disk. Most of what you learn about working on the floppy drive will also work on your home or work computer when you use drive C (or other hard drives).

Now you'll open the My Computer window.

To open the My Computer window and explore the contents of your Data Disk:

1. Open the My Computer window.

2. Click the **3½ Floppy (A:)** icon and then press the **Enter** key. A window appears showing the contents of drive A; maximize this window if necessary. See Figure 2-13.

Figure 2-13   CONTENTS OF DATA DISK

icons show contents
of floppy disk

information about
the disk in drive A

three-letter file
extensions might
appear on your screen
for some or all files

TROUBLE? If the window appears before you press the Enter key, don't worry. Windows 2000 can be configured to use different keyboard and mouse combinations to open windows. You'll learn about these configuration issues shortly.

TROUBLE? If you see a list of filenames instead of icons, click View on the menu bar and then click Large Icons on the menu.

Changing the Appearance of the My Computer Window

Windows 2000 offers several different options that control how toolbars, icons, and buttons appear in the My Computer window. To make the My Computer window look the same as it does in the figures in this book, you need to ensure three things: that only the Address and Standard toolbars are visible, that files and other objects are displayed using large icons, and that the configuration of Windows 2000 uses the default setting. Setting your computer to match the figures will make it easier for you to follow the steps.

Controlling the Toolbar Display

The My Computer window, in addition to displaying a Standard toolbar, allows you to display the same toolbars that can appear on the Windows 2000 taskbar, such as the Address toolbar or the Links toolbar. These toolbars make it easy to access the Web from the My Computer window. In this tutorial, however, you need to see only the Address and Standard toolbars.

To display only the Address and Standard toolbars:

1. Click **View**, point to **Toolbars**, and then examine the Toolbars submenu. The Standard Buttons and Address Bar options should be preceded by a check mark. The Links and Radio options should not be checked. Follow the steps below to ensure that you have check marks next to the correct options.

2. If the Standard Buttons and Address Bar options *are not checked*, then click them to select them (you will have to repeat Step 1 to view the Toolbars submenu to do this for each option).

3. If the Links or Radio options *are checked,* then click them to deselect them (you will have to repeat Step 1 to view the Toolbars submenu to do this for each option).

4. Click **View** and then point to **Toolbars** one last time and verify that your Toolbars submenu and the toolbar display look like Figure 2-14.

Figure 2-14	CHECKING VIEW OPTIONS

TROUBLE? If the check marks are distributed differently than in Figure 2-14, repeat Steps 1–4 until the correct options are checked.

TROUBLE? If your toolbars are not displayed as shown in Figure 2-14 (for example, both the Standard and Address toolbars might be on the same line, or the Standard toolbar might be above the Address toolbar), you can easily rearrange them. To move a toolbar, drag the vertical bar at the far left of the toolbar. By dragging that vertical bar, you can drag the toolbar left, right, up, or down.

Changing the Icon Display

Windows 2000 provides five ways to view the contents of a disk—Large Icons, Small Icons, List, Details, and Thumbnails. Figure 2-15 shows examples of these five styles.

Figure 2-15	VIEWING STYLES

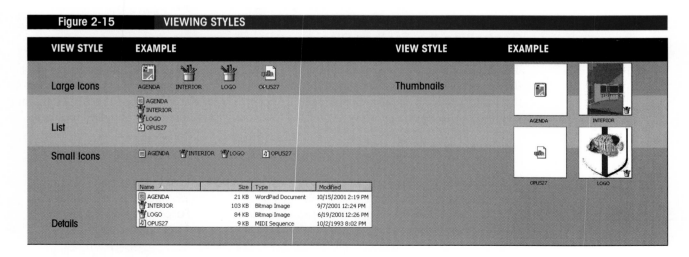

The default view, **Large Icons view**, displays a large icon and title for each file. The icon provides a visual cue to the type of the file, as Figure 2-16 illustrates. You can also get this same information with the smaller icons displayed in the **Small Icons** and **List** views, but in less screen space. In Small Icons and List views, you can see more files and folders at one time, which is helpful when you have many files in one location.

Figure 2-16	TYPICAL ICONS IN WINDOWS 2000

FILE AND FOLDER ICONS

	Text documents that you can open using the Notepad accessory are represented by notepad icons.
	Graphic image documents that you can open using the Paint accessory are represented by drawing instruments.
	Word-processed documents that you can open using the WordPad accessory are represented by a formatted notepad icon, unless your computer designates a different word-processing program to open files created with WordPad.
	Word-processed documents that you can open using a program such as Microsoft Word are represented by formatted document icons.
	Files created by programs that Windows does not recognize are represented by the Windows logo.
	A folder icon represents folders.
	Certain folders created by Windows 2000 have a special icon design related to the folder's purpose.

PROGRAM ICONS

	Icons for programs usually depict an object related to the function of the program. For example, an icon that looks like a calculator represents the Calculator accessory.
	Non-Windows programs are represented by the icon of a blank window.

All of the three icon views (Large Icons, Small Icons, and List) help you quickly identify a file and its type, but what if you want more information about a set of files? **Details view** shows more information than the Large Icon, Small Icon, and List views. Details view shows the file icon, the filename, the file size, the program you used to create the file, and the date and time the file was created or last modified.

Finally, if you have graphic files, you may want to use **Thumbnails view**, which displays a small "preview" image of the graphic, so that you can quickly see not only the filename, but also which picture or drawing the file contains. Thumbnails view is great for browsing a large collection of graphic files, but switching to this view can be time-consuming, since Windows 2000 has to create all of the preview images.

To see how easy it is to switch from one view to another, try displaying the contents of drive A in Details view.

To view a detailed list of files:

1. Click **View** and then click **Details** to display details for the files on your disk, as shown in Figure 2-17. Your files might be listed in a different order.

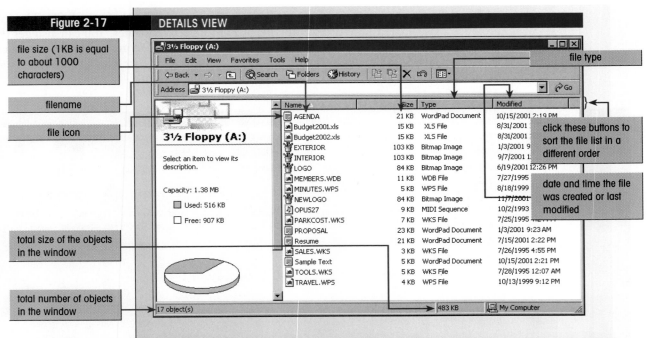

Figure 2-17   DETAILS VIEW

file size (1KB is equal to about 1000 characters)

filename

file icon

total size of the objects in the window

total number of objects in the window

file type

click these buttons to sort the file list in a different order

date and time the file was created or last modified

2. Look at the file sizes. Do you see that Exterior and Interior are the largest files?

3. Look at the dates and times the files were modified. Which is the oldest file?

One of the advantages that Details view has over other views is that you can sort the file list by filename, size, type, or the date the file was last modified. This helps if you're working with a large file list and you're trying to locate a specific file.

To sort the file list by type:

1. Click the **Type** button at the top of the list of files.

   The files are now sorted in alphabetical order by type, starting with the "Bitmap Image" files and ending with the "XLS File" files. This would be useful if, for example, you were looking for all the .doc files (those created with Microsoft Word), because they would all be grouped together under "M" for "Microsoft Word."

2. Click the **Type** button again.

   The sort order is reversed with the "XLS File" files now at the top of the list.

3. Click the **Name** button at the top of the file list.

   The files are now sorted in alphabetical order by filename.

Now that you have looked at the file details, switch back to Large Icon view.

To switch to Large Icon view:

1. Click **View** and then click **Large Icons** to return to the large icon display.

Restoring the My Computer Default Settings

Windows 2000 provides other options in working with your files and windows. These options fall into two general categories: Classic style and Web style. **Classic style** is a mode of working with windows and files that resembles earlier versions of the Windows operating system. **Web style** allows you to work with your windows and files in the same way you work with Web pages on the World Wide Web. For example, to open a file in Classic style, you can double-click the file icon (a **double-click** is clicking the left mouse button twice quickly) or click the file icon once and press the Enter key. To open a file in Web style, you would simply click the file icon once, and the file would open. You could also create your own style, choosing elements of both the Classic and Web styles, and add in a few customized features of your own.

In order to simplify matters, this book will assume that you're working in the Default style, that is the configuration that Windows 2000 uses when it is initially installed. No matter what changes you make to the configuration of Windows 2000, you can always revert back to the Default style. Try switching back to Default style now.

To switch to the Default style:

1. Click **Tools** and then click **Folder Options** on the menu.

2. If it is not already selected, click the **General** tab.

   The General sheet displays general options for working with files and windows. Take some time to look over the list of options available.

3. Click the **Restore Defaults** button.

4. Click the **View** tab.

   The View sheet displays options that control the appearance of files and other objects. You should set these options to their default values as well.

5. Click the **Restore Defaults** button.

6. Click the **OK** button to close the Folder Options dialog box.

Working **with Folders and Directories**

Up to now, you've done a little work with files and windows, but before going further you should look at some of the terminology used to describe these tasks. Any location where you can store files on a computer is referred to as a **directory**. The main directory of a disk is sometimes called the **root directory**, or the **top-level directory**. All of the files on your Data Disk are currently in the root directory of your floppy disk.

If too many files are stored in a directory, the list of files becomes very long and difficult to manage. You can divide a directory into **subdirectories,** also called **folders**. The number of files for each folder then becomes much fewer and easier to manage. A folder within a folder is called a **subfolder**. The folder that contains another folder is called the **parent folder**.

All of these objects exist in a **hierarchy**, which begins with your desktop and extends down to each subfolder. Figure 2-18 shows part of a typical hierarchy of Windows 2000 objects.

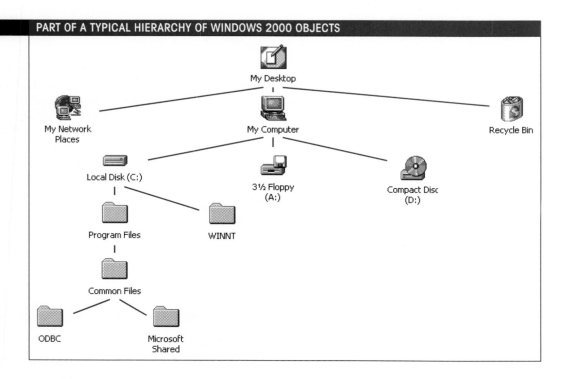

Figure 2-18 PART OF A TYPICAL HIERARCHY OF WINDOWS 2000 OBJECTS

Creating a Folder

You've already seen folder icons in the various windows you've previously opened. Now, you'll create your own folder called Practice to hold your documents.

> *To create a Practice folder:*
>
> **1.** Click **File** and then point to **New** to display the submenu.
>
> **2.** Click **Folder**. A folder icon with the label "New Folder" appears.
>
> **3.** Type **Practice** as the name of the folder.
>
> TROUBLE? If nothing happens when you type the folder name, it's possible that the folder name is no longer selected. Right-click the Practice folder, click Rename, and then repeat Step 3.
>
> **4.** Press the **Enter** key.
>
> The folder is now named "Practice" and is the selected item on your Data Disk.
>
> **5.** Click a blank area next to the Practice folder to deselect it.

Navigating Through the Windows 2000 Hierarchy

Now that you've created a subfolder, how do you move into it? You've seen that to view the contents of a file, you open it. To move into a subfolder, you open it in the same way.

To view the contents of the Practice folder:

1. Click the **Practice** folder and press the **Enter** key.

2. The Practice folder opens. Because there are no files in the folder, there are no items to display. You'll change that shortly.

You've seen that to navigate through the devices and folders on your computer, you open My Computer and then click the icons representing the objects you want to explore. But what if you want to move back to the root directory? The Standard toolbar, which stays the same regardless of which folder or object is open, includes buttons that help you navigate through the hierarchy of drives, directories, folders, subfolders and other objects in your computer. Figure 2-19 summarizes the navigation buttons on the Standard toolbar.

Figure 2-19		NAVIGATION BUTTONS
BUTTON	**ICON**	**DESCRIPTION**
Back	⇐	Returns you to the folder, drive, directory, or object you were most recently viewing. The button is active only when you have viewed more than one window in the current session.
Forward	⇒	Reverses the effect of the Back button.
Up	⬆	Moves you up one level in the hierarchy of directories, drives, folders, and other objects on your computer.

You can return to your floppy's root directory by using the Back or the Up button. Try both of these techniques now.

To move up to the root directory:

1. Click the **Back** button ⇐.

Windows 2000 moves you back to the previous window, in this case the root directory of your Data Disk.

2. Click the **Forward** button ⇒.

The Forward button reverses the effect of the Back button and takes you to the Practice folder.

3. Click the **Up** button ⬆.

You move up one level in hierarchy of Windows 2000 objects, going to the root directory of the Data Disk.

Another way of moving around in the Windows 2000 hierarchy is through the Address toolbar. By clicking the Address list arrow, you can view a list of the objects in the top part of the Windows 2000 hierarchy (see Figure 2-20). This gives you a quick way of moving to the top without having to navigate through the intermediate levels.

| Figure 2-20 | A HIERARCHY OF OBJECTS DISPLAYED IN THE ADDRESS LIST BOX |

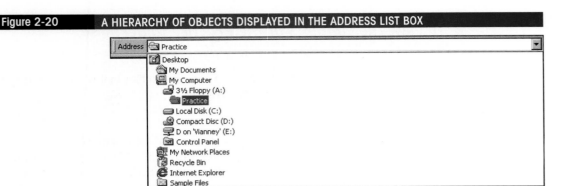

Now that you know how to move among the folders and devices on your computer, you can practice manipulating files. The better you are at working with the hierarchy of files and folders on your computer, the more organized the hierarchy will be, and the easier it will be to find the files you need.

Working with Files

As you've seen, the Practice folder doesn't contain any files. In the next set of steps, you will place a file from the root directory into it.

Moving and Copying a File

If you want to place a file into a folder from another location, you can either move the file or copy it. **Moving** a file takes it out of its current location and places it in the new location. **Copying** places the file in both locations. Windows 2000 provides several different techniques for moving and copying files. One way is to make sure that both the current and the new location are visible on your screen and then hold down the right mouse button and drag the file from the old location to the new location. A menu will then appear, and you can then select whether you want to move the file to the new location or make a copy in the new location. The advantage of this technique is that you are never confused as to whether you copied the file or merely moved it. Try this technique now by placing a copy of the Agenda file in the Practice folder.

To copy the Agenda file:

1. Point to the **Agenda** file in the root directory of your Data Disk and press the *right* mouse button.

2. With the right mouse button still pressed down, drag the **Agenda** file icon to the **Practice** folder icon; when the Practice folder icon turns blue, release the button.

3. A menu appears, as shown in Figure 2-21. Click **Copy Here**.

Figure 2-21 **COPYING A FILE**

TROUBLE? If you release the mouse button by mistake before dragging the Agenda icon to the Practice folder, the Agenda shortcut menu opens. Press the Esc key and then repeat Steps 1 and 2.

4. Double-click the **Practice** folder.

The Agenda file should now appear in the Practice folder.

Note that the "Move Here" command was also part of the menu. In fact, the command was in boldface, indicating that it is the default command whenever you drag a document from one location to another on the same drive. This means that if you were to drag a file from one location to another on the same drive using the left mouse button (instead of the right), the file would be moved and not copied.

Renaming a File

You will often find that you want to change the name of files as you change their content or as you create other files. You can easily rename a file by using the Rename option on the file's shortcut menu or by using the file's label.

Practice using this feature by renaming the Agenda file "Practice Agenda," since it is now in the Practice folder.

To rename the Agenda file:

1. Right-click the **Agenda** icon.

2. Click **Rename**. After a moment the filename is highlighted and a box appears around it.

3. Type **Practice Agenda** and press the **Enter** key.

> TROUBLE? If you make a mistake while typing and you haven't pressed the Enter key yet, you can press the Backspace key until you delete the mistake, then complete Step 3. If you've already pressed the Enter key, repeat Steps 1-3 to rename the file a second time.
>
> The file appears with a new name.

Deleting a File

You should periodically delete files you no longer need so that your folders and disks don't get cluttered. You delete a file or folder by deleting its icon. Be careful when you delete a folder, because you also delete all the files it contains! When you delete a file from a hard drive on your computer, the filename is deleted from the directory but the file contents are held in the Recycle Bin. The Recycle Bin is an area on your hard drive that holds deleted files until you remove them permanently; an icon on the desktop allows you easy access to the Recycle Bin. If you change your mind and want to retrieve a file deleted from your hard drive, you can recover it by using the Recycle Bin. However, once you've emptied the Recycle Bin, you can no longer recover the files that were in it.

When you delete a file from a floppy disk or a disk that exists on another computer on your network, it does not go into the Recycle Bin. Instead, it is deleted as soon as its icon disappears—and you can't recover it.

Try deleting the Practice Agenda file from your Data Disk. Because this file is on a floppy disk and not on the hard disk, it will not go into the Recycle Bin, and if you change your mind you won't be able to get it back.

To delete the Practice Agenda file:

1. Right-click the icon for the Practice Agenda file.
2. Click **Delete** on the menu that appears.
3. Windows 2000 asks if you're sure that you want to delete this file. Click the **Yes** button.
4. Click the **Close** button ☒ to close the My Computer window.

If you like using your mouse, another way of deleting a file is to drag its icon to the Recycle Bin on the desktop. Be aware that if you're dragging a file from your floppy disk or a network disk, the file will *not* be placed in the Recycle Bin—it will still be permanently deleted.

Other Copying and Moving Techniques

As was noted earlier, there are several ways of moving and copying. As you become more familiar with Windows 2000, you will no doubt settle on the technique you like best. Figure 2-22 describes some of the other ways of moving and copying files.

Figure 2-22	METHODS FOR MOVING AND COPYING FILES	
METHOD	**TO MOVE**	**TO COPY**
Cut, copy, and paste	Select the file icon. Click **Edit** on the menu bar and **Cut** on the menu bar. Move to the new location. Click **Edit** and **Paste**.	Select the file icon. Click **Edit** on the menu bar and **Copy** on the menu bar. Move to the new location. Click **Edit** and **Paste**.
Drag and drop	Click the file icon. Drag and drop the icon in the new location.	Click the file icon. Hold down the Ctrl key and drag and drop the icon in the new location.
Right-click, drag and drop	With the right mouse button pressed down, drag the file icon to the new location. Release the mouse button and click **Move Here** on the menu.	With the right mouse button pressed down, drag the file icon to the new location. Release the mouse button and click **Copy Here** on the menu.
Move to folder and copy to folder	Click the file icon. Click **Edit** on the menu bar and **Move to Folder** on the menu bar. Select the new location in the Browse for Folder dialog box.	Click the file icon. Click **Edit** on the menu bar and **Copy to Folder** on the menu bar. Select the new location in the Browse for Folder dialog box.

The techniques shown in Figure 2-22 are primarily for document files. Because a program might not work correctly if moved into a new location, the techniques for moving program files are slightly different. See the Windows 2000 online Help for more information on moving or copying a program file.

Copying an Entire Floppy Disk

You can have trouble accessing the data on your floppy disk if the disk is damaged, is exposed to magnetic fields, or picks up a computer virus. To avoid losing all your data, it is a good idea to make a copy of your floppy disk.

If you wanted to make a copy of an audiocassette, your cassette player would need two cassette drives. You might wonder, therefore, how your computer can make a copy of your disk if you have only one floppy disk drive. Figure 2-23 illustrates how the computer uses only one disk drive to make a copy of a disk.

Figure 2-23	USING ONE DISK DRIVE TO COPY A DISK

1. First, the computer copies the data from your original disk into memory.

2. Once the data is in memory, you remove your original disk from the drive and replace it with your copy disk.

3. The computer moves the data from memory onto your copy disk.

Memory

Data

Original Disk

Original Disk

Memory

Copy Disk

Copy Disk

Memory

Data

Copy Disk

REFERENCE WINDOW   **RW**

Copying a Disk
- Insert the disk you want to copy in drive A.
- In My Computer, right-click the 3½ Floppy (A:) icon, and then click Copy Disk.
- Click Start to begin the copy process.
- When prompted, remove the disk you want to copy, place your second disk in drive A, and then click OK.

If you have an extra floppy disk, you can make a copy of your Data Disk now. Make sure you copy the disk regularly so that as you work through the tutorials in this book it will stay updated.

To copy your Data Disk:

1. Write your name and "Windows 2000 Disk 1 Data Disk Copy" on the label of your second disk. Make sure the disk is blank and formatted.

   TROUBLE? If you aren't sure if the disk is blank, place it in the disk drive and open the 3½ Floppy (A:) window to view its contents. If the disk contains files you need, get a different disk. If it contains files you don't need, you could format the disk now, using the steps you learned at the beginning of this tutorial.

2. Make sure your original Data Disk is in drive A and the My Computer window is open.

3. Right-click the **3½ Floppy (A:)** icon, and then click **Copy Disk**. The Copy Disk dialog box opens.

4. Click the **Start** button and then the **OK** button to begin the copy process.

5. When the message "Insert the disk you want to copy to (destination disk)..." appears, remove your Data Disk and insert your Windows 2000 Disk 1 Data Disk Copy in drive A.

6. Click the **OK** button. When the copy is complete, you will see the message "Copy completed successfully." Click the **Close** button.

7. Close the My Computer window.

8. Remove your disk from the drive.

As you finish copying your disk, Shannon emphasizes the importance of making copies of your files frequently, so you won't risk losing important documents for your distance learning course. If your original Data Disk were damaged, you could use the copy you just made to access the files.

Keeping copies of your files is so important that Windows 2000 includes a program called Backup that automates the process of duplicating and storing data. In the Projects at the end of the tutorial you'll have an opportunity to explore the difference between what you just did in copying a disk and the way in which a program such as the Windows 2000 Backup program helps you safeguard data.

Session 2.2 QUICK CHECK

1. If you want to find out about the storage devices and printers connected to your computer, what window could you open?

2. If you have only one floppy disk drive on your computer, it is usually identified by the letter _____ .

3. The letter C is typically used for the _____ drive of a computer.

4. What information does Details view supply about a list of folders and files?

5. The main directory of a disk is referred to as the _____ directory.

6. What is the topmost object in the hierarchy of Windows 2000 objects?

7. If you have one floppy disk drive, but you have two disks, can you copy the files on one floppy disk to the other?

REVIEW ASSIGNMENTS

1. **Opening, Editing, and Printing a Document** In this tutorial you learned how to create a document using WordPad. You also learned how to save, open, and print a document. Practice these skills by copying the document called **Resume** into the Practice folder on your Data Disk. Rename the file **Woods Resume**. This document is a resume for Jamie Woods. Make the changes shown in Figure 2-24. Save your revisions in Word for Windows 6.0 format, preview, and then print the document. Close WordPad.

Figure 2-24

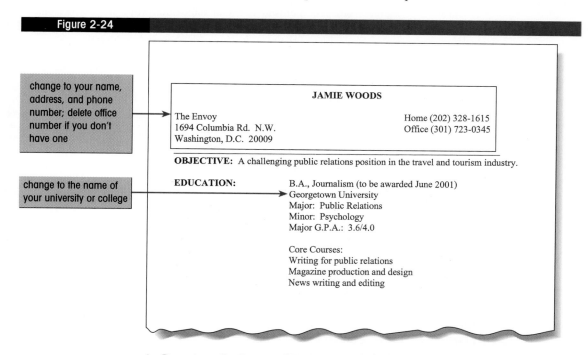

change to your name, address, and phone number; delete office number if you don't have one

change to the name of your university or college

JAMIE WOODS

The Envoy
1694 Columbia Rd. N.W.
Washington, D.C. 20009

Home (202) 328-1615
Office (301) 723-0345

OBJECTIVE: A challenging public relations position in the travel and tourism industry.

EDUCATION: B.A., Journalism (to be awarded June 2001)
Georgetown University
Major: Public Relations
Minor: Psychology
Major G.P.A.: 3.6/4.0

Core Courses:
Writing for public relations
Magazine production and design
News writing and editing

2. **Creating, Saving, and Printing a Letter** Use WordPad to write a one-page letter to a relative or a friend. Save the document in the Practice folder on your Data Disk with the name **Letter**. Use the Print Preview feature to look at the format of your finished letter, then print it, and be sure to sign it. Close WordPad.

3. **Managing Files and Folders** Using the copy of the disk you made at the end of the tutorial, complete steps a through f below to practice your file-management skills, and then answer the questions below.

    a. Create a folder called Spreadsheets on your Data Disk.
    b. Move the files **Parkcost**, **Budget2001**, **Budget2002**, and **Sales** into the Spreadsheets folder.
    c. Create a folder called Park Project.
    d. Move the files **Proposal**, **Members**, **Tools**, **Logo**, and **Newlogo** into the Park Project folder.
    e. Delete the file called **Travel**.
    f. Switch to the Details view and write out your answers to Questions 1 through 5:
        1. What is the largest file or files in the Park Project folder?
        2. What is the newest file or files in the Spreadsheets folder?
        3. How many files (don't include folders) are in the root directory of your Data Disk?
        4. How are the Opus and Exterior icons different? Judging from the appearance of the icons, what would you guess these two files contain?
        5. Which file in the root directory has the most recent date?

4. **More Practice with Files and Folders** For this assignment, you need a third blank disk. Complete steps a through g below to practice your file-management skills.

    a. Write "Windows 2000 Tutorial 2 Assignment 4" on the label of the blank disk, and then format the disk if necessary.
    b. Create another copy of your original Data Disk, using the Assignment 4 disk. Refer to the section "Creating Your Data Disk" in Session 2.2.
    c. Create three folders on the Assignment 4 Data Disk you just created: Documents, Budgets, and Graphics.
    d. Move the files **Interior**, **Exterior**, **Logo**, and **Newlogo** to the Graphics folder.
    e. Move the files **Travel**, **Members**, and **Minutes** to the Documents folder.
    f. Move **Budget2001** and **Budget2002** to the Budgets folder.
    g. Switch to Details view and write out your answers to Questions 1 through 6:
        1. What is the largest file or files in the Graphics folder?
        2. How many word-processed documents are in the root directory? *Hint*: These documents will appear with the WordPad, Microsoft Word, or some other word-processing icon, depending on what software you have installed.
        3. What is the newest file or files in the root directory (don't include folders)?
        4. How many files in all folders are 5 KB in size?
        5. How many files in the root directory are WKS files? *Hint*: Look in the Type column to identify WKS files.
        6. Do all the files in the Graphics folder have the same icon? What type are they?

5. **Searching for a File** Windows 2000 Help includes a topic that discusses how to search for files on a disk without looking through all the folders. Start Windows Help, then locate this topic, and answer Questions a through c:

    a. To display the Search dialog box, you must click the _____ button, then point to _____ on the menu, and finally click _____ on the submenu.
    b. Do you need to type in the entire filename to find the file?
    c. How do you perform a case-sensitive search?

6. **Help with Files and Folders** In Tutorial 2 you learned how to work with Windows 2000 files and folders. What additional information on this topic does Windows 2000 Help provide? Use the Start button to access Help. Use the Index tab to locate topics related to files and folders. Find at least two tips or procedures for working with files and folders that were not covered in the tutorial. Write out the tip in your own words and include the title of the Help screen that contains the information.

7. **Formatting Text** You can use a word processor such as WordPad to format text, that is, to give it a specific look and feel by using bold, italics, and different fonts, and by applying other features. Using WordPad, type the title and words to one of your favorite songs and

then save the document on your Data Disk (make sure you use your original Data Disk) with the filename Song.

a. Select the title, and then click the Center ![Center button], Bold ![Bold button], and Italic ![Italic button] buttons on the toolbar.
b. Click the Font list arrow and select a different font. Repeat this step several times with different fonts until you locate a font that is appropriate for the song.
c. Experiment with other formatting options until you find a look you like for your document. Save and print the final version.

PROJECTS

1. Formatting a floppy disk removes all the data on a disk. Answer the following questions using full sentences:
   a. What other method did you learn in this tutorial for removing data from a disk?
   b. If you wanted to remove all data from a disk, which method would you use? Why?
   c. What method would you use if you wanted to remove only one file? Why?

2. A friend who is new to computers is trying to learn how to enter text into WordPad. She has just finished typing her first paragraph when she notices a mistake in the first sentence. She can't remember how to fix a mistake, so she asks you for help. Write the set of steps she should try.

3. Computer users usually develop habits about how they access their files and programs. Follow the steps below to practice methods of opening a file, and then evaluate which method you would be likely to use and why.
   a. Using WordPad, create a document containing the words to a favorite poem, and save it on your Data Disk with the name Poem.
   b. Close WordPad and return to the desktop.
   c. Open the document using a document-centric approach.
   d. After a successful completion of step c, close the program and reopen the same document using another approach.
   e. Write the steps you used to complete steps c and d of this assignment. Then write a paragraph discussing which approach is most convenient when you are starting from the desktop, and indicate what habits you would develop if you owned your own computer and used it regularly.

 4. The My Computer window gives you access to the objects on your computer. In this tutorial you used My Computer to access your floppy drive so you could view the contents of your Data Disk. The My Computer window gives you access to other objects too. Open My Computer and write a list of the objects you see, including folders. Then open each icon and write a two-sentence description of the contents of each window that opens.

Explore 5. In this tutorial you learned how to copy a disk to protect yourself in the event of data loss. If you had your own computer with an 80 MB hard drive that was being used to capacity, it would take many 1.44 MB floppy disks to copy the contents of the entire hard drive. Is copying to floppy disks a reasonable method to use for protecting the data on your hard disk? Why, or why not?
   a. As mentioned at the end of the tutorial, Windows 2000 also includes an accessory called Backup that helps you safeguard your data. Backup doesn't just copy the data—it organizes it so that it takes up much less space than if you simply copied it. This program might not be installed on your computer, but if it is, try starting it (click the Start button, point to Programs, point to Accessories, point to System Tools, and then click Backup) and opening the Help files to learn what you can about how it functions. If it is not installed, skip Part a.
   b. Look up the topic of backups in a computer concepts textbook or in computer trade magazines. You could also interview experienced computer owners to find out which method they use to protect their data. When you have finished researching the concept of the backup, write a single-page essay that explains the difference between copying and backing up files, and evaluates which method is preferable for backing up large amounts of data, and why.

Using Files

LAB ASSIGNMENTS

Using Files   In this Lab you manipulate a simulated computer to view what happens in memory and on disk when you create, save, open, revise, and delete files. Understanding what goes on "inside the box" will help you quickly grasp how to perform basic file operations with most application software. See the Read This Before You Begin page for instructions on starting the Using Files Course Lab.

1. Click the Steps button to learn how to use the simulated computer to view the contents of memory and disk when you perform basic file operations. As you proceed through the Steps, answer all of the Quick Check questions that appear. After you complete the Steps, you will see a Quick Check Summary Report. Follow the instructions on the screen to print this report.

2. Click the Explore button and use the simulated computer to perform the following tasks:
   a. Create a document containing your name and the city in which you were born. Save this document as NAME.
   b. Create another document containing two of your favorite foods. Save this document as FOODS.
   c. Create another file containing your two favorite classes. Call this file CLASSES.
   d. Open the FOOD file and add another one of your favorite foods. Save this file without changing its name.
   e. Open the NAME file. Change this document so that it contains your name and the name of your school. Save this as a new document called SCHOOL.
   f. Write down how many files are on the simulated disk and the exact contents of each file.
   g. Delete all the files.

3. In Explore, use the simulated computer to perform the following tasks.
   a. Create a file called MUSIC that contains the name of your favorite CD.
   b. Create another document that contains eight numbers and call this file LOTTERY.
   c. You didn't win the lottery this week. Revise the contents of the LOTTERY file, but save the revision as LOTTERY2.
   d. Revise the MUSIC file so that it also contains the name of your favorite musician or composer, and save this file as MUSIC2.
   e. Delete the MUSIC file.
   f. Write down how many files are on the simulated disk and the exact contents of each file.

QUICK | CHECK ANSWERS

Session 2.1
1. file
2. Formatting
3. True
4. insertion point
5. a list of recently opened files and objects
6. The Files of Type list box could be set to display files of a different type than the one you're looking for.
7. From the Print Preview window, using the Print button on the toolbar, and using the Print command from the File menu. If you want to print multiple copies of a file, use either the Print button from the Print Preview window or the Print command from the File menu—both of these techniques will display the Print dialog box containing the options you need to set.

Session 2.2
1. My Computer
2. A
3. hard
4. filename, size, type, and date modified
5. root or top-level
6. the Desktop
7. yes

New Perspectives on

MICROSOFT®
OFFICE XP

Read This Before You Begin

To the Student

Data Disks

To complete this tutorial and the Review Assignments, you need one Data Disk. Your instructor will either provide you with the Data Disk or ask you to make your own.

If you are making your own Data Disk, you will need **one** blank, formatted high-density disk. You will need to copy a set of files and/or folders from a file server, standalone computer, or the Web onto your disk. Your instructor will tell you which computer, drive letter, and folder contain the files you need. You could also download the files by going to www.course.com and following the instructions on the screen.

The information below shows you which folder goes on your disk, so that you will have enough disk space to complete the tutorial and Review Assignments:

Data Disk 1

Write this on the disk label:
Data Disk 1: Introducing Office XP

Put this folder on the disk:
Tutorial.01

When you begin the tutorial, be sure you are using the correct Data Disk. Refer to the "File Finder" chart at the back of this text for more detailed information on which files are used in the tutorial. See the inside front or inside back cover of this book for more information on Data Disk files, or ask your instructor or technical support person for assistance.

Using Your Own Computer

If you are going to work through this tutorial using your own computer, you need:

- **Computer System** Microsoft Windows 98, NT, 2000 Professional, or higher must be installed on your computer. This book assumes a typical installation of Microsoft Office XP.

- **Data Disk** You will not be able to complete this tutorial or Review Assignments using your own computer until you have your Data Disk.

Visit Our World Wide Web Site

Additional materials designed especially for you are available on the World Wide Web.
Go to www.course.com/NewPerspectives.

To the Instructor

The Data Disk Files are available on the Instructor's Resource Kit for this title. Follow the instructions in the Help file on the CD-ROM to install the programs to your network or standalone computer. For information on creating the Data Disk, see the "To the Student" section above.

You are granted a license to copy the Data Disk Files to any computer or computer network used by students who have purchased this book.

OBJECTIVES

In this tutorial you will:

- Explore the programs that comprise Microsoft Office

- Explore the benefits of integrating data between programs

- Start programs and switch between them

- Use personalized menus and toolbars

- Save and close a file

- Open an existing file

- Print a file

- Get Help

- Close files and exit programs

INTRODUCING MICROSOFT OFFICE XP

Preparing Promotional Materials for Delmar Office Supplies

CASE

Delmar Office Supplies

Delmar Office Supplies, a company in Wisconsin founded by Nicole Delmar in 1996, sells recycled office supplies to businesses and home-based offices around the world. The demand for quality recycled papers, reconditioned toner cartridges, and renovated office furniture has been growing each year. Nicole and all her employees use Microsoft Office XP, which provides everyone in the company the power and flexibility to store a variety of information, create consistent documents, and share data. In this tutorial, you'll review some of the latest documents the company's employees have created using Microsoft Office XP.

Exploring **Microsoft Office XP**

Microsoft Office XP, or simply **Office**, is a collection of the most popular Microsoft programs: Word, Excel, PowerPoint, Access, and Outlook. Each Office program contains valuable tools to help you accomplish many tasks, such as composing reports, analyzing data, preparing presentations, and compiling information.

Microsoft Word 2002, or simply **Word**, is a **word processing program** you use to create text documents. The files you create in Word are called **documents**. Word offers many special features that help you compose and update all types of documents, ranging from letters and newsletters to reports, fliers, faxes, and even books—all in attractive and readable formats. You also can use Word to create, insert, and position figures, tables, and other graphics to enhance the look of your documents. Figure 1 shows a business letter that a sales representative composed with Word.

Figure 1	LETTER COMPOSED IN A WORD DOCUMENT

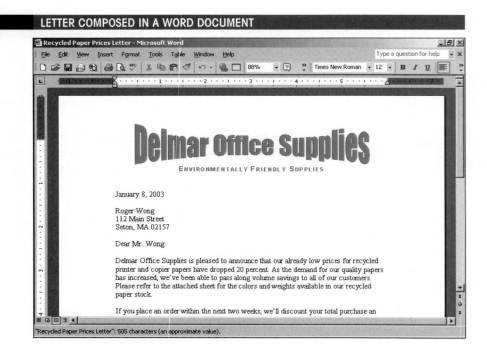

Microsoft Excel 2002, or simply **Excel**, is a **spreadsheet program** you use to display, organize, and analyze numerical information. You can do some of this in Word with tables, but Excel provides many more tools for performing calculations than Word does. Its graphics capabilities also enable you to display data visually. You might, for example, generate a pie chart or bar chart to help readers quickly see the significance of and the connections between information. The files you create in Excel are called **workbooks**. Figure 2 shows an Excel workbook with a line chart that the Operations Department uses to track the company's financial performance.

Figure 2 FINANCIAL DATA IN AN EXCEL WORKBOOK

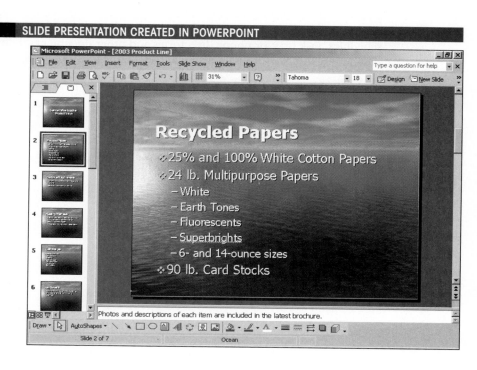

Microsoft PowerPoint 2002, or simply **PowerPoint**, is a **presentation graphics program** you use to create a collection of "slides" that can contain text, charts, pictures, and so on. The files you create in PowerPoint are called **presentations**. You can show these presentations on your computer monitor, project them onto a screen as a slide show, print them, share them over the Internet, or display them on the World Wide Web. You also can use PowerPoint to generate presentation-related documents such as audience handouts, outlines, and speakers' notes. Figure 3 shows an effective slide presentation the Sales Department created with PowerPoint to promote the latest product line.

Figure 3 SLIDE PRESENTATION CREATED IN POWERPOINT

Microsoft Access 2002, or simply **Access**, is a **database program** you use to enter, organize, display, and retrieve related information. The files you create in Access are called **databases**. With Access you can create data entry forms to make data entry easier, and you can create professional reports to improve the readability of your data. Figure 4 shows a table in an Access database with customer names and addresses compiled by the Sales Department.

Figure 4	CUSTOMER ADDRESSES COMPILED IN AN ACCESS DATABASE

Microsoft Access - [Shipping Information : Table]

File   Edit   View   Insert   Format   Records   Tools   Window   Help   Type a question for help

Customer Num	Name	Street	City	State/Prov	Postal Code
201	Wonder Supplies	5499 Alpine Lane	Gardner	MA	01440
285	The Best Supplies	2837 Commonwealth Avenue	Cambridge	MA	02142
129	Office World	95 North Bay Boulevard	Warwick	RI	02287
135	Supplies Plus	2840 Cascade Road	Laconia	NH	03246
104	American Office	Pond Hill Road	Millinocket	ME	04462
515	Pens and Paper	8200 Baldwin Boulevard	Burlington	VT	05406
165	Pen and Ink	1935 Snow Street	Nagatuck	CT	06770
423	Wonderful World of Work	H 1055	Budapest	Hungary	1/A
83	Sophia's Supplies	87 Weeping Willow Road	Brooklyn	NY	11201
17	Supplies and More	132-A Old Country Road	Bellport	NY	11763
322	Supply Closet	114 Lexington	Plattsburgh	NY	12901
302	Blackburg's Stationers	4489 Perlman Avenue	Blacksburg	VA	24060
136	Home Office Needs	4090 Division Stret NW	Fort Lauderdale	FL	33302
131	Supplies 4 U	14832 Old Bedford Trail	Mishawaka	IN	46544
122	VIP Stationery	8401 E. Fletcher Road	Clare	MI	48617
164	Supply Depot	1355 39th Street	Roscommon	MI	48653
325	Max Office Supplies	56 Four Mile Road	Grand Rapids	MI	49505
133	Supply Your Office	2874 Western Avenue	Sioux Falls	SD	57057
107	A+ Supplies	82 Mix Avenue	Bonners Ferry	ID	83805
203	Discount Supplies	28320 Fruitland Street	Studio City	CA	94106
536	One Stop Shop	31 Union Street	San Francisco	CA	94123
82	Supply Stop	2159 Causewayside	Edinburgh	Scotland	EH9 1PH
202	Office Products	3130 Edgwood Parkway	Thunder Bay	Ontario	L5B 1X2
407	Paper and More	44 Tower Lane	Leeds	England	LS12 3SD
394	The Office Store	397 Pine Road	Toronto	Ontario	M4J1B5

Record: 1 of 25

Datasheet View   NUM

Microsoft Outlook 2002, or simply **Outlook**, is an **information management program** you use to send, receive, and organize e-mail; plan your schedule; arrange meetings; organize contacts; create a to-do list; and jot down notes. You also can use Outlook to print schedules, task lists, or phone directories and other documents. Figure 5 shows how Nicole Delmar uses Outlook to plan her schedule and create a to-do list.

Figure 5   **CALENDAR AND TASKS IN OUTLOOK**

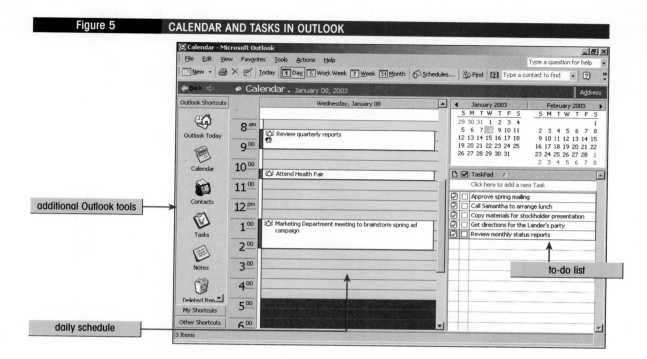

additional Outlook tools

to-do list

daily schedule

Although each Office program individually is a strong tool, their potential is even greater when used together.

Integrating Programs

One of the main advantages of Office is **integration**, the ability to share information between programs. Integration ensures consistency and accuracy, and it saves time because you don't have to re-enter the same information in several Office programs. The staff at Delmar Office Supplies uses the integration features of Office daily, including the following examples:

■ The Accounting Department created an Excel bar chart on the last two years' fourth-quarter results, which they inserted into the quarterly financial report, created in Word. They added a hyperlink to the Word report that employees can click to open the Excel workbook and view the original data. See Figure 6.

Figure 6 | **WORD DOCUMENT WITH AN EXCEL CHART**

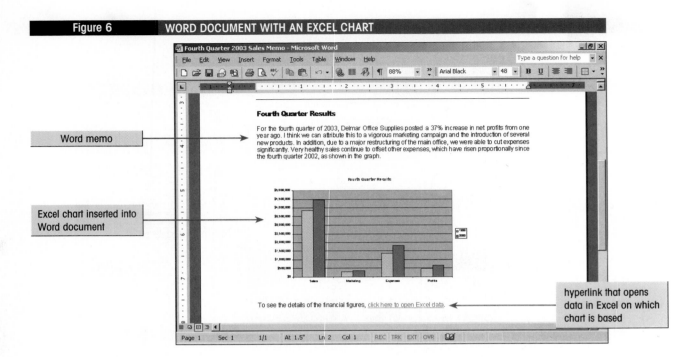

Word memo

Excel chart inserted into Word document

hyperlink that opens data in Excel on which chart is based

■ An Excel pie chart of sales percentages by divisions of Delmar Office Supplies can be duplicated on a PowerPoint slide. The slide is part of the Operations Department's presentation to stockholders. See Figure 7.

Figure 7 | **POWERPOINT PRESENTATION WITH AN EXCEL CHART**

PowerPoint slide

pie chart created in Excel

■ An Access database or an Outlook contact list that stores the names and addresses of customers can be combined with a form letter that the Marketing Department created in Word, to produce a mailing promoting the company's newest products. See Figure 8.

Figure 8   **WORD LETTER WITH ACCESS OR OUTLOOK DATA**

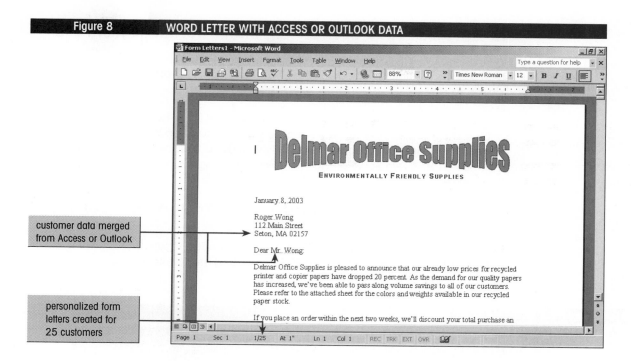

customer data merged
from Access or Outlook

personalized form
letters created for
25 customers

These are just a few examples of how you can take information from one Office program and integrate it into another.

Starting Office Programs

All Office programs start the same way—from the Programs menu on the Start button. You select the program you want, and then the program starts so you can immediately begin to create new files or work with existing ones.

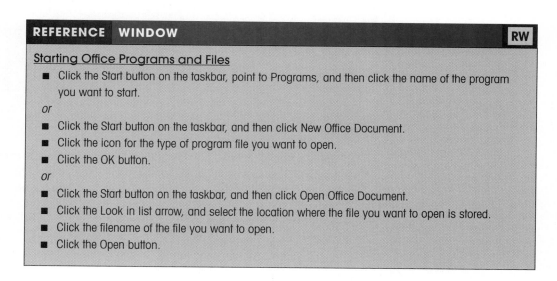

REFERENCE WINDOW   **RW**

Starting Office Programs and Files

- Click the Start button on the taskbar, point to Programs, and then click the name of the program you want to start.

or

- Click the Start button on the taskbar, and then click New Office Document.
- Click the icon for the type of program file you want to open.
- Click the OK button.

or

- Click the Start button on the taskbar, and then click Open Office Document.
- Click the Look in list arrow, and select the location where the file you want to open is stored.
- Click the filename of the file you want to open.
- Click the Open button.

You'll start Excel using the Start button.

To start Excel and open a new, blank workbook from the Start menu:

1. Make sure your computer is on and the Windows desktop appears on your screen.

   TROUBLE? Don't worry if your screen differs slightly from those shown in the figures. The figures in this book were created while running Windows 2000 in its default settings, but Office runs equally well using Windows 98 or later or Windows NT 4 with Service Pack 5. These operating systems share the same basic user interface.

2. Click the **Start** button on the taskbar, and then point to **Programs** to display the Programs menu.

3. Point to **Microsoft Excel** on the Programs menu. See Figure 9. Depending on how your computer is set up, your desktop and menu might contain different icons and commands.

Figure 9	START MENU WITH PROGRAMS MENU DISPLAYED

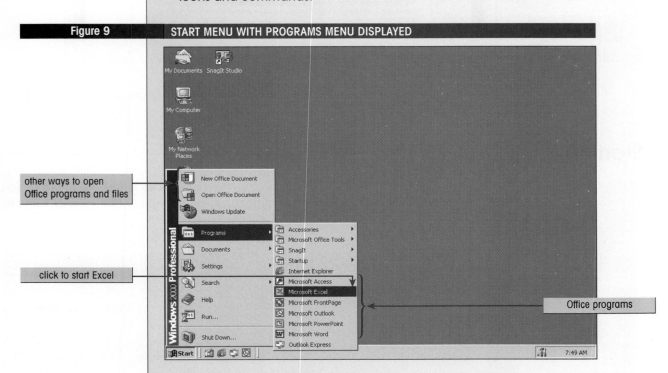

other ways to open Office programs and files

click to start Excel

Office programs

TROUBLE? If you don't see Microsoft Excel on the Programs menu, point to Microsoft Office, and then point to Microsoft Excel. If you still don't see Microsoft Excel, ask your instructor or technical support person for help.

4. Click **Microsoft Excel** to start Excel and open a new, blank workbook. See Figure 10.

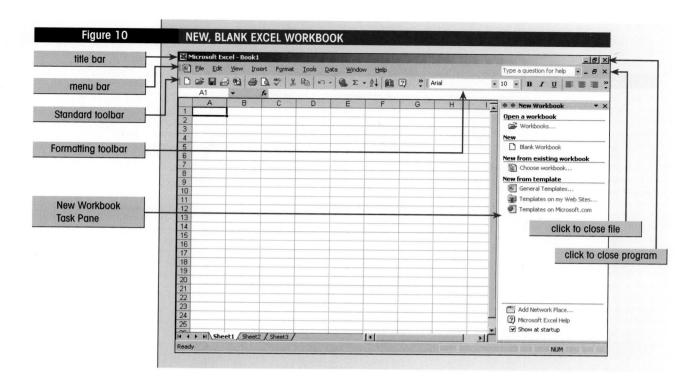

Figure 10   **NEW, BLANK EXCEL WORKBOOK**

- title bar
- menu bar
- Standard toolbar
- Formatting toolbar
- New Workbook Task Pane
- click to close file
- click to close program

An alternate method for starting programs with a blank file is to click the New Office Document command on the Start menu; the kind of file you choose determines which program opens. You'll use this method to start Word and open a new, blank document.

To start Word and open a new, blank document with the New Office Document command:

1. Leaving Excel open, click the **Start** button on the taskbar, and then click **New Office Document**. The New Office Document dialog box opens, providing another way to start Office programs. See Figure 11.

Figure 11   **NEW OFFICE DOCUMENT DIALOG BOX**

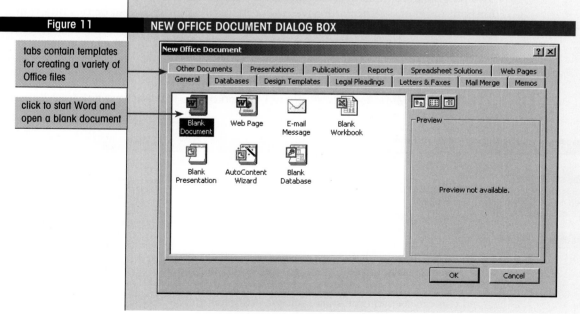

- tabs contain templates for creating a variety of Office files
- click to start Word and open a blank document

2. If necessary, click the **General** tab, click the **Blank Document** icon, and then click the **OK** button. Word opens with a new, blank document. See Figure 12.

Figure 12	NEW, BLANK DOCUMENT IN WORD

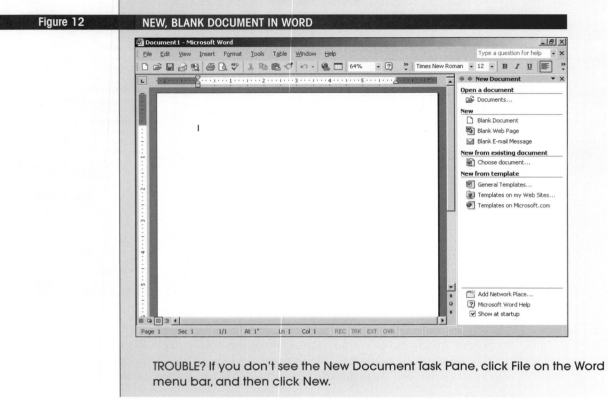

TROUBLE? If you don't see the New Document Task Pane, click File on the Word menu bar, and then click New.

You've tried two ways to start a program. There are several methods for performing most tasks in Office. This flexibility enables you to use Office in the way that fits how you like to work.

Switching Between Open Programs and Files

Two programs are running at the same time—Excel and Word. The taskbar contains buttons for both programs. When you have two or more programs running, or two files within the same program open, you can use the taskbar buttons to switch from one program or file to another. The employees at Delmar Office Supplies often work in several programs at once.

To switch between Word and Excel:

1. Click the **Microsoft Excel – Book1** button on the taskbar to switch from Word to Excel. See Figure 13.

Figure 13	EXCEL AND WORD PROGRAMS OPENED

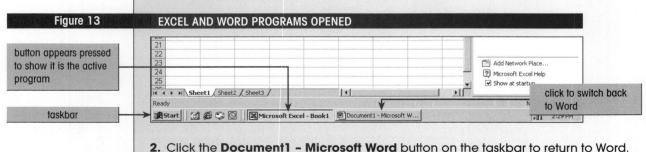

2. Click the **Document1 – Microsoft Word** button on the taskbar to return to Word.

As you can see, you can start multiple programs and switch between them in seconds.

The Office programs also share many features, so once you've learned one program, it's easy to learn the others. One of the most visible similarities among all the programs is the "personalized" menus and toolbars.

Using **Personalized Menus and Toolbars**

In each Office program, you perform tasks using a menu command, a toolbar button, or a keyboard shortcut. A **menu command** is a word on a menu that you click to execute a task; a **menu** is a group of related commands. For example, the File menu contains commands for managing files, such as the Open command and the Save command. A **toolbar** is a collection of **buttons** that correspond to commonly used menu commands. For example, the Standard toolbar contains an Open button and a Save button. **Keyboard shortcuts** are combinations of keys you press to perform a command. For example, Ctrl+S is the keyboard shortcut for the Save command (you hold down the Ctrl key while you press the S key). Keyboard shortcuts are displayed to the right of many menu commands.

When you first use a newly installed Office program, the menus and toolbars display only the basic and most commonly used commands and buttons, streamlining the program window. The other commands and buttons are available, but you have to click an extra button to see them (the double-arrow button on a menu and the Toolbar Options button on a toolbar). As you select commands and click buttons, the ones you use often are put on the short, personalized menu and on the visible part of the toolbars. The ones you don't use remain available on the full menus and toolbars. This means that the Office menus and toolbars might display different commands and buttons on each person's computer.

To view a personalized and full menu:

1. Click **Insert** on the Word menu bar to display the short, personalized menu. See Figure 14. The Bookmark command, for example, does not appear on the short menu.

| Figure 14 | SHORT, PERSONALIZED MENU |

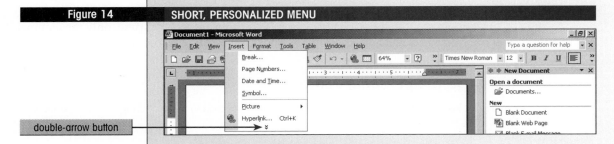

double-arrow button

TROUBLE? If the Insert menu displays different commands than shown in Figure 14, you need to reset the menus. Click Tools on the menu bar, click Customize (you might need to pause until the full menu appears to see that command), and then click the Options tab in the Customize dialog box. Click the Always show full menus check box to remove the check mark if necessary, and then click the Show full menus after a short delay check box to insert a check mark if necessary. Click the Reset my usage data button, and then click the Yes button to confirm that you want to reset the commands. Click the Close button. Repeat Step 1.

You can display the full menu in one of three ways: (1) pause until the full menu appears, which might happen as you read this; (2) click the double-arrow button at the bottom of the menu; or (3) double-click the menu name on the menu bar.

2. Pause until the full Insert menu appears, as shown in Figure 15. The Bookmark command and other commands are now visible.

Figure 15	EXPANDED, FULL MENU

commands with light border appear on short menu

commands with dark border appear only on full menu

3. Click the **Bookmark** command. A dialog box opens when you click a command whose name is followed by an ellipsis (...). In this case, the Bookmark dialog box opens.

4. Click the **Cancel** button to close the Bookmark dialog box.

5. Click **Insert** on the menu bar again to display the short, personalized menu. The Bookmark command appears on the short, personalized menu because you used it.

6. Press the **Esc** key to close the menu.

As you can see, the menu changed based on your actions. Over time, only the commands you use frequently will appear on the personalized menu. The toolbars work similarly.

To use the personalized toolbars:

1. Observe that the Standard and Formatting toolbars appear side by side below the menu bar.

TROUBLE? If the toolbars appear on two rows, you need to reset them. Click Tools on the menu bar, click Customize, and then click the Options tab in the Customize dialog box. Click the Show Standard and Formatting toolbars on two rows check box to remove the check mark. Click the Reset my data usage button, and then click the Yes button to confirm you want to reset the commands. Click the Close button. Repeat Step 1.

The Formatting toolbar sits to the right of the Standard toolbar. You can see most of the Standard toolbar buttons, but only a few Formatting toolbar buttons.

2. Click the **Toolbar Options** button at the right side of the Standard toolbar. See Figure 16.

Figure 16 TOOLBAR OPTIONS LIST

Toolbar Options button

Bullets button

click to move toolbars onto separate rows

drag from here to resize side-by-side toolbars

TROUBLE? If you see different buttons on the Toolbar Options list, your side-by-side toolbars might be resized differently than the ones shown in Figure 16. Continue with Step 3.

3. Click the **Bullets** button. The Bullets button moves to the visible part of the Formatting toolbar, and another button is moved onto the Toolbar Options list to make room for the new button.

TROUBLE? If the Bullets button already appears on the Formatting toolbar, click another button on the Toolbar Options list. Then click that same button again in Step 4 to turn off that formatting.

4. Click again to turn off the Bullets formatting.

Some people like that the menus and toolbars change to meet their work habits. Others prefer to see all the menu commands or to display the toolbars on different rows so that all the buttons are always visible. You'll change the toolbar setting now.

To turn off the personalized toolbars:

1. Click the **Toolbar Options** button at the right side of the Standard toolbar.

2. Click the **Show Buttons on Two Rows command**. The toolbars move to separate rows (the Standard toolbar on top) and you can see all the buttons on each toolbar.

You can easily access any button on the toolbars with one mouse click. The drawback is that the toolbars take up more space in the program window.

Using Speech Recognition

Another way to perform tasks in Office is with your voice. Office's **speech recognition technology** enables you to say the names of the toolbar buttons, menus, menu commands, dialog box items, and so forth, rather than clicking the mouse or pressing keys to select them. The Language toolbar includes the Speech Balloon, which displays the voice command equivalents of a selected button or command. If you switch from Voice mode to Dictation mode, you can dictate the contents of your files rather than typing the text or numbers. For better accuracy, complete the Training Wizard, which helps Office learn your vocal quality, rate of talking, and speech patterns. To start using speech recognition, click Tools on the menu bar in any Office program, and then click Speech. The first time you start this feature, the Training Wizard guides you through the setup process.

Saving and Closing a File

As you create and modify Office files, your work is stored only in the computer's temporary memory, not on disk. If you were to exit the programs, turn off your computer, or experience a power failure, your work would be lost. To prevent losing work, frequently save your file to a disk—at least every ten minutes. You can save files to the hard disk located inside your computer or to portable storage disks, such as CD-ROMs, Zip disks, or floppy disks.

The first time you save a file, you need to name it. This name is called a **filename**. When you choose a filename, select a descriptive one that accurately reflects the content of the document, workbook, presentation, or database, such as "Shipping Options Letter" or "Fourth Quarter Financial Analysis." Filenames can include a maximum of 255 letters, numbers, hyphens, or spaces in any combination. Office appends a **file extension** to the filename, which identifies the program in which that file was created. The file extensions are .doc for Word, .xls for Excel, .ppt for PowerPoint, and .mdb for Access. Whether you see file extensions depends on how Windows is set up for your computer.

You also need to decide where you'll save the file—on which disk and in what folder. Choose a logical location that you'll remember whenever you want to use the file again.

REFERENCE WINDOW   **RW**

Saving a File
- Click the Save button on the Standard toolbar (*or* click File on the menu bar, and then click Save or Save As).
- Click the Save in list arrow, and then select the location where you want to save the file.
- Type a filename in the File name text box.
- Click the Save button.
- To resave the named file to the same location, click the Save button on the Standard toolbar (*or* click File on the menu bar, and then click Save).

Nicole has asked you to start working on the agenda for the stockholder meeting. You enter text in a Word document by typing. After you type some text, you'll save the file.

To enter text in a document:

1. Type **Delmar Office Supplies**, and then press the **Enter** key. The text you typed appears on one line in the Word document.

   TROUBLE? If you make a typing error, press the Backspace key to delete the incorrect letters, and then retype the text.

2. Type **Stockholder Meeting Agenda**, and then press the **Enter** key. The text you typed appears on the second line.

The two lines of text you typed are not yet saved on disk. You'll do that now.

To save a file for the first time:

1. Insert your Data Disk in the appropriate drive.

> **TROUBLE?** If you don't have a Data Disk, you need to get one before you can proceed. Your instructor or technical support person will either give you one or ask you to make your own by following the instructions on the "Read This Before You Begin" page at the beginning of this tutorial. See your instructor or technical support person for more information.

2. Click the **Save** button 🖫 on the Standard toolbar. The Save As dialog box opens. See Figure 17. The first few words of the first line appear in the File name text box, as a suggested filename. You'll replace this with a more descriptive filename.

Figure 17	SAVE AS DIALOG BOX

location where file will be saved; click arrow to choose another location

folder within selected location

shortcuts to locations on your computer

type filename here

> **TROUBLE?** If the .doc file extension appears after the filename, then your computer is configured to show file extensions. Just continue with Step 3.

3. Type **Stockholder Meeting Agenda** in the File name text box.

4. Click the **Save in** list arrow, and then click the drive that contains your Data Disk.

5. Double-click the **Tutorial.01** folder in the list box, and then double-click the **Tutorial** folder. This is the location where you want to save the document.

6. Click the **Save** button. The Save As dialog box closes, and the name of your file appears in the program window title bar.

The saved file includes everything in the document at the time you saved. Any edits or additions you then make to the document exist only in the computer's memory and are not saved in the file on the disk. As you work, remember to save frequently so that the file is updated to reflect the latest content of the document.

Because you already named the document and selected a storage location, the second and subsequent times you save, the Save As dialog box doesn't open. If you wanted to save a copy of the file with a different filename or to a different location, you would reopen the Save As dialog box by clicking File on the menu bar, and then clicking Save As. The previous version of the file remains on your disk as well.

You need to add your name to the agenda. Then you'll save your changes and close the file. You can close a file by clicking the Close command on the File menu or by clicking the Close Window button in the upper-right corner of the menu bar.

> ### To modify, save, and close a file:
>
> **1.** Type your name, and then press the **Enter** key. The text you typed appears on the next line.
>
> **2.** Click the **Save** button on the Standard toolbar.
>
> The updated document is saved to the file. When you're done with a file, you can close it. Although you can keep multiple files open at one time, you should close any file you are no longer working on to conserve system resources.
>
> **3.** Click the **Close Window** button ☒ on the Word menu bar to close the document. Word is still running, but no documents are open.
>
> TROUBLE? If a dialog box opens and asks whether you want to save the changes you made to the document, you modified the document since you last saved. Click the Yes button to save the current version and close it.

Opening a File

Once you have a program open, you can create additional new files for the open programs or you can open previously created and saved files. You can do both of these from the New Task Pane. The New Task Pane enables you to create new files and open existing ones. The name of the Task Pane varies, depending on the program you are using: Word has the New Document Task Pane, Excel has the New Workbook Task Pane, PowerPoint has the New Presentation Task Pane, and Access has the New File Task Pane.

When you want to work on a previously created file, you must open it first. Opening a file transfers a copy of the file from the storage disk (either a hard disk or a portable disk) to the computer's memory and displays it on your screen. The file is then in your computer's memory and on the disk.

> **REFERENCE WINDOW** **RW**
>
> <u>Opening an Existing or New File</u>
> - Click File on the menu bar, click New, and then (depending on the program) click the More documents, More workbooks, More presentations, or More files link in the New Task Pane (*or* click the Open button on the Standard toolbar *or* click File on the menu bar, and then click Open).
> - Click the Look in list arrow, and then select the storage location of the file you want to open.
> - Click the filename of the file you want to open.
> - Click the Open button.
> *or*
> - Click File on the menu bar, click New, and then (depending on the program) click the Blank Document, Blank Workbook, Blank Presentation, or Blank Database link in the New Task Pane (*or* click the New button on the Standard toolbar).

Nicole asks you to print the agenda. To do that, you'll reopen the file. Because Word is still open, you'll use the New Document Task Pane.

To open an existing file:

1. If necessary, click **File** on the menu bar, and then click **New** to display the New Document Task Pane. See Figure 18.

Figure 18	NEW DOCUMENT TASK PANE

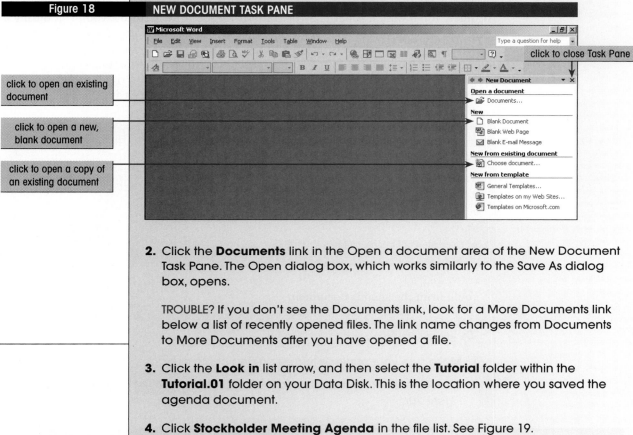

click to open an existing document

click to open a new, blank document

click to open a copy of an existing document

click to close Task Pane

2. Click the **Documents** link in the Open a document area of the New Document Task Pane. The Open dialog box, which works similarly to the Save As dialog box, opens.

   TROUBLE? If you don't see the Documents link, look for a More Documents link below a list of recently opened files. The link name changes from Documents to More Documents after you have opened a file.

3. Click the **Look in** list arrow, and then select the **Tutorial** folder within the **Tutorial.01** folder on your Data Disk. This is the location where you saved the agenda document.

4. Click **Stockholder Meeting Agenda** in the file list. See Figure 19.

Figure 19	OPEN DIALOG BOX

files in this folder are displayed below

agenda file to open and print

---

5. Click the **Open** button. The file you saved earlier reopens in the Word program window, and the New Document Task Pane closes.

After the file is open, you can view, edit, print, or resave it.

Printing a File

At times, you'll want a paper copy of your Office file. The first time you print during each computer session, you should use the Print menu command to open the Print dialog box so you can verify or adjust the printing settings. You can select a printer, the number of copies to print, the portion of the file to print, and so forth; the printing settings vary slightly from program to program. For subsequent print jobs you can use the Print button to print without opening the dialog box, if you want to use the same default settings.

REFERENCE WINDOW	RW

Printing a File
- Click File on the menu bar, and then click Print.
- Verify the print settings in the Print dialog box.
- Click the OK button.

or
- Click the Print button on the Standard toolbar.

You'll print the agenda document.

To print a file:

1. Make sure your printer is turned on and contains paper.

2. Click **File** on the menu bar, and then click **Print**. The Print dialog box opens. See Figure 20.

Figure 20   PRINT DIALOG BOX

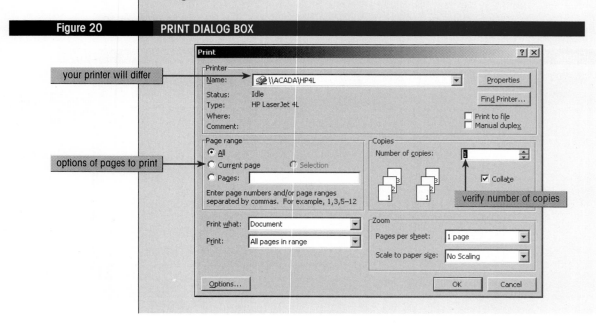

3. Verify that the correct printer appears in the Name list box. If the wrong printer appears, click the **Name** list arrow, and then click the correct printer from the list of available printers.

4. Verify that **1** appears in the Number of copies text box.

5. Click the **OK** button to print the document. See Figure 21.

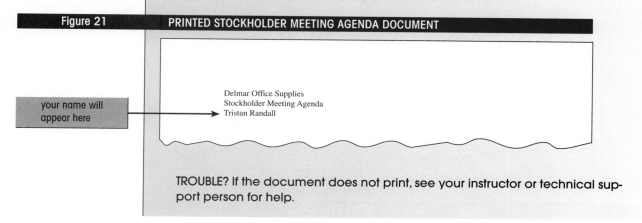

| Figure 21 | PRINTED STOCKHOLDER MEETING AGENDA DOCUMENT |

your name will appear here

Delmar Office Supplies
Stockholder Meeting Agenda
Tristan Randall

TROUBLE? If the document does not print, see your instructor or technical support person for help.

Another important aspect of Office is the ability to get help right from your computer.

Getting Help

If you don't know how to perform a task or want more information about a feature, you can turn to Office itself for information on how to use it. This information, referred to simply as **Help**, is like a huge encyclopedia stored on your computer. You can access it in a variety of ways.

There are two fast and simple methods you can use to get Help about objects you see on the screen. First, you can position the mouse pointer over a toolbar button to view its **ScreenTip**, a yellow box with the button's name. Second, you can click the **What's This?** command on the Help menu to change the pointer to ⌖?, which you can click on any toolbar button, menu command, dialog box option, worksheet cell, or anything else you can see on your screen to view a brief description of that item.

For more in-depth help, you can use the **Ask a Question** box, located on the menu bar of every Office program, to find information in the Help system. You simply type a question using everyday language about a task you want to perform or a topic you need help with, and then press the Enter key to search the Help system. The Ask a Question box expands to show Help topics related to your query. You click a topic to open a Help window with step-by-step instructions that guide you through a specific procedure and explanations of difficult concepts in clear, easy-to-understand language. For example, you might ask how to format a cell in an Excel worksheet; a list of Help topics related to the words you typed will appear. The Help window also has Contents, Answer Wizard, and Index tabs, which you can use to look up information directly from the Help window.

If you prefer, you can ask questions of the **Office Assistant**, an interactive guide to finding information from the Help system. In addition, the Office Assistant can provide Help topics and tips on tasks as you work. For example, it might offer a tip when you select a menu command instead of clicking the corresponding toolbar button. You can turn on or off the tips, depending on your personal preference.

REFERENCE WINDOW   RW

Getting Help from the Ask a Question Box
- Click in the Ask a Question box on the menu bar.
- Type your question, and then press the Enter key.
- Click a Help topic.
- Read the information in the Help window. For more information, click other topics or links.
- Click the Close button in the Help window title bar.

You'll use the Ask a Question box to obtain more information about Help.

To use the Ask a Question box:

1. Click in the **Ask a Question** box on the menu bar, and then type **How do I search help?**.

2. Press the **Enter** key to retrieve a list of topics, as shown in Figure 22.

Figure 22   ASK A QUESTION BOX WITH HELP TOPICS

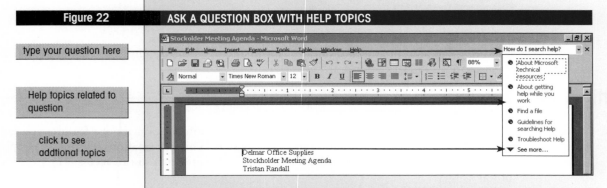

type your question here

Help topics related to question

click to see addtional topics

3. Click the **See more** link, review the additional Help topics, and then click the **See previous** link.

4. Click **About getting help while you work** to open the Help window and learn more about the various ways to obtain assistance in Office. See Figure 23.

Figure 23   HELP WINDOW

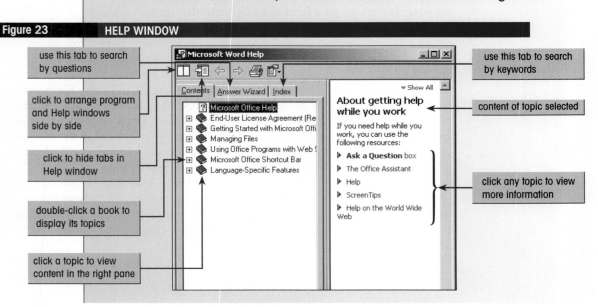

use this tab to search by questions

click to arrange program and Help windows side by side

click to hide tabs in Help window

double-click a book to display its topics

click a topic to view content in the right pane

use this tab to search by keywords

content of topic selected

click any topic to view more information

5. Click **Help** in the right pane to display information about that topic.

6. Click the other links about Help features and read the information.

7. When you're done, click the **Close** button ☒ in the Help window title bar to return to the Word window.

The Help features enable the staff at Delmar Office Supplies to get answers to questions they have about any task or procedure when they need it. The more you practice getting information from the Help system, the more effective you will be at using Office to its full potential.

Exiting Programs

Whenever you finish working with a program, you should exit it. As with many other aspects of Office, you can exit programs with a button or from a menu. You'll use both methods to close Word and Excel.

To exit a program:

1. Click the **Close** button ☒ in the upper-right corner of the screen to exit Word. Word exits, and the Excel window is visible again on your screen.

   TROUBLE? If a dialog box opens, asking whether you want to save the document, you may have inadvertently made a change to the document. Click the No button.

2. Click **File** on the menu bar, and then click **Exit**. The Excel program exits.

Exiting programs after you are done using them keeps your Windows desktop uncluttered for the next person using the computer, frees up your system's resources, and prevents data from being lost accidentally.

QUICK CHECK

1. Which Office program would you use to write a letter?
2. Which Office programs could you use to store customer names and addresses?
3. What is integration?
4. Explain the difference between Save As and Save.
5. What is the purpose of the New Task Pane?
6. When would you use the Ask a Question box?

REVIEW ASSIGNMENTS

Before the stockholders meeting at Delmar Office Supplies, you'll open and print documents for the upcoming presentation.

1. Start PowerPoint using the Start button and the Programs menu.

2. Use the Ask a Question box to learn how to change the toolbar buttons from small to large, and then do it. Use the same procedure to change the buttons back to regular size. Close the Help window when you're done.

3. Open a blank Excel workbook using the New Office Document command on the Start menu.

Explore

4. Switch to the PowerPoint window using the taskbar, and then close the presentation but leave open the PowerPoint program. (*Hint:* Click the Close Window button in the menu bar.)

Explore

5. Open a new, blank PowerPoint presentation from the New Presentation Task Pane. (*Hint:* Click Blank Presentation in the New area of the New Presentation Task Pane.)

6. Close the PowerPoint presentation and program using the Close button in the PowerPoint title bar; do not save changes if asked.

Explore

7. Open a copy of the Excel **Finances** workbook located in the **Review** folder within the **Tutorial.01** folder on your Data Disk using the New Workbook Task Pane. (*Hint:* Click File on the Excel menu bar and then click New to open the Task Pane. Click Choose Workbook in the New from existing workbook area of the New Workbook Task Pane; the dialog box functions similarly to the Open dialog box.)

8. Type your name, and then press the Enter key to insert your name at the top of the worksheet.

9. Save the worksheet as **Delmar Finances** in the **Review** folder within the **Tutorial.01** folder on your Data Disk.

10. Print one copy of the worksheet using the Print command on the File menu.

11. Exit Excel using the File menu.

Explore

12. Open the **Letter** document located in the **Review** folder within the **Tutorial.01** folder on your Data Disk using the Open Office Document command on the Start menu.

13. Use the Save As command to save the document with the filename **Delmar Letter** in the **Review** folder within the **Tutorial.01** folder on your Data Disk.

Explore

14. Press and hold the Ctrl key, press the End key, and then release both keys to move the insertion point to the end of the letter, and then type your name.

15. Use the Save button on the Standard toolbar to save the change to the Delmar Letter document.

16. Print one copy of the document, and then close the document.

17. Exit the Word program using the Close button on the title bar.

QUICK CHECK ANSWERS

1. Word
2. Access or Outlook
3. the ability to share information between programs
4. Save As enables you to change the filename and save location of a file. Save updates a file to reflect its latest contents using its current filename and location.
5. enables you to create new files and open existing files
6. when you don't know how to perform a task or want more information about a feature

New Perspectives on

MICROSOFT®
ACCESS 2002

Read This Before You Begin

To the Student

Data Disks

To complete the Level I tutorials, Review Assignments, and Case Problems, you need six Data Disks. Your instructor will either provide you with these Data Disks or ask you to make your own.

If you are making your own Data Disks, you will need **six** blank, formatted high-density disks. You will need to copy a set of files and/or folders from a file server, standalone computer, or the Web onto your disks. Your instructor will tell you which computer, drive letter, and folders contain the files you need. You could also download the files by going to **www.course.com** and following the instructions on the screen.

The information below shows you which folders go on each of your disks, so that you will have enough disk space to complete all the tutorials, Review Assignments, and Case Problems:

Data Disk 1
Write this on the disk label:
Data Disk 1: Access 2002 Tutorial Files
Put this folder on the disk:
Tutorial

Data Disk 2
Write this on the disk label:
Data Disk 2: Access 2002 Review Assignments
Put this folder on the disk:
Review

Data Disk 3
Write this on the disk label:
Data Disk 3: Access 2002 Case Problem 1
Put this folder on the disk:
Cases

Data Disk 4
Write this on the disk label:
Data Disk 4: Access 2002 Case Problem 2
Put this folder on the disk:
Cases

Data Disk 5
Write this on the disk label:
Data Disk 5: Access 2002 Case Problem 3
Put this folder on the disk:
Cases

Data Disk 6
Write this on the disk label:
Data Disk 6: Access 2002 Case Problem 4
Put this folder on the disk:
Cases

When you begin each tutorial, be sure you are using the correct Data Disk. Refer to the "File Finder" chart at the back of this text for more detailed information on which files are used in which tutorials, and make sure you carefully read the note above the chart. See the inside front or inside back cover of this book for more information on Data Disk files, or ask your instructor or technical support person for assistance.

Course Labs

The Access Level I tutorials feature an interactive Course Lab to help you understand database concepts. There are Lab Assignments at the end of Tutorial 1 that relate to this Lab.

To start a Lab, click the **Start** button on the Windows taskbar, point to **Programs**, point to **Course Labs**, point to **New Perspectives Course Labs**, and then click the name of the Lab you want to use.

Using Your Own Computer

If you are going to work through this book using your own computer, you need:

- **Computer System** Microsoft Windows 98, NT, 2000 Professional, or higher must be installed on your computer. This book assumes a typical installation of Microsoft Access.

- **Data Disks** You will not be able to complete the tutorials or exercises in this book using your own computer until you have your Data Disks.

- **Course Labs** See your instructor or technical support person to obtain the Course Lab software for use on your own computer.

Visit Our World Wide Web Site

Additional materials designed especially for you are available on the World Wide Web.
Go to www.course.com/NewPerspectives.

To the Instructor

The Data Disk Files and Course Labs are available on the Instructor's Resource Kit for this title. Follow the instructions in the Help file on the CD-ROM to install the programs to your network or standalone computer. For information on creating Data Disks or the Course Labs, see the "To the Student" section above.

You are granted a license to copy the Data Files and Course Labs to any computer or computer network used by students who have purchased this book.

OBJECTIVES

In this tutorial you will:

- Define the terms field, record, table, relational database, primary key, and foreign key

- Open an existing database

- Identify the components of the Access and Database windows

- Open and navigate a table

- Learn how Access saves a database

- Open an existing query, and create, sort, and navigate a new query

- Create and navigate a form

- Create, preview, and navigate a report

- Learn how to manage a database by backing up, restoring, compacting, and converting a database

LAB

Databases

INTRODUCTION
TO MICROSOFT
ACCESS 2002

*Viewing and Working with a Table
Containing Employer Data*

CASE

Northeast Seasonal Jobs International (NSJI)

During her high school and college years, Elsa Jensen spent her summers working as a lifeguard for some of the most popular beaches on Cape Cod, Massachusetts. Throughout those years, Elsa met many foreign students who had come to the United States to work for the summer, both at the beaches and at other seasonal businesses, such as restaurants and hotels. Elsa formed friendships with several students and kept in contact with them beyond college. Through discussions with her friends, Elsa realized that foreign students often have a difficult time finding appropriate seasonal work, relying mainly on "word-of-mouth" references to locate jobs. Elsa became convinced that there must be an easier way.

Several years ago, Elsa founded Northeast Seasonal Jobs, a small firm located in Boston that served as a job broker between foreign students seeking part-time, seasonal work and resort businesses located in New England. Recently Elsa expanded her business to include resorts in the eastern provinces of Canada, and consequently she changed her company's name to Northeast Seasonal Jobs International (NSJI). At first the company focused mainly on summer employment, but as the business continued to grow, Elsa increased the scope of operations to include all types of seasonal opportunities, including foliage tour companies in the fall and ski resorts in the winter.

Elsa depends on computers to help her manage all areas of NSJI's operations, including financial management, sales, and information management. Several months ago the company upgraded to Microsoft Windows and **Microsoft Access 2002** (or simply **Access**), a computer program used to enter, maintain, and retrieve related data in a format known as a database. Elsa and her staff use Access to maintain data such as information about employers, positions they have available for seasonal work, and foreign students seeking employment. Elsa recently created a database named Seasonal to track the company's employer customers and data about their available positions. She asks for your help in completing and maintaining this database.

SESSION 1.1

In this session, you will learn key database terms and concepts, open an existing database, identify components of the Access and Database windows, open and navigate a table, and learn how Access saves a database.

Introduction to Database Concepts

Before you begin working on Elsa's database and using Access, you need to understand a few key terms and concepts associated with databases.

Organizing Data

Data is a valuable resource to any business. At NSJI, for example, important data includes employers' names and addresses, and available positions and wages. Organizing, storing, maintaining, retrieving, and sorting this type of data are critical activities that enable a business to find and use information effectively. Before storing data on a computer, however, you first must organize the data.

Your first step in organizing data is to identify the individual fields. A **field** is a single characteristic or attribute of a person, place, object, event, or idea. For example, some of the many fields that NSJI tracks are employer ID, employer name, employer address, employer phone number, position, wage, and start date.

Next, you group related fields together into tables. A **table** is a collection of fields that describe a person, place, object, event, or idea. Figure 1-1 shows an example of an Employer table consisting of four fields: EmployerID, EmployerName, EmployerAddress, and PhoneNumber.

Figure 1-1	DATA ORGANIZATION FOR A TABLE OF EMPLOYERS

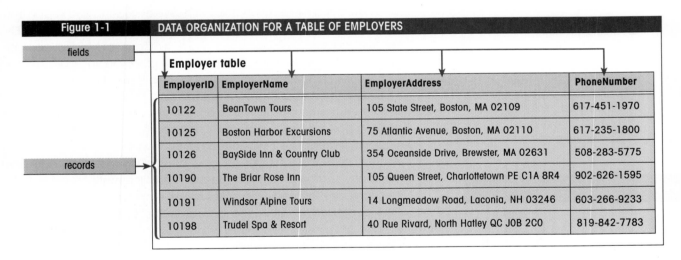

Employer table

EmployerID	EmployerName	EmployerAddress	PhoneNumber
10122	BeanTown Tours	105 State Street, Boston, MA 02109	617-451-1970
10125	Boston Harbor Excursions	75 Atlantic Avenue, Boston, MA 02110	617-235-1800
10126	BaySide Inn & Country Club	354 Oceanside Drive, Brewster, MA 02631	508-283-5775
10190	The Briar Rose Inn	105 Queen Street, Charlottetown PE C1A 8R4	902-626-1595
10191	Windsor Alpine Tours	14 Longmeadow Road, Laconia, NH 03246	603-266-9233
10198	Trudel Spa & Resort	40 Rue Rivard, North Hatley QC J0B 2C0	819-842-7783

The specific value, or content, of a field is called the **field value**. In Figure 1-1, the first set of field values for EmployerID, EmployerName, EmployerAddress, and PhoneNumber are, respectively: 10122; BeanTown Tours; 105 State Street, Boston, MA 02109; and 617-451-1970. This set of field values is called a **record**. In the Employer table, the data for each employer is stored as a separate record. Figure 1-1 shows six records; each row of field values is a record.

Databases and Relationships

A collection of related tables is called a **database**, or a **relational database**. NSJI's Seasonal database contains two related tables: the Employer and NAICS tables, which Elsa created. (The NAICS table contains North American Industry Classification System codes, which are used to classify businesses by the type of activity in which they are engaged.) In Tutorial 2, you will create a Position table to store information about the available positions at NSJI's employer clients.

Sometimes you might want information about employers and their available positions. To obtain this information, you must have a way to connect records in the Employer table to records in the Position table. You connect the records in the separate tables through a **common field** that appears in both tables.

In the sample database shown in Figure 1-2, each record in the Employer table has a field named EmployerID, which is also a field in the Position table. For example, BaySide Inn & Country Club is the third employer in the Employer table and has an EmployerID of 10126. This same EmployerID field value, 10126, appears in three records in the Position table. Therefore, BaySide Inn & Country Club is the employer with these three positions available.

| Figure 1-2 | DATABASE RELATIONSHIP BETWEEN TABLES FOR EMPLOYERS AND POSITIONS |

Employer table

EmployerID	EmployerName	EmployerAddress	PhoneNumber
10122	BeanTown Tours	105 State Street, Boston, MA 02109	617-451-1970
10125	Boston Harbor Excursions	75 Atlantic Avenue, Boston, MA 02110	617-235-1800
10126	BaySide Inn & Country Club	354 Oceanside Drive, Brewster, MA 02631	508-283-5775
10190	The Briar Rose Inn	105 Queen Street, Charlottetown PE C1A 8R4	902-626-1595
10191	Windsor Alpine Tours	14 Longmeadow Road, Laconia, NH 03246	603-266-9233
10198	Trudel Spa & Resort	40 Rue Rivard, North Hatley QC J0B 2C0	819-842-7783

primary keys

common field

three positions for BaySide Inn & Country Club

foreign key

Position table

PositionID	PositionTitle	EmployerID	Hours/Week
2040	Waiter/Waitress	10126	32
2045	Tour Guide	10122	24
2053	Host/Hostess	10190	24
2066	Lifeguard	10198	32
2073	Pro Shop Clerk	10126	24
2078	Ski Patrol	10191	30
2079	Day Care	10191	35
2082	Reservationist	10125	40
2111	Kitchen Help	10126	32

Each EmployerID in the Employer table must be unique, so that you can distinguish one employer from another and identify the employer's specific positions available in the Position table. The EmployerID field is referred to as the primary key of the Employer table. A **primary key** is a field, or a collection of fields, whose values uniquely identify each record in a table. In the Position table, PositionID is the primary key.

When you include the primary key from one table as a field in a second table to form a relationship between the two tables, it is called a **foreign key** in the second table, as shown in Figure 1-2. For example, EmployerID is the primary key in the Employer table and a foreign key in the Position table. Although the primary key EmployerID has unique values in the Employer table, the same field as a foreign key in the Position table does not have unique values. The EmployerID value 10126, for example, appears three times in the Position table because the BaySide Inn & Country Club has three available positions. Each foreign key value, however, must match one of the field values for the primary key in the other table. In the example shown in Figure 1-2, each EmployerID value in the Position table must match an EmployerID value in the Employer table. The two tables are related, enabling users to connect the facts about employers with the facts about their employment positions.

Relational Database Management Systems

To manage its databases, a company purchases a database management system. A **database management system (DBMS)** is a software program that lets you create databases and then manipulate data in them. Most of today's database management systems, including Access, are called relational database management systems. In a **relational database management system**, data is organized as a collection of tables. As stated earlier, a relationship between two tables in a relational DBMS is formed through a common field.

A relational DBMS controls the storage of databases on disk by carrying out data creation and manipulation requests. Specifically, a relational DBMS provides the following functions, which are illustrated in Figure 1-3:

- It allows you to create database structures containing fields, tables, and table relationships.
- It lets you easily add new records, change field values in existing records, and delete records.
- It contains a built-in query language, which lets you obtain immediate answers to the questions you ask about your data.
- It contains a built-in report generator, which lets you produce professional-looking, formatted reports from your data.
- It provides protection of databases through security, control, and recovery facilities.

| Figure 1-3 | RELATIONAL DATABASE MANAGEMENT SYSTEM |

A company such as NSJI benefits from a relational DBMS because it allows users working in different departments to share the same data. More than one user can enter data into a database, and more than one user can retrieve and analyze data that was entered by others. For example, NSJI will store only one copy of the Employer table, and all employees will be able to use it to meet their specific requests for employer information.

Finally, unlike other software programs, such as spreadsheets, a DBMS can handle massive amounts of data and can easily form relationships among multiple tables. Each Access database, for example, can be up to two gigabytes in size and can contain up to 32,768 objects (tables, queries, and so on).

Opening **an Existing Database**

Now that you've learned some database terms and concepts, you're ready to start Access and open the Seasonal database.

To start Access and open the Seasonal database:

1. Click the **Start** button on the taskbar, point to **Programs**, and then point to **Microsoft Access**. See Figure 1-4.

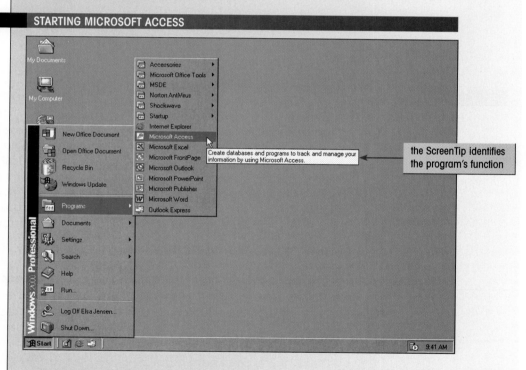

Figure 1-4   STARTING MICROSOFT ACCESS

the ScreenTip identifies the program's function

TROUBLE? If your screen differs slightly from the figure, don't worry. Although the figures in this tutorial were created on a computer running Windows 2000 in its default settings, the different Windows operating systems share the same basic user interface, and Microsoft Access runs equally well using Windows 98, Windows NT, or Windows 2000.

TROUBLE? If you don't see the Microsoft Access option on the Programs menu, you might need to click the double arrow on the Programs menu to display more options. If you still cannot find the Microsoft Access option, ask your instructor or technical support person for help.

2. Click **Microsoft Access** to start Access. After a short pause, the Access copyright information appears in a message box and remains on the screen until the Access window opens. See Figure 1-5.

| Figure 1-5 | MICROSOFT ACCESS WINDOW |

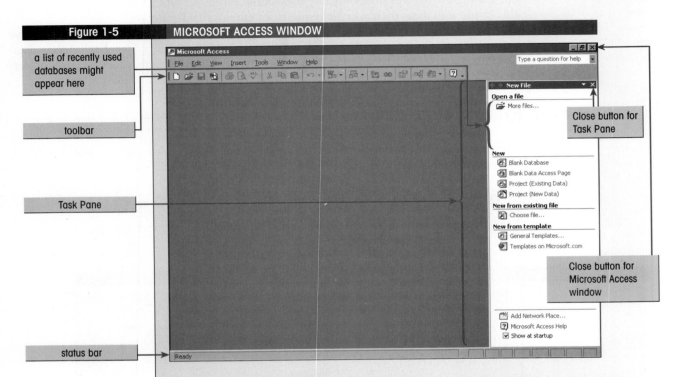

a list of recently used databases might appear here

toolbar

Task Pane

status bar

Close button for Task Pane

Close button for Microsoft Access window

When you start Access, the Access window contains a Task Pane that allows you to create a new database or to open an existing database. You can click the "Blank Database" option in the "New" section of the Task Pane to create a new database on your own, or you can click the "General Templates" option in the "New from template" section of the Task Pane to let Access guide you through the steps for creating one of the standard databases provided by Microsoft. In this case, you need to open an existing database.

To open an existing database, you can select the name of a database in the list of recently opened databases (if the list appears), or you can click the "More files" option to open a database not listed. You need to open an existing database—the Seasonal database on your Data Disk.

3. Make sure you have created your copy of the Access Data Disk, and then place your Data Disk in the appropriate disk drive.

TROUBLE? If you don't have a Data Disk, you need to get one before you can proceed. Your instructor will either give you one or ask you to make your own. (See your instructor for more information.) In either case, be sure that you have made a backup copy of your Data Disk before you begin working, so that the original Data Files will be available on the copied disk in case you need to start over because of an error or problem.

4. In the "Open a file" section of the Task Pane, click the **More files** option. The Open dialog box is displayed. See Figure 1-6.

Figure 1-6   OPEN DIALOG BOX

Look in list box

click to display the list
of available drives
and folders

TROUBLE? The list of folders and files on your screen might be different from the
list in Figure 1-6.

5. Click the **Look in** list arrow, and then click the drive that contains your Data Disk.

6. Click **Tutorial** in the list box (if necessary), and then click the **Open** button to
display a list of the files in the Tutorial folder.

7. Click **Seasonal** in the list box, and then click the **Open** button. The Seasonal
database opens in the Access window. See Figure 1-7.

Figure 1-7   ACCESS AND DATABASE WINDOWS

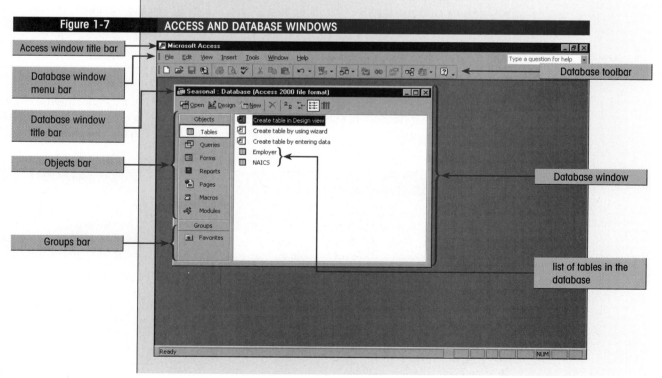

Access window title bar

Database window
menu bar

Database window
title bar

Objects bar

Groups bar

Database toolbar

Database window

list of tables in the
database

> **TROUBLE?** The filename on your screen might be Seasonal.mdb instead of Seasonal, depending on your computer's default settings. The extension ".mdb" identifies the file as a Microsoft Access database.
>
> **TROUBLE?** If Tables is not selected in the Objects bar of the Database window, click it to display the list of tables in the database.

Before you can begin working with the database, you need to become familiar with the components of the Access and Database windows.

The Access and Database Windows

The **Access window** is the program window that appears when you start the program. The **Database window** appears when you open a database; this window is the main control center for working with an open Access database. Except for the Access window title bar, all screen components now on your screen are associated with the Database window (see Figure 1-7). Most of these screen components—including the title bars, window sizing buttons, menu bar, toolbar, and status bar—are the same as the components in other Windows programs.

Notice that the Database window title bar includes the notation "(Access 2000 file format)." By default, databases that you create in Access 2002 use the Access 2000 database file format. This feature ensures that you can use and share databases originally created in Access 2002 without converting them to Access 2000, and vice versa. (You'll learn more about database file formats and converting databases later in this tutorial.)

The Database window provides a variety of options for viewing and manipulating database objects. Each item in the **Objects bar** controls one of the major object groups—such as tables, queries, forms, and reports—in an Access database. The **Groups bar** allows you to organize different types of database objects into groups, with shortcuts to those objects, so that you can work with them more easily. The Database window also provides buttons for quickly creating, opening, and managing objects, as well as shortcut options for some of these tasks.

Elsa has already created the Employer and NAICS tables in the Seasonal database. She asks you to open the Employer table and view its contents.

Opening an Access Table

As noted earlier, tables contain all the data in a database. Tables are the fundamental objects for your work in Access. To view, add, change, or delete data in a table, you first open the table. You can open any Access object by using the Open button in the Database window.

REFERENCE WINDOW   **RW**

Opening an Access Object
- In the Objects bar of the Database window, click the type of object you want to open.
- If necessary, scroll the object list box until the object name appears, and then click the object name.
- Click the Open button in the Database window.

You need to open the Employer table, which is one of two tables in the Seasonal database.

To open the Employer table:

1. In the Database window, click **Employer** to select it.

2. Click the **Open** button in the Database window. The Employer table opens in Datasheet view on top of the Database and Access windows. See Figure 1-8.

Figure 1-8	EMPLOYER TABLE DISPLAYED IN DATASHEET VIEW

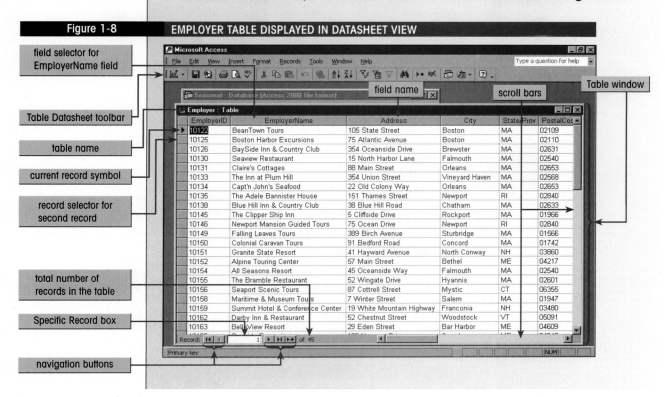

Datasheet view shows a table's contents as a **datasheet** in rows and columns, similar to a table or spreadsheet. Each row is a separate record in the table, and each column contains the field values for one field in the table. Each column is headed by a field name inside a field selector, and each row has a record selector to its left. Clicking a **field selector** or a **record selector** selects that entire column or row (respectively), which you then can manipulate. A field selector is also called a **column selector**, and a record selector is also called a **row selector**.

Navigating an Access Datasheet

When you first open a datasheet, Access selects the first field value in the first record. Notice that this field value is highlighted and that a darkened triangle symbol, called the current record symbol, appears in the record selector to the left of the first record. The **current record symbol** identifies the currently selected record. Clicking a record selector or field value in another row moves the current record symbol to that row. You can also move the pointer over the data on the screen and click one of the field values to position the insertion point.

The Employer table currently has 13 fields and 45 records. To view fields or records not currently visible in the datasheet, you can use the horizontal and vertical scroll bars shown in Figure 1-8 to navigate through the data. The **navigation buttons**, also shown in Figure 1-8, provide another way to move vertically through the records. Figure 1-9 shows which record becomes the current record when you click each navigation button. The **Specific Record box**, which appears between the two sets of navigation buttons, displays the current record number. The total number of records in the table appears to the right of the navigation buttons.

Figure 1-9	NAVIGATION BUTTONS

NAVIGATION BUTTON	RECORD SELECTED	NAVIGATION BUTTON	RECORD SELECTED
⏮	First Record	⏭	Last Record
◀	Previous Record	▶*	New Record
▶	Next Record		

Elsa suggests that you use the various navigation techniques to move through the Employer table and become familiar with its contents.

To navigate the Employer datasheet:

1. Click the right scroll arrow in the horizontal scroll bar a few times to scroll to the right and view the remaining fields in the Employer table.

2. Drag the scroll box in the horizontal scroll bar all the way to the left to return to the previous display of the datasheet.

3. Click the **Next Record** navigation button ▶ . The second record is now the current record, as indicated by the current record symbol in the second record selector. Also, notice that the second record's value for the EmployerID field is highlighted, and "2" (for record number 2) appears in the Specific Record box.

4. Click the **Last Record** navigation button ⏭ . The last record in the table, record 45, is now the current record.

5. Click the **Previous Record** navigation button ◀ . Record 44 is now the current record.

6. Click the **First Record** navigation button ⏮ . The first record is now the current record.

Saving a Database

Notice the Save button 🖫 on the Table Datasheet toolbar. Unlike the Save buttons in other Windows programs, this Save button does not save the active document (database) to your disk. Instead, you use the Save button to save the design of an Access object, such as a table, or to save datasheet format changes. Access does not have a button or option you can use to save the active database.

Access saves changes to the active database to your disk automatically, when a record is changed or added and when you close the database. If your database is stored on a disk in drive A, you should never remove the disk while the database file is open. If you remove the disk, Access will encounter problems when it tries to save the database, which might damage the database.

Now that you've viewed the Employer table, you can exit Access.

To exit Access:

1. Click the **Close** button ☒ on the Access window title bar. The Employer table and the Seasonal database close, Access closes, and you return to the Windows desktop.

Now that you've become familiar with Access and the Seasonal database, in the next session, you'll be ready to work with the data stored in the database.

Session 1.1 QUICK CHECK

1. A(n) _____ is a single characteristic of a person, place, object, event, or idea.

2. You connect the records in two separate tables through a(n) _____ that appears in both tables.

3. The _____, whose values uniquely identify each record in a table, is called a(n) _____ when it is placed in a second table to form a relationship between the two tables.

4. In a table, the rows are also called _____, and the columns are also called _____.

5. The _____ identifies the selected record in an Access table.

6. Describe two methods for navigating through a table.

SESSION 1.2

In this session, you will open an existing query and create and navigate a new query; create and navigate a form; and create, preview, and navigate a report. You will also learn how to manage databases by backing up and restoring, compacting and repairing, and converting databases.

Working with Queries

A **query** is a question you ask about the data stored in a database. In response to a query, Access displays the specific records and fields that answer your question. When you create a query, you tell Access which fields you need and what criteria Access should use to select the records. Then Access displays only the information you want, so you don't have to navigate through the entire database for the information.

Before creating a new query, you will open a query that Elsa created recently so that she could view information in the Employer table in a different way.

Opening an Existing Query

Queries that you create and save appear in the Queries list of the Database window. To see the results of a query, you simply open, or run, the query. Elsa created and saved a query named "Contacts" in the Seasonal database. This query shows all the fields from the Employer table, but in a different order. Elsa suggests that you open this query to see its results.

To open the Contacts query:

1. Insert your Data Disk into the appropriate disk drive.

2. Start Access, and then click the **More files** option in the Task Pane to display the Open dialog box.

3. Click the **Look in** list arrow, click the drive that contains your Data Disk, click **Tutorial** in the list box, and then click the **Open** button to display the list of files in the Tutorial folder.

4. Click **Seasonal** in the list box, and then click the **Open** button.

5. Click **Queries** in the Objects bar of the Database window to display the Queries list. The Queries list box contains one object—the Contacts query. See Figure 1-10.

Figure 1-10	LIST OF QUERIES IN THE SEASONAL DATABASE

Now you will run the Contacts query by opening it.

6. Click **Contacts** to select it, and then click the **Open** button in the Database window. Access displays the results of the query in Datasheet view. See Figure 1-11.

Figure 1-11	RESULT OF RUNNING THE CONTACTS QUERY

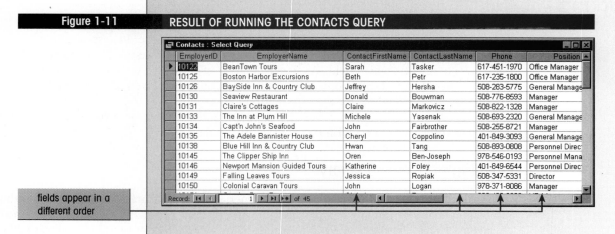

Notice that the query displays the fields from the Employer table, but in a different order. For example, the first and last names of each contact, as well as the contact's phone number, appear next to the employer name. This arrangement lets Elsa view pertinent contact information without having to scroll through the table. Rearranging the display of table data is one task you can perform with queries, so that table information appears in a different order to suit how you want to work with the information.

7. Click the **Close** button **X** on the Query window title bar to close the Contacts query.

Even though a query can display table information in a different way, the information still exists in the table as it was originally entered. If you opened the Employer table, it would still show the fields in their original order.

Zack Ward, the director of marketing at NSJI, wants a list of all employers so that his staff can call them to check on their satisfaction with NSJI's services and recruits. He doesn't want the list to include all the fields in the Employer table (such as PostalCode and NAICSCode). To produce this list for Zack, you need to create a query using the Employer table.

Creating, Sorting, and Navigating a Query

You can design your own queries or use an Access **Query Wizard**, which guides you through the steps to create a query. The Simple Query Wizard allows you to select records and fields quickly, and it is an appropriate choice for producing the employer list Zack wants. You can choose this Wizard either by clicking the New button, which opens a dialog box from which you can choose among several different Wizards to create your query, or by double-clicking the "Create query by using wizard" option, which automatically starts the Simple Query Wizard.

To start the Simple Query Wizard:

1. Double-click **Create query by using wizard**. The first Simple Query Wizard dialog box opens. See Figure 1-12.

| Figure 1-12 | FIRST SIMPLE QUERY WIZARD DIALOG BOX |

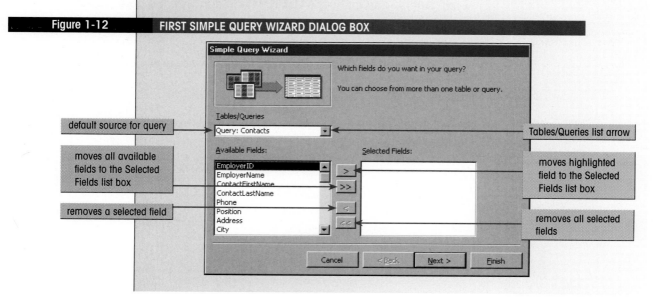

Because Contacts is the only query object currently in the Seasonal database, it is listed in the Tables/Queries box by default. You need to base the query you're creating on the Employer table.

2. Click the **Tables/Queries** list arrow, and then click **Table: Employer** to select the Employer table as the source for the new query. The Available Fields list box now lists the fields in the Employer table.

You need to select fields from the Available Fields list to include them in the query. To select fields one at a time, click a field and then click the > button. The selected field moves from the Available Fields list box on the left to the Selected Fields list box on the right. To select all the fields, click the >> button. If you change your mind or make a mistake, you can remove a field by clicking it in the Selected Fields list box and then clicking the < button. To remove all selected fields, click the << button.

Each Wizard dialog box contains buttons on the bottom that allow you to move to the previous dialog box (Back button), move to the next dialog box (Next button), or cancel the creation process (Cancel button) and return to the Database window. You can also finish creating the object (Finish button) and accept the Wizard's defaults for the remaining options.

Zack wants his list to include data from only the following fields: EmployerName, City, State/Prov, ContactFirstName, ContactLastName, and Phone. You need to select these fields to include them in the query.

To create the query using the Simple Query Wizard:

1. Click **EmployerName** in the Available Fields list box, and then click the > button. The EmployerName field moves to the Selected Fields list box.

2. Repeat Step 1 for the fields **City**, **State/Prov**, **ContactFirstName**, **ContactLastName**, and **Phone**, and then click the **Next** button. The second, and final, Simple Query Wizard dialog box opens and asks you to choose a name for your query. This name will appear in the Queries list in the Database window. You'll change the suggested name (Employer Query) to "Employer List."

3. Click at the end of the highlighted name, use the Backspace key to delete the word "Query," and then type **List**. Now you can view the query results.

4. Click the **Finish** button to complete the query. Access displays the query results in Datasheet view.

5. Click the **Maximize** button on the Query window title bar to maximize the window. See Figure 1-13.

| Figure 1-13 | QUERY RESULTS |

The datasheet displays the six selected fields for each record in the Employer table. The fields are shown in the order you selected them, from left to right.

The records are currently listed in order by the primary key field (EmployerID from the Employer table). This is true even though the EmployerID field is not included in the display of the query results. Zack prefers the records listed in order by state or province, so that his staff members can focus on all records for the employers in a particular state or province. To display the records in the order Zack wants, you need to sort the query results by the State/Prov field.

To sort the query results:

1. Click to position the insertion point anywhere in the State/Prov column. This establishes the State/Prov column as the current field.

2. Click the **Sort Ascending** button on the Query Datasheet toolbar. Now the records are sorted in ascending alphabetical order by the values in the State/Prov field. All the records for Connecticut (CT) are listed first, followed by the records for Massachusetts (MA), Maine (ME), and so on.

   Notice that the navigation buttons are located at the bottom of the window. You navigate through a query datasheet in the same way that you navigate through a table datasheet.

3. Click the **Last Record** navigation button. The last record in the query datasheet, for the Darby Inn & Restaurant, is now the current record.

4. Click the **Previous Record** navigation button. Record 44 in the query datasheet is now the current record.

5. Click the **First Record** navigation button ⏮ . The first record is now the current record.

6. Click the **Close Window** button ✕ on the menu bar to close the query.

   A dialog box opens and asks if you want to save changes to the design of the query. This box opens because you changed the sort order of the query results.

7. Click the **Yes** button to save the query design changes and return to the Database window. Notice that the Employer List query now appears in the Queries list box. In addition, because you maximized the Query window, now the Database window is also maximized. You need to restore the window.

8. Click the **Restore Window** button 🗗 on the menu bar to restore the Database window.

The query results are not stored in the database; however, the query design is stored as part of the database with the name you specified. You can re-create the query results at any time by running the query again. You'll learn more about creating and running queries in Tutorial 3.

After Zack views the query results, Elsa then asks you to create a form for the Employer table so that her staff members can use the form to enter and work with data in the table easily.

Creating **and Navigating a Form**

A **form** is an object you use to maintain, view, and print records in a database. Although you can perform these same functions with tables and queries, forms can present data in many customized and useful ways.

In Access, you can design your own forms or use a Form Wizard to create your forms automatically. A **Form Wizard** is an Access tool that asks you a series of questions, and then creates a form based on your answers. The quickest way to create a form is to use an **AutoForm Wizard**, which places all the fields from a selected table (or query) on a form automatically, without asking you any questions, and then displays the form on the screen.

Elsa wants a form for the Employer table that will show all the fields for one record at a time, with fields listed one below another in a column. This type of form will make it easier for her staff to focus on all the data for a particular employer. You'll use the AutoForm: Columnar Wizard to create the form.

To create the form using an AutoForm Wizard:

1. Click **Forms** in the Objects bar of the Database window to display the Forms list. The Forms list box does not contain any forms yet.

2. Click the **New** button in the Database window to open the New Form dialog box. See Figure 1-14.

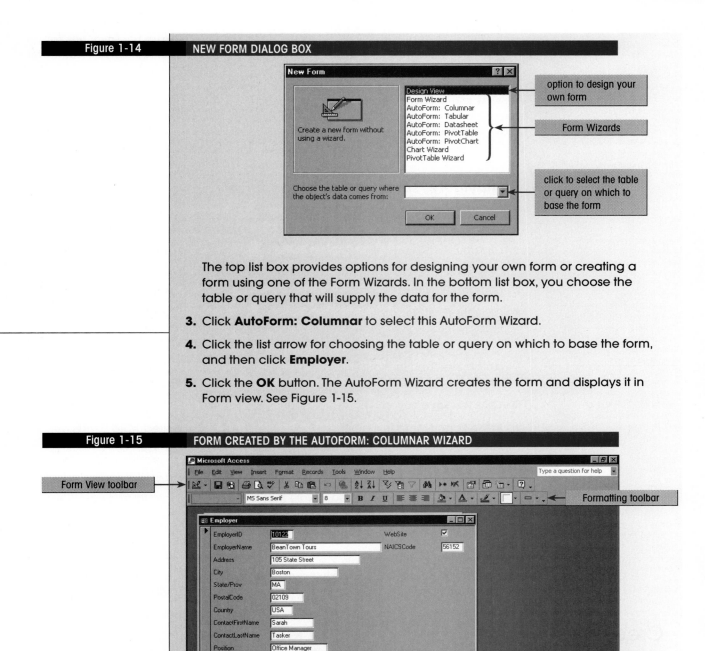

Figure 1-14   **NEW FORM DIALOG BOX**

option to design your own form

Form Wizards

click to select the table or query on which to base the form

The top list box provides options for designing your own form or creating a form using one of the Form Wizards. In the bottom list box, you choose the table or query that will supply the data for the form.

3. Click **AutoForm: Columnar** to select this AutoForm Wizard.

4. Click the list arrow for choosing the table or query on which to base the form, and then click **Employer**.

5. Click the **OK** button. The AutoForm Wizard creates the form and displays it in Form view. See Figure 1-15.

Figure 1-15   **FORM CREATED BY THE AUTOFORM: COLUMNAR WIZARD**

Form View toolbar

Formatting toolbar

TROUBLE? The background of your form might look different from the one shown in Figure 1-15, depending on your computer's settings. If so, don't worry. You will learn how to change the form's style later in this text. For now, continue with the tutorial.

The form displays one record at a time in the Employer table. Access displays the field values for the first record in the table and selects the first field value (EmployerID). Each field name appears on a separate line (spread over two columns) and on the same line as its field value, which appears in a box. The widths of the boxes are different to accommodate the different sizes of the displayed field values; for example, compare the small box for the State/Prov field value with the larger box for the EmployerName field value. The AutoForm: Columnar Wizard automatically placed the field names and values on the form and supplied the background style.

To view and maintain data using a form, you must know how to move from field to field and from record to record. Notice that the Form window contains navigation buttons, similar to those available in Datasheet view, which you can use to display different records in the form. You'll use these now to navigate through the form; then you'll save and close the form.

To navigate, save, and close the form:

1. Click the **Next Record** navigation button ▶ . The form now displays the values for the second record in the Employer table.

2. Click the **Last Record** navigation button ▶❙ to move to the last record in the table. The form displays the information for record 45, Lighthouse Tours.

3. Click the **Previous Record** navigation button ◀ to move to record 44.

4. Click the **First Record** navigation button ❙◀ to return to the first record in the Employer table.

   Next, you'll save the form with the name "Employer Data" in the Seasonal database. Then the form will be available for later use. You'll learn more about creating and customizing forms in Tutorial 4.

5. Click the **Save** button 🖫 on the Form View toolbar. The Save As dialog box opens.

6. In the Form Name text box, click at the end of the highlighted word "Employer," press the **spacebar**, type **Data**, and then press the **Enter** key. Access saves the form as Employer Data in the Seasonal database and closes the dialog box.

7. Click the **Close** button ✖ on the Form window title bar to close the form and return to the Database window. Note that the Employer Data form is now listed in the Forms list box.

After attending a staff meeting, Zack returns with another request. He wants the same employer list you produced earlier when you created the Employer List query, but he'd like the information presented in a more readable format. You'll help Zack by creating a report.

Creating, Previewing, and Navigating a Report

A **report** is a formatted printout (or screen display) of the contents of one or more tables in a database. Although you can print data appearing in tables, queries, and forms, reports provide you with the greatest flexibility for formatting printed output. As with forms, you can design your own reports or use a Report Wizard to create reports automatically.

Zack wants a report showing the same information contained in the Employer List query that you created earlier. However, he wants the data for each employer to be grouped together, with one employer record below another, as shown in the report sketch in Figure 1-16.

Figure 1-16   **SKETCH OF ZACK'S REPORT**

Employer List

EmployerName   _____
City   _____
State/Prov   ____
ContactFirstName   _____
ContactLastName   _____
Phone   _____

EmployerName   _____
City   _____
State/Prov   ____
ContactFirstName   _____
ContactLastName   _____
Phone   _____

To produce the report for Zack, you'll use the AutoReport: Columnar Wizard, which is similar to the AutoForm: Columnar Wizard you used earlier when creating the Employer Data form.

To create the report using the AutoReport: Columnar Wizard:

1. Click **Reports** in the Objects bar of the Database window, and then click the **New** button in the Database window to open the New Report dialog box, which is similar to the New Form dialog box you saw earlier.

2. Click **AutoReport: Columnar** to select this Wizard for creating the report.

   Because Zack wants the same data as in the Employer List query, you need to choose that query as the basis for the report.

3. Click the list arrow for choosing the table or query on which to base the report, and then click **Employer List**.

4. Click the **OK** button. The AutoReport Wizard creates the report and displays it in Print Preview, which shows exactly how the report will look when printed.

   To view the report better, you'll maximize the window and change the Zoom setting so that you can see the entire page.

5. Click the **Maximize** button 🔲 on the Report window title bar, click the **Zoom** list arrow (to the right of the value 100%) on the Print Preview toolbar, and then click **Fit**. The entire first page of the report is displayed in the window. See Figure 1-17.

Figure 1-17	FIRST PAGE OF THE REPORT IN PRINT PREVIEW

report title taken from query name

fields grouped for each record

page navigation buttons

lines separate records

TROUBLE? The fonts used in your report might look different from the ones shown in Figure 1-17, depending on your computer's settings. If so, don't worry. You will learn how to change the report's style later in this text.

Each field from the Employer List query appears on its own line, with the corresponding field value to the right and in a box. Horizontal lines separate one record from the next, visually grouping all the fields for each record. The name of the query—Employer List—appears as the report's title.

Notice that the Print Preview window provides page navigation buttons at the bottom of the window, similar to the navigation buttons you've used to move through records in a table, query, and form. You use these buttons to move through the pages of a report.

6. Click the **Next Page** navigation button ▶ . The second page of the report is displayed in Print Preview.

7. Click the **Last Page** navigation button ▶I to move to the last page of the report. Note that this page contains the fields for only one record. Also note that the box in the middle of the navigation buttons displays the number "12"; there are 12 pages in this report.

TROUBLE? Depending on the printer you are using, your report might have more or fewer pages. If so, don't worry. Different printers format reports in different ways, sometimes affecting the total number of pages.

8. Click the **First Page** navigation button I◀ to return to the first page of the report.

At this point, you could close the report without saving it because you can easily re-create it at any time. In general, it's best to save an object—report, form, or query—only if you anticipate using the object frequently or if it is time-consuming to create, because these objects use considerable storage space on your disk. However, Zack wants to show the report to his staff members, so he asks you to save it.

To close and save the report:

1. Click the **Close Window** button ⊠ on the menu bar. *Do not* click the Close button on the Print Preview toolbar.

   TROUBLE? If you clicked the Close button on the Print Preview toolbar, you switched to Design view. Simply click the Close Window button ⊠ on the menu bar, and then continue with the steps.

   A dialog box opens and asks if you want to save the changes to the report design.

2. Click the **Yes** button. The Save As dialog box opens.

3. Click to the right of the highlighted text in the Report Name text box, press the **spacebar** once, type **Report**, and then click the **OK** button. Access saves the report as "Employer List Report" and returns to the Database window.

You'll learn more about creating and customizing reports in Tutorial 4.

Managing a Database

One of the main tasks involved in working with database software is managing your databases and the data they contain. By managing your databases, you can ensure that they operate in the most efficient way, that the data they contain is secure, and that you can work with the data effectively. Some of the activities involved in database management include backing up and restoring a database, compacting and repairing a database, and converting a database for use in other versions of Access.

Backing Up and Restoring a Database

You make a backup copy of a database file to protect your database against loss or damage. You can make the backup copy using one of several methods: Windows Explorer, My Computer, Microsoft Backup, or other backup software. If you back up your database file to a floppy disk, and the file size exceeds the size of the disk, you cannot use Windows Explorer or My Computer; you must use Microsoft Backup or some other backup software so that you can copy the file over more than one disk.

To restore a backup database file, choose the same method you used to make the backup copy. For example, if you used the Microsoft Backup tool (which is one of the System Tools available from the Programs menu and Accessories submenu in Windows 2000), you must choose the Restore option for this tool to copy the database file to your database folder. If the existing database file and the backup copy have the same name, restoring the backup copy might replace the existing file. If you want to save the existing file, rename it before you restore it.

Compacting and Repairing a Database

Whenever you open an Access database and work in it, the size of the database increases. Likewise, when you delete records and when you delete or replace database objects—such as queries, forms, and reports—the space that had been occupied on the disk by the deleted or replaced records or objects does not become available for other records or objects. To make the space available, you must compact the database. **Compacting** a database rearranges the data and objects in a database to decrease its file size. Unlike making a copy of a database file, which you do to protect your database against loss or damage, you compact a database to make it smaller, thereby making more space available on your disk and speeding up the process of opening and closing the database. Figure 1-18 illustrates the compacting process; the orange colored elements in the figure represent database records and objects.

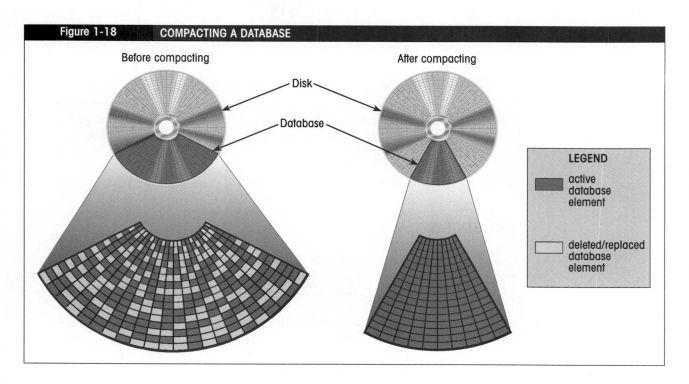

Figure 1-18   COMPACTING A DATABASE

Before compacting · After compacting · Disk · Database

LEGEND
active database element
deleted/replaced database element

When you compact a database, Access repairs the database at the same time. In many cases, Access detects that a database is damaged when you try to open it and gives you the option to compact and repair it at that time. If you think your database might be damaged because it is behaving unpredictably, you can use the "Compact and Repair Database" option to fix it. With your database file open, point to the Database Utilities option on the Tools menu, and then choose the Compact and Repair Database option.

Compacting a Database Automatically

Access also allows you to set an option for your database file so that every time you close the database, it will be compacted automatically.

REFERENCE | WINDOW   **RW**

Compacting a Database Automatically

- Make sure the database file you want to compact automatically is open.
- Click Tools on the menu bar, and then click Options.
- Click the General tab in the Options dialog box.
- Click the Compact on Close check box to select it.
- Click the OK button.

You'll set the compact option now for the Seasonal database. Then, every time you subsequently close the Seasonal database, Access will compact the database file for you. After setting this option, you'll exit Access.

To set the option for compacting the Seasonal database:

1. Make sure the Seasonal Database window is open on your screen.

2. Click **Tools** on the menu bar, and then click **Options**. The Options dialog box opens.

3. Click the **General** tab in the dialog box, and then click the **Compact on Close** check box to select it. See Figure 1-19.

Figure 1-19	GENERAL TAB OF THE OPTIONS DIALOG BOX

Compact on Close
option is selected

4. Click the **OK** button to set the option.

5. Click the **Close** button ⊠ on the Access window title bar to exit Access. When you exit, Access closes the Seasonal database file and compacts it automatically.

Converting an Access 2000 Database

Another important database management task is converting a database so that you can work with it in a different version of Access. As noted earlier in this tutorial, the default file format for databases you create in Access 2002 is Access 2000. This enables you to work with the database in either the Access 2000 or 2002 versions of the software, without having to convert it. This compatibility makes it easy for multiple users working with different versions of the software to share the same database and work more efficiently.

Sometimes, however, you might need to convert an Access 2000 database to another version. For example, if you needed to share an Access 2000 database with a colleague who worked on a laptop computer with Access 97 installed on it, you could convert the Access 2000 database to the Access 97 format. Likewise, you might want to convert an Access 2000 database to the Access 2002 file format if the database becomes very large in size. Access 2002 is enhanced so that large databases run faster in the Access 2002 file format, making it more efficient for you to work with the information contained in them.

To convert a database, follow these steps:

1. Make sure the database you want to convert is closed and the Access window is open.

2. Click Tools on the menu bar, point to Database Utilities, point to Convert Database, and then choose the format you want to convert to—To Access 97 File Format, To Access 2000 File Format, or To Access 2002 File Format.

3. In the Database to Convert From dialog box, select the name of the database you want to convert, and then click the Convert button.

4. In the Convert Database Into dialog box, enter a new name for the converted database in the File name text box, and then click the Save button.

After converting a database, you can use it in the version of Access to which you converted the file. Note, however, that when you convert to a previous file format, such as converting from the Access 2000 file format to the Access 97 file format, you might lose some of the advanced features of the newer version and you might need to make some adjustments to the converted database.

With the Employer and NAICS tables in place, Elsa can continue to build the Seasonal database and use it to store, manipulate, and retrieve important data for NSJI. In the following tutorials, you'll help Elsa complete and maintain the database, and you'll use it to meet the specific information needs of other NSJI employees.

Session 1.2 QUICK | CHECK

1. A(n) _____ is a question you ask about the data stored in a database.

2. Unless you specify otherwise, the records resulting from a query are listed in order by the _____.

3. The quickest way to create a form is to use a(n) _____.

4. Describe the form created by the AutoForm: Columnar Wizard.

5. After creating a report, the AutoReport Wizard displays the report in _____.

6. _____ a database rearranges the data and objects in a database to decrease its file size.

REVIEW ASSIGNMENTS

In the Review Assignments, you'll work with the **Seasons** database, which is similar to the database you worked with in the tutorial. Complete the following:

1. Make sure your Data Disk is in the disk drive.

2. Start Access and open the **Seasons** database, which is located in the Review folder on your Data Disk.

Explore ▷ 3. Open the Microsoft Access Help window, and then display the Contents tab. Double-click the topic "Microsoft Access Help" (if necessary), and then double-click the topic "Queries," and then click "About types of queries." Read the displayed information, and then click "Select queries." Read the displayed information. In the Contents tab, double-click the topic "Forms," and then click the topic "About forms." Read the displayed information. In the Contents tab, scroll down and double-click the topic "Reports and Report Snapshots," and then click the topic "About reports." Read the displayed information. When finished reading all the topics, close the Microsoft Access Help window. Use Notepad, Word, or some other text editor to write a brief summary of what you learned.

Explore ▷ 4. Use the "Ask a Question" box to ask the following question: "How do I rename an object?" Click the topic "Rename a database object" and read the displayed information. Close the Microsoft Access Help window. Then, in the **Seasons** database, rename the **Table1** table as **Employers**.

5. Open the **Employers** table.

Explore ▷ 6. Open the Microsoft Access Help window, and then display the Index tab. Type the keyword "print" in the Type keywords text box, and then click the Search button. Click the topic "Set page setup options for printing" and then click "For a table, query, form, or report." Read the displayed information. Close the Microsoft Access Help window. Set the option for printing in landscape orientation, and then print the first page only of the **Employers** table datasheet. Close the **Employers** table.

Explore ▷ 7. Use the Simple Query Wizard to create a query that includes the City, EmployerName, ContactFirstName, ContactLastName, and Phone fields (in that order) from the **Employers** table. Name the query **Employer Phone List**. Sort the query results in ascending order by City. Set the option for printing in landscape orientation, and then print the second page only of the query results. Close and save the query.

8. Use the AutoForm: Columnar Wizard to create a form for the **Employers** table.

Explore ▷ 9. Use context-sensitive Help to find out how to move to a particular record and display it in the form. Click the What's This? command from the Help menu, and then use the Help pointer to click the number 1 in the Specific Record box at the bottom of the form. Read the displayed information. Click to close the Help box, and then use the Specific Record box to move to record 42 (for Whitney's Resort & Spa) in the **Employers** table.

Explore ▷ 10. Print the form for the current record (42). (*Hint:* Click the Selected Record(s) option in the Print dialog box to print the current record.)

11. Save the form as **Employer Info**, and then close the form.

Explore ▷ 12. Use the AutoReport: Tabular Wizard to create a report based on the **Employers** table. Print the first page of the report, and then close and save the report as **Employers**.

13. Set the option for compacting the **Seasons** database on close.

Explore ▶   14. Convert the **Seasons** database to Access 2002 file format, saving the converted file as **Seasons2002** in the Review folder. Then convert the **Seasons** database to Access 97 file format, saving the converted file as **Seasons97** in the Review folder. Using Windows Explorer or My Computer, view the contents of your Review folder, and note the file sizes of the three versions of the **Seasons** database. Describe the results.

   15. Exit Access.

CASE PROBLEMS

Case 1. Lim's Video Photography   Several years ago, Youngho Lim left his position at a commercial photographer's studio and started his own business, Lim's Video Photography, located in San Francisco, California. Youngho quickly established a reputation as one of the area's best videographers, specializing in digital video photography. Youngho offers customers the option of storing edited videos on CD or DVD. His video shoots include weddings and other special events, as well as recording personal and commercial inventories for insurance purposes.

As his business continues to grow, Youngho relies on Access to keep track of information about clients, contracts, and so on. Youngho recently created an Access database named **Videos** to store data about his clients. You'll help Youngho complete and maintain the **Videos** database. Complete the following:

   1. Make sure your Data Disk is in the disk drive.

   2. Start Access and open the **Videos** database, which is located in the Cases folder on your Data Disk.

   3. Open the **Client** table, print the table datasheet, and then close the table.

   4. Use the Simple Query Wizard to create a query that includes the ClientName, Phone, and City fields (in that order) from the **Client** table. Name the query **Client List**. Print the query results, and then close the query.

Explore ▶   5. Use the AutoForm: Tabular Wizard to create a form for the **Contract** table. Print the form, save it as **Contract Info**, and then close it.

Explore ▶   6. Use the AutoReport: Columnar Wizard to create a report based on the **Contract** table. Maximize the Report window and change the Zoom setting to Fit. Use the Two Pages button on the Print Preview toolbar to view the first two pages of the report in Print Preview. Print the first page of the report, and then close and save it as **Contracts**.

   7. Set the option for compacting the **Videos** database on close.

Explore ▶   8. Convert the **Videos** database to Access 2002 file format, saving the converted file as **Videos2002** in the Cases folder. Then convert the **Videos** database to Access 97 file format, saving the converted file as **Videos97** in the Cases folder. Using Windows Explorer or My Computer, view the contents of your Cases folder, and note the file sizes of the three versions of the **Videos** database. Describe the results.

   9. Exit Access.

Case 2. DineAtHome.course.com   After working as both a concierge in a local hotel and a manager of several restaurants, Claire Picard founded DineAtHome.course.com in Naples, Florida. Her idea for this e-commerce company was a simple one: to provide people with an easy-to-use, online service that would allow them to order meals from one or more area restaurants and have the meals delivered to their homes. DineAtHome acts as a sort of broker between restaurants and customers. The participating restaurants offer everything from simple fare to gourmet feasts. Claire's staff performs a variety of services, from simply picking up and delivering the meals to providing linens and table service for more formal occasions.

Claire created the **Meals** database in Access to maintain information about participating restaurants and their menu offerings. She needs your help in working with this database. Complete the following:

1. Make sure your Data Disk is in the disk drive.

2. Start Access and open the **Meals** database, which is located in the Cases folder on your Data Disk.

Explore 3. Open the **Restaurant** table, print the table datasheet in landscape orientation, and then close the table.

4. Use the Simple Query Wizard to create a query that includes the RestaurantName, OwnerFirstName, OwnerLastName, and City fields (in that order) from the **Restaurant** table. Name the query **Owner List**.

Explore 5. Sort the query results in descending order by the City field. (*Hint*: Use a toolbar button.)

Explore 6. Use the "Ask a Question" box to ask the following question: "How do I select multiple records?" Click the topic "Select fields and records," and then click the topic "Select fields and records in a datasheet." Read the displayed information, and then close the Help window. Select the four records with "Marco Island" as the value in the City field, and then print just the selected records. (*Hint:* Use the Selected Record(s) option in the Print dialog box to print them.) Close the query, and save your changes to the design.

Explore 7. Use the AutoForm: Columnar Wizard to create a form for the **Restaurant** table. Use context-sensitive Help to find out how to move to a particular record and display it in the form. Click the What's This? command from the Help menu, and then use the Help pointer to click the number 1 in the Specific Record box at the bottom of the form. Read the displayed information. Click to close the Help box, use the Specific Record box to move to record 11 (for The Gazebo), and then print the form for the current record only. (*Hint:* Use the Selected Record(s) option in the Print dialog box to print the current record.) Save the form as **Restaurant Info**, and then close the form.

8. Use the AutoReport: Columnar Wizard to create a report based on the **Restaurant** table. Maximize the Report window and change the Zoom setting to Fit.

Explore 9. Use the View menu to view all eight pages of the report at the same time in Print Preview.

10. Print just the first page of the report, and then close and save the report as **Restaurants**.

11. Set the option for compacting the **Meals** database on close.

Explore 12. Convert the **Meals** database to Access 2002 file format, saving the converted file as **Meals2002** in the Cases folder. Then convert the **Meals** database to Access 97 file format, saving the converted file as **Meals97** in the Cases folder. Using Windows Explorer or My Computer, view the contents of your Cases folder, and note the file sizes of the three versions of the **Meals** database. Describe the results.

13. Exit Access.

Case 3. Redwood Zoo The Redwood Zoo is a small zoo located in the picturesque city of Gig Harbor, Washington, on the shores of Puget Sound. The zoo is ideally situated, with the natural beauty of the site providing the perfect backdrop for the zoo's varied exhibits. Although there are larger zoos in the greater Seattle area, the Redwood Zoo is considered to have some of the best exhibits of marine animals. The newly constructed polar bear habitat is a particular favorite among patrons.

Michael Rosenfeld is the director of fundraising activities for the Redwood Zoo. The zoo relies heavily on donations to fund both ongoing exhibits and temporary displays, especially those involving exotic animals. Michael created an Access database named **Redwood** to keep track of information about donors, their pledges, and the status of funds. You'll help Michael maintain the **Redwood** database. Complete the following:

1. Make sure your Data Disk is in the disk drive.

2. Start Access and open the **Redwood** database, which is located in the Cases folder on your Data Disk.

3. Open the **Donor** table, print the table datasheet, and then close the table.

Explore ▸ 4. Use the Simple Query Wizard to create a query that includes all the fields in the **Donor** table *except* the MI field. (*Hint*: Use the >> and < buttons to select the necessary fields.) Name the query **Donors**.

Explore ▸ 5. Sort the query results in descending order by the Class field. (*Hint*: Use a toolbar button.) Print the query results, and then close and save the query.

Explore ▸ 6. Use the AutoForm: Columnar Wizard to create a form for the **Fund** table. Use context-sensitive Help to find out how to move to a particular record and display it in the form. Click the What's This? command from the Help menu, and then use the Help pointer to click the number 1 in the Specific Record box at the bottom of the form. Read the displayed information. Click to close the Help box, use the Specific Record box to move to record 7 (Polar Bear Park), and then print the form for the current record only. (*Hint*: Use the Selected Record(s) option in the Print dialog box to print the current record.) Save the form as **Fund Info**, and then close it.

7. Use the AutoReport: Columnar Wizard to create a report based on the **Donor** table. Maximize the Report window and change the Zoom setting to Fit.

Explore ▸ 8. Use the View menu to view all seven pages of the report at the same time in Print Preview.

9. Print just the first page of the report, and then close and save the report as **Donors**.

10. Set the option for compacting the **Redwood** database on close.

Explore ▸ 11. Convert the **Redwood** database to Access 2002 file format, saving the converted file as **Redwood2002** in the Cases folder. Then convert the **Redwood** database to Access 97 file format, saving the converted file as **Redwood97** in the Cases folder. Using Windows Explorer or My Computer, view the contents of your Cases folder, and note the file sizes of the three versions of the **Redwood** database. Describe the results.

12. Exit Access.

Case 4. Mountain River Adventures   Several years ago, Connor and Siobhan Dempsey moved to Boulder, Colorado, drawn by their love of the mountains and their interest in outdoor activities of all kinds. This interest led them to form the Mountain River Adventures center. The center began as a whitewater rafting tour provider, but quickly grew to encompass other activities, such as canoeing, hiking, camping, fishing, and rock climbing.

From the beginning, Connor and Siobhan have used computers to help them manage all aspects of their business. They recently installed Access and created a database named **Trips** to store information about clients, equipment, and the types of guided tours they provide. You'll work with the **Trips** database to manage this information. Complete the following:

1. Make sure your Data Disk is in the disk drive.

2. Start Access and open the **Trips** database, which is located in the Cases folder on your Data Disk.

3. Open the **Client** table.

Explore ▶ 4. Print the **Client** table datasheet in landscape orientation, and then close the table.

5. Use the Simple Query Wizard to create a query that includes the ClientName, City, State/Prov, and Phone fields (in that order) from the **Client** table. Name the query **Client Info**.

Explore ▶ 6. Sort the query results in descending order by State/Prov. (*Hint*: Use a toolbar button.)

7. Print the query results, and then close and save the query.

Explore ▶ 8. Use the AutoForm: Columnar Wizard to create a form for the **Client** table. Use context-sensitive Help to find out how to move to a particular record and display it in the form. Click the What's This? command from the Help menu, and then use the Help pointer to click the number 1 in the Specific Record box at the bottom of the form. Read the displayed information. Click to close the Help box, use the Specific Record box to move to record 18, and then print the form for the current record only. (*Hint:* Use the Selected Record(s) option in the Print dialog box to print the current record.) Save the form as **Client Info**, and then close it.

Explore ▶ 9. Use the AutoReport: Tabular Wizard to create a report based on the **Client** table. Maximize the Report window and change the Zoom setting to Fit. Use the Two Pages button on the Print Preview toolbar to view both pages of the report in Print Preview. Print the first page of the report in landscape orientation, and then close and save the report as **Clients**.

10. Set the option for compacting the **Trips** database on close.

Explore ▶ 11. Convert the **Trips** database to Access 2002 file format, saving the converted file as **Trips2002** in the Cases folder. Then convert the **Trips** database to Access 97 file format, saving the converted file as **Trips97** in the Cases folder. Using Windows Explorer or My Computer, view the contents of your Cases folder, and note the file sizes of the three versions of the **Trips** database. Describe the results.

12. Exit Access.

LAB ASSIGNMENTS

These Lab Assignments are designed to accompany the interactive Course Lab called Databases. To start the Databases Lab, click the Start button on the Windows taskbar, point to Programs, point to Course Labs, point to New Perspectives Course Labs, and then click Databases. If you do not see Course Labs on your Programs menu, see your instructor or technical support person.

Databases   This Databases Lab demonstrates the essential concepts of file and database management systems. You will use the Lab to search, sort, and report the data contained in a file of classic books.

1. Click the Steps button to review basic database terminology and to learn how to manipulate the classic books database. As you proceed through the Steps, answer all of the Quick Check questions that appear. After you complete the Steps, you will see a Quick Check summary report. Follow the instructions on the screen to print this report.

2. Click the Explore button. Make sure you can apply basic database terminology to describe the classic books database by answering the following questions:
   a. How many records does the file contain?
   b. How many fields does each record contain?

    c. What are the contents of the Catalog # field for the book written by Margaret Mitchell?

    d. What are the contents of the Title field for the record with Thoreau in the Author field?

    e. Which field has been used to sort the records?

3. In Explore, manipulate the database as necessary to answer the following questions:

    a. When the books are sorted by title, what is the first record in the file?

    b. Use the Search button to search for all the books in the West location. How many do you find?

    c. Use the Search button to search for all the books in the Main location that are checked in. What do you find?

4. Use the Report button to print out a report that groups the books by Status and sorts them by Title. On your report, circle the four field names. Draw a box around the summary statistics showing which books are currently checked in and which books are currently checked out.

INTERNET ASSIGNMENTS

Student Union

The purpose of the Internet Assignments is to challenge you to find information on the Internet that you can use to create effective documents. The actual assignments are updated and maintained on the Course Technology Web site. Log on to the Internet and use your Web browser to go to the Student Union on the New Perspectives Series site at **www.course.com/NewPerspectives/studentunion**. Click the Online Companions link, and then click the link for this text.

QUICK CHECK ANSWERS

Session 1.1

1. field

2. common field

3. primary key; foreign key

4. records; fields

5. current record symbol

6. Use the horizontal and vertical scroll bars to view fields or records not currently visible in the datasheet; use the navigation buttons to move vertically through the records.

Session 1.2

1. query

2. primary key

3. AutoForm Wizard

4. The form displays each field name to the left of its field value, which appears in a box; the widths of the boxes represent the size of the fields.

5. Print Preview

6. Compacting

In this tutorial you will:

- Learn the guidelines for designing databases and setting field properties

- Create a new database

- Create and save a table

- Define fields and specify a table's primary key

- Add records to a table

- Modify the structure of a table

- Delete, move, and add fields

- Change field properties

- Copy records and import tables from another Access database

- Delete and change records

CREATING
AND MAINTAINING
A DATABASE

Creating the Northeast Database, and Creating, Modifying, and Updating the Position Table

CASE

Northeast Seasonal Jobs International (NSJI)

The Seasonal database contains two tables—the Employer table and the NAICS table. These tables store data about NSJI's employer customers and the NAICS codes for pertinent job positions, respectively. Elsa Jensen also wants to track information about each position that is available at each employer's place of business. This information includes the position title and wage. Elsa asks you to create a third table, named Position, in which to store the position data.

Because this is your first time creating a new table, Elsa suggests that you first create a new database, named "Northeast," and then create the new Position table in this database. This will keep the Seasonal database intact. Once the Position table is completed, you then can import the Employer and NAICS tables from the Seasonal database into your new Northeast database.

Some of the position data Elsa needs is already stored in another NSJI database. After creating the Position table and adding some records to it, you'll copy the records from the other database into the Position table. Then you'll maintain the Position table by modifying it and updating it to meet Elsa's specific data requirements.

SESSION 2.1

In this session, you will learn the guidelines for designing databases and setting field properties. You'll also learn how to create a new database, create a table, define the fields for a table, select the primary key for a table, and save the table structure.

Guidelines for Designing Databases

A database management system can be a useful tool, but only if you first carefully design the database so that it meets the needs of its users. In database design, you determine the fields, tables, and relationships needed to satisfy the data and processing requirements. When you design a database, you should follow these guidelines:

■ **Identify all the fields needed to produce the required information.** For example, Elsa needs information about employers, NAICS codes, and positions. Figure 2-1 shows the fields that satisfy these information requirements.

Figure 2-1	ELSA'S DATA REQUIREMENTS

EmployerID	ContactFirstName
PositionID	ContactLastName
PositionTitle	Position
EmployerName	Wage
Address	Hours/Week
City	NAICSCode
State/Prov	NAICSDesc
PostalCode	StartDate
Country	EndDate
Phone	ReferredBy
Openings	WebSite

■ **Group related fields into tables.** For example, Elsa grouped the fields relating to employers into the Employer table and the fields related to NAICS codes into the NAICS table. The other fields are grouped logically into the Position table, which you will create, as shown in Figure 2-2.

Figure 2-2	ELSA'S FIELDS GROUPED INTO TABLES

Employer table	NAICS table	Position table
EmployerID	NAICSCode	PositionID
EmployerName	NAICSDesc	PositionTitle
Address		Wage
City		Hours/Week
State/Prov		Openings
PostalCode		ReferredBy
Country		StartDate
ContactFirstName		EndDate
ContactLastName		
Position		
Phone		
WebSite		

■ **Determine each table's primary key.** Recall that a primary key uniquely identifies each record in a table. Although a primary key is not mandatory in Access, it's usually a good idea to include one in each table. Without a primary key, selecting the exact record that you want can be a problem. For some tables, one of the fields, such as a Social Security or credit card number, naturally serves the function of a primary key. For other tables, two or more fields might be needed to function as the primary key. In these cases, the primary key is referred to as a **composite key**. For example, a school grade table would use a combination of student number and course code to serve as the primary key. For a third category of tables, no single field or combination of fields can uniquely identify a record in a table. In these cases, you need to add a field whose sole purpose is to serve as the table's primary key.

For Elsa's tables, EmployerID is the primary key for the Employer table, NAICSCode is the primary key for the NAICS table, and PositionID will be the primary key for the Position table.

■ **Include a common field in related tables.** You use the common field to connect one table logically with another table. For example, Elsa's Employer and Position tables will include the EmployerID field as a common field. Recall that when you include the primary key from one table as a field in a second table to form a relationship, the field is called a foreign key in the second table; therefore, the EmployerID field will be a foreign key in the Position table. With this common field, Elsa can find all positions available at a particular employer; she can use the EmployerID value for an employer and search the Position table for all records with that EmployerID value. Likewise, she can determine which employer has a particular position available by searching the Employer table to find the one record with the same EmployerID value as the corresponding value in the Position table.

■ **Avoid data redundancy.** Data redundancy occurs when you store the same data in more than one place. With the exception of common fields to connect tables, you should avoid redundancy because it wastes storage space and can cause inconsistencies, if, for instance, you type a field value one way in one table and a different way in the same table or in a second table. Figure 2-3, which contains portions of potential data to be stored in the Employer and Position tables, shows an example of incorrect database design that has data redundancy in the Position table; the EmployerName field is redundant, and one value was entered incorrectly, in three different ways.

Figure 2-3	INCORRECT DATABASE DESIGN WITH DATA REDUNDANCY

Employer table

EmployerID	EmployerName	Address	Phone
10122	BeanTown Tours	105 State Street, Boston, MA 02109	617-451-1970
10125	Boston Harbor Excursions	75 Atlantic Avenue, Boston, MA 02110	617-235-1800
10126	BaySide Inn & Country Club	354 Oceanside Drive, Brewster, MA 02631	508-283-5775
10190	The Briar Rose Inn	105 Queen Street, Charlottetown PE C1A 8R4	902-626-1595
10191	Windsor Alpine Tours	14 Longmeadow Road, Laconia, NH 03246	603-266-9233
10198	Trudel Spa & Resort	40 Rue Rivard, North Hatley QC J0B 2C0	819-842-7783

data redundancy

Position table

PositionID	EmployerID	EmployerName	PositionTitle	Hours/Week
2040	10126	DaySide Inn & Country Club	Waiter/Waitress	32
2045	10122	BeanTown Tours	Tour Guide	24
2053	10190	The Briar Rose Inn	Host/Hostess	24
2066	10198	Trudel Spa & Resort	Lifeguard	32
2073	10126	Baside Inn & Country Club	Pro Shop Clerk	24
2078	10191	Windsor Alpine Tours	Ski Patrol	30
2079	10191	Windsor Alpine Tours	Day Care	35
2082	10125	Boston Harbor Excursions	Reservationist	40
2111	10126	BaySide Inn Club	Kitchen Help	32

inconsistent data

■ **Determine the properties of each field.** You need to identify the **properties**, or characteristics, of each field so that the DBMS knows how to store, display, and process the field values. These properties include the field's name, maximum number of characters or digits, description, valid values, and other field characteristics. You will learn more about field properties later in this tutorial.

The Position table you need to create will contain the fields shown in Figure 2-2, plus the EmployerID field as a foreign key. Before you create the new Northeast database and the Position table, you first need to learn some guidelines for setting field properties.

Guidelines for Setting Field Properties

As just noted, the last step of database design is to determine which values to assign to the properties, such as the name and data type, of each field. When you select or enter a value for a property, you **set** the property. Access has rules for naming fields, choosing data types, and setting other properties for fields.

Naming Fields and Objects

You must name each field, table, and other object in an Access database. Access then stores these items in the database, using the names you supply. It's best to choose a field or object name that describes the purpose or contents of the field or object, so that later you can easily remember what the name represents. For example, the three tables in the Northeast database will be named Employer, NAICS, and Position, because these names suggest their contents.

The following rules apply to naming fields and objects:

- A name can be up to 64 characters long.
- A name can contain letters, numbers, spaces, and special characters, except for a period (.), exclamation mark (!), accent grave (`), and square brackets ([ ]).
- A name cannot start with a space.
- A table or query name must be unique within a database. A field name must be unique within a table, but it can be used again in another table.

In addition, experienced users of databases follow these conventions for naming fields and objects:

- Capitalize the first letter of each word in the name.
- Avoid extremely long names because they are difficult to remember and reference.
- Use standard abbreviations, such as Num for Number, Amt for Amount, and Qty for Quantity.
- Do not use spaces in field names because these names will appear in column headings on datasheets and on labels in forms and reports. By not using spaces, you'll be able to show more fields in these objects at one time.

Assigning Field Data Types

You must assign a data type for each field. The **data type** determines what field values you can enter for the field and what other properties the field will have. For example, the Position table will include a StartDate field, which will store date values, so you will assign the date/time data type to this field. Then Access will allow you to enter and manipulate only dates or times as values in the StartDate field.

Figure 2-4 lists the 10 data types available in Access, describes the field values allowed for each data type, explains when you should use each data type, and indicates the field size of each data type.

Figure 2-4	DATA TYPES FOR FIELDS	
DATA TYPE	**DESCRIPTION**	**FIELD SIZE**
Text	Allows field values containing letters, digits, spaces, and special characters. Use for names, addresses, descriptions, and fields containing digits that are not used in calculations.	0 to 255 characters; 50 characters default
Memo	Allows field values containing letters, digits, spaces, and special characters. Use for long comments and explanations.	1 to 65,535 characters; exact size is determined by entry
Number	Allows positive and negative numbers as field values. Numbers can contain digits, a decimal point, commas, a plus sign, and a minus sign. Use for fields that you will use in calculations, except calculations involving money.	1 to 15 digits
Date/Time	Allows field values containing valid dates and times from January 1, 100 to December 31, 9999. Dates can be entered in mm/dd/yy (month, day, year) format, several other date formats, or a variety of time formats, such as 10:35 PM. You can perform calculations on dates and times, and you can sort them. For example, you can determine the number of days between two dates.	8 bytes
Currency	Allows field values similar to those for the number data type. Unlike calculations with number data type decimal values, calculations performed using the currency data type are not subject to round-off error.	Accurate to 15 digits on the left side of the decimal separator and to 4 digits on the right side

Figure 2-4	DATA TYPES FOR FIELDS, CONTINUED	
DATA TYPE	**DESCRIPTION**	**FIELD SIZE**
AutoNumber	Consists of integers with values controlled by Access. Access automatically inserts a value in the field as each new record is created. You can specify sequential numbering or random numbering, which guarantees a unique field value, so that such a field can serve as a table's primary key.	9 digits
Yes/No	Limits field values to yes and no, on and off, or true and false. Use for fields that indicate the presence or absence of a condition, such as whether an order has been filled or whether an employee is eligible for the company dental plan.	1 character
OLE Object	Allows field values that are created in other programs as objects, such as photographs, video images, graphics, drawings, sound recordings, voice-mail messages, spreadsheets, and word-processing documents. These objects can be linked or embedded.	1 gigabyte maximum; exact size depends on object size
Hyperlink	Consists of text used as a hyperlink address. A hyperlink address can have up to three parts: the text that appears in a field or control; the path to a file or page; and a location within the file or page. Hyperlinks help you to connect your application easily to the Internet or an intranet.	Up to 64,000 characters total for the three parts of a hyperlink data type
Lookup Wizard	Creates a field that lets you look up a value in another table or in a predefined list of values.	Same size as the primary key field used to perform the lookup

Setting Field Sizes

The **Field Size** property defines a field value's maximum storage size for text, number, and AutoNumber fields only. The other data types have no Field Size property because their storage size is either a fixed, predetermined amount or is determined automatically by the field value itself, as shown in Figure 2-4. A text field has a default field size of 50 characters; you can also set its field size by entering a number from 0 to 255. For example, the PositionTitle and ReferredBy fields in the Position table will be text fields with a size of 30 each.

When you use the number data type to define a field, you should set the field's Field Size property based on the largest value that you expect to store in that field. Access processes smaller data sizes faster using less memory, so you can optimize your database's performance and its storage space by selecting the correct field size for each field. For example, it would be wasteful to use the Long Integer setting when defining a field that will store only whole numbers ranging from 0 to 255, because the Long Integer setting will use four bytes of storage space. A better choice would be the Byte setting, which uses one byte of storage space to store the same values. Field Size property settings for number fields are as follows:

- **Byte:** Stores whole numbers (numbers with no fractions) from 0 to 255 in one byte
- **Integer:** Stores whole numbers from −32,768 to 32,767 in two bytes
- **Long Integer** (default): Stores whole numbers from −2,147,483,648 to 2,147,483,647 in four bytes
- **Single:** Stores positive and negative numbers to precisely seven decimal places and uses four bytes
- **Double:** Stores positive and negative numbers to precisely 15 decimal places and uses eight bytes
- **Replication ID:** Establishes a unique identifier for replication of tables, records, and other objects and uses 16 bytes
- **Decimal:** Stores positive and negative numbers to precisely 28 decimal places and uses 12 bytes

Elsa documented the design for the new Position table by listing each field's name, data type, size (if applicable), and description, as shown in Figure 2-5. Note that Elsa assigned the text data type to the PositionID, PositionTitle, EmployerID, and ReferredBy fields; the currency data type to the Wage field; the number data type to the Hours/Week and Openings fields; and the date/time data type to the StartDate and EndDate fields.

Figure 2-5	DESIGN FOR THE POSITION TABLE		
Field Name	**Data Type**	**Field Size**	**Description**
PositionID	Text	4	Primary key
PositionTitle	Text	30	
EmployerID	Text	5	Foreign key
Wage	Currency		Rate per hour
Hours/Week	Number	Integer	Work hours per week
Openings	Number	Integer	Number of openings
ReferredBy	Text	30	
StartDate	Date/Time		Month and day
EndDate	Date/Time		Month and day

With Elsa's design in place, you're ready to create the new Northeast database and the Position table.

Creating a New Database

Access provides two ways for you to create a new database: using a Database Wizard or creating a blank database. When you use a Wizard, the Wizard guides you through the database creation process and provides the necessary tables, forms, and reports for the type of database you choose—all in one operation. Using a Database Wizard is an easy way to start creating a database, but only if your data requirements closely match one of the supplied templates. When you choose to create a blank database, you need to add all the tables, forms, reports, and other objects after you create the database file. Creating a blank database provides the most flexibility, allowing you to define objects in the way that you want, but it does require that you define each object separately. Whichever method you choose, you can always modify or add to your database after you create it.

The following steps outline the process for creating a new database using a Database Wizard:

1. If necessary, click the New button on the Database toolbar to display the Task Pane.

2. In the "New from template" section of the Task Pane, click General Templates. The Templates dialog box opens.

3. Click the Databases tab, and then choose the Database Wizard that most closely matches the type of database you want to create. Click the OK button.

4. In the File New Database dialog box, choose the location in which to save the new database, specify its name, and then click the Create button.

5. Complete each of the Wizard dialog boxes, clicking the Next button to move through them after making your selections.

6. Click the Finish button when you have completed all the Wizard dialog boxes.

None of the Database Wizards matches the requirements of the new Northeast database, so you'll use the Blank Database option to create it.

To create the Northeast database:

1. Place your Data Disk in the appropriate disk drive, and then start Access.

2. In the New section of the Task Pane, click **Blank Database**. The File New Database dialog box opens. This dialog box is similar to the Open dialog box.

3. Click the **Save in** list arrow, and then click the drive that contains your Data Disk.

4. Click **Tutorial** in the list box, and then click the **Open** button.

5. In the File name text box, double-click the text **db1** to select it, and then type **Northeast**.

    TROUBLE? Your File name text box might contain an entry other than "db1." Just select whatever text is in this text box, and continue with the steps.

6. Click the **Create** button. Access creates the Northeast database in the Tutorial folder on your Data Disk, and then displays the Database window for the new database with the Tables object selected.

Now you can create the Position table in the Northeast database.

Creating a Table

Creating a table consists of naming the fields and defining the properties for the fields, specifying a primary key (and a foreign key, if applicable) for the table, and then saving the table structure. You will use Elsa's design (Figure 2-5) as a guide for creating the Position table in the Northeast database.

To begin creating the Position table:

1. Click the **New** button in the Database window. The New Table dialog box opens. See Figure 2-6.

Figure 2-6	NEW TABLE DIALOG BOX

click to design your own table

other ways to define a table

TROUBLE? If the Task Pane opens and displays "New File" at the top, you clicked the New button on the Database toolbar instead of the New button in the Database window. Click the Close button to close the Task Pane, and then repeat Step 1.

In Access, you can create a table from entered data (Datasheet View), define your own table (Design View), use a Wizard to automate the table creation process (Table Wizard), or use a Wizard to import or link data from another database or other data source (Import Table or Link Table). For the Position table, you will define your own table.

2. Click **Design View** in the list box, and then click the **OK** button. The Table window opens in Design view. (Note that you can also double-click the "Create table in Design view" option in the Database window to open the Table window in Design view.) See Figure 2-7.

Figure 2-7	TABLE WINDOW IN DESIGN VIEW

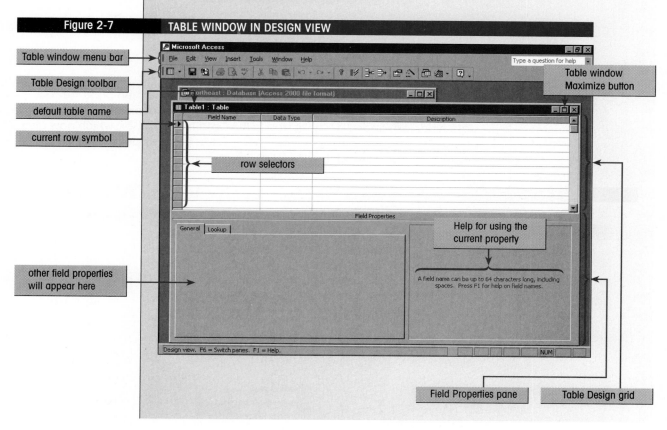

You use Design view to define or modify a table structure or the properties of the fields in a table. If you create a table without using a Wizard, you enter the fields and their properties for your table directly in the Table window in Design view.

Defining Fields

Initially, the default table name, Table1, appears on the Table window title bar, the current row symbol is positioned in the first row selector of the Table Design grid, and the insertion point is located in the first row's Field Name box. The purpose or characteristics of the current property (Field Name, in this case) appear in the right side of the Field Properties pane. You can display more complete information about the current property by pressing the F1 key.

You enter values for the Field Name, Data Type, and Description field properties in the Table Design grid. You select values for all other field properties, most of which are optional, in the Field Properties pane. These other properties will appear when you move to the first row's Data Type text box.

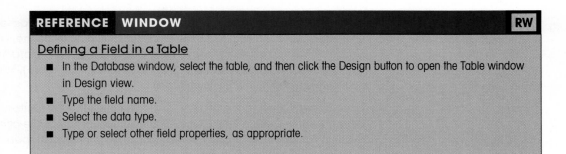

REFERENCE WINDOW   **RW**

<u>Defining a Field in a Table</u>
- In the Database window, select the table, and then click the Design button to open the Table window in Design view.
- Type the field name.
- Select the data type.
- Type or select other field properties, as appropriate.

The first field you need to define is PositionID.

To define the PositionID field:

1. Type **PositionID** in the first row's Field Name text box, and then press the **Tab** key (or press the **Enter** key) to advance to the Data Type text box. The default data type, Text, appears highlighted in the Data Type text box, which now also contains a list arrow, and field properties for a text field appear in the Field Properties pane. See Figure 2-8.

Figure 2-8   **TABLE WINDOW AFTER ENTERING THE FIRST FIELD NAME**

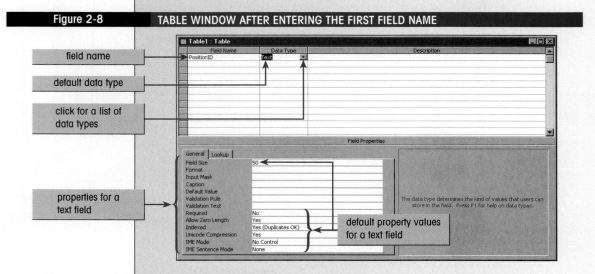

Notice that the right side of the Field Properties pane now provides an explanation for the current property, Data Type.

TROUBLE? If you make a typing error, you can correct it by clicking the mouse to position the insertion point, and then using either the Backspace key to delete characters to the left of the insertion point or the Delete key to delete characters to the right of the insertion point. Then type the correct text.

Because the PositionID numbers will not be used in calculations, you will assign the text data type (as opposed to the number data type) to the PositionID field.

2. Press the **Tab** key to accept Text as the data type and to advance to the Description text box.

Next you'll enter the Description property value as "Primary key." You can use the Description property to enter an optional description for a field to explain its purpose or usage. A field's Description property can be up to 255 characters long, and its value appears on the status bar when you view the table datasheet.

3. Type **Primary key** in the Description text box.

   Notice the Field Size property for the text field. The default setting of "50" is displayed. You need to change this number to "4" because all PositionID values at NSJI contain only 4 digits. (Refer to the Access Help system for a complete description of all the properties available for the different data types.)

4. Double-click the number **50** in the Field Size property box to select it, and then type **4**. The definition of the first field is completed. See Figure 2-9.

Figure 2-9	PositionID FIELD DEFINED

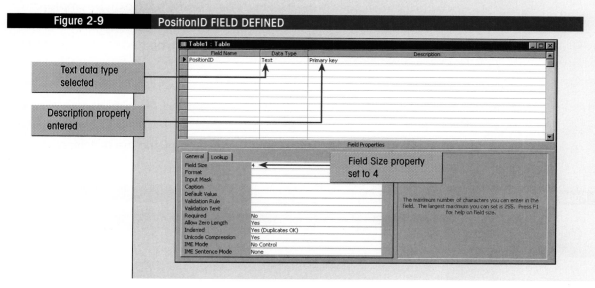

Text data type selected

Description property entered

Field Size property set to 4

Elsa's Position table design shows PositionTitle as the second field. You will define PositionTitle as a text field with a Field Size of 30, which is a sufficient length for any title values that will be entered.

To define the PositionTitle field:

1. Place the insertion point in the second row's Field Name text box, type **PositionTitle** in the text box, and then press the **Tab** key to advance to the Data Type text box.

2. Press the **Tab** key to accept Text as the field's data type.

   According to Elsa's design (Figure 2-5), you do not need to enter a description for this field. If you've assigned a descriptive field name and the field does not fulfill a special function (such as primary key), you usually do not enter a value for the optional Description property. PositionTitle is a field that does not require a value for its Description property.

   Next, you'll change the Field Size property to 30. Note that when defining the fields in a table, you can move between the Table Design grid and the Field Properties pane of the Table window by pressing the F6 key.

3. Press the **F6** key to move to the Field Properties pane. The current entry for the Field Size property, 50, is highlighted.

4. Type **30** to set the Field Size property. You have completed the definition of the second field.

The third field in the Position table is the EmployerID field. Recall that this field will serve as the foreign key in the Position table, allowing you to relate data from the Position table to data in the Employer table. The field must be defined in the same way in both tables—that is, a text field with a field size of 5.

To define the EmployerID field:

1. Place the insertion point in the third row's Field Name text box, type **EmployerID** in the text box, and then press the **Tab** key to advance to the Data Type text box.

2. Press the **Tab** key to accept Text as the field's data type and to advance to the Description text box.

3. Type **Foreign key** in the Description text box.

4. Press the **F6** key to move to the Field Properties pane. The current entry for the Field Size property, 50, is highlighted.

5. Type **5** to set the Field Size property. You have completed the definition of the third field. See Figure 2-10.

Figure 2-10	TABLE WINDOW AFTER DEFINING THE FIRST THREE FIELDS

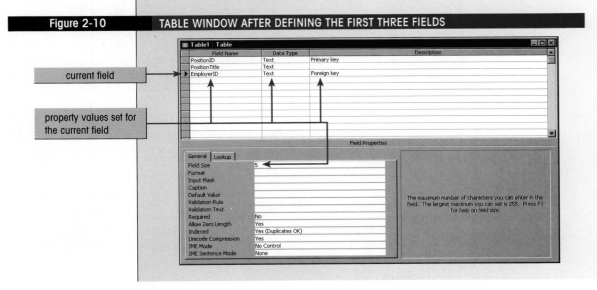

The fourth field is the Wage field, which will display values in the currency format.

To define the Wage field:

1. Place the insertion point in the fourth row's Field Name text box, type **Wage** in the text box, and then press the **Tab** key to advance to the Data Type text box.

2. Click the **Data Type** list arrow, click **Currency** in the list box, and then press the **Tab** key to advance to the Description text box.

3. Type **Rate per hour** in the Description text box.

   Elsa wants the Wage field values to be displayed with two decimal places, and she does not want any value to be displayed by default for new records. So, you need to set the Decimal Places and Default Value properties accordingly.

4. Click the **Decimal Places** text box to position the insertion point there. A list arrow appears on the right side of the Decimal Places text box.

   When you position the insertion point or select text in many Access text boxes, Access displays a list arrow, which you can click to display a list box with options. You can display the list arrow and the list box simultaneously if you click the text box near its right side.

5. Click the **Decimal Places** list arrow, and then click **2** in the list box to specify two decimal places for the Wage field values.

   Next, notice the Default Value property, which specifies the value that will be automatically entered into the field when you add a new record. Currently this property has a setting of 0. Elsa wants the Wage field to be empty (that is, to contain *no* default value) when a new record is added. Therefore, you need to change the Default Value property to the setting "Null." Setting the Default Value property to "Null" tells Access to display no value in the Wage field, by default.

6. Select **0** in the Default Value text box either by dragging the pointer or double-clicking the mouse, and then type **Null**.

The next two fields in the Position table—Hours/Week and Openings—are number fields with a field size of Integer. Also, for each of these fields, Elsa wants the values displayed with no decimal places, and she does not want a default value displayed for the fields when new records are added. You'll define these two fields next.

To define the Hours/Week and Openings fields:

1. Position the insertion point in the fifth row's Field Name text box, type **Hours/Week** in the text box, and then press the **Tab** key to advance to the Data Type text box.

2. Click the **Data Type** list arrow, click **Number** in the list box, and then press the **Tab** key to advance to the Description text box.

3. Type **Work hours per week** in the Description text box.

4. Click the right side of the **Field Size** text box, and then click **Integer** to choose this setting. Recall that the Integer field size stores whole numbers in two bytes.

5. Click the right side of the **Decimal Places** text box, and then click **0** to specify no decimal places.

6. Select the value **0** in the Default Value text box, and then type **Null**.

7. Repeat Steps 1 through 6 to define the **Openings** field as the sixth field in the Position table. For the Description, enter the text **Number of openings**.

According to Elsa's design (Figure 2-5), the final three fields to be defined in the Position table are ReferredBy, a text field, and StartDate and EndDate, both date/time fields. You'll define these three fields next.

To define the ReferredBy, StartDate, and EndDate fields:

1. Position the insertion point in the seventh row's Field Name text box, type **ReferredBy** in the text box, press the **Tab** key to advance to the Data Type text box, and then press the **Tab** key again to accept the default Text data type.

2. Change the default Field Size of 50 to **30** for the ReferredBy field.

3. Position the insertion point in the eighth row's Field Name text box, type **StartDate**, and then press the **Tab** key to advance to the Data Type text box.

4. Click the **Data Type** list arrow, click **Date/Time** to select this type, press the **Tab** key, and then type **Month and day** in the Description text box.

   Elsa wants the values in the StartDate field to be displayed in a format showing only the month and day, as in the following example: 03/11. You use the Format property to control the display of a field value.

5. In the Field Properties pane, click the right side of the **Format** text box to display the list of predefined formats. As noted in the right side of the Field Properties pane, you can either choose a predefined format or enter a custom format.

   TROUBLE? If you see a list arrow instead of a list of predefined formats, click the list arrow to display the list.

   None of the predefined formats matches the layout Elsa wants for the StartDate values. Therefore, you need to create a custom date format. Figure 2-11 shows some of the symbols available for custom date and time formats. (A complete description of all the custom formats is available in Help.)

Figure 2-11	SYMBOLS FOR SOME CUSTOM DATE FORMATS

SYMBOL	DESCRIPTION
/	date separator
d	day of the month in one or two numeric digits, as needed (1 to 31)
dd	day of the month in two numeric digits (01 to 31)
ddd	first three letters of the weekday (Sun to Sat)
dddd	full name of the weekday (Sunday to Saturday)
w	day of the week (1 to 7)
ww	week of the year (1 to 53)
m	month of the year in one or two numeric digits, as needed (1 to 12)
mm	month of the year in two numeric digits (01 to 12)
mmm	first three letters of the month (Jan to Dec)
mmmm	full name of the month (January to December)
yy	last two digits of the year (01 to 99)
yyyy	full year (0100 to 9999)

Elsa wants the dates to be displayed with a two-digit month (mm) and a two-digit day (dd). You'll enter this custom format now.

6. Click the **Format** list arrow to close the list of predefined formats, and then type **mm/dd** in the Format text box. See Figure 2-12.

Figure 2-12   SPECIFYING THE CUSTOM DATE FORMAT

current field

custom date format entered

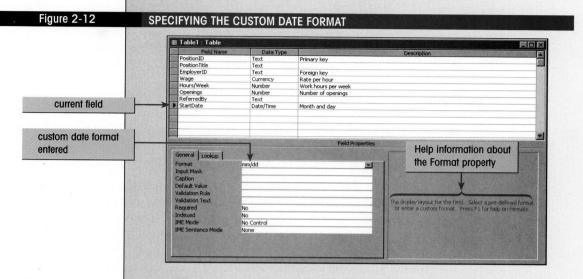

Next, you'll define the ninth and final field, EndDate. This field will have the same definition and properties as the StartDate field.

7. Place the insertion point in the ninth row's Field Name text box, type **EndDate**, and then press the **Tab** key to advance to the Data Type text box.

You can select a value from the Data Type list box as you did for the StartDate field. Alternately, you can type the property value in the text box or type just the first character of the property value.

8. Type **d**. The value in the ninth row's Data Type text box changes to "date/Time," with the letters "ate/Time" highlighted. See Figure 2-13.

Figure 2-13   SELECTING A VALUE FOR THE DATA TYPE PROPERTY

"d" typed

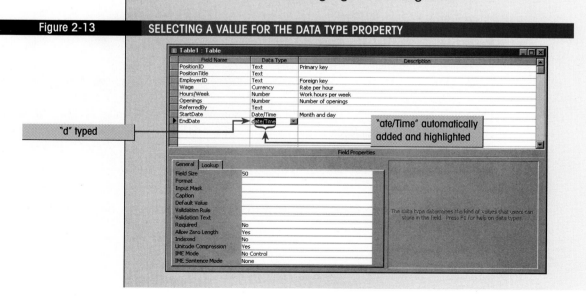

9. Press the **Tab** key to advance to the Description text box, and then type **Month and day**. Note that Access changes the value for the Data Type property to Date/Time.

10. In the Format text box, type **mm/dd** to specify the custom date format for the EndDate field.

You've finished defining the fields for the Position table. Next, you need to specify the primary key for the table.

Specifying the Primary Key

Although Access does not require a table to have a primary key, including a primary key offers several advantages:

- A primary key uniquely identifies each record in a table.
- Access does not allow duplicate values in the primary key field. If a record already exists with a PositionID value of 1320, for example, Access prevents you from adding another record with this same value in the PositionID field. Preventing duplicate values ensures the uniqueness of the primary key field.
- When a primary key has been specified, Access forces you to enter a value for the primary key field in every record in the table. This is known as **entity integrity**. If you do not enter a value for a field, you have actually given the field what is known as a **null value**. You cannot give a null value to the primary key field because entity integrity prevents Access from accepting and processing that record.
- Access stores records on disk in the same order as you enter them but displays them in order by the field values of the primary key. If you enter records in no specific order, you are ensured that you will later be able to work with them in a more meaningful, primary key sequence.
- Access responds faster to your requests for specific records based on the primary key.

REFERENCE WINDOW   **RW**

Specifying a Primary Key for a Table

- In the Table window in Design view, click the row selector for the field you've chosen to be the primary key.
- If the primary key will consist of two or more fields, press and hold down the Ctrl key, and then click the row selector for each additional primary key field.
- Click the Primary Key button on the Table Design toolbar.

According to Elsa's design, you need to specify PositionID as the primary key for the Position table.

To specify PositionID as the primary key:

1. Position the pointer on the row selector for the PositionID field until the pointer changes to a ➡ shape. See Figure 2-14.

Figure 2-14	SPECIFYING PositionID AS THE PRIMARY KEY

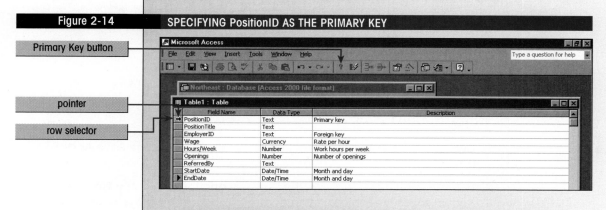

2. Click the mouse button. The entire first row of the Table Design grid is highlighted.

3. Click the **Primary Key** button ⌨ on the Table Design toolbar, and then click a row other than the first to deselect the first row. A key symbol appears in the row selector for the first row, indicating that the PositionID field is the table's primary key. See Figure 2-15.

Figure 2-15	PositionID SELECTED AS THE PRIMARY KEY

TROUBLE? Your insertion point might be in a different location from the one shown in the figure, depending on where you clicked to deselect the first row.

If you specify the wrong field as the primary key, or if you later change your mind and do not want the designated primary key field to be the table's primary key, you can select the field and then click the Primary Key button on the Table Design toolbar again, which will remove the key symbol and the primary key designation from the field. Then you can choose another field to be the primary key, if necessary.

You've defined the fields for the Position table and specified its primary key, so you can now save the table structure.

Saving the Table Structure

The last step in creating a table is to name the table and save the table's structure on disk. Once the table is saved, you can use it to enter data in the table.

> ### REFERENCE WINDOW   RW
>
> **Saving a Table Structure**
> - Click the Save button on the Table Design toolbar.
> - Type the name of the table in the Table Name text box of the Save As dialog box.
> - Click the OK button (or press the Enter key).

According to Elsa's plan, you need to save the table you've defined as "Position."

To name and save the Position table:

1. Click the **Save** button 🖫 on the Table Design toolbar. The Save As dialog box opens.

2. Type **Position** in the Table Name text box, and then press the **Enter** key. Access saves the table with the name Position in the Northeast database on your Data Disk. Notice that Position now appears instead of Table1 in the Table window title bar.

Recall that in Tutorial 1 you set the Compact on Close option for the Seasonal database so that it would be compacted automatically each time you closed it. Now you'll set this option for your new Northeast database, so that it will be compacted automatically.

To set the option for compacting the Northeast database automatically:

1. Click **Tools** on the menu bar, and then click **Options**. The Options dialog box opens.

2. Click the **General** tab in the dialog box, and then click the **Compact on Close** check box to select it.

3. Click the **OK** button to set the option.

The Position table is now complete. In Session 2.2, you'll continue to work with the Position table by entering records in it, modifying its structure, and maintaining data in the table. You will also import two tables, Employer and NAICS, from the Seasonal database into the Northeast database.

Session 2.1 QUICK CHECK

1. What guidelines should you follow when designing a database?
2. What is the purpose of the Data Type property for a field?
3. For which three types of fields can you assign a field size?

4. In Design view, which key do you press to move between the Table Design grid and the Field Properties pane?

5. You use the _____ property to control the display of a field value.

6. A(n) _____ value, which results when you do not enter a value for a field, is not permitted for a primary key.

SESSION 2.2

In this session, you will add records to a table; modify the structure of an existing table by deleting, moving, and adding fields and changing field properties; copy records from another Access database; import tables from another Access database; and update an existing database by deleting and changing records.

Adding Records to a Table

You can add records to an Access table in several ways. A table datasheet provides a simple way for you to add records. As you learned in Tutorial 1, a datasheet shows a table's contents in rows and columns. Each row is a separate record in the table, and each column contains the field values for one field in the table. If you are currently working in Design view, you first must change from Design view to Datasheet view in order to view the table's datasheet.

Elsa asks you to add the two records shown in Figure 2-16 to the Position table. These two records contain data for positions that have recently become available at two employers.

Figure 2-16	RECORDS TO BE ADDED TO THE POSITION TABLE							
PositionID	PositionTitle	EmployerID	Wage	Hours/Week	Openings	ReferredBy	StartDate	EndDate
2021	Waiter/Waitress	10155	9.50	30	1	Sue Brown	6/30	9/15
2017	Tour Guide	10149	15.00	20	1	Ed Curran	9/21	11/1

To add the records in the Position table datasheet:

1. If you took a break after the previous session, make sure that Access is running and that the Position table of the Northeast database is open in Design view. To open the table in Design view from the Database window, right-click the **Position** table, and then click **Design View** on the shortcut menu.

   Access displays the fields you defined for the Position table in Design view. Now you need to switch to Datasheet view so that you can enter the two records for Elsa.

2. Click the **View** button for Datasheet view ▦ on the Table Design toolbar. The Table window opens in Datasheet view. See Figure 2-17.

Figure 2-17   TABLE WINDOW IN DATASHEET VIEW

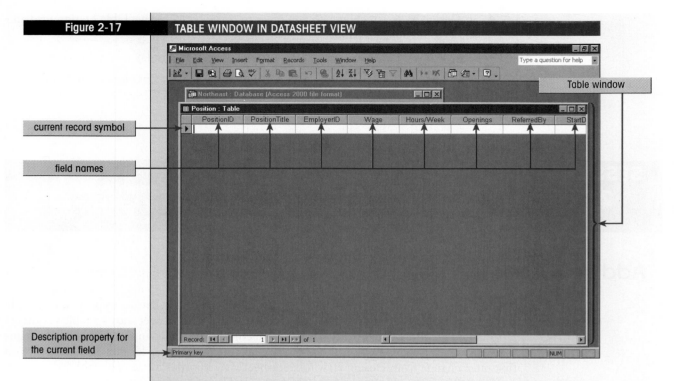

The table's nine field names appear at the top of the datasheet. Some of the field names might not be visible. The current record symbol in the first row's record selector identifies the currently selected record, which contains no data until you enter the first record. The insertion point is located in the first row's PositionID field, whose Description property appears on the status bar.

3. Type **2021**, which is the first record's PositionID field value, and then press the **Tab** key. Each time you press the Tab key, the insertion point moves to the right to the next field in the record. See Figure 2-18.

Figure 2-18   DATASHEET FOR POSITION TABLE AFTER ENTERING THE FIRST FIELD VALUE

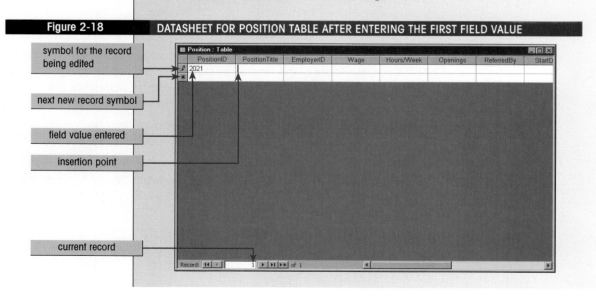

TROUBLE? If you make a mistake when typing a value, use the Backspace key to delete characters to the left of the insertion point or the Delete key to delete characters to the right of the insertion point. Then type the correct value. If you want to correct a value by replacing it entirely, double-click the value to select it, and then type the correct value.

The pencil symbol in the first row's record selector indicates that the record is being edited. The star symbol in the second row's record selector identifies the second row as the next one available for a new record. Notice that all the fields are initially empty; this occurs because you set the Default Value property for the fields (as appropriate) to Null.

4. Type **Waiter/Waitress** in the PositionTitle field, and then press the **Tab** key. The insertion point moves to the EmployerID field.

5. Type **10155** and then press the **Tab** key. The insertion point moves to the right side of the Wage field.

   Recall that the PositionID, PositionTitle, and EmployerID fields are all text fields and that the Wage field is a currency field. Field values for text fields are left-aligned in their boxes, and field values for number, date/time, and currency fields are right-aligned in their boxes.

6. Type **9.5** and then press the **Tab** key. Access displays the field value with a dollar sign and two decimal places ($9.50), as specified by the currency format. You do not need to type the dollar sign, commas, or decimal point (for whole dollar amounts) because Access adds these symbols automatically for you.

7. In the Hours/Week field, type **30**, press the **Tab** key, type **1** in the Openings field, and then press the **Tab** key.

8. Type **Sue Brown** in the ReferredBy field, and then press the **Tab** key. Depending on your monitor's resolution and size, the display of the datasheet might shift so that the next field, StartDate, is completely visible.

9. Type **6/30** in the StartDate field, and then press the **Tab** key. Access displays the value as 06/30, as specified by the custom date format (mm/dd) you set for this field. The insertion point moves to the final field in the table, EndDate.

10. Type **9/15** in the EndDate field, and then press the **Tab** key. Access displays the value as 09/15, shifts the display of the datasheet back to the left, stores the first completed record in the Position table, removes the pencil symbol from the first row's record selector, advances the insertion point to the second row's PositionID text box, and places the current record symbol in the second row's record selector.

    Now you can enter the values for the second record.

11. Refer to Figure 2-16, and repeat Steps 3 through 10 to add the second record to the table. Access saves the record in the Position table, and moves the insertion point to the beginning of the third row. See Figure 2-19.

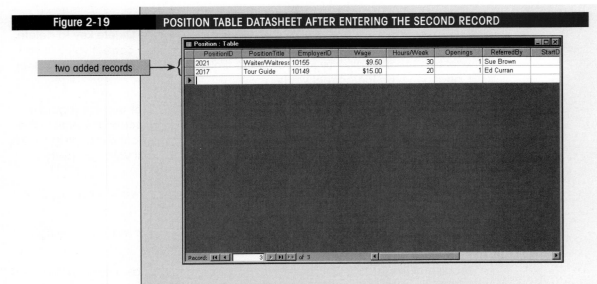

| Figure 2-19 | POSITION TABLE DATASHEET AFTER ENTERING THE SECOND RECORD |

two added records

Notice that "Record 3 of 3" appears around the navigation buttons, even though the table contains only two records. Access is anticipating that you will enter a new record, which would be the third of three records in the table. If you moved the insertion point to the second record, the display would change to "Record 2 of 2."

Notice that the two records are currently listed in the order in which you entered them. However, once you close the table or change to another view, and then redisplay the table datasheet, the records will be listed in primary key order by the values in the PositionID field.

Modifying the Structure of an Access Table

Even a well-designed table might need to be modified. For example, the government at all levels and competitors place demands on a company to track more data and to modify the data it already tracks. Access allows you to modify a table's structure in Design view: you can add and delete fields, change the order of fields, and change the properties of the fields.

After holding a meeting with her staff members and reviewing the structure of the Position table and the format of the field values in the datasheet, Elsa has several changes she wants you to make to the table. First, she has decided that it's not necessary to keep track of the name of the person who originally requested a particular position, so she wants you to delete the ReferredBy field. Also, she thinks that the Wage field should remain a currency field, but she wants the dollar signs removed from the displayed field values in the datasheet. She also wants the Openings field moved to the end of the table. Finally, she wants you to add a new yes/no field, named Experience, to the table to indicate whether the available position requires that potential recruits have prior experience in that type of work. The Experience field will be inserted between the Hours/Week and StartDate fields. Figure 2-20 shows Elsa's modified design for the Position table.

Figure 2-20	MODIFIED DESIGN FOR THE POSITION TABLE			
Field Name	Data Type	Field Size	Description	
PositionID	Text	4	Primary key	
PositionTitle	Text	30		
EmployerID	Text	5	Foreign key	
Wage	Currency		Rate per hour	
Hours/Week	Number	Integer	Work hours per week	
Experience	Yes/No		Experience required	
StartDate	Date/Time		Month and day	
EndDate	Date/Time		Month and day	
Openings	Number	Integer	Number of openings	

You'll begin modifying the table by deleting the ReferredBy field.

Deleting a Field

After you've defined a table structure and added records to the table, you can delete a field from the table structure. When you delete a field, you also delete all the values for the field from the table. Therefore, you should make sure that you need to delete a field and that you delete the correct field.

REFERENCE WINDOW   **RW**

Deleting a Field from a Table Structure
■ In the Table window in Design view, right-click the row selector for the field you want to delete, to select the field and display the shortcut menu.
■ Click Delete Rows on the shortcut menu.

You need to delete the ReferredBy field from the Position table structure.

To delete the ReferredBy field:

1. Click the **View** button for Design view ⌐ on the Table Datasheet toolbar. The Table window for the Position table opens in Design view.

2. Position the pointer on the row selector for the ReferredBy field until the pointer changes to a ➡ shape.

3. Right-click to select the entire row for the ReferredBy field and display the short-cut menu, and then click **Delete Rows**.

   A dialog box opens asking you to confirm the deletion.

4. Click the **Yes** button to close the dialog box and to delete the field and its values from the table. See Figure 2-21.

Figure 2-21   **TABLE STRUCTURE AFTER DELETING ReferredBy FIELD**

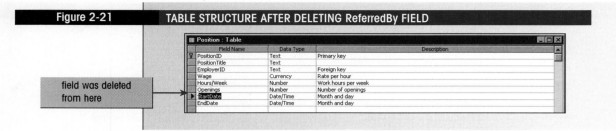

field was deleted
from here

You have deleted the ReferredBy field in the Table window, but the change doesn't take place in the table on disk until you save the table structure. Because you have other modifications to make to the table, you'll wait until you finish them all before saving the modified table structure to disk.

Moving a Field

To move a field, you use the mouse to drag it to a new location in the Table window in Design view. Your next modification to the Position table structure is to move the Openings field to the end of the table, as Elsa requested.

To move the Openings field:

1. Click the **row selector** for the Openings field to select the entire row.

2. Place the pointer in the row selector for the Openings field, click the ⇗ pointer, and then drag the ⇗ pointer to the row selector below the EndDate row selector. See Figure 2-22.

Figure 2-22   **MOVING A FIELD IN THE TABLE STRUCTURE**

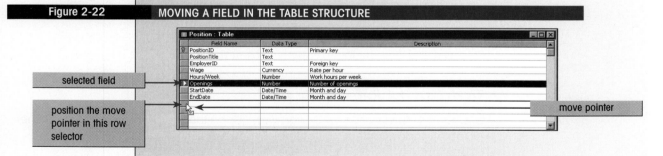

selected field

position the move
pointer in this row
selector

move pointer

3. Release the mouse button. Access moves the Openings field below the EndDate field in the table structure.

   TROUBLE? If the Openings field did not move, repeat Steps 1 through 3, making sure you firmly hold down the mouse button during the drag operation.

Adding a Field

Next, you need to add the Experience field to the table structure between the Hours/Week and StartDate fields. To add a new field between existing fields, you must insert a row. You begin by selecting the field that will be below the new field you want to insert.

To add the Experience field to the Position table:

1. Right-click the **row selector** for the StartDate field to select this field and display the shortcut menu, and then click **Insert Rows**. Access adds a new, blank row between the Hours/Week and StartDate fields. See Figure 2-23.

Figure 2-23   **AFTER INSERTING A ROW IN THE TABLE STRUCTURE**

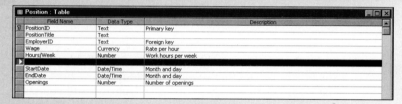

You'll define the Experience field in the new row of the Position table. Access will add this new field to the Position table structure between the Hours/Week and StartDate fields.

2. Click the **Field Name** text box for the new row, type **Experience**, and then press the **Tab** key.

The Experience field will be a yes/no field that will specify whether prior work experience is required for the position.

3. Type **y**. Access completes the data type as "yes/No."

4. Press the **Tab** key to select the yes/no data type and to move to the Description text box.

Notice that Access changes the value in the Data Type text box from "yes/No" to "Yes/No."

5. Type **Experience required** in the Description text box.

Elsa wants the Experience field to have a Default Value property value of "No," so you need to set this property.

6. In the Field Properties pane, click the **Default Value** text box, type **no**, and then click somewhere outside of the Default Value text box to deselect the value. Notice that Access changes the Default Value property value from "no" to "No." See Figure 2-24.

Figure 2-24	EXPERIENCE FIELD ADDED TO THE POSITION TABLE

new field

Default Value property
set to "No"

TROUBLE? Your insertion point might be in a different location from the one shown in the figure, depending on where you clicked to deselect the value.

You've completed adding the Experience field to the Position table in Design view. As with the other changes you've made in Design view, however, the Experience field is not added to the Position table in the Northeast database until you save the changes to the table structure.

Changing Field Properties

Elsa's last modification to the table structure is to remove the dollar signs from the Wage field values displayed in the datasheet—repeated dollar signs are unnecessary and they clutter the datasheet. As you learned earlier when defining the StartDate and EndDate fields, you use the Format property to control the display of a field value.

To change the Format property of the Wage field:

1. Click the **Description** text box for the Wage field. The Wage field is now the current field.

2. Click the right side of the **Format** text box to display the Format list box. See Figure 2-25.

Figure 2-25   **FORMAT LIST BOX FOR THE WAGE FIELD**

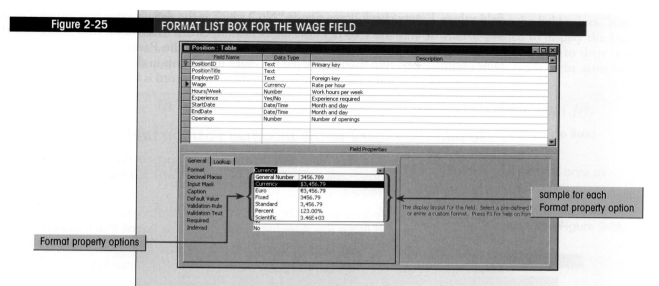

Format property options

Currency
General Number   3456.789
Currency $3,456.79
Euro   €3,456.79
Fixed   3456.79
Standard   3,456.79
Percent   123.00%
Scientific   3.46E+03

sample for each Format property option

The display layout for the field. Select a pre-defined or enter a custom format. Press F1 for help on for

To the right of each Format property option is a field value whose appearance represents a sample of the option. The Standard option specifies the format Elsa wants for the Wage field.

3. Click **Standard** in the Format list box to accept this option for the Format property.

Elsa wants you to add a third record to the Position table datasheet. Before you can add the record, you must save the modified table structure, and then switch to the Position table datasheet.

To save the modified table structure, and then switch to the datasheet:

1. Click the **Save** button 🖫 on the Table Design toolbar. The modified table structure for the Position table is stored in the Northeast database. Note that if you forget to save the modified structure and try to close the table or switch to another view, Access will prompt you to save the table before you can continue.

2. Click the **View** button for Datasheet view 🔲 on the Table Design toolbar. The Position table datasheet opens. See Figure 2-26.

Figure 2-26   **DATASHEET FOR THE MODIFIED POSITION TABLE**

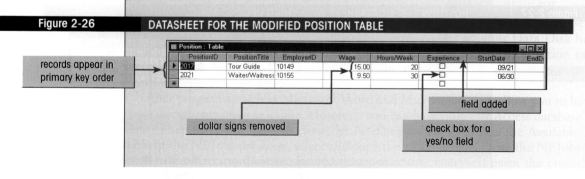

records appear in primary key order

dollar signs removed

field added

check box for a yes/no field

Notice that the ReferredBy field no longer appears in the datasheet, the Openings field is now the rightmost column (you might need to scroll the datasheet to see it), the Wage field values do not contain dollar signs, and the Experience field appears between the Hours/Week and StartDate fields. The Experience column contains check boxes to represent the yes/no

To copy the records from the Available Positions table:

1. Click the **Close** button ☒ on the Table window title bar to close the Position table. A message box opens asking if you want to save the changes to the layout of the Position table. This box appears because you resized the datasheet columns to their best fit.

2. Click the **Yes** button in the message box.

3. Click ☒ on the Database window title bar to close the Northeast database.

4. Click the **Open** button 🗁 on the Database toolbar to display the Open dialog box.

5. If necessary, display the list of files on your Data Disk, and then open the **Tutorial** folder.

6. Open the database file named **NEJobs**. The Database window opens. Notice that the NEJobs database contains only one table, the Available Positions table. This table contains the records you need to copy.

7. Click **Available Positions** in the Tables list box (if necessary), and then click the **Open** button in the Database window. The datasheet for the Available Positions table opens. See Figure 2-29. Note that this table contains a total of 62 records.

Figure 2-29	DATASHEET FOR THE NEJobs DATABASE'S AVAILABLE POSITIONS TABLE

click here to select all records

total number of records in the table

Elsa wants you to copy all the records in the Available Positions table. You can select all records by clicking the row selector for the field name row.

8. Click the **row selector** for the field name row (see Figure 2-29). All the records in the table are now highlighted, which means that Access has selected all of them.

9. Click the **Copy** button 🖺 on the Table Datasheet toolbar. All the records are copied to the Windows Clipboard.

   TROUBLE? If a Clipboard panel opens in the Task Pane, click its Close button to close it, and then continue with Step 10.

10. Click ☒ on the Table window title bar. A dialog box opens asking if you want to save the data you copied to the Windows Clipboard.

11. Click the **Yes** button in the dialog box. The dialog box closes, and then the table closes.

12. Click ☒ on the Database window title bar to close the NEJobs database.

To finish copying and pasting the records, you must open the Position table and paste the copied records into the table.

To paste the copied records into the Position table:

1. Click **File** on the menu bar, and then click **Northeast** in the list of recently opened databases. The Database window opens, showing the tables for the Northeast database.

2. In the Tables list box, click **Position** (if necessary), and then click the **Open** button in the Database window. The datasheet for the Position table opens.

You must paste the records at the end of the table.

3. Click the **row selector** for row four, which is the next row available for a new record.

4. Click the **Paste** button 🛍 on the Table Datasheet toolbar. A dialog box opens asking if you are sure you want to paste the records (62 in all).

5. Click the **Yes** button. All the records are pasted from the Windows Clipboard, and the pasted records remain highlighted. See Figure 2-30. Notice that the table now contains a total of 65 records—the three original records plus the 62 copied records.

Figure 2-30	TABLE AFTER COPYING AND PASTING RECORDS

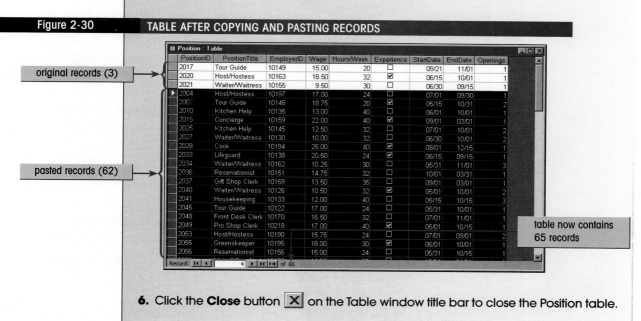

6. Click the **Close** button ☒ on the Table window title bar to close the Position table.

Importing a Table from Another Access Database

When you import a table from one Access database to another, you place a copy of the table—including its structure, field definitions, and field values—in the database into which you import it. There are two ways to import a table from another Access database into your current database: using the Get External Data option on the File menu, or using the Import Table Wizard, which is available in the New Table dialog box. You'll use both methods to import the two tables from the Seasonal database into your Northeast database.

To import the Employer and NAICS tables:

1. Make sure the Northeast Database window is open on your screen.

2. Click **File** on the menu bar, position the pointer on the double-arrow at the bottom of the File menu to display the full menu (if necessary), point to **Get External Data**, and then click **Import**. The Import dialog box opens. This dialog box is similar to the Open dialog box.

3. Display the list of files in your Tutorial folder, click **Seasonal**, and then click the **Import** button. The Import Objects dialog box opens. See Figure 2-31.

| Figure 2-31 | IMPORT OBJECTS DIALOG BOX |

table objects in the
Seasonal database

The Tables tab of the dialog box lists both tables in the Seasonal database—Employer and NAICS. Note that you can import other objects as well (queries, forms, reports, and so on).

4. Click **Employer** in the list of tables, and then click the **OK** button. The Import Objects dialog box closes, and the Employer table is now listed in the Northeast Database window.

Now you'll use the Import Table Wizard to import the NAICS table. (Note that you could also use the Select All button in the Import Objects dialog box to import all the objects listed on the current tab at the same time.)

5. Click the **New** button in the Database window, click **Import Table** in the New Table dialog box, and then click the **OK** button. The Import dialog box opens.

6. If necessary, display the list of files in your Tutorial folder, click **Seasonal**, and then click the **Import** button. The Import Objects dialog box opens, again displaying the tables in the Seasonal database.

7. Click **NAICS** in the list of tables, and then click the **OK** button to import the NAICS table into the Northeast database.

Now that you have all the records in the Position table and all three tables in the Northeast database, Elsa examines the records to make sure they are correct. She finds one record in the Position table that she wants you to delete and another record that needs changes to its field values.

Updating a Database

Updating, or **maintaining**, a database is the process of adding, changing, and deleting records in database tables to keep them current and accurate. You've already added records to the Position table. Now Elsa wants you to delete and change records.

Deleting Records

To delete a record, you need to select the record in Datasheet view, and then delete it using the Delete Record button on the Table Datasheet toolbar or the Delete Record option on the shortcut menu.

REFERENCE WINDOW   **RW**

Deleting a Record

- In the Table window in Datasheet view, click the row selector for the record you want to delete, and then click the Delete Record button on the Table Datasheet toolbar (or right-click the row selector for the record, and then click Delete Record on the shortcut menu).
- In the dialog box asking you to confirm the deletion, click the Yes button.

Elsa asks you to delete the record whose PositionID is 2015 because this record was entered in error; the position for this record does not exist. The fourth record in the table has a PositionID value of 2015. This record is the one you need to delete.

To delete the record:

1. Open the Position table in Datasheet view.

2. Right-click the **row selector** for row four. Access selects the fourth record and displays the shortcut menu. See Figure 2-32.

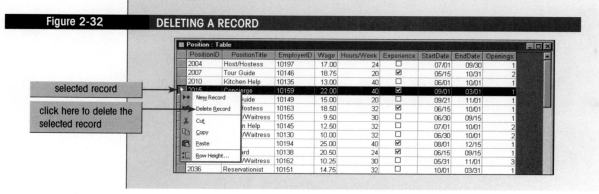

Figure 2-32   **DELETING A RECORD**

selected record

click here to delete the selected record

3. Click **Delete Record** on the shortcut menu. Access deletes the record and opens a dialog box asking you to confirm the deletion. Because the deletion of a record is permanent and cannot be undone, Access prompts you to make sure that you want to delete the record.

TROUBLE? If you selected the wrong record for deletion, click the No button. Access ends the deletion process and continues to display the selected record. Repeat Steps 2 and 3 to delete the correct record.

4. Click the **Yes** button to confirm the deletion and close the dialog box.

Elsa's final update to the Position table involves changes to field values in one of the records.

Changing Records

To change the field values in a record, you first must make the record the current record. Then you position the insertion point in the field value to make minor changes or select the field value to replace it entirely. In Tutorial 1, you used the mouse with the scroll bars and the navigation buttons to navigate through the records in a datasheet. You can also use keystroke combinations and the F2 key to navigate a datasheet and to select field values.

The **F2 key** is a toggle that you use to switch between navigation mode and editing mode:

- In **navigation mode**, Access selects an entire field value. If you type while you are in navigation mode, your typed entry replaces the highlighted field value.
- In **editing mode**, you can insert or delete characters in a field value based on the location of the insertion point.

Figure 2-33 shows some of the navigation mode and editing mode keystroke techniques.

Figure 2-33	NAVIGATION MODE AND EDITING MODE KEYSTROKE TECHNIQUES	
PRESS	**TO MOVE THE SELECTION IN NAVIGATION MODE**	**TO MOVE THE INSERTION POINT IN EDITING MODE**
←	Left one field value at a time	Left one character at a time
→	Right one field value at a time	Right one character at a time
Home	Left to the first field value in the record	To the left of the first character in the field value
End	Right to the last field value in the record	To the right of the last character in the field value
↑ or ↓	Up or down one record at a time	Up or down one record at a time and switch to navigation mode
Tab or Enter	Right one field value at a time	Right one field value at a time and switch to navigation mode
Ctrl + Home	To the first field value in the first record	To the left of the first character in the field value
Ctrl + End	To the last field value in the last record	To the right of the last character in the field value

The record Elsa wants you to change has a PositionID field value of 2125. Some of the values were entered incorrectly for this record, and you need to enter the correct values.

To modify the record:

1. Make sure the PositionID field value for the fourth record is still highlighted, indicating that the table is in navigation mode.

2. Press **Ctrl + End**. Access displays records from the end of the table and selects the last field value in the last record. This field value is for the Openings field.

3. Press the **Home** key. The first field value in the last record is now selected. This field value is for the PositionID field.

4. Press the ↑ key. The PositionID field value for the previous record (PositionID 2125) is selected. This record is the one you need to change.

   Elsa wants you to change these field values in the record: PositionID to 2124, EmployerID to 10163, Wage to 14.50, Experience to "Yes" (checked), and EndDate to 10/15.

5. Type **2124**, press the **Tab** key twice, type **10163**, press the **Tab** key, type **14.5**, press the **Tab** key twice, press the **spacebar** to insert a check mark in the Experience check box, press the **Tab** key twice, and then type **10/15**. The changes to the record are complete. See Figure 2-34.

| Figure 2-34 | TABLE AFTER CHANGING FIELD VALUES IN A RECORD |

field values changed

2115	Gift Shop Clerk	10154	13.00	25	☐	05/01	09/30	1
2117	Housekeeping	10220	13.50	30	☐	06/30	09/30	3
2118	Greenskeeper	10218	17.00	32	☐	05/01	11/01	1
2120	Lifeguard	10154	19.00	32	☑	06/15	09/30	2
2122	Kitchen Help	10151	13.00	35	☐	09/01	03/31	3
2123	Main Office Clerk	10170	14.50	32	☐	07/01	11/15	1
2124	Kitchen Help	10163	14.50	40	☑	06/01	10/15	2
2127	Waiter/Waitress	10185	10.50	40	☐	12/01	05/01	1

Record: |◀ ◀ [63] ▶ ▶| ▶* of 64

You've completed all of Elsa's updates to the Position table. Now you can exit Access.

6. Click the **Close** button ☒ on the Access window title bar to close the Position table and the Northeast database, and to exit Access.

Elsa and her staff members approve of the revised table structure for the Position table. They are confident that the table will allow them to easily track position data for NSJI's employer customers.

Session 2.2 QUICK CHECK

1. What does a pencil symbol in a datasheet's row selector represent? A star symbol?

2. What is the effect of deleting a field from a table structure?

3. How do you insert a field between existing fields in a table structure?

4. A field with the _____ data type can appear in the table datasheet as a check box.

5. Describe the two ways in which you can display the Import dialog box, so that you can import a table from one Access database to another.

6. In Datasheet view, what is the difference between navigation mode and editing mode?

REVIEW ASSIGNMENTS

Elsa needs a database to track data about the students recruited by NSJI and about the recruiters who find jobs for the students. She asks you to create the database by completing the following:

1. Make sure your Data Disk is in the appropriate disk drive, and then start Access.

2. Create a new, blank database named **Recruits** and save it in the Review folder on your Data Disk.

Explore

3. Use the Table Wizard to create a new table named **Recruiter** in the **Recruits** database, as follows:

   a. Base the new table on the Employees sample table, which is one of the sample tables in the Business category.

   b. Add the following fields to your table (in the order shown): SocialSecurityNumber, Salary, FirstName, MiddleName, and LastName.

   c. Click SocialSecurityNumber in the "Fields in my new table" list, and then use the Rename Field button to change the name of this field to SSN. Click the Next button.

   d. Name the new table **Recruiter**, and choose the option for setting the primary key yourself. Click the Next button.

   e. Specify SSN as the primary key field and accept the default data type. Click the Next button.

   f. In the final Table Wizard dialog box, click the Finish button to display the table in Datasheet view. (*Note:* The field names appear with spaces between words; this is how the Table Wizard is set up to format these field names when they appear in Datasheet view.)

4. Add the recruiter records shown in Figure 2-35 to the **Recruiter** table. (*Note:* You do not have to type the dashes in the SSN field values or commas in the Salary field values; the Table Wizard formatted these fields so that these symbols are entered automatically for you.)

Figure 2-35

SSN	Salary	First Name	Middle Name	Last Name
892-77-1201	40,000	Kate	Teresa	Foster
901-63-1554	38,500	Paul	Michael	Kirnicki
893-91-0178	40,000	Ryan	James	DuBrava

5. Make the following changes to the structure of the **Recruiter** table:

   a. Move the Salary field so that it appears after the LastName field.

   b. Add a new field between the LastName and Salary fields, using the following properties:

Field Name:	BonusQuota
Data Type:	Number
Description:	Number of recruited students needed to receive bonus
Field Size:	Byte
Decimal Places:	0

   c. Change the format of the Salary field so that commas are displayed, dollar signs are not displayed, and no decimal places are displayed in the field values.

   d. Save the revised table structure.

6. Use the **Recruiter** datasheet to update the database as follows:

   a. Enter these BonusQuota values for the three records: 60 for Kate Foster; 60 for Ryan DuBrava; and 50 for Paul Kirnicki.

   b. Add a record to the **Recruiter** datasheet with the following field values:

SSN:	899-40-2937
First Name:	Sonia
Middle Name:	Lee
Last Name:	Xu
BonusQuota:	50
Salary:	39,250

7. Close the **Recruiter** table, and then set the option for compacting the **Recruits** database on close.

8. Elsa created a database with her name as the database name. The **Recruiter Employees** table in that database has the same format as the **Recruiter** table you created. Copy all the records from the **Recruiter Employees** table in the **Elsa** database (located in the Review folder on your Data Disk) to the end of the **Recruiter** table in the **Recruits** database.

Explore ▶ 9. Because you added a number of records to the database, its size has increased. Compact the database manually using the Compact and Repair Database option.

10. Delete the MiddleName field from the **Recruiter** table structure, and then save the table structure.

11. Resize all columns in the datasheet for the **Recruiter** table to their best fit.

12. Print the **Recruiter** table datasheet, and then save and close the table.

13. Create a table named **Student** using the Import Table Wizard. The table you need to import is named **Student**, which is one of the tables in the **Elsa** database located in the Review folder on your Data Disk.

14. Make the following modifications to the structure of the **Student** table in the **Recruits** database:
   a. Enter the following Description property values:
      StudentID: Primary key
      SSN: Foreign key value of the recruiter for this student
   b. Change the Field Size property for both the FirstName field and the LastName field to 15.
   c. Move the BirthDate field so that it appears between the Nation and Gender fields.
   d. Change the format of the BirthDate field so that it displays only two digits for the year instead of four.
   e. Save the table structure changes. (Answer "Yes" to any warning messages about property changes and lost data.)

15. Switch to Datasheet view, and then resize all columns in the datasheet to fit the data.

16. Delete the record with the StudentID DRI9901 from the **Student** table.

17. Save, print, and then close the **Student** datasheet.

18. Close the **Recruits** database, and then exit Access.

CASE PROBLEMS

Case 1. Lim's Video Photography Youngho Lim uses the **Videos** database to maintain information about the clients, contracts, and events for his video photography business. Youngho asks you to help him maintain the database by completing the following:

1. Make sure your Data Disk is in the appropriate disk drive.

2. Start Access and open the **Videos** database located in the Cases folder on your Data Disk.

Explore ▶ 3. Use Design view to create a table using the table design shown in Figure 2-36.

Figure 2-36

Field Name	Data Type	Description	Field Size	Other Properties
Shoot#	Number	Primary key	Long Integer	Decimal Places: 0 Default Value: Null
ShootType	Text		2	
ShootTime	Date/Time			Format: Medium Time
Duration	Number	# of hours	Single	Default Value: Null
Contact	Text	Person who booked shoot	30	
Location	Text		30	
ShootDate	Date/Time			Format: mm/dd/yyyy
Contract#	Number	Foreign key	Integer	Decimal Places: 0 Default Value: Null

4. Specify Shoot# as the primary key, and then save the table as **Shoot**.

5. Add the records shown in Figure 2-37 to the **Shoot** table.

Figure 2-37

Shoot#	ShootType	ShootTime	Duration	Contact	Location	ShootDate	Contract#
927032	AP	4:00 PM	3.5	Ellen Quirk	Elm Lodge	9/27/2003	2412
103031	HP	9:00 AM	3.5	Tom Bradbury	Client's home	10/30/2003	2611

6. Youngho created a database named **Events** that contains a table with shoot data named **Shoot Events**. The **Shoot** table you created has the same format as the **Shoot Events** table. Copy all the records from the **Shoot Events** table in the **Events** database (located in the Cases folder on your Data Disk) to the end of the **Shoot** table in the **Videos** database.

7. Modify the structure of the **Shoot** table by completing the following:

   a. Delete the Contact field.

   b. Move the ShootDate field so that it appears between the ShootType and ShootTime fields.

8. Switch to Datasheet view and resize all columns in the datasheet for the **Shoot** table to their best fit.

9. Use the **Shoot** datasheet to update the database as follows:

   a. For Shoot# 421032, change the ShootTime value to 7:00 PM, and change the Location value to Le Bistro.

   b. Add a record to the **Shoot** datasheet with the following field values:

      Shoot#:   913032
      ShootType: SE
      ShootDate: 9/13/2003
      ShootTime: 1:00 PM
      Duration: 2.5
      Location: High School football field
      Contract#:   2501

10. Switch to Design view, and then switch back to Datasheet view so that the records appear in primary key sequence by Shoot#. Resize any datasheet columns to their best fit, as necessary.

11. Print the **Shoot** table datasheet, and then save and close the table.

Explore   12. Create a table named **ShootDesc**, based on the data shown in Figure 2-38 and according to the following steps:

Figure 2-38

ShootType	ShootDesc
AP	Anniversary Party
BM	Bar/Bat Mitzvah
BP	Birthday Party
CP	Insurance Commercial Property
DR	Dance Recital
GR	Graduation
HP	Insurance Home Property
LS	Legal Services
RC	Religious Ceremony
SE	Sports Event
WE	Wedding

   a. Select the Datasheet View option in the New Table dialog box.

   b. Enter the 11 records shown in Figure 2-38. (Do *not* enter the field names at this point.)

   c. Switch to Design view, supply the table name, and then answer "No" if asked if you want to create a primary key.

   d. Type the following field names and set the following properties for the two text fields:
     ShootType
      Description: Primary key
      Field Size: 2
     ShootDesc
      Description: Description of shoot
      Field Size: 30
   e. Specify the primary key, save the table structure changes, and then switch back to Datasheet view. If you receive any warning messages, answer "Yes" to continue.
   f. Resize both datasheet columns to their best fit; then save, print, and close the datasheet.

13. Close the **Videos** database, and then exit Access.

Case 2. DineAtHome.course.com   Claire Picard uses the **Meals** database to track information about local restaurants and orders placed at the restaurants by the customers of her e-commerce business. You'll help her maintain this database by completing the following:

1. Make sure your Data Disk is in the appropriate disk drive.

2. Start Access and open the **Meals** database located in the Cases folder on your Data Disk.

3. Use Design view to create a table using the table design shown in Figure 2-39.

Figure 2-39

Field Name	Data Type	Description	Field Size	Other Properties
Order#	Number	Primary key	Long Integer	Decimal Places: 0 Default Value: Null
Restaurant#	Number	Foreign key	Long Integer	Decimal Places: 0
OrderAmt	Currency	Total amount of order		Format: Fixed

4. Specify Order# as the primary key, and then save the table as **Order**.

5. Add the records shown in Figure 2-40 to the **Order** table.

Figure 2-40

Order#	Restaurant#	OrderAmt
3117	131	155.35
3123	115	45.42
3020	120	85.50

Explore

6. Modify the structure of the **Order** table by adding a new field between the Restaurant# and OrderAmt fields, with the following properties:
    Field Name: OrderDate
    Data Type: Date/Time
    Format: Long Date

7. Use the revised **Order** datasheet to update the database as follows:
   a. Enter the following OrderDate values for the three records: 1/15/03 for Order# 3020, 4/2/03 for Order# 3117, and 5/1/03 for Order# 3123.
   b. Add a new record to the **Order** datasheet with the following field values:
     Order#:   3045
     Restaurant#:   108
     OrderDate: 3/16/03
     OrderAmt: 50.25

8. Claire created a database named **Customer** that contains a table with order data named **Order Records**. The **Order** table you created has the same format as the **Order Records** table. Copy all the records from the **Order Records** table in the **Customer** database (located in the Cases folder on your Data Disk) to the end of the **Order** table in the **Meals** database.

9. Resize all columns in the datasheet for the **Order** table to their best fit.

10. For Order# 3039, change the OrderAmt value to 87.30.

11. Delete the record for Order# 3068.

12. Print the **Order** table datasheet, and then save and close the table.

13. Close the **Meals** database, and then exit Access.

Case 3. Redwood Zoo Michael Rosenfeld continues to track information about donors, their pledges, and the status of funds to benefit the Redwood Zoo. Help him maintain the **Redwood** database by completing the following:

1. Make sure your Data Disk is in the appropriate disk drive.

2. Start Access and open the **Redwood** database located in the Cases folder on your Data Disk.

3. Create a table named **Pledge** using the Import Table Wizard. The table you need to import is named **Pledge Records**, which is located in the **Pledge** database in the Cases folder on your Data Disk.

Explore ▶ 4. After importing the **Pledge Records** table, use the shortcut menu to rename the table to **Pledge** in the Database window.

Explore ▶ 5. Modify the structure of the **Pledge** table by completing the following:

    a. Enter the following Description property values:

        Pledge#:   Primary key

        DonorID: Foreign key

        FundCode: Foreign key

    b. Change the format of the PledgeDate field to mm/dd/yyyy.

    c. Change the Data Type of the TotalPledged field to Currency with the Standard format.

    d. Specify a Default Value of B for the PaymentMethod field.

    e. Specify a Default Value of F for the PaymentSchedule field.

    f. Save the modified table structure.

6. Switch to Datasheet view, and then resize all columns in the datasheet to their best fit.

7. Use the **Pledge** datasheet to update the database as follows:

    a. Add a new record to the **Pledge** table with the following field values:

        Pledge#:   2695

        DonorID: 59045

        FundCode: P15

        PledgeDate: 7/11/2003

        TotalPledged: 1000

        PaymentMethod: B

        PaymentSchedule: M

    b. Change the TotalPledged value for Pledge# 2499 to 150.

    c. Change the FundCode value for Pledge# 2332 to B03.

8. Print the **Pledge** table datasheet, and then save and close the table.

9. Close the **Redwood** database, and then exit Access.

Case 4. Mountain River Adventures Connor and Siobhan Dempsey use the **Trips** database to track the data about the guided tours they provide. You'll help them maintain this database by completing the following:

1. Make sure your Data Disk is in the appropriate disk drive.

2. Start Access and open the **Trips** database located in the Cases folder on your Data Disk.

Explore ▶ 3. Use the Import Spreadsheet Wizard to create a new table named **Rafting Trip**. The data you need to import is contained in the **Rafting** workbook, which is a Microsoft Excel file located in the Cases folder on your Data Disk.

    a. Select the Import Table option in the New Table dialog box.

    b. Change the entry in the Files of type list box to display the list of Excel workbook files in the Cases folder.

   c. Select the **Rafting** file and then click the Import button.

   d. In the Import Spreadsheet Wizard dialog boxes, choose the Sheet1 worksheet; choose the option for using column headings as field names; select the option for choosing your own primary key; specify Trip# as the primary key; and enter the table name (**Rafting Trip**). Otherwise, accept the Wizard's choices for all other options for the imported data.

4. Open the **Rafting Trip** table and resize all datasheet columns to their best fit.

5. Modify the structure of the **Rafting Trip** table by completing the following:

   a. For the Trip# field, enter a Description property of "Primary key", change the Field Size to Long Integer, and set the Decimal Places property to 0.

   b. For the River field, change the Field Size to 45.

   c. For the TripDistance field, enter a Description property of "Distance in miles", change the Field Size to Integer, and set the Decimal Places property to 0.

   d. For the TripDays field, enter a Description property of "Number of days for the trip", and change the Field Size to Single.

   e. For the Fee/Person field, change the Data Type to Currency and set the Format property to Fixed.

   f. Save the table structure. If you receive any warning messages about lost data or integrity rules, click the Yes button.

6. Use the **Rafting Trip** datasheet to update the database as follows:

   a. For Trip# 3142, change the TripDistance value to 20.

   b. Add a new record to the **Rafting Trip** table with the following field values:

Trip#:	3675
River:	Colorado River (Grand Canyon)
TripDistance:	110
TripDays:	2.5
Fee/Person:	215

   c. Delete the record for Trip# 3423.

7. Print the **Rafting Trip** table datasheet, and then close the table.

8. Use Design view to create a new table named **Booking** using the table design shown in Figure 2-41.

Figure 2-41

Field Name	Data Type	Description	Field Size	Other Properties
Booking#	Number	Primary key	Long Integer	Decimal Places: 0 Default Value: Null
Client#	Number	Foreign key	Integer	Decimal Places: 0
TripDate	Date/Time			Format: Short Date
Trip#	Number	Foreign key	Long Integer	Decimal Places: 0
People	Number	Number of people in the group	Byte	Decimal Places: 0

9. Specify Booking# as the primary key, and then save the table as **Booking**.

10. Add the records shown in Figure 2-42 to the **Booking** table.

Figure 2-42

Booking#	Client#	TripDate	Trip#	People
410	330	6/5/03	3529	4
403	315	7/1/03	3107	7
411	311	7/5/03	3222	5

11. Connor created a database named **Groups** that contains a table with booking data named **Group Info**. The **Booking** table you created has the same format as the **Group Info** table. Copy all the records from the **Group Info** table in the **Groups** database (located in the Cases folder on your Data Disk) to the end of the **Booking** table in the **Trips** database.

12. Resize all columns in the **Booking** datasheet to their best fit.

13. Print the **Booking** datasheet, and then save and close the table.

14. Close the **Trips** database, and then exit Access.

INTERNET ASSIGNMENTS

Student Union

The purpose of the Internet Assignments is to challenge you to find information on the Internet that you can use to create effective documents. The actual assignments are updated and maintained on the Course Technology Web site. Log on to the Internet and use your Web browser to go to the Student Union on the New Perspectives Series site at **www.course.com/NewPerspectives/studentunion**. Click the Online Companions link, and then click the link for this text.

QUICK CHECK ANSWERS

Session 2.1

1. Identify all the fields needed to produce the required information, group related fields into tables, determine each table's primary key, include a common field in related tables, avoid data redundancy, and determine the properties of each field.

2. The Data Type property determines what field values you can enter for the field and what other properties the field will have.

3. text, number, and AutoNumber fields

4. F6

5. Format

6. null

Session 2.2

1. the record being edited; the next row available for a new record

2. The field and all its values are removed from the table.

3. In Design view, right-click the row selector for the row above which you want to insert the field, click Insert Rows on the shortcut menu, and then define the new field.

4. yes/no

5. Make sure the database into which you want to import a table is open, click the File menu, point to Get External Data, and then click Import; or, click the New button in the Database window, click Import Table in the New Table dialog box, and then click the OK button.

6. In navigation mode, the entire field value is selected, and anything you type replaces the field value; in editing mode, you can insert or delete characters in a field value based on the location of the insertion point.

OBJECTIVES

In this tutorial you will:

- Learn how to use the Query window in Design view

- Create, run, and save queries

- Update data using a query

- Define a relationship between two tables

- Sort data in a query

- Filter data in a query

- Specify an exact match condition in a query

- Change a datasheet's appearance

- Use a comparison operator to match a range of values

- Use the And and Or logical operators

- Use multiple undo and redo

- Perform calculations in a query using calculated fields, aggregate functions, and record group calculations

QUERYING A DATABASE

Retrieving Information About Employers and Their Positions

CASE

Northeast Seasonal Jobs International (NSJI)

At a recent company meeting, Elsa Jensen and other NSJI employees discussed the importance of regularly monitoring the business activity of the company's employer clients. For example, Zack Ward and his marketing staff track employer activity to develop new strategies for promoting NSJI's services. Matt Griffin, the manager of recruitment, needs to track information about available positions, so that he can find student recruits to fill those positions. In addition, Elsa is interested in analyzing other aspects of the business, such as the wage amounts paid for different positions at different employers. All of these informational needs can be satisfied by queries that retrieve information from the Northeast database.

SESSION 3.1

In this session, you will use the Query window in Design view to create, run, and save queries; update data using a query; define a one-to-many relationship between two tables; sort data with a toolbar button and in Design view; and filter data in a query datasheet.

Introduction to Queries

As you learned in Tutorial 1, a query is a question you ask about data stored in a database. For example, Zack might create a query to find records in the Employer table for only those employers located in a specific state or province. When you create a query, you tell Access which fields you need and what criteria Access should use to select the records.

Access provides powerful query capabilities that allow you to:

- display selected fields and records from a table
- sort records
- perform calculations
- generate data for forms, reports, and other queries
- update data in the tables in a database
- find and display data from two or more tables

Most questions about data are generalized queries in which you specify the fields and records you want Access to select. These common requests for information, such as "Which employers are located in Quebec?" or "How many waiter/waitress positions are available?" are called **select queries**. The answer to a select query is returned in the form of a datasheet. The result of a query is also referred to as a **recordset**, because the query produces a set of records that answers your question.

More specialized, technical queries, such as finding duplicate records in a table, are best formulated using a Query Wizard. A Query Wizard prompts you for information by asking a series of questions and then creates the appropriate query based on your answers. In Tutorial 1, you used the Simple Query Wizard to display only some of the fields in the Employer table; Access provides other Query Wizards for more complex queries. For common, informational queries, it is easier for you to design your own query than to use a Query Wizard.

Zack wants you to create a query to display the employer ID, employer name, city, contact first name, contact last name, and Web site information for each record in the Employer table. He needs this information for a market analysis his staff is completing on NSJI's employer clients. You'll open the Query window to create the query for Zack.

Query Window

You use the Query window in Design view to create a query. In Design view, you specify the data you want to view by constructing a query by example. When you use **query by example** (**QBE**), you give Access an example of the information you are requesting. Access then retrieves the information that precisely matches your example.

For Zack's query, you need to display data from the Employer table. You'll begin by starting Access, opening the Northeast database, and displaying the Query window in Design view.

To start Access, open the Northeast database, and open the Query window in Design view:

1. Place your Data Disk in the appropriate disk drive.

2. Start Access and open the **Northeast** database located in the Tutorial folder on your Data Disk. The Northeast database is displayed in the Database window.

3. Click **Queries** in the Objects bar of the Database window, and then click the **New** button. The New Query dialog box opens. See Figure 3-1.

Figure 3-1   NEW QUERY DIALOG BOX

You'll design your own query instead of using a Query Wizard.

4. If necessary, click **Design View** in the list box.

5. Click the **OK** button. Access opens the Show Table dialog box on top of the Query window. (Note that you could also have double-clicked the "Create query in Design view" option in the Database window.) Notice that the title bar of the Query window shows that you are creating a select query.

The query you are creating will retrieve data from the Employer table, so you need to add this table to the Select Query window.

6. Click **Employer** in the Tables list box (if necessary), click the **Add** button, and then click the **Close** button. Access places the Employer table's field list in the Select Query window and closes the Show Table dialog box.

To display more of the fields you'll be using for creating queries, you'll maximize the Select Query window.

7. Click the **Maximize** button on the Select Query window title bar. See Figure 3-2.

Figure 3-2   **SELECT QUERY IN DESIGN VIEW**

View button for Datasheet view

field list

design grid

Run button

Query Type button shows select query

In Design view, the Select Query window contains the standard title bar, the menu bar, the status bar, and the Query Design toolbar. On the toolbar, the Query Type button shows a select query; the icon on this button changes according to the type of query you are creating. The title bar on the Select Query window displays the query type (Select Query) and the default query name (Query1). You'll change the default query name to a more meaningful one later when you save the query.

The Select Query window in Design view contains a field list and the design grid. The **field list** contains the fields for the table you are querying. The table name appears at the top of the list box, and the fields are listed in the order in which they appear in the table. You can scroll the field list to see more fields; or, you can expand the field list to display all the fields and the complete field names by resizing the field list box.

In the **design grid**, you include the fields and record selection criteria for the information you want to see. Each column in the design grid contains specifications about a field you will use in the query. You can choose a single field for your query by dragging its name from the field list to the design grid in the lower portion of the window. Alternatively, you can double-click a field name to place it in the next available design grid column.

When you are constructing a query, you can see the query results at any time by clicking the View button or the Run button on the Query Design toolbar. In response, Access displays the datasheet, which contains the set of fields and records that results from answering, or **running**, the query. The order of the fields in the datasheet is the same as the order of the fields in the design grid. Although the datasheet looks just like a table datasheet and appears in Datasheet view, a query datasheet is temporary, and its contents are based on the criteria you establish in the design grid. In contrast, a table datasheet shows the permanent data in a table. However, you can update data while viewing a query datasheet, just as you can when working in a table datasheet or form.

If the query you are creating includes every field from the specified table, you can use one of the following three methods to transfer all the fields from the field list to the design grid:

■ Click and drag each field individually from the field list to the design grid. Use this method if you want the fields in your query to appear in an order that is different from the order in the field list.

■ Double-click the asterisk in the field list. Access places the table name followed by a period and an asterisk (as in "Employer.*") in the design grid, which signifies that the order of the fields will be the same in the query as it is in the field list. Use this method if you don't need to sort the query or specify conditions for the records you want to select. The advantage of using this method is that you do not need to change the query if you add or delete fields from the underlying table structure. Such changes are reflected automatically in the query.

■ Double-click the field list title bar to highlight all the fields, and then click and drag one of the highlighted fields to the design grid. Access places each field in a separate column and arranges the fields in the order in which they appear in the field list. Use this method when you need to sort your query or include record selection criteria.

Now you'll create and run Zack's query to display selected fields from the Employer table.

Creating and Running a Query

The default table datasheet displays all the fields in the table, in the same order as they appear in the table. In contrast, a query datasheet can display selected fields from a table, and the order of the fields can be different from that of the table.

Zack wants the Employer table's EmployerID, EmployerName, City, ContactFirstName, ContactLastName, and WebSite fields to appear in the query results. You'll add each of these fields to the design grid.

To select the fields for the query, and then run the query:

1. Drag **EmployerID** from the Employer field list to the design grid's first column Field text box, and then release the mouse button. See Figure 3-3.

Figure 3-3	FIELD ADDED TO THE DESIGN GRID

drag field from here

release mouse button here

indicates that the field will appear in the datasheet

In the design grid's first column, the field name EmployerID appears in the Field text box, the table name Employer appears in the Table text box, and the check mark in the Show check box indicates that the field will be displayed in the datasheet when you run the query. Sometimes you might not want to display a field and its values in the query results. For example, if you are creating a query to show all employers located in Massachusetts, and you assign the name "Employers in Massachusetts" to the query, you do not need to include the State/Prov field value for each record in the query results—every State/Prov field value would be "MA" for Massachusetts. Even if you choose not to include a field in the display of the query results, you can still use the field as part of the query to select specific records or to specify a particular sequence for the records in the datasheet.

2. Double-click **EmployerName** in the Employer field list. Access adds this field to the second column of the design grid.

3. Scrolling the Employer field list as necessary, repeat Step 2 for the **City**, **ContactFirstName**, **ContactLastName**, and **WebSite** fields to add these fields to the design grid in that order.

   TROUBLE? If you double-click the wrong field and accidentally add it to the design grid, you can remove the field from the grid. Select the field's column by clicking the pointer ↓ on the bar above the Field text box for the field you want to delete, and then press the Delete key (or click Edit on the menu bar, and then click Delete Columns).

   Having selected the fields for Zack's query, you now can run the query.

4. Click the **Run** button ❗ on the Query Design toolbar. Access runs the query and displays the results in Datasheet view. See Figure 3-4.

| Figure 3-4 | DATASHEET DISPLAYED AFTER RUNNING THE QUERY |

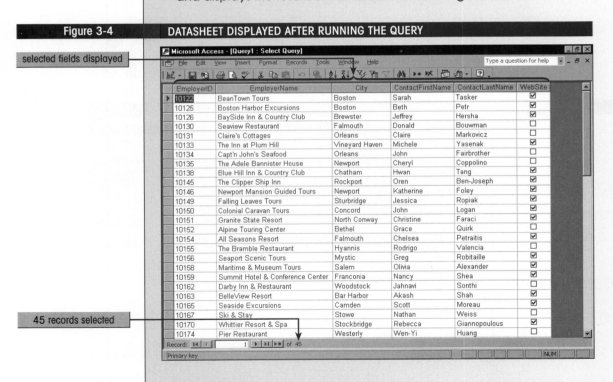

selected fields displayed

45 records selected

The six fields you added to the design grid appear in the datasheet, and the records are displayed in primary key sequence by EmployerID. Access selected a total of 45 records for display in the datasheet.

Zack asks you to save the query as "Employer Analysis" so that he can easily retrieve the same data again.

5. Click the **Save** button 🖫 on the Query Datasheet toolbar. The Save As dialog box opens.

6. Type **Employer Analysis** in the Query Name text box, and then press the **Enter** key. Access saves the query with the specified name in the Northeast database on your Data Disk and displays the name in the title bar.

When viewing the results of the query, Zack noticed a couple of changes that need to be made to the data in the Employer table. The Adele Bannister House recently developed a Web site, so the WebSite field for this record needs to be updated. In addition, the contact information has changed for the Alpine Touring Center.

Updating Data Using a Query

Although a query datasheet is temporary and its contents are based on the criteria in the query design grid, you can update the data in a table using a query datasheet. In this case, Zack has changes he wants you to make to records in the Employer table. Instead of making the changes in the table datasheet, you can make them in the Employer Analysis query datasheet. The underlying Employer table will be updated with the changes you make.

To update data using the Employer Analysis query datasheet:

1. For the record with EmployerID 10135 (The Adele Bannister House), click the check box in the WebSite field to place a check mark in it.

2. For the record with EmployerID 10152 (Alpine Touring Center), change the ContactFirstName field value to **Mary** and change the ContactLastName field value to **Grant**.

3. Click the **Close Window** button ☒ on the menu bar to close the query. Note that the Employer Analysis query appears in the list of queries.

4. Click the **Restore Window** button 🗗 on the menu bar to return the Database window to its original size.

Now you will check the Employer table to verify that the changes you made in the query datasheet were also made to the Employer table records.

5. Click **Tables** in the Objects bar of the Database window, click **Employer** in the list of tables, and then click the **Open** button. The Employer table datasheet opens.

6. For the record with EmployerID 10135, scroll the datasheet to the right to verify that the WebSite field contains a check mark. For the record with EmployerID 10152, scroll to the right to see the new contact information (Mary Grant).

7. Click the **Close** button ☒ on the Employer table window to close it.

Matt also wants to view specific information in the Northeast database. However, he needs to see data from both the Employer table and the Position table at the same time. To view data from two tables at the same time, you need to define a relationship between the tables.

Defining Table Relationships

One of the most powerful features of a relational database management system is its ability to define relationships between tables. You use a common field to relate one table to another. The process of relating tables is often called performing a **join**. When you join tables that have a common field, you can extract data from them as if they were one larger table. For example, you can join the Employer and Position tables by using the EmployerID field in both tables as the common field. Then you can use a query, a form, or a report to extract selected data from each table, even though the data is contained in two separate tables, as shown in Figure 3-5. In the Positions query shown in Figure 3-5, the PositionID, PositionTitle, and Wage columns are fields from the Position table, and the EmployerName and State/Prov columns are fields from the Employer table. The joining of records is based on the common field of EmployerID. The Employer and Position tables have a type of relationship called a one-to-many relationship.

Figure 3-5	ONE-TO-MANY RELATIONSHIP AND SAMPLE QUERY

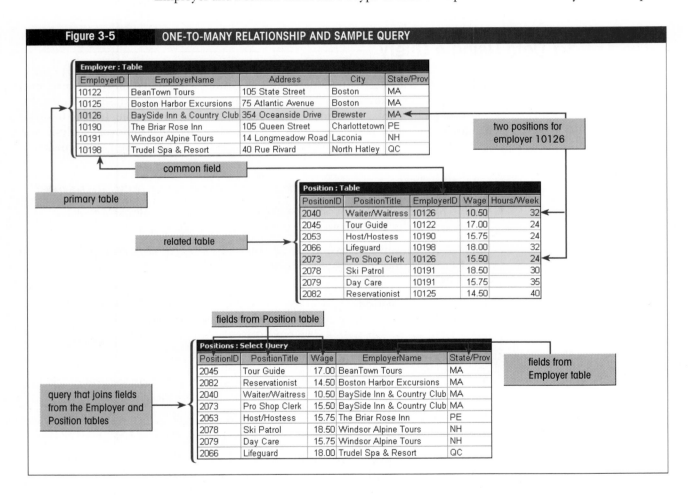

One-to-Many Relationships

A **one-to-many relationship** exists between two tables when one record in the first table matches zero, one, or many records in the second table, and when one record in the second table matches exactly one record in the first table. For example, as shown in Figure 3-5, employers 10126 and 10191 each have two available positions, and employers 10122, 10125, 10190, and 10198 each have one available position. Every position has a single matching employer.

Access refers to the two tables that form a relationship as the primary table and the related table. The **primary table** is the "one" table in a one-to-many relationship; in Figure 3-5, the Employer table is the primary table because there is only one employer for each available position. The **related table** is the "many" table; in Figure 3-5, the Position table is the related table because there can be many positions offered by each employer.

Because related data is stored in two tables, inconsistencies between the tables can occur. Consider the following scenarios:

- Matt adds a position record to the Position table for a new employer, Glen Cove Inn, using EmployerID 10132. Matt did not first add the new employer's information to the Employer table, so this position does not have a matching record in the Employer table. The data is inconsistent, and the position record is considered to be an **orphaned** record.

- Matt changes the EmployerID in the Employer table for BaySide Inn & Country Club from 10126 to 10128. Two orphaned records for employer 10126 now exist in the Position table, and the database is inconsistent.

- Matt deletes the record for Boston Harbor Excursions, employer 10125, in the Employer table because this employer is no longer an NSJI client. The database is again inconsistent; one record for employer 10125 in the Position table has no matching record in the Employer table.

You can avoid these problems by specifying referential integrity between tables when you define their relationships.

Referential Integrity

Referential integrity is a set of rules that Access enforces to maintain consistency between related tables when you update data in a database. Specifically, the referential integrity rules are as follows:

- When you add a record to a related table, a matching record must already exist in the primary table, thereby preventing the possibility of orphaned records.

- If you attempt to change the value of the primary key in the primary table, Access prevents this change if matching records exist in a related table. However, if you choose the **cascade updates** option, Access permits the change in value to the primary key and changes the appropriate foreign key values in the related table, thereby eliminating the possibility of inconsistent data.

- When you delete a record in the primary table, Access prevents the deletion if matching records exist in a related table. However, if you choose the **cascade deletes** option, Access deletes the record in the primary table and also deletes all records in related tables that have matching foreign key values.

Now you'll define a one-to-many relationship between the Employer and Position tables so that you can use fields from both tables to create a query that will retrieve the information Matt needs. You will also define a one-to-many relationship between the NAICS (primary) table and the Employer (related) table.

Defining a Relationship Between Two Tables

When two tables have a common field, you can define a relationship between them in the Relationships window. The **Relationships window** illustrates the relationships among a database's tables. In this window, you can view or change existing relationships, define new relationships between tables, and rearrange the layout of the tables in the window.

You need to open the Relationships window and define the relationship between the Employer and Position tables. You'll define a one-to-many relationship between the two tables, with Employer as the primary table and Position as the related table, and with EmployerID as the common field (the primary key in the Employer table and a foreign key in the Position table). You'll also define a one-to-many relationship between the NAICS and Employer tables, with NAICS as the primary table and Employer as the related table, and with NAICSCode as the common field (the primary key in the NAICS table and a foreign key in the Employer table).

To define the one-to-many relationship between the Employer and Position tables:

1. Click the **Relationships** button on the Database toolbar. The Show Table dialog box opens on top of the Relationships window. See Figure 3-6.

| Figure 3-6 | SHOW TABLE DIALOG BOX |

add these two tables

Relationships button

You must add each table participating in a relationship to the Relationships window.

2. Click **Employer** (if necessary), and then click the **Add** button. The Employer field list is added to the Relationships window.

3. Click **Position**, and then click the **Add** button. The Position field list is added to the Relationships window.

4. Click the **Close** button in the Show Table dialog box to close it and reveal the entire Relationships window.

   To form the relationship between the two tables, you drag the common field of EmployerID from the primary table to the related table. Then Access opens the Edit Relationships dialog box, in which you select the relationship options for the two tables.

5. Click **EmployerID** in the Employer field list, and drag it to **EmployerID** in the Position field list. When you release the mouse button, the Edit Relationships dialog box opens. See Figure 3-7.

Figure 3-7	EDIT RELATIONSHIPS DIALOG BOX

primary table → **Table/Query:** Employer   **Related Table/Query:** Position ← related table

EmployerID   EmployerID ← common field

referential integrity option → □ Enforce Referential Integrity

cascade options → □ Cascade Update Related Fields   □ Cascade Delete Related Records

Relationship Type: One-To-Many ← type of relationship

Create   Cancel   Join Type..   Create New..

The primary table, related table, and common field appear at the top of the dialog box. The type of relationship, One-To-Many, appears at the bottom of the dialog box. When you click the Enforce Referential Integrity check box, the two cascade options become available. If you select the Cascade Update Related Fields option, Access will change the appropriate foreign key values in the related table when you change a primary key value in the primary table. If you select the Cascade Delete Related Records option, when you delete a record in the primary table, Access will delete all records in the related table that have a matching foreign key value.

6. Click the **Enforce Referential Integrity** check box, click the **Cascade Update Related Fields** check box, and then click the **Cascade Delete Related Records** check box. **Note:** You should select this option with caution because you might inadvertently delete records you do not want deleted.

7. Click the **Create** button to define the one-to-many relationship between the two tables and to close the dialog box. The completed relationship appears in the Relationships window. See Figure 3-8.

Figure 3-8	DEFINED RELATIONSHIP IN THE RELATIONSHIPS WINDOW

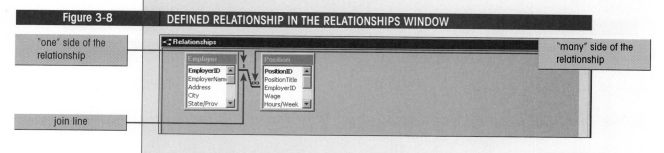

"one" side of the relationship

"many" side of the relationship

join line

Relationships

Employer: **EmployerID**, EmployerName, Address, City, State/Prov

Position: **PositionID**, PositionTitle, EmployerID, Wage, Hours/Week

The **join line** connects the EmployerID fields, which are common to the two tables. The common field joins the two tables, which have a one-to-many relationship. The "one" side of the relationship has the digit 1 at its end, and the "many" side of the relationship has the infinity symbol ∞ at its end. The two tables are still separate tables, but you can use the data in them as if they were one table.

Now you need to define the one-to-many relationship between the NAICS and Employer tables. In this relationship, NAICS is the primary ("one") table because there is only one code for each employer. Employer is the related ("many") table because there are multiple employers with the same NAICS code.

To define the one-to-many relationship between the NAICS and Employer tables:

1. Click the **Show Table** button on the Relationship toolbar. The Show Table dialog box opens on top of the Relationships window.

2. Click **NAICS** in the list of tables, click the **Add** button, and then click the **Close** button to close the Show Table dialog box. The NAICS field list appears in the Relationships window to the right of the Position field list. To make it easier to define the relationship, you'll move the NAICS field list below the Employer and Position field lists.

3. Click the NAICS field list title bar and drag the list until it is below the Position table (see Figure 3-9), and then release the mouse button.

4. Scroll the Employer field list until the NAICSCode field is visible. Because the NAICS table is the primary table in this relationship, you need to drag the NAICSCode field from the NAICS field list to the Employer field list. Notice that the NAICSCode field in the NAICS table appears in a bold font; this indicates that the field is the table's primary key. On the other hand, the NAICSCode field in the Employer table is not bold, which is a reminder that this field is the foreign key in this table.

5. Click and drag the **NAICSCode** field in the NAICS field list to the **NAICSCode** field in the Employer field list. When you release the mouse button, the Edit Relationships dialog box opens.

6. Click the **Enforce Referential Integrity** check box, click the **Cascade Update Related Fields** check box, and then click the **Cascade Delete Related Records** check box. You now have selected all the necessary relationship options.

7. Click the **Create** button to define the one-to-many relationship between the two tables and close the dialog box. The completed relationship appears in the Relationships window. See Figure 3-9.

| Figure 3-9 | BOTH RELATIONSHIPS DEFINED |

With both relationships defined, you have connected the data among the three tables in the Northeast database.

8. Click the **Save** button on the Relationship toolbar to save the layout in the Relationships window.

9. Click the **Close** button on the Relationships window title bar. The Relationships window closes, and you return to the Database window.

Creating a Multi-table Query

Now that you have joined the Employer and Position tables, you can create a query to produce the information Matt wants. To help him determine his recruiting needs, Matt wants a query that displays the EmployerName, City, and State/Prov fields from the Employer table and the Openings, PositionTitle, StartDate, and EndDate fields from the Position table.

To create, run, and save the query using the Employer and Position tables:

1. Click **Queries** in the Objects bar of the Database window, and then double-click **Create query in Design view**. The Show Table dialog box opens on top of the Query window in Design view.

   You need to add the Employer and Position tables to the Query window.

2. Click **Employer** in the Tables list box (if necessary), click the **Add** button, click **Position**, click the **Add** button, and then click the **Close** button. The Employer and Position field lists appear in the Query window, and the Show Table dialog box closes. Note that the one-to-many relationship that exists between the two tables is shown in the Query window. Also, notice that the join line is thick at both ends; this signifies that you selected the option to enforce referential integrity. If you had not selected this option, the join line would be thin at both ends and neither the "1" nor the infinity symbol would appear, even though there is a one-to-many relationship between the two tables.

   You need to place the EmployerName, City, and State/Prov fields from the Employer field list into the design grid, and then place the Openings, PositionTitle, StartDate, and EndDate fields from the Position field list into the design grid.

3. Double-click **EmployerName** in the Employer field list to place EmployerName in the design grid's first column Field text box.

4. Repeat Step 3 to add the **City** and **State/Prov** fields from the Employer table, so that these fields are placed in the second and third columns of the design grid.

5. Repeat Step 3 to add the **Openings**, **PositionTitle**, **StartDate**, and **EndDate** fields (in that order) from the Position table, so that these fields are placed in the fourth through seventh columns of the design grid.

   The query specifications are completed, so you now can run the query.

6. Click the **Run** button 🔳 on the Query Design toolbar. Access runs the query and displays the results in the datasheet.

7. Click the **Maximize** button 🔲 on the Query window title bar. See Figure 3-10.

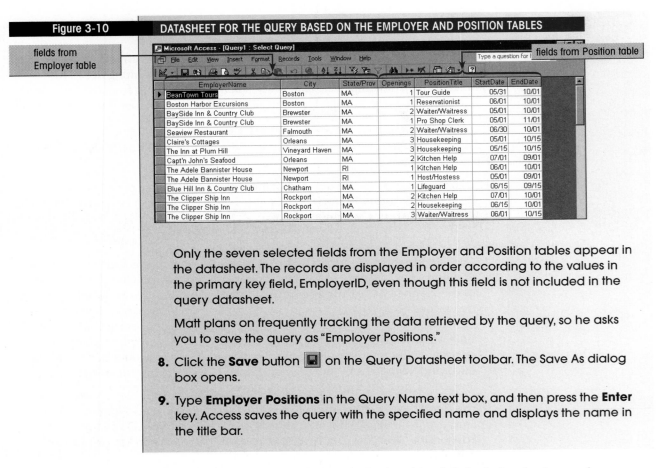

Figure 3-10   DATASHEET FOR THE QUERY BASED ON THE EMPLOYER AND POSITION TABLES

fields from Employer table

fields from Position table

Only the seven selected fields from the Employer and Position tables appear in the datasheet. The records are displayed in order according to the values in the primary key field, EmployerID, even though this field is not included in the query datasheet.

Matt plans on frequently tracking the data retrieved by the query, so he asks you to save the query as "Employer Positions."

8. Click the **Save** button 🖫 on the Query Datasheet toolbar. The Save As dialog box opens.

9. Type **Employer Positions** in the Query Name text box, and then press the **Enter** key. Access saves the query with the specified name and displays the name in the title bar.

Matt decides he wants the records displayed in alphabetical order by employer name. Because the query displays data in order by the field value of EmployerID, which is the primary key for the Employer table, you need to sort the records by EmployerName to display the data in the order Matt wants.

Sorting Data in a Query

Sorting is the process of rearranging records in a specified order or sequence. Sometimes you might need to sort data before displaying or printing it to meet a specific request. For example, Matt might want to review position information arranged by the StartDate field because he needs to know which positions are available earliest in the year. On the other hand, Elsa might want to view position information arranged by the Openings field for each employer, because she monitors employer activity for NSJI.

When you sort data in a query, you do not change the sequence of the records in the underlying tables. Only the records in the query datasheet are rearranged according to your specifications.

To sort records, you must select the **sort key**, which is the field used to determine the order of records in the datasheet. In this case, Matt wants the data sorted by the employer name, so you need to specify the EmployerName field as the sort key. Sort keys can be text, number, date/time, currency, AutoNumber, yes/no, or Lookup Wizard fields, but not memo, OLE object, or hyperlink fields. You sort records in either ascending (increasing) or descending (decreasing) order. Figure 3-11 shows the results of each type of sort for different data types.

Figure 3-11	SORTING RESULTS FOR DIFFERENT DATA TYPES	
DATA TYPE	ASCENDING SORT RESULTS	DESCENDING SORT RESULTS
Text	A to Z	Z to A
Number	lowest to highest numeric value	highest to lowest numeric value
Date/Time	oldest to most recent date	most recent to oldest date
Currency	lowest to highest numeric value	highest to lowest numeric value
AutoNumber	lowest to highest numeric value	highest to lowest numeric value
Yes/No	yes (check mark in check box) then no values	no then yes values

Access provides several methods for sorting data in a table or query datasheet and in a form. One method, clicking a toolbar sort button, lets you sort the displayed records quickly.

Using a Toolbar Button to Sort Data

The **Sort Ascending** and **Sort Descending** buttons on the toolbar allow you to sort records immediately, based on the values in the selected field. First you select the column on which you want to base the sort, and then you click the appropriate sort button on the toolbar to rearrange the records in either ascending or descending order. Unless you save the datasheet or form after you've sorted the records, the rearrangement of records is temporary.

Recall that in Tutorial 1 you used the Sort Ascending button to sort query results by the State/Prov field. You'll use this same button to sort the Employer Positions query results by the EmployerName field.

To sort the records using a toolbar sort button:

1. Click any visible EmployerName field value to establish the field as the current field (if necessary).

2. Click the **Sort Ascending** button on the Query Datasheet toolbar. The records are rearranged in ascending order by employer name. See Figure 3-12.

Figure 3-12	SORTING RECORDS ON A SINGLE FIELD IN A DATASHEET

Sort Ascending button

Sort Descending button

records sorted in ascending order by EmployerName

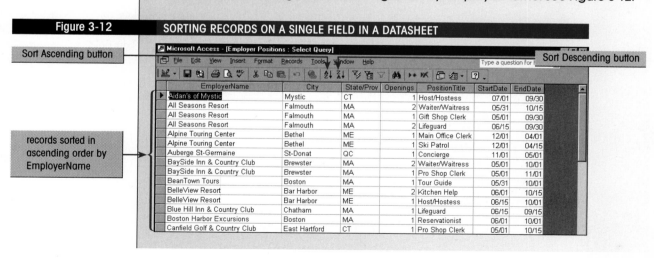

After viewing the query results, Matt decides that he'd prefer to see the records arranged by the value in the PositionTitle field, so that he can identify the types of positions he needs to fill. He also wants to display the records in descending order according to the value of the Openings field, so that he can easily see how many openings there are for each position. To do this you need to sort using two fields.

Sorting Multiple Fields in Design View

Sort keys can be unique or nonunique. A sort key is **unique** if the value of the sort key field for each record is different. The EmployerID field in the Employer table is an example of a unique sort key because each employer record has a different value in this field. A sort key is **nonunique** if more than one record can have the same value for the sort key field. For example, the PositionTitle field in the Position table is a nonunique sort key because more than one record can have the same PositionTitle value.

When the sort key is nonunique, records with the same sort key value are grouped together, but they are not in a specific order within the group. To arrange these grouped records in a specific order, you can specify a **secondary sort key**, which is a second sort key field. The first sort key field is called the **primary sort key**. Note that the primary sort key is *not* the same as a table's primary key field. A table has at most one primary key, which must be unique, whereas any field in a table can serve as a primary sort key.

Access lets you select up to 10 different sort keys. When you use the toolbar sort buttons, the sort key fields must be in adjacent columns in the datasheet. You highlight the adjacent columns, and Access sorts first by the first column and then by each other highlighted column in order from left to right.

Matt wants the records sorted first by the PositionTitle field and then by the Openings field. The two fields are adjacent, but not in the correct left-to-right order, so you cannot use the toolbar buttons to sort them. You could move the Openings field to the right of the PositionTitle field in the query datasheet. However, you can specify only one type of sort—either ascending or descending—for selected columns in the query datasheet. This is not what Matt wants; he wants the PositionTitle field values to be sorted in ascending alphabetical order and the Openings field values to be sorted in descending order.

In this case, you need to specify the sort keys for the query in Design view. Any time you want to sort on multiple fields that are nonadjacent or in the wrong order, but do not want to rearrange the columns in the query datasheet to accomplish the sort, you must specify the sort keys in Design view.

In the Query window in Design view, Access first uses the sort key that is leftmost in the design grid. Therefore, you must arrange the fields you want to sort from left to right in the design grid, with the primary sort key being the leftmost sort key field. In Design view, multiple sort fields do not have to be adjacent to each other, as they do in Datasheet view; however, they must be in the correct left-to-right order.

REFERENCE WINDOW   **RW**

Sorting a Query Datasheet

■ In the query datasheet, select the column or adjacent columns on which you want to sort.
■ Click the Sort Ascending button or the Sort Descending button on the Query Datasheet toolbar.
or
■ In Design view, position the fields serving as sort keys from left (primary sort key) to right, and then select the sort order for each sort key.

To achieve the results Matt wants, you need to switch to Design view, move the Openings field to the right of the EndDate field, and then specify the sort order for the two fields.

To select the two sort keys in Design view:

1. Click the **View** button for Design view 🔲 on the Query Datasheet toolbar to open the query in Design view.

   First, you'll move the Openings field to the right of the EndDate field. Remember, in Design view, the sort fields do not have to be adjacent, and non-sort key fields can appear between sort key fields. So, you will move the Openings field to the end of the query design, following the EndDate field.

2. If necessary, click the right arrow in the design grid's horizontal scroll bar a few times to scroll to the right so that both the Openings and EndDate fields are completely visible.

3. Position the pointer in the Openings field selector until the pointer changes to a ⬇ shape, and then click to select the field. See Figure 3-13.

Figure 3-13   SELECTED OPENINGS FIELD

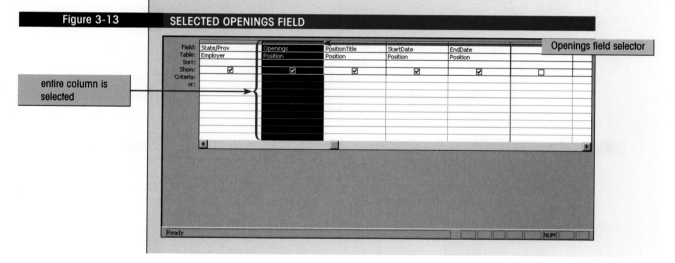

Openings field selector

entire column is selected

4. Position the pointer in the Openings field selector, and then click and drag the pointer ⏳ to the right until the vertical line on the right of the EndDate field is highlighted. See Figure 3-14.

Figure 3-14	DRAGGING THE FIELD IN THE DESIGN GRID

5. Release the mouse button. The Openings field moves to the right of the EndDate field.

The fields are now in the correct order for the sort. Next, you need to specify an ascending sort order for the PositionTitle field and a descending sort order for the Openings field.

6. Click the right side of the **PositionTitle Sort** text box to display the list arrow and the sort options, and then click **Ascending**. You've selected an ascending sort order for the PositionTitle field, which will be the primary sort key. The PositionTitle field is a text field, and an ascending sort order will display the field values in alphabetical order.

7. Click the right side of the **Openings Sort** text box, click **Descending**, and then click in one of the empty text boxes to the right of the Openings field to deselect the setting. You've selected a descending sort order for the Openings field, which will be the secondary sort key, because it appears to the right of the primary sort key (PositionTitle) in the design grid. See Figure 3-15.

Figure 3-15	SELECTING TWO SORT KEYS IN DESIGN VIEW

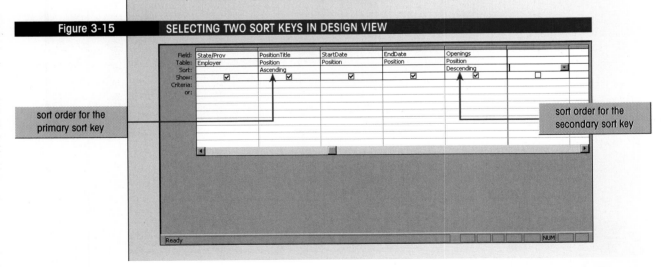

You have finished your query changes, so now you can run the query and then save the modified query with the same query name.

8. Click the **Run** button [!] on the Query Design toolbar. Access runs the query and displays the query datasheet. The records appear in ascending order, based on the values of the PositionTitle field. Within groups of records with the same PositionTitle field value, the records appear in descending order by the values of the Openings field. See Figure 3-16.

Figure 3-16 | **DATASHEET SORTED ON TWO FIELDS**

primary sort key

secondary sort key

records shown in descending order by Openings

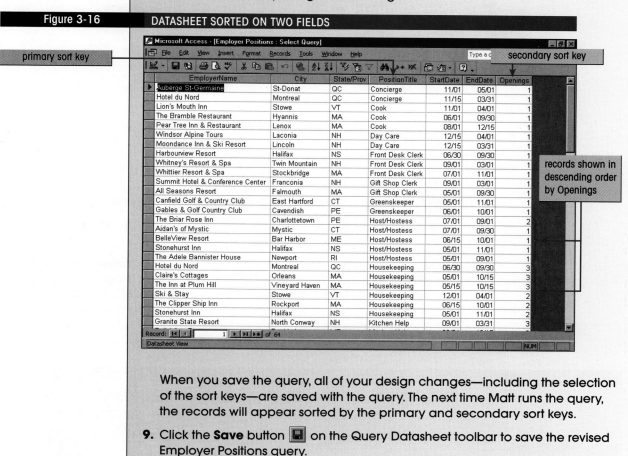

When you save the query, all of your design changes—including the selection of the sort keys—are saved with the query. The next time Matt runs the query, the records will appear sorted by the primary and secondary sort keys.

9. Click the **Save** button [💾] on the Query Datasheet toolbar to save the revised Employer Positions query.

Matt wants to concentrate on the positions in the datasheet with a start date sometime in May, to see how many recruits he will need to fill these positions. Selecting only the records with a StartDate field value in May is a temporary change that Matt wants in the datasheet, so you do not need to switch to Design view and change the query. Instead, you can apply a filter.

Filtering Data

A **filter** is a set of restrictions you place on the records in an open datasheet or form to *temporarily* isolate a subset of the records. A filter lets you view different subsets of displayed records so that you can focus on only the data you need. Unless you save a query or form with a filter applied, an applied filter is not available the next time you run the query or open the form.

The simplest technique for filtering records is Filter By Selection. **Filter By Selection** lets you select all or part of a field value in a datasheet or form, and then display only those records that contain the selected value in the field. Another technique for filtering records is to use **Filter By Form**, which changes your datasheet to display empty fields. Then you can select a value from the list arrow that appears when you click any blank field to apply a filter that selects only those records containing that value.

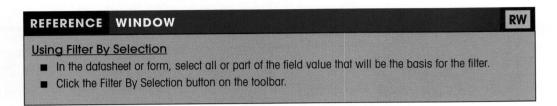

REFERENCE WINDOW   RW

Using Filter By Selection
- In the datasheet or form, select all or part of the field value that will be the basis for the filter.
- Click the Filter By Selection button on the toolbar.

For Matt's request, you need to select just the beginning digits "05" in the StartDate field, to view all the records with a May start date, and then use Filter By Selection to display only those query records with this same partial value.

To display the records using Filter By Selection:

1. In the query datasheet, locate the first occurrence of a May date in the StartDate field, and then select **05** in that field value.

2. Click the **Filter By Selection** button 🇻 on the Query Datasheet toolbar. Access displays the filtered results. Only the 17 query records that have a StartDate field value with the beginning digits "05" appear in the datasheet. The status bar's display (FLTR), the area next to the navigation buttons, and the selected Remove Filter button on the toolbar all indicate that the records have been filtered. See Figure 3-17.

Figure 3-17	USING FILTER BY SELECTION

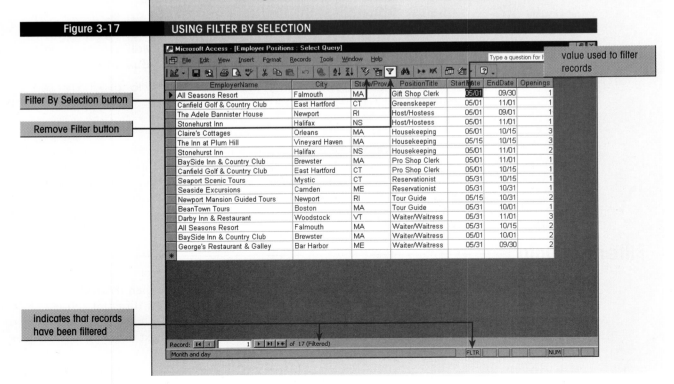

TROUBLE? If you are unable to select only the digits "05" in the StartDate field because the entire field value (including a four-digit year) is displayed when you click in the field, your Windows date settings might be affecting the display of the field values. In this case, you can either read through the remaining steps on this page without completing them, or ask your instructor for assistance.

Next, Matt wants to view only those records with a StartDate value of 05/01, because he needs to fill those positions before the other May positions. So, you need to filter by the complete field value of 05/01.

3. Click in any StartDate field value of **05/01**, and then click 🦅. The filtered display now shows only the 9 records with a value of 05/01 in the StartDate field.

Now you can redisplay all the query records by clicking the Remove Filter button; this button works as a toggle to switch between the filtered and nonfiltered displays.

4. Click the **Remove Filter** button ▼ on the Query Datasheet toolbar. Access redisplays all the records in the query datasheet.

5. Click the **Save** button 🖫 on the Query Datasheet toolbar, and then click the **Close Window** button ✕ on the menu bar to save and close the query and return to the Database window.

6. Click the **Restore Window** button 🗗 on the menu bar to return the Database window to its original size.

The queries you've created will help NSJI employees retrieve just the information they want to view. In the next session, you'll continue to create queries to meet their information needs.

Session 3.1 QUICK CHECK

1. What is a select query?

2. Describe the field list and the design grid in the Query window in Design view.

3. How are a table datasheet and a query datasheet similar? How are they different?

4. The _____ is the "one" table in a one-to-many relationship, and the _____ is the "many" table in the relationship.

5. _____ is a set of rules that Access enforces to maintain consistency between related tables when you update data in a database.

6. For a date/time field, how do the records appear when sorted in ascending order?

7. When must you define multiple sort keys in Design view instead of in the query datasheet?

8. A(n) _____ is a set of restrictions you place on the records in an open datasheet or form to isolate a subset of records temporarily.

SESSION 3.2

In this session, you will specify an exact match condition in a query, change a datasheet's appearance, use a comparison operator to match a range of values, use the And and Or logical operators to define multiple selection criteria for queries, use multiple undo and redo, and perform calculations in queries.

Defining Record Selection Criteria for Queries

Matt wants to display employer and position information for all positions with a start date of 07/01, so that he can plan his recruitment efforts accordingly. For this request, you could create a query to select the correct fields and all records in the Employer and Position tables, select a StartDate field value of 07/01 in the query datasheet, and then click the Filter By Selection button to filter the query results to display only those positions starting on July 1. However, a faster way of displaying the data Matt needs is to create a query that displays the selected fields and only those records in the Employer and Position tables that satisfy a condition.

Just as you can display selected fields from a database in a query datasheet, you can display selected records. To tell Access which records you want to select, you must specify a condition as part of the query. A **condition** is a criterion, or rule, that determines which records are selected. To define a condition for a field, you place the condition in the field's Criteria text box in the design grid.

A condition usually consists of an operator, often a comparison operator, and a value. A **comparison operator** asks Access to compare the value in a database field to the condition value and to select all the records for which the relationship is true. For example, the condition >15.00 for the Wage field selects all records in the Position table having Wage field values greater than 15.00. Figure 3-18 shows the Access comparison operators.

Figure 3-18	ACCESS COMPARISON OPERATORS	
OPERATOR	**MEANING**	**EXAMPLE**
=	equal to (optional; default operator)	="Hall"
<	less than	<#1/1/99#
<=	less than or equal to	<=100
>	greater than	>"C400"
>=	greater than or equal to	>=18.75
<>	not equal to	<>"Hall"
Between ... And...	between two values (inclusive)	Between 50 And 325
In ()	in a list of values	In ("Hall", "Seeger")
Like	matches a pattern that includes wildcards	Like "706*"

Specifying an Exact Match

For Matt's request, you need to create a query that will display only those records in the Position table with the value 07/01 in the StartDate field. This type of condition is called an **exact match** because the value in the specified field must match the condition exactly in order for the record to be included in the query results. You'll use the Simple Query Wizard to create the query, and then you'll specify the exact match condition.

To create the query using the Simple Query Wizard:

1. If you took a break after the previous session, make sure that Access is running, the Northeast database is open, and the Queries object is selected in the Database window.

2. Double-click **Create query by using wizard**. Access opens the first Simple Query Wizard dialog box, in which you select the tables (or queries) and fields for the query.

3. Click the **Tables/Queries** list arrow, and then click **Table: Position**. The fields in the Position table appear in the Available Fields list box. Except for the PositionID and EmployerID fields, you will include all fields from the Position table in the query.

4. Click the >> button. All the fields from the Available Fields list box move to the Selected Fields list box.

5. Scroll up and click **PositionID** in the Selected Fields list box, click the < button to move the PositionID field back to the Available Fields list box, click **EmployerID** in the Selected Fields list box, and then click the < button to move the EmployerID field back to the Available Fields list box.

   Matt also wants certain information from the Employer table included in the query results. Because he wants the fields from the Employer table to appear in the query datasheet to the right of the fields from the Position table fields, you need to click the last field in the Selected Fields list box so that the new Employer fields will be inserted below it in the list.

6. Click **Openings** in the Selected Fields list box.

7. Click the **Tables/Queries** list arrow, and then click **Table: Employer**. The fields in the Employer table now appear in the Available Fields list box. Notice that the fields you selected from the Position table remain in the Selected Fields list box.

8. Click **EmployerName** in the Available Fields list box, and then click the > button to move EmployerName to the Selected Fields list box, below the Openings field.

9. Repeat Step 8 to move the **State/Prov**, **ContactFirstName**, **ContactLastName**, and **Phone** fields into the Selected Fields list box. (Note that you can also double-click a field to move it from the Available Fields list box to the Selected Fields list box.)

10. Click the **Next** button to open the second Simple Query Wizard dialog box, in which you choose whether the query will display records from the selected tables or a summary of those records. Summary options show calculations such as average, minimum, maximum, and so on. Matt wants to view the details for the records, not a summary.

11. Make sure the **Detail (shows every field of every record)** option button is selected, and then click the **Next** button to open the last Simple Query Wizard dialog box, in which you choose a name for the query and complete the Wizard. You need to enter a condition for the query, so you'll want to modify the query's design.

12. Type **July 1 Positions**, click the **Modify the query design** option button, and then click the **Finish** button. Access saves the query as July 1 Positions and opens the query in Design view. See Figure 3-19.

Figure 3-19	QUERY IN DESIGN VIEW

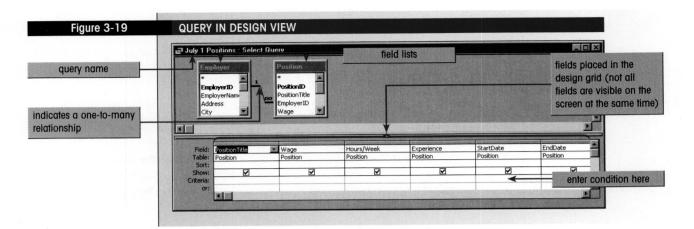

The field lists for the Employer and Position tables appear in the top portion of the window, and the join line indicating a one-to-many relationship connects the two tables. The selected fields appear in the design grid. Not all of the fields are visible in the grid; to see the other selected fields, you need to scroll to the right using the horizontal scroll bar.

To display the information Matt wants, you need to enter the condition for the StartDate field in its Criteria text box. Matt wants to display only those records with a start date of 07/01.

To enter the exact match condition, and then run the query:

1. Click the **StartDate Criteria** text box, type **7/01**, and then press the **Enter** key. The condition changes to #7/01/2003#.

   TROUBLE? If your date is displayed with a two-digit year, or if it shows a different year, don't worry. You can customize Windows to display different date formats.

   Access automatically placed number signs (#) before and after the condition. You must place date and time values inside number signs when using these values as selection criteria. If you omit the number signs, however, Access will include them automatically.

2. Click the **Run** button ! on the Query Design toolbar. Access runs the query and displays the selected field values for only those records with a StartDate field value of 07/01. A total of 9 records are selected and displayed in the datasheet. See Figure 3-20.

   TROUBLE? If your query does not produce the results shown in Figure 3-20, you probably need to specify the year "01" as part of the StartDate criteria. To do so, return to the query in Design view, enter the criteria "7/01/01" for the StartDate, and then repeat Step 2.

| Figure 3-20 | DATASHEET DISPLAYING SELECTED FIELDS AND RECORDS |

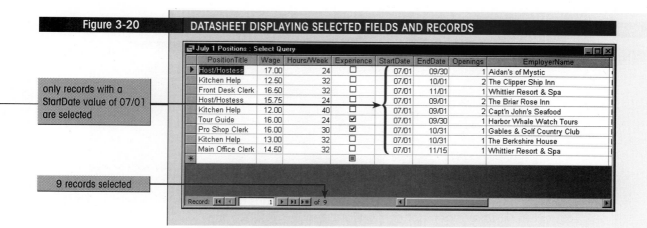

only records with a
StartDate value of 07/01
are selected

9 records selected

Matt would like to see more fields and records on the screen at one time. He asks you to maximize the datasheet, change the datasheet's font size, and resize all the columns to their best fit.

Changing a Datasheet's Appearance

You can change the characteristics of a datasheet, including the font type and size of text in the datasheet, to improve its appearance or readability. As you learned in Tutorial 2, you can also resize the datasheet columns to view more columns on the screen at the same time.

You'll maximize the datasheet, change the font size from the default 10 points to 8, and then resize the datasheet columns.

To change the font size and resize columns in the datasheet:

1. Click the **Maximize** button on the Query window title bar.

2. Click **Format** on the menu bar, and then click **Font** to open the Font dialog box.

3. Scroll the Size list box, click **8**, and then click the **OK** button. The font size for the entire datasheet changes to 8.

   Next you need to resize the columns to their best fit, so that each column is just wide enough to fit the longest value in the column. Instead of resizing each column individually, as you did in Tutorial 2, you'll select all the columns and resize them at the same time.

4. Position the pointer in the PositionTitle field selector. When the pointer changes to a ↓ shape, click to select the entire column.

5. Click the right arrow on the horizontal scroll bar until the Phone field is fully visible, and then position the pointer in the Phone field selector until the pointer changes to a ↓ shape.

6. Press and hold the **Shift** key, and then click the mouse button. All the columns are selected. Now you can resize all of them at once.

7. Position the pointer at the right edge of the Phone field selector until the pointer changes to a ↔ shape. See Figure 3-21.

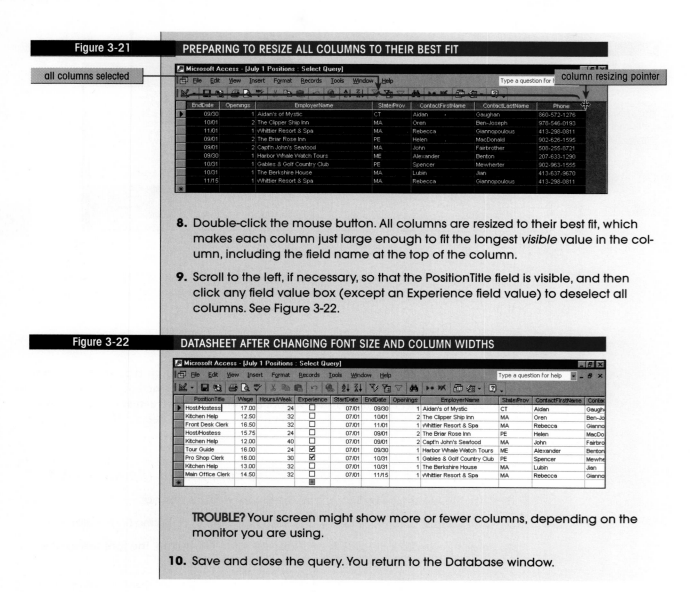

Figure 3-21   **PREPARING TO RESIZE ALL COLUMNS TO THEIR BEST FIT**

all columns selected

column resizing pointer

8. Double-click the mouse button. All columns are resized to their best fit, which makes each column just large enough to fit the longest *visible* value in the column, including the field name at the top of the column.

9. Scroll to the left, if necessary, so that the PositionTitle field is visible, and then click any field value box (except an Experience field value) to deselect all columns. See Figure 3-22.

Figure 3-22   **DATASHEET AFTER CHANGING FONT SIZE AND COLUMN WIDTHS**

TROUBLE? Your screen might show more or fewer columns, depending on the monitor you are using.

10. Save and close the query. You return to the Database window.

After viewing the query results, Matt decides that he would like to see the same fields, but only for those records whose Wage field value is equal to or greater than 17.00. He needs this information when he recruits students who will require a higher wage per hour for the available positions. To create the query needed to produce these results, you need to use a comparison operator to match a range of values—in this case, any Wage value greater than or equal to 17.00.

Using a Comparison Operator to Match a Range of Values

Once you create and save a query, you can click the Open button to run it again, or you can click the Design button to change its design. Because the design of the query you need to create next is similar to the July 1 Positions query, you will change its design, run the query to test it, and then save the query with a new name, which keeps the July 1 Positions query intact.

To change the July 1 Positions query design to create a new query:

1. Click the **July 1 Positions** query in the Database window (if necessary), and then click the **Design** button to open the July 1 Positions query in Design view.

2. Click the **Wage Criteria** text box, type **>=17**, and then press the **Tab** key three times. See Figure 3-23.

Figure 3-23	CHANGING A QUERY'S DESIGN TO CREATE A NEW QUERY

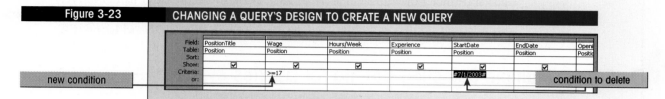

Matt's new condition specifies that a record will be selected only if its Wage field value is 17.00 or higher. Before you run the query, you need to delete the condition for the StartDate field.

3. With the StartDate field condition highlighted, press the **Delete** key. Now there is no condition for the StartDate field.

4. Click the **Run** button ⚫ on the Query Design toolbar. Access runs the query and displays the selected fields for only those records with a Wage field value greater than or equal to 17.00. A total of 19 records are selected. See Figure 3-24.

Figure 3-24	RUNNING THE MODIFIED QUERY

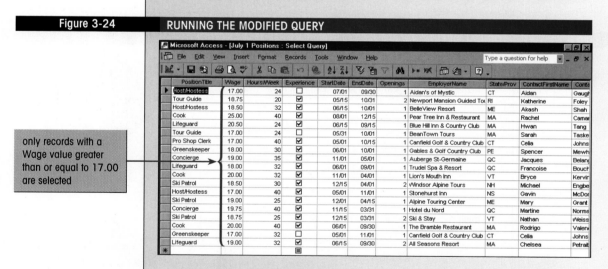

So that Matt can display this information again, as necessary, you'll save the query as High Wage Amounts.

5. Click **File** on the menu bar, click the double-arrow at the bottom of the menu to display the full menu (if necessary), and then click **Save As** to open the Save As dialog box.

6. In the text box for the new query name, type **High Wage Amounts**. Notice that the As text box specifies that you are saving the data as a query.

7. Click the **OK** button to save the query using the new name. The new query name appears in the title bar.

8. Close the Query window and return to the Database window.

Elsa asks Matt for a list of the positions with a start date of 07/01 for only the employers in Prince Edward Island. She wants to increase NSJI's business activity throughout eastern Canada (Prince Edward Island in particular), especially in the latter half of the year. To produce this data, you need to create a query containing two conditions—one for the position's start date and another to specify only the employers in Prince Edward Island (PE).

Defining **Multiple Selection Criteria for Queries**

Multiple conditions require you to use **logical operators** to combine two or more conditions. When you want a record selected only if two or more conditions are met, you need to use the **And logical operator**. In this case, Elsa wants to see only those records with a StartDate field value of 07/01 *and* a State/Prov field value of PE. If you place conditions in separate fields in the *same* Criteria row of the design grid, all conditions in that row must be met in order for a record to be included in the query results. However, if you place conditions in *different* Criteria rows, a record will be selected if at least one of the conditions is met. If none of the conditions is met, Access does not select the record. When you place conditions in different Criteria rows, you are using the **Or logical operator**. Figure 3-25 illustrates the difference between the And and Or logical operators.

Figure 3-25	LOGICAL OPERATORS And AND Or FOR MULTIPLE SELECTION CRITERIA

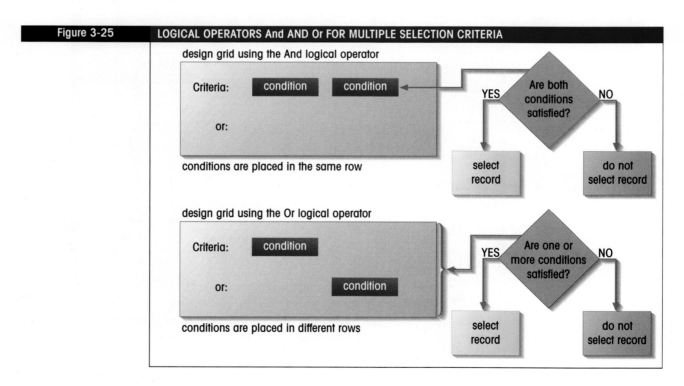

The And Logical Operator

To create Elsa's query, you need to modify the existing July 1 Positions query to show only the records for employers located in Prince Edward Island and offering positions starting on 07/01. For the modified query, you must add a second condition in the same Criteria row. The existing condition for the StartDate field finds records for positions that start on July 1; the new condition "PE" in the State/Prov field will find records for employers in Prince Edward Island. Because the conditions appear in the same Criteria row, the query will select records only if both conditions are met.

After modifying the query, you'll save it and then rename it as "PE July 1 Positions," overwriting the July 1 Positions query, which Matt no longer needs.

To modify the July 1 Positions query and use the And logical operator:

1. With the Queries object selected in the Database window, click **July 1 Positions** (if necessary), and then click the **Design** button to open the query in Design view.

2. Scroll the design grid to the right, click the **State/Prov Criteria** text box, type **PE**, and then press the ↓ key. See Figure 3-26.

| Figure 3-26 | QUERY TO FIND POSITIONS IN PE THAT START ON 07/01 |

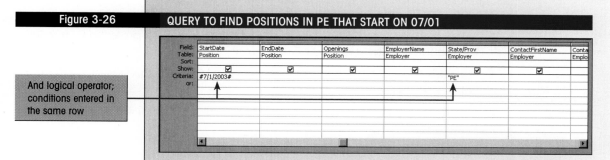

And logical operator; conditions entered in the same row

Notice that Access added quotation marks around the entry "PE"; you can type the quotation marks when you enter the condition, but if you forget to do so, Access will add them for you automatically.

The condition for the StartDate field is already entered, so you can run the query.

3. Run the query. Access displays in the datasheet only those records that meet both conditions: a StartDate field value of 07/01 and a State/Prov field value of PE. Two records are selected. See Figure 3-27.

| Figure 3-27 | RESULTS OF QUERY USING THE AND LOGICAL OPERATOR |

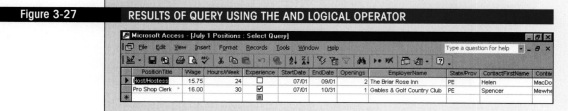

Now you can save the changes to the query and rename it.

4. Save and close the query. You return to the Database window.

5. Right-click **July 1 Positions** in the Queries list box, and then click **Rename** on the shortcut menu.

6. Click to position the insertion point to the left of the word "July," type **PE**, press the **spacebar**, and then press the **Enter** key. The query name is now PE July 1 Positions.

Using Multiple Undo and Redo

In previous versions of Access, you could not undo certain actions. Now Access allows you to undo and redo multiple actions when you are working in Design view for tables, queries, forms, reports, and so on. For example, when working in the Query window in Design view, if you specify multiple selection criteria for a query, you can use the multiple undo feature to remove the criteria—even after you run and save the query.

To see how this feature works, you will reopen the PE July 1 Positions query in Design view, delete the two criteria, and then reinsert them using multiple undo.

To modify the PE July 1 Positions query and use the multiple undo feature:

1. Open the **PE July 1 Positions** query in Design view.

2. Select the StartDate Criteria value, **#7/1/2003#**, and then press the **Delete** key. The StartDate Criteria text box is now empty.

3. Press the **Tab** key four times to move to and select **"PE"**, the State/Prov Criteria value, and then press the **Delete** key.

4. Run the query. Notice that the results display all records for the fields specified in the query design grid.

5. Switch back to Design view.

   Now you will use multiple undo to reverse the edits you made and reinsert the two conditions.

6. Click the **list arrow** for the Undo button ↰ on the Query Design toolbar. A menu appears listing the actions you can undo. See Figure 3-28.

Figure 3-28	USING MULTIPLE UNDO

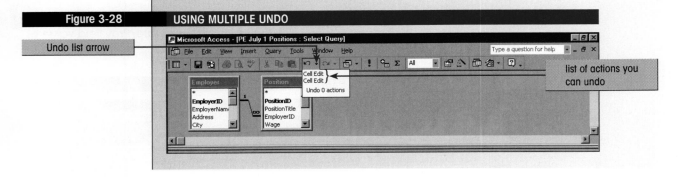

Undo list arrow

list of actions you can undo

Two items, both named "Cell Edit," are listed in the Undo list box. These items represent the two changes you made to the query design—first deleting the StartDate condition and then deleting the State/Prov condition. If you select an action that is below other items in the list, you will undo all the actions above the one you select, in addition to the one you select. Currently no actions are selected, so the list box indicates "Undo 0 actions."

7. Position the pointer over the second occurrence of **Cell Edit** in the list. Notice that both undo actions are highlighted, and the list box indicates that you can undo two actions.

8. Click the second occurrence of **Cell Edit**. Both actions are "undone," and the two conditions are redisplayed in the query design grid. The multiple undo feature makes it easy for you to test different criteria for a query and, when necessary, to undo your actions based on the query results.

   Notice that the Redo button and list arrow are now available. You can redo the actions you've just undone.

9. Click the **list arrow** for the Redo button [⟳] on the Query Design toolbar. The Redo list box indicates that you can redo the two cell edits.

10. Click the **list arrow** for the Redo button [⟳] again to close the Redo list box without selecting any option.

11. Close the query. Click the **No** button in the message box that opens, asking if you want to save your changes. You return to the Database window.

Matt has another request for information. He knows that it can be difficult to find student recruits for positions that offer fewer than 30 hours of work per week or that require prior work experience. So that his staff can focus on such positions, Matt wants to see a list of those positions that provide less than 30 hours of work or that require experience. To create this query, you need to use the Or logical operator.

The Or Logical Operator

For Matt's request, you need a query that selects a record when either one of two conditions is satisfied or when both conditions are satisfied. That is, a record is selected if the Hours/Week field value is less than 30 *or* if the Experience field value is "Yes" (checked). You will enter the condition for the Hours/Week field in one Criteria row and the condition for the Experience field in another Criteria row, thereby using the Or logical operator.

To display the information Matt wants to view, you'll create a new query containing the EmployerName and City fields from the Employer table and the PositionTitle, Hours/Week, and Experience fields from the Position table. Then you'll specify the conditions using the Or logical operator.

To create the query and use the Or logical operator:

1. In the Database window, double-click **Create query in Design view**. The Show Table dialog box opens on top of the Query window in Design view.

2. Click **Employer** in the Tables list box (if necessary), click the **Add** button, click **Position**, click the **Add** button, and then click the **Close** button. The Employer and Position field lists appear in the Query window and the Show Table dialog box closes.

3. Double-click **EmployerName** in the Employer field list to add the EmployerName field to the design grid's first column Field text box.

4. Repeat Step 3 to add the **City** field from the Employer table, and then add the **PositionTitle**, **Hours/Week**, and **Experience** fields from the Position table.

   Now you need to specify the first condition, <30, in the Hours/Week field.

5. Click the **Hours/Week Criteria** text box, type **<30** and then press the **Tab** key.

   Because you want records selected if either of the conditions for the Hours/Week or Experience fields is satisfied, you must enter the condition for the Experience field in the "or" row of the design grid.

6. Press the ↓ key, and then type **Yes** in the "or" text box for Experience. See Figure 3-29.

Figure 3-29	QUERY WINDOW WITH THE OR LOGICAL OPERATOR

Field:	EmployerName	City	PositionTitle	Hours/Week	Experience	
Table:	Employer	Employer	Position	Position	Position	
Sort:						
Show:	✓	✓	✓	✓	✓	☐
Criteria:				<30		
or:					Yes	

Or logical operator; conditions entered in different rows

7. Run the query. Access displays only those records that meet either condition: an Hours/Week field value less than 30 or an Experience field value of "Yes" (checked). A total of 35 records are selected.

   Matt wants the list displayed in alphabetical order by EmployerName. The first record's EmployerName field is highlighted, indicating the current field.

8. Click the **Sort Ascending** button ⸻ on the Query Datasheet toolbar.

9. Resize all datasheet columns to their best fit. Scroll through the entire datasheet to make sure that all values are completely displayed. Deselect all columns when you are finished resizing them, and then return to the top of the datasheet. See Figure 3-30.

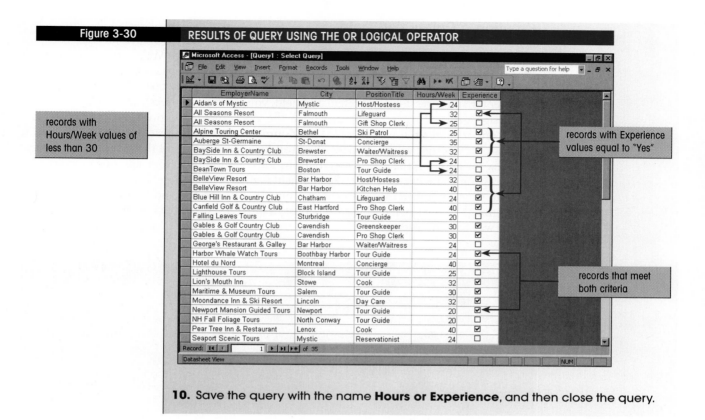

Figure 3-30   **RESULTS OF QUERY USING THE OR LOGICAL OPERATOR**

records with Hours/Week values of less than 30

records with Experience values equal to "Yes"

records that meet both criteria

10. Save the query with the name **Hours or Experience**, and then close the query.

Next, Elsa wants to use the Northeast database to perform calculations. She is considering offering a 2% bonus per week to the student recruits in higher paid positions, based on employer recommendation, and she wants to know exactly what these bonuses would be.

Performing Calculations

In addition to using queries to retrieve, sort, and filter data in a database, you can use a query to perform calculations. To perform a calculation, you define an **expression** containing a combination of database fields, constants, and operators. For numeric expressions, the data types of the database fields must be number, currency, or date/time; the constants are numbers such as .02 (for the 2% bonus); and the operators can be arithmetic operators (+ – * /) or other specialized operators. In complex expressions, you can enclose calculations in parentheses to indicate which one should be performed first. In expressions without parentheses, Access calculates in the following order of precedence: multiplication and division before addition and subtraction. When operators have equal precedence, Access calculates them in order from left to right.

To perform a calculation in a query, you add a calculated field to the query. A **calculated field** is a field that displays the results of an expression. A calculated field appears in a query datasheet or in a form or report; however, it does not exist in a database. When you run a query that contains a calculated field, Access evaluates the expression defined by the calculated field and displays the resulting value in the datasheet, form, or report.

Creating a Calculated Field

To produce the information Elsa wants, you need to open the High Wage Amounts query and create a calculated field that will multiply each Wage field value by each Hours/Week value, and then multiply that amount by .02 to determine the 2% weekly bonus Elsa is considering.

To enter an expression for a calculated field, you can type it directly in a Field text box in the design grid. Alternately, you can open the Zoom box or Expression Builder and use either one to enter the expression. The **Zoom box** is a large text box for entering text, expressions, or other values. **Expression Builder** is an Access tool that contains an expression box for entering the expression, buttons for common operators, and one or more lists of expression elements, such as table and field names. Unlike a Field text box, which is too small to show an entire expression at one time, the Zoom box and Expression Builder are large enough to display lengthy expressions. In most cases, Expression Builder provides the easiest way to enter expressions.

REFERENCE WINDOW   **RW**

Using Expression Builder

- Open the query in Design view.
- In the design grid, position the insertion point in the Field text box of the field for which you want to create an expression.
- Click the Build button on the Query Design toolbar.
- Use the expression elements and common operators to build the expression, or type the expression directly.
- Click the OK button.

You'll begin by copying, pasting, and renaming the High Wage Amounts query, keeping the original query intact. You'll name the new query "High Wages with Bonus." Then you'll modify this query in Design view to show only the information Elsa wants to view.

To copy the High Wage Amounts query and paste the copy with a new name:

1. Right-click the **High Wage Amounts** query in the list of queries, and then click **Copy** on the shortcut menu.

2. Right-click an empty area of the Database window, and then click **Paste** on the shortcut menu. The Paste As dialog box opens.

3. Type **High Wages with Bonus** in the Query Name text box, and then press the **Enter** key. The new query appears in the query list, along with the original High Wage Amounts query.

Now you're ready to modify the High Wages with Bonus query to create the calculated field for Elsa.

To modify the High Wages with Bonus query:

1. Open the **High Wages with Bonus** query in Design view.

Elsa wants to see only the EmployerName, PositionTitle, and Wage fields in the query results. First, you'll delete the unnecessary fields, and then you'll move the EmployerName field so that it appears first in the query results.

2. Scroll the design grid to the right until the Hours/Week and EmployerName fields are visible at the same time.

3. Position the pointer on the Hours/Week field until the pointer changes to a ⬇ shape, click and hold down the mouse button, drag the mouse to the right to highlight the Hours/Week, Experience, StartDate, EndDate, and Openings fields, and then release the mouse button.

4. Press the **Delete** key to delete the five selected fields.

5. Repeat Steps 3 and 4 to delete the State/Prov, ContactFirstName, ContactLastName, and Phone fields from the query design grid.

Next you'll move the EmployerName field to the left of the PositionTitle field so that the Wage values will appear next to the calculated field values in the query results.

6. Scroll the design grid back to the left (if necessary), select the **EmployerName** field, and then use the pointer 🔓 to drag the field to the left of the PositionTitle field. See Figure 3-31.

| Figure 3-31 | MODIFIED QUERY BEFORE ADDING THE CALCULATED FIELD |

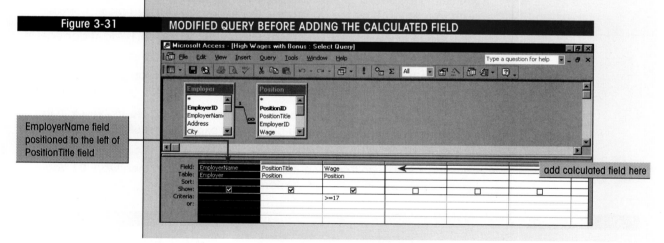

Now you're ready to use Expression Builder to enter the calculated field in the High Wages with Bonus query.

To add the calculated field to the High Wages with Bonus query:

1. Position the insertion point in the Field text box to the right of the Wage field, and then click the **Build** button 🔨 on the Query Design toolbar. The Expression Builder dialog box opens. See Figure 3-32.

Figure 3-32   INITIAL EXPRESSION BUILDER DIALOG BOX

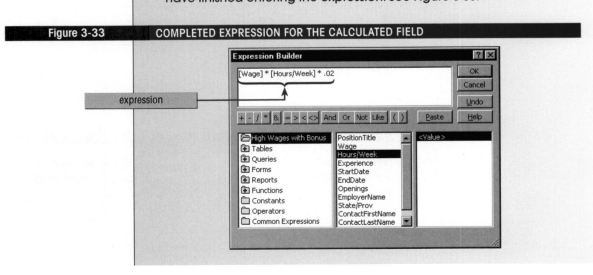

You use the common operators and expression elements to help you build an expression. Note that the High Wages with Bonus query is already selected in the list box on the lower left; the fields included in the original version of the query are listed in the center box.

The expression for the calculated field will multiply the Wage field values by the Hours/Week field values, and then multiply that amount by the numeric constant .02 (which represents a 2% bonus). To include a field in the expression, you select the field and then click the Paste button. To include a numeric constant, you simply type the constant in the expression.

2. Click **Wage** in the field list, and then click the **Paste** button. [Wage] appears in the expression box.

To include the multiplication operator in the expression, you click the asterisk (*) button.

3. Click the * button in the row of common operators, click **Hours/Week** in the field list, and then click the **Paste** button. The expression multiplies the Wage values by the Hours/Week values.

4. Click the * button in the row of common operators, and then type **.02**. You have finished entering the expression. See Figure 3-33.

Figure 3-33   COMPLETED EXPRESSION FOR THE CALCULATED FIELD

Note that you also could have typed the expression directly into the expression box, instead of clicking the field names and the operator.

5. Click the **OK** button. Access closes the Expression Builder dialog box and adds the expression to the design grid in the Field text box for the calculated field.

   Next, you need to specify a name for the calculated field as it will appear in the query results.

6. Press the **Home** key to position the insertion point to the left of the expression.

   You'll enter the name WeeklyBonus, which is descriptive of the field's contents; then you'll run the query.

7. Type **WeeklyBonus**:. *Make sure you include the colon following the field name. The colon is needed to separate the field name from its expression.*

8. Run the query. Access displays the query datasheet, which contains the three specified fields and the calculated field with the name "WeeklyBonus." Resize all datasheet columns to their best fit. See Figure 3-34.

Figure 3-34	DATASHEET DISPLAYING THE CALCULATED FIELD

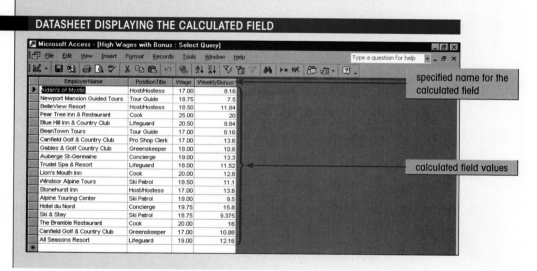

Notice the WeeklyBonus value for Ski & Stay; the value appears with three decimal places (9.375). Currency values should have only two decimal places, so you need to format the WeeklyBonus calculated field so that all values appear in the Fixed format with two decimal places.

To format the calculated field:

1. Switch to Design view.

2. Right-click the **WeeklyBonus** calculated field in the design grid to open the shortcut menu, and then click **Properties**. The property sheet for the selected field opens. The property sheet for a field provides options for changing the display of field values in the datasheet.

3. Click the right side of the **Format** text box to display the list of formats, and then click **Fixed**.

4. Click the right side of the **Decimal Places** text box, and then click **2**.

5. Click in the **Description** text box to deselect the Decimal Places setting. See Figure 3-35.

| Figure 3-35 | PROPERTY SHEET SETTINGS TO FORMAT THE CALCULATED FIELD |

Now that you have formatted the calculated field, you can run the query.

6. Close the Field Properties window, and then save and run the query. The value for Ski & Stay now correctly appears as 9.38.

7. Close the query.

Elsa prepares a report on a regular basis that includes a summary of information about the wages paid to student recruits. She lists the minimum hourly wage paid, the average wage amount, and the maximum hourly wage paid. She asks you to create a query to determine these statistics from data in the Position table.

Using Aggregate Functions

You can calculate statistical information, such as totals and averages, on the records selected by a query. To do this, you use the Access aggregate functions. **Aggregate functions** perform arithmetic operations on selected records in a database. Figure 3-36 lists the most frequently used aggregate functions. Aggregate functions operate on the records that meet a query's selection criteria. You specify an aggregate function for a specific field, and the appropriate operation applies to that field's values for the selected records.

Figure 3-36	FREQUENTLY USED AGGREGATE FUNCTIONS	
AGGREGATE FUNCTION	**DETERMINES**	**DATA TYPES SUPPORTED**
Avg	Average of the field values for the selected records	AutoNumber, Currency, Date/Time, Number
Count	Number of records selected	AutoNumber, Currency, Date/Time, Memo, Number, OLE Object, Text, Yes/No
Max	Highest field value for the selected records	AutoNumber, Currency, Date/Time, Number, Text
Min	Lowest field value for the selected records	AutoNumber, Currency, Date/Time, Number, Text
Sum	Total of the field values for the selected records	AutoNumber, Currency, Date/Time, Number

To display the minimum, average, and maximum of all the wage amounts in the Position table, you will use the Min, Avg, and Max aggregate functions for the Wage field.

To calculate the minimum, average, and maximum of all wage amounts:

1. Double-click **Create query in Design view**, click **Position**, click the **Add** button, and then click the **Close** button. The Position field list is added to the Query window and the Show Table dialog box closes.

   To perform the three calculations on the Wage field, you need to add the field to the design grid three times.

2. Double-click **Wage** in the Position field list three times to add three copies of the field to the design grid.

   You need to select an aggregate function for each Wage field. When you click the Totals button on the Query Design toolbar, a row labeled "Total" is added to the design grid. The Total row provides a list of the aggregate functions that you can select.

3. Click the **Totals** button Σ on the Query Design toolbar. A new row labeled "Total" appears between the Table and Sort rows in the design grid. See Figure 3-37.

Figure 3-37	TOTAL ROW INSERTED IN THE DESIGN GRID

In the Total row, you specify the aggregate function you want to use for a field.

4. Click the right side of the first column's **Total** text box, and then click **Min**. This field will calculate the minimum amount of all the Wage field values.

   When you run the query, Access automatically will assign a datasheet column name of "MinOfWage" for this field. You can change the datasheet column name to a more descriptive or readable name by entering the name you want in the Field text box. However, you must also keep the field name Wage in the Field text box, because it identifies the field whose values will be calculated. The Field text box will contain the datasheet column name you specify followed by the field name (Wage) with a colon separating the two names.

5. Position the insertion point to the left of Wage in the first column's Field text box, and then type **MinimumWage**:. Be sure that you type the colon.

6. Click the right side of the second column's **Total** text box, and then click **Avg**. This field will calculate the average of all the Wage field values.

7. Position the insertion point to the left of Wage in the second column's Field text box, and then type **AverageWage**:.

8. Click the right side of the third column's **Total** text box, and then click **Max**. This field will calculate the maximum amount of all the Wage field values.

9. Position the insertion point to the left of Wage in the third column's Field text box, and then type **MaximumWage**:.

   The query design is completed, so you can run the query.

10. Run the query. Access displays one record containing the three aggregate function values. The single row of summary statistics represents calculations based on the 64 records selected by the query.

   You need to resize the three columns to their best fit to see the column names.

11. Resize all columns to their best fit, and then position the insertion point in the field value in the first column. See Figure 3-38.

Figure 3-38	RESULTS OF THE QUERY USING AGGREGATE FUNCTIONS

12. Save the query as **Wage Statistics**, and then close the query.

Elsa also wants her report to include the same wage statistics (minimum, average, and maximum) for each type of position. She asks you to display the wage statistics for each different PositionTitle value in the Position table.

Using Record Group Calculations

In addition to calculating statistical information on all or selected records in selected tables, you can calculate statistics for groups of records. For example, you can determine the number of employers in each state or province, or the average wage amount by position.

To create a query for Elsa's latest request, you can modify the current query by adding the PositionTitle field and assigning the Group By operator to it. The **Group By operator** divides the selected records into groups based on the values in the specified field. Those records with the same value for the field are grouped together, and the datasheet displays one record for each group. Aggregate functions, which appear in the other columns of the design grid, provide statistical information for each group.

You need to modify the current query to add the Group By operator for the PositionTitle field. This will display the statistical information grouped by position for the 64 selected records in the query. As you did earlier, you will copy the Wage Statistics query and paste it with a new name, keeping the original query intact, to create the new query.

To copy and paste the query, and then add the PositionTitle field with the Group By operator:

1. Right-click the **Wage Statistics** query in the list of queries, and then click **Copy** on the shortcut menu.

2. Right-click an empty area of the Database window, and then click **Paste** on the shortcut menu.

3. Type **Wage Statistics by Position** in the Query Name text box, and then press the **Enter** key.

Now you're ready to modify the query design.

4. Open the **Wage Statistics by Position** query in Design view.

5. Double-click **PositionTitle** in the Position field list to add the field to the design grid. Group By, which is the default option in the Total row, appears for the PositionTitle field.

You've completed the query changes, so you can run the query.

6. Run the query. Access displays 16 records—one for each PositionTitle group. Each record contains the three aggregate function values and the PositionTitle field value for the group. Again, the summary statistics represent calculations based on the 64 records selected by the query. See Figure 3-39.

Figure 3-39	AGGREGATE FUNCTIONS GROUPED BY PositionTitle

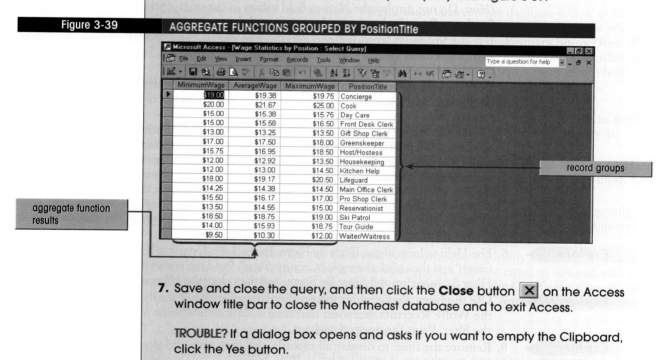

aggregate function results

record groups

7. Save and close the query, and then click the **Close** button ✕ on the Access window title bar to close the Northeast database and to exit Access.

TROUBLE? If a dialog box opens and asks if you want to empty the Clipboard, click the Yes button.

The queries you've created and saved will help Elsa, Zack, Matt, and other employees to monitor and analyze the business activity of NSJI's employer customers. Now any NSJI staff member can run the queries at any time, modify them as needed, or use them as the basis for designing new queries to meet additional information requirements.

Session 3.2 QUICK CHECK

1. A(n) _____ is a criterion, or rule, that determines which records are selected for a query datasheet.

2. In the design grid, where do you place the conditions for two different fields when you use the And logical operator? The Or logical operator?

5. Use Design view to create a select query based on the **Restaurant** and **Order** tables. For all orders placed on 03/21/2003, display the Order#, OrderAmt, OrderDate, and RestaurantName fields. Save the query as **March 21 Orders**, and then run the query. Switch to Design view, modify the query so that the OrderDate values do not appear in the query results, and then save the modified query. Run the query, print the query results, and then close the query.

6. Use Design view to create a select query based on the **Restaurant** table. For all restaurants that have a Website and are located in Naples, display the RestaurantName, OwnerFirstName, OwnerLastName, and Phone fields. Save the query as **Naples Restaurants with Websites**, run the query, print the query results, and then close the query.

7. Use Design view to create a select query based on the **Restaurant** and **Order** tables. For all orders placed on 03/14/2003 or 03/15/2003, display the fields OrderDate, OrderAmt, RestaurantName, and Restaurant# (from the **Restaurant** table). Display the results in ascending order by OrderDate and then in descending order by OrderAmt. Save the query as **Selected Dates**, run the query, print the query datasheet, and then close the query.

Explore

8. Use the **Order** table to display the highest, lowest, total, average, and count of the OrderAmt field for all orders. Then do the following:

   a. Specify column names of HighestOrder, LowestOrder, TotalOrders, AverageOrder, and #Orders. Use the property sheet for each column (except #Orders) to format the results as Fixed with two decimal places. Save the query as **Order Statistics**, and then run the query. Resize all datasheet columns to their best fit, save the query, and then print the query results.

   b. Change the query to display the same statistics grouped by RestaurantName. (*Hint*: Use the Show Table button on the Query Design toolbar to add the **Restaurant** table to the query.) Save the query as **Order Statistics by Restaurant**. Run the query, print the query results, and then close the query.

9. Close the **Meals** database, and then exit Access.

Case 3. Redwood Zoo Michael Rosenfeld wants to find specific information about the donors and their pledge amounts for the Redwood Zoo. You'll help them find the information in the **Redwood** database by completing the following:

1. Make sure your Data Disk is in the appropriate disk drive, start Access, and then open the **Redwood** database located in the Cases folder on your Data Disk.

Explore

2. Define the necessary one-to-many relationships between the database tables, as follows: between the primary **Donor** table and the related **Pledge** table, and between the primary **Fund** table and the related **Pledge** table. (*Hint*: Add all three tables to the Relationships window, and then define the two relationships.) Select the referential integrity option and both cascade options for each relationship.

3. Use Design view to create a select query that, for all pledges with a TotalPledged field value of greater than 200, displays the DonorID (from the **Donor** table), FirstName, LastName, Pledge#, TotalPledged, and FundName fields. Sort the query in ascending order by TotalPledged. Save the query as **Large Pledges**, and then run the query.

4. Use the **Large Pledges** datasheet to update the **Pledge** table by changing the TotalPledged field value for Pledge# 2976 to 750. Print the query datasheet, and then close the query.

5. Use Design view to create a select query that, for all donors who pledged less than $150 or who donated to the Whale Watchers fund, displays the Pledge#, PledgeDate, TotalPledged, FirstName, and LastName fields. Save the revised query as **Pledged or Whale Watchers**, run the query, and then print the query datasheet. Change the query to select all donors who pledged less than $150 and who donated to the Whale Watchers fund. Save the revised query as **Pledged and Whale Watchers**, and then run the query. Close the query.

Explore

6. Use Design view to create a select query that displays the DonorID (from the **Donor** table), TotalPledged, PaymentMethod, PledgeDate, and FundName fields. Save the query as **Pledges after Costs**. Create a calculated field named Overhead that displays the results of multiplying the TotalPledged field values by 15% (to account for overhead costs). Save the query, and then create a second calculated field named NetPledge that displays the results of subtracting the Overhead field values from the TotalPledged field values.

Format the calculated fields as Fixed. Display the results in ascending order by TotalPledged. Save the modified query, and then run the query. Resize all datasheet columns to their best fit, print the query results, and then save and close the query.

Explore

7. Use the **Pledge** table to display the sum, average, and count of the TotalPledged field for all pledges. Then do the following:
   a. Specify column names of TotalPledge, AveragePledge, and #Pledges.
   b. Change properties so that the values in the TotalPledge and AveragePledge columns display two decimal places and the Fixed format.
   c. Save the query as **Pledge Statistics**, run the query, resize all datasheet columns to their best fit, and then print the query datasheet. Save the query.
   d. Change the query to display the sum, average, and count of the TotalPledged field for all pledges by FundName. (*Hint*: Use the Show Table button on the Query Design toolbar to add the **Fund** table to the query.) Save the query as **Pledge Statistics by Fund**, run the query, print the query datasheet, and then close the query.

8. Close the **Redwood** database, and then exit Access.

Case 4. Mountain River Adventures Connor and Siobhan Dempsey want to analyze data about their clients and the rafting trips they take. Help them query the **Trips** database by completing the following:

1. Make sure your Data Disk is in the appropriate disk drive, start Access, and then open the **Trips** database located in the Cases folder on your Data Disk.

Explore

2. Define the necessary one-to-many relationships between the database tables, as follows: between the primary **Client** table and the related **Booking** table, and between the primary **Rafting Trip** table and the related **Booking** table. (*Hint*: Add all three tables to the Relationships window, and then define the two relationships.) Select the referential integrity option and both cascade options for each relationship.

3. For all clients, display the ClientName, City, State/Prov, Booking#, and TripDate fields. Save the query as **Client Trip Dates**, and then run the query. Resize all datasheet columns to their best fit. In Datasheet view, sort the query results in ascending order by the TripDate field. Print the query datasheet, and then save and close the query.

4. For all clients from Colorado (CO), display the ClientName, City, State/Prov, Trip#, People, and TripDate fields. Sort the query in ascending order by City. Save the query as **Colorado Clients**, and then run the query. Modify the query to remove the display of the State/Prov field values from the query results. Save the modified query, run the query, print the query datasheet, and then close the query.

Explore

5. For all clients who are not from Colorado or who are taking a rafting trip in the month of July 2003, display the ClientName, City, State/Prov, Booking#, TripDate, and Trip# fields. (*Hint*: Refer to Figure 3-18 to determine the correct comparison operators to use.) Sort the query in descending order by TripDate. Save the query as **Out of State or July**, run the query, and then print the query datasheet. Change the query to select all clients who are not from Colorado and who are taking a rafting trip in the month of July 2003. Sort the query in ascending order by State/Prov. Save the query as **Out of State and July**, run the query, print the query datasheet, and then close the query.

6. For all bookings, display the Booking#, TripDate, Trip# (from the **Booking** table), River, People, and Fee/Person fields. Save the query as **Trip Cost**. Then create a calculated field named TripCost that displays the results of multiplying the People field values by the Fee/Person field values. Display the results in descending order by TripCost. Run the query, resize all datasheet columns to their best fit, print the query datasheet, and then save and close the query.

Explore

7. Use the **Rafting Trip** table to determine the minimum, average, and maximum Fee/Person for all trips. Use the Ask a Question box to ask the question, "What is a caption?" and then locate and click the topic "Change a field name in a query." Read the displayed information, and then click and read the subtopic "Change a field's caption."

Close the Help window. Set the Caption property of the three fields to Lowest Fee, Average Fee, and Highest Fee, respectively. Also set the properties so that the results of the three fields are displayed as Fixed with two decimal places. Save the query as **Fee Statistics**, run the query, resize all datasheet columns to their best fit, print the query datasheet, and then save the query again. Revise the query to show the fee statistics grouped by People. (*Hint*: Use the Show Table button on the Query Design toolbar to display the Show Table dialog box.) Save the revised query as **Fee Statistics by People**, run the query, print the query datasheet, and then close the query.

Explore

8. Use the Ask a Question box to ask the following question: "How do I create a Top Values query?" Click the topic "Show only the high or low values in a query." Read the displayed information, and then close the Help window. Open the **Trip Cost** query in Design view, and then modify the query to display only the top five values for the TripCost field. Save the query as **Top Trip Cost**, run the query, print the query datasheet, and then close the query.

9. Close the **Trips** database, and then exit Access.

INTERNET ASSIGNMENTS

Student Union

The purpose of the Internet Assignments is to challenge you to find information on the Internet that you can use to create effective documents. The actual assignments are updated and maintained on the Course Technology Web site. Log on to the Internet and use your Web browser to go to the Student Union on the New Perspectives Series site at **www.course.com/NewPerspectives/studentunion**. Click the Online Companions link, and then click the link for this text.

QUICK CHECK ANSWERS

Session 3.1

1. a general query in which you specify the fields and records you want Access to select
2. The field list contains the table name at the top of the list box and the table's fields listed in the order in which they appear in the table; the design grid displays columns that contain specifications about a field you will use in the query.
3. A table datasheet and a query datasheet look the same, appearing in Datasheet view, and can be used to update data in a database. A table datasheet shows the permanent data in a table, whereas a query datasheet is temporary and its contents are based on the criteria you establish in the design grid.
4. primary table; related table
5. Referential integrity
6. oldest to most recent date
7. when you want to perform different types of sorts (both ascending and descending, for example) on multiple fields, and when you want to sort on multiple fields that are nonadjacent or in the wrong order, but you do not want to rearrange the columns in the query datasheet to accomplish the sort
8. filter

Session 3.2

1. condition
2. in the same Criteria row; in different Criteria rows
3. expression
4. A calculated field appears in a query datasheet, form, or report but does not exist in a database, as does a table field.
5. a function that performs an arithmetic operation on selected records in a database
6. Group By

OBJECTIVES

In this tutorial you will:

- Create a form using the Form Wizard

- Change a form's AutoFormat

- Find data using a form

- Preview and print selected form records

- Maintain table data using a form

- Check the spelling of table data using a form

- Create a form with a main form and a subform

- Create a report using the Report Wizard

- Insert a picture in a report

- Preview and print a report

CREATING FORMS AND REPORTS

Creating a Position Data Form, an Employer Positions Form, and an Employers and Positions Report

CASE

Northeast Seasonal Jobs International (NSJI)

Elsa Jensen wants to continue enhancing the Northeast database to make it easier for NSJI employees to find and maintain data. In particular, she wants the database to include a form based on the Position table to make it easier for employees to enter and change data about available positions. She also wants the database to include a form that shows data from both the Employer and Position tables at the same time. This form will show the position information for each employer along with the corresponding employer data, providing a complete picture of NSJI's employer clients and their available positions.

In addition, Zack Ward would like the database to include a formatted report of employer and position data so that his marketing staff members will have printed output when completing market analyses and planning strategies for selling NSJI's services to employer clients. He wants the information to be formatted attractively, perhaps by including a picture or graphic image on the report for visual interest.

In this session, you will create a form using the Form Wizard, change a form's AutoFormat, find data using a form, preview and print selected form records, maintain table data using a form, and check the spelling of table data using a form.

Creating a Form Using the Form Wizard

As you learned in Tutorial 1, a form is an object you use to maintain, view, and print records in a database. In Access, you can design your own forms or use a Form Wizard to create them for you automatically.

Elsa asks you to create a new form that her staff can use to view and maintain data in the Position table. In Tutorial 1, you used the AutoForm Wizard to create the Employer Data form in the Seasonal database. The AutoForm Wizard creates a form automatically, using all the fields in the selected table or query. To create the form for the Position table, you'll use the Form Wizard. The **Form Wizard** allows you to choose some or all of the fields in the selected table or query, choose fields from other tables and queries, and display the selected fields in any order on the form. You can also apply an existing style to the form to format its appearance quickly.

To open the Northeast database and activate the Form Wizard:

1. Place your Data Disk in the appropriate disk drive.

2. Start Access and open the **Northeast** database located in the Tutorial folder on your Data Disk.

3. Click **Forms** in the Objects bar of the Database window.

4. Click the **New** button in the Database window. The New Form dialog box opens.

5. Click **Form Wizard**, click the list arrow for choosing a table or query, click **Position** to select this table as the source for the form, and then click the **OK** button. The first Form Wizard dialog box opens. See Figure 4-1.

Figure 4-1	FIRST FORM WIZARD DIALOG BOX

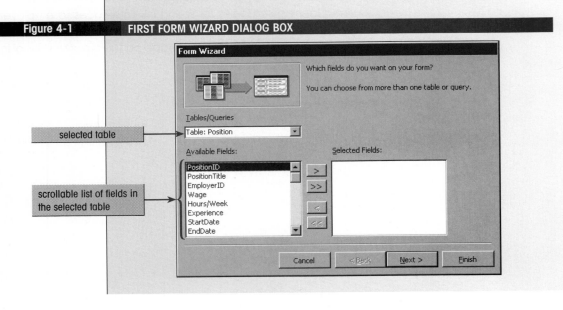

selected table

scrollable list of fields in the selected table

Elsa wants the form to display all the fields in the Position table, but in a different order. She would like the Experience field to appear at the bottom of the form so that it stands out more, making it easier to determine if a position requires prior work experience.

To finish creating the form using the Form Wizard:

1. Click **PositionID** in the Available Fields list box (if necessary), and then click the ⟩ button to move the field to the Selected Fields list box.

2. Repeat Step 1 to select the **PositionTitle, EmployerID, Wage, Hours/Week, StartDate, EndDate, Openings,** and **Experience** fields, in that order. Remember, you can also double-click a field to move it from the Available Fields list box to the Selected Fields list box.

3. Click the **Next** button to display the second Form Wizard dialog box, in which you select a layout for the form. See Figure 4-2.

| Figure 4-2 | CHOOSING A LAYOUT FOR THE FORM |

The layout choices are Columnar, Tabular, Datasheet, Justified, PivotTable, and PivotChart. A sample of the selected layout appears on the left side of the dialog box.

4. Click each of the option buttons and review the corresponding sample layout.

The Tabular and Datasheet layouts display the fields from multiple records at one time, whereas the Columnar and Justified layouts display the fields from one record at a time. The PivotTable and PivotChart layouts display summary and analytical information. Elsa thinks the Columnar layout is the appropriate arrangement for displaying and updating data in the table, so you'll choose this layout.

5. Click the **Columnar** option button (if necessary), and then click the **Next** button. Access displays the third Form Wizard dialog box, in which you choose a style for the form. See Figure 4-3.

Figure 4-3	CHOOSING A STYLE FOR THE FORM

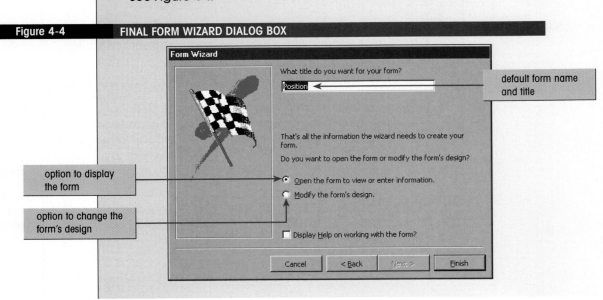

A sample of the selected style appears in the box on the left. If you choose a style, which is called an **AutoFormat**, and decide you'd prefer a different one after the form is created, you can change it.

TROUBLE? Don't worry if a different form style is selected in your dialog box instead of the one shown in Figure 4-3. The dialog box displays the most recently used style, which might be different on your computer.

6. Click each of the styles and review the corresponding sample.

Elsa likes the Expedition style and asks you to use it for the form.

7. Click **Expedition** and then click the **Next** button. Access displays the final Form Wizard dialog box and shows the Position table's name as the default form name. "Position" is also the default title that will appear in the form's title bar. See Figure 4-4.

Figure 4-4	FINAL FORM WIZARD DIALOG BOX

You'll use "Position Data" as the form name and, because you don't need to change the form's design at this point, you'll display the form.

8. Click the insertion point to the right of Position in the text box, press the **spacebar**, type **Data**, and then click the **Finish** button. The completed form opens in Form view. See Figure 4-5.

Figure 4-5	COMPLETED FORM FOR THE POSITION TABLE

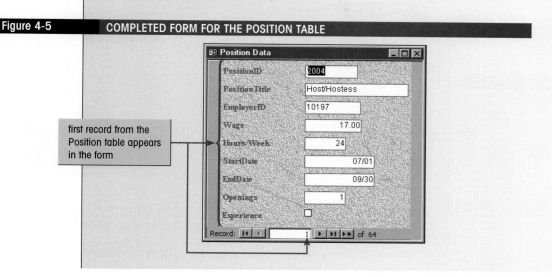

first record from the Position table appears in the form

After viewing the form, Elsa decides that she doesn't like the form's style; the background makes the field names a bit difficult to read. She asks you to change the form's style.

Changing a Form's AutoFormat

You can change a form's appearance by choosing a different AutoFormat for the form. As you learned when you created the Position Data form, an AutoFormat is a predefined style for a form (or report). The AutoFormats available for a form are the ones you saw when you selected the form's style using the Form Wizard. To change an AutoFormat, you must switch to Design view.

REFERENCE WINDOW   **RW**

Changing a Form's AutoFormat
- Display the form in Design view.
- Click the AutoFormat button on the Form Design toolbar to open the AutoFormat dialog box.
- In the Form AutoFormats list box, click the AutoFormat you want to apply to the form, and then click the OK button.

To change the AutoFormat for the Position Data form:

1. Click the **View** button for Design view 🔲 on the Form View toolbar. The form is displayed in Design view. See Figure 4-6.

| Figure 4-6 | FORM DISPLAYED IN DESIGN VIEW |

TROUBLE? If your screen displays any window other than those shown in Figure 4-6, click the Close button ⊠ on the window's title bar to close it.

You use Design view to modify an existing form or to create a form from scratch. In this case, you need to change the AutoFormat for the Position Data form.

2. Click the **AutoFormat** button 🖫 on the Form Design toolbar. The AutoFormat dialog box opens.

3. Click the **Options** button to display the AutoFormat options. See Figure 4-7.

| Figure 4-7 | AUTOFORMAT DIALOG BOX |

A sample of the selected AutoFormat appears to the right of the Form AutoFormats list box. The options at the bottom of the dialog box let you apply the selected AutoFormat or just its font, color, or border.

Elsa decides that she prefers the Standard AutoFormat, because its field names and field values are easy to read.

4. Click **Standard** in the Form AutoFormats list box, and then click the **OK** button. The AutoFormat dialog box closes, the Standard AutoFormat is applied to the form, and the Form window in Design view becomes the active window.

5. Click the **View** button for Form view 🖳 on the Form Design toolbar. The form is displayed in Form view with the new AutoFormat. See Figure 4-8.

| Figure 4-8 | FORM DISPLAYED WITH THE NEW AUTOFORMAT |

You have finished modifying the format of the form and can now save it.

6. Click the **Save** button 🖫 on the Form View toolbar to save the modified form.

Elsa wants to use the Position Data form to view some data in the Position table. To view data, you need to navigate through the form. As you learned in Tutorial 1, you navigate through a form in the same way that you navigate through a table datasheet. Also, the navigation mode and editing mode keystroke techniques you used with datasheets in Tutorial 2 are the same when navigating a form.

To navigate through the Position Data form:

1. Press the **Tab** key to move to the PositionTitle field value, and then press the **End** key to move to the Experience field. Because the Experience field is a yes/no field, its value is not highlighted; instead, a dotted outline appears around the field name to indicate that it is the current field.

2. Press the **Home** key to move back to the PositionID field value. The first record in the Position table still appears in the form.

3. Press **Ctrl + End** to move to the Experience field for record 64, which is the last record in the table. The record number for the current record appears in the Specific Record box between the navigation buttons at the bottom of the form.

4. Click the **Previous Record** navigation button ◄ to move to the Experience field in record 63.

5. Press the ↑ key twice to move to the EndDate field in record 63.

6. Click the insertion point between the numbers "1" and "5" in the EndDate field value to switch to editing mode, press the **Home** key to move the insertion point to the beginning of the field value, and then press the **End** key to move the insertion point to the end of the field value.

7. Click the **First Record** navigation button [◄] to move to the EndDate field value in the first record. The entire field value is highlighted because you have switched from editing mode to navigation mode.

8. Click the **Next Record** navigation button [►] to move to the EndDate field value in record 2, the next record.

Elsa asks you to display the records for The Clipper Ship Inn, whose EmployerID is 10145, because she wants to review the available positions for this employer.

Finding Data Using a Form

The **Find** command lets you search for data in a form or datasheet so you can display only those records you want to view. You choose a field to serve as the basis for the search by making that field the current field; then you enter the value you want Access to match in the Find and Replace dialog box. You can use the Find command by clicking the toolbar Find button or by using the Edit menu.

REFERENCE WINDOW | **RW**

Finding Data in a Form or Datasheet
- Make the field you want to search the current field.
- Click the Find button on the toolbar to open the Find and Replace dialog box.
- In the Find What text box, type the field value you want to find.
- Complete the remaining options, as necessary, to specify the type of search to conduct.
- Click the Find Next button to begin the search.
- Click the Find Next button to continue searching for the next match.
- Click the Cancel button to stop the search operation.

You need to find all records in the Position table for The Clipper Ship Inn, whose EmployerID is 10145.

To find the records using the Position Data form:

1. Click in the **EmployerID** field value box. This is the field that you will search for matching values.

2. Click the **Find** button [🔍] on the Form View toolbar. The Find and Replace dialog box opens. Note that the Look In list box shows the name of the field that Access will search (in this case, the current EmployerID field), and the Match list box indicates that Access will find values that match the entire entry in the field. You could choose to match only part of a field value or only the beginning of each field value.

3. If the Find and Replace dialog box covers the form, move the dialog box by dragging its title bar. If necessary, move the Position Data form window so that you can see both the dialog box and the form at the same time. See Figure 4-9.

Figure 4-9	FIND AND REPLACE DIALOG BOX

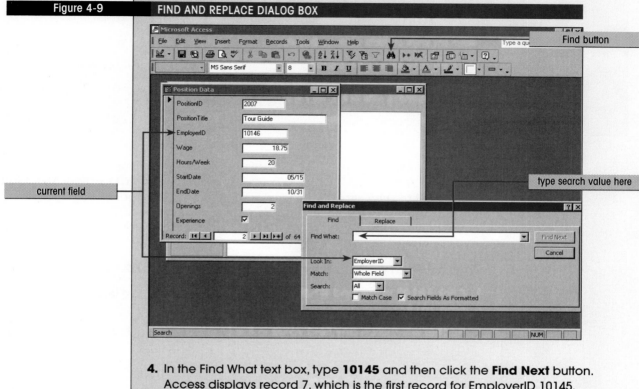

4. In the Find What text box, type **10145** and then click the **Find Next** button. Access displays record 7, which is the first record for EmployerID 10145.

5. Click the **Find Next** button. Access displays record 47, which is the second record for EmployerID 10145.

6. Click the **Find Next** button. Access displays record 48, which is the third record for EmployerID 10145.

7. Click the **Find Next** button. Access displays a dialog box informing you that the search is finished.

8. Click the **OK** button to close the dialog box.

The search value you enter can be an exact value, such as the EmployerID 10145 you just entered, or it can include wildcard characters. A **wildcard character** is a placeholder you use when you know only part of a value or when you want to start or end with a specific character or match a certain pattern. Figure 4-10 shows the wildcard characters you can use when finding data.

Figure 4-10	WILDCARD CHARACTERS	
WILDCARD CHARACTER	**PURPOSE**	**EXAMPLE**
*	Match any number of characters. It can be used as the first and/or last character in the character string.	th* finds *the, that, this, therefore,* and so on
?	Match any single alphabetic character.	a?t finds *act, aft, ant, apt,* and *art*
[]	Match any single character within the brackets.	a[fr]t finds *aft* and *art* but not *act, ant,* and *apt*
!	Match any character not within brackets.	a[!fr]t finds *act, ant,* and *apt* but not *aft* and *art*
-	Match any one of a range of characters. The range must be in ascending order (a to z, not z to a).	a[d-p]t finds *aft, ant,* and *apt* but not *act* and *art*
#	Match any single numeric character.	#72 finds *072, 172, 272, 372,* and so on

Elsa wants to view the position records for two employers: George's Restaurant & Galley (EmployerID 10180) and Moondance Inn & Ski Resort (EmployerID 10185). Matt Griffin, the manager of recruitment, knows of some student recruits with prior work experience who are interested in working for these employers. Elsa wants to see which positions, if any, require experience. You'll use the * wildcard character to search for these employers' positions.

To find the records using the * wildcard character:

1. Click **10145** in the Find What text box to select the entire value, and then type **1018***.

   Access will match any field value in the EmployerID field that starts with the digits 1018.

2. Click the **Find Next** button. Access displays record 64, which is the first record found for EmployerID 10185. Note that the Experience field value is unchecked, indicating that this position does not require experience.

3. Click the **Find Next** button. Access displays record 25, which is the first record found for EmployerID 10180. Again, the Experience field value is unchecked.

4. Click the **Find Next** button. Access displays record 42, which is the second record found for EmployerID 10185. In this case, the Experience field value is checked, indicating that this position requires prior work experience.

5. Click the **Find Next** button. Access displays a dialog box informing you that the search is finished.

6. Click the **OK** button to close the dialog box.

7. Click the **Cancel** button to close the Find and Replace dialog box.

Of the three positions, only one requires experience—PositionID 2089. Elsa asks you to use the form to print the data for record 42, which is for PositionID 2089, so that she can give the printout to Matt.

Previewing and Printing Selected Form Records

Access prints as many form records as can fit on a printed page. If only part of a form record fits on the bottom of a page, the remainder of the record prints on the next page. Access allows you to print all pages or a range of pages. In addition, you can print the currently selected form record.

Before printing record 42, you'll preview the form record to see how it will look when printed. Notice that the current record number (in this case, 42) appears in the Specific Record box at the bottom of the form.

To preview the form and print the data for record 42:

1. Click the **Print Preview** button on the Form View toolbar. The Print Preview window opens, showing the form records for the Position table in miniature. If you clicked the Print button now, all the records for the table would be printed, beginning with the first record.

2. Click the **Maximize** button on the form's title bar.

3. Click the **Zoom** button on the Print Preview toolbar, and then use the vertical scroll bar to view the entire page. Each record from the Position table appears in a separate form. See Figure 4-11.

Figure 4-11	PRINT PREVIEW WINDOW DISPLAYING FORM RECORDS

Zoom button

form's Restore Window button

form records

4. Click the **Restore Window** button on the Print Preview menu bar, and then click the **Close** button on the Print Preview toolbar to return to the table in Form view.

The record that you need to print, PositionID 2089, appears in the form. To print selected records you need to use the Print dialog box.

5. Click **File** on the menu bar, and then click **Print**. The Print dialog box opens.

6. Click the **Selected Record(s)** option button to print the current form record (record 42).

7. Click the **OK** button to close the dialog box and to print the selected record.

Elsa has identified several updates, as shown in Figure 4-12, that she wants you to make to the Position table. You'll use the Position Data form to update the data in the Position table.

Figure 4-12	UPDATES TO THE POSITION TABLE

PositionID	Update Action
2033	Change Hours/Week to 35
	Change StartDate to 6/30
2072	Delete record
2130	Add new record for PositionID 2130:
	PositionTitle = Housekeeping
	EmployerID = 10151
	Wage = 12.50
	Hours/Week = 30
	StartDate = 6/1
	EndDate = 10/15
	Openings = 2
	Experience = No

Maintaining **Table Data Using a Form**

Maintaining data using a form is often easier than using a datasheet, because you can concentrate on all the changes required to a single record at one time. You already know how to navigate a form and find specific records. Now you'll make the changes Elsa requested to the Position table, using the Position Data form.

First, you'll update the record for PositionID 2033.

To change the record using the Position Data form:

1. Make sure the Position Data form is displayed in Form view.

When she reviewed the position data to identify possible corrections, Elsa noted that 10 is the record number for PositionID 2033. If you know the number of the record you want to display, you can type the number in the Specific Record box and press the Enter key to go directly to that record.

2. Select **42** in the Specific Record box, type **10**, and then press the **Enter** key. Record 10 (PositionID 2033) is now the current record.

You need to change the Hours/Week field value to 35 and the StartDate field value to 6/30 for this record.

3. Click the insertion point to the left of the number 2 in the Hours/Week field value, press the **Delete** key twice, and then type **35**. Note that the pencil symbol appears in the upper-left corner of the form, indicating that the form is in editing mode.

4. Press the **Tab** key to move to and select the StartDate field value, type **6/30**, and then press the **Enter** key. See Figure 4-13.

Figure 4-13   POSITION RECORD AFTER CHANGING FIELD VALUES

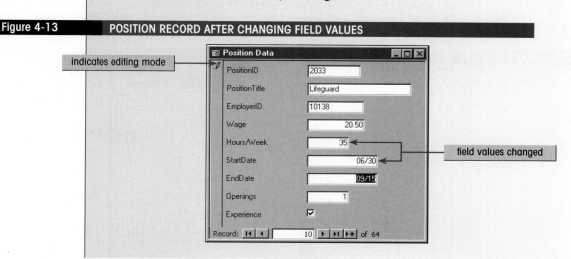

You have completed the changes for PositionID 2033. Elsa's next update is to delete the record for PositionID 2072. The employer client recently informed Elsa that a full-time, permanent employee has been hired for this position, so it is no longer available for student recruits.

To delete the record using the Position Data form:

1. Click anywhere in the PositionID field value to make it the current field.

2. Click the **Find** button 🔍 on the Form View toolbar. The Find and Replace dialog box opens.

3. Type **2072** in the Find What text box, click the **Find Next** button, and then click the **Cancel** button. The record for PositionID 2072 is now the current record.

4. Click the **Delete Record** button 🗙 on the Form View toolbar. A dialog box opens, asking you to confirm the record deletion.

5. Click the **Yes** button. The dialog box closes, and the record for PositionID 2072 is deleted from the table.

Elsa's final maintenance change is to add a record for a new position available at the Granite State Resort.

To add the new record using the Position Data form:

1. Click the **New Record** button ▶✳ on the Form View toolbar. Record 64, the next record available for a new record, becomes the current record. All field value boxes are empty, and the insertion point is positioned at the beginning of the field value box for PositionID.

2. Refer to Figure 4-14 and enter the value shown for each field. Press the **Tab** key to move from field to field.

Figure 4-14	COMPLETED FORM FOR THE NEW RECORD

TROUBLE? Compare your screen with Figure 4-14. If any field value is wrong, correct it now, using the methods described earlier for editing field values.

3. After entering the value for Openings, press the **Tab** key twice (if necessary). Record 65, the next record available for a new record, becomes the current record, and the record for PositionID 2130 is saved in the Position table.

You've completed Elsa's changes to the Position table, so you can close the Position Data form.

4. Click the **Close** button ☒ on the form's title bar. The form closes and you return to the Database window. Notice that the Position Data form is listed in the Forms list box.

Checking the Spelling of Table Data Using a Form

You can check the spelling of table data using a table or query datasheet or a form that displays the table data. The Spelling feature searches through the data and identifies any words that are not included in its dictionary. Sometimes the word is misspelled, and you can correct it; other words are spelled correctly, but they are not listed in the spelling dictionary.

Elsa wants to make sure that the position data contains no spelling errors. You'll use the Position Data form to check the spelling of data in the Position table.

To check the spelling of data using the Position Data form:

1. Double-click **Position Data** to open the form in Form view. The form displays data for the first record.

2. Click the **Spelling** button 📖 on the Form View toolbar. The Spelling dialog box opens, identifying the word "Reservationist" as not in its dictionary. See Figure 4-15.

Figure 4-15	SPELLING DIALOG BOX

TROUBLE? If the word "Reservationist" is not identified by the Spelling feature, it was probably added to your dictionary. Just continue with the steps.

Note that the dialog box provides buttons for ignoring the word or changing it to one of the suggested alternatives, plus an option for ignoring all entries in the selected field (PositionTitle, in this case). The word is spelled correctly, so you will ignore all occurrences of this word in the Position table.

3. Click the **Ignore All** button. Next, the Spelling dialog box identifies the word "Greenskeeper" as not in its dictionary, and suggests the spelling should be two words, "Greens keeper." You'll change to the suggested spelling.

4. Click the **Change All** button. All occurrences of the word "Greenskeeper" are changed to the words "Greens keeper" in the Position table.

   A dialog box opens, informing you that the spell check is complete.

5. Click the **OK** button to close the dialog box.

6. Close the form.

You can customize how the Spelling feature works in Access by changing the settings on the Spelling tab of the Options dialog box, which you open by choosing Options from the Tools menu. For example, you can choose another language for the main dictionary, and you can create custom dictionaries to contain words or phrases specific to the type of data in your database. Adding frequently used words to a custom dictionary will prevent the Spelling feature from identifying those words as not in its dictionary, thereby speeding up the spell check process.

The Position Data form will enable Elsa and her staff to enter and maintain data easily in the Position table. In the next session, you'll create another form for working with data in both the Position and Employer tables at the same time. You'll also create a report showing data from both tables.

Session 4.1 QUICK CHECK

1. Describe the difference between creating a form using the AutoForm Wizard and creating a form using the Form Wizard.

2. What is an AutoFormat, and how do you change one for an existing form?

3. Which table record is displayed in a form when you press Ctrl + End while you are in navigation mode?

4. You can use the Find command to search for data in a form or _____.

5. Which wildcard character matches any single alphabetic character?

6. How many form records does Access print by default on a page?

SESSION 4.2	In this session, you will create a form with a main form and a subform, modify a form in Design view, create a report using the Report Wizard, insert a picture in a report, and preview and print a report.

Elsa would like you to create a form so that she can view the data for each employer and its available positions at the same time. The type of form you need to create will include a main form and a subform.

Creating a Form with a Main Form and a Subform

To create a form based on two tables, you must first define a relationship between the two tables. In Tutorial 3, you defined a one-to-many relationship between the Employer (primary) and Position (related) tables, so you are ready to create the form based on both tables.

When you create a form containing data from two tables that have a one-to-many relationship, you actually create a main form for data from the primary table and a subform for data from the related table. Access uses the defined relationship between the tables to join the tables automatically through the common field that exists in both tables.

Elsa and her staff will use the form when contacting employers about their available positions. The main form will contain the employer ID and name, contact first and last names, and phone number for each employer. The subform will contain the position ID and title, wage, hours/week, experience, start and end dates, and number of openings for each position.

You'll use the Form Wizard to create the form.

To create the form using the Form Wizard:

1. If you took a break after the previous session, make sure that Access is running and the Northeast database is open.

2. Make sure the Forms object is selected in the Database window, and then click the **New** button. The New Form dialog box opens.

When creating a form based on two tables, you first choose the primary table and select the fields you want to include in the main form; then you choose the related table and select fields from it for the subform.

3. Click **Form Wizard**, click the list arrow for choosing a table or query, click **Employer** to select this table as the source for the main form, and then click the **OK** button. The first Form Wizard dialog box opens, in which you select fields in the order you want them to appear on the main form.

Elsa wants the form to include only the EmployerID, EmployerName, ContactFirstName, ContactLastName, and Phone fields from the Employer table.

4. Click **EmployerID** in the Available Fields list box (if necessary), and then click the > button to move the field to the Selected Fields list box.

5. Repeat Step 4 for the **EmployerName**, **ContactFirstName**, **ContactLastName**, and **Phone** fields.

The EmployerID field will appear in the main form, so you do not have to include it in the subform. Otherwise, Elsa wants the subform to include all the fields from the Position table.

6. Click the **Tables/Queries** list arrow, and then click **Table: Position**. The fields from the Position table appear in the Available Fields list box. The quickest way to add the fields you want to include is to move all the fields to the Selected Fields list box, and then to remove the only field you don't want to include (EmployerID).

7. Click the >> button to move all the fields from the Position table to the Selected Fields list box.

8. Click **Position.EmployerID** in the Selected Fields list box, and then click the < button to move the field back to the Available Fields list box. Note that the table name (Position) is included in the field name to distinguish it from the same field (EmployerID) in the Employer table.

9. Click the **Next** button. The next Form Wizard dialog box opens. See Figure 4-16.

| Figure 4-16 | CHOOSING A MAIN/SUBFORM FORMAT |

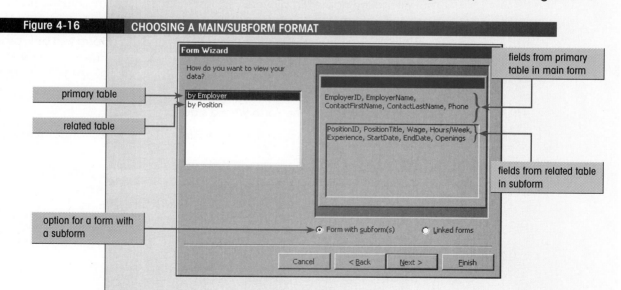

In this dialog box, the list box on the left shows the order in which you will view the selected data: first by data from the primary Employer table, and then by data from the related Position table. The form will be displayed as shown in the right side of the dialog box, with the fields from the Employer table at the top in the main form, and the fields from the Position table at the bottom in the sub-form. The selected option button specifies a main form with a subform. The Linked forms option creates a form structure where only the main form fields are displayed. A button with the subform's name on it appears on the main form; you can click this button to display the associated subform records.

The default options shown in Figure 4-16 are correct for creating a form with Employer data in the main form and Position data in the subform.

To finish creating the form:

1. Click the **Next** button. The next Form Wizard dialog box opens, in which you choose the subform layout.

   The Tabular layout displays subform fields as a table, whereas the Datasheet layout displays subform fields as a table datasheet. The PivotTable and PivotChart layouts display summary and analytical information. The layout choice is a matter of personal preference. You'll use the Datasheet layout.

2. Click the **Datasheet** option button (if necessary), and then click the **Next** button. The next Form Wizard dialog box opens, in which you choose the form's style.

   Elsa wants all forms in the Northeast database to have the same style, so you will choose Standard, which is the same style you applied to the Position Data form.

3. Click **Standard** (if necessary), and then click the **Next** button. The next Form Wizard dialog box opens, in which you choose names for the main form and the subform.

   You will use the name "Employer Positions" for the main form and the name "Position Subform" for the subform.

4. Click the insertion point to the right of the last letter in the Form text box, press the **spacebar**, and then type **Positions**. The main form name is now Employer Positions. Note that the default subform name, Position Subform, is the name you want, so you don't need to change it.

   You have answered all the Form Wizard's questions.

5. Click the **Finish** button. After a few moments, the completed form opens in Form view.

   Some of the columns in the subform are not wide enough to display the field names entirely. You need to resize the columns to their best fit.

6. Double-click the pointer ✛ at the right edge of each column in the subform, scrolling the subform to the right, as necessary, to display additional columns. Scroll the subform all the way back to the left. The columns are resized to their best fit. See Figure 4-17.

| Figure 4-17 | MAIN FORM WITH SUBFORM IN FORM VIEW |

In the main form, Access displays the fields from the first record in the Employer table in columnar format. The records in the main form appear in primary key sequence by EmployerID. EmployerID 10122 has one related record in the Position table; this record is shown in the subform datasheet. The form shows that BeanTown Tours has one available position for a Tour Guide.

Notice that the subform is not wide enough to display all the fields from the Position table. Although the subform includes a horizontal scroll bar, which allows you to view the other fields, Elsa wants all the fields from the Position table to be visible in the subform at the same time. Even if you maximized the Form window, the subform would still not display all of the fields. You need to widen the main form and the subform in Design view.

Modifying a Form in Design View

Just as you use Design view to modify the format and content of tables and queries, you use Design view to modify a form. You can change the fields that are displayed on a form, and modify their size, location, format, and so on. You need to open the Employer Positions form in Design view and resize the Position subform to display all the fields at the same time.

To widen the Position subform:

1. Click the **View** button for Design view on the Form View toolbar to display the form in Design view.

2. Click the **Maximize** button to enlarge the window. See Figure 4-18.

Figure 4-18	FORM DISPLAYED IN DESIGN VIEW

3. Click the **Form Header** bar for the subform (refer to Figure 4-18) to select the subform. Notice that small boxes appear around the subform's border. These boxes, which are called **handles**, indicate that the subform is selected and can be manipulated. See Figure 4-19.

Figure 4-19	SUBFORM SELECTED IN DESIGN VIEW

4. Position the pointer on the right-center sizing handle so it changes to a ↔ shape, and then click and drag the handle to the right to the **6.5**-inch mark on the horizontal ruler. See Figure 4-20.

Figure 4-20   **RESIZING THE POSITION SUBFORM**

widen the subform
to this mark

resizing pointer

5. Release the mouse button. The subform section is resized. Notice that the main form section is also resized.

6. Switch back to Form view. Notice that all the field names in the Position Subform are now visible.

7. Click the **Restore Window** button 🗗 on the menu bar to restore the form to its original size. Now you need to resize the Form window in Form view so that all the fields will be displayed when the Form window is not maximized.

8. Position the pointer on the right edge of the form so it changes to a ⟷ shape, and then click and drag the right edge of the form to resize it so that it matches the form shown in Figure 4-21.

Figure 4-21   **FORM WITH ALL SUBFORM FIELDS VISIBLE**

9. Save the modified form.

Two sets of navigation buttons appear at the bottom of the Form view window. You use the top set of navigation buttons to select records from the related table in the subform, and the bottom set to select records from the primary table in the main form.

You'll use the navigation buttons to view different records.

To navigate to different main form and subform records:

1. Click the **Last Record** navigation button ▶❘ in the main form. Record 45 in the Employer table for Lighthouse Tours becomes the current record in the main form. The subform shows that this employer has one available Tour Guide position.

2. Click the **Previous Record** navigation button ◀ in the main form. Record 44 in the Employer table for Harbor Whale Watch Tours becomes the current record in the main form.

3. Select **44** in the Specific Record box for the main form, type **32**, and then press the **Enter** key. Record 32 in the Employer table for Windsor Alpine Tours becomes the current record in the main form. This employer has two available positions.

4. Click the **Last Record** navigation button ▶❘ in the subform. Record 2 in the Position table becomes the current record in the subform.

   You have finished your work with the form, so you can close it.

5. Close the form. Notice that both the main form, Employer Positions, and the subform, Position Subform, appear in the Forms list box.

Zack would like a report showing data from both the Employer and Position tables so that all the pertinent information about employer clients and their positions is available in one place. To satisfy Zack's request, you'll create the report using the Report Wizard.

Creating a Report Using the Report Wizard

As you learned in Tutorial 1, a report is a formatted printout of the contents of one or more tables in a database. In Access, you can create your own reports or use the Report Wizard to create them for you. Like the Form Wizard, the **Report Wizard** asks you a series of questions and then creates a report based on your answers. Whether you use the Report Wizard or design your own report, you can change the report's design after you create it.

Zack wants you to create a report that includes selected employer data from the Employer table and all the available positions from the Position table for each employer. Zack has sketched a design of the report he wants (Figure 4-22). Like the Employer Positions form you just created, which includes a main form and a subform, the report will be based on both tables, which are joined in a one-to-many relationship through the common EmployerID field. As shown in the sketch in Figure 4-22, the selected employer data from the primary Employer table includes the employer ID and name, city, state or province, contact first and last names, and phone number. Below the data for each employer, the report will include the position ID and title, wage, hours/week, experience, start and end dates, and openings data from the related Position table. The set of field values for each position is called a **detail record**.

| Figure 4-22 | REPORT SKETCH FOR THE EMPLOYERS AND POSITIONS REPORT |

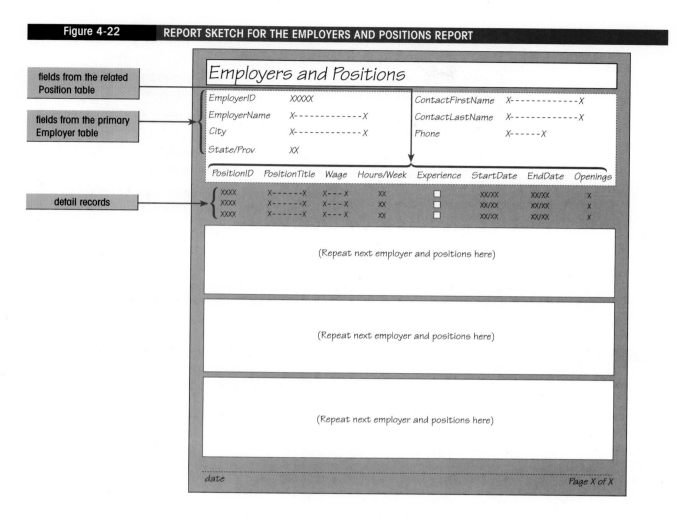

You'll use the Report Wizard to create the report according to the design in Zack's sketch.

To start the Report Wizard and select the fields to include in the report:

1. Click **Reports** in the Objects bar of the Database window to display the Reports list box. You have not yet created any reports.

2. Click the **New** button in the Database window. The New Report dialog box opens.

As was the case when you created the form with a subform, initially you can choose only one table or query to be the data source for the report. Then you can include data from other tables. You will select the primary Employer table in the New Report dialog box.

3. Click **Report Wizard**, click the list arrow for choosing a table or query, and then click **Employer**.

4. Click the **OK** button. The first Report Wizard dialog box opens.

In the first Report Wizard dialog box, you select fields in the order you want them to appear on the report. Zack wants the EmployerID, EmployerName, City,

State/Prov, ContactFirstName, ContactLastName, and Phone fields from the Employer table to appear on the report.

5. Click **EmployerID** in the Available Fields list box (if necessary), and then click the > button. The field moves to the Selected Fields list box.

6. Repeat Step 5 to add the **EmployerName**, **City**, **State/Prov**, **ContactFirstName**, **ContactLastName**, and **Phone** fields to the report.

7. Click the **Tables/Queries** list arrow, and then click **Table: Position**. The fields from the Position table appear in the Available Fields list box.

The EmployerID field will appear on the report with the employer data, so you do not have to include it in the detail records for each position. Otherwise, Zack wants all the fields from the Position table to be included in the report.

8. Click the >> button to move all the fields from the Available Fields list box to the Selected Fields list box.

9. Click **Position.EmployerID** in the Selected Fields list box, click the < button to move the selected field back to the Available Fields list box, and then click the **Next** button. The second Report Wizard dialog box opens. See Figure 4-23.

Figure 4-23   CHOOSING A GROUPED OR UNGROUPED REPORT

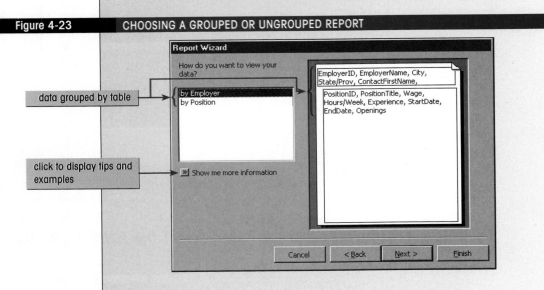

You can choose to arrange the selected data grouped by table, which is the default, or ungrouped. For a grouped report, the data from a record in the primary table appears as a group, followed on subsequent lines of the report by the joined records from the related table. For the report you are creating, data from a record in the Employer table appears in a group, followed by the related records for each employer from the Position table. An example of an ungrouped report would be a report of records from the Employer and Position tables in order by PositionID. Each position and its associated employer data would appear together on one or more lines of the report; the data would not be grouped by table.

You can display tips and examples for the choices in the Report Wizard dialog box by clicking the "Show me more information" button ⤐.

To display tips about the options in the Report Wizard dialog box:

1. Click the ⟫ button. The Report Wizard Tips dialog box opens. Read the information shown in the dialog box.

   You can display examples of different grouping methods by clicking the ⟫ button ("Show me examples").

2. Click ⟫. The Report Wizard Examples dialog box opens. See Figure 4-24.

Figure 4-24   REPORT WIZARD EXAMPLES DIALOG BOX

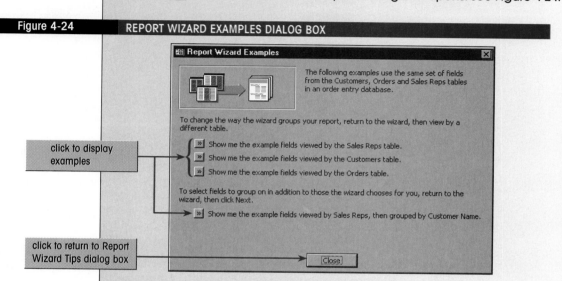

click to display examples

click to return to Report Wizard Tips dialog box

You can display examples of different grouping methods by clicking the ⟫ buttons.

3. Click each ⟫ button in turn, review the displayed example, and then click the **Close** button to return to the Report Wizard Examples dialog box.

4. Click the **Close** button to return to the Report Wizard Tips dialog box, and then click the **Close** button to return to the second Report Wizard dialog box.

The default options shown on your screen are correct for the report Zack wants, so you can continue responding to the Report Wizard questions.

To finish creating the report using the Report Wizard:

1. Click the **Next** button. The next Report Wizard dialog box opens, in which you choose additional grouping levels.

   Two grouping levels are shown: one for an employer's data, and the other for an employer's positions. Grouping levels are useful for reports with multiple levels, such as those containing monthly, quarterly, and annual totals, or for those containing city and country groups. Zack's report contains no further grouping levels, so you can accept the default options.

2. Click the **Next** button. The next Report Wizard dialog box opens, in which you choose the sort order for the detail records. See Figure 4-25.

Figure 4-25 CHOOSING THE SORT ORDER FOR DETAIL RECORDS

The records from the Position table for an employer represent the detail records for Zack's report. He wants these records to appear in increasing, or ascending, order by the value in the PositionID field. The Ascending option is already selected by default. To change to descending order, you simply click this button, which acts as a toggle between the two sort orders. Also, notice that you can sort on multiple fields, as you can with queries.

3. Click the **1** list arrow, click **PositionID**, and then click the **Next** button. The next Report Wizard dialog box opens, in which you choose a layout and page orientation for the report. See Figure 4-26.

Figure 4-26 CHOOSING THE REPORT LAYOUT AND PAGE ORIENTATION

A sample of each layout appears in the box on the left.

4. Click each layout option and examine each sample that appears.

You'll use the Outline 2 layout option because it resembles the layout shown in Zack's sketch of the report. Also, because of the number of fields in the Position table, the information would fit better in a wide format; therefore, you'll choose the landscape orientation.

5. Click the **Outline 2** option button, click the **Landscape** option button, and then click the **Next** button. The next Report Wizard dialog box opens, in which you choose a style for the report.

A sample of the selected style, or AutoFormat, appears in the box on the left. You can always choose a different AutoFormat after you create the report, just as you can when creating a form. Zack likes the appearance of the Corporate AutoFormat, so you'll choose this one for your report.

6. Click **Corporate** (if necessary), and then click the **Next** button. The last Report Wizard dialog box opens, in which you choose a report name, which also serves as the printed title on the report.

According to Zack's sketch, the report title you need to specify is "Employers and Positions."

7. Type **Employers and Positions** and then click the **Finish** button. The Report Wizard creates the report based on your answers and saves it as an object in the Northeast database. Then Access opens the Employers and Positions report in Print Preview.

To view the report better, you need to maximize the Report window.

8. Click the **Maximize** button 🔲 on the Employers and Positions title bar.

To view the entire page, you need to change the Zoom setting.

9. Click the **Zoom** list arrow on the Print Preview toolbar, and then click **Fit**. The first page of the report is displayed in Print Preview. See Figure 4-27.

| Figure 4-27 | REPORT DISPLAYED IN PRINT PREVIEW |

Zoom list arrow

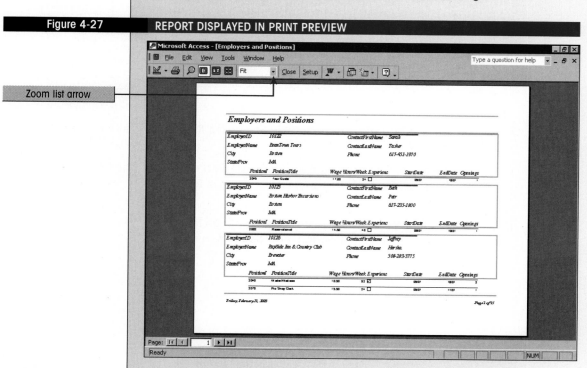

When a report is displayed in Print Preview, you can use the pointer to toggle between a full-page display and a close-up display of the report. Zack asks you to check the report to see if any adjustments need to be made. For example, some of the field titles or values might not be displayed completely, or you might need to move fields to enhance the report's appearance. To do so, you need to view a close-up display of the report.

To view a close-up display of the report and make any necessary corrections:

1. Click the pointer ⊕ at the top center of the report. The display changes to show a close-up view of the report. See Figure 4-28.

Figure 4-28	CLOSE-UP VIEW OF THE REPORT

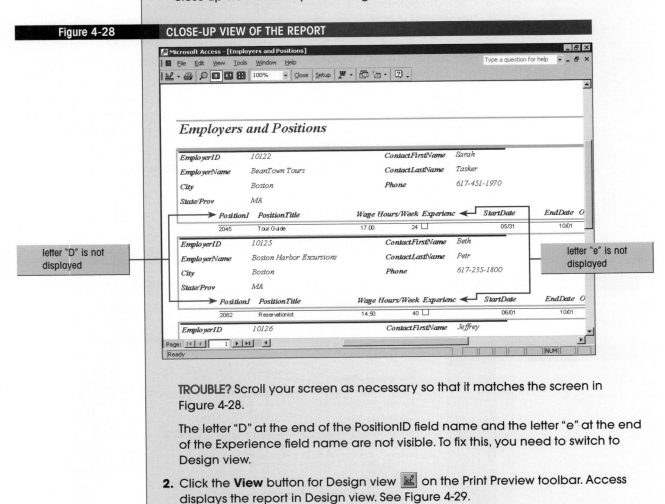

letter "D" is not displayed

letter "e" is not displayed

TROUBLE? Scroll your screen as necessary so that it matches the screen in Figure 4-28.

The letter "D" at the end of the PositionID field name and the letter "e" at the end of the Experience field name are not visible. To fix this, you need to switch to Design view.

2. Click the **View** button for Design view ⊻ on the Print Preview toolbar. Access displays the report in Design view. See Figure 4-29.

Figure 4-29   REPORT DISPLAYED IN DESIGN VIEW

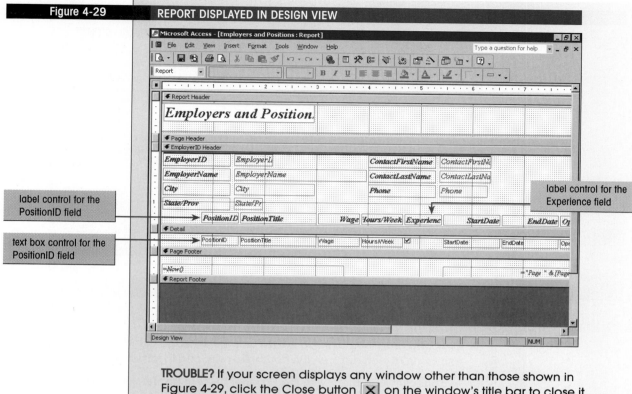

label control for the
PositionID field

text box control for the
PositionID field

label control for the
Experience field

TROUBLE? If your screen displays any window other than those shown in Figure 4-29, click the Close button ⊠ on the window's title bar to close it.

You use the Report window in Design view to modify existing reports and to create custom reports.

Each item on a report in Design view is called a **control**. For example, the PositionID field consists of two controls: the label "PositionID," which appears on the report to identify the field value, and the PositionID text box, in which the actual field value appears. You need to widen the label control for the PositionID field so that the entire field name is visible in the report.

3. Click the label control for the PositionID field to select it. Handles appear on the border around the control, indicating that the control is selected and can be manipulated.

4. Position the pointer on the center-left handle of the PositionID label control until the pointer changes to a ⟷ shape. See Figure 4-30.

| Figure 4-30 | RESIZING THE PositionID LABEL CONTROL |

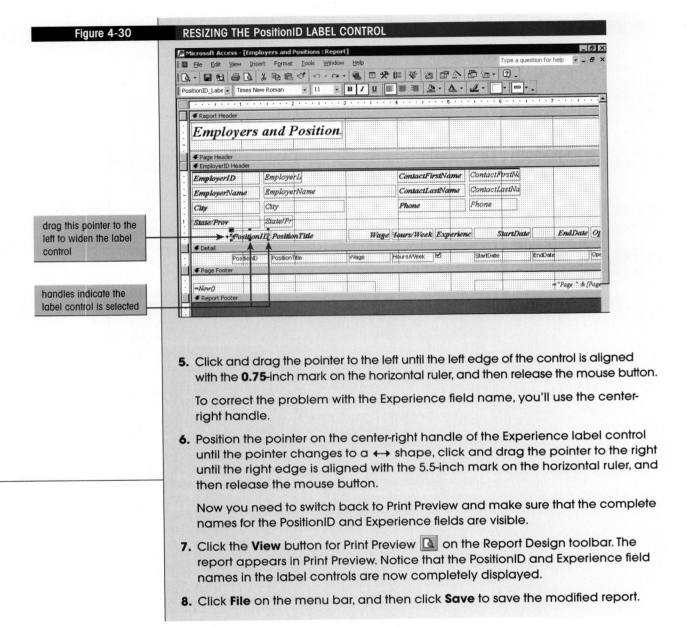

drag this pointer to the left to widen the label control

handles indicate the label control is selected

5. Click and drag the pointer to the left until the left edge of the control is aligned with the **0.75**-inch mark on the horizontal ruler, and then release the mouse button.

   To correct the problem with the Experience field name, you'll use the center-right handle.

6. Position the pointer on the center-right handle of the Experience label control until the pointer changes to a ↔ shape, click and drag the pointer to the right until the right edge is aligned with the 5.5-inch mark on the horizontal ruler, and then release the mouse button.

   Now you need to switch back to Print Preview and make sure that the complete names for the PositionID and Experience fields are visible.

7. Click the **View** button for Print Preview [🔍] on the Report Design toolbar. The report appears in Print Preview. Notice that the PositionID and Experience field names in the label controls are now completely displayed.

8. Click **File** on the menu bar, and then click **Save** to save the modified report.

Zack decides that he wants the report to include a graphic image to the right of the report title, for visual interest. You can add the graphic to the report by inserting a picture.

Inserting a Picture in a Report

In Access, you can insert a picture or other graphic image in a report or form to enhance the appearance of the report or form. Sources of graphic images include files created in Microsoft Paint and other drawing programs, and scanned files. The file containing the picture you need to insert is named Globe, and it is located in the Tutorial folder on your Data Disk.

To insert the picture in the report:

1. Click the **Close** button on the Print Preview toolbar to display the report in Design view. See Figure 4-31.

Figure 4-31   INSERTING A PICTURE IN DESIGN VIEW

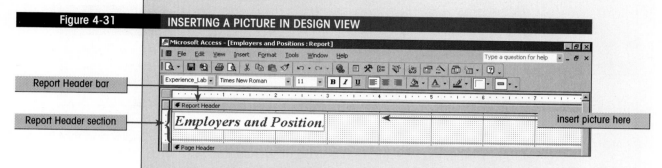

Report Header bar

Report Header section

insert picture here

Zack wants the picture to appear on the first page of the report only; therefore, you need to insert the picture in the Report Header section (see Figure 4-31). Any text or picture placed in this section appears once at the beginning of the report.

2. Click the **Report Header** bar to select this section of the report. The bar is high-lighted to indicate that the section is selected.

3. Click **Insert** on the menu bar, and then click **Picture**. The Insert Picture dialog box opens. If necessary, open the **Tutorial** folder on your Data Disk. See Figure 4-32.

Figure 4-32   INSERT PICTURE DIALOG BOX

picture file

4. Click **Globe** to select the picture for the report, and then click the **OK** button. The picture is inserted in the left side of the Report Header section, covering some of the report title text. See Figure 4-33.

Figure 4-33 — PICTURE INSERTED IN THE REPORT

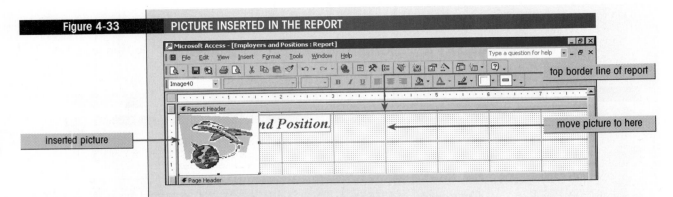

Notice that handles appear around the picture's border, indicating that the picture is selected and can be manipulated.

Zack wants the picture to appear to the right of the report title, so you need to move the picture using the mouse.

5. Position the pointer on the picture until the pointer changes to a 🖐 shape, and then click and drag the mouse to move the picture to the right so that its left edge aligns with the 4-inch mark on the horizontal ruler and its top edge is just below the top border line above the report title (see Figure 4-33).

6. Release the mouse button. The picture appears in the new position. Notice that the height of the Report Header section increased slightly to accommodate the picture. See Figure 4-34.

Figure 4-34 — REPOSITIONED PICTURE IN THE REPORT

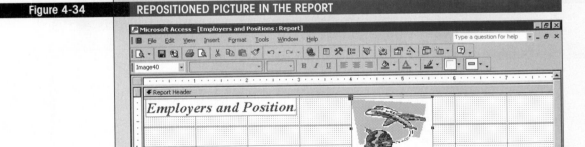

TROUBLE? If your picture appears in a different location from the one shown in Figure 4-34, use the pointer 🖐 to reposition the picture until it is in approximately the same position shown in the figure. Be sure that the top edge of the picture is below the top border line of the report.

7. Switch to Print Preview. The report now includes the inserted picture. If necessary, click the **Zoom** button 🔍 on the Print Preview toolbar to display the entire report page. See Figure 4-35.

Figure 4-35   PRINT PREVIEW OF REPORT WITH PICTURE

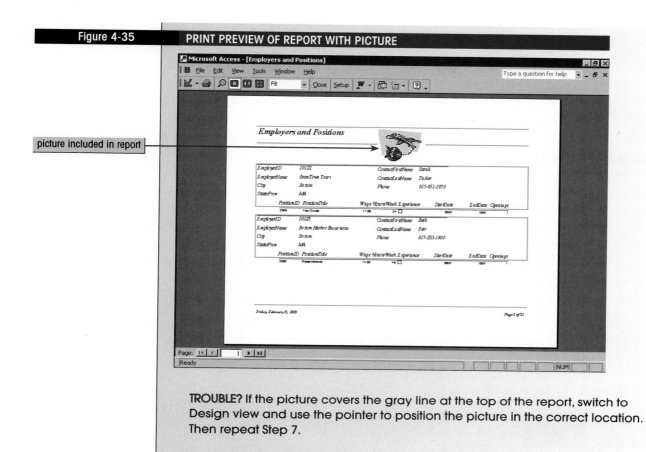

picture included in report

TROUBLE? If the picture covers the gray line at the top of the report, switch to Design view and use the pointer to position the picture in the correct location. Then repeat Step 7.

8. Save the modified report.

The report is now completed. You'll print just the first page of the report so that Zack can review the report layout and the inserted picture.

To print page 1 of the report:

1. Click **File** on the menu bar, and then click **Print**. The Print dialog box opens.

2. In the Print Range section, click the **Pages** option button. The insertion point now appears in the From text box so that you can specify the range of pages to print.

3. Type **1** in the From text box, press the **Tab** key to move to the To text box, and then type **1**. These settings specify that only page 1 of the report will be printed.

4. Click the **OK** button. The Print dialog box closes, and the first page of the report is printed.

Zack approves of the report layout and contents, so you can close the report.

5. Click the **Close Window** button ⊠ on the menu bar.

TROUBLE? If you click the Close button on the Print Preview toolbar by mistake, you switch to Design view. Click the Close Window button ⊠ on the menu bar.

6. Exit Access.

Elsa is satisfied that the forms you created—the Position Data form and the Employer Positions form—will make it easier to enter, view, and update data in the Northeast database. The Employers and Positions report presents important information about NSJI's employer clients in an attractive and professional format, which will help Zack and his staff in their marketing efforts.

Session 4.2 QUICK CHECK

1. In a form that contains a main form and a subform, what data is displayed in the main form and what data is displayed in the subform?

2. Describe how you use the navigation buttons to move through a form containing a main form and a subform.

3. When you use the Report Wizard, the report name is also used as the _____.

4. Each item on a report in Design view is called a(n) _____.

5. To insert a picture in a report, the report must be displayed in _____.

6. Any text or pictures placed in the _____ section of a report will appear only on the first page of the report.

REVIEW ASSIGNMENTS

Elsa wants to enhance the **Recruits** database with forms and reports, and she asks you to complete the following:

1. Make sure your Data Disk is in the appropriate disk drive, start Access, and then open the **Recruits** database located in the Review folder on your Data Disk.

2. If your **Recruits** database is stored on drive A, you will need to delete the files **Seasons97.mdb** and **Seasons2002.mdb** from your disk so you will have enough room to complete the steps. If your database is stored on a hard or network drive, no action is necessary.

3. Use the Form Wizard to create a form based on the **Student** table. Select all fields for the form, the Columnar layout, the SandStone style, and the title **Student Data** for the form.

4. Use the form you created in the previous step to print the fifth form record. Change the AutoFormat to Sumi Painting, save the changed form, and then print the fifth form record again.

5. Use the **Student Data** form to update the **Student** table as follows:

   a. Use the Find command to move to the record with StudentID STO1323. Change the field values for FirstName to Nathaniel, City to Perth, and BirthDate to 4/2/85 for this record.

   b. Use the Find command to move to the record with StudentID KIE2760, and then delete the record.

   c. Add a new record with the following field values:
   StudentID: SAN2540
   FirstName: Pedro
   LastName: Sandes

City:	Barcelona
Nation:	Spain
BirthDate:	5/1/85
Gender:	M
SSN:	977-07-1798

   d. Print only this form record, and then close the form.

Explore

6. Use the AutoForm: Columnar Wizard to create a form based on the **Salaries with Raises** query. Save the form as **Salaries with Raises**, and then close the form.

Explore

7. Use the Form Wizard to create a form containing a main form and a subform. Select the FirstName, LastName, and SSN fields from the **Recruiter** table for the main form, and select all fields except SSN from the **Student** table for the subform. Use the Datasheet layout and the Sumi Painting style. Specify the title **Recruiter Students** for the main form and the title **Student Subform** for the subform. Resize all columns in the subform to their best fit. Use Design view to resize the main form and the subform so that all fields are visible in the subform at the same time. Resize the Form window in Form view, as necessary, so that all fields are visible at the same time. Print the fourth main form record and its subform records. Save and close the form.

Explore

8. Use the Report Wizard to create a report based on the primary **Recruiter** table and the related **Student** table. Select all fields from the **Recruiter** table, and select all fields from the **Student** table except SSN, in the following order: FirstName, LastName, City, Nation, BirthDate, Gender, StudentID. In the third Report Wizard dialog box, specify the Nation field as an additional grouping level. Sort the detail records in ascending order by City. Choose the Align Left 2 layout and the Formal style for the report. Specify the title **Recruiters and Students** for the report.

Explore

9. Display the **Recruiters and Students** report in Design view and maximize the Report window. In the Nation Header section, change the Student_FirstName label control to "FirstName" and change the Student_LastName label control to "LastName." Widen both the Gender and StudentID label controls so that the labels are fully visible in the report. (*Hint*: You can resize the Gender control to both the left and the right, and the borders of adjacent controls can touch each other.)

10. Insert the **Travel** picture, which is located in the Review folder on your Data Disk, in the Report Header section of the **Recruiters and Students** report. Position the picture so that its left edge aligns with the 4-inch mark on the horizontal ruler and its top edge is just below the top border line of the report.

11. Print only the first page of the report, and then close and save the modified report.

12. If your database is stored on drive A, you will need to turn off the Compact on Close feature before closing the **Recruits** database because there isn't enough room on the disk to compact the database. If your database is stored on a hard or network drive, no action is necessary.

13. Close the **Recruits** database, and then exit Access.

CASE PROBLEMS

Case 1. Lim's Video Photography Youngho Lim wants the **Videos** database to include forms and reports that will help him track and view information about his clients and their video shoot events. You'll create the necessary forms and reports by completing the following:

1. Make sure your Data Disk is in the appropriate disk drive, start Access, and then open the **Videos** database located in the Cases folder on your Data Disk.

2. Use the Form Wizard to create a form based on the **Client** table. Select all fields for the form, the Columnar layout, and the Blends style. Specify the title **Client Data** for the form.

3. Change the AutoFormat for the **Client Data** form to Standard.

4. Use the Find command to move to the record with Client# 338, and then change the Address field value for this record to 2150 Brucewood Avenue.

5. Use the **Client Data** form to add a new record with the following field values:

   Client#:   351
   ClientName: Peters, Amanda
   Address: 175 Washington Street
   City: Berkeley
   State: CA
   Zip: 94704
   Phone: 510-256-1007

   Print only this form record, and then save and close the form.

6. Use the Form Wizard to create a form containing a main form and a subform. Select all the fields from the **Client** table for the main form, and select all fields except Client# from the **Contract** table for the subform. Use the Tabular layout and the Standard style. Specify the title **Contracts by Client** for the main form and the title **Contract Subform** for the subform.

7. Print the seventh main form record and its subform records, and then close the **Contracts by Client** form.

8. Use the Report Wizard to create a report based on the primary **Client** table and the related **Contract** table. Select all the fields from the **Client** table, and select all the fields from the **Contract** table except Client#. Sort the detail records in ascending order by Contract#. Choose the Align Left 2 layout and the Casual style. Specify the title **Client Contracts** for the report.

9. Insert the **Camcord** picture, which is located in the Cases folder on your Data Disk, in the Report Header section of the **Client Contracts** report. Position the picture so that its left edge aligns with the 4-inch mark on the horizontal ruler and its top edge is just below the top border line of the report.

10. Print only the first page of the report, and then close and save the modified report.

11. Close the **Videos** database, and then exit Access.

Case 2. DineAtHome.course.com Claire Picard continues her work with the **Meals** database to track and analyze the business activity of the restaurants she works with and their customers. To help her, you'll enhance the **Meals** database by completing the following:

1. Make sure your Data Disk is in the appropriate disk drive, start Access, and then open the **Meals** database located in the Cases folder on your Data Disk.

2. Use the Form Wizard to create a form containing a main form and a subform. Select the Restaurant#, RestaurantName, City, Phone, and Website fields from the **Restaurant** table for the main form, and select all fields except Restaurant# from the **Order** table for the subform. Use the Datasheet layout and the Industrial style. Specify the title **Restaurant Orders** for the main form and the title **Order Subform** for the subform. Resize all columns in the subform to their best fit. Print the first main form record and its displayed subform records.

3. For the form you just created, change the AutoFormat to SandStone, save the changed form, and then print the first main form record and its subform records.

4. Navigate to the third record in the subform for the first main record, and then change the OrderAmt field value to 107.80.

5. Use the Find command to move to the record with the Restaurant# 118, and then delete the record. Answer Yes to any warning messages about deleting the record.

Explore
6. Use the appropriate wildcard character to find all records with the word "House" anywhere in the restaurant name. (*Hint*: You must enter the wildcard character before and after the text you are searching for.) How many records did you find? Close the **Restaurant Orders** form.

Explore
7. Use the Report Wizard to create a report based on the primary **Restaurant** table and the related **Order** table. Select the Restaurant#, RestaurantName, Street, City, OwnerFirstName, and OwnerLastName fields from the **Restaurant** table, and select all fields from the **Order** table except Restaurant#. In the third Report Wizard dialog box, specify the OrderDate field as an additional grouping level. Sort the detail records by OrderAmt in *descending* order. Choose the Align Left 1 layout and the Bold style for the report. Specify the title **Orders by Restaurants** for the report.

8. Insert the **Server** picture, which is located in the Cases folder on your Data Disk, in the Report Header section of the **Orders by Restaurants** report. Leave the picture in its original position at the left edge of the Report Header section.

Explore
9. Use the Ask a Question box to ask the following question: "How do I move a control in front of or behind other controls?" Click the topic "Move one or more controls to a new position," and then click the subtopic "Move a control in front of or behind other controls." Read the information and then close the Help window. Make sure the **Server** picture is still selected, and then move it behind the Orders by Restaurants title.

Explore
10. Use the Ask a Question box to ask the following question: "How do I change the background color of a control?" Click the topic "Change the background color of a control or section." Read the information and then close the Help window. Select the Orders by Restaurant title object, and then change its background color to Transparent.

11. Display the report in Print Preview. Print just the first page of the report, and then close and save the report.

12. Close the **Meals** database, and then exit Access.

Case 3. Redwood Zoo Michael Rosenfeld wants to create forms and reports for the **Redwood** database. You'll help him create these database objects by completing the following:

1. Make sure your Data Disk is in the appropriate disk drive, start Access, and then open the **Redwood** database located in the Cases folder on your Data Disk.

2. If your **Redwood** database is stored on drive A, you will need to delete the files **Redwood97.mdb** and **Redwood2002.mdb** from your disk so you will have enough room to complete the steps. If your database is stored on a hard or network drive, no action is necessary.

3. Use the Form Wizard to create a form based on the **Pledge** table. Select all fields for the form, the Columnar layout, and the Blueprint style. Specify the title **Pledge Info** for the form.

4. Use the **Pledge Info** form to update the **Pledge** table as follows:

   a. Use the Find command to move to the record with Pledge# 2490, and then change the FundCode to B11 and the TotalPledged amount to 75.

   b. Add a new record with the following values:

Pledge#:	2977
DonorID:	59021
FundCode:	M23
PledgeDate:	12/15/2003
TotalPledged:	150
PaymentMethod:	C
PaymentSchedule:	S

   c. Print just this form record.

   d. Delete the record with Pledge# 2900.

5. Change the AutoFormat of the **Pledge Info** form to Expedition, save the changed form, and then use the form to print the last record in the **Pledge** table. Close the form.

6. Use the Form Wizard to create a form containing a main form and a subform. Select all the fields from the **Donor** table for the main form, and select the Pledge#, FundCode, PledgeDate, and TotalPledged fields from the **Pledge** table for the subform. Use the Tabular layout and the Expedition style. Specify the title **Donors and Pledges** for the main form and the title **Pledge Subform** for the subform.

7. Display record 11 in the main form. Print the current main form record and its subform records, and then close the **Donors and Pledges** form.

Explore   8. Use the Report Wizard to create a report based on the primary **Donor** table and the related **Pledge** table. Select the DonorID, FirstName, LastName, and Class fields from the **Donor** table, and select all fields from the **Pledge** table except DonorID. In the third Report Wizard dialog box, specify the FundCode field as an additional grouping level. Sort the detail records in *descending* order by TotalPledged. Choose the Align Left 2 layout, Landscape orientation, and the Soft Gray style. Specify the title **Donors and Pledges** for the report.

9. Insert the **Animals** picture, which is located in the Cases folder on your Data Disk, in the Report Header section of the **Donors and Pledges** report. Position the picture so that its left edge aligns with the 4-inch mark on the horizontal ruler and its top edge is just below the top border line of the report.

Explore   10. Use the Ask a Question box to ask the following question: "How do I add a special effect to an object?" Click the topic "Make a control appear raised, sunken, shadowed, chiseled, or etched." Read the information, and then close the Help window. Add the Shadowed special effect to the **Animals** picture, and then save the report.

Explore   11. Print only pages 1 and 7 of the report, and then close it.

12. If your database is stored on drive A, you will need to turn off the Compact on Close feature before closing the **Redwood** database because there isn't enough room on the disk to compact the database. If your database is stored on a hard or network drive, no action is necessary.

13. Close the **Redwood** database, and then exit Access.

Case 4. Mountain River Adventures   Connor and Siobhan Dempsey want to create forms and reports that will help them track and analyze data about their customers and the rafting trips they take. Help them enhance the **Trips** database by completing the following:

1. Make sure your Data Disk is in the appropriate disk drive, start Access, and then open the **Trips** database located in the Cases folder on your Data Disk.

2. Use the Form Wizard to create a form containing a main form and a subform. Select the Client#, ClientName, City, State/Prov, and Phone fields from the **Client** table for the main form, and select all fields except Client# from the **Booking** table for the subform. Use the Datasheet layout and the Standard style. Specify the title **Clients and Bookings** for the main form and the title **Booking Subform** for the subform. Resize all columns in the subform to their best fit. Print the ninth main form record and its subform records.

3. For the form you just created, change the AutoFormat to Stone, save the changed form, and then print the ninth main form record and its subform records.

4. Navigate to the second record in the subform for the ninth main record, and then change the People field value to 7.

5. Use the Find command to move to the record with Client# 330, and then delete the record. Answer Yes to any warning messages about deleting the record.

6. Use the appropriate wildcard character to find all records with a City value that begins with the letter "D." How many records did you find? Close the form.

7. Use the Report Wizard to create a report based on the primary **Client** table and the related **Booking** table. Select all fields from the **Client** table, and select all fields except Client# from the **Booking** table. Sort the detail records by the TripDate field in ascending order. Choose the Outline 1 layout and the Compact style. Specify the title **Client Bookings** for the report.

Explore ▶ 8. Display the **Client Bookings** report in Design view, and then widen the Phone text box control so that the Phone field values are completely displayed in the report.

9. Insert the **Raft** picture, which is located in the Cases folder on your Data Disk, in the Report Header section of the **Client Bookings** report. Position the picture so that its left edge aligns with the 2-inch mark on the horizontal ruler and its top edge is just below the top border line of the report. (If the picture blocks part of the bottom border line of the header, that is fine.)

Explore ▶ 10. Insert the same **Raft** picture in the Report Footer section of the **Client Bookings** report. (Items placed in the Report Footer section appear only once, at the end of the report.) Position the picture so that its right edge aligns with the right edge of the report, at approximately the 6.5-inch mark on the horizontal ruler. Save the report.

Explore ▶ 11. View the first two pages of the report in Print Preview at the same time. (*Hint*: Use a toolbar button.) Use the Page navigation buttons to move through the report, displaying two pages at a time. Print only the first and last pages of the report, and then close the report.

12. Close the **Trips** database, and then exit Access.

INTERNET ASSIGNMENTS

Student Union

The purpose of the Internet Assignments is to challenge you to find information on the Internet that you can use to create effective documents. The actual assignments are updated and maintained on the Course Technology Web site. Log on to the Internet and use your Web browser to go to the Student Union on the New Perspectives Series site at **www.course.com/NewPerspectives/studentunion**. Click the Online Companions link, and then click the link for this tutorial.

QUICK | CHECK ANSWERS

Session 4.1

1. The AutoForm Wizard creates a form automatically using all the fields in the selected table or query; the Form Wizard allows you to choose some or all of the fields in the selected table or query, choose fields from other tables and queries, and display fields in any order on the form.

2. An AutoFormat is a predefined style for a form (or report). To change a form's AutoFormat, display the form in Design view, click the AutoFormat button on the Form Design toolbar, click the new AutoFormat in the Form AutoFormats list box, and then click the OK button.

3. the last record in the table

4. datasheet

5. the question mark (?)

6. as many form records as can fit on a printed page

Session 4.2

1. The main form displays the data from the primary table, and the subform displays the data from the related table.

2. You use the top set of navigation buttons to select and move through records from the related table in the subform, and the bottom set to select and move through records from the primary table in the main form.

3. report title

4. control

5. Design view

6. Report Header

New Perspectives on

MICROSOFT®
ACCESS 2002

Read This Before You Begin

To the Student

Data Disks

To complete the Level II tutorials, Review Assignments, and Case Problems, you will need to store your Data Disk files on your computer's hard drive or on a personal network drive. Your instructor will either provide you with these Data Disk files or ask you to obtain them.

If you are obtaining your own Data Disk files, you will need to copy a set of files and/or folders from a file server, standalone computer, or the Web onto your drives. Your instructor will tell you which computer, drive letter, and folders contain the files you need. You could also download the files by going to www.course.com and following the instructions on the screen.

If you will store your original Data Disk files on floppy disks, you will need **two** blank, formatted high-density disks. The information below shows you which folders go on each of your disks. After making your Data Disks, you can copy the files to your hard drive or personal network drive, and then retain the Data Disks as a backup.

Data Disk 1

Write this on the disk label:
Data Disk 1: Access 2002 Tutorial Files (Tutorials 5-7)
Access 2002 Review Assignments (Tutorials 5-7)

Put these folders on the disk:
Tutorial
Review

Data Disk 2

Write this on the disk label:
Data Disk 2: Access 2002 Case Problems 1-5 (Tutorials 5-7)

Put this folder on the disk:
Cases

When you begin each tutorial, be sure you are using the correct files. Refer to the "File Finder" chart at the back of this text for more detailed information on which files are used in which tutorials. These Access Level II tutorials use the same files for Tutorials 5-7. If you are completing the Level III tutorials (Tutorials 8-11), you will need to obtain new Data Disk files for those tutorials. See the inside front or inside back cover of this book for more information on Data Disk files, or ask your instructor or technical support person for assistance.

Using Your Own Computer

If you are going to work through this book using your own computer, you need:

■ **Computer System** Microsoft Windows 98, NT, 2000 Professional, or higher must be installed on your computer. This book assumes a typical installation of Microsoft Access. You will also need Microsoft Internet Explorer 5.0 or higher (or another comparable Web browser), Microsoft Excel, and Microsoft Word to complete Tutorial 7.

■ **Data Disk Files** You will not be able to complete the tutorials or exercises in this book using your own computer until you have your Data Disk files.

Visit Our World Wide Web Site

Additional materials designed especially for you are available on the World Wide Web.
Go to www.course.com/NewPerspectives.

To the Instructor

The Data Disk files are available on the Instructor's Resource Kit for this title. Follow the instructions in the Help file on the CD-ROM to install the files to your network or standalone computer. For information on creating Data Disks, see the "To the Student" section above.

You are granted a license to copy the Data Files to any computer or computer network used by students who have purchased this book.

In this tutorial you will:

- Create a Lookup Wizard field in a table

- Display related table records in a subdatasheet

- Create an input mask for a table field

- Define data validation criteria

- Use the In, Like, and Not operators in queries

- Use both the And and Or logical operators in the same query

- Create a parameter query

- Design and create a custom form

- Add, select, move, resize, delete, and rename controls

- Add form headers and footers

- Add a graphic image to a form

- Use Control Wizards to create a multi-page form with a subform

- Use Filter By Form

ENHANCING

A TABLE'S DESIGN, AND CREATING ADVANCED QUERIES AND CUSTOM FORMS

Making the Jobs Database Easy to Use

CASE

Northeast Seasonal Jobs International (NSJI)

Several years ago, Elsa Jensen founded Northeast Seasonal Jobs International (NSJI), a small Boston firm that serves as a job broker between foreign students seeking part-time, seasonal work and resort businesses located in New England and the eastern provinces of Canada. At first the company focused mainly on summer employment, but as the business continued to grow, Elsa increased the scope of operations to include all types of seasonal opportunities, including foliage tour companies in the fall and ski resorts in the winter.

Elsa incorporated the use of computers in all aspects of the business, including financial management, payroll, accounts payable, and student recruitment. Her company developed the Jobs database of employer and position data and uses **Microsoft Access 2002** (or simply **Access**) to manage it.

The Jobs database contains tables, queries, forms, and reports that Zack Ward, director of marketing, and Matt Griffin, manager of recruitment, use to track employers and their positions.

Elsa, Zack, and Matt are pleased with the information they get from the Jobs database. They are interested in taking better advantage of the power of Access to make the database easier to use and to create more sophisticated queries and custom forms. For example, Zack wants to obtain lists of employers with certain area codes, and Matt needs a list of positions in a specified state or province. Elsa wants to change the design of the Employer table. She wants to make entering the NAICS code value for an Employer record easier, improve the appearance of Phone field values, verify the correct entry of country values, and learn more about subdatasheets. (NAICS codes are the North American Industry Classification System codes used to classify businesses by the type of activity in which they are engaged.) In this tutorial, you'll make the necessary modifications and customizations to the Jobs database.

SESSION 5.1

In this session, you will change the NAICSCode field in the Employer table to a Lookup Wizard field, display related Position table records as a subdatasheet in the Employer table, create an input mask for the Phone field in the Employer table, and specify data validation values for the Country field in the Employer table. You will also create a pattern match query, a list-of-values query, and a query selecting nonmatching values. Finally, you will construct complex selection criteria using the And with Or operators, and you'll create a parameter query.

Creating a Lookup Wizard Field

The Employer table in the Jobs database contains information about the seasonal businesses with available jobs that NSJI fills with qualified foreign students. Elsa wants to make entering data in the table easier for her staff. In particular, data entry is easier if they do not need to remember the correct NAICS code for each employer. So, Elsa wants to change the NAICSCode field in the Employer table to a Lookup Wizard field. A **Lookup Wizard field** lets the user select a value from a list of possible values. For the NAICSCode field, the user will be able to select from the list of NAICS codes in the NAICS table rather than having to remember the correct code. The NAICSCode field in the Employer table will store the NAICS code, but the NAICS code description will appear in Datasheet view. This arrangement makes entering codes easier for the user and guarantees that the NAICS code is valid.

Elsa asks you to change the NAICSCode field in the Employer table to a Lookup Wizard field. You begin by opening the Jobs database and then opening the Employer table in Design view.

To change the NAICSCode field to a Lookup Wizard field:

1. Make sure you have created your copy of the Access Data Disk, and then place your Data Disk in the appropriate disk drive.

   TROUBLE? If you don't have a Data Disk, you need to get one before you can proceed. Your instructor or technical support person will either give you one or ask you to make your own. (See your instructor for information.) In either case, make sure you have a copy of your Data Disk before you begin, so that the original Data Disk files are available on the copied disk in case you need to start over because of an error or problem.

   TROUBLE? If you are not sure which disk drive to use for your Data Disk, read the "Read This Before You Begin" page on page AC 5.02 or ask your instructor for help.

2. Start Access, open the **Jobs** database located in the Tutorial folder on your Data Disk, and then open the **Employer** table in Design view.

3. Scroll down (if necessary) to the NAICSCode field, click the right side of the **Data Type** text box for the NAICSCode field, and then click **Lookup Wizard**. The first Lookup Wizard dialog box opens. See Figure 5-1.

Figure 5-1   **FIRST LOOKUP WIZARD DIALOG BOX**

make sure this option is selected

This dialog box lets you specify a list of allowed values for the NAICSCode field in a record in the Employer table. You can specify a table or query from which users select the value, or you can enter a new list of values. You want the NAICSCode value to come from the NAICS table.

4. Make sure the option for looking up the values in a table or query is selected, and then click the **Next** button to display the next Lookup Wizard dialog box.

5. Make sure **Table: NAICS** is selected, and then click the **Next** button to display the next Lookup Wizard dialog box. See Figure 5-2.

Figure 5-2   **SELECTING THE NAICS TABLE FIELDS**

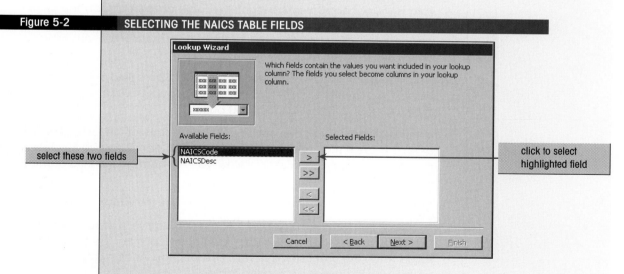

select these two fields

click to select highlighted field

This dialog box lets you select the lookup fields from the NAICS table. You need to select the NAICSCode field because it's the common field that links the NAICS and Employer tables. You also must select the NAICSDesc field because Elsa wants the user to be able to select from a list of NAICS descriptions when entering a new employer record.

6. Click the ⟩ button to select the NAICSCode field from the NAICS table so the lookup column will include it, click the ⟩ button to select the NAICSDesc field, and then click the **Next** button. See Figure 5-3.

Figure 5-3	ADJUSTING THE WIDTH OF THE LOOKUP FIELD

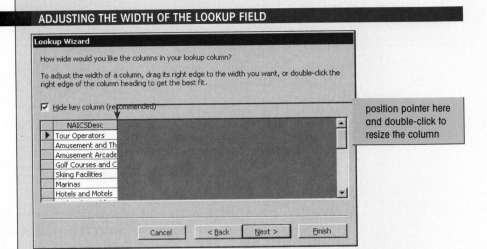

In this dialog box, you can adjust the width of the NAICSDesc column. This column will appear when a user enters a NAICSCode for the employer in the Employer table. The user can select a NAICSDesc, and Access will enter the correct NAICSCode for the selected NAICSDesc value automatically. The selected "Hide key column (recommended)" option means that the list of NAICSCode values will not appear in the Employer table datasheet; only the list of NAICSDesc values will appear. If you uncheck this option, both lists of field values will appear in the Employer table datasheet when you select a value for the field.

7. Place the pointer on the right edge of the NAICSDesc field column heading. When the pointer changes to a ↔ shape, double-click to resize the column to fit the data, and then click the **Next** button.

In this dialog box, you can specify the field name for the lookup field. The default value is the current field name, NAICSCode. Because the field will show NAICS descriptions in Datasheet view, you will change the field name to NAICSDesc.

8. Type **NAICSDesc** in the text box, and then click the **Finish** button.

To create the Lookup Wizard field, Access must save the table design and create the necessary relationship, so Access can enter the correct NAICSCode value when the user selects a NAICS description. Access displays a dialog box asking you to confirm saving the table.

9. Click the **Yes** button. Access creates the Lookup Wizard field, and you return to the Employer table in Design view. See Figure 5-4.

Figure 5-4   **LOOKUP WIZARD FIELD DEFINED**

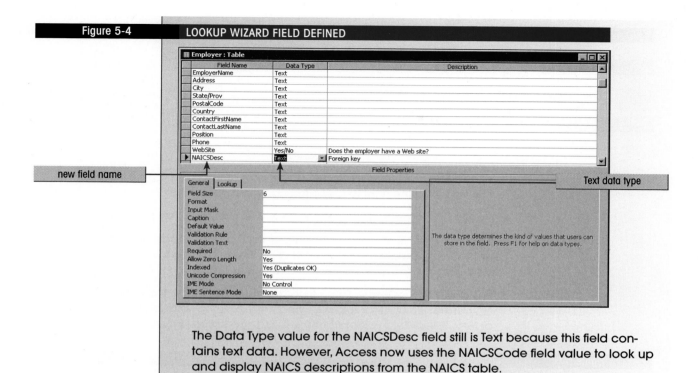

new field name

Text data type

The Data Type value for the NAICSDesc field still is Text because this field contains text data. However, Access now uses the NAICSCode field value to look up and display NAICS descriptions from the NAICS table.

Elsa just discovered that the NAICSCode field value stored in the Employer table for Boston Harbor Excursions is incorrect. She asks you to test the new Lookup Wizard field to select the correct code. To do so, you need to switch to Datasheet view.

To change the NAICSCode Lookup Wizard field value:

1. Switch to Datasheet view.

The NAICSCode field values, which now have NAICSDesc for a column heading in the datasheet, are in column 13. After you scroll to the right to view the NAICSDesc column, you'll no longer be able to verify that you're changing the correct field value because the EmployerID and EmployerName fields will be hidden. You'll freeze those two columns so they'll remain visible in the datasheet as you scroll to the right.

2. Click the **EmployerID** column selector, press and hold down the **Shift** key, click the **EmployerName** column selector to select both columns, and then release the **Shift** key.

3. Click **Format** on the menu bar, click **Freeze Columns**, and then click anywhere in the datasheet to deselect the first two columns. A dark vertical line now separates the two leftmost columns from the other columns. The line indicates that these two columns will remain visible no matter where you scroll in the datasheet. See Figure 5-5.

Figure 5-5   **FREEZING THE FIRST TWO DATASHEET COLUMNS**

frozen columns

dark vertical line

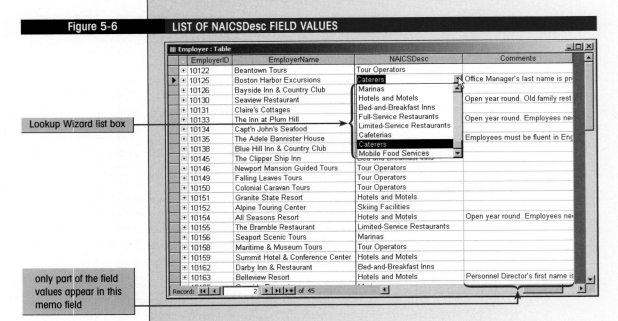

You'll scroll to the right to make the rightmost columns in the datasheet visible.

4. Scroll to the right until you see the NAICSDesc and Comments columns.

Because NAICSDesc field values replaced the NAICSCode field values in column 13, you should resize the column to its best fit before you change the NAICSDesc field value for Boston Harbor Excursions.

5. Resize the NAICSDesc column to its best fit, double-click **Caterers** in the NAICSDesc column for record 2, and then click the list arrow to display the list of NAICSDesc field values from the NAICS table. See Figure 5-6.

Figure 5-6   **LIST OF NAICSDesc FIELD VALUES**

Lookup Wizard list box

only part of the field values appear in this memo field

6. Click **Marinas** to select this field value. The list box closes and Marinas appears in the NAICSDesc text box. However, it is the value 71393, which is the NAICSCode field value for Marinas, that is stored in the Employer table for this column.

The Comments column is a memo field that NSJI staff members use to store explanations about the employer, its contact, and its positions. The Comments field values are partially hidden because the datasheet column is not wide enough. You'll increase the datasheet row height so more of the Comments field values will be visible.

7. Place the pointer between the row selectors for rows 2 and 3, and, when the pointer changes to a ✛ shape, drag the edge down to the approximate position shown in Figure 5-7. Note that you could have increased the row height by placing the pointer between any two row selectors.

| Figure 5-7 | DATASHEET ROWS RESIZED |

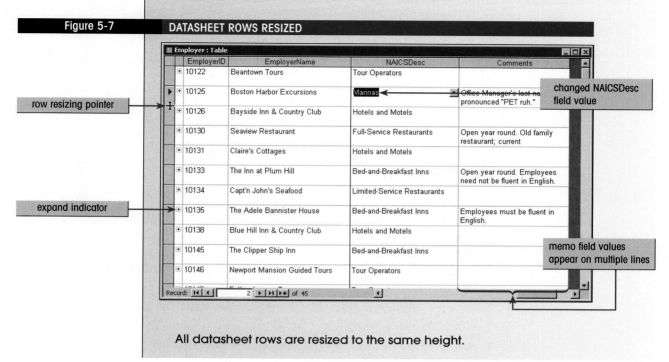

All datasheet rows are resized to the same height.

Elsa notices that a plus symbol appears to the left of the EmployerID field in the Employer table datasheet and asks what function it serves. You investigate and find that when you defined the one-to-many relationship between the Employer and Position tables in Tutorial 3, Access automatically added plus symbols to the Employer datasheet. These plus symbols let you view an employer's related Position table records in a subdatasheet.

Displaying **Related Records in a Subdatasheet**

For tables such as the Employer and Position tables, which have a one-to-many relationship, you can display records from the related table—the Position table in this case—as a **subdatasheet** in the primary table's datasheet—the Employer table in this case. When you first open a table (or query) datasheet, its subdatasheets are not expanded. To display the position subdatasheet for a specific employer, you click the **expand indicator** ➕ in the row for that employer. Next, you'll display the position subdatasheet for Beantown Tours.

To display Position table records in a subdatasheet:

1. Click the **expand indicator** ➕ for Beantown Tours, which is EmployerID 10122. The subdatasheet for Beantown Tours opens. See Figure 5-8.

Figure 5-8	POSITION SUBDATASHEET EXPANDED

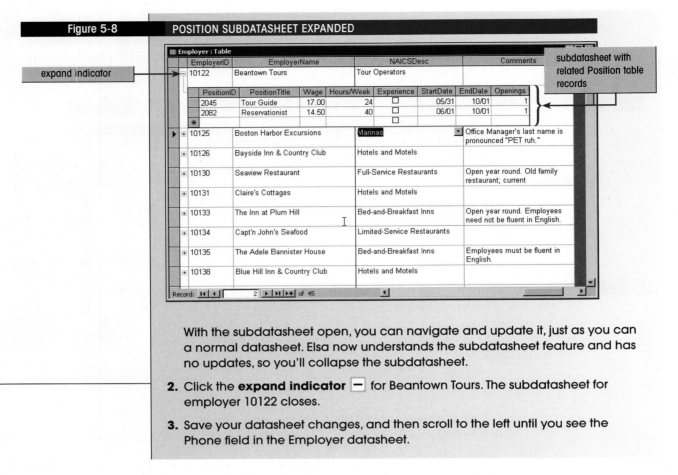

expand indicator

subdatasheet with related Position table records

With the subdatasheet open, you can navigate and update it, just as you can a normal datasheet. Elsa now understands the subdatasheet feature and has no updates, so you'll collapse the subdatasheet.

2. Click the **expand indicator** — for Beantown Tours. The subdatasheet for employer 10122 closes.

3. Save your datasheet changes, and then scroll to the left until you see the Phone field in the Employer datasheet.

Elsa asks you to change the appearance of the Phone field in the Employer table to a standard telephone number format.

Using the Input Mask Wizard

The Phone field in the Employer table is a 10-digit number that's difficult to read because it appears with none of the special formatting characters usually associated with a telephone number. For example, the Phone field value for Beantown Tours, which appears as 6174511970, would be more readable in any of the following formats: 617-451-1970, 617.451.1970, 617/451-1970, or (617) 451-1970. Elsa asks you to use the 617-451-1970 style for the Phone field.

Elsa wants hyphens to appear as literal display characters whenever users enter Phone field values. **Literal display characters** are the special characters that automatically appear in specific positions of a field value; users don't need to type literal display characters. To include these characters, you need to create an **input mask**, a predefined format used to enter and display data in a field. An easy way to create an input mask is to use the **Input Mask Wizard**, an Access tool that guides you in creating a predefined format for a field. You must use the Input Mask Wizard in Design view.

To use the Input Mask Wizard for the Phone field:

1. Switch to Design view, and then click the **Field Name** text box for the Phone field to make it the current field and to display its Field Properties options.

2. Click the **Input Mask** text box in the Field Properties pane. A Build button [...] appears to the right of the Input Mask text box.

3. Click the **Build** button [...] next to the Input Mask text box. The first Input Mask Wizard dialog box opens. See Figure 5-9.

Figure 5-9	INPUT MASK WIZARD DIALOG BOX

TROUBLE? If a dialog box opens and tells you that this feature is not installed, insert your Office XP CD into the correct drive, and then click the Yes button. If you do not have an Office XP CD, ask your instructor or technical support person for help.

You can scroll the Input Mask list box, select the input mask you want, and then enter representative values to practice using the input mask.

4. If necessary, click **Phone Number** in the Input Mask list box to select it.

5. Click the far left side of the **Try It** text box. (___) ___-___ appears in the Try It text box. As you type a phone number, Access replaces the underscores, which are placeholder characters.

   TROUBLE? If your insertion point is not immediately to the right of the left parenthesis, press the Left Arrow key until it is.

6. Type **9876543210** to practice entering a sample phone number. The input mask makes the typed value appear as (987) 654-3210.

7. Click the **Next** button. The next Input Mask Wizard dialog box opens. In it, you can change the input mask and placeholder character. Because changing an input mask is easier after the Input Mask Wizard finishes, you'll accept all Wizard defaults.

8. Click the **Finish** button. The Input Mask Wizard creates the default phone number input mask, placing it in the Input Mask text box for the Phone field. See Figure 5-10.

Figure 5-10	INPUT MASK CREATED BY THE INPUT MASK WIZARD

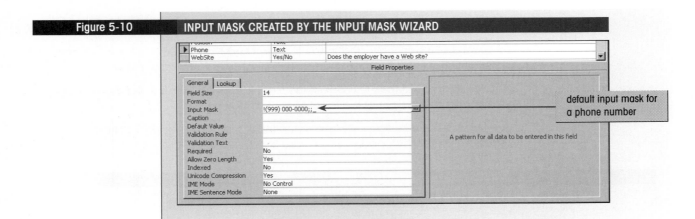

The characters preceding the first semicolon represent the input mask. The symbols in the default phone number input mask of !(999) 000-0000;;_ have the meanings shown in Figure 5-11.

Figure 5-11	INPUT MASK CHARACTERS

INPUT MASK CHARACTER	DESCRIPTION
!	Causes the input mask to display from right to left, rather than the default of left to right. Characters typed in the mask always fill in from left to right.
9	Digit or space can be entered. Entry is not required.
0	Digit only can be entered. Entry is required.
;;	The character between the first and second semicolon determines whether to store in the database the literal display characters such as the hyphen and parentheses. If left blank or set to a value of 1, do not store the literal characters. If set to a value of 0, store the literal characters.
_ (underscore)	Placeholder character because it follows the second semicolon.
( ) -	Literal display characters

Elsa wants to view the Phone field with the default input mask before you change it for her.

To view and change the input mask for the Phone field:

1. Save your table design changes, and then switch to Datasheet view.

2. Scroll the table to the right until the Phone field is visible. The Phone field values now have the format specified by the input mask.

3. Switch to Design view.

   The input mask changed from !(999) 000-0000;;_ to !\(999") "000\-0000;;_. The backslash character (\) causes the character that follows it to appear as a literal character. Characters enclosed in quotation marks also appear as literal characters.

4. Change the input mask to **!999\-000\-0000;;_** in the Input Mask text box for the Phone field.

5. Save your table design changes, and then switch to Datasheet view.

6. Scroll the table to the right until the Phone field is visible. The Phone field values now have the format Elsa requested. See Figure 5-12.

Figure 5-12	AFTER CHANGING THE PHONE FIELD INPUT MASK

Phone field with input mask

		EmployerID	EmployerName	Position	Phone	WebSite	NAICSDes
▶	+	10122	Beantown Tours	Office Manager	617-451-1970	☑	Tour Operators
	+	10125	Boston Harbor Excursions	Office Manager	617-235-1800	☑	Marinas
	+	10126	Bayside Inn & Country Club	General Manager	508-283-5775	☑	Hotels and Motels
	+	10130	Seaview Restaurant	Manager	508-776-8593	☐	Full-Service Restaur
	+	10131	Claire's Cottages	Manager	508-822-1328	☐	Hotels and Motels
	+	10133	The Inn at Plum Hill	General Manager	508-693-2320	☑	Bed-and-Breakfast I

Employer : Table

Elsa wants to limit the entry of Country field values in the Employer table to Canada and USA because NSJI employer clients are located in only these two countries. She's concerned that typing errors might produce incorrect query results and cause other problems. To provide this data-entry capability, you'll set validation properties for the Country field.

Defining **Data Validation Criteria**

To prevent a user from entering a value other than Canada or USA, you can set the Validation Rule and the Validation Text properties for the Country field in the Employer table. The **Validation Rule** property value specifies the valid values that users can enter in a field. The **Validation Text** property value will be displayed in a dialog box if the user enters an invalid value (in this case, a value other than Canada or USA). After you set these two Country field properties in the Employer table, Access will prevent users from entering an invalid Country field value in all current and future forms and queries.

You'll now set the Validation Rule and Validation Text properties for the Country field in the Employer table.

To set the Validation Rule and Validation Text properties for the Country field:

1. Switch to Design view, and then click the **Country Field Name** text box to make that row the current row.

To make sure that the only values entered in the Country field are Canada or USA, you'll specify a list of valid values in the Validation Rule text box.

2. Click the **Validation Rule** text box, type **Canada or USA**, and then press the **Tab** key.

When you pressed the Tab key, the Validation Rule changed to "Canada" Or "USA". You can set the Validation Text property to a value that appears in a dialog box that opens if a user enters a value not listed in the Validation Rule text box.

3. Type **Must be Canada or USA** in the Validation Text text box. See Figure 5-13.

Figure 5-13	VALIDATION PROPERTIES FOR THE COUNTRY FIELD

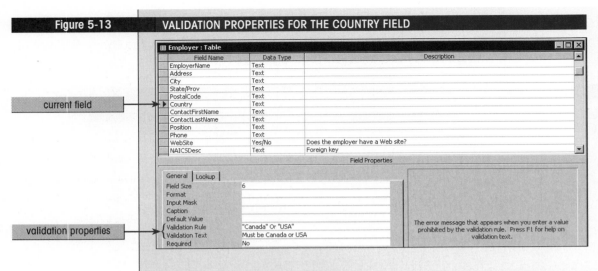

current field

validation properties

You can now save the table design changes and then test the validation properties.

4. Save your table design changes, and click the **Yes** button when asked if you want to test the existing Country field values in the Employer table against the new validation rule.

Next, you'll test the validation rule.

5. Switch to Datasheet view, and then scroll the table to the right until the Country field is visible.

6. Double-click **USA** in the first row's Country field text box, type **Spain**, and then press the **Tab** key. A dialog box opens containing the message "Must be Canada or USA," which is the Validation Text property setting you created in Step 3.

7. Click the **OK** button, and then click the **Undo typing** button ![undo] on the Table Datasheet toolbar. The first row's Country field value again has its original value, USA.

8. Close the Employer table, and click the **Yes** button if asked to save the table design changes.

You defined the validation criteria for the Country field and completed your design changes to the Employer table. You are now ready to create the queries that Elsa, Matt, and Zack requested. You are already familiar with queries that use an exact match or a range of values (for example, queries that use the >= and < comparison operators) to select records. Access provides many other operators for creating select queries. These operators let you create more complicated queries that are difficult or impossible to create with exact match or range of values selection criteria.

Elsa, Matt, and Zack created a list of questions they want to answer using the Jobs database:

- Which employers have the 508 area code?
- What is the employer information for employers located in Maine (ME), New Hampshire (NH), or Vermont (VT)?
- What is the position information for all positions *except* those positions with the titles Lifeguard or Ski Patrol?

- What is the position information for those Waiter/Waitress or Kitchen Help positions located in Massachusetts (MA) or New Hampshire (NH)?
- What is the position information for positions in a particular state or province? For this query, the user needs to be able to specify the state or province.

Next, you will create the queries necessary to answer these questions. To do so, you'll use the Query window in Design view.

Using a Pattern Match in a Query

Zack wants to view the records for all employers within the 508 area code. He plans to travel in their area next week and wants to contact them. To answer Zack's question, you can create a query that uses a pattern match. A **pattern match** selects records with a value for the selected field that matches the pattern of the simple condition value, in this case, employers with the 508 area code. You do this using the Like comparison operator.

The **Like comparison operator** selects records by matching field values to a specific pattern that includes one or more of these wildcard characters: asterisk (*), question mark (?), and number symbol (#). The asterisk represents any string of characters, the question mark represents any single character, and the number symbol represents any single digit. Using a pattern match is similar to using an exact match, except that a pattern match includes wildcard characters.

To create the query, you must first place the Employer table field list in the Query window in Design view.

> ### To create the pattern match query in Design view:
>
> 1. Click **Queries** in the Objects bar of the Database window, and then click the **New** button. The New Query dialog box opens.
>
> 2. Click **Design View** in the list box (if necessary), and then click the **OK** button. The Show Table dialog box opens on top of the Query window.
>
> 3. Click **Employer** in the Tables list box (if necessary), click the **Add** button, and then click the **Close** button. Access places the Employer table field list in the Query window.
>
> 4. Double-click the **title bar** of the Employer field list to highlight all the fields, and then drag one of the highlighted fields to the first column's Field text box in the design grid. Access places each field in a separate column in the design grid, in the same order that the fields appear in the table. See Figure 5-14.

Figure 5-14	ADDING THE FIELDS FOR THE QUERY

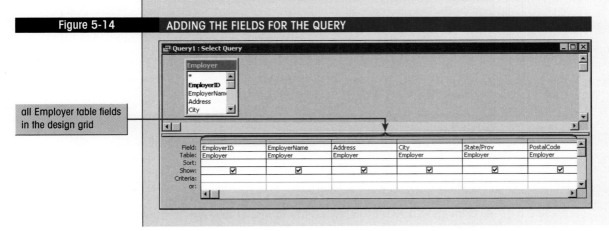

all Employer table fields in the design grid

TROUBLE? If Employer.* appears in the first column's Field text box, you dragged the * from the field list instead of one of the highlighted fields. Press the Delete key, and then repeat Step 4.

Now you will enter the pattern match condition Like "508*" for the Phone field. Access will select records with a Phone field value of 508 in positions one through three. The asterisk (*) wildcard character specifies that any characters can appear in the remaining positions of the field value.

To specify records that match the specified pattern:

1. Scroll the design grid until the Phone field is visible.

2. Click the **Phone Criteria** text box, and then type **Like "508*"**. See Figure 5-15. (*Note*: If you omit the Like operator, Access automatically adds it when you run the query.)

Figure 5-15	RECORD SELECTION BASED ON MATCHING A SPECIFIC PATTERN

pattern match selection criterion

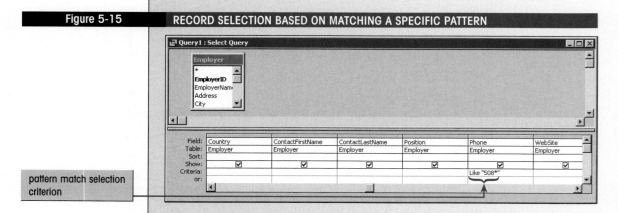

3. Click the **Run** button [!] on the Query Design toolbar, scroll the window until the Phone field is visible, and then reduce the row height, as shown in Figure 5-16. The query results display the nine records with the area code 508 in the Phone field.

Figure 5-16	EMPLOYER RECORDS FOR AREA CODE 508

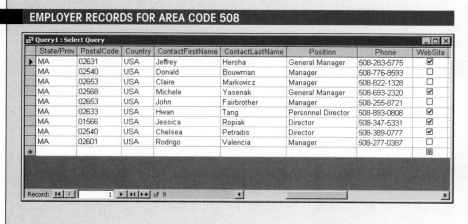

Now you can save the query.

4. Click the **Save** button [💾] on the Query Datasheet toolbar. The Save As dialog box opens.

> **5.** Type **508 Area Code** in the Query Name text box, and then press the **Enter** key. Access saves the query in the Jobs database on your Data Disk.

Next, Zack asks you to create a query that displays information about employers in the states of Maine (ME), New Hampshire (NH), or Vermont (VT). He wants a printout of the employer data for his administrative aide, who will contact these employers. To produce the results Zack wants, you'll create a query using a list-of-values match.

Using a List-of-Values Match in a Query

A **list-of-values match** selects records whose value for the selected field matches one of two or more simple condition values. You could accomplish this by including several Or conditions in the design grid, but the In comparison operator provides an easier way to do this. The **In comparison operator** lets you define a condition with two or more values. If a record's field value matches one value from the list of defined values, then Access selects and includes that record in the query results.

To display the information Zack requested, you want records selected if their State/Prov field value equals ME, NH, or VT. These are the values you will use with the In comparison operator.

> *To create the query using a list-of-values match:*
>
> **1.** Switch to Design view.
>
>   First you need to delete the condition for the previous query you created.
>
> **2.** Click the **Phone Criteria** text box, press the **F2** key to highlight the entire condition, and then press the **Delete** key to remove the condition.
>
>   Now you can enter the criteria for the new query using the In comparison operator. When you use this operator, you must enclose the list of values you want to match within parentheses and separate the values with commas. In addition, for Text data types you must enclose each value in quotation marks, but you don't use the quotation marks for Number data type fields.
>
> **3.** Scroll the design grid to the left to display the State/Prov column, click the **State/Prov Criteria** text box, and then type **In ("ME","NH","VT")**. See Figure 5-17.

Figure 5-17	RECORD SELECTION BASED ON MATCHING FIELD VALUES TO A LIST OF VALUES

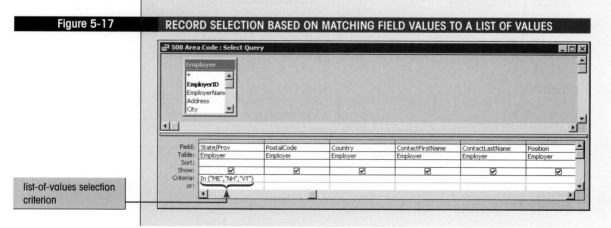

list-of-values selection criterion

4. Run the query. Access displays the query results, which show the 14 records with ME, NH, or VT in the State/Prov field.

Now you can print the query results for Zack. Because Zack doesn't need this information again, you don't have to save this query.

5. Click the **Print** button 🖨 on the Query Datasheet toolbar, and then close the query without saving your design changes.

Matt recruited several students who qualify for any position except Lifeguard and Ski Patrol. You can provide Matt with this information by creating a query with a nonmatching condition.

Using a Nonmatching Value in a Query

A **nonmatching value** selects records whose value for the selected field does not match the simple condition value. You create the selection criterion using the Not logical operator. The **Not logical operator** negates a criterion. For example, if you enter Not = "CT" in the Criteria text box for the State/Prov field in the Employer table, the query results show records that do not have the State/Prov field value CT; that is, records of all employers not located in Connecticut.

To create Matt's query, you will combine the Not operator with the In operator to select positions whose PositionTitle field value is not in the list ("Lifeguard","Ski Patrol"). The Weekly Wages query has the fields that Matt needs to see in the query results.

To create the query using a nonmatching value:

1. Open the **Weekly Wages** query in Design view.

2. Click the **PositionTitle Criteria** text box, and then type **Not In ("Lifeguard","Ski Patrol")** for the condition. See Figure 5-18.

Figure 5-18	RECORD SELECTION BASED ON NOT MATCHING A LIST OF VALUES

negation operator with list-of-values selection criterion

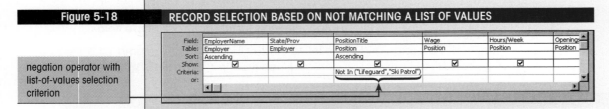

TROUBLE? Your screen might show only part of the criterion in the PositionTitle Criteria text box.

3. Run the query. Access displays only those records with a PositionTitle field value that is not Lifeguard and is not Ski Patrol. The query results include a total of 58 of the 64 position records.

4. Scroll down the datasheet to make sure that no Lifeguard and Ski Patrol positions appear in your results.

Matt wants a printed copy of the query results.

5. Switch to Print Preview, and use the navigation buttons to preview the report. Notice that two pages are required to print all seven columns, so you'll change to landscape orientation.

6. Click the **Setup** button on the Print Preview toolbar to open the Page Setup dialog box, click the **Page** tab, click the **Landscape** option button, and then click the **OK** button.

7. Print the query results.

   Now you can close the query without saving it, because Matt does not need to run this query again.

8. Close the query without saving your design changes.

You now are ready to create the query to answer Matt's question about Waiter/Waitress or Kitchen Help positions located in Massachusetts (MA) or New Hampshire (NH).

Using Both the And and Or Operators in the Same Query

Matt wants to see the employer names, states/provinces, position titles, wages, hours per week, number of openings, and weekly wages for employers in Massachusetts or New Hampshire that have openings for Waiter/Waitress or Kitchen Help positions. To create this query, you must use both the And and the Or logical operators to create two compound conditions. That is, you will create conditions that select records for employers located in Massachusetts *or* in New Hampshire *and* have Waiter/Waitress positions *or* Kitchen Help positions. Because Matt wants to see the same fields used in the Weekly Wages query, you will use this query as the basis for your new query.

To create the query using the And logical operator with the Or logical operator:

1. Open the **Weekly Wages** query in Design view.

   Matt wants to view data for employers in Massachusetts (MA) or New Hampshire (NH). You have several choices for specifying the required Or logical operator. One choice is to type "MA" in the State/Prov Criteria text box and then type "NH" in the State/Prov or text box. A second choice is to type "MA" Or "NH" in the State/Prov Criteria text box. A third choice, and the one you'll use, is the In comparison operator.

2. Click the **State/Prov Criteria** text box, type **In (MA,NH)** and then press the **Enter** key. The State/Prov condition changed to In ("MA","NH") because Access adds quotation marks automatically to fields defined with the Text data type.

   To use the And logical operator, you need to enter the condition for the PositionTitle field in the same row as the State/Prov condition. This time you'll use the Or logical operator for the condition in the PositionTitle column.

3. Type **"Waiter/Waitress" Or "Kitchen Help"** in the PositionTitle Criteria text box, and then press the **Enter** key. See Figure 5-19.

Figure 5-19	AND WITH OR CONDITIONS IN THE DESIGN GRID

first Or condition using the In comparison operator

second Or condition using the Or logical operator

both conditions in the same row for the And condition

TROUBLE? Your screen might show only part of the criterion in the PositionTitle Criteria text box.

4. Run the query. Access displays the query results. See Figure 5-20.

Figure 5-20	RESULTS OF QUERY USING AND WITH OR

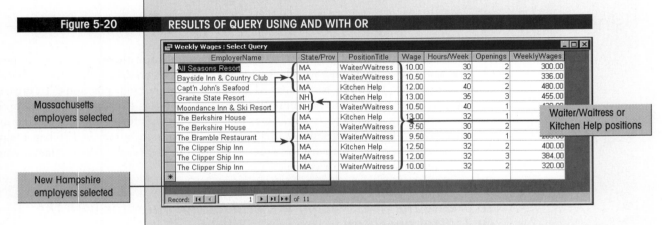

Massachusetts employers selected

New Hampshire employers selected

Waiter/Waitress or Kitchen Help positions

The query results show records for employers in Massachusetts or New Hampshire that have either Waiter/Waitress or Kitchen Help positions. Next, you'll save the query with a new name (to keep the original query intact), and then you'll close the query.

5. Click **File** on the menu bar, click **Save As**, type **MA and NH Special Positions** in the Save Query text box, and then press the **Enter** key.

6. Close the query.

TROUBLE? If necessary, scroll the Queries list box to the left to display all the queries.

You are now ready to create the query to satisfy Matt's request for information about positions in a particular state or province.

Creating a Parameter Query

Matt's final query asks for records in the Weekly Wages query for employers in a particular state or province. For this query, he wants to specify the state or province, such as RI (Rhode Island), QC (Quebec), or NS (Nova Scotia).

To create this query, you will modify the existing Weekly Wages query. You could create a simple condition using an exact match for the State/Prov field, but you would need to change it in Design view every time you run the query. Instead, you will create a parameter query. A **parameter query** prompts you for information when the query runs. In this case, you want to create a query that prompts you for the state or province of the employers to select from the table. You enter the prompt in the Criteria text box for the State/Prov field.

When Access runs the query, it will open a dialog box and prompt you to enter the state or province. Access then creates the query results, just as if you had changed the criteria in Design view.

REFERENCE WINDOW   **RW**

Creating a Parameter Query

■ Create a select query that includes all fields to appear in the query results. Also choose the sort keys and set the criteria that do not change when you run the query.

■ Decide which fields will use prompts when the query runs. In the Criteria text box for each of these fields, type the prompt you want to appear in a message box when you run the query, and enclose the prompt in brackets.

Now you can open the Weekly Wages query in Design view and change its design to create the parameter query.

To create the parameter query based on an existing query:

1. Open the **Weekly Wages** query in Design view.

Next you must enter the criteria for the parameter query. In this case, Matt wants the query to prompt users to enter the state or province for the position information they want to view. So, you need to enter the prompt in the Criteria text box for the State/Prov field. Brackets must enclose the text of the prompt.

2. Click the **State/Prov Criteria** text box, type **[Enter the state or province:]** and then press the **Enter** key. See Figure 5-21.

Figure 5-21	SPECIFYING THE PROMPT FOR THE PARAMETER QUERY

Field:	EmployerName	State/Prov	PositionTitle	Wage	Hours/Week	Openings
Table:	Employer	Employer	Position	Position	Position	Position
Sort:	Ascending		Ascending			
Show:	☑	☑	☑	☑	☑	
Criteria:		[Enter the state or province:]				
or:						

prompt text

TROUBLE? Your screen might show only part of the criterion in the State/Prov Criteria text box.

3. Run the query. Access displays a dialog box prompting you for the name of the state or province. See Figure 5-22.

Figure 5-22	ENTER PARAMETER VALUE DIALOG BOX

The text you specified in the Criteria text box of the State/Prov field appears above a text box, in which you must type a State/Prov field value. You must enter the value so that it matches the spelling of a State/Prov field value in the table, but you can enter the value in either lowercase or uppercase letters. Matt wants to see all positions in Nova Scotia (NS).

4. Type **NS**, and then press the **Enter** key. Access displays the data for the three positions in Nova Scotia. See Figure 5-23.

Figure 5-23	RESULTS OF THE PARAMETER QUERY

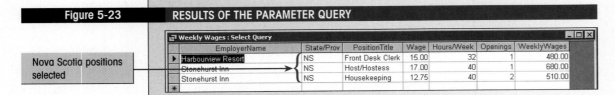

Matt plans to run this query frequently to monitor available positions by state or province, so he asks you to save it with a new name.

5. Click **File** on the menu bar, and then click **Save As**. The Save As dialog box opens.

6. Press the **End** key, press the **spacebar**, type **Parameter**, press the **Enter** key, and then close the query.

The Employer table design changes you made and the queries you created will make the Jobs database easier to use. In the next session, you will create a custom form for the database to help NSJI employees enter and maintain data more easily.

Session 5.1 QUICK CHECK

1. What is a Lookup Wizard field?

2. What is a subdatasheet?

3. A(n) _____ is a predefined format you use to enter data in a field.

   4. Define the Validation Rule property, and give an example of when you would use it.

   5. Define the Validation Text property, and give an example of when you would use it.

   6. Which comparison operator selects records based on a specific pattern?

   7. What is the purpose of the asterisk (*) in a pattern match query?

   8. When do you use the In comparison operator?

   9. How do you negate a selection criterion?

   10. When do you use a parameter query?

SESSION 5.2

In this session, you will create a custom form for employer information. You will work in Design view to add form controls; select, move, resize, delete, and rename the controls; create a form header with a title and a picture; and add color to the background of the form.

Creating a Custom Form

Elsa has been using the Employer Positions form to enter and view information about NSJI's employers and their positions. She likes having the information on a single form, but she prefers to display all fields from the Employer table instead of only a few. Also, Elsa would prefer to have the fields rearranged and a picture added to the form. To make the form easier to read, she wants the employer and position information on separate pages, like the tabs in a dialog box. She asks you to create a new form to display information this way. Because this form differs significantly from the Employer Positions form, you will create a new custom form.

To create a **custom form**, you can modify an existing form or design and create a form from scratch. In either case, you create a custom form in the Form window in Design view. You can design a custom form to match a paper form, to display some fields side by side and others top to bottom, to highlight certain sections with color, or to add special buttons and list boxes. A multi-page form displays the form on more than one page on a single screen. Each page is labeled with a tab; by clicking a tab, you can display the information on that page.

Designing a Custom Form

Whether you want to create a simple or complex custom form, planning the form's content and appearance first is always best. Figure 5-24 shows Elsa's design for the custom form she wants you to create.

| Figure 5-24 | ELSA'S DESIGN FOR THE MULTI-PAGE CUSTOM FORM |

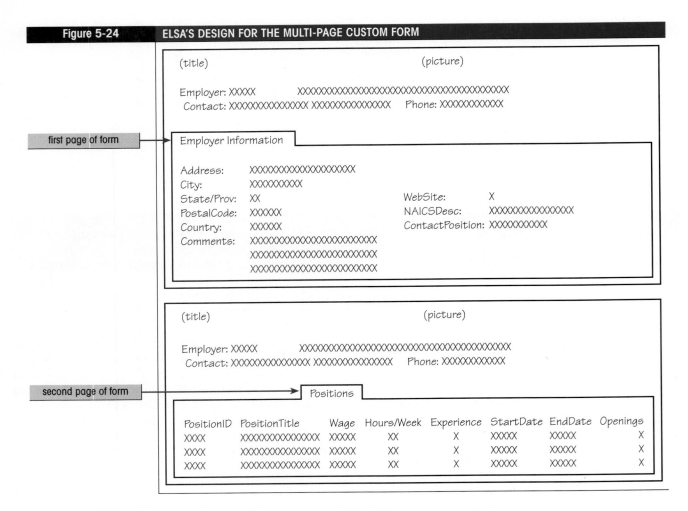

Notice that the top of the form displays a title and picture. Below these items are field values from the Employer table—the first employer line displays the EmployerID and EmployerName field values; and the second employer line displays the ContactFirstName, ContactLastName, and Phone field values. Also, notice that Elsa's form contains two pages. The first page, labeled "Employer Information," displays the employer's address information, comments, and miscellaneous information. The second page, labeled "Positions," displays position information for the employer. Each field value from the Employer table is to appear in a text box, with identifying labels placed to the left of most field values. Each label will be the value of the field's Caption property (if any) or the field name. In Elsa's form design, a series of Xs indicates the locations and approximate lengths of each field value. For example, the five Xs following the Employer field label indicate that the field value (for the EmployerID field) is approximately five characters. The Position table fields appear in a **subform**, a separate form contained within another form, on the second page. Unlike the Employer table data, which appears on the first page with identifying labels to the left of the field values in text boxes, the Position table data appears in datasheet format with identifying labels above field values.

With the design for the custom form in place, you are ready to create it. You could use an AutoForm Wizard or the Form Wizard to create a basic form and then customize it in Design view. However, to create the form Elsa wants, you would need to make many modifications to a basic form, so you will design the entire form directly in Design view.

The Form Window in Design View

You use the Form window in Design view to create and modify forms. To create Elsa's custom form, you'll create a blank form based on the Employer table and then add the Position table fields in a subform.

REFERENCE WINDOW   **RW**

Creating a Form in Design View
- In the Database window, click Forms in the Objects bar to display the Forms list.
- Click the New button to open the New Form dialog box, and then click Design View.
- Select the table or query on which to base the form, and then click the OK button.
- Place the necessary controls in the Form window in Design view. Modify the size, position, and other control properties as necessary.
- Click the Save button on the Form Design toolbar, and then enter a name for the form.

Now you'll create a blank form based on the Employer table.

To create a blank form in Design view:

1. If you took a break after the previous session, make sure that Access is running and that the **Jobs** database from the Tutorial folder on your Data Disk is open.

2. Click **Forms** in the Objects bar of the Database window, and then click the **New** button. The New Form dialog box opens.

3. Click **Design View** (if necessary), click the list arrow for choosing a table or query, click **Employer**, and then click the **OK** button. Access opens the Form window in Design view.

4. Click the **Maximize** button 🔲 on the Form window to maximize the window. See Figure 5-25.

Figure 5-25	FORM WINDOW IN DESIGN VIEW

View button

Formatting toolbar

rulers

Detail section

grid

Field List button

Toolbox button

Form Design toolbar

field list

toolbox docked under Formatting toolbar

TROUBLE? If the rulers, grid, or toolbox do not appear, click View on the menu bar, and then click Ruler, Grid, or Toolbox to display the missing component. If the grid is still invisible, ask your instructor or technical support person for assistance. If the toolbox is not positioned as in Figure 5-25, click the Toolbox window's title bar and then drag it to the position shown.

TROUBLE? If the field list is not visible, click the Field List button 📠 on the Form Design toolbar to display it. If the field list is not positioned as in Figure 5-25, click the field list title bar and then drag it to the position shown. If necessary, resize the field list window so it matches the one shown Figure 5-25.

TROUBLE? If the Form Design toolbar or the Formatting toolbar does not appear, click View on the menu bar, point to Toolbars, and then click Form Design or Formatting (Form/Report) to display the missing toolbar.

TROUBLE? If the Form Design and Formatting toolbars appear on the same line, drag the Formatting toolbar's move handle 🔢 below the Form Design toolbar to the position shown in Figure 5-25.

The Form window in Design view contains the tools necessary to create a custom form. You create the form by placing objects on the blank form in the window. Each object—such as a text box, list box, rectangle, or command button—that you place on a form is called a **control**. You can place three kinds of controls on a form:

- A **bound control** is linked, or bound, to a field in the underlying table or query. You use a bound control to display table field values.

- An **unbound control** is not linked to a field in the underlying table or query. You use an unbound control to display text, such as a form title or instructions; to display lines and rectangles; or to display graphics and pictures created using other software programs. An unbound control that displays text is called a **label**.

■ A **calculated control** displays a value calculated using data from one or more fields.

To create a bound control, you use the Field List button on the Form Design toolbar to display a list of fields available from the underlying table or query. Then you drag fields from the field list box to the Form window, and place the bound controls where you want them to appear on the form.

To place other controls on a form, you use the buttons on the toolbox. The **toolbox** is a specialized toolbar containing buttons that represent the tools you use to place controls on a form or report. ScreenTips are available for each tool. If you want to show or hide the toolbox, click the Toolbox button on the Form Design toolbar. Figure 5-26 describes the tools available on the toolbox. (*Note:* You'll learn about Control Wizards later in this tutorial.)

Figure 5-26		SUMMARY OF BUTTONS AVAILABLE ON THE TOOLBOX FOR A FORM OR REPORT	
BUTTON	**BUTTON NAME**	**PURPOSE ON A FORM OR A REPORT**	**CONTROL WIZARD AVAILABLE?**
	Bound Object Frame	Display a frame for enclosing a bound OLE object stored in an Access database table	Yes
	Check Box	Display a check box control bound to a yes/no field	Yes
	Combo Box	Display a control that combines the features of a list box and a text box; you can type in the text box or select an entry in the list box to add a value to an underlying field	Yes
	Command Button	Display a control button you can use to link to an action, such as finding a record, printing a record, or applying a form filter	Yes
	Control Wizards	Activate Control Wizards for certain other toolbox tools	No
	Image	Display a graphic image	Yes
	Label	Display text, such as title or instructions; an unbound control	No
	Line	Display a line	No
	List Box	Display a control that contains a scrollable list of values	Yes
	More Controls	Display a list of all available controls	No
	Option Button	Display an option button control bound to a yes/no field	Yes
	Option Group	Display a group frame containing toggle buttons, options buttons, or check boxes	Yes
	Page Break	Begin a new screen on a form or a new page on a report	No
	Rectangle	Display a rectangle	No
	Select Objects	Select, move, size, and edit controls	No
	Subform/Subreport	Display data from a related table	Yes
	Tab Control	Display a tab control with multiple pages	No
	Text Box	Display a label attached to a text box that contains a bound control or a calculated control	No
	Toggle Button	Display a toggle button control bound to a yes/no field	Yes
	Unbound Object Frame	Display a frame for enclosing an unbound OLE object, such as a Microsoft Excel spreadsheet	Yes

The Form window in Design view also contains a **Detail section**, which appears as a light gray rectangle. In this section, you place the fields, labels, and values for your form. You can change the size of the Detail section by dragging its edges. The **grid** consists of the dots that appear in the Detail section to help you position controls precisely on a form.

Rulers at the top and left edge of the Detail section define the horizontal and vertical dimensions of the form and serve as guides for placing controls on a form.

Your first task is to add bound controls to the Detail section for the EmployerID, EmployerName, ContactFirstName, ContactLastName, and Phone fields from the Employer table.

Adding Fields to a Form

When you add a bound control to a form, Access adds a text box and, to its left, a label. The text box displays the field values from the underlying table or query on which the form is based, and the label identifies the values. To create a bound control, you display the field list by clicking the Field List button on the Form Design toolbar. Then you select one or more fields from the field list and drag the fields to place them on the form. You select a single field by clicking that field. You select two or more fields by holding down the Ctrl key and clicking each field; you select all fields by double-clicking the field list title bar.

Next, you will add bound controls to the Detail section for five of the fields in the field list.

To add bound controls from the Employer table to the grid:

1. Click **EmployerID** in the field list, press and hold the **Ctrl** key, click (scrolling as necessary) **EmployerName**, **ContactFirstName**, **ContactLastName**, and **Phone** in the field list, and then release the **Ctrl** key. You selected all five fields.

2. Click one highlighted field and then drag it to the form's Detail section. Release the mouse button when the pointer is positioned at the 1.5-inch mark on the horizontal ruler and at the top of the Detail section. Access adds five bound controls—one for the each of the five selected fields in the Employer field list—in the Detail section of the form. See Figure 5-27.

| Figure 5-27 | ADDING TEXT BOXES AND ATTACHED LABELS AS BOUND CONTROLS TO A FORM |

TROUBLE? You do not need to place your controls in exactly the same position as the controls in Figure 5-27. However, you should place them in approximately the same position. If you did not position the bound controls properly in the Detail section, click the Undo button on the Form Design toolbar to delete the text boxes and labels from the Detail section. Then repeat Step 2 to add and position the bound controls.

3. Click the **Close** button ☒ on the field list to close it.

Comparing the form's Detail section with Elsa's design, notice that you need only three of the five labels, so you'll delete two labels.

4. Click the darker gray area outside the Detail section to deselect all controls.

5. Right-click the **EmployerName label** to select it, and then click **Cut** on the shortcut menu.

6. Repeat Step 5 to delete the **ContactLastName label**.

Working on a form in Design view might seem awkward at first. With practice you will become comfortable with creating a custom form. Remember that you can always click the Undo button one or more times immediately after you make one or more errors or make undesired form adjustments.

Comparing the form's Detail section with Elsa's design, notice that you need to arrange the labels and text boxes in two rows. To do so, you must select and move the controls.

Selecting and Moving Controls

Five text boxes now appear in the form's Detail section, one below the other. Each text box is a bound control linked to a field in the underlying table. Three text boxes have labels attached to their left. Each text box and each label is a control on the form. When you select a control, square boxes appear on its corners and edges. Called **sizing handles**, these boxes let you move or resize the control. The handle in a control's upper-left corner is its **move handle**, which you use to move the control.

> **REFERENCE WINDOW**   **RW**
>
> Selecting and Moving Controls
> - Click the control to select it. To select several controls at once, press and hold down the Shift key while clicking each control. Handles appear around all selected controls.
> - To move a single selected control, drag the control's move handle to its new position.
> - To move a group of selected controls, click any selected control (but do not click any of its handles), and then drag the group of selected controls to its new position.

For Elsa's custom form, you must select the EmployerID and ContactFirstName controls and move them to the far left edge of the Detail section. Each control consists of a field-value text box and a corresponding label to its left.

To select the EmployerID and ContactFirstName controls:

1. Hold down the **Shift** key, click the **EmployerID** text box, click the **ContactFirstName** text box, and then release the **Shift** key. Move handles, which are the larger handles, appear on the upper-left corners of the two selected text boxes and their attached labels. Sizing handles also appear, but only on the two text boxes. See Figure 5-28.

Figure 5-28	SELECTING TWO BOUND CONTROLS

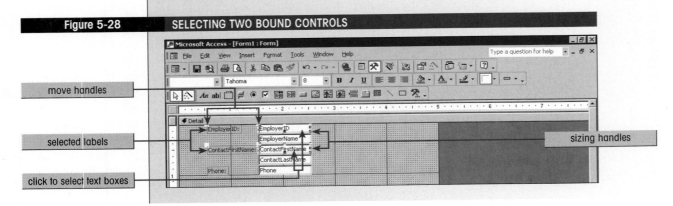

move handles

selected labels

sizing handles

click to select text boxes

You can move a text box and its attached label together. To move them, place the pointer anywhere on the border of the text box, but not on a move handle or a sizing handle. When the pointer changes to a ✋ shape, you can drag the text box and its attached label to the new location. As you move the controls, their outline moves to show you the changing position.

You can also move either the text box or its label individually. If you want to move the text box but not its label, for example, place the pointer on the text box's move handle. When the pointer changes to a ☝ shape, drag the text box to the new location. You use the label's move handle in a similar way to move just the label.

You'll now arrange the controls to match Elsa's design.

To rearrange the controls in the Detail section:

1. Position the pointer on the EmployerID text box, but not on a move handle or a sizing handle. When the pointer changes to a ✋ shape, drag the control as far left as you can, and then release the mouse button. When the EmployerID and ContactFirstName labels reach the left edge of the Detail section, you won't be able to move the labels and text boxes any further left. See Figure 5-29.

Figure 5-29	AFTER MOVING THE EmployerID AND ContactFirstName BOUND CONTROLS

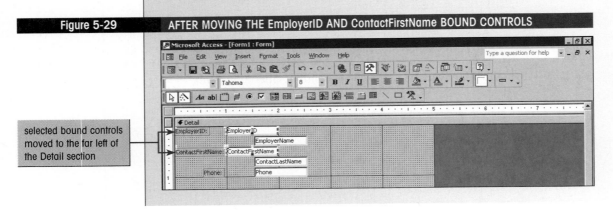

selected bound controls moved to the far left of the Detail section

Next, you'll move the EmployerName text box to the right of the EmployerID text box.

2. Click the **EmployerName** text box, and then position the pointer on its move handle. When the pointer changes to a 👆 shape, drag the control to the top of the Detail section, so its left edge is on the 2.125-inch mark on the horizontal ruler, and then release the mouse button.

TROUBLE? If other form controls moved with the EmployerName text box, these other controls were also selected when you moved the EmployerName text box. To return the controls to their original positions, click the Undo button 🔄 on the Form Design toolbar, and then click the gray area outside the Detail section to deselect all selected controls. Repeat Step 2 to move the EmployerName text box.

According to Elsa's design, the three labels should be captioned "Employer:", "Contact:", and "Phone:". Before you finish arranging the controls in the Detail section, you'll modify the label text. To change the label text, you'll change each label's caption.

Changing a Label's Caption

The text in a label on a form is defined by the column name used for the associated text box in the underlying table or query. If you want the label to display different text, you need to change the label's Caption property value.

REFERENCE WINDOW   **RW**

Changing a Label's Caption
- Right-click the label to select it and to display the shortcut menu, and then click Properties to display the property sheet.
- If necessary, click the All tab to display the All page of the property sheet.
- Edit the existing label in the Caption text box, or double-click the Caption text box to select the current value, and then type a new caption.
- Click the property sheet Close button to close it.

EmployerID, ContactFirstName, and Phone are the field names in the Employer table for the three bound controls in the report that still have attached labels. The "Phone:" label in the report matches Elsa's form design, but Elsa wants the other two labels to be "Employer:" and "Contact:", so you'll change the Caption property for these two labels.

To change the Caption property value for the two labels:

1. Right-click the **EmployerID label** to select it and to display the shortcut menu, and then click **Properties** on the shortcut menu. The property sheet for the EmployerID label opens.

2. If necessary, click the property sheet title bar and drag the property sheet down to the lower-right corner of your screen, so that all controls in the Detail section are visible.

3. If necessary, click the **All** tab to display all properties for the selected EmployerID label.

   TROUBLE? If you do not see the word "Label" on your title bar or if EmployerID: is not the Caption property value, then you selected the wrong control in Step 1. Click the EmployerID label to change to the property sheet for this control.

4. Position the insertion point between the "D" and the colon in EmployerID: in the Caption text box, and then press the **Backspace** key twice. The Caption property value should now be Employer:. See Figure 5-30.

Figure 5-30	CHANGING THE CAPTION PROPERTY FOR THE LABEL

Name property value

object type

property sheet

Object list box

Name property value

Caption property value

   TROUBLE? The property sheet title bar, the Object list box, and the Name property on your screen might have a value other than the one shown in Figure 5-30. Also, if your label's position slightly differs from the position shown in the figure, some property values on your screen, such as the Left and Top property values, might differ. These differences cause no problems.

   The property sheet title bar displays the object type (Label) and the Name property value (Label5—yours might differ). For most form controls, Access sets the Name property to the object type followed by a number; you can set the Name property to another value at any time.

5. Click the **ContactFirstName label** to select it. The property sheet now displays the properties for the ContactFirstName label, and the EmployerID label in the Detail section now displays Employer:.

6. Change the Caption property value for the label to **Contact:**.

7. Click the **Close** button ⊠ on the property sheet to close it. The ContactFirstName label in the Detail section now displays Contact:.

   As you create a form, you should periodically check your progress by displaying the form in Form view. You might find you want to make adjustments to your form in Design view. Next, you'll save the current form design and then view the form in Form view.

To save the form and switch to Form view:

1. Click the **Save** button 🖫 on the Form Design toolbar. The Save As dialog box opens.

2. Type **Employer Information Multi-page**, and then press the **Enter** key. Access saves the form in the Jobs database.

3. Click the **View** button for Form view 🖳 on the Form Design toolbar. Access closes the Form window in Design view and displays the form in Form view. See Figure 5-31.

| Figure 5-31 | FORM WINDOW IN FORM VIEW |

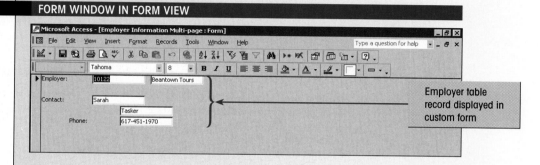

Access displays the EmployerID, EmployerName, ContactFirstName, ContactLastName, and Phone field values for the first record in the Employer table (Beantown Tours). You can use the navigation buttons to view other records from the table in the form.

4. Click the **Last Record** navigation button ▶❙ to view record 45 in the Employer table (Lighthouse Tours), and then click the **Previous Record** navigation button ◀ to view record 44 (Harbor Whale Watchers).

Form view reveals that you need to make some adjustments to the form design. The EmployerID, ContactFirstName, ContactLastName, and Phone text boxes are too large for the field values they contain; and the EmployerName text box is too small for the field value it contains. To correct these design problems, you will resize all five text boxes in Design view.

Resizing Controls

A selected control displays seven sizing handles: one on each side of the control and one at each corner except the upper-left corner. The upper-left corner displays the move handle. Positioning the pointer over a sizing handle changes the pointer to a two-headed arrow; the directions in which the arrows point indicate in which direction you can resize the selected control. When you drag a sizing handle, you resize the control. As you resize the control, a thin line appears between the sizing handle to guide you in completing the task accurately.

> **REFERENCE WINDOW** **RW**
>
> **Resizing a Control**
> - Click the control to select it and display the sizing handles.
> - Place the pointer over the sizing handle you want, and then drag the edge of the control until it is the size you want.

You'll begin by resizing the EmployerID text box, which is much larger than necessary to display the five-digit EmployerID field value. Then you'll resize the other four controls appropriately.

To resize the text boxes:

1. Switch to Design view, and then click the **EmployerID** text box to select it.

2. Place the pointer on the middle-right handle. When the pointer changes to a ←→ shape, drag the right border horizontally to the left until the text box is approximately the size shown in Figure 5-32.

   TROUBLE? If you accidentally change the vertical size of the text box, click the Undo button on the Form Design toolbar, and then repeat Step 2.

   Now you will move the EmployerName control to its correct position and then resize the EmployerName text box.

3. Click the **EmployerName** text box to select it. Place the pointer on the EmployerName text box, but not on a move handle or a sizing handle. When the pointer changes to a 🖐 shape, drag the control to the left until its left edge is at the 1.75-inch mark on the horizontal ruler.

4. Place the pointer on the middle-right handle of the EmployerName text box control. When the pointer changes to a ←→ shape, drag the right border horizontally to the right until the right edge of the text box is at the 3.75-inch mark on the horizontal ruler. See Figure 5-32.

| Figure 5-32 | EmployerID AND EmployerName CONTROLS MOVED AND RESIZED |

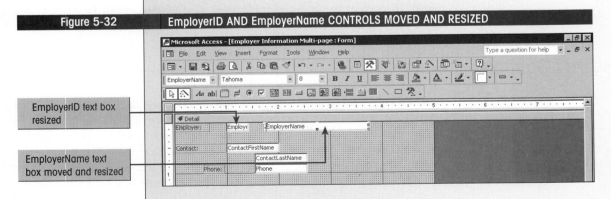

EmployerID text box resized

EmployerName text box moved and resized

Next, you'll move and resize the remaining controls on the form.

5. Select the **ContactFirstName** text box, move it and its attached label up until their top edges are at the 0.25-inch mark on the vertical ruler, and then drag the right edge of the ContactFirstName text box to the left until its right edge is at the 1.75-inch mark on the horizontal ruler. See Figure 5-33.

6. Select the **ContactLastName** text box, move it until its top edge is at the 0.25-inch mark on the vertical ruler and its left edge is at the 1.875-inch mark on the horizontal ruler, and then drag the right edge of the ContactLastName text box to the left until its right edge is at the 2.75-inch mark on the horizontal ruler. See Figure 5-33.

7. Select the **Phone** text box, and then move it and its attached label up until their top edges are at the 0.25-inch mark on the vertical ruler and the left edge of the label is at the 3-inch mark on the horizontal ruler. See Figure 5-33.

8. Place the pointer on the **Phone** text box move handle and, when the pointer changes to a 🖑 shape, drag the control to the left to the 3.5-inch mark on the horizontal ruler. Make sure the top edge of the control remains at the 0.25-inch mark on the vertical ruler. See Figure 5-33.

9. Resize the Phone text box by dragging its right edge to the left to the 4.25-inch mark on the horizontal ruler. See Figure 5-33.

Figure 5-33	AFTER MOVING AND RESIZING ALL CONTROLS

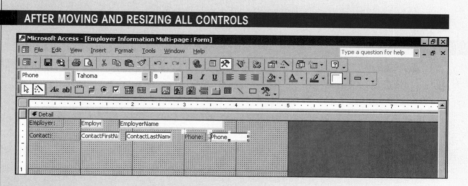

10. Save your design changes, and then switch to Form view to view the controls on the form. Navigate through the first several records, and notice that the text boxes are now the appropriate sizes for displaying the field values.

Now you will add the title and picture to the top of the form.

Using Form Headers and Form Footers

The Form Header and Form Footer sections let you add titles, instructions, command buttons, and other information to the top and bottom of your form, respectively. Controls placed in the Form Header or Form Footer sections remain on the screen whenever the form is displayed; they do not change when the contents of the Detail section change. To add either a header or footer to your form, you must first add both the Form Header and Form Footer sections as a pair to the Form window in Design view. If your form needs one of these sections but not the other, you can remove a section by setting its height to zero, which is the same method you would use to remove any form section.

REFERENCE   WINDOW   **RW**

Adding and Removing Form Header and Form Footer Sections

- Display the form in Design view.
- Click View on the menu bar, and then click Form Header/Footer to add a Form Header section and a Form Footer section to the form.
- To remove a Form Header or Form Footer section, drag its bottom edge up until the section area disappears.

Elsa's design includes a title and a picture at the top of the form. Because these two controls will not change as you navigate through the form records, you will add them to a Form Header section in the form.

To add Form Header and Form Footer sections to the form:

1. Switch to Design view.

2. Click **View** on the menu bar, and then click **Form Header/Footer**. Access inserts a Form Header section above the Detail section and a Form Footer section below the Detail section. See Figure 5-34.

| Figure 5-34 | ADDING THE FORM HEADER AND FORM FOOTER SECTIONS |

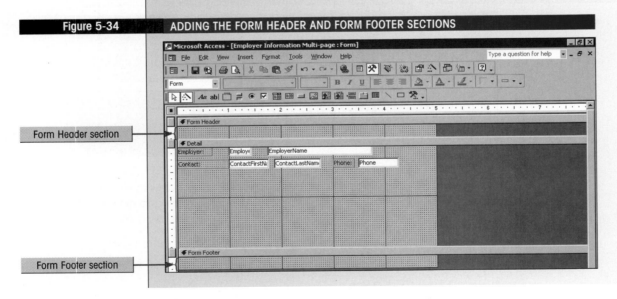

Elsa's form design does not include any items on the bottom of each form, so you don't need the Form Footer section. You'll remove it by changing its height to zero.

To remove the Form Footer section:

1. Place the pointer at the bottom edge of the Form Footer section. When the pointer changes to a ✛ shape, drag the bottom edge of the section up until it disappears. Even though the words "Form Footer" remain, the area defining the section is set to zero, so the section will not appear in the form. If a future form design change makes adding controls to the Form Footer section necessary, you can restore the section by using the pointer to drag its bottom edge back down.

You can now add the title to the Form Header section using the Label tool on the toolbox.

Adding a Label to a Form

The form design shows a title at the top of the form. You can add a title or other text to a form by using the Label tool on the toolbox.

REFERENCE WINDOW   **RW**

Adding a Label to a Form
- If necessary, click the Toolbox button on the Form Design toolbar to display the toolbox.
- Click the Label tool on the toolbox.
- Place the pointer at the position for the upper-left corner of the label.
- Click the mouse button. Access places a box in the form where the label will appear.
- Type the text for the label in the label box.
- Click anywhere outside the label box to deselect it.

You'll begin by placing a label box for the title in the Form Header section.

To place a label on the form:

1. Click the **Label** tool [Aa] on the toolbox.

2. Move the pointer to the Form Header section. The pointer changes to a ⁺A shape.

3. Position the center of the + portion of the pointer on the grid dot in the upper-left corner of the Form Header section. This is the location for the upper-left corner of the label.

4. Click the mouse button. Access inserts a small label box in the Form Header section and places the insertion point in the label box.

5. Type **NSJI Employer Information** in the label box, and then click anywhere outside the label box to deselect it. See Figure 5-35.

| Figure 5-35 | LABEL PLACED IN THE FORM HEADER SECTION |

Label tool

label added

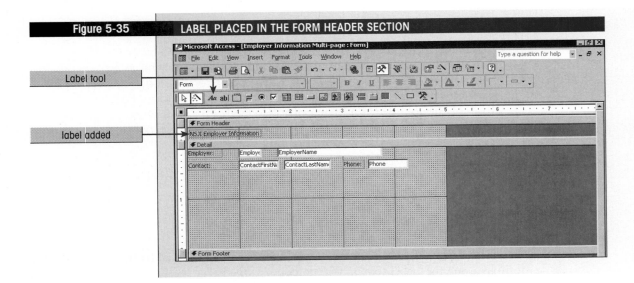

Elsa wants the title to be prominent on the form, so you will change the format of the label text to increase its font size and change its font weight to bold. You do this by using the buttons on the Formatting toolbar.

To change the font size and weight for the title:

1. Click the title label control to select it. Sizing handles appear on the control.

2. Click the **Font Size** list arrow on the Formatting toolbar, and then click **14**.

3. Click the **Bold** button **B** on the Formatting toolbar. See Figure 5-36.

| Figure 5-36 | SETTING THE PROPERTIES FOR THE TITLE LABEL CONTROL |

Bold button

label font size and weight changed

Font size list arrow

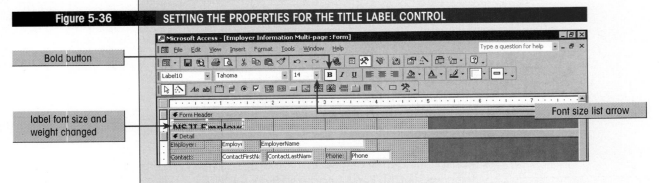

The label control now displays the title in 14-point, bold text. However, the label control is not large enough to display the entire title. You need to resize the label control so that it is large enough to display all the text. You could use the sizing handles to resize the label. However, using the Format menu is faster.

4. Click **Format** on the menu bar, point to **Size**, and then click **To Fit**. The resized label control displays the entire title. In addition, the Form Header's size automatically increased to accommodate the new label size. See Figure 5-37.

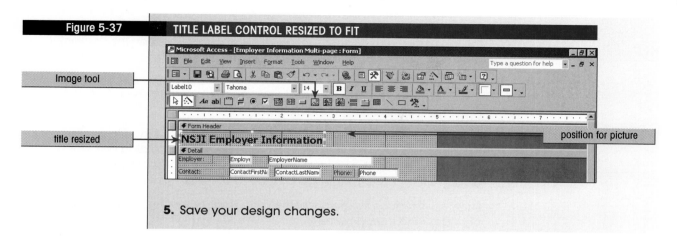

Figure 5-37 · **TITLE LABEL CONTROL RESIZED TO FIT**

Image tool

title resized

position for picture

5. Save your design changes.

Elsa also wants a picture at the top of the form. You will now add the picture to the Form Header section.

Adding a Picture to a Form

Access lets you use files and data created by other software programs. To enhance the appearance of a form or report, for example, you can include a picture or another graphic image on the form or report. To do so, you use the Image tool on the toolbox.

REFERENCE WINDOW   **RW**

Adding a Picture to a Form

- Display the form in Design view.
- If necessary, click the Toolbox button on the Form Design toolbar to display the toolbox.
- Click the Image tool on the toolbox.
- Place the pointer at the position for the upper-left corner of the picture.
- Click the mouse button. Access places an outline in the form and opens the Insert Picture dialog box.
- If necessary, use the Look in list box to locate the picture file you want.
- Click the name of the picture file, and then click the OK button.

Elsa's picture was created in a graphics program and saved in a file named Plane. Now you'll add this picture to the upper-right of the form.

To place the picture on the form:

1. Click the **Image** tool 🖾 on the toolbox.

2. Move the pointer to the Form Header section. The pointer changes to a ⁺🖾 shape.

3. Using the ruler as a guide, position the + portion of the pointer slightly below the top of the Form Header section, at the 3.25-inch mark on the horizontal ruler. (See Figure 5-37 for the correct position.) This is the location for the upper-left corner of the picture.

4. Click the mouse button. Access places an outline in the Form Header section and opens the Insert Picture dialog box.

5. Make sure **Tutorial** appears in the Look in list box, click **Plane** to select the picture file, and then click the **OK** button. The Insert Picture dialog box closes, and Access inserts the picture on the form. The Form Header section automatically enlarges to accommodate the image.

   Now, you'll reduce the height of the Form Header section, save your form changes, and then view the form.

6. Drag the bottom edge of the Form Header section up to the 0.875-inch mark on the vertical ruler.

7. Save your form changes, and then switch to Form view to view the form. See Figure 5-38.

| Figure 5-38 | VIEWING THE FORM WITH THE NEW HEADER |

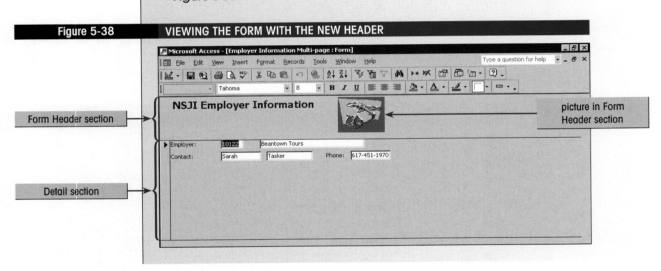

Elsa views the form and confirms that you correctly placed, formatted, and sized the title and picture. However, she wants you to change the background color of the form to dark teal to match the outline color of the picture, so that the picture will blend in better with the form.

Changing the Background Color of a Form Control

You can change the background color of a form or of a specific section or control on the form by using tools available in Design view.

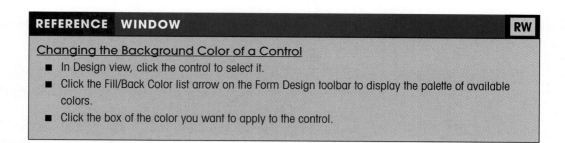

REFERENCE WINDOW   RW

Changing the Background Color of a Control
- In Design view, click the control to select it.
- Click the Fill/Back Color list arrow on the Form Design toolbar to display the palette of available colors.
- Click the box of the color you want to apply to the control.

You need to change the background color of the Form Header and Detail sections of the form to match the outline color of the picture. This will cause the picture to blend in with the form.

To change the background color of the Detail and Form Header sections:

1. Switch to Design view.

2. Click an empty area of the Detail section to make the Detail section the selected control.

3. Click the list arrow for the **Fill/Back Color** button 🎨 on the Formatting toolbar. Access displays the palette of available colors. See Figure 5-39.

Figure 5-39	CHANGING THE BACKGROUND COLOR OF THE FORM SECTIONS

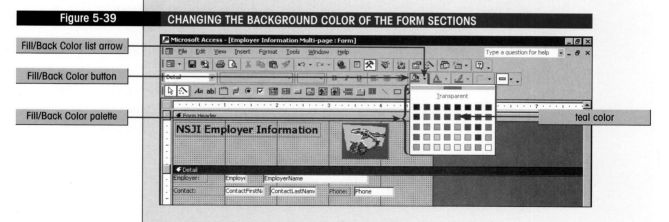

Fill/Back Color list arrow

Fill/Back Color button

Fill/Back Color palette

teal color

4. Click the **teal** box in the color palette, the box in row 2, column 5. (See Figure 5-39.) The background color of the Detail section changes to teal.

Now you need to apply the same color to the Form Header section. To do so, you do not have to redisplay the color palette; once you select a color from the palette, you can apply the color to other objects by simply clicking the Fill/Back Color button.

5. Click an empty area of the Form Header section to make the Form Header section the selected control.

6. Click the **Fill/Back Color** button 🎨 (not the list arrow) on the Formatting toolbar. The Form Header section now appears with the teal background.

Now you can save the form and view your changes in Form view.

7. Save your design changes, and then switch to Form view to view the form. See Figure 5-40.

Figure 5-40   FORM WITH NEW BACKGROUND COLOR

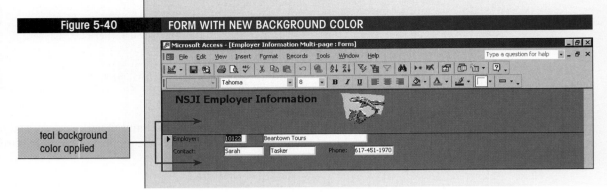

teal background
color applied

In the next session, you will add the two pages to the form to display employer address and miscellaneous information on one page and the position information on the other.

Session 5.2 QUICK CHECK

1. What is the difference between a bound control and an unbound control?

2. The _____ consists of the dots that appear in the Detail section to help you position controls precisely on a form.

3. The _____ is a specialized toolbar containing buttons that represent the tools you use to place controls on a form or a report.

4. The handle in an object's upper-left corner is the _____ handle.

5. How do you move a selected control and its label at the same time?

6. How do you change a label's caption?

7. How do you resize a control?

8. What is the Form Header section?

9. How do you add a picture created using another software program to a form?

SESSION 5.3

In this session, you will create a multi-page form and use Control Wizards to add a subform. You will also use the custom form to filter the data and save the filter as a query.

Creating a Multi-page Form Using Tab Controls

You can create a multi-page form in two ways: by inserting a page break control in the form or by using a tab control. If you insert a page break control in a form, the user can move between pages by pressing the Page Up and Page Down keys. If you use a tab control, the control appears with tabs at the top, with one tab for each page. The user can switch between pages by clicking the tabs.

Elsa wants to include a tab control with two pages on the Employer Information Multi-page form. The first page of the tab control will contain employer information, such as the employer address from the Employer table. The second page of the tab control will contain a subform with position information for that employer.

First, you will resize the Detail section of the form to make room for the tab control.

To resize the Detail section:

1. If you took a break after the previous session, make sure that Access is running, that the **Jobs** database from the Tutorial folder on your Data Disk is open, that the **Employer Information Multi-page** form is open in Form view, and that the window is maximized.

2. Switch to Design view.

3. Place the pointer on the right edge of the Detail section. When the pointer changes to a ◀▶ shape, drag the section's edge to the right until it is at the 6.5-inch mark on the horizontal ruler.

Now you can place the tab control on the form.

To place the tab control on the form:

1. Click the **Tab Control** tool 🔲 on the toolbox.

2. Position the + portion of the pointer at the left edge of the Detail section, approximately 0.5-inch below the top of the Detail section, and then click the mouse button. (Refer to Figure 5-41 for the correct position of the tab control.) Access places a tab control in the Detail section.

   Now you will resize the tab control so that it is wide enough to display the remaining fields for the form.

3. Drag the middle-right sizing handle of the tab control to the right until it is three grid dots from the right edge of the form. See Figure 5-41.

Figure 5-41	TAB CONTROL PLACED IN THE DETAIL SECTION AND RESIZED

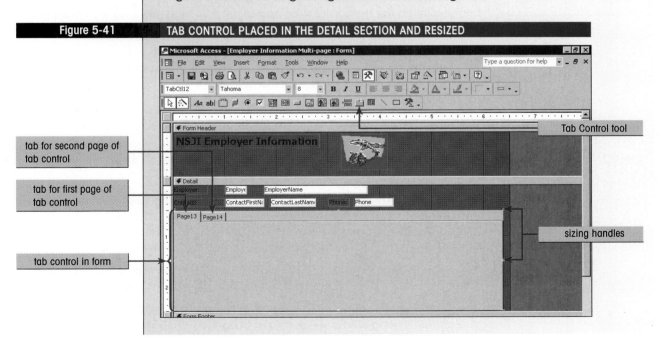

tab for second page of tab control

tab for first page of tab control

tab control in form

Tab Control tool

sizing handles

TROUBLE? The page tabs on your screen might show different page numbers in the labels, depending on how you completed the previous steps. This does not affect the form. Just continue with the tutorial.

The top of the tab control displays two tabs. Each tab indicates a separate page on the form. On the first page, you will place the controls for the fields from the Employer table. On the second page, you will place a subform displaying the fields from the Position table for that employer. The user can move between the two pages by clicking the tabs.

First, you'll add the fields from the Employer table to the first page of the tab control.

To add the fields from the Employer table to the tab control:

1. Click the **Field List** button 🗐 on the Form Design toolbar to display the field list.

2. Click the **Address** field in the field list, scroll to the end of the field list, press and hold down the **Shift** key, click the **Comments** field, and then release the **Shift** key. You selected all fields in the list, except EmployerID and EmployerName.

   The ContactFirstName, ContactLastName, and Phone fields are already in the form, so you'll remove these three fields from your selection.

3. Press and hold down the **Ctrl** key, click the **ContactFirstName** field, click the **ContactLastName** field, click the **Phone** field, and then release the **Ctrl** key.

   Next, you'll drag the selected fields to the first page of the tab control. When you drag the fields over the central portion of the tab control, the central portion changes color and the area near the borders remains gray; as you drag the fields near a tab control border, the entire tab control turns gray again. The area that changes color shows you where you can release the mouse button to make sure the bound controls fit within the tab control.

4. Drag the selected fields to the tab control, and release the mouse button when the tab control changes color and when the pointer is approximately at the 1-inch mark on the horizontal ruler and at the 0.75-inch mark on the vertical ruler, making sure the pointer is still positioned in the area that changes color.

   Text boxes for the selected fields are added in a column to the tab control with each text box's associated label to its left. To fit all the added bound controls to the tab control, Access increased the height of the tab control at its bottom automatically.

5. Close the field list, and then click a blank area of the tab control to deselect the bound controls.

   Now you need to move and resize the controls to match Elsa's form design.

6. Click the **NAICSDesc** text box to select it, and then position the pointer on one of its borders. When the pointer changes to a 🖑 shape, drag the bound control up and to the right until the left edge of the outline is at the 3-inch mark on the horizontal ruler and the top edge is at the 1.5-inch mark on the vertical ruler. Refer to Figure 5-42 for help in positioning the bound control.

   Next, you'll resize the NAICSDesc text box and align the top of the NAICSDesc bound control with the top of the PostalCode bound control.

7. Place the pointer on the middle-right handle of the **NAICSDesc** text box. When the pointer changes to a ←→ shape, drag the right border to the right until the right edge of the text box is at the 5.75-inch mark on the horizontal ruler.

8. Press and hold down the **Shift** key, click the **PostalCode** text box, click the **NAICSDesc label** (the PostalCode text box and the NAICSDesc text box and label should all have handles on their borders), click the **PostalCode** label, release the **Shift** key, click **Format** on the menu bar, point to **Align**, and then click **Top**. You aligned the top edges of the two bound controls.

   TROUBLE? If the NAICSDesc label is not aligned with the other three controls, deselect all controls, select the NAICSDesc label and the PostalCode label, click Format on the menu bar, point to Align, and then click Top.

   All the labels, except the WebSite label, have colons, so you'll add the colon to its caption, and then resize the label to fit.

9. Open the property sheet for the **WebSite label**, add a colon at the end of the control's Caption property, close the property sheet, and then size the control to fit.

   Unlike the other labels, the WebSite label is to the right of its associated text box, so you'll move the two WebSite controls independently.

10. Make sure the WebSite label is still selected, and then position the pointer on its move handle in the upper-left corner. When the pointer changes to a 🖑 shape, drag the label above the NAICSDesc label, align their left edges, and then align the bottom edges of the WebSite and State/Prov labels. (See Figure 5-42.)

11. Click the **WebSite** text box, move the control above the NAICSDesc text box, align the two controls on their left edges, and then align the top edges of the WebSite label and the WebSite text box. (See Figure 5-42.)

12. Move, resize, and align the remaining controls. Use Figure 5-42 as a guide for positioning, sizing, and aligning the controls. Make sure to use the Align command on the Format menu to position pairs or larger groups of controls, aligning the controls on their top, left, or other edges.

| Figure 5-42 | EMPLOYER FIELDS PLACED IN THE TAB CONTROL |

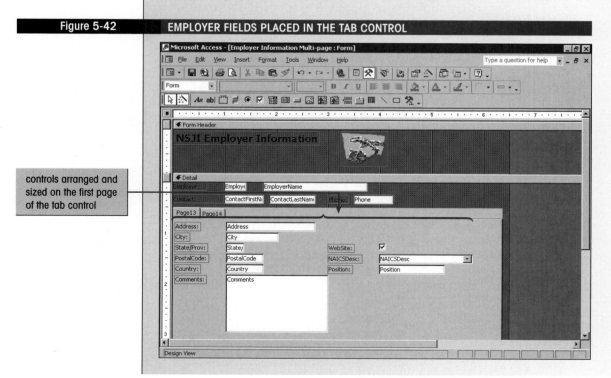

controls arranged and sized on the first page of the tab control

TROUBLE? You do not have to position your controls exactly where the controls appear in Figure 5-42. However, you should place them in approximately the same position. If you placed the controls incorrectly, move, resize, and align them now.

Elsa refers back to her form design and identifies two more changes. The Position label needs its Caption property changed to "ContactPosition:". Also, you must size the Employer and Contact labels above the tab control to fit and then move them to the right so that they are closer to their associated text boxes. Finally, Elsa's design shows these labels as right-aligned. To align them, you will select all labels in a column and use the shortcut menu.

REFERENCE WINDOW **RW**

Aligning Controls on a Form
- Select the objects you want to align.
- Right-click any one of the selected controls to display the shortcut menu.
- Point to Align, and then click the alignment you want.

Now you can change the Position label's Caption property and then resize, move, and align the two labels above the tab control.

To change the Caption property and then resize, move, and right-align the labels:

1. Open the property sheet for the **Position label**, set the Caption property to **ContactPosition:**, close the property sheet, and then size the control to fit.

2. Deselect all controls, press and hold down the **Shift** key, click the **Employer label**, click the **Contact label**, release the **Shift** key, and then size both controls to fit.

3. Place the pointer on the Employer label's move handle in the upper-left corner. When the pointer changes to a ✋ shape, drag the **Employer label** to the right until its left edge is at the 0.375-inch mark on the horizontal ruler. Refer to Figure 5-43 for help in positioning the label.

4. Make sure the Employer and Contact labels are still selected, and then right-click either of the selected label boxes to display the shortcut menu.

5. Point to **Align**, and then click **Right**. Access aligns the right edges of the label boxes. See Figure 5-43.

Figure 5-43   SIZING AND ALIGNING LABEL BOXES

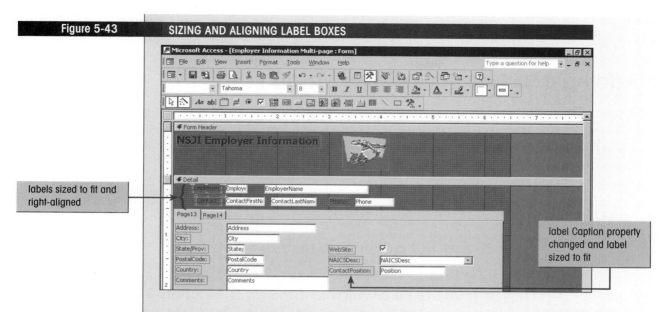

labels sized to fit and right-aligned

label Caption property changed and label sized to fit

TROUBLE? If the text boxes also were aligned, click the Undo button [↶] on the Form Design toolbar, make sure that you select only the Employer and Contact labels (and that no other controls have sizing handles), and then repeat Steps 4 and 5.

6. Save your design changes, and then switch to Form view to view the form. See Figure 5-44.

Figure 5-44   FIRST RECORD IN FORM VIEW

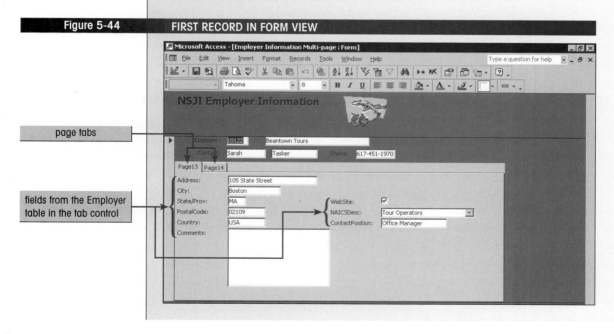

page tabs

fields from the Employer table in the tab control

You are now ready to add the Position table fields as a subform on the second page of the tab control.

Adding a Subform Using Control Wizards

You use the Subform/Subreport tool on the toolbox to add a subform to a form. If you want help when defining the subform, you can select one of the Access Control Wizards. A **Control Wizard** asks a series of questions and then uses your answers to create a control on a form or report. Access offers Control Wizards for the Combo Box, List Box, Option Group, Command Button, and Subform/Subreport tools, among others.

You will use the Subform/Subreport Wizard to add the subform for the Position table records to the second page of the tab control.

To add the subform to the tab control:

1. Switch to Design view.

2. Make sure the **Control Wizards** tool on the toolbox is selected.

3. Click the tab for the second page (the tab on the right) to select it.

4. Click the **Subform/Subreport** tool on the toolbox.

5. Position the + portion of the pointer near the upper-left corner of the tab control, just below the 1-inch mark on the vertical ruler and at the 0.5-inch mark on the horizontal ruler, and then click the mouse button. Access places a subform control in the tab control and opens the first SubForm Wizard dialog box.

You can use an existing table, query, or form as the source for a new subform. You'll use the Position table as the basis for the new subform.

To use the SubForm Wizard to add the subform to the form:

1. Make sure the **Use existing Tables and Queries** option button is selected, and then click the **Next** button. Access opens the next SubForm Wizard dialog box. This dialog box lets you select a table or query as the basis for the subform and then select the fields from that table or query.

2. Click the **Tables/Queries** list arrow to display the list of tables and queries in the Jobs database, and then click **Table: Position**. The Available Fields list box shows the fields in the Position table. See Figure 5-45.

| Figure 5-45 | SELECTING THE TABLE AND FIELDS FOR THE SUBFORM |

Elsa's design includes all fields from the Position table in the subform, except the EmployerID field, which is already placed on the form from the Employer table.

3. Click the >> button to move all available fields to the Selected Fields list box, click **EmployerID** in the Selected Fields list box, click the < button, and then click the **Next** button. See Figure 5-46.

| Figure 5-46 | SELECTING THE LINKING FIELD |

This dialog box lets you select the link between the Employer table and the Position table. EmployerID, as the common field between the two tables, links the two tables. Access uses the EmployerID field to display a record in the main form, which displays data from the Employer table, and to select and display the related records for that employer in the subform, which displays data from the Position table.

4. Make sure the **Choose from a list** option button is selected and that the first link is highlighted, and then click the **Next** button. The next SubForm Wizard dialog box lets you specify a name for the subform.

5. Type **Employer Information Subform** and then click the **Finish** button. Access inserts a subform object in the tab control. This is where the Position records will appear.

6. Maximize the Form window, and then close the field list.

7. Save your form changes, and then switch to Form view.

    The tab control shows the employer information on the first page. You can view the position information for the employer by clicking the second page tab.

8. Click the page tab on the right to display the position information. The subform displays the position data in a datasheet. See Figure 5-47.

| Figure 5-47 | VIEWING THE SUBFORM ON THE TAB CONTROL |

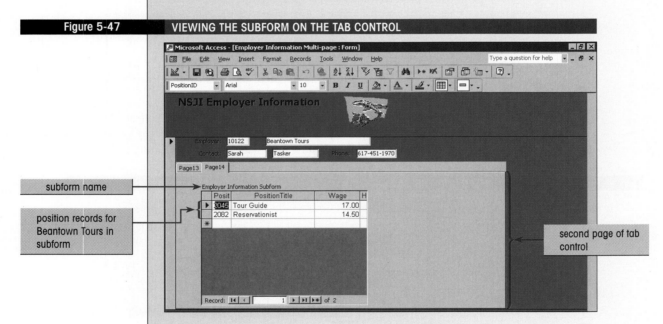

subform name

position records for Beantown Tours in subform

second page of tab control

TROUBLE? If the size of the columns in your datasheet differs, don't worry. You'll resize all columns to their best fit later.

After viewing the form, Elsa identifies several modifications she wants you to make. The subform is not properly sized and the columns in the subform are not sized to their best fit. She wants you to resize the subform and its columns, so that the columns are entirely visible. Also, she asks you to delete the Employer Information Subform label and to edit the labels for the tabs in the tab control, so that they indicate the contents of each page.

You can resize the subform and edit the labels in Design view. Then you can resize the subform columns in Form view. You'll begin by resizing the subform and editing the labels in Design view.

To resize the subform, delete its label, and edit the labels for the tabs:

1. Switch to Design view. Notice that in Design view, the subform data does not appear in a datasheet as it does in Form view. That difference causes no problem; you should ignore it.

2. If necessary, scroll down until you see the bottom of the subform. If necessary, click the right tab to select it.

   If you click a tab, you select the tab control, and sizing handles appear on its edges. If you want to select a subform positioned in a tab control, you should click the right or bottom edge of the subform; sizing handles disappear from the tab control and appear on the edges of the subform, indicating that it's selected.

3. Select and then resize the subform on the right and left, so that the subform extends horizontally from the 0.25-inch mark to the 6.25-inch mark on the horizontal ruler. Then drag the bottom of the subform up to the 3-inch mark on the vertical ruler.

4. Click anywhere in the light gray area of the tab control to deselect the subform, right-click the label for the subform control (make sure the subform no longer has sizing handles), and then click **Cut** on the shortcut menu to delete the label.

   Next, you'll change the labels on the tabs. To do so, you need to set the Caption property for each tab.

5. Right-click the subform page tab, and then click **Properties** on the shortcut menu to open the property sheet.

6. Click the **All** tab (if necessary), and then type **Positions** in the Caption text box. See Figure 5-48.

Figure 5-48	SETTING THE CAPTION PROPERTY VALUE FOR THE PAGE TAB

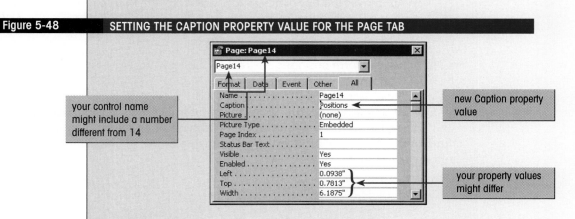

your control name might include a number different from 14

new Caption property value

your property values might differ

7. Click the page tab on the left, set the Caption property to **Employer Information**, and then close the property sheet.

Now you can view the form, and then resize the columns in the subform.

To view the form and resize the columns in the subform:

1. Switch to Form view, and then click the **Positions** tab. The second page of the multi-page form displays the Position table records for Beantown Tours.

   Before you resize the columns in the Positions subform, you'll change the font size in the subform datasheet.

2. Make sure the PositionID field in the datasheet is the current field, and then change the font size to **9**. All text in the datasheet changes to Arial 9.

3. Resize all datasheet columns to their best fit. The form is complete. See Figure 5-49.

Figure 5-49	POSITION COLUMNS AFTER RESIZING

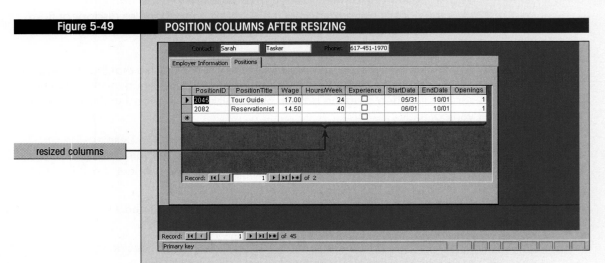

resized columns

4. Practice navigating through the Employer and Position table records using the form. When you finish, click the **Employer Information** tab, and then click the main form's **First Record** navigation button ◄ to display the employer information for Beantown Tours.

   Now you can save the completed form.

5. Save your form changes.

Elsa has a new request. She wants to see information for all employers in Massachusetts and Rhode Island that are tour operators. She wants to view this information using the Employer Information Multi-page form. To display the results she wants, you need to use a filter with the form.

Using a Filter with a Form

Recall that a **filter** is a set of criteria that describes the records you want to see, in a datasheet or a form, and their sequence. A filter is like a query, but it applies only to the current datasheet or form. If you want to use a filter at another time, you can save the filter as a query.

Four filter tools let you specify and apply filters: Filter By Selection, Filter By Form, Filter For Input, and Advanced Filter/Sort. With Filter By Selection, Filter By Form, and Filter For Input, you specify the record selection criteria directly in the form. **Filter By Selection** finds records that match a particular field value or a portion of a field value. **Filter By Form** and **Filter For Input** find records that match multiple selection criteria using the same Access logical and comparison operators used in queries. After applying a filter by selection or by form or for input, you can use the Sort Ascending or Sort Descending toolbar buttons to rearrange the records, if necessary.

Advanced Filter/Sort lets you specify multiple selection criteria and specify a sort order for selected records in the Advanced Filter/Sort window, in the same way you specify record selection criteria and sort orders for a query in Design view.

To produce the results Elsa wants, you'll use Filter By Form.

Using Filter By Form

Because the Employer Information Multi-page form already shows all the employer information, you can use Filter By Form to display information for only employers in Massachusetts and Rhode Island that are tour operators.

REFERENCE WINDOW   **RW**

Selecting Records Using Filter By Form
- Open the form in Form view.
- Click the Filter By Form button on the Form View toolbar.
- Enter a simple selection criterion or an And condition in the first form, using the text boxes for the appropriate fields.
- If there is an Or condition, click the Or tab and enter the Or condition in the second form. Continue to enter Or conditions on separate forms by using the Or tab.
- Click the Apply Filter button on the Filter/Sort toolbar.

To answer Elsa's question, the multiple selection criteria you will enter are: Massachusetts *and* Tour Operators *or* Rhode Island *and* Tour Operators.

To select the records using Filter By Form:

1. Click the **Filter By Form** button 🔳 on the Form View toolbar. Access displays a blank form. See Figure 5-50.

Figure 5-50	BLANK FORM FOR FILTER BY FORM

Clear Grid button

Or tab

enter selection criteria for first And condition on blank form

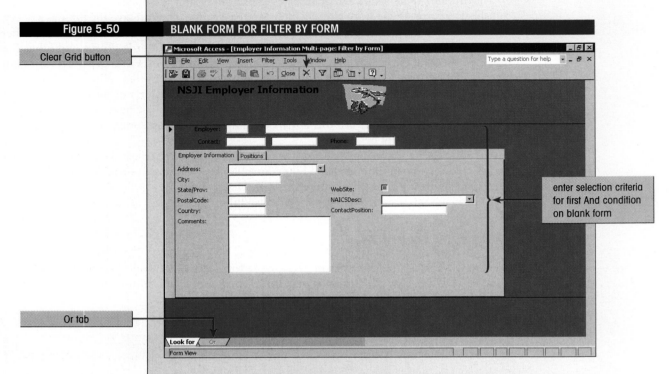

On this blank form, you specify multiple selection criteria by entering conditions in the text boxes for the fields in a record. If you enter criteria in more than one field, you create the equivalent of an And condition—Access selects any record that matches all criteria. To create an Or condition, you enter the criteria for the first part of the condition in the field on the first (Look for) blank form, and then click the Or tab to display a new blank form. You enter the criteria for the second part of the condition on the "Or" blank form. Access selects any record that matches all criteria on the Look for form *or* all criteria on the Or form.

2. Click the **State/Prov** text box, click the list arrow that appears, and then click **MA**. Access adds the criterion "MA" to the State/Prov text box.

3. Click the **NAICSDesc** list arrow, and then click **Tour Operators**. Access adds the criterion "Tour Operators" to the NAICSDesc text box.

   You specified the logical operator (And) for the condition "Massachusetts and Tour Operators." To add the rest of the criteria, you need to display the Or form.

4. Click the **Or** tab to display a second blank form. The insertion point is in the text box for the NAICSDesc field. Notice that a third tab, also labeled "Or," is now available in case you need to specify another Or condition.

5. Click the **NAICSDesc** list arrow, and then click **Tour Operators**.

6. Click the **State/Prov** text box, click the list arrow, and then click **RI**. The form now contains the second And condition: "Rhode Island and Tour Operators." See Figure 5-51.

Figure 5-51	COMPLETED FILTER BY FORM

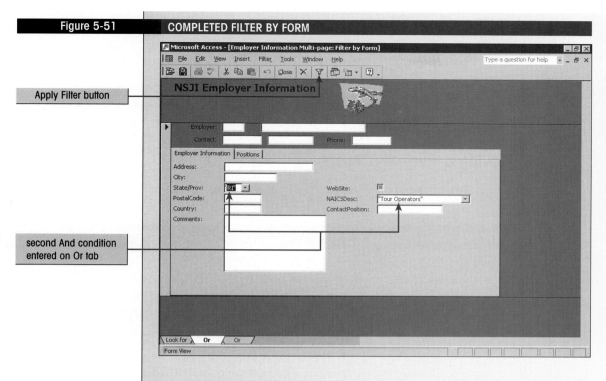

Apply Filter button

second And condition
entered on Or tab

Combined with the Look for form, you now have the Or condition, and the complete Filter By Form conditions.

7. Click the **Apply Filter** button on the Filter/Sort toolbar. Access applies the filter and displays the first record that matches the selection criteria (Beantown Tours, a tour operator in Massachusetts). The bottom of the screen shows that the filter selected six records. See Figure 5-52.

Figure 5-52	FIRST RECORD THAT MATCHES THE SELECTION CRITERIA

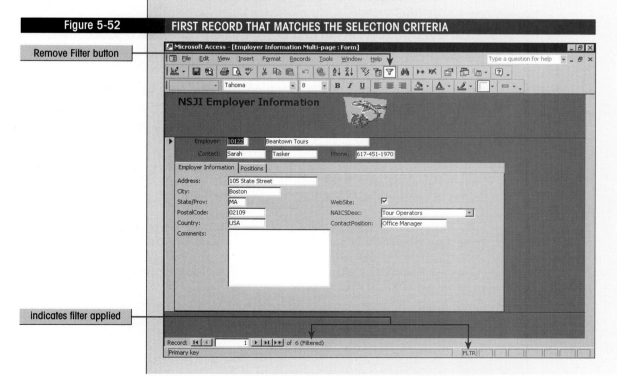

Remove Filter button

indicates filter applied

8. Click the main form's **Next Record** navigation button ▶ to display the second selected record (Newport Mansion Guided Tours, a tour operator in Rhode Island).

Now that you defined the filter, you can save it as a query, so that Elsa can easily view this information in the future.

Saving a Filter as a Query

By saving a filter as a query, you can reuse the filter in the future by opening the saved query.

REFERENCE WINDOW	RW

Saving a Filter as a Query

- Create a filter using Filter By Selection, Filter By Form, Filter For Input, or Advanced Filter/Sort.
- Click the Save As Query button on the Filter/Sort toolbar to open the Save As Query dialog box.
- Type the name for the query, and then press the Enter key (or click the OK button).

Next, you'll save the filter you just created as a query named "Tour Operators in MA and RI."

To close the Form window and view the query list:

1. Click the **Filter By Form** button 🗐 on the Form View toolbar. Access displays the form with the selection criteria.

2. Click the **Save As Query** button 🖫 on the Filter/Sort toolbar. The Save As Query dialog box opens.

3. Type **Tour Operators in MA and RI** in the Query Name text box, and then press the **Enter** key. Access saves the filter as a query in the Jobs database and closes the dialog box.

Now you can clear the selection criteria, close the Filter by Form window, and return to Form view.

4. Click the **Clear Grid** button ⊠ on the Filter/Sort toolbar. Access removes the selection criteria from the forms.

5. Click the **Close Window** button ⊠ on the menu bar to close the Filter by Form window and return to Form view. The filter is still in effect in this window, so you need to remove it.

TROUBLE? If a dialog box opens and asks if you want to save your form changes, click the Yes button.

6. Click the **Remove Filter** button ▽ on the Form View toolbar. The bottom of the screen shows that 45 records are available.

Next, to check that you saved the filter as a query, you'll close the Form window and view the list of queries on the Queries tab.

To close the Form window and view the query list:

1. Click the **Close Window** button ⊠ on the menu bar.

2. Click **Queries** in the Objects bar of the Database window to display the Queries list box. The query "Tour Operators in MA and RI" is now listed.

The next time Elsa wants to view the records selected by this query, she can apply the query to the form. If she simply runs the query, she will see the selected records, but they will not be shown in the Employer Information Multi-page form. Instead, she can open the form and apply the saved query to select the records she wants to view in the form.

Applying a Filter Saved as a Query

To see how to apply a query as a filter to a form, you will open the Employer Information Multi-page form and apply the Tour Operators in MA and RI query as a filter.

REFERENCE WINDOW   **RW**

Applying a Filter Saved as a Query

- Open the form to which you want to apply the filter.
- Click the Filter By Form button on the Form View toolbar.
- Click the Load from Query button on the Filter/Sort toolbar.
- Select the query you want to apply. Access loads the saved query into the Filter by Form window.
- Click the Apply Filter button on the Filter/Sort toolbar.

Now you'll open the Employer Information Multi-page form and apply the Tour Operators in MA and RI query as a filter.

To apply the filter saved as a query:

1. Open the **Employer Information Multi-page** form in Form view.

2. Click the **Filter By Form** button 🖼 on the Form View toolbar.

   TROUBLE? If your Filter by Form window already has the filter applied, skip to Step 5.

3. Click the **Load from Query** button 🖼 on the Filter/Sort toolbar. Access opens the Applicable Filter dialog box. See Figure 5-53.

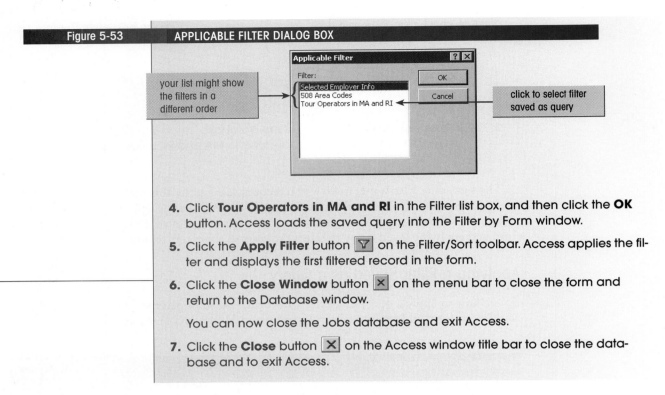

Figure 5-53 | APPLICABLE FILTER DIALOG BOX

your list might show the filters in a different order

click to select filter saved as query

4. Click **Tour Operators in MA and RI** in the Filter list box, and then click the **OK** button. Access loads the saved query into the Filter by Form window.

5. Click the **Apply Filter** button on the Filter/Sort toolbar. Access applies the filter and displays the first filtered record in the form.

6. Click the **Close Window** button on the menu bar to close the form and return to the Database window.

   You can now close the Jobs database and exit Access.

7. Click the **Close** button on the Access window title bar to close the database and to exit Access.

The design changes you made to the Employer table and the new queries and form that you created will make it much easier for Elsa, Matt, and Zack to enter, retrieve, and view information in the Jobs database.

Session 5.3 QUICK CHECK

1. Describe how you would use a Control Wizard to add a tab control to a form.

2. How do you align a group of labels?

3. What is the purpose of Filter By Form?

4. How do you reuse a filter?

5. What is the difference between opening a query and applying a query to a form?

REVIEW ASSIGNMENTS

The **Students** database contains information about NSJI's recruiters and overseas students. The **Recruiter** table in the database contains records of the recruiters employed by NSJI to find students for seasonal work and match them with NSJI's client employers. The **Student** table contains student information. The database contains several other objects, including queries, forms, and reports. Elsa wants you to make changes to the design of the **Student** table, create some new queries, and create a custom form. Complete the following:

1. Make sure your Data Disk is in the appropriate disk drive, start Access, and then open the **Students** database in the Review folder on your Data Disk.

2. Open the **Student** table in Design view. Change the SSN field data type to Lookup Wizard. Look up values in the **Recruiter** table; select the SSN, FirstName, and LastName fields from the **Recruiter** table; use the label RecruiterName; and accept all other Lookup Wizard default choices. View the **Student** table datasheet, resize the RecruiterName column to its best fit, and then save and close the table.

3. Define data validation criteria for the Gender field in the **Student** table. Acceptable field values for the Gender field are F and M. Use the message, "Value must be F or M", to notify a user who enters an invalid Gender field value. Save your table changes, test the data validation criteria for the Gender field, and verify that the Lookup Wizard feature of the RecruiterName field works properly. Make sure the field values are the same as they were before you tested.

4. Modify the first record in the **Student** table datasheet by changing the FirstName, LastName, BirthDate, and Gender field values to your name, birth date, and gender. Close the table.

5. Use the Input Mask Wizard to add an input mask to the SSN field in the **Recruiter** table. Select the Social Security Number input mask, and then click the Finish button. Change the default input mask to 000\-00\-0000. Test the input mask by typing over an existing SSN field value, being sure not to change the value by pressing the Esc key after you type the last digit in the SSN field. Close the table.

6. Create a query to find all records in the **Student** table in which the Nation field value starts with either the letter A or the letter I. Include all fields in the query results. Save the query as **Students from Selected Countries**, run the query, and then print the query results. Keep the query open.

Explore

7. Modify the query you created in Step 6. Use the modified query to find all records in the **Student** table in which the Nation field value starts with neither the letter A nor the letter S. Save the query as **Students from Selected Countries Modified**, run the query, print the query results, and then close the query.

8. Create a query to find all records from the **Recruiter** table in which the BonusQuota field value is 40, 50, or 60. Use a list-of-values match for the selection criteria. Include all fields in the query results. Save the query as **Selected Bonus Quotas**, run the query, print the query results, and then close the query.

9. Create a query to select all records in the **Student** table for females from Australia or Germany. Display the FirstName, LastName, City, Nation, and Gender fields in the query results. Sort the query in ascending order by LastName. Save the query as **Females from Australia or Germany**, run the query, print the query results, and then close the query.

10. Create a parameter query to select the **Student** table records for a Nation field value that the user specifies. Include all fields in the query results. Save the query as **Nation Parameter**. Run the query and enter Ireland as the Nation field value. Print the query results and then close the query.

11. Use Figure 5-54 and the following steps to create a multi-page form based on the **Recruiter** and **Student** tables.

Figure 5-54

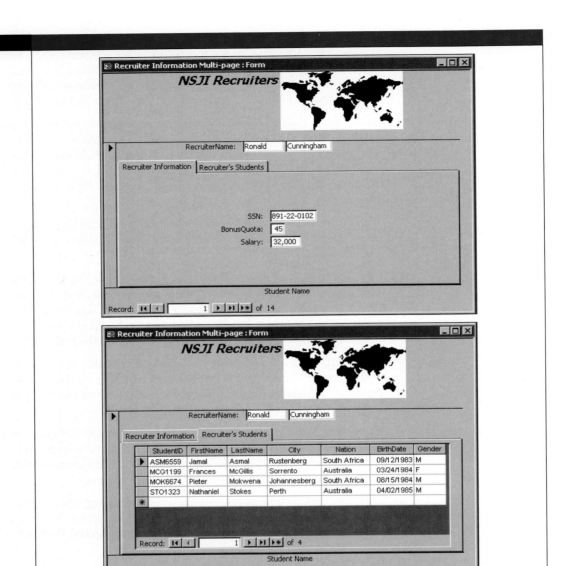

a. Place the FirstName and LastName fields from the **Recruiter** table at the top of the Detail section. Delete the LastName label and change the caption for the FirstName label to RecruiterName:.

b. Insert a Form Header section and a Form Footer section in the form. Place a title label in the Form Header section. Enter the title NSJI Recruiters, and change its font to 14-point bold italic.

c. Place the **WorldMap** picture in the Form Header section to the right of the title. The file containing this picture is in the Review folder on your Data Disk.

d. Place a label in the Form Footer section, and type your name in the label.

e. Place a tab control below the Recruiter Name label in the Detail section. On the first page of the tab control, place the remaining fields from the **Recruiter** table. Set the Caption property for each label, align the labels on the right, and move them closer to the text boxes. Resize the text boxes to appropriate widths.

f. On the second page of the tab control, place a subform based on the **Student** table, include all fields from the table in the subform, and use SSN as the link field. Save the subform as **NSJI Student Subform**.

g. Change the Caption property for each tab, and delete the subform label.

h. Resize the form, the tab control, and the subform. You might need to resize one or more of these controls again as you complete the remaining steps.

Explore

i. In Form view, hide the RecruiterName column in the subform datasheet.

j. In Form view, change the text in the subform datasheet to 8 points, and then resize all datasheet columns to their best fit.

k. Save the form as **Recruiter Information Multi-page**.

l. View the form, and then print both pages for record 10. (*Hint:* Print the selected record after selecting one tab, and then repeat the procedure for the other tab.)

12. Use Filter By Form with the **Recruiter Information Multi-page** form to select all records in which the bonus quota is 40 and the salary is either 28,500 or 29,000. Apply the filter. How many records are selected?

13. Print the first page of the first selected record. Save the filter as a query named **Recruiter Information Multi-page Filter**. Close the filter and then close the form.

14. Close the **Students** database, and then exit Access.

CASE PROBLEMS

Case 1. Lim's Video Photography Youngho Lim owns a videography business, Lim's Video Photography. Located in San Francisco, California, the company specializes in digital video photography and offers customers the option of storing edited videos on CD or DVD. His video shoots include weddings and other special events, as well as recording personal and commercial inventories for insurance purposes. Youngho created an Access database named **Clients** to store data about his clients. He asks you to make changes to the design of the **Client** and **Shoot** tables in this database, to create several new queries, and to create a new form. You'll do so by completing the following steps.

1. Make sure your Data Disk is in the appropriate disk drive, start Access, and then open the **Clients** database in the Cases folder on your Data Disk.

2. Open the **Shoot** table in Design view. Change the ShootType field data type to Lookup Wizard. Look up values in the **ShootDesc** table, select the ShootType and ShootDesc fields from the **ShootDesc** table, use the label ShootDesc, and accept all other Lookup Wizard default choices. View the **Shoot** table datasheet, resize the ShootDesc column to its best fit, and then save and close the table.

3. Use the Input Mask Wizard to add an input mask to the Phone field in the **Client** table. Select the Phone Number input mask, and then click the Finish button. Change the default input mask to 999\/000\-0000. Test the input mask by typing over an existing Phone field value, being sure not to change the value by pressing the Esc key after you type the last digit in the Phone field.

4. Change the first record in the **Client** table datasheet so the ClientName field value is your name in the format: last name, comma, space, first name. Close the table.

5. Create a query to find all records in the **Client** table in which the Phone field value begins with 415. Include all fields from the **Client** table in the query results. Save the query as **415 Area Codes**, run the query, print the query results, and then close the query.

6. Create a query to find all records in the **Shoot** table in which the ShootDesc field value is AP, BP, or WE. Use a list-of-values match for the selection criterion, and include all fields from the **Shoot** table in the query results. Sort the query in ascending order by ShootDate and then in ascending order by ShootTime. Save the query as **Milestone Celebrations**, run the query, and then print the query results in landscape orientation. Keep the query open.

7. Modify the query you created in Step 6. Use the modified query to find all records in the **Shoot** table in which the ShootDesc value is not any of: AP, BP, or WE. Save the query as **Not Milestone Celebrations**, run the query, print the query results in landscape orientation, and then close the query.

8. Create a parameter query to select the **Shoot** table records for a ShootType field value that the user specifies. (*Hint:* Use the ShootDesc field from the Shoot table as the parameter field.) Include all fields from the **Shoot** table and the ContractAmt field from the **Contract** table in the query results. Save the query as **Shoot Type Parameter**. Run the query and enter SE as the ShootType field value. Print the query results in landscape orientation, and then close the query.

9. Use Figure 5-55 and the following steps to create a multi-page form based on the **Client** and **Contract** tables.

Figure 5-55

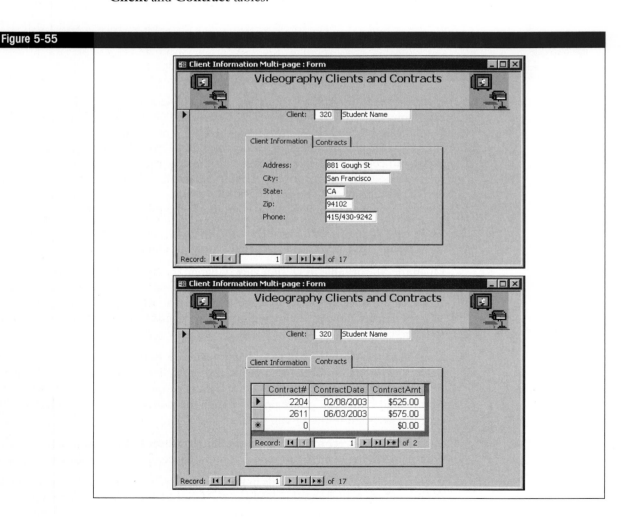

    a. Place the Client# and ClientName fields from the **Client** table at the top of the Detail section. Delete the ClientName label, and change the caption for the Client# label to Client:.

    b. Insert a Form Header section, but not a Form Footer section, in the form. Place a title label in the Form Header section. Enter the title and change its font to 12 points and bold.

    c. Place the **TVandVCR** picture in the Form Header section to the right of the title. The file containing this picture is in the Cases folder on your Data Disk. Next, copy the picture, paste it to the left of the title, and then resize the section.

    d. Place a tab control below the Client label in the Detail section. On the first page of the tab control, place the remaining fields from the **Client** table. Resize the text boxes to appropriate widths.

    e. On the second page of the tab control, place a subform based on the **Contract** table, and include all fields except the Client# field from the table in the subform. Save the subform as **Contract Subform**.

    f. Change the Caption property for each tab, and delete the subform label.

    g. Resize the form, the tab control, and the subform. In Form view, resize all datasheet columns to their best fit.

    h. Save the form as **Client Information Multi-page**.

    i. View the form, print both pages for the first record, and then close the form.

10. Close the **Clients** database, and then exit Access.

Case 2. DineAtHome.course.com   DineAtHome.course.com in Naples, Florida, is an online service that lets people order meals from one or more area restaurants and delivers the meals to their homes. Participating restaurants offer everything from simple fare to gourmet feasts. Claire Picard, founder and owner, and her staff perform a variety of services, from simply picking up and delivering the meals to providing linens and table service for more formal occasions. Claire created the **Delivery** database to maintain information about participating restaurants and orders placed by customers. To make the database easier to use, Claire wants you to make changes to its design, create several queries, and design two new forms. To do so, you'll complete the following steps.

1. Make sure your Data Disk is in the appropriate disk drive, start Access, and then open the **Delivery** database in the Cases folder on your Data Disk.

2. Use the Input Mask Wizard to add an input mask to the OrderDate field in the **Order** table. Select the Short Date input mask, and then click the Finish button. Modify the default Short Date input mask by changing the two slashes to dashes. Next, set the Format property for the OrderDate field to mm-dd-yyyy. Test the input mask by typing over an existing OrderDate field value, being sure not to change the value by pressing the Esc key after you type the last digit in the OrderDate field. Resize the OrderDate column to its best fit, and then save and close the table.

3. Define data validation criteria for the DeliveryCharge field in the **Restaurant** table. Acceptable field values for the DeliveryCharge field are 0, 8, 10, and 15. Enter the message, "Value must be 0, 8, 10, or 15", so it appears if a user enters an invalid DeliveryCharge field value. Save your table changes and then test the data validation criteria for the DeliveryCharge field; make sure the field values are the same as they were before you tested.

4. Modify the first record in the **Restaurant** table datasheet by changing the OwnerFirstName and OwnerLastName field values to your name. Close the table.

5. Create a query to find all records in the **Order** table in which the Restaurant# field value is 108, 115, or 133. Use a list-of-values match for the selection criterion, and include all fields from the **Order** table in the query results. Sort the query in descending order by OrderAmt. Save the query as **Selected Restaurants**, run the query, and then print the query results. Keep the query open.

6. Modify the query you created in Step 5. Use the modified query to find all records in the **Order** table in which the Restaurant# field value is not any of: 108, 115, or 133. Save the query as **Selected Restaurants Modified**, run the query, print the query results, and then close the query.

7. Modify the **Marco Island Restaurants** query to select all records in which the City field value is Marco Island or Naples and the TakeoutOnly field value is No. Save the query as **Marco Island and Naples Restaurants**, run the query, print the query results, and then close the query.

8. Create a parameter query to select the **Restaurant** table records for a City field value that the user specifies. Include all fields from the **Restaurant** table in the query results, except for the State, Website, and TakeoutOnly fields. Save the query as **Restaurant City Parameter**. Run the query and enter Naples as the City field value. Print the first page of the query results in landscape orientation, and then close the query.

Explore ▷ 9. Create a custom form based on the **Large Orders** query. Display all fields from the query in the form. Create your own design for the form. Add a label to the bottom of the Detail section, and enter your name in the label. Change the label's font so that your name appears in bold blue text. Change the OrderAmt text box format so that the field value appears in bold red text. Save the form as **Large Orders**. In Form view, print the first record.

10. Use Filter By Form with the **Large Orders** form to select all orders placed in Naples or East Naples for more than $110. Apply the filter. How many records are selected?

11. Print the first selected record. Save the filter as a query named **Large Orders Filter**. Close the form.

12. Create a multi-page custom form named **Restaurant Multi-page** based on the **Restaurant** and **Order** tables by completing the following steps.
    a. Place a title label in the Detail section at the top of the form. Enter the title Restaurants. Change the title label font to 24-point bold Bookman Old Style, and then resize the title label to fit.
    b. Place the **PlaceSet** picture at the top of the form to the right of the title label. The file containing this picture is in the Cases folder on your Data Disk.
    c. Place the Restaurant# and RestaurantName fields below the title label and picture.

Explore ▷   d. Change the Restaurant# and RestaurantName label and text box formats so that the label and field values appear as red text set in 12-point, bold Bookman Old Style. Make sure each control box is appropriately sized.
    e. On the first page of the tab control, display the other fields from the **Restaurant** table. Make sure all field text boxes are left-aligned, all labels are right-aligned, and each field text box is appropriately sized. Change the Caption property for the first tab to Restaurant Information.
    f. On the second page of the tab control, display all fields from the **Order** table, except for Restaurant#, in a subform named **Order Multi-page Subform**. Resize the subform, change the Caption property for the second tab to Order Information, delete the subform label, and then resize the subform columns to their best fit in Form view.
    g. View the form, print both pages for the first record, and then save and close the form.

Explore ▷ 13. Open the **Restaurant Multi-page** form, and save it as **Enhanced Restaurant Multi-page**. Make and save the following changes to the design of the new form.
    a. Change the background color of the form's Detail section to light blue.
    b. Use the Line/Border Width button to place a border (weight 2) around the title label.
    c. Use the Font/Fore Color button to change the color of the title label to red.
    d. Print both pages of the finished form for the first record, save your changes, and then close the form.

14. Close the **Delivery** database, and then exit Access.

Case 3. Redwood Zoo The Redwood Zoo is a small zoo located in the picturesque city of Gig Harbor, Washington, on the shores of Puget Sound. The Redwood Zoo has some of the best exhibits of marine animals in the United States. Its newly constructed polar bear habitat is a particular favorite among patrons. The zoo relies heavily on donations to fund both permanent exhibits and temporary displays, especially those involving exotic animals. Michael Rosenfeld, director of fundraising activities, created the **Donors** database to track information about donors, their pledges, and the status of funds. Michael wants you to make changes to the database design, create several queries, and design two new forms. To do so, you'll complete the following steps.

1. Make sure your Data Disk is in the appropriate disk drive, start Access, and then open the **Donors** database in the Cases folder on your Data Disk.

2. Open the **Pledge** table in Design view. Change the FundCode field data type to Lookup Wizard. Look up values in the **Fund** table, select the FundCode and FundName fields from the **Fund** table, use the label FundName, and accept all other Lookup Wizard default choices. View the **Pledge** table datasheet, resize the FundName column to its best fit, and then save and close the table.

3. Define data validation criteria for the Class field in the **Donor** table. Acceptable field values for the Class field are B, D, and P. Enter the message, "Value must be B, D, or P", that appears if a user enters an invalid Class field value. Save your table changes and then test the data validation criteria for the Class field; make sure the field values are the same as they were before you tested.

4. Modify the first record in the **Donor** table datasheet by changing the Title, FirstName, MI, and LastName field values to your title and name. Close the table.

5. Create a query to find all records in the **Pledge** table in which the PaymentSchedule field value is M, Q, or S. Use a list-of-values match for the selection criterion, and include all fields from the **Pledge** table in the query results. Save the query as **Selected Payment Schedules**, run the query, and then print the query results in landscape orientation. Keep the query open.

6. Modify the query you created in Step 5. Use the modified query to find all records in the **Pledge** table in which the PaymentSchedule field value is not any of: M, Q, or S. Save the query as **Selected Payment Schedules Modified**, run the query, print the query results in landscape orientation, and then close the query.

7. Create a query to select all records from the **Pledge** table with fund codes of B11 or P15 in which the payment method is either C or E. (*Hint:* Use the FundName field from the Pledge table to set the criterion for fund codes.) Display all fields in the query results. Save the query as **Paid Bear Fund Pledges**, run the query, print the query results in landscape orientation, and then close the query.

8. Create a parameter query to select the **Pledge** table records for a FundCode field value that the user specifies. (*Hint:* Use the FundName field from the Pledge table as the parameter field.) Include all fields from the **Pledge** table in the query results. Save the query as **Fund Code Parameter**. Run the query and enter W13 as the FundCode field value. Print the query results in landscape orientation, and then close the query.

Explore 9. Create a custom form based on the **Costs** query. Display all fields in the form. Use your own design for the form. Change the FundName label and text box format, so the label and field values appear in 12-point bold, blue text on a yellow background. Add your name to the bottom of the form. Save the form as **Costs**, view the form, print the first record, and then close the form.

10. Close the **Donors** database, and then exit Access.

Case 4. Mountain River Adventures Connor and Siobhan Dempsey own Mountain River Adventures center, which offers clients their choice of outdoor activities, including white-water rafting, canoeing, hiking, camping, fishing, and rock climbing. To track their clients and bookings, they created the **Outdoors** database. Connor and Siobhan want you to make changes to the design of the database, create several queries, and design two new forms. To do so, you'll complete the following steps.

1. Make sure your Data Disk is in the appropriate disk drive, start Access, and then open the **Outdoors** database in the Cases folder on your Data Disk.

2. Open the **Booking** table in Design view. Change the Trip# field data type to Lookup Wizard. Look up values in the **Rafting Trip** table; select the Trip#, River, and Fee/Person fields from the **Rafting Trip** table; use the label River; and accept all other Lookup Wizard default choices. View the **Booking** table datasheet, resize the River column to its best fit, and then save and close the table.

3. Use the Input Mask Wizard to add an input mask to the Phone field in the **Client** table. Select the Phone Number input mask, and then click the Finish button. Change the default input mask to 999\-000\-0000. Test the input mask by typing over an existing Phone field value, being sure not to change the value by pressing the Esc key after you type the last digit in the Phone field.

4. Change the first record in the **Client** table datasheet, so the ClientName field value is your name in the format: last name, comma, space, first name. Close the table.

5. Create a query to find all records in the **Rafting Trip** table in which the River field value starts with the word Arkansas. Include all fields in the query results. Save the query as **Arkansas Trips**, run the query, and then print the query results. Keep the query open.

6. Modify the query you created in Step 5. Use the modified query to find all records in the **Rafting Trip** table in which the River field value starts with a word other than Arkansas. Save the query as **Non-Arkansas Trips**, run the query, print the query results, and then close the query.

7. Create a query to find all records in the **Client** table where the State/Prov field value is NE, UT, or WY. Use a list-of-values match for the selection criterion, and include all fields from the **Client** table in the query results. Save the query as **Selected Clients**, run the query, print the query results in landscape orientation, and then close the query.

8. Create a parameter query to select the **Client** table records for a State/Prov field value that the user specifies. Include all fields from the **Client** table in the query results. Save the query as **State/Prov Parameter**. Run the query and enter CO as the State/Prov field value. Print the query results in landscape orientation, and then close the query.

Explore

9. Create a custom form based on the **Costs** query. Display all fields in the form. Use your own design for the form, but place the title "Booked Trips," the **Kayak** picture (found in the Cases folder on your Data Disk), and your name in the Form Header section. Change the Booking# label and text box format so that the label and field value appear in 12-point bold text on a light blue background. Save the form as **Costs**, view the form, and then print the first form record.

10. Use Filter By Form with the **Costs** form to select all records that have a Fee/Person value of over $100 or include trips on the Arkansas River. Apply the filter. How many records does the filter select?

11. Print the first record. Save the filter as a query named **Costs Filter**, and then close the form.

12. Create a multi-page custom form named **Client Multi-page** based on the **Client** and **Booking** tables by completing the following steps.

    a. Place the ClientName field in the Detail section of the form.
    b. On the first page of a tab control, display the other fields from the **Client** table. Make sure each field text box is an appropriate size. Change the Caption property for the first tab to Client Information.
    c. On the second page of the tab control, display all fields from the **Booking** table in a subform named **Booking Multi-page Subform**. Resize the subform, change the Caption property for the second tab to Booking Information, delete the subform label, and resize the subform columns to their best fit.
    d. View the form, print both pages for the first record, and then save and close the form.

13. Make a copy of the **Client Multi-page** form, and save it as **Client Multi-page Enhanced**. Make the following changes to the design of the new form.

    a. Change the background color of the Detail section of the form (except the subform) to light blue.
    b. Use the Line/Border Width button to place a border (weight 2) around the ClientName label and field-value text box. Change the font size and weight for these controls, so that they stand out. Resize these controls, if necessary.
    c. Use the Font/Fore Color button to change the color of the Phone field value to red.
    d. Use the Special Effect button on the Form Design toolbar to change the display of the **Booking Multi-page Subform** subform to raised.
    e. Print both pages of the finished form for the first record, and then save and close the form.

14. Close the **Outdoors** database, and then exit Access.

Explore

Case 5. eACH Internet Auction Site Chris and Pat Aquino own a successful ISP (Internet service provider) and want to expand their business to host an Internet auction site. The auction site will let sellers offer items for sale, such as antiques, first-edition books, vintage dolls, coins, art, stamps, glass bottles, autographs, and sports memorabilia. After a seller posts an item for sale, the auction site sells it to the buyer who places the highest bid. Before people can sell and bid on items, they must register with the auction site. Each item will be listed by subcategory within a general category, so bidders can easily find items of interest. For example, the general category of antiques might consist of several subcategories, including ancient world, musical instruments, and general.

Chris and Pat registered their Web site name eACH, which stands for *e*lectronic *A*uction *C*ollectibles *H*ost. Now they need to create a database to track people registered, items for sale, and bids received for those items. The process of creating a complete database—including all fields, tables, relationships, queries, forms, and other database objects—for eACH is an enormous undertaking. So you start with just a few database components, and then you will create additional objects in subsequent tutorials.

Complete the following steps to create the database and its initial objects:

1. Read the appendix titled "Relational Databases and Database Design" at the end of this book.

2. Use your Web browser to gather information about other Internet auction sites, so that you become familiar with common rules and requirements, categories and subcategories, fields and their attributes, and entities. (*Hint:* Yahoo (www.yahoo.com) lists names of several auction sites, and eBay (www.ebay.com) is a popular Internet auction site.)

3. The initial database structure includes the following relations and fields.

    a. The **Category** relation includes a unique category number and a category (the category name or description).
    b. The **Subcategory** relation includes a unique subcategory number, subcategory name or description, and a category number.

    c. The **Registrant** relation includes a unique registrant number, last name, first name, middle initial, phone number, e-mail address, optional user ID, and password. Each person registers once and then can sell and bid on items.

    d. The **Item** relation includes a unique item number, the registrant who's selling the item, the subcategory number, a title (a short item description), a description (a fuller item description), a quantity (the number of identical items being sold separately, if there are more than one), a minimum bid amount in whole dollars, a duration (the number of days the site will accept bids for the item), an optional reserve price amount in whole dollars (the lowest sale price acceptable to the seller; this is not made available to bidders), and the date and time bidding started on the item.

4. Use the information in Step 3 to draw an entity-relationship diagram showing the entities (relations) and the relationships between the entities.

5. Build on Steps 3 and 4, creating on paper the initial database design for the eACH system. For each relation, identify all primary and foreign keys. For each field, determine attributes, such as data type, field size, and validation rules.

6. Create the database structure using Access. Use the database name **eACH**, and save the database in the Cases folder on your Data Disk. Create the tables with their fields. Be sure to set each field's properties correctly, select a primary key for each table, and then define the relationships between appropriate tables.

7. For each table, create a form that you'll use to view, add, edit, and delete records in that table.

8. For tables with one-to-many relationships, create a form with a main form for the primary table and a subform for the related table.

9. Design test data for each table in the database. You can research Internet auction sites to collect realistic values for categories, subcategories, and other fields, if necessary. Make sure your test data covers common situations. For example, your text data should include at least two sellers with multiple items for sale, one seller selling items in the same subcategory, another seller selling items in different subcategories, and at least one seller who currently has no items for sale. Each table should have at least 10 records. Include your name as one of the registrants, and include at least two items that you're selling.

10. Add the test data to your tables using the forms you created in Steps 7 and 8.

11. Open each table datasheet, resize all datasheet columns to their best fit, and then print each datasheet.

12. Set the option so Access compacts the **eACH** database when you close it.

13. Use the Input Mask Wizard to add an appropriate input mask to one field in any table. Print the table's datasheet after adding the input mask.

14. Define data validation criteria for any one field in any table. Make sure to set both the Validation Rule and the Validation Text properties for the field.

15. For one of the foreign key fields in one of the tables, change the field's data type to Lookup Wizard. (*Hint*: Before you change the data type to Lookup Wizard, you must delete the relationship for which the field serves as the foreign key.) If necessary, resize the table datasheet, and then print the datasheet.

16. Create, test, save, and print one parameter query.

17. Close the **eACH** database, and then exit Access.

INTERNET ASSIGNMENTS

Student Union

The purpose of the Internet Assignments is to challenge you to find information on the Internet that you can use to create effective documents. The actual assignments are updated and maintained on the Course Technology Web site. Log on to the Internet and use your Web browser to go to the Student Online Companion to accompany this text at **www.course.com/NewPerspectives/studentunion**. Click the Online Companions link, and then click the link for this tutorial.

QUICK CHECK ANSWERS

Session 5.1

1. A Lookup Wizard field lets you select a value from a list of possible values, making data entry easier.
2. If two tables have a one-to-many relationship, when you display the primary table in Datasheet view, you can use a subdatasheet to display and edit the records from the related table.
3. input mask
4. The Validation Rule property specifies the valid values that users can enter in a field. For example, you could use this property to specify that users can enter only positive numeric values in a numeric field.
5. The Validation Text property value appears in a message box if the user violates the validation rule. For example, you could display the message, "Must be a positive integer", if the user enters a value less than or equal to zero.
6. Like
7. The asterisk is a wildcard that represents any string of characters in a pattern match query.
8. Use the In comparison operator to define a condition with two or more values.
9. Use the Not logical operator to negate a condition.
10. Use a parameter query when you want to prompt the user to enter the selection criterion when the query runs.

Session 5.2

1. A bound control is linked to a field in the underlying table or query; an unbound control is not.
2. grid
3. toolbox
4. move
5. Position the pointer anywhere on the border of the control (except not on a move or sizing handle), and then drag the control and its attached label.
6. Right-click the label, click Properties on the shortcut menu, click the All tab, edit the existing label in the Caption text box, or double-click it to select the current value, and then type a new caption.

7. Select the control, position the pointer on a sizing handle, and then drag the pointer in the appropriate direction to the new location.

8. The Form Header section lets you add titles, instructions, command buttons, and other information to the top of your form. This section of the form does not change as you navigate through the records.

9. Open the form in Design view, click the Image tool on the toolbox, position the pointer at the location for the upper-left corner of the picture, click the mouse button, select the picture file, and then click the OK button.

Session 5.3

1. Open the form in Design view, click the Tab Control tool on the toolbox, position the pointer in the form at the location for the upper-left corner of the tab control, and then click the mouse button.

2. Click a label, press and hold down the Shift key, click the other labels, release the Shift key, click Format on the menu bar, point to Align, and then click the appropriate alignment option.

3. Filter By Form finds records that match multiple selection criteria using the same Access logical and comparison operators that you use in queries.

4. Save the filter as a query, and then apply the query to an open form.

5. Opening a query runs the query and displays the results in Datasheet view. Applying a query to a form opens the query and displays the results in the open form.

In this tutorial you will:

- Design and create a custom report

- Assign a conditional value to a calculated field

- Sort and group data in a report

- Add, move, resize, and align controls in a report

- Modify control properties

- Add a subreport to a main report

- Add lines to a report

- Hide duplicate values in a report

- Add calculated controls to a report

- Calculate group and overall totals in a report

- Define conditional formatting rules

- Use domain aggregate functions

- Add the date, page numbers, and title to a report

- Create and modify mailing labels

CREATING CUSTOM REPORTS

Creating a Potential Income Report

CASE

Northeast Seasonal Jobs International (NSJI)

At a recent staff meeting, Elsa Jensen indicated that she would like a new report created for the Jobs database. She wants a printed list of all positions for all NSJI employer clients. She also wants subtotals of the placement fee and potential income amounts from each employer and a grand total for all potential income amounts.

In this tutorial, you will create the report for Elsa. In building the report, you will use many Access report customization features—such as grouping data, adding a subreport, calculating totals, and adding lines to separate report sections. These features will enhance Elsa's report and make it easier to read.

SESSION 6.1

In this session, you will create a custom report. You will review two existing queries and create a new query that includes calculated fields and assigns conditional values. You will also add a Group Header section to the report and specify the sorting and grouping fields for the records. Finally, you will add, move, resize, and align controls in the report and change their captions and Can Grow properties.

Creating a Custom Report

A **report** is the formatted, printed contents of one or more tables from a database. Although you can format and print data using datasheets, queries, and forms, reports offer you greater flexibility and provide a more professional, custom appearance. For example, NSJI can create customized reports for billing statements and mailing labels.

An Access report is divided into sections. Each report can have the seven different sections described in Figure 6-1.

Figure 6-1	ACCESS REPORT SECTIONS
REPORT SECTION	**DESCRIPTION**
Report Header	Appears once at the beginning of a report. Use it for report titles, company logos, report introductions, and cover pages.
Page Header	Appears at the top of each page of a report. Use it for column headings, report titles, page numbers, and report dates. If your report has a Report Header section, it precedes the first Page Header section.
Group Header	Appears at the beginning of each new group of records. Use it to print the group name and the field value that all records in the group have in common. A report can have up to 10 grouping levels.
Detail	Appears once for each record in the underlying table or query. Use it to print selected fields from the table or query and to print calculated values.
Group Footer	Appears at the end of each group of records. It is usually used to print totals for the group.
Report Footer	Appears once at the end of the report. Use it for report totals and other summary information.
Page Footer	Appears at the bottom of each page of a report. Use it for page numbers and brief explanations of symbols or abbreviations. If your report has a Report Footer section, it precedes the Page Footer section on the last page of the report.

You don't have to include all seven sections in a report. When you design your report, you determine which sections to include and what information to place in each section. Figure 6-2 shows a sample report produced from the Jobs database; it includes all seven sections.

Figure 6-2	SAMPLE REPORT SHOWING THE SEVEN SECTIONS OF A REPORT

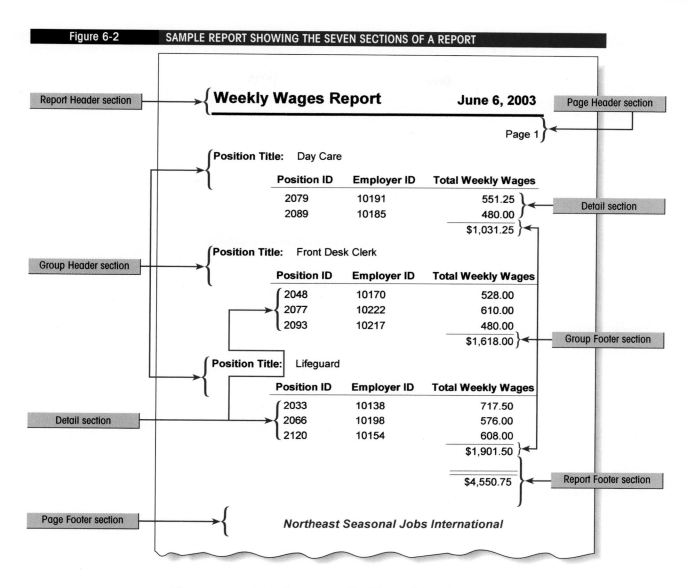

The report you need to create for Elsa will list the records for all employers and their positions. Elsa wants the report to group employers by values in the NAICSDesc field. The report will contain four sections:

- A Page Header section will show the current date, report title, and page number.
- A Group Header section will print the NAICS description and code.
- A Detail section will list all field values from the Employer table. Records within each NAICS group will appear in ascending order by employer name. Then for each employer's positions, the position title and ID, number of openings, and placement fee amount will print in ascending order by position title.
- A Report Footer section will print the grand total of the potential income amount.

From your work with AutoReport and the Report Wizard, you know that, by default, Access places the report title in the Report Header section and the date and page number in the Page Footer section. Elsa prefers the date, report title, and page number to appear at the top of each page, so you need to place this information in the Page Header section.

You could use the Report Wizard to create the report and then modify the report to match the report design. However, because you need to customize several components of the report, you will create the report in Design view. When you modify a report created by AutoReport or the Report Wizard, or design and create your own report, you produce a **custom report**. You should create a custom report whenever AutoReport or the Report Wizard cannot automatically create the specific report you need.

Designing a Custom Report

Before you create a custom report, you should first plan the report's contents and appearance. Figure 6-3 shows the design of the report you will create for Elsa.

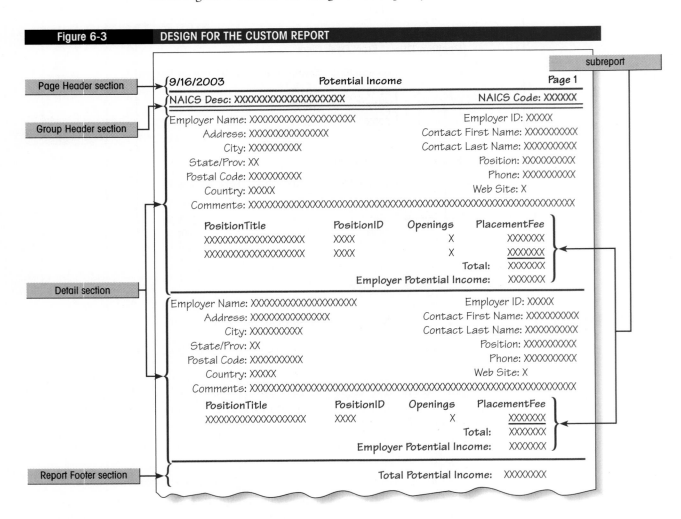

Figure 6-3   **DESIGN FOR THE CUSTOM REPORT**

The Page Header section contains the report title ("Potential Income") centered between the current date on the left and the page number on the right. A thick blue horizontal line separates this section from the rest of the report page.

The NAICS description and code will appear in the Group Header section. Two thin, blue horizontal lines separate this section from the Detail section that follows.

In the Detail section, a series of Xs indicates the locations and relative lengths of the field values. The label for a field value will print to its left in the top portion of the Detail section and above the field value in the bottom portion of the Detail section. Employers with specific

NAICS codes will print in ascending order by employer name; a thick blue horizontal line will print at the bottom of the Detail section to separate each employer and its positions from the next employer's data. The position data in the Detail section will appear in a **subreport**, a report contained within another report.

The PlacementFee field in the Detail section is a calculated field based on the Openings, Hours/Week, and Wage field values in the Position table. The total for an employer's PlacementFee field values will appear in the Detail section after the employer's positions. Finally, two potential income values—a subtotal in the Detail section for each employer's positions and an overall total in the Report Footer section—will be calculated fields.

Reviewing and Creating Queries for a Custom Report

How does NSJI make the money it needs to run its business? It charges its employer clients a fee for each position filled. NSJI calculates this placement fee by multiplying the weekly wages for a position by two. Because the database does not contain a position's weekly wage amount, NSJI calculates the weekly wage value by multiplying the Hours/Week and Wage fields in the Position table. In addition to the placement fee, NSJI charges each employer a one-time search fee based on the total number of openings filled. For fewer than three openings filled, NSJI charges a $500 search fee; NSJI reduces the search fee to $200 if it fills three or more openings. Combining the search fee with the total placement fees for an employer produces the total income from the employer. The report you'll create for Elsa will show the placement fees and total income for each employer with the assumption that NSJI will fill all available openings for all positions. For this reason, the employer and overall income printed are considered potential income amounts.

The source data for a report (or form) can come from a single table, from a single query based on one or more tables, or from multiple tables and/or queries. Your report will contain data from the Employer, NAICS, and Position tables, but the report requirements are complicated enough that you'll need a total of three queries to supply the needed data. Elsa has already created two queries: the NAICS and Employers query and the Potential Placement Fees query. You'll create the third: the Potential Income by Employer query.

The first existing query, the NAICS and Employers query, lists all fields from the NAICS and Employer tables. This query will supply the data for the report's Group Header section and for the employer data in the Detail section.

The second existing query, the Potential Placement Fees query, lists the PositionID, PositionTitle, Openings, and EmployerID fields from the Position table. This query will provide the source data for the report's Detail section subreport, which is where the position data for an employer will print. The subreport also includes the PlacementFee column, which will print the calculated results of multiplying the Openings, Hours/Week, and Wage fields in the Position table by two. You can create a calculated field on a form or report, but then you wouldn't be able to calculate subtotals by employer and a grand total for the calculated field. However, you can calculate totals on a form or report for any field, including calculated fields, from a table or query used as the basis for the form or report. Because Elsa wants subtotals by employer for the PlacementFee field values on her report, the existing Potential Placement Fees query already includes the PlacementFee calculated field.

In most situations, the two existing queries would be the only data sources needed for Elsa's report. However, the report will list all employers, even those with no currently available positions. Elsa's report will not print the subreport for these employers for two reasons. First, printing a position-related column heading line and a subtotal in the subreport without any detail position data doesn't make sense and wouldn't look attractive. Second, for those employers without positions, Access will generate a data error for the subreport subtotals because Access doesn't let you calculate statistics when there are no records upon which to base the calculations. Because the subreport will not be printed for all employers, Access will generate a data error if you base your calculation for the grand total potential income on the individual employer potential incomes. Thus, you'll create a third query to serve as the source for the grand total of the new report's potential income value.

The query you'll create will be based on data from the Position table. It will be a statistical query, which you'll save as Potential Income by Employer, that will list the total number of openings, total placement fees, and total potential income by employer for those clients with available positions.

Before creating the new query, you'll review the two queries that Elsa already created for the report.

To review the NAICS and Employers query:

1. Place your Data Disk in the appropriate disk drive.

2. Start Access and open the **Jobs** database located in the Tutorial folder on your Data Disk.

3. Maximize the Database window, and then open the **NAICS and Employers** query. Forty-five records—one for each record in the Employer table—appear in the recordset.

4. Scroll right to view the fields in the recordset, and then switch to Design view. See Figure 6-4.

Figure 6-4   **NAICS AND EMPLOYERS QUERY IN DESIGN VIEW**

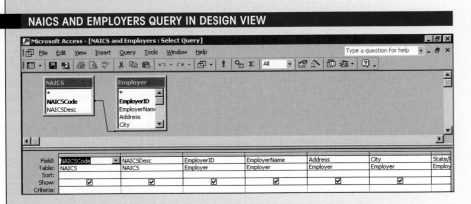

The NAICS and Employer tables are the source tables for the query. Both fields from the NAICS table—NAICSCode and NAICSDesc—appear in the design grid, as do all fields from the Employer table, except for the common NAICSCode field, which would be redundant if included in the query.

5. Close the query, and then restore the Database window.

Next, you'll review the design and recordset for the Potential Placement Fees query, the second query Elsa developed for the new report.

To review the Potential Placement Fees query:

1. Open the **Potential Placement Fees** query in Design view. The PositionID, PositionTitle, Openings, and EmployerID fields from the Position table appear in the design grid, along with the PlacementFee field, a calculated field.

2. Right-click the **PlacementFee Field** text box, click **Zoom** on the shortcut menu, and then position the insertion point to the right of the expression in the Zoom dialog box. See Figure 6-5.

Figure 6-5	CALCULATED FIELD IN THE ZOOM DIALOG BOX

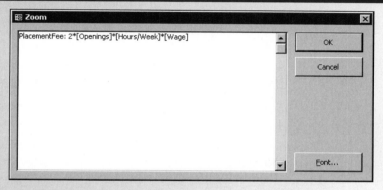

The **Zoom dialog box** has a large text box for entering text, expressions, and other values. The PlacementFee calculated field entry in the Zoom dialog box determines an employer's placement fee for a position by multiplying the weekly wages (Hours/Week field times the Wage field) by two, and then multiplying by the number of openings (Openings field) for the position.

3. Click the **OK** button, and then run the query. The recordset displays the four fields from the Position table and the calculated field, PlacementFee. See Figure 6-6.

Figure 6-6	RECORDSET DISPLAYING THE CALCULATED FIELD

calculated field

4. Close the query, and then click the **No** button when asked if you want to save design changes to the query.

Next, you'll create the final query needed for Elsa's report.

Assigning a Conditional Value to a Calculated Field

You'll create the Potential Income by Employer query to list the total number of openings, total placement fees, and total potential income by employer. For the total potential income field calculation, you'll need to add either $200 (if the total number of openings is three or greater) or $500 (if the total number of openings is less than three) to an employer's total placement fees. To permit the calculated field to be one of two values based on a condition, you'll use the IIf function. The **IIf function** lets you assign one value to a calculated field or control if a condition is true, and a second value if the condition is false. The format of the IIf function you'll use is: *IIf (TotalOpenings>=3, PlacementFee+200, PlacementFee+500)*. You interpret this function as: If the TotalOpenings field value is greater than or equal to 3, then set the calculated field value equal to the sum of the PlacementFee field value and 200; otherwise, set the calculated field value equal to the sum of the PlacementFee field value and 500.

Now you are ready to create the statistical query.

To create the Potential Income by Employer query:

1. Double-click **Create query in Design view**, double-click **Position** in the Show Table dialog box, and then click the **Close** button.

   You need to add the EmployerID and Openings fields from the Position field list to the design grid, change the query to a statistical query, and then add two calculated fields—one to calculate the placement fees for an employer, and the other to calculate the potential income from the employer.

2. Add the **EmployerID** field to the first column of the design grid, add the **Openings** field to the second column of the design grid, and then click the **Totals** button Σ on the Query Design toolbar.

   Because you need the statistics grouped by employer, you'll use the default Group By operator for the EmployerID field. For the Openings field, you need to determine the total number of openings, so you'll use the Sum aggregate function and then enter the field name TotalOpenings.

3. Click the right side of the **Openings Total** text box, click **Sum**, position the insertion point to the left of Openings in the second column's Field text box, and then type **TotalOpenings:** (Make sure you type the colon.)

   Next, you'll add to the design grid's third column the PlacementFee calculated field that determines an employer's total placement fee. Once again, you'll use the Sum aggregate function for the calculated field that will multiply the product of the Openings, Hours/Week, and Wage fields in the Position table by two.

4. Right-click the **Field** text box in the third column, and then click **Zoom** on the shortcut menu.

   Because brackets must enclose field names containing spaces or special characters, you'll need to enclose the expression's Hours/Week field in brackets. If you omit brackets for other field names, Access adds them automatically when you close the Zoom dialog box.

5. Type **PlacementFee: 2*Openings*[Hours/Week]*Wage**. See Figure 6-7.

| Figure 6-7 | EXPRESSION FOR THE PlacementFee CALCULATED FIELD |

TROUBLE? If your calculated field differs from that shown in Figure 6-7, correct it so it matches.

The expression for the PlacementFee calculated field is the same as the expression in Elsa's Potential Placement Fees query for its PlacementFee calculated field.

6. Click the **OK** button, click the right side of the **PlacementFee Total** text box, and then click **Sum**.

Finally, you'll add to the design grid's fourth column the PotentialIncome calculated field that will determine an employer's total potential income using the IIf function.

7. Right-click the **Field** text box in the fourth column, click **Zoom** on the shortcut menu, and then type **PotentialIncome: IIf (TotalOpenings>=3, PlacementFee+200, PlacementFee+500)**. See Figure 6-8.

| Figure 6-8 | EXPRESSION FOR THE PotentialIncome CALCULATED FIELD |

For calculated fields that include functions, such as the IIf function, you must set the field's Total property to Expression.

8. Click the **OK** button, click the right side of the **PotentialIncome Total** text box, scroll down the list, and then click **Expression**.

9. Save the query as **Potential Income by Employer**, run the query, resize each column in the recordset to its best fit, and then deselect the columns. The recordset displays the statistical query that includes the two calculated fields for each employer with available positions in the Position table. See Figure 6-9.

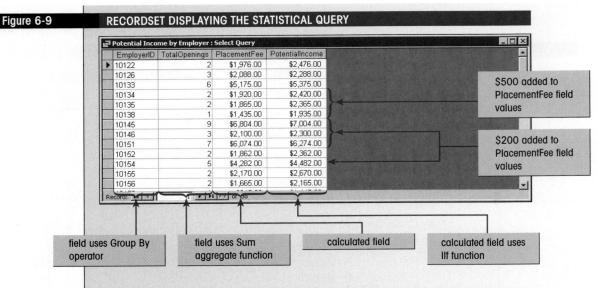

| Figure 6-9 | RECORDSET DISPLAYING THE STATISTICAL QUERY |

Potential Income by Employer : Select Query

EmployerID	TotalOpenings	PlacementFee	PotentialIncome
10122	2	$1,976.00	$2,476.00
10126	3	$2,088.00	$2,288.00
10133	6	$5,175.00	$5,375.00
10134	2	$1,920.00	$2,420.00
10135	2	$1,865.00	$2,365.00
10138	1	$1,435.00	$1,935.00
10145	9	$6,804.00	$7,004.00
10146	3	$2,100.00	$2,300.00
10151	7	$6,074.00	$6,274.00
10152	2	$1,862.00	$2,362.00
10154	5	$4,282.00	$4,482.00
10155	2	$2,170.00	$2,670.00
10156	2	$1,665.00	$2,165.00

$500 added to PlacementFee field values

$200 added to PlacementFee field values

field uses Group By operator

field uses Sum aggregate function

calculated field

calculated field uses IIf function

Records 4, 5, and 6 have PotentialIncome field values of $500 more than their PlacementFee field values because their TotalOpenings field values are less than three. Records with TotalOpenings field values equal to three or greater, such as records 7, 8, 9, and 11, have PotentialIncome field values of $200 more than their PlacementFee field values.

10. Save and then close the query.

You are now ready to create Elsa's report. To do so, you need to display a blank report in Design view.

Report Window in Design View

The Report window in Design view is similar to the Form window in Design view, which you used in Tutorial 5 to create a custom form.

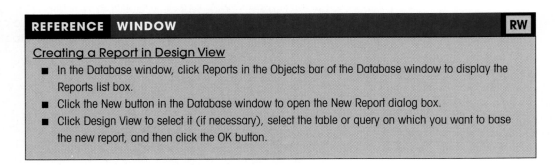

| REFERENCE | WINDOW | RW |

Creating a Report in Design View

- In the Database window, click Reports in the Objects bar of the Database window to display the Reports list box.
- Click the New button in the Database window to open the New Report dialog box.
- Click Design View to select it (if necessary), select the table or query on which you want to base the new report, and then click the OK button.

The main source for the report you are creating is the NAICS and Employers query that you reviewed earlier in this tutorial. To begin, you need to create a blank report in Design view.

To create a blank report in Design view:

1. Click **Reports** in the Objects bar of the Database window to display the Reports list box, and then click the **New** button in the Database window to open the New Report dialog box.

2. Click **Design View** (if necessary), click the list arrow to display the list of tables and queries in the Jobs database, scroll down and click **NAICS and Employers** to select this query as the basis for your report, and then click the **OK** button. The Report window in Design view opens and displays a blank report.

3. Click the **Maximize** button 🔲 on the Report window. See Figure 6-10.

Figure 6-10	REPORT WINDOW IN DESIGN VIEW

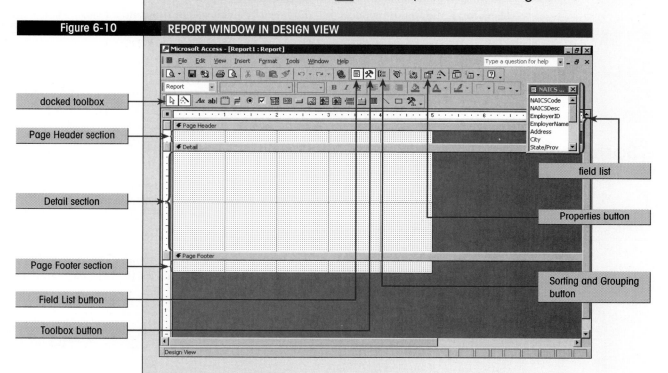

docked toolbox

Page Header section

Detail section

Page Footer section

Field List button

Toolbox button

field list

Properties button

Sorting and Grouping button

TROUBLE? If the rulers, grid, or toolbox do not appear, click View on the menu bar, and then click Ruler, Grid, or Toolbox to display the missing component. If the grid still does not appear, see your instructor or technical support person for assistance. If the toolbox is not positioned as shown in Figure 6-10, click the Toolbox window's title bar, and then drag it into position.

TROUBLE? If the field list does not appear, click the Field List 📄 button on the Report Design toolbar to display it. If the field list is not positioned and sized as shown in Figure 6-10, click the field list title bar, and then drag it to the position shown; use the mouse to resize the field list.

TROUBLE? If the Report Design toolbar or the Formatting toolbar does not appear, click View, point to Toolbars, and then click Report Design or Formatting (Form/Report) to display the missing toolbar.

> **TROUBLE?** If the Report Design and Formatting toolbars appear as one toolbar or if the Formatting toolbar is positioned above the Report Design toolbar, drag the Formatting toolbar move handle ▌ below the Report Design toolbar to the position shown in Figure 6-10.

Notice that the Report window in Design view has many of the same components as the Form window in Design view. For example, the Report Design toolbar includes a Properties button, a Field List button, and a Toolbox button. Both windows also have horizontal and vertical rulers, a grid, and a Formatting toolbar.

Unlike the Form window in Design view, which initially displays only the Detail section on a blank form, the Report window also displays a Page Header section and a Page Footer section. Reports often contain these sections, so Access automatically includes them in a blank report.

According to Elsa's plan for the report (see Figure 6-3), the NAICSDesc and NAICSCode fields from the NAICS and Employers query will appear in a Group Header section, and the remaining 13 fields from the query will appear in the Detail section. Before you can add the NAICSDesc and NAICSCode fields to the report, you need to create the Group Header section by specifying the NAICSDesc field as a grouping field.

Sorting and Grouping Data in a Report

Access lets you organize records in a report by sorting them using one or more sort keys. Each sort key can also be a grouping field. If you specify a sort key as a **grouping field**, you can include a Group Header section and a Group Footer section for the group. A Group Header section typically includes the name of the group, and a Group Footer section typically includes a count or subtotal for records in that group.

You use the Sorting and Grouping button on the Report Design toolbar to select sort keys and grouping fields for a report. Each report can have up to 10 sort fields, and any of its sort fields can also be grouping fields.

REFERENCE WINDOW   **RW**

Sorting and Grouping Data in a Report
- Display the report in Design view.
- Click the Sorting and Grouping button on the Report Design toolbar.
- Click the first Field/Expression list arrow in the Sorting and Grouping dialog box, and select the field to use as the primary sort key. In the Sort Order text box, select the sort order.
- Repeat the previous step to select secondary sorting keys and their sort orders as necessary.
- To group data, click the field in the Field/Expression text box by which you want to group records. In the Group Properties section, set the grouping options for the field.
- Click the Close button on the Sorting and Grouping dialog box to close it.

Elsa wants records listed in ascending order based on the NAICSDesc field; the NAICSDesc and NAICSCode field values print at the beginning of each NAICSDesc group. For these reasons, you need to specify the NAICSDesc field as both the primary sort key and the grouping field. Elsa also wants the employer data listed in ascending order by EmployerName within each NAICSDesc group. So, you need to specify the EmployerName field as the secondary sort key.

To select the sort keys and the group field:

1. Click the **Sorting and Grouping** button 📇 on the Report Design toolbar. The Sorting and Grouping dialog box opens.

   The top section of the Sorting and Grouping dialog box lets you specify the sort keys for the records in the Detail section. For each sort key, the Group Properties section of the dialog box lets you designate the sort key as a grouping field and specify whether you want a Group Header section, a Group Footer section, and other options for the group.

2. Click the list arrow in the first **Field/Expression** text box to display the list of available fields, and then click **NAICSDesc**. Ascending is the default sort order in the Sort Order text box, so you do not need to change this setting.

   You can now designate NAICSDesc as a grouping field and specify that you want a Group Header section for this group. This section will contain the NAICS description and code labels and field values.

3. Click the right side of the **Group Header** text box to display a list arrow and a list of values, and then click **Yes**. Access adds a Group Header section named NAICSDesc Header to the Report window. See Figure 6-11.

Figure 6-11	ADDING A GROUP HEADER SECTION

Notice the symbol placed to the left of the Field/Expression text box for NAICSDesc. That symbol indicates that you designated NAICSDesc as a grouping field.

You can now specify the secondary sort key and its sort order.

4. Click the right side of the second **Field/Expression** text box to display the list of fields, and then click **EmployerName**. Once again, you do not need to change the default sort order, so you've finished setting the sorting and grouping options for the main report.

5. Close the Sorting and Grouping dialog box.

Now that you've created the NAICSDesc Header section, you can add the fields from the field list to the correct sections of the report.

Adding Fields to a Report

Your next task is to add bound controls to the Group Header and Detail sections for all the fields from the NAICS and Employers query. Recall that a bound control displays field values from the table or query on which a form or report is based. You add bound controls to a report in the same way that you add them to a form.

REFERENCE WINDOW   **RW**

Adding Fields to a Report

- Display the report in Design view.
- If necessary, click the Field List button on the Report Design toolbar to display the field list.
- To place a single field on the report, position the pointer on the field name in the field list, drag the field name to the report, and then release the mouse button when the pointer is positioned correctly.
- To place all fields on the report, double-click the field list title bar to highlight them. Click anywhere in the highlighted area of the field list, and then drag the fields to the report. Release the mouse button when the pointer is positioned correctly.

First, you need to add bound controls for the NAICSCode and NAICSDesc fields to the Group Header section. Then you'll add bound controls for the other fields to the Detail section.

To add bound controls for all fields in the field list:

1. Click **NAICSCode** in the field list, hold down the **Shift** key, click **NAICSDesc** in the field list, and then release the **Shift** key to highlight both fields.

2. Click anywhere in the highlighted area of the field list (except the title bar), and then drag the fields to the NAICSDesc Header section. Release the mouse button when the pointer ⬚ is positioned at the top of the NAICSDesc Header section and at the 3-inch mark on the horizontal ruler. You've added bound controls for the two selected fields. Each bound control consists of a text box and an attached label positioned to the left of the text box. See Figure 6-12. Notice that the text boxes are left aligned near the 3-inch mark; the labels are also left aligned.

   TROUBLE? If you did not position the bound controls properly in the NAICSDesc Header section, click the Undo button 🔄 on the Report Design toolbar, and then repeat Step 2. However, if the positioning of your controls differs just slightly from those shown in Figure 6-12, leave them where they are because you'll move all the controls later in this tutorial.

3. Double-click the field list title bar to highlight all the fields in the NAICS and Employers field list.

4. Hold down the **Ctrl** key, click **NAICSCode** in the field list, click **NAICSDesc** in the field list, and then release the **Ctrl** key. You've highlighted all fields in the field list, except the NAICSCode and NAICSDesc fields.

5. Drag the highlighted fields to the Detail section. Release the mouse button when the pointer ⬚ is positioned at the top of the Detail section and at the 3-inch mark on the horizontal ruler. You've added bound controls to the Detail section for the 13 selected fields. See Figure 6-12.

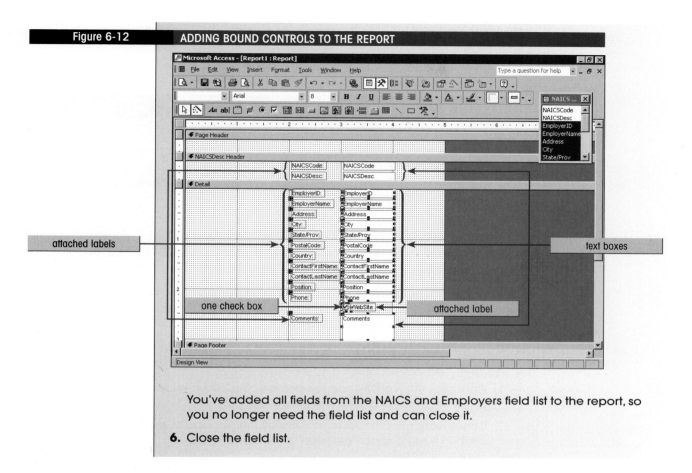

Figure 6-12   ADDING BOUND CONTROLS TO THE REPORT

You've added all fields from the NAICS and Employers field list to the report, so you no longer need the field list and can close it.

6. Close the field list.

Performing operations in the Report window in Design view will become easier with practice. Remember, you can always click the Undo button one or more times immediately after you make report design changes that produce unsatisfactory results. You can also click the Print Preview button at any time to view your progress on the report.

Working with Controls

Two text boxes now appear in a column in the NAICSDesc Header section, and 12 text boxes and one check box now appear in a column in the Detail section. Each box is a bound control linked to a field in the underlying query and has an attached label box. The label boxes appear to the left of the text boxes and to the right of the check box. The labels identify the contents of the text boxes and the check box; the text boxes and check box will display the field values from the database.

According to Elsa's plan for the report (see Figure 6-3), all multi-word labels, such as EmployerName and ContactFirstName, have spaces between the separate words—for example, EmployerName appears in the plan as Employer Name. You'll change the text of these labels by changing each label's Caption property.

Changing the Caption Property

Each label has a **Caption property** that controls the text that appears in the label. The default Caption property value for a bound control is the field name followed by a colon. Other controls, such as buttons and tab controls, have Caption properties as well. You can change the value of a Caption property for a control by using the property sheet for that control. You should change the Caption property value for a control when the default value is difficult to read or understand.

REFERENCE WINDOW RW

Changing the Caption Property for a Label
- Right-click the label to select it and to display the shortcut menu, and then click Properties to open the property sheet.
- Click the All tab (if necessary), click the Caption text box, and then press the F2 key to select the current Caption property value.
- Type the new Caption property value.
- Click the Close button to close the property sheet.

The default Caption property values for several labels in the report do not match Elsa's report design. You need to change the Caption property for nine labels—two labels in the NAICSDesc Header section and seven labels in the Detail section.

To change the Caption property for the labels:

1. Right-click the **NAICSCode label** in the NAICSDesc Header section, and then click **Properties** to display the property sheet for the NAICSCode label.

2. If necessary, click the **All** tab to display the All page of the property sheet. You need to insert a space between "NAICS" and "Code."

    TROUBLE? If the property sheet blocks any controls in the report, drag the property sheet title bar down and to the right.

3. Position the insertion point between "NAICS" and "Code," and then press the **spacebar**. See Figure 6-13.

Figure 6-13   CHANGING THE CAPTION PROPERTY VALUE

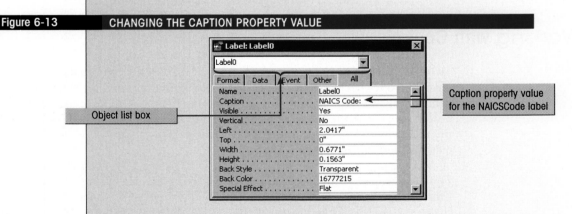

TROUBLE? The property sheet title bar, the Object list box, the Name property, and the label measurements on your screen might have values different than those shown in Figure 6-13. This causes no problems.

4. Click the **NAICSDesc label** in the NAICSDesc Header section to select it. The property sheet changes to show the properties for the NAICSDesc label.

5. Edit the text of the Caption property so that it displays the value **NAICS Desc:**.

6. Repeat Steps 4 and 5 for the EmployerID, EmployerName, PostalCode, ContactFirstName, ContactLastName, and WebSite labels. Change the Caption property to **Employer ID:**, **Employer Name:**, **Postal Code:**, **Contact First Name:**, **Contact Last Name:**, and **Web Site:**, respectively.

7. Close the property sheet.

8. Click an empty area of the grid to deselect any selected controls.

According to Elsa's report design, you need to reposition all labels and text boxes in the report. You'll also resize several text boxes, and you'll resize all labels to their best fit.

Moving and Resizing Controls

Just like with forms, you can move a text box and its attached label as a pair in the Report window. You can also move or resize any individual control or multiple selected controls. When you select a control, a move handle appears in its upper-left corner. This is the handle you use to reposition the selected control. Around its border, a selected control also displays sizing handles, which you can use to resize a control in different directions.

REFERENCE WINDOW   **RW**

Moving and Resizing Controls

- In Design view, click the control to select it.
- To move a control, position the pointer on the control's move handle, and then drag the control to its new location.
- To resize a control, position the pointer on one of the control's sizing handles, and then drag the sizing handle until the control is the proper size.

You need to resize all labels to their best fit, and then reposition the text boxes, check box, and labels to match the report's design.

To resize the labels and move the controls in the NAICSDesc Header and Detail sections:

1. Click the **NAICSCode label**, hold down the **Shift** key, click all other labels in the NAICSDesc Header and Detail sections, and then release the **Shift** key. You've selected all the labels.

2. Click **Format** on the menu bar, point to **Size**, and then click **To Fit**. Access resizes all the label boxes to fit the captions.

   Next, you'll reposition all controls in the NAICSDesc Header and Detail sections.

3. Click an empty area of the grid to deselect all selected controls.

4. Click the **NAICSDesc label** in the NAICSDesc Header section, position the pointer on the move handle in the upper-left corner of the label so it changes to a ☝ shape, and then drag the label to the upper-left corner of the NAICSDesc Header section.

5. Click the **NAICSDesc** text box in the NAICSDesc Header section, position the pointer on the move handle in the upper-left corner of the text box so it changes to a 🖐 shape, and then drag the text box to the position shown in Figure 6-14.

6. Refer to Figure 6-14 and use the procedures in Steps 4 and 5 to move the other labels and text boxes in the NAICSDesc Header and Detail sections to match the figure as closely as possible. The report's width will widen automatically from 5 inches to approximately 5.5 inches when you move the NAICSCode text box in the NAICSDesc Header section. See Figure 6-14.

Figure 6-14   AFTER MOVING THE CONTROLS IN THE REPORT WINDOW

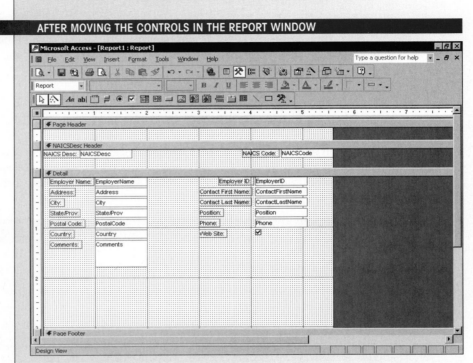

You've made many modifications to the report design and should save the report before proceeding.

To save the report design:

1. Click the **Save** button 🖫 on the Report Design toolbar. The Save As dialog box opens.

2. Type **Potential Income** in the Report Name text box, and then press the **Enter** key. The dialog box closes, and Access saves the report in the Jobs database.

Next, you'll resize four text boxes—the NAICSDesc, EmployerName, Address, and Comments text boxes—so their field-value contents will be completely visible. Because the Comments field in the Employer table is a memo field, the Comments text box is a special case; comments about an employer can range from none to many lines of text. Thus, you'll need to resize the Comments text box for the minimal case of one line, but you want the text box to expand to display the entire field value when multiple lines are needed. Setting the Can Grow property of the Comments text box to Yes will do exactly this. The **Can Grow property**, when set to Yes, expands a text box vertically to fit the field value when the report is printed.

To resize the text boxes and set the Can Grow property:

1. Click the **Comments** text box in the Detail section, position the pointer on its middle-right sizing handle so it changes to a ↔ shape, and then drag the right border to the right to the 5.5-inch mark on the horizontal ruler.

2. Position the pointer on the middle-bottom sizing handle of the Comments text box so it changes to a ↕ shape, and then drag the bottom border up until it's the same height as the bottom of the Comments label.

3. Refer to Figure 6-15 and repeat Step 1 to resize the width of the **EmployerName** and **Address** text boxes in the Detail section and the width of the **NAICSDesc** text box in the NAICSDesc Header section.

Figure 6-15	AFTER RESIZING FOUR TEXT BOXES

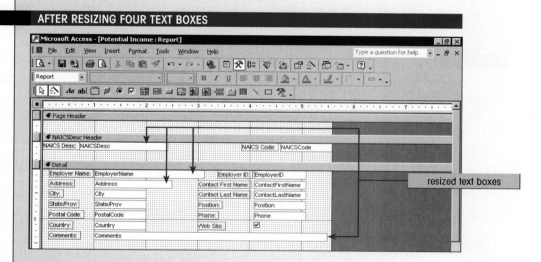

4. Click the **Comments** text box, press the **F4** key to open the property sheet, set the Can Grow property to **Yes**, and then close the property sheet.

Now you need to align the two columns of labels in the Detail section on their right edges.

Aligning Controls

You can align controls in a report or form using the **Align** command, which provides different options for aligning controls. For example, if you select controls in a column, you can use the Align Left option to align the left edges of the controls. Similarly, if you select controls in a row, you can use the Align Top option to align the top edges of the controls. The Align Right and Align Bottom options work the same way. A fifth option, Align To Grid, aligns selected controls with the grid dots in the Report window. To match Elsa's report design, you will use the Align Right option to align the labels in the Detail section. Then you'll save the modified report and preview it to see what it will look like when printed.

To align the labels in the Detail section and then save and preview the report:

1. Click an empty area of the grid to deselect all controls.

2. Click the **EmployerName label** in the Detail section, hold down the **Shift** key, click each of the six labels below the EmployerName label, and then release the **Shift** key. This action selects the seven labels in the left column of the Detail section in preparation for aligning them on their right edges.

3. Right-click one selected label, point to **Align** on the shortcut menu, and then click **Right** to right-align the selected labels on the right.

4. Repeat Steps 1 through 3 for the six labels in the right column of the Detail section to right-align them, and then click an empty area of the grid to deselect all controls. See Figure 6-16.

Figure 6-16	AFTER RIGHT-ALIGNING THE LABELS IN THE DETAIL SECTION

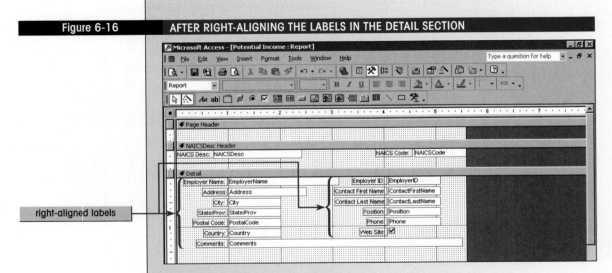

right-aligned labels

As you create a report, you should periodically save your modifications to the report and preview your progress.

5. Save your report design changes, and then switch to Print Preview.

6. Scroll the Print Preview window so that you can see more of the report on the screen. The field values for the first two employers follow the first pair of NAICS field values. See Figure 6-17.

Figure 6-17   REPORT IN PRINT PREVIEW

7. Navigate to Seaview Restaurant (page 7 or 8 of the Print Preview window). Notice that the Comments field value for Seaview Restaurant displays three lines of text, verifying that the Can Grow property is properly set for the field.

8. Click the **Close** button on the Print Preview toolbar to return to the Report window in Design view.

You have completed your initial work on the report. In the next session, you will continue developing the report according to Elsa's design.

Session 6.1 QUICK CHECK

1. Describe the seven sections of an Access report.

2. What is a custom report?

3. The _____ function lets you assign one value to a calculated field if a condition is true and a second value if the condition is false.

4. What does the Report window in Design view have in common with the Form window in Design view? How do the two windows differ?

5. What is a grouping field?

6. What is the Caption property for a control, and when would you change it?

7. The _____ property, when set to Yes, expands a text box vertically to fit the field value when a report is printed.

8. How do you right-align controls in a column?

SESSION 6.2

In this session, you will continue creating the Potential Income report. You will add a subreport to the Detail section, add a Group Footer section to the subreport, specify grouping and sorting fields for the subreport, and then add a line and group totals to the Group Footer section. Finally, you will define conditional formatting rules and use a domain aggregate function to add a grand total to the Report Footer section.

Adding a Subreport Using Control Wizards

According to Elsa's design, the Potential Income report uses a subreport in the Detail section to include an employer's position information. Similar to a subform, a Control Wizard can help you create a subreport. You will use the Subform/Subreport Wizard to add the subreport based on the data from the Potential Placement Fees query, which Elsa created and you reviewed at the beginning of Session 6.1.

To add the subreport to the report's Detail section:

1. If you took a break after the previous session, make sure that Access is running, that the **Jobs** database from the Tutorial folder on your Data Disk is open, and that the **Potential Income** report is open in Design view in a maximized window.

2. Make sure the **Control Wizards** tool on the toolbox is selected, and then click the **Subform/Subreport** tool on the toolbox.

3. Position the + portion of the pointer near the left edge of the Detail section, just below the 1.5-inch mark on the vertical ruler and in the third column of grid dots, and then click the mouse button. Access places a subreport control in the Detail section and opens the first SubReport Wizard dialog box.

   TROUBLE? If a dialog box opens and tells you that Microsoft can't start this Wizard, place your Office XP CD in the correct drive, and then click the Yes button. If you do not have this CD, ask your instructor or technical support person for help.

4. Make sure the **Use existing Tables and Queries** option button is selected, and then click the **Next** button. Access opens the next SubReport Wizard dialog box, from which you select the table or query on which the subreport is based and the fields from that table or query.

   You'll select all fields from the Potential Placement Fees query.

5. Click the **Tables/Queries** list arrow to display the list of tables and queries in the Jobs database, click **Query: Potential Placement Fees**, click the >> button to select all fields from the query, and then click the **Next** button to open the next SubReport Wizard dialog box.

   In this dialog box, you select the link between the main report and the subreport. You want to use the default option, which uses the EmployerID field as the common field between the two queries—the main report's NAICS and Employers source query includes the common field; so does the subreport's Potential Placement Fees source query.

6. Make sure the **Choose from a list** option button is selected and the first link is highlighted, and then click the **Next** button. The next SubReport Wizard dialog box lets you specify a name for the subreport.

7. Type **Potential Income Subreport**, and then click the **Finish** button. Access inserts a subreport control, which is where an employer's position records will appear, in the Detail section of the main report.

8. Save your report changes, maximize the Report window, and then close the field list. See Figure 6-18.

| Figure 6-18 | AFTER ADDING THE SUBREPORT TO THE MAIN REPORT |

9. Switch to Print Preview to review the report. See Figure 6-19.

| Figure 6-19 | PRINT PREVIEW OF THE SUBREPORT IN THE MAIN REPORT |

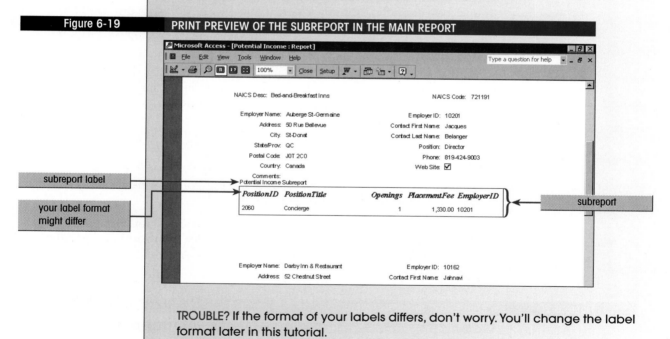

TROUBLE? If the format of your labels differs, don't worry. You'll change the label format later in this tutorial.

Based on Elsa's report design, you'll need to make several changes to the subreport.

Modifying a Subreport

In Elsa's report design (see Figure 6-3), the subreport includes columns for the PositionTitle, PositionID, Openings, and PlacementFee columns, but not for the EmployerID column. Also, the PositionTitle controls appear to the left of the PositionID controls. In addition, a line appears above the placement fee total. Before you open the subreport to modify it based on Elsa's report design, you'll delete the subreport label and change some subreport properties.

The subreport label does not appear in Elsa's report design, so you'll delete the label. In addition, you'll set the subreport's Can Shrink and Border Style properties. The **Can Shrink property**, when set to Yes, reduces the height of a control that contains no data to eliminate blank lines in the printed report. You'll set the subreport's Can Shrink property to Yes. When an employer has no available positions, Elsa wants to avoid printing the blank space occupied by the empty subreport. Finally, the subreport includes a rectangular border by default; Elsa's report design does not include this border. You'll set the **Border Style property**, which specifies a control's border type, to Transparent, so that the rectangle is invisible.

To delete the subreport label and set the Can Shrink and Border Style properties:

1. Switch to Design view, right-click the subreport label, and then click **Cut** on the shortcut menu to delete the label.

2. Right-click the subreport border to select it, and then click **Properties** to open the property sheet for the subreport.

3. If necessary, click the **Format** tab.

4. Set the Can Shrink property to **Yes**, set the Border Style property to **Transparent**, and then close the property sheet.

You could modify the subreport in the Report window of the Potential Income report. However, because the subreport is a separate report and making the subreport changes is easier in a separate window, you'll open the subreport in Design view in a new window. Then you'll modify the subreport design to match Elsa's design.

To open the subreport in Design view and modify the subreport design:

1. If the subreport is not the currently selected control, click the subreport border. Sizing handles appear around the subreport.

2. Move the pointer to the subreport border; when the pointer changes to a ✋ shape, right-click the mouse button, and then click **Subreport in New Window** on the shortcut menu. The Potential Income Subreport report opens in Design view. See Figure 6-20.

| Figure 6-20 | SUBREPORT IN DESIGN VIEW |

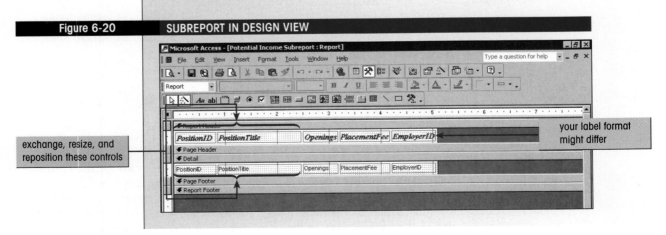

exchange, resize, and reposition these controls

your label format might differ

TROUBLE? If the labels in your Report Header section have different font properties than the labels shown in Figure 6-20, select the five labels, and then change their properties to match. Figure 6-20 shows labels set in 11-point, bold, italic, Times New Roman font; if you need to change these properties, use the buttons on the Formatting toolbar.

TROUBLE? If the label captions in your Report Header section are not blue, select the five labels, open the property sheet, click the Fore Color text box, click the Build button ... next to the Fore Color text box, click the blue color (row 5, column 5), click the OK button, and then close the property sheet.

Unlike the main report, which initially contained Detail, Page Header, and Page Footer sections when you created a blank report, the subreport contains a Report Header section and a Detail section. (Although the Page Header, Page Footer, and Report Footer sections appear in the subreport, their heights are set to zero. As a result, these three sections do not appear in Print Preview or in the printed subreport.) Labels appear as column headings in the Report Header section, and field-value text boxes appear in the Detail section.

To match Elsa's design, you'll reduce the widths of the PositionID and PositionTitle controls so that you can exchange their positions, and then you'll resize and reposition the four controls.

3. Click an empty area of the grid to deselect any selected controls (if necessary), click the **PositionTitle label**, hold down the **Shift** key, click the **PositionTitle** text box, release the **Shift** key to select both controls, and then use the middle-right sizing handle of either control to reduce the widths of the selected controls to approximately 0.5 inches.

4. Click a blank area of the Report Header section to deselect the PositionTitle controls, and then repeat Step 3 for the **PositionID label** and the **PositionID** text box.

5. Position the pointer on the PositionID text box; when the pointer changes to a 🖑 shape, drag the two selected controls to the right of the PositionTitle controls.

6. Refer to Figure 6-21 to resize and reposition the PositionID label and text box and the PositionTitle label and text box.

| Figure 6-21 | AFTER EXCHANGING, RESIZING, AND REPOSITIONING CONTROLS |

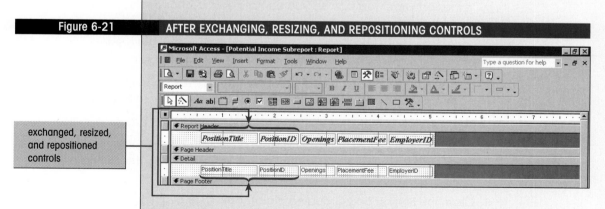

exchanged, resized, and repositioned controls

Because the EmployerID label and field value appear in the main report's Detail section, you need to prevent them from printing in the subreport by setting their Visible property. You use the **Visible property** to show or hide a control.

7. Use the Shift key to select the **EmployerID label** and the **EmployerID** text box.

8. Press the **F4** key to open the property sheet. The text "Multiple selection" in the property sheet title bar and the empty Object list box both indicate that you'll set properties for two or more controls. See Figure 6-22.

Figure 6-22	PROPERTY SHEET FOR MULTIPLE CONTROLS

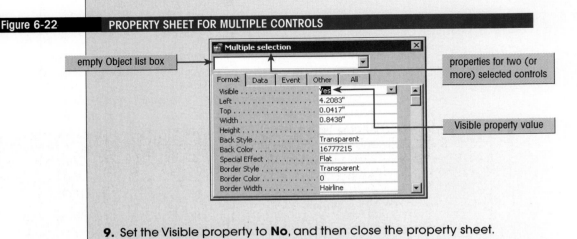

empty Object list box

properties for two (or more) selected controls

Visible property value

9. Set the Visible property to **No**, and then close the property sheet.

Elsa's report design includes subreport totals for the placement fee and employer potential income amounts, so you need to add a Group Footer section for the EmployerID field to the subreport. Thus, EmployerID will be the primary sort key using an ascending sort order. Because Elsa wants the positions to print in ascending order by the position titles for an employer, the PositionTitle field will be the secondary sort key.

To select the sort keys and the group field for the subreport:

1. Click the **Sorting and Grouping** button 〔≣〕 on the Report Design toolbar to open the Sorting and Grouping dialog box.

2. Click the list arrow in the first **Field/Expression** text box to display the list of available fields, and then click **EmployerID**. Ascending is the default sort order in the Sort Order text box, so you do not need to change this setting.

   You can now designate EmployerID as a grouping field and specify that you want a Group Footer section for this group. This section will contain the employer totals for the placement fee and potential income amounts.

3. Click the right side of the **Group Footer** text box, and then click **Yes**. Access adds a Group Footer section named EmployerID Footer to the Report window.

   You can now specify the secondary sort key and its sort order.

4. Click the right side of the second **Field/Expression** text box to display the list of fields, and then click **PositionTitle**. You've finished setting the sorting and grouping options for the subreport.

5. Close the Sorting and Grouping dialog box.

Next, you'll add a line to the EmployerID Footer section to separate the detail placement fees from the employer placement fee total.

Adding Lines to a Report

You can use lines in a report to improve the report's readability and to group related information. The **Line tool** on the toolbox lets you add a line to a report or form.

REFERENCE WINDOW **RW**

Adding a Line to a Report
- Display the report in Design view.
- Click the Line tool on the toolbox.
- Position the pointer where you want the line to begin.
- Drag the pointer to the position for the end of the line, and then release the mouse button. If you want to ensure that you draw a straight horizontal or vertical line, hold down the Shift key before and during the drag operation.
- To make small adjustments to the line length, select the line, hold down the Shift key, and then press an arrow key. To make small adjustments in the placement of a line, select the line, hold down the Ctrl key, and then press an arrow key.

You will add a horizontal line to the top of the EmployerID Footer section under the PlacementFee text box to separate the total employer placement fee from the column of individual placement fees for the employer on the printed report.

To add a line to the report:

1. Click the **Line** tool 🖿 on the toolbox.

2. Position the pointer in the EmployerID Footer section. The pointer changes to a +🖿 shape.

3. Position the pointer's plus symbol (+) near the top of the EmployerID Footer section at the 3.75-inch mark on the horizontal ruler.

4. Drag a horizontal line from left to right, so the end of the line aligns with the right edge of the PlacementFee text box in the Detail section, and then release the mouse button. See Figure 6-23.

| Figure 6-23 | ADDING A LINE TO THE REPORT |

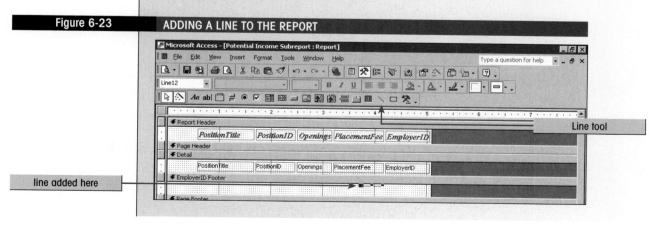

line added here

Line tool

TROUBLE? If the line is not straight or not positioned correctly, click the Undo button on the Report Design toolbar, and then repeat Steps 1 through 4. If the line is not the correct length, hold down the Shift key, and press one or more of the arrow keys until the line's length is the same as that of the line shown in Figure 6-23.

Next, you'll move the line to the top of the EmployerID Footer section.

5. Hold down the **Ctrl** key, and then press the ↑ key until the line reaches the top of the EmployerID Footer section.

TROUBLE? If the line jumps up to the bottom of the Detail section, hold down the Ctrl key and press the ↓ key until the line moves back to the top of the EmployerID Footer section.

Elsa asks you to remove the excess space above and below the five controls in the Detail section and to reduce the height of the Detail section.

6. Select all five controls in the Detail section and place the pointer on a selected control; when the pointer changes to a ✋ shape, drag the controls straight up to the top of the Detail section.

7. Position the pointer on the bottom edge of the Detail section; when the pointer changes to a ✛ shape, drag the bottom edge up until it touches the bottom of the text boxes in the Detail section.

8. Save your subreport design changes.

Recall that the subreport's primary sort key is the EmployerID field and the secondary sort key is the PositionTitle field. For employers with several positions, it's possible that two or more positions could have the same PositionTitle field value. In these cases, Elsa wants the PositionTitle field value printed for the first position but not for subsequent positions because she believes that would make the position data easier to read.

Hiding **Duplicate Values in a Report**

You use the **Hide Duplicates property** to hide a control on a report when the control's value is the same as that of the preceding record.

REFERENCE WINDOW	RW
Hiding Duplicate Values in a Report	
■ Display the report in Design view.	
■ Open the property sheet for the field whose duplicate values you want to hide, set the Hide Duplicates property to Yes, and then close the property sheet.	

Your next change is to hide duplicate PositionTitle field values in the Detail section.

To hide the duplicate PositionTitle field values:

1. Click an empty area of the grid to deselect all controls.

2. Open the property sheet for the PositionTitle text box.

3. Click the **Format** tab (if necessary), click the right side of the **Hide Duplicates** text box, and then click **Yes**. See Figure 6-24.

Figure 6-24	HIDING DUPLICATE FIELD VALUES

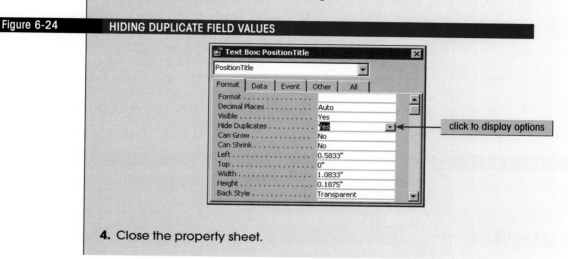

click to display options

4. Close the property sheet.

You are now ready to calculate the group totals for the placement fee and employer potential income amounts.

Calculating Group Totals

Elsa wants the report to print each employer's subtotals for the placement fee and potential income amounts. To calculate subtotals and overall totals in a report, you use the **Sum function**. You place the Sum function in a Group Footer section to print each group's total. When placed in the Report Footer section, the Sum function prints the overall total. The format for the Sum function is =Sum([*fieldname*]). To create the appropriate text boxes in the footer sections, you use the Text Box tool on the toolbox.

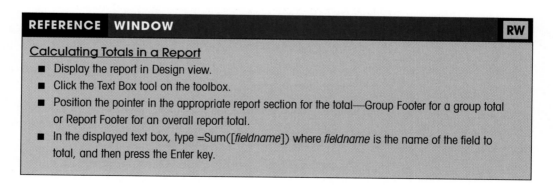

REFERENCE WINDOW   **RW**

Calculating Totals in a Report
- Display the report in Design view.
- Click the Text Box tool on the toolbox.
- Position the pointer in the appropriate report section for the total—Group Footer for a group total or Report Footer for an overall report total.
- In the displayed text box, type =Sum([*fieldname*]) where *fieldname* is the name of the field to total, and then press the Enter key.

To add the group totals to your report, you need to increase the height of the EmployerID Footer section to make room for the two text boxes that will contain the calculated fields. Then you need to add text boxes for the two calculated fields.

To resize the group footer section and add the two calculated fields for the group totals:

1. Use the ⊥ pointer to increase the height of the EmployerID Footer section until the bottom of the section is at the 0.5-inch mark on the vertical ruler.

   Next, you'll add the first calculated field that will print the employer placement fee total.

2. Click the **Text Box** tool [abl] on the toolbox.

3. Position the pointer in the EmployerID Footer section, and click when the pointer's plus symbol (+) is positioned at the top of the section and aligns vertically with the left edge of the PlacementFee text box. Access adds a text box with an attached label box to its left. Inside the text box is the description "Unbound." Recall that an unbound control is a control that is not linked to a database table field. See Figure 6-25.

Figure 6-25	ADDING A TEXT BOX IN THE FOOTER SECTION

Text Box tool

resized section

label (your caption format might differ)

text box for the calculated field

TROUBLE? The label on your screen might have a caption other than the one shown in Figure 6-25. That causes no problems.

You'll now add the Sum function to the text box, which contains the name Unbound, and then set its Format property to Standard, which will print the values with two decimal places.

4. Right-click the **Unbound** text box, click **Properties** on the shortcut menu, click the **All** tab, type **=Sum([PlacementFee])** in the Control Source text box, set the Format property to **Standard**, and then close the property sheet.

   Now add a text box for the second calculated field. You'll use the IIf function for this calculated field.

5. Repeat Steps 2 and 3, clicking when the pointer's plus symbol (+) is positioned in the EmployerID Footer section two grid dots below the other text box and vertically aligned with its left edge.

6. Open the property sheet for the **Unbound** text box, right-click the **Control Source** text box, click **Zoom** on the shortcut menu, and then type **=IIf (Sum (Openings) >= 3, Sum (PlacementFee) + 200, Sum (PlacementFee) + 500)** in the Zoom box. See Figure 6-26.

Figure 6-26	CALCULATION FOR THE EMPLOYER POTENTIAL INCOME

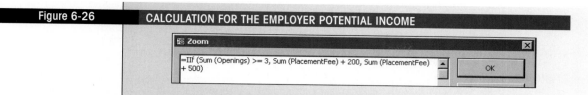

The calculation is the same one you used in the Potential Income by Employer query, except it includes the Sum function. Depending on whether the total number of openings for an employer is three or more, either $200 or $500 is added to the employer total placement fee.

Next, you'll set the calculated field's Format property to Standard.

7. Click the **OK** button, set the Format property to **Standard**, and then close the property sheet.

8. Save your design changes, and then switch to Print Preview. See Figure 6-27.

Figure 6-27	PRINT PREVIEW OF THE SUBREPORT

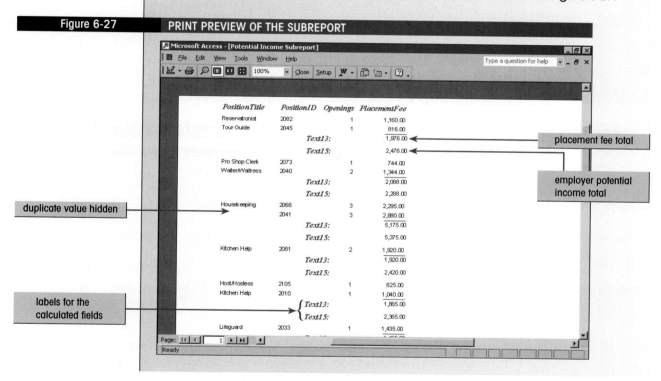

You still need to make several modifications to the subreport. The decimal points for the two calculated fields don't line up with the PlacementFee field values, so you'll need to resize the text boxes for the calculated fields. You'll set the Caption property for both labels, and then you'll resize and reposition them. Finally, Elsa wants to make it easier to use the report to find potential income amounts for employers with low- and high-income potential (under $2000 and over $5000, respectively).

First, you'll resize the text boxes and modify the properties for the two labels.

To resize the text boxes and modify the label properties:

1. Switch to Design view, and then click an empty area of the grid to deselect all controls.

2. Select both text boxes in the EmployerID Footer section.

3. Position the pointer on the middle-right sizing handle of either selected control so it changes to a ↔ shape, and then drag the right borders to the left so that they align with the right border of the PlacementFee text box in the Detail section.

4. Using the middle-left sizing handle, repeat Step 3 to drag the left borders of the selected controls to the right until they are just to the right of the 3.5-inch mark on the horizontal ruler. (See Figure 6-28.)

5. Deselect the controls, open the property sheet for the top label in the EmployerID Footer section, set its Caption property to **Total:**, and then change its font size to **8** and make sure its font is **Times New Roman**, bold, and italic.

6. Click the bottom label in the EmployerID Footer section, set its Caption property to **Employer Potential Income:**, change its font size to **8** and make sure its font is **Times New Roman**, bold, and italic. Close the property sheet.

7. Resize and reposition both labels to match the labels shown in Figure 6-28, and then reduce the height of the EmployerID Footer section.

Figure 6-28	AFTER MODIFYING THE FOOTER LABELS AND TEXT BOXES

labels' final placement and appearance

text boxes' final placement

TROUBLE? If the label captions in your EmployerID Footer section are not blue, select the two labels, open the property sheet, click the Fore Color text box, click the Build button [...] next to the Fore Color text box, click the blue color (row 5, column 5), click the **OK** button, and then close the property sheet and deselect the controls.

Your final subreport modification will allow Elsa to more easily find employer potential income amounts under $2000 and over $5000.

Defining **Conditional Formatting Rules**

One way to make employer potential income amounts easier to spot on the report is to use conditional formatting for the calculated field's text box in the EmployerID Footer section.

Conditional formatting lets you change the format of a report or form control based on the control's value. For example, you can change the calculated field's font style or color when its value is more than $5000 and change the field's font to a different style or color when its value is less than $2000. All other values for the control print in the default font style or color. You can define up to a maximum of three conditional formats for each control.

REFERENCE   WINDOW   **RW**

Defining Conditional Formatting for a Control
- In Design view, right-click the control to select it, and then click Conditional Formatting on the shortcut menu.
- Select and enter the conditions, and then select the format options to be used.
- For a second or third conditional format, click the Add button.
- Click the OK button.

You will use bold text for employer potential income amounts over $5000 and bold, italic text for values under $2000.

To define conditional formatting for the potential income amounts:

1. Right-click the **Employer Potential Income** text box in the EmployerID Footer section, and then click **Conditional Formatting** on the shortcut menu. The Conditional Formatting dialog box opens. See Figure 6-29.

Figure 6-29   CONDITIONAL FORMATTING DIALOG BOX

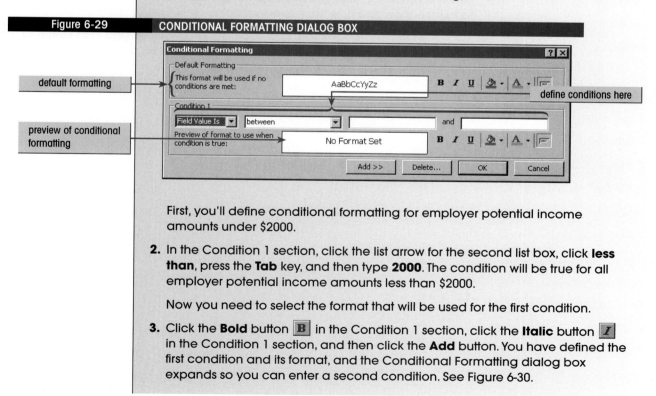

First, you'll define conditional formatting for employer potential income amounts under $2000.

2. In the Condition 1 section, click the list arrow for the second list box, click **less than**, press the **Tab** key, and then type **2000**. The condition will be true for all employer potential income amounts less than $2000.

Now you need to select the format that will be used for the first condition.

3. Click the **Bold** button **B** in the Condition 1 section, click the **Italic** button *I* in the Condition 1 section, and then click the **Add** button. You have defined the first condition and its format, and the Conditional Formatting dialog box expands so you can enter a second condition. See Figure 6-30.

Figure 6-30	AFTER DEFINING THE FIRST CONDITIONAL FORMAT

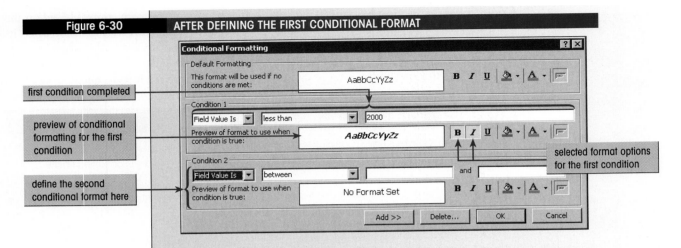

first condition completed

preview of conditional formatting for the first condition

define the second conditional format here

selected format options for the first condition

Next, you'll define the conditional formatting for employer potential income amounts over $5000.

4. In the Condition 2 section, click the list arrow for the second list box, click **greater than**, press the **Tab** key, and then type **5000**. The condition will be true for all employer potential income amounts greater than $5000.

5. In the Condition 2 section, click **B**. You have defined the second condition and its format.

You've finished defining the conditional formats for the employer potential income amounts. Next, you'll accept the conditional formats, save your work, and then show Elsa how the subreport looks.

6. Click the **OK** button, save your subreport design changes, and then switch to Print Preview to verify that the default format and the two conditional formats produce the results you expected. See Figure 6-31.

Figure 6-31   PRINT PREVIEW SHOWING CONDITIONAL FORMATS

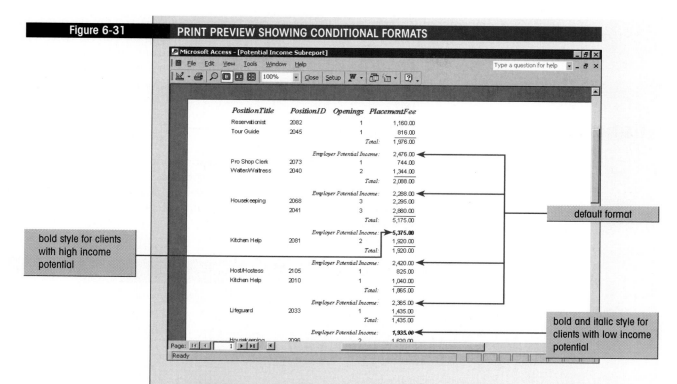

bold style for clients with high income potential

default format

bold and italic style for clients with low income potential

7. Preview the remaining pages of the report to verify that the two conditional formats are correct.

You've completed the subreport design, so you'll return to Design view and close the subreport.

8. Switch to Design view, and then click the **Close Window** button ⊠ on the menu bar. The subreport closes, and you return to Design view for the main report.

Now that you've completed the subreport, you'll check the progress of your report design in Print Preview.

9. Switch to Print Preview. The Group Header and Detail sections are displayed for the first employer. See Figure 6-32.

Figure 6-32   PRINT PREVIEW OF THE MAIN REPORT

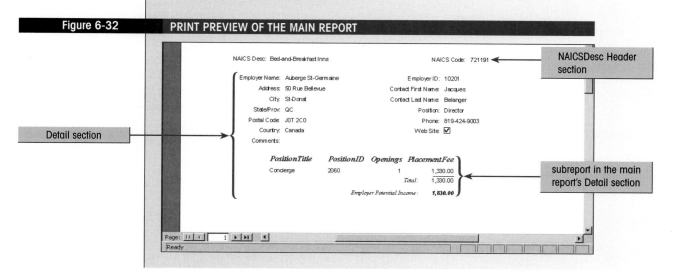

Detail section

NAICSDesc Header section

subreport in the main report's Detail section

Comparing your report with Elsa's report design (see Figure 6-3), you can see that you've completed most of the work. Your remaining tasks include adding the current date, report title, and page number to the Page Header section; adding horizontal lines to all three sections of the main report; and adding a calculated field for the total potential income.

First, you'll add the calculated field to the Report Footer section.

Using Domain Aggregate Functions

When you print a report, anything contained in the Report Footer section appears once at the end of the report. This section is often used to display overall totals. Elsa wants the report to print an overall total based on the employer potential income amounts. To include information in the Report Footer, you must first add both a Report Header section and a Report Footer section to the report.

REFERENCE WINDOW   **RW**

Adding and Removing Report Header and Report Footer Sections
- Display the report in Design view.
- To add the Report Header and Report Footer sections, click View on the menu bar, and then click Report Header/Footer.
- To remove a Report Header or Report Footer section, drag the bottom edge of that section up until the section area disappears.

Before adding the total potential income amount to the report, you need to add Report Header and Report Footer sections. Also, because you will not place any controls in the Report Header and Page Footer sections, you will remove these two sections.

To add Report Header and Report Footer sections and remove report sections:

1. Switch to Design view.

2. Click **View** on the menu bar, and then click **Report Header/Footer**. Access places a Report Header section at the top of the Report window and a Report Footer section at the bottom.

3. Scrolling vertically as necessary, use the ✛ pointer to decrease the height of the Report Header and Page Footer sections to 0, and to decrease the height of the Detail section to 2.5 inches. The new height of the Detail section will allow sufficient room to add a horizontal line in this section below the subreport control. See Figure 6-33.

Figure 6-33   REPORT SECTIONS ADDED AND REMOVED

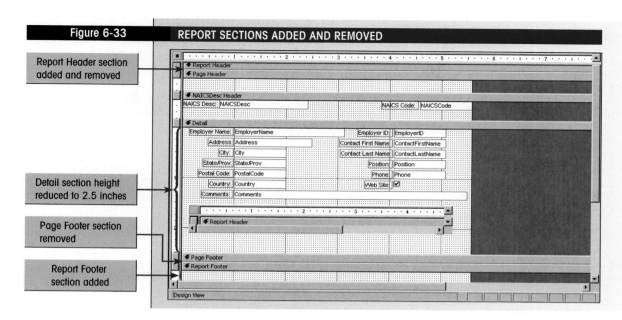

Report Header section added and removed

Detail section height reduced to 2.5 inches

Page Footer section removed

Report Footer section added

The subreport does not appear for those employers without available positions. Recall from Session 6.1 that this causes Access to generate a data error if you attempt to base your calculation for the total potential income amount on the individual employer potential incomes. For that reason, you created the Potential Income by Employer query in Session 6.1. To calculate the total potential income amount for Elsa, you'll use the Potential Income by Employer query as the data source and a domain aggregate function to perform the calculation.

Domain aggregate functions provide statistical information about a set of records (recordset), or **domain**. The set of records can be those records defined in a table or a query. Figure 6-34 describes the available domain aggregate functions. You use aggregate functions, such as the Sum function you used in the subreport, when the fields you're using for the function are bound fields that appear in text boxes in the report. In contrast, you use domain aggregate functions when the source data you're using for the function appear in a table or query recordset.

Figure 6-34   DOMAIN AGGREGATE FUNCTIONS

DOMAIN AGGREGATE FUNCTION	DESCRIPTION
DAvg	Calculates the average of the specified field values from the selected recordset.
DCount	Calculates the number of records with nonnull values in the specified field from the selected recordset.
DFirst	Provides the value in the specified field from the first physical record in the selected recordset.
DLast	Provides the value in the specified field from the last physical record in the selected recordset.
DLookup	Provides the value in the specified field from the selected recordset based on the specified criteria.
DMax	Provides the maximum value of the specified field from the selected recordset.
DMin	Provides the minimum value of the specified field from the selected recordset.
DStDev	Estimates a population sample standard deviation of the specified field from the selected recordset.
DStDevP	Estimates a population standard deviation of the specified field from the selected recordset.
DSum	Calculates the sum of the specified field values from the selected recordset.
DVar	Estimates a population sample variance of the specified field from the selected recordset.
DVarP	Estimates a population variance of the specified field from the selected recordset.

To calculate the total potential income amount, you use the **DSum domain aggregate function**. You place the DSum function in a text box in the Report Footer section to print the overall total. The format for the DSum function is =DSum("expression", "domain", "criteria").

REFERENCE WINDOW   **RW**

Using a Domain Aggregate Function in a Report
- Display the report in Design view.
- Add a text box to the Report Footer section.
- In the text box, set the Control Source property to =*DFunction*("*expression*", "*domain*", "*criteria*"), where *DFunction* is the domain aggregate function, *expression* is the field name, *domain* is the table or query name, and the optional *criteria* is a condition.

You need to add a text box for the DSum function in the Report Footer section.

To add a text box in the Report Footer section and add the DSum function:

1. Click the **Text Box** tool abl on the toolbox, position the pointer in the Report Footer section, and click when the pointer's plus symbol (+) is at the top of the Report Footer section and approximately at the 3.5-inch mark on the horizontal ruler. Access adds a text box with an attached label box to its left.

   You can now enter the DSum function for the text box.

2. Open the property sheet for the **Unbound** text box, click the **All** tab (if necessary), right-click the **Control Source** text box, and then click **Zoom** on the shortcut menu.

3. Type **=DSum("PotentialIncome", "[Potential Income by Employer]")** in the Zoom box. See Figure 6-35.

| Figure 6-35 | TOTAL POTENTIAL INCOME CALCULATION |

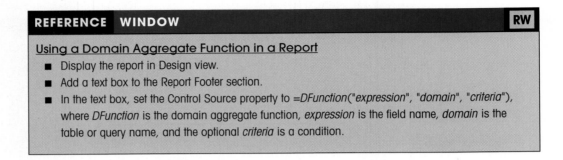

The DSum function will calculate the total of all the PotentialIncome field values in the Potential Income by Employer recordset.

Because Elsa wants the calculated value to print as a money field, you'll set the calculated field's Format and Decimal Places properties.

4. Click the **OK** button to close the Zoom box, set the Format property to **Currency**, and then set the Decimal Places property to **2**.

   Next, you'll set the label's Caption property, and then you'll format it similar to the other labels in the subreport—with blue, bold, italic Times New Roman font.

5. Click the label in the Report Footer section, and then set the Caption property to **Total Potential Income:**.

6. Scroll down the property sheet, click the **Fore Color** text box, and then click the **Build** button [...] next to the Fore Color text box. Access displays the palette of available colors. See Figure 6-36.

Figure 6-36   **CHANGING THE LABEL'S FONT COLOR**

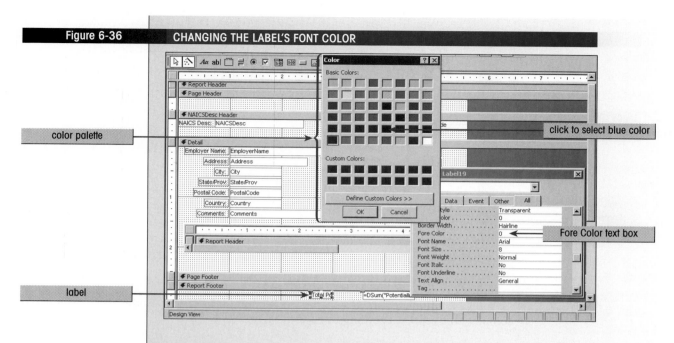

color palette

click to select blue color

Fore Color text box

label

7. Click the blue box in the color palette in row 5 and column 5 (see Figure 6-36), click the **OK** button, and then close the property sheet. The label text color changes to blue.

8. Click the **Bold** button **B** on the Formatting toolbar, click the **Italic** button *I* on the Formatting toolbar, click the **Font** list arrow on the Formatting toolbar, and then scroll down and click **Times New Roman**.

   Now you need to resize and reposition the label and text box in the Report Footer section.

9. Refer to Figure 6-37 to resize and reposition the DSum text box in the Report Footer section, and to size to fit and reposition the label in the Report Footer section.

Figure 6-37   **FINAL SIZES AND POSITIONS OF REPORT FOOTER CONTROLS**

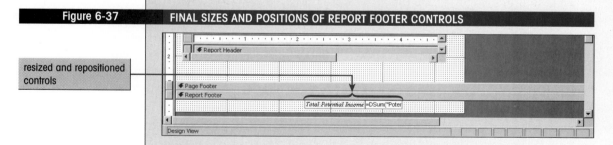

resized and repositioned controls

10. Save your report design changes, switch to Print Preview, and then navigate to the last page of the report. The total potential income and its associated label appear below the information for the last employer and its one available position. See Figure 6-38.

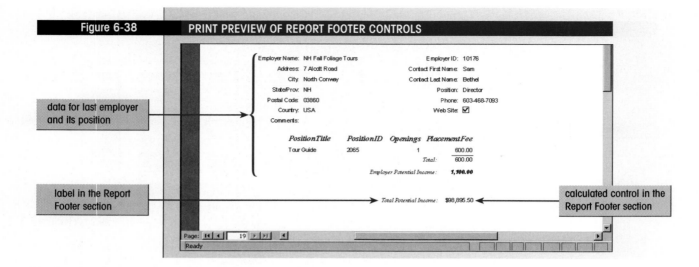

Figure 6-38   PRINT PREVIEW OF REPORT FOOTER CONTROLS

data for last employer and its position

label in the Report Footer section

calculated control in the Report Footer section

You have completed the Report Footer section of the report. In the next session, you will complete the report according to Elsa's design.

Session 6.2 QUICK CHECK

1. The _____ property, when set to Yes, reduces the height of a control that contains no data to eliminate blank lines from the printed report.

2. When you use Control Wizards to create a subreport, which non-empty sections does the Wizard create automatically?

3. You use the _____ property to show or hide a control.

4. To make small adjustments in the placement of a selected line, hold down the Ctrl key, and press a(n) _____ key.

5. Why might you want to hide duplicate values in a report?

6. What is the maximum number of conditional formats you can define for a control?

7. What is a domain?

SESSION 6.3

In this session, you will complete the Potential Income report. You will add a title and line, and add the date and page number to the Page Header section of the main report. You will also add lines to separate sections of the report visually. Finally, you will create and modify mailing labels.

Adding the Date to a Report

According to Elsa's design, the Potential Income report must include the date in the Page Header section. To add the date to a report, you insert the Date function in a text box. The **Date function** is a type of calculated control that prints the current date on a report. The format of the Date function is =Date(). The equals sign (=) indicates that what follows it is a calculated control; Date is the name of the function; and the parentheses () indicate a function rather than simple text.

REFERENCE WINDOW   **RW**

Adding the Date to a Report
- Display the report in Design view.
- Click the Text Box tool on the toolbox, position the pointer where you want the date to appear, and then click to place the text box in the report.
- Click the text box, type =Date(), and then press the Enter key.

You need to insert the Date function in the Page Header section so that the current date will print on each page of the report.

To add the Date function to the Page Header section:

1. If you took a break after the previous session, make sure that Access is running, that the **Jobs** database from the Tutorial folder on your Data Disk is open, and that the **Potential Income** report is open in a maximized Print Preview window.

2. Switch to Design view.

3. Click the **Text Box** tool [abl] on the toolbox, and then position the pointer in the Page Header section. The pointer changes to a $^+$[abl] shape.

4. Position the pointer's plus symbol (+) in the second row of grid dots in the Page Header section at the 1-inch mark on the horizontal ruler (see Figure 6-38), and then click the mouse button. Access adds a text box with an attached label box to its left.

5. Click the **Unbound** text box to position the insertion point and remove the word "Unbound," and then type **=Date**() and press the **Enter** key. See Figure 6-39.

Figure 6-39 | ADDING THE CURRENT DATE TO THE REPORT

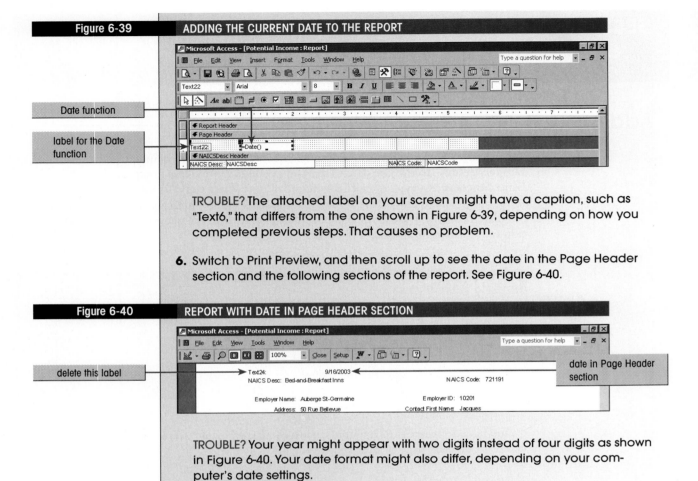

TROUBLE? The attached label on your screen might have a caption, such as "Text6," that differs from the one shown in Figure 6-39, depending on how you completed previous steps. That causes no problem.

6. Switch to Print Preview, and then scroll up to see the date in the Page Header section and the following sections of the report. See Figure 6-40.

Figure 6-40 | REPORT WITH DATE IN PAGE HEADER SECTION

TROUBLE? Your year might appear with two digits instead of four digits as shown in Figure 6-40. Your date format might also differ, depending on your computer's date settings.

When you print or preview the report, the current date appears instead of the Date function you entered in the text box. The date label is unnecessary, so you can delete it. You'll also move the text box to the left edge of the Page Header section and then left-align the date in the text box.

To delete the Date label and move and left-align the Date text box:

1. Switch to Design view.

2. Right-click the **Date label** located at the far left of the Page Header section, and then click **Cut** on the shortcut menu to delete the label.

3. Click the **Date** text box, drag its move handle to the left edge of the Page Header section, and then click the **Align Left** button 📄 on the Formatting toolbar to left-align the date in the text box.

4. Save your report design changes.

You are now ready to add page numbers to the Page Header section.

Adding **Page Numbers to a Report**

You can print page numbers in a report by including an expression in the Page Header or Page Footer section. You can type the expression in an unbound control, just as you did for the Date function, or you can use the Page Numbers option on the Insert menu. The inserted page number expression automatically prints the correct page number on each page of a report.

REFERENCE WINDOW   **RW**

Adding Page Numbers to a Report
- Display the report in Design view.
- Click the section in which you want to place page numbers.
- Click Insert on the menu bar, and then click Page Numbers.
- Select the formatting, position, and alignment options you want.
- Click the OK button to place the page number expression in the report.

Elsa wants the page number to be printed at the right side of the Page Header section, on the same line with the date. You'll use the Page Numbers option to insert the page number in the report.

To add page numbers in the Page Header section:

1. Click an empty area of the Page Header section to deselect the Date text box.

2. Click **Insert** on the menu bar, and then click **Page Numbers**. The Page Numbers dialog box opens.

   You use the Format options to specify the format of the page number. Elsa wants page numbers to appear as Page 1, Page 2, and so on. This is the Page N format option. You use the Position options to place the page numbers at the top of the page in the Page Header section or at the bottom of the page in the Page Footer section. Elsa's design shows page numbers at the top of the page.

3. Make sure that the **Page N** option button in the Format section and that the **Top of Page [Header]** option button in the Position section are both selected.

   The report design shows page numbers at the right side of the page. You can specify this placement in the Alignment list box.

4. Click the **Alignment** list arrow, and then click **Right**.

5. Make sure that the **Show Number on First Page** check box is checked, so the page number prints on the first page and all other pages as well. See Figure 6-41.

| Figure 6-41 | COMPLETED PAGE NUMBERS DIALOG BOX |

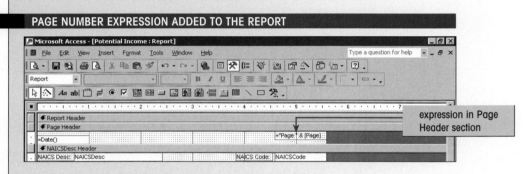

click to select format → Format: ⊙ Page N ○ Page N of M

click to select position on page → Position: ⊙ Top of Page [Header] ○ Bottom of Page [Footer]

indicates page number will be printed on all pages → Alignment: Right ☑ Show Number on First Page

click to display alignment options

6. Click the **OK** button. The text box shown in Figure 6-42 appears in the upper-right corner of the Page Header section. The expression ="Page " & [Page] in the text box means that the printed report will show the word "Page" followed by a space and the page number.

| Figure 6-42 | PAGE NUMBER EXPRESSION ADDED TO THE REPORT |

expression in Page Header section

Elsa wants the word "Page," the page number, and the date to be bold. You could select both controls and then set both to bold at the same time. Or you could select one of the two controls, set it to bold, and then duplicate the formatting for the other control. To duplicate a control's formatting, you can use the Format Painter. The **Format Painter** lets you copy the format of a control to other controls in the report. With the Format Painter, creating several controls with the same font style, size, color, and special effect is easy.

Elsa's report design also shows the page number's bottom edge aligned with the date in the Page Header section.

To use the Format Painter and to align controls:

1. Click the **Date** text box to select it, and then click the **Bold** button **B** on the Formatting toolbar to change the date to bold.

2. Click the **Format Painter** button on the Report Design toolbar.

3. Click the **Page Number** text box. The Format Painter automatically formats the Page Number text box like the Date text box, changing its font to bold.

   You'll now align the bottom border of the Date and Page Number text boxes.

4. Hold down the **Shift** key, click the **Page Number** text box, release the **Shift** key, click **Format** on the menu bar, point to **Align**, and then click **Bottom**. The bottom borders of the text boxes are now aligned.

5. Switch to Print Preview. See Figure 6-43.

Figure 6-43	DATE AND PAGE NUMBER IN THE PAGE HEADER SECTION

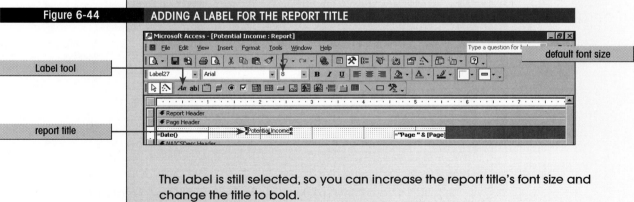

date → 9/16/2003 ... Page 1 ← page number
NAICS Desc: Bed-and-Breakfast Inns   NAICS Code: 721191
Employer Name: Auberge St-Germaine   Employer ID: 10201

Now you are ready to add the title to the Page Header section.

Adding a Title to a Report

Elsa's report design includes the title "Potential Income," which you'll add to the Page Header section. To emphasize the report title, Elsa asks you to change it to bold and increase its font size from 8 points, the default, to 14 points.

To add the title to the Page Header section:

1. Switch to Design view.

2. Click the **Label** tool [Aa] on the toolbox, and then position the pointer in the Page Header section. The pointer changes to a ⁺A shape.

3. Position the pointer's plus symbol (+) at the top of the Page Header section and at the 1.75-inch mark on the horizontal ruler, and then click the mouse button. Access places a very narrow text box in the Page Header section. When you start typing in this text box, it will expand to accommodate the text.

4. Type **Potential Income**, and then press the **Enter** key. See Figure 6-44.

Figure 6-44	ADDING A LABEL FOR THE REPORT TITLE

Label tool
default font size
report title
Potential Income
=Date()   ="Page " & [Page]

The label is still selected, so you can increase the report title's font size and change the title to bold.

5. Click the **Font Size** list arrow on the Formatting toolbar, click **14**, and then click the **Bold** button [B] on the Formatting toolbar. The font size and style of the report title change from 8 points to 14 points and to bold. The label box is now too small to display the entire report title, so you will need to resize the label box.

6. Click **Format** on the menu bar, point to **Size**, and then click **To Fit** to resize the report title text box.

Elsa wants to see how the report looks, so you'll switch to Print Preview to check the report against her design.

7. Save your report design changes, switch to Print Preview and, if necessary, scroll the Print Preview window to see more of the report. See Figure 6-45.

Figure 6-45	REPORT TITLE IN THE PAGE HEADER SECTION

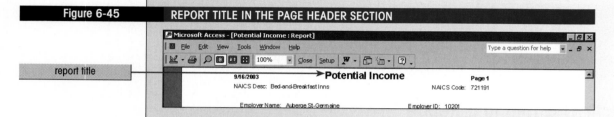

report title

8. Review the first several pages of the report in Print Preview. Notice that the NAICSDesc Header section on page 5 appears near the bottom of the page, and the first employer name within this group appears at the top of the next page. See Figure 6-46.

Figure 6-46	GROUP HEADER SECTION ORPHANED FROM GROUP'S FIRST EMPLOYER

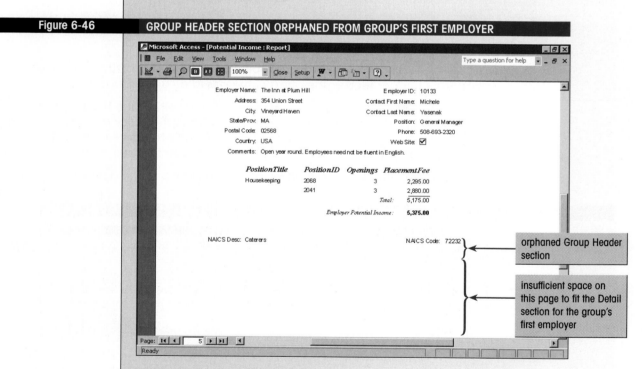

orphaned Group Header section

insufficient space on this page to fit the Detail section for the group's first employer

TROUBLE? If your Print Preview screen for page 5 doesn't match the one shown in Figure 6-46, navigate through the remaining Print Preview pages to find a similar Group Header section with the same problem. Depending on your printer driver, you might not find a similar Group Header section; in this case, simply continue with the tutorial.

The Group Header section shown in Figure 6-46 is an example of an orphaned header section. An **orphaned header section** appears by itself at the bottom of a page. Elsa prefers to see the NAICSDesc Header printed at the top of a page, just before the first employer name in the group. To do this, you'll set the Keep Together property for the NAICSDesc Header section. The **Keep Together property** prints a group header on a page only if there is enough room on the page to print the first detail record for the group; otherwise, the group header prints at the top of the next page.

Now you'll set the Keep Together property for the NAICSDesc Header section.

To set the Keep Together property for the NAICSDesc Header section:

1. Switch to Design view.

2. Click the **Sorting and Grouping** button [≡] on the Report Design toolbar to open the Sorting and Grouping dialog box. The NAICSDesc field is selected.

3. Click the right side of the **Keep Together** text box, and then click **With First Detail**. The NAICSDesc Header section will now print on a page only if the first detail record for the group can also print on the page.

4. Close the Sorting and Grouping dialog box.

5. Switch to Print Preview, and then navigate through the Print Preview pages to verify that the orphaned header section problem no longer exists.

6. Switch to Design view.

To make your report look like Elsa's report design, your final task is to add blue horizontal lines to the Page Header, NAICSDesc Header, and Detail sections. You'll first increase the height of the Page Header section so it will be easier to add the line below the three controls in the section.

To add lines to the report:

1. Use the ╪ pointer to increase the height of the Page Header section to the 0.5-inch mark on the vertical ruler. The new height of the Page Header section will allow sufficient room to add a horizontal line in this section below the three controls.

   You can now add a line under the controls in the Page Header section. If you want to make sure you draw a straight horizontal line, press the Shift key before you start drawing the line and release the Shift key after you've created the line.

2. Click the **Line** tool [◣] on the toolbox, position the pointer at the left edge of the Page Header section and on the bottom border of the Date text box, and then draw a horizontal line from left to right, ending at the 5-inch mark on the horizontal ruler.

   Elsa's report design shows a thick blue line in the Page Header section, so you'll now change the line to match the design.

3. Click the list arrow for the **Line/Border Color** button [▨] on the Formatting toolbar, and then click the dark blue box in the color palette in row 1 and column 6. The line's color changes to dark blue.

4. Click the list arrow for the **Line/Border Width** button ⬜ on the Formatting toolbar, and then click width **3**. The line changes to a thick blue line. See Figure 6-47.

Figure 6-47

AFTER ADDING A THICK BLUE LINE IN THE PAGE HEADER SECTION

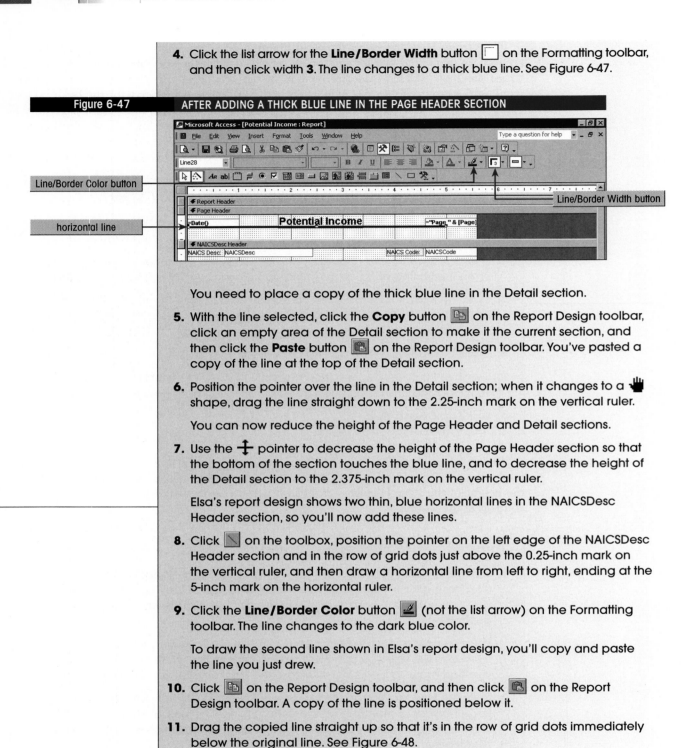

You need to place a copy of the thick blue line in the Detail section.

5. With the line selected, click the **Copy** button 🗐 on the Report Design toolbar, click an empty area of the Detail section to make it the current section, and then click the **Paste** button 🗐 on the Report Design toolbar. You've pasted a copy of the line at the top of the Detail section.

6. Position the pointer over the line in the Detail section; when it changes to a ✋ shape, drag the line straight down to the 2.25-inch mark on the vertical ruler.

You can now reduce the height of the Page Header and Detail sections.

7. Use the ✛ pointer to decrease the height of the Page Header section so that the bottom of the section touches the blue line, and to decrease the height of the Detail section to the 2.375-inch mark on the vertical ruler.

Elsa's report design shows two thin, blue horizontal lines in the NAICSDesc Header section, so you'll now add these lines.

8. Click ╲ on the toolbox, position the pointer on the left edge of the NAICSDesc Header section and in the row of grid dots just above the 0.25-inch mark on the vertical ruler, and then draw a horizontal line from left to right, ending at the 5-inch mark on the horizontal ruler.

9. Click the **Line/Border Color** button 🖉 (not the list arrow) on the Formatting toolbar. The line changes to the dark blue color.

To draw the second line shown in Elsa's report design, you'll copy and paste the line you just drew.

10. Click 🗐 on the Report Design toolbar, and then click 🗐 on the Report Design toolbar. A copy of the line is positioned below it.

11. Drag the copied line straight up so that it's in the row of grid dots immediately below the original line. See Figure 6-48.

Figure 6-48   ADDING LINES TO THE REPORT

horizontal line

two horizontal lines

copied horizontal line

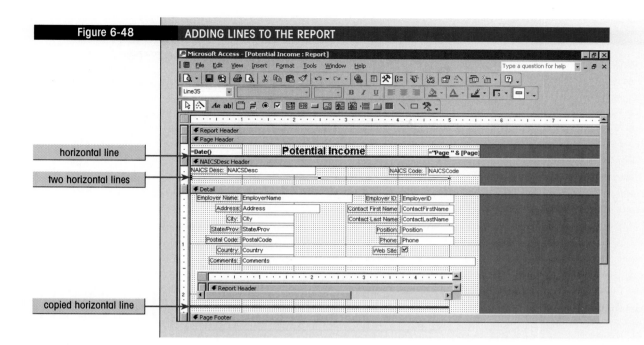

The Potential Income report is finished. You can now save the report and then preview its pages.

To save and preview the report:

1. Save your report changes, and then switch to Print Preview to display the first page of the report. See Figure 6-49.

Figure 6-49   PRINT PREVIEW OF PAGE 1 OF THE FINAL REPORT

Group Header section

Detail section for the first employer

Page Header section

subreport

start of Detail section for the second employer

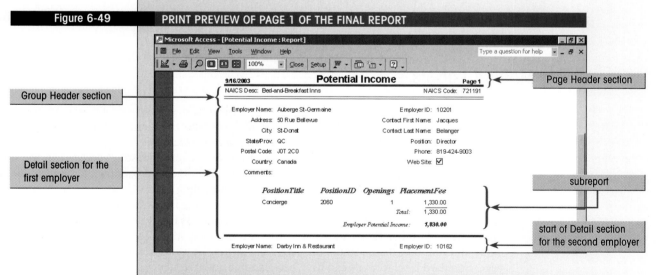

2. Use the navigation buttons to view the other pages of the report. In particular, note the information for Seaview Restaurant, which appears on approximately page 5. For this employer, the Comments field's Can Grow property has expanded its text box vertically to display its three lines of text. Also, because Seaview Restaurant has no available positions, the subreport's Can Shrink property removed the blank space for this control. See Figure 6-50.

Figure 6-50	CAN GROW AND CAN SHRINK PROPERTIES

Can Shrink property removed blank space for the subreport

Can Grow property expanded the Comments field text box vertically

3. Navigate to the last Print Preview page to view the overall total at the end of the report.

4. Click the **Close Window** button [X] on the menu bar to close the report and return to the Database window.

Now that you've finished the Potential Income report, Elsa wants you to create mailing labels that can be used in mass mailings to NSJI's employer clients.

Creating Mailing Labels

Elsa needs a set of mailing labels printed for all employers, so she can mail a marketing brochure and other materials to them. The Employer table contains the name and address information that will serve as the source data for the labels. Each mailing label will have the same format: contact name on the first line; employer name on the second line; street address on the third line; city, state or province, and postal code on the fourth line; and country on the fifth line. In addition, Elsa wants the NSJI logo to appear on each mailing label.

You could create a custom report to produce the mailing labels, but using the Label Wizard is an easier and faster way to produce them. The **Label Wizard** provides templates for hundreds of standard label formats, each of which is uniquely identified by a label manufacturer's name and number; these templates specify the dimensions and arrangement of labels on each page. Standard label formats can have between one and five labels across a page; the number of labels printed on a single page also varies. Elsa's mailing labels are Avery number C2163; each sheet has 1.5-inch by 3.9-inch labels arranged in two columns and six rows on the page.

REFERENCE WINDOW   **RW**

Creating Mailing Labels and Other Labels
- In the Database window, click Reports in the Objects bar of the Database window to display the Reports list box.
- Click the New button in the Database window to open the New Report dialog box.
- Click Label Wizard to select it, select the table or query that contains the source data for the mailing labels, and then click the OK button.
- Select the label manufacturer and its product number, and then click the Next button.
- Select the label font, color, and style, and then click the Next button.
- Construct the label content by selecting the fields from the data source and specifying their placement and spacing on the label, and then click the Next button.
- Select the sort fields, click the Next button, specify the report name, and then click the Finish button.

You'll use the Label Wizard to create a report to produce mailing labels for all employer clients.

To use the Label Wizard to create the mailing label report:

1. Make sure that **Reports** is selected in the Objects bar of the Database window, and then click the **New** button in the Database window to open the New Report dialog box.

2. Click **Label Wizard**, click the list arrow to display the list of tables and queries in the Jobs database, click **Employer** to select this table as the basis for your report, and then click the **OK** button. The first Label Wizard dialog box opens and asks you to select the standard or custom label you'll use.

3. Make sure that the **English** option button is selected in the Unit of Measure section, that the **Sheet feed** option button is selected in the Label Type section, that **Avery** is selected in the Filter by manufacturer list box, and then click **C2163** in the Product number list box. See Figure 6-51.

Figure 6-51	SELECTING A STANDARD LABEL

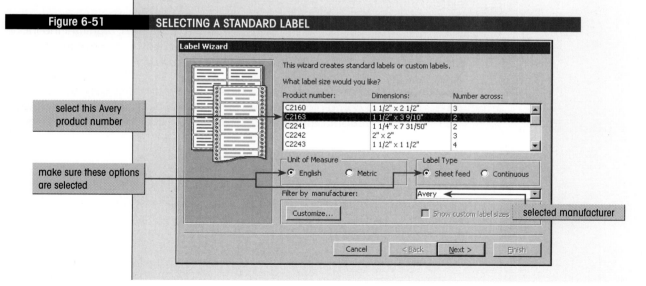

Because you've filtered the labels by Avery as the manufacturer, the top list box shows the Avery product number, dimensions, and number of labels across the page for each of its standard label formats. If your label manufacturer or its labels do not appear in the list box, you can create your own custom format for them. You can display the dimensions in the list in either inches or millimeters by choosing the appropriate option in the Unit of Measure section. You can also specify in the Label Type section whether the labels are on individual sheets or are continuous forms.

4. Click the **Next** button to open the second Label Wizard dialog box, in which you choose font specifications for the labels.

   Elsa wants the labels to use 10-point Arial with a medium font weight and without italics or underlines. The font weight determines how light or dark the characters will print; you can choose from nine values ranging from thin to heavy.

5. If necessary, select **Arial** for the Font name, **10** for the Font size, and **Medium** for the Font weight; make sure the Italic and the Underline check boxes are unchecked and that black is the Text color; and then click the **Next** button to open the third Label Wizard dialog box, from which you select the data to appear on the labels.

   As you select fields from the Available fields list box or type text for the label, the Prototype label box shows the format for the label. Elsa wants the mailing labels to print the ContactFirstName and ContactLastName fields on the first line; the EmployerName field on the second line; the Address field on the third line; the City, State/Prov, and PostalCode fields on the fourth line; and the Country field on the fifth line. One space will separate the ContactFirstName and ContactLastName fields, the City and State/Prov fields, and the State/Prov and PostalCode fields.

6. Scroll down and click **ContactFirstName** in the Available fields list box, click the ☐ > button to move the field to the Prototype label box, press the **spacebar**, click **ContactLastName** in the Available fields list box (if necessary), and then click the ☐ > button (see Figure 6-52). The braces around the field names in the Prototype label box indicate that the name represents a field rather than text that you entered.

   TROUBLE? If you select the wrong field or type the wrong text, highlight the incorrect item in the Prototype label box, press the Delete key to remove the item, and then select the correct field or type the correct text.

7. Press the **Enter** key to move to the next line in the Prototype label box, and then use Figure 6-52 to complete the entries in the Prototype label box. Make sure you press the spacebar after selecting the City field and the State/Prov field.

Figure 6-52   COMPLETED LABEL PROTOTYPE

8. Click the **Next** button to open the fourth Label Wizard dialog box, in which you choose the sort keys for the labels.

   Elsa wants the PostalCode to be the primary sort key and the EmployerName to be the secondary sort key.

9. Select the **PostalCode** field as the primary sort key, select the **EmployerName** field as the secondary sort key, and then click the **Next** button to open the last Label Wizard dialog box, in which you enter a name for the report.

10. Type **Employer Mailing Labels**, and then click the **Finish** button. Access saves the report as Employer Mailing Labels and then opens the Report window in Print Preview.

11. Click the **Zoom** list arrow on the Print Preview toolbar, and then click **Fit**. The first page of the report appears. Note that two columns of labels appear across the page. See Figure 6-53.

Figure 6-53	PREVIEWING THE MAILING LABELS

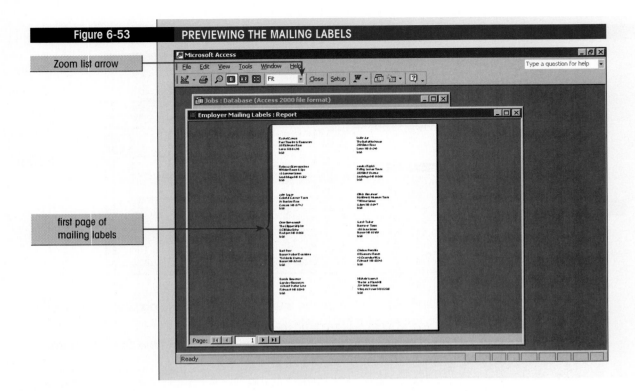

Zoom list arrow

first page of
mailing labels

Elsa wants the NSJI logo to appear on each mailing label, but first you'll review the mailing labels more closely to see if Elsa has other changes for you to make.

To preview the mailing label report in greater detail:

1. Click the **Zoom** list arrow on the Print Preview toolbar, and then click **75%** to preview the report in greater detail. See Figure 6-54.

Figure 6-54	PREVIEWING THE LABEL CONTENT AND SEQUENCE

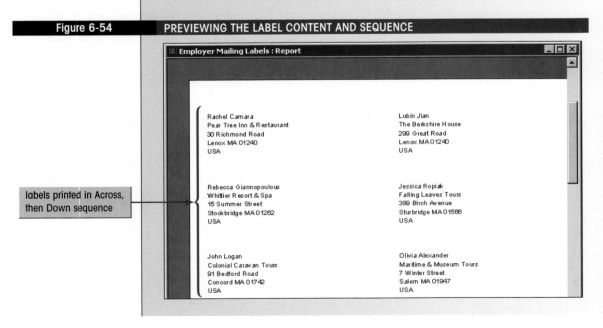

labels printed in Across,
then Down sequence

The Employer Mailing Labels report is a **multiple-column report**, one that prints the same collection of data fields in two or more sets across the page. The labels will print in ascending PostalCode order and then in ascending EmployerName order. The first label will print in the upper-left corner on the first page, the second label will print to its right, the third label will print under the first label, and so on. This style of multiple-column report is the "across, then down" layout. Instead, Elsa wants the labels to print with the "down, then across" layout—the first label prints, the second label prints under the first, and so on. After the bottom label in the first column is printed, the next label is printed at the top of the second column. The "down, then across" layout is also called **newspaper-style columns**, or **snaking columns**.

Elsa also wants the NSJI logo to print above the employer name and address information, so you'll add the logo as a picture in the report.

To change the layout and to add a picture to the mailing label report:

1. Switch to Design view. The Detail section, the only section in the report, is sized for a single label.

   First, you'll change the layout to snaking columns.

2. Click **File** on the menu bar, click **Page Setup**, and then click the **Columns** tab. The Page Setup dialog box displays the Columns options for the report. See Figure 6-55.

Figure 6-55	COLUMNS OPTIONS IN THE PAGE SETUP DIALOG BOX

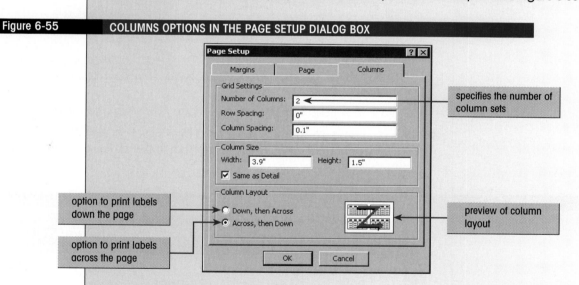

specifies the number of column sets

option to print labels down the page

option to print labels across the page

preview of column layout

The Columns options in the Page Setup dialog box let you change the properties of a multiple-column report. In the Grid Settings section, you specify the number of column sets and the row and column spacing between the column sets. In the Column Size section, you specify the width and height of each column set. In the Column Layout section, you select between the "Down, then Across" and the "Across, then Down" layouts.

You can now change the layout for the labels.

3. Click the **Down, then Across** option button, and then click the **OK** button.

   Because Elsa wants the NSJI logo printed above the employer data, you'll select all controls and move them down the Detail section.

4. Click **Edit** on the menu bar, and then click **Select All** to select all controls in the Detail section.

5. Position the pointer over one of the selected controls; when the pointer changes to a 🖑 shape, drag the controls straight down the Detail section until the top border of the top control is at the 0.375-inch mark on the vertical ruler.

   Next, you'll add the NSJI logo above the employer information. You could add the logo to the report in the same way you added a picture to a form by using the Image tool on the toolbox. Instead, you'll use the Picture option on the Insert menu.

6. Click an empty area of the grid to deselect all controls, click **Insert** on the menu bar, and then click **Picture**. The Insert Picture dialog box opens.

7. Make sure **Tutorial** appears in the Look in list box, click **NSJILogo** to select the picture file, and then click the **OK** button. The Insert Picture dialog box closes and the picture is inserted in the upper-left corner of the Detail section.

8. Move the picture straight to the right until its left edge is at the 2-inch mark on the horizontal ruler. See Figure 6-56.

Figure 6-56   FINAL DESIGN FOR THE MAILING LABELS

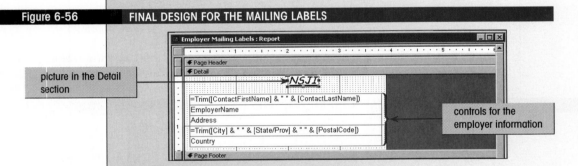

picture in the Detail section

controls for the employer information

You've finished Elsa's changes, so you can now save and preview the report.

9. Save your report design changes, and then switch to Print Preview. The logo will print on each label, and the labels appear in the snaking-columns layout. See Figure 6-57.

Figure 6-57   THE COMPLETED LABELS IN PRINT PREVIEW

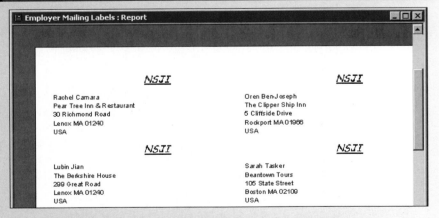

Because you've finished Elsa's reports, you can now close the Jobs database and exit Access.

10. Click the **Close** button ☒ on the Access window title bar to close the Jobs database and to exit Access.

Elsa is very pleased with the two new reports, which will provide her with improved information and help expedite her written communications with NSJI's employer clients.

Session 6.3 QUICK CHECK

1. What do you type in a text box control to print the current date?

2. How do you insert a page number in the Page Header section?

3. You can use the _____ to copy the format of a control to other controls.

4. The Keep Together property prints a group header on a page only if there is enough room on the page to print the first _____ record for the group.

5. What is a multiple-column report?

REVIEW ASSIGNMENTS

Elsa wants you to create a custom report for the **Students** database that prints all recruiters and the students they've recruited. You will create the report by completing the following steps.

1. Make sure your Data Disk is in the appropriate disk drive, start Access, and then open the **Students** database in the Review folder on your Data Disk.

2. Create a custom report based on the **Recruiter** table. Figure 6-58 shows a sample of the completed report. Refer to the figure as a guide as you complete Steps 3 through 7.

Figure 6-58

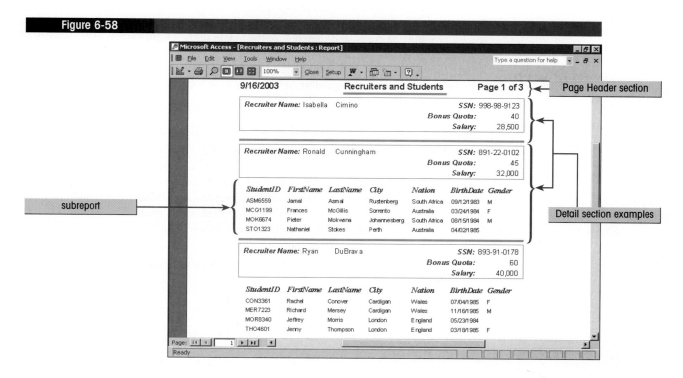

3. Use the **Recruiter** table as the source for the main report.

4. Make the following modifications to the main report:

a. Include the following sections in the main report: Page Header, Detail, and Page Footer.

b. At the top center of the Page Header section, enter the report title and format it with dark blue, 12-point, bold Arial font. Use the same format for the current date at the left edge of the section and for the page number at the right edge of the section. Use the "Page N of M" format for page numbers. Add a red line with a 3-point border width below the report title.

c. Type your name in the top center of the Page Footer section with the same format that you used for the report title, and then save the report as **Recruiters and Students**.

d. Add all fields from the **Recruiter** table to the Detail section, using Figure 6-58 as a guide.

e. Delete the LastName label. Change the caption for the FirstName label to "Recruiter Name:", change the caption for the BonusQuota label to "Bonus Quota:", and resize both labels to fit.

f. Change all labels and text boxes in the Detail section to 10-point Arial font; format all the labels with dark blue, bold, italic font; and then size all labels to fit.

Explore ▶ g. Draw a rectangle around the recruiter controls in the Detail section, and then change the rectangle's border color to red. Use the Send to Back option on the Format menu to position the rectangle.

h. Sort the recruiter records in ascending order by the LastName field, and then in ascending order by the FirstName field.

5. Use the following instructions to add a subreport using Control Wizards to the Detail section:

a. Select all fields from the **Student** table, link the main report and subreport using the SSN field, and name the subreport **Student Subreport**.

b. Delete the subreport label.

c. Open the subreport in a new window, and then delete the RecruiterName label and text box.

d. Resize all labels to their best fit.

e. By switching between Design view and Print Preview, resize each text box so that it's just wide enough to display the entire field value, and move and resize the labels and text boxes as necessary.

f. Left-align all text boxes and their corresponding labels.

g. Move all text boxes straight up to the top of the Detail section to eliminate all extra blank space above the text boxes, and then reduce the height of the Detail section until the bottom of the section touches the bottom of the text boxes.

h. Reduce the subreport's width until the right edge touches the right edge of the Gender controls.

i. Sort the student records in ascending order by the LastName field, and then in ascending order by the FirstName field.

j. Hide duplicate values for the Gender field.

k. Save the subreport design changes, and then close the subreport.

6. Make the following modifications to the main report:

a. By switching between Design view and Print Preview, reduce the width of the subreport control in the Detail section from the right as much as possible (approximately 6 inches or less).

b. Set the subreport border style to Transparent, and set its Can Shrink property to Yes.

c. Add a red line with a 3-point border width below the subreport control.

Explore ▶ d. Set the Can Shrink property of the Detail section to Yes. (*Hint*: Click the Detail section bar to make the entire section the current control.)

7. Save your report design changes, switch to Print Preview, print the report's first page, and then close the report.

8. Close the **Students** database, and then exit Access.

CASE PROBLEMS

Case 1. Lim's Video Photography Youngho Lim wants you to create a custom report and mailing labels for the **Clients** database. The custom report will be based on the results of two queries you will create. You will create the queries, the custom report, and the mailing labels by completing the following steps.

1. Make sure your Data Disk is in the appropriate disk drive, start Access, and then open the **Clients** database in the Cases folder on your Data Disk.

2. Create two queries for the custom report following these instructions:
   a. For the first query, select (in order) the ShootDesc field from the **ShootDesc** table; and then select the ShootDate, Duration, Location, and Contract# fields from the **Shoot** table. Sort the query in ascending order by the Contract# field. Save the query as **Shoot Data**, run and print the query, and then close the query.
   b. For the second query, select all fields from the **Client** table; and then select all fields, except the Client# field, from the **Contract** table. Sort the query in ascending order by the Contract# field. Save the query as **Clients and Contracts**, run the query, print it in landscape orientation, and then close the query.

3. Create a custom report based on the **Clients and Contracts** query. Figure 6-59 shows a sample of the completed report. Refer to the figure as a guide as you complete Steps 4 through 8.

Figure 6-59

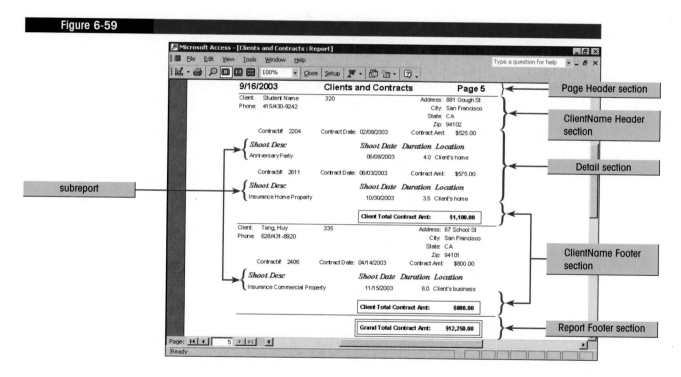

4. Use the **Clients and Contracts** query as the source for the main report.

5. Make the following modifications to the main report:
   a. You'll be directed to include the following sections in your report: Page Header, ClientName Header, Detail, ClientName Footer, Page Footer, and Report Footer.
   b. At the top center of the Page Header section, enter the report title and format it with Arial 12-point, bold font. Use the same format for the current date at the left edge of the section and for the page number at the right edge of the section. Below the controls in the Page Header section, add a dark blue line running from the left edge of the section to approximately the 5-inch mark on the horizontal ruler.
   c. Enter your name in the top center of the Page Footer section with the same format that you used for the report title, and then save the report as **Clients and Contracts**.

    d. Sort the main report records in ascending order by the ClientName field, and then in ascending order by the Contract# field. Add Group Header and Group Footer sections for the ClientName field, and set its Keep Together property to "Whole Group."

    e. Add the ClientName, Client#, Phone, Address, City, State, and Zip fields from the **Clients and Contracts** query to the ClientName Header section. Delete the Client# label, and change the caption for the ClientName label to "Client:". Resize and reposition the labels and text boxes in the ClientName Header section as shown in Figure 6-59, positioning the Client# text box to the right of the ClientName text box.

    f. Add the Contract#, ContractDate, and ContractAmt fields from the **Clients and Contracts** query to the Detail section. Change the ContractDate label to "Contract Date:" and the ContractAmt label to "Contract Amt:". Resize and reposition the labels and text boxes in the Detail section as shown in Figure 6-59.

6. Use the following instructions to add a subreport using Control Wizards to the Detail section:

    a. Select all fields from the **Shoot Data** query, link the main report and subreport using the Contract# field, and name the subreport **Shoot Subreport**.

    b. Open the subreport in a new window, and then delete the Contract# label and text box.

    c. Change the ShootDesc label to "Shoot Desc" and the ShootDate label to "Shoot Date".

    d. By switching between Design view and Print Preview, resize each text box so that it's just wide enough to display the entire field value.

    e. Resize and reposition the labels in the Report Header section and the text boxes in the Detail section until they're positioned as shown in Figure 6-59.

    f. Move all text boxes straight up to the top of the Detail section to eliminate all extra blank space above the text boxes, and then reduce the height of the Detail section until the bottom of the section touches the bottom of the text boxes.

    g. If necessary, reduce the subreport's width until its right edge touches the right edge of the Location controls.

    h. Sort the subreport records in ascending order by the ShootDate field.

    i. Save the subreport design changes, and then close the subreport.

7. Make the following modifications to the main report:

    a. Delete the subreport label.

    b. By switching between Design view and Print Preview, reduce the width of the subreport control in the Detail section from the right as much as possible.

    c. Set the subreport border style to Transparent, and set its Can Shrink property to Yes.

    d. Reduce the height of the Detail section to just below the subreport control, and then reduce the width of the main report as much as possible.

    e. Add a text box to the ClientName Footer section, enter the function to calculate the total of the ContractAmt field values, format the calculated field as currency, change the label caption to "Client Total Contract Amt:", and then format both controls as bold. Resize and reposition the controls in the ClientName Footer section as shown in Figure 6-59.

Explore   f. Draw a rectangle around the controls in the ClientName Footer section, and then change the rectangle's border color to dark blue. Use the Send to Back option on the Format menu to position the rectangle.

    g. Add the Report Footer section, but not the Report Header section, to the main report. Add a text box to the Report Footer section, enter the function to calculate the total of the ContractAmt field values, and format the calculated field as currency. Change the label caption to "Grand Total Contract Amt:", and then format both controls as bold. Resize and reposition the controls in the Report Footer section as shown in Figure 6-59.

Explore   h. Draw a rectangle around the controls in the Report Footer section, and then change the rectangle's border color to dark blue. Use the Send to Back option on the Format menu to position the rectangle. Draw a second rectangle around the first rectangle, and then set its properties to match the properties for the inner rectangle.

    i. Add a dark blue line below the controls in the ClientName Footer section. Start the line at the left edge of the section and end it at approximately the 5-inch mark on the horizontal ruler.

j. If necessary, reduce the height of the ClientName Footer and Report Footer sections to the bottom of the controls in the section.

8. Save your report design changes, switch to Print Preview, print the first and last pages of the report, and then close the report.

9. Use the following instructions to create the mailing labels:
   a. Use the **Client** table as the source for the mailing labels.
   b. Use Durable 1452 labels, and use the default font and color. (*Hint*: Make sure the Metric option button is selected in the Unit of Measure section.)
   c. For the prototype label, place ClientName on the first line; Address on the second line; and City, a space, State, a space, and Zip on the third line.
   d. Sort by Zip and then by ClientName, and then enter the report name **Client Labels**.
   e. Print the first page of the report, and then close the report.

10. Close the **Clients** database, and then exit Access.

Case 2. DineAtHome.course.com   Claire Picard wants you to create a custom report and mailing labels for the **Delivery** database. The custom report will be based on the results of a query you will create. You will create the query, the custom report, and the mailing labels by completing the following steps.

1. Make sure your Data Disk is in the appropriate disk drive, start Access, and then open the **Delivery** database in the Cases folder on your Data Disk.

2. Create a new query based on the **Restaurant** and **Order** tables. Select all fields from the **Restaurant** table, and select all fields except Restaurant# from the **Order** table. Add a calculated field named BillTotal that adds the OrderAmt and DeliveryCharge fields; use the IIf function to add an additional $2 to the BillTotal field if the City field value is Naples. Save the query as **Restaurant Orders**, and then close it.

3. Create a custom report based on the **Restaurant Orders** query. Figure 6-60 shows a sample of the completed report. Refer to the figure as a guide as you create the report.

Figure 6-60

a. Sort the report records in ascending order by the RestaurantName field, and then in ascending order by the OrderDate field. Add Group Header and Group Footer sections for the RestaurantName field, and set its Keep Together property to "Whole Group."

b. In the RestaurantName Header section, add all fields from the **Restaurant Orders** query, except for the three **Order** table fields. Delete the Restaurant# label. Change the caption for the RestaurantName label to "Restaurant:", and then resize the label to fit. Resize and reposition the labels and text boxes as shown in Figure 6-60, placing the Restaurant# and RestaurantName text boxes to the right of the Restaurant label.

c. Add a red line to the RestaurantName Header section in the row of grid dots below the bottom controls. Start the line at the left edge of the section and end it at the 5-inch mark on the horizontal ruler. Save the report as **Restaurant Orders**.

Explore ▷   d. From the **Restaurant Orders** query, add the OrderDate, Order#, and BillTotal fields to the Detail section. Cut the three labels in the Detail section and paste them into the RestaurantName Header section. (*Hint*: Select the three labels, click the Cut button on the Report Design toolbar, click the RestaurantName Header bar, and then click the Paste button on the Report Design toolbar.) Change the captions for the OrderDate and BillTotal labels, resize them to fit, reposition the three labels, and then delete the colons from the label captions.

e. Add a second red line to the RestaurantName Header section in the row of grid dots below the three labels, and then reduce the height of the section to the row of grid dots below the line.

Explore ▷   f. Resize the three text boxes in the Detail section, move the text boxes to the top of the section, and then reduce the height of the section to the bottom of the text boxes. Define conditional formatting rules for the BillTotal field—use bold and italic font for values between 100 and 150, use bold for values between 150.01 and 200, and use a bold, dark blue font and a light yellow fill for values over 200. Set the BillTotal field's Format property to Fixed and its Decimal Places property to 2.

g. At the top center of the Page Header section, enter the report title and format it with 12-point Arial bold font. Use the same format for the current date at the left edge of the section and for the page number at the right edge of the section. Add a red line with a 4-point border width under the controls in the Page Header section. Start the line at the left edge of the section and end it at the 5-inch mark on the horizontal ruler. Reduce the height of the section to the row of grid dots below the line.

h. Add a text box to the RestaurantName Footer section, enter the function to calculate the total of the BillTotal field values, format the calculated field as Standard, and then change the label caption to "Subtotal Bill Total:". Add a short red line at the top of the section, above the calculated field; then add a red line with a 4-point border width below the controls in the section. Extend the line from the left edge of the section to the 5-inch mark on the horizontal ruler. Reduce the height of the section to the row of grid dots below the line.

i. Add the Report Footer section, but not the Report Header section, to the report. Add a text box to the Report Footer section, enter the function to calculate the total of the BillTotal field values, format the calculated field as Standard, and then change the label caption to "Grand Total Bill Total:". Resize and reposition the controls in the Report Footer. Add a red line with a 4-point border width below the controls in the section. Start the line at the left edge of the section and end it at the 5-inch mark on the horizontal ruler. See Figure 6-61.

Figure 6-61

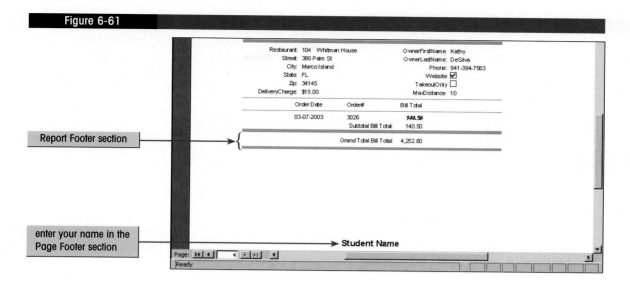

Report Footer section

enter your name in the Page Footer section

j. Enter your name in the top center of the Page Footer section with the same format you used for the report title.

4. Save your report design changes, switch to Print Preview, print the last page of the report, and then close the report.

5. Use the following instruction to create the mailing labels:
    a. Use the **Restaurant** table as the source for the mailing labels.
    b. Use Avery C2160 labels, and use the default font and color. (*Hint*: Make sure the English option button is selected in the Unit of Measure section.)
    c. For the prototype label, place OwnerFirstName, a space, and OwnerLastName on the first line; RestaurantName on the second line; Street on the third line; and City, a space, State, a space, and Zip on the fourth line.
    d. Sort by Zip and then by RestaurantName, and then type the report name **Restaurant Labels**.
    e. Select all controls in the Detail section, and then move them straight down until the top border of the top selected control is at the 0.75-inch mark on the vertical ruler.
    f. Add the **DineLogo** picture, located in the Cases folder on your Data Disk, to the upper-left corner of the Detail section.
    g. Save your report design changes, print the first page of the report, and then close the report.

6. Close the **Delivery** database, and then exit Access.

Case 3. Redwood Zoo Michael Rosenfeld asks you to create a custom report for the **Donors** database so that he can better track pledges made by donors to the zoo's funds. You'll create the report by completing the following.

1. Make sure your Data Disk is in the appropriate disk drive, start Access, and then open the **Donors** database in the Cases folder on your Data Disk.

2. Create a new query based on the **Donor** and **Pledge** tables. Select the FirstName and LastName fields from the **Donor** table; then select the FundName, PledgeDate, TotalPledged, and PaymentMethod fields from the **Pledge** table. Save the query as **Donor Pledges**, and then close it.

3. Create a custom report based on the **Fund** table. Figure 6-62 shows the completed report. Refer to the figure as a guide as you complete Steps 4 through 8.

Figure 6-62

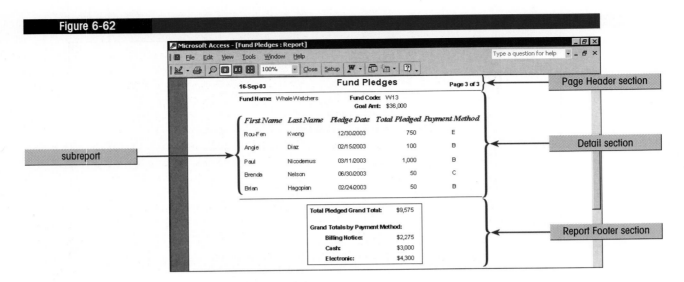

4. Use the **Fund** table as the source for the main report.

5. Make the following modifications to the main report:
   a. Sort the report records in ascending order by the FundName field.
   b. At the top center of the Page Header section, enter the report title and format it with 13-point Arial bold font. Add the current date at the left edge of the section, change it to bold, and then set the Format property to Medium Date. Add the page number at the right edge of the section, using the "Page N of M" format for the page numbers, and then change it to bold. Add a line to the section below the controls. Extend the line from the left edge of the current date text box to the right edge of the page number text box. If necessary, reduce the height of the Page Header section to the bottom of the controls in the section.
   c. Type your name in the top center of the Page Footer section with the same format you used for the report title, and then save the report as **Fund Pledges**.
   d. Add the three fields from the **Fund** table to the Detail section. Change the captions for the labels so that there's one space between each word, and make sure the labels are bold. Resize the labels to fit, and then resize and reposition the labels and text boxes in the Detail section as shown in Figure 6-62.

6. Use the following instructions to add a subreport using Control Wizards to the Detail section:
   a. Select all fields from the **Donor Pledges** query, link the main report and subreport using the FundCode field, and name the subreport **Fund Pledges Subreport**.
   b. Open the subreport in a new window, and then delete the FundName label and text box.
   c. Change the label captions by adding one space between each word, and then resize the labels to fit. Resize and reposition the labels and text boxes in the subreport as shown in Figure 6-62.
   d. If necessary, reduce the subreport width until its right edge touches the right edge of the PaymentMethod controls.
   e. Save the subreport design changes, and then close the subreport.

7. Make the following modifications to the main report:
   a. Delete the subreport label.
   b. By switching between Design view and Print Preview, reduce the width of the subreport control in the Detail section from the right as much as possible.
   c. Set the subreport border style to Transparent, and set its Can Shrink property to Yes.
   d. To the Detail section below the subreport, add a line that's the same length as the line in the Page Header section.
   e. Reduce the height of the Detail section to just below the line you drew below the subreport control, and then reduce the width of the main report as much as possible.

f. Add the Report Footer section, but not the Report Header section, to the main report. Add a text box to the Report Footer section, and then enter the DSum function to calculate the total of the TotalPledged field values from the **Donor Pledges** query. Format the calculated field as Currency with zero decimal places, and then change the label caption's text to "Total Pledged Grand Total:"and its font to bold. Resize and reposition the two controls in the Report Footer section, as shown in Figure 6-62.

Explore

g. Add a label below the two controls in the Report Footer section, using the caption value "Grand Totals by Payment Method:" and changing the text to bold. Below the label in the Report Footer section, add three text boxes. For each text box, enter the DSum function to calculate the total of the TotalPledged field values from the **Donor Pledges** query for each of the three PaymentMethod field values: B for a billing notice, C for cash, and E for electronic. (*Hint*: Use the same DSum function you used in Step 7f, but include the third optional *criteria* condition in the function. For example, use "PaymentMethod='B'" as the condition to calculate the total of the TotalPledged field values from billing notices as a payment method.) Set the captions for the three labels, format the text boxes as Currency with zero decimal places, and then resize and reposition the labels and text boxes.

Explore

h. Draw a rectangle around the controls in the Report Footer section, and then use the Send to Back option on the Format menu to position the rectangle.

i. If necessary, reduce the height of each section in the main report, and then reduce the width of the main report.

8. Save your report design changes, switch to Print Preview, print the first and last pages of the report, and then close the report.

9. Close the **Donors** database, and then exit Access.

Case 4. Mountain River Adventures   Connor and Siobhan Dempsey want you to create a custom report and mailing labels for the **Outdoors** database. You will create the custom report and the mailing labels by completing the following steps.

1. Make sure your Data Disk is in the appropriate disk drive, start Access, and then open the **Outdoors** database in the Cases folder on your Data Disk.

2. Create a new query based on the **Rafting Trip** and **Booking** tables. Select all fields from the **Rafting Trip** table, and select all fields except River from the **Booking** table. Add a calculated field named TripFee that multiples the Fee/Person and People fields; use the IIf function to reduce the TripFee by 10% if the People field value is greater than six. Set the calculated field's Format property to Standard. Save the query as **Booked Rafting Trips**, and then close it.

3. Complete Steps 4 through 8 to create a custom report based on the **Client** table, saving the report as **Booked Trips**.

4. Use the **Client** table as the source for the main report.

5. Make the following modifications to the main report:
   a. Change the page orientation to landscape, and then change the width of the report to 7.5 inches.
   b. Sort the report records in ascending order by the Client# field.
   c. At the top center of the Page Header section, enter the report title of Booked Trips, and format it with 12-point Arial bold font. Use the same format for the current date at the left edge of the section and for the page number at the right edge of the section. Add a black line with a 3-point border width to underline the controls in the Page Header section. Extend the line from the left edge of the section to approximately the 7.5-inch mark on the horizontal ruler. If necessary, reduce the height of the Page Header section to the bottom of the controls in the section.
   d. In the top center of the Page Footer section, type your name. Use the same format for your name that you used for the report title, and then save the report.
   e. Add the eight fields from the **Client** table to the Detail section. Move the Client#, ClientName, Address, and City labels and text boxes in a column to the left. Move the State/Prov, and PostalCode, Country, and Phone labels and text boxes in a column to the right. Right-align the labels and left-align the text boxes.

6. Use the following instructions to add a subreport using Control Wizards to the Detail section:
   a. Select all fields from the **Booked Rafting Trips** query, link the main report and subreport using the Client# field, and name the subreport **Booked Trips Subreport**.
   b. Open the subreport in a new window, and then delete the Client# label and text box. Format the TripFee text box as Standard.
   c. Make sure the subreport page orientation is landscape, set its width to approximately 7.5 inches, and then resize and reposition its labels and text boxes. Switch between Print Preview and Design view to make sure that the labels and text boxes are aligned and that all field values are fully visible.
   d. Move all text boxes straight up to the top of the Detail section to eliminate all extra blank space above the text boxes, and then reduce the height of the Detail section until its bottom edge touches the bottom edges of the text boxes.
   e. Sort the subreport records in ascending order by the Client# field, and then sort in ascending order by the TripDate field. Add a Group Footer section for the Client# field, and set its Keep Together property to "Whole Group."
   f. Add a text box to the Client# Footer section, enter the function to calculate the total of the TripFee field values, format the calculated field as Standard, and then change the label caption to "Subtotal Trip Fee:". At the top of the section, add a short black line above the calculated field; then below the controls in the section, add a black line with a 3-point border width that extends from the left edge of the section to the 7.5-inch mark on the horizontal ruler. Reduce the height of the section to the row of grid dots below the line.
   g. Save the subreport design changes, and then close the subreport.

7. Make the following modifications to the main report:
   a. Delete the subreport label.
   b. Change the width of the subreport control in the Detail section so that it extends from the left edge of the section to the 7.5-inch mark on the horizontal ruler.
   c. Set the subreport border style to Transparent, and set its Can Shrink property to Yes.
   d. Reduce the height of the Detail section to just below the subreport control.
   e. Add the Report Footer section, but not the Report Header section, to the main report. Add a text box to the Report Footer section, and then enter the DSum function to calculate the total of the TripFee field values from the **Booked Rafting Trips** query. Format the calculated field as Standard with two decimal places, and then change the label caption to "Grand Total Trip Fee:". Change the label font to 11-point Times New Roman, change its style to bold and italic, and change its color to blue. Resize and reposition the two controls in the Report Footer section so that the calculated field right-aligns with the subtotal amount.

Explore
   f. In the Report Footer section, add two text boxes below the text box you added in Step 7e. In the first text box that you added, use the DAvg function to calculate the average of the TripFee field values from the **Booked Rafting Trips** query. Format the DAvg text box as Standard with two decimal places. In the other text box, use the DCount function to calculate the total number of trips booked. (*Hints*: The DAvg and DCount functions use the same format as the DSum function. You can use the TripFee field for the DCount function.) Format the DCount text box as Standard with zero decimal places. Use the label captions "Average Trip Fee:" and "Total Trips:", and then change the labels to bold. Resize and reposition the labels and text boxes in the Report Footer section.
   g. If necessary, reduce the height of the Report Footer section in the main report.

8. Save your report design changes, switch to Print Preview, print the first and last pages of the report, and then close the report.

9. Use the following instructions to create the mailing labels:
   a. Use the **Client** table as the source for the mailing labels.
   b. Use Avery C2163 labels, and use the default font and color settings. (*Hint*: Make sure the English option button is selected in the Unit of Measure section.)
   c. For the prototype label, place ClientName on the first line; Address on the second line; City, a space, State/Prov, a space, and PostalCode on the third line; and Country on the fourth line.
   d. Sort by PostalCode and then by ClientName, and then enter the report name **Client Labels**.

e. Change the column layout to "Down, then Across," print the first page of the report, and then save and close the report.

10. Close the **Outdoors** database, and then exit Access.

Explore

Case 5. eACH Internet Auction Site Chris and Pat Aquino want you to continue developing their Internet auction site for collectibles. Their auction site is now a proven success, with tens of thousands of bids placed daily. However, their costs have increased because they've had to install additional servers and high-speed communication lines to support the growing traffic at eACH. Income they earn from eACH offsets their costs—they charge a seller $2 to post an item plus an additional 3% of the item's final sale price. The number of items for sale varies dramatically each day, so Chris and Pat want you to design and then create a custom report to project income from the **eACH** database; the basis for the report will be a query you'll need to create. You will create the necessary query and report by completing the following steps.

1. Make sure your Data Disk is in the appropriate drive, start Access, and then open the **eACH** database in the Cases folder on your Data Disk.

2. Create a select query based on all four tables in the database. Display the subcategory name from the **Subcategory** table; the category name from the **Category** table; the title from the **Item** table; the seller's last name and first name from the **Registrant** table; and the minimum bid from the **Item** table, in that order. Create a calculated field named ProjectedIncome that displays the results of adding $2 to 3% of the minimum bid. Format the calculated field as Standard with two decimal places. Sort the query in descending order by the ProjectedIncome field. Save the query as **Projected Income**, run the query, resize all columns to their best fit, print the query in landscape orientation, and then save and close the query.

3. On a piece of paper, sketch the design for a custom report based on the **Projected Income** query. The report must include at least the following features:
   a. A Page Header section that includes the report title, the current date, the page number, and column headings.
   b. A Group Header section that includes the subcategory name and category name, both sorted in ascending order.
   c. A Detail section that includes the title, seller's first name and last name, minimum bid, and ProjectedIncome field. (Hide duplicate values for the title.)
   d. A Group Footer section that includes an appropriate label and totals by subcategory for the minimum bid and ProjectedIncome field.
   e. A Report Footer section that includes an appropriate label and totals for the minimum bid and ProjectedIncome field.

4. Building on Step 3, create, test, and print the custom report. Save the report as **Projected Income Based on Minimum Bid**. You might need to add records to your tables and modify existing records so that you have enough data and a sufficient level of variety to test your report features.

5. Close the **eACH** database, and then exit Access.

INTERNET ASSIGNMENTS

Student Union

The purpose of the Internet Assignments is to challenge you to find information on the Internet that you can use to create effective documents. The actual assignments are updated and maintained on the Course Technology Web site. Log on to the Internet and use your Web browser to go to the Student Online Companion to accompany this text at **www.course.com/NewPerspectives/studentunion**. Click the Online Companions link, and then click the link for this tutorial.

QUICK CHECK ANSWERS

Session 6.1

1. The Report Header section appears once at the beginning of a report. The Page Header section appears at the top of each page of a report. The Group Header section appears once at the beginning of a new group of records. The Detail section appears once for each record in the underlying table or query. The Group Footer section appears once at the end of a group of records. The Report Footer section appears once at the end of a report. The Page Footer section appears at the bottom of each page of a report.

2. A custom report is a report you make by modifying a report created by AutoReport or the Report Wizard, or by creating a report from scratch in Design view.

3. IIf

4. The Report window in Design view has many of the same components as the Form window in Design view, including a Properties button, a Field List button, and a Toolbox button on the toolbar. Both windows also have horizontal and vertical rulers, a grid, and a Formatting toolbar. Unlike the Form window in Design view, which initially displays only the Detail section on a blank form, the Report window also displays a Page Header section and a Page Footer section.

5. A grouping field is a field from the underlying table or query by which records are grouped in a report.

6. The Caption property for a control determines the text displayed for the control. You would change the Caption property value for a control when the default value is difficult to read or understand.

7. Can Grow

8. Click a control, hold down the Shift key, click the other controls, release the Shift key, right-click a selected control, point to Align, and then click Right.

Session 6.2

1. Can Shrink

2. Report Header and Detail sections

3. Visible

4. arrow

5. Hiding duplicate values makes a report easier to read; duplicate values clutter the report.

6. three

7. a recordset or set of records

Session 6.3

1. =Date()

2. Click Insert on the menu bar; click Page Numbers; specify the format, position, and alignment of the page number; and then click the OK button.

3. Format Painter

4. detail

5. A multiple-column report prints the same collection of data fields in two or more sets across the page.

INTEGRATING
ACCESS WITH THE WEB AND WITH OTHER PROGRAMS

Creating Web-Enabled and Integrated Information for the Jobs Database

CASE

Northeast Seasonal Jobs International (NSJI)

Elsa Jensen, Zack Ward, and Matt Griffin are pleased with the design and contents of the Jobs database. Their work has been made much easier because they are able to quickly obtain the information they need from the database. Matt feels that others in the company would benefit from gaining access to the Jobs database. Elsa asks Matt if he can make information in the database available to employees using the company network. That way, employees could obtain company information using their desktop and portable computers rather than using printouts and paper forms.

Zack mentions that most employees, such as the recruiters, do not need access to the entire database, nor should they be able to make changes to all the database objects. He proposes publishing the necessary Access data on the company's intranet, or internal network, as Web pages.

In this tutorial, you will use Access to make objects in the Jobs database available to employees on NSJI's internal network. You will use Access to import and export XML files and integrate Access with other Office programs.

SESSION 7.1

In this session, you will export an Access query to an HTML document and then view the HTML document using a Web browser. You'll use a Wizard to create a data access page for an Access table, and use your Web browser to update the data and to sort and filter records on the data access page. Finally, you'll create a custom data access page.

Using the Web

The **World Wide Web** (**WWW**), commonly called the **Web**, is a vast collection of digital documents available over the **Internet**, which is a worldwide network consisting of millions of interconnected computers. Each electronic document on the Web is called a **Web page**. Individuals and companies store their Web pages on special computers called **Web servers**. Each Web page is assigned an Internet address called a **Uniform Resource Locator** (**URL**); the URL identifies where the Web page is stored—the location of both the Web server and the Web page filename on that server. To view a Web page, you start a special program called a **Web browser**, such as Microsoft Internet Explorer or Netscape Navigator. After you start the Web browser, you enter the Web page's URL. The Web browser uses the URL to find and retrieve the Web page, and then displays it on your computer screen.

Each Web page contains the necessary instructions for your Web browser to display its text and graphics. These instructions, called **tags**, describe how text is formatted, position graphic images, and set the document's background color and other visual characteristics of the Web page. Certain tags, called **hyperlinks**, link one Web page to another. When you click hyperlink text, the linked page opens. Hyperlinks connect Web pages throughout the Internet, and these connections form the Web. Hyperlinks are the primary means of navigation on the Web.

Most Web pages are created using a programming language called **HTML** (**HyperText Markup Language**). You can create a Web page by typing all the necessary HTML code into a text document, called an **HTML document**, and saving the document with the .htm or .html file extension. Some programs, including Access, have built-in tools that convert objects to HTML documents for viewing on the Web.

When you use Access to create a Web page, the page can be either static or dynamic. A **static Web page** shows the state of the database object at the time the page was created. Any subsequent changes made to the database object, such as updates to field values in records, are not reflected in a static Web page. A **dynamic Web page** is updated automatically each time the page is viewed and therefore reflects the current state of the database at that time. When you use a browser to open a Web page created from an Access database, you cannot make changes to the database using a static Web page, but you can change database data for certain types of dynamic Web pages. The type of Web page you create depends on how you want other users to be able to share and manipulate its information. In this tutorial, you'll work with both static and dynamic Web pages.

Exporting an Access Query to an HTML Document

Matt has asked you to create an HTML document for the Employer Positions query. He wants this data to be available to the recruiters when they work outside the office to interview and screen students for available positions. The recruiters will access the company's intranet from laptop computers connected to telephone lines. The recruiters usually wait until they have completed all interviews for available positions before matching qualified applicants with appropriate jobs. For this reason, the recruiters only need to reference the available positions data, so Matt asks you to create a static Web page for the recruiters to use as a resource during the interview process.

Creating the necessary HTML document is not as difficult as it might appear at first. You will use the Export command on the shortcut menu, which automatically converts the selected database object to an HTML document.

REFERENCE   WINDOW   **RW**

Exporting an Access Object to an HTML Document
- In the Database window, right-click the object (table, query, form, or report) you want to export, and then click Export on the shortcut menu.
- Enter the filename in the File name text box, and then select the location where you want to save the file.
- Click the Save as type list arrow, and then click HTML Documents.
- Click the Save formatted check box (if using a template), and then click the Export button.
- Select the template (if necessary), and then click the OK button.

To complete the following steps, you need to use Access and a Web browser. The steps in this tutorial are written for Internet Explorer, the Web browser used at NSJI. If you use Navigator or another browser, the steps you need to complete will be slightly different.

You'll export the Employer Positions query as an HTML document.

To export the Employer Positions query as an HTML document:

1. Place your Data Disk in the appropriate disk drive, start Access, and then open the **Jobs** database in the Tutorial folder on your Data Disk.

2. Click **Queries** in the Objects bar of the Database window, right-click **Employer Positions** to display the shortcut menu, and then click **Export**. The Export dialog box opens, displaying the type and name of the object you are exporting in its title bar—in this case, the Employer Positions query.

   In this dialog box you specify the filename for the exported file and its type and location. You'll save the Employer Positions query as an HTML document in the Tutorial folder on your Data Disk.

3. Make sure the Save in list box displays the **Tutorial** folder on your Data Disk.

4. Click the **Save as type** list arrow, and then scroll down the list and click **HTML Documents**. The query name is added to the File name text box automatically. See Figure 7-1.

Figure 7-1	EXPORT DIALOG BOX

folder to use on the Data Disk

option for saving the object as a datasheet

default name for HTML document

selected file type

The Save formatted option lets you save the object formatted as a datasheet. If you do not choose this option, the object will appear without the field names as column headings. Matt wants the query saved in datasheet format.

5. Click the **Save formatted** check box, and then click the **Export** button. The HTML Output Options dialog box opens.

This dialog box lets you specify an HTML template or use the default format when saving the object. An **HTML template** is a file that contains HTML instructions for creating a Web page with both text and graphics, together with special instructions that tell Access where to place the Access data on the Web page. Matt used a text-editing program to create an HTML template, named NSJI-Tbl, that you'll use. This template will automatically include the NSJI logo in all Web pages created with it. You need to locate Matt's template file on your Data Disk.

6. Make sure the **Select a HTML Template** check box is checked, and then click the **Browse** button. The HTML Template to Use dialog box opens.

7. If necessary, use the Look in list box to display the contents of the **Tutorial** folder on your Data Disk, click **NSJI-Tbl**, and then click the **OK** button. Access closes the HTML Template to Use dialog box, returns to the HTML Output Options dialog box, and displays the location and filename for the HTML template. See Figure 7-2.

| Figure 7-2 | HTML OUTPUT OPTIONS DIALOG BOX |

your path to the NSJI-Tbl template might differ

data encoding options if you're not using a template

TROUBLE? If NSJI-Tbl does not appear in the Tutorial folder on your Data Disk when you open the HTML Template to Use dialog box, click the Cancel button to return to the HTML Output Options dialog box so you can specify the template file manually. In the HTML Template text box, type the full path to the NSJI-Tbl.htm file in the Tutorial folder on your Data Disk.

8. Click the **OK** button. The HTML Output Options dialog box closes, and the HTML document named Employer Positions is saved in the Tutorial folder on your Data Disk.

Now you can view the Web page.

Viewing an HTML Document Using Internet Explorer

Matt asks to see the Web page you created. You can view the HTML document that you created using any Web browser. You'll view it using Internet Explorer next.

REFERENCE   WINDOW   **RW**

Viewing an HTML Document in a Web Browser

■ If necessary, click View on the menu bar, point to Toolbars, and then click Web to display the Web toolbar.
■ Click the Go button on the Web toolbar, and then click Open Hyperlink.
■ Use the Browse button to select the file to open, and then click the Open button.
■ Click the OK button.

You can now view the Employer Positions query Web page.

To view the Employer Positions query Web page:

1. If necessary, click **View** on the menu bar, point to **Toolbars**, and then click **Web**. Access displays the Web toolbar. See Figure 7-3.

Figure 7-3   DISPLAYING THE WEB TOOLBAR

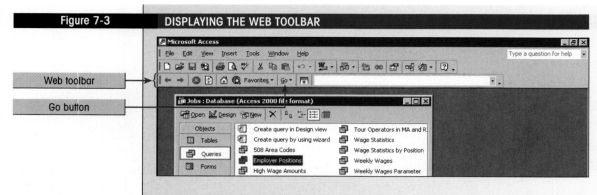

Web toolbar

Go button

TROUBLE? If the Database and Web toolbars appear on the same line or the Web toolbar appears above the Database toolbar, drag the Web toolbar's move handle ▐ below the Database toolbar to the position shown in Figure 7-3.

2. Click the **Go** button on the Web toolbar, and then click **Open Hyperlink**. Access opens the Open Internet Address dialog box, in which you can specify or browse for the URL of the Web page or the path and filename of the HTML document you want to view.

3. Click the **Browse** button. Access opens the Browse dialog box.

4. Make sure the Look in list box displays the **Tutorial** folder on your Data Disk, click **Employer Positions** in the list, and then click the **Open** button. The Browse dialog box closes, and the Address text box in the Open Internet Address dialog box now displays the path and filename for the Employer Positions HTML document. See Figure 7-4.

Figure 7-4   OPEN INTERNET ADDRESS DIALOG BOX

path to the Employer Positions HTML document (yours might differ)

5. Click the **OK** button. Internet Explorer starts and opens the Employer Positions Web page. See Figure 7-5.

TROUBLE? If a dialog box opens and tells you that an unexpected error has occurred, click the OK button, click the Start button on the taskbar, point to Programs, click Internet Explorer, type the path to the Employer Positions.html file in the Tutorial folder in the Address bar, and then press the Enter key.

| Figure 7-5 | EMPLOYER POSITIONS QUERY IN THE INTERNET EXPLORER WINDOW |

HTML document filename appears as the Web page title

graphic supplied by template

records from the Employer Positions query

address for the Employer Positions Web page (yours might differ)

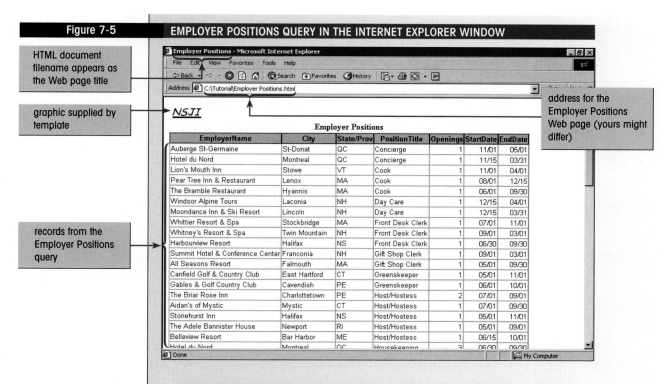

NSJI

Employer Positions

EmployerName	City	State/Prov	PositionTitle	Openings	StartDate	EndDate
Auberge St-Germaine	St-Donat	QC	Concierge	1	11/01	05/01
Hotel du Nord	Montreal	QC	Concierge	1	11/15	03/31
Lion's Mouth Inn	Stowe	VT	Cook	1	11/01	04/01
Pear Tree Inn & Restaurant	Lenox	MA	Cook	1	08/01	12/15
The Bramble Restaurant	Hyannis	MA	Cook	1	06/01	09/30
Windsor Alpine Tours	Laconia	NH	Day Care	1	12/15	04/01
Moondance Inn & Ski Resort	Lincoln	NH	Day Care	1	12/15	03/31
Whittier Resort & Spa	Stockbridge	MA	Front Desk Clerk	1	07/01	11/01
Whitney's Resort & Spa	Twin Mountain	NH	Front Desk Clerk	1	09/01	03/01
Harbourview Resort	Halifax	NS	Front Desk Clerk	1	06/30	09/30
Summit Hotel & Conference Center	Franconia	NH	Gift Shop Clerk	1	09/01	03/01
All Seasons Resort	Falmouth	MA	Gift Shop Clerk	1	05/01	09/30
Canfield Golf & Country Club	East Hartford	CT	Greenskeeper	1	05/01	11/01
Gables & Golf Country Club	Cavendish	PE	Greenskeeper	1	06/01	10/01
The Briar Rose Inn	Charlottetown	PE	Host/Hostess	2	07/01	09/01
Aidan's of Mystic	Mystic	CT	Host/Hostess	1	07/01	09/30
Stonehurst Inn	Halifax	NS	Host/Hostess	1	05/01	11/01
The Adele Bannister House	Newport	RI	Host/Hostess	1	05/01	09/01
Belleview Resort	Bar Harbor	ME	Host/Hostess	1	06/15	10/01
Hotel du Nord	Montreal	QC	Housekeeping	3	06/30	09/30

TROUBLE? If another program opens, such as Microsoft Word, then Internet Explorer might not be installed on your computer. If the title bar on your screen displays "Microsoft Word," you can continue with the steps, but your screens will look different from those shown in the figures.

TROUBLE? If your computer has Navigator installed as its default browser, Navigator will start automatically and open the Employer Positions Web page. If Navigator opens, your screens will look slightly different from those shown in the figures.

TROUBLE? If a Web browser is not installed on your computer, ask your instructor or technical support person for help.

Changes that NSJI employees make to the Jobs database will not appear in the Employer Positions Web page that you created because it is a static page—that is, it reflects the state of the Employer Positions query in the Jobs database at the time you created it. If data in the Employer Positions query changes, Matt will have to export the Employer Positions Web page again.

Because this static Web page is not linked to the Employer Positions query on which it is based, you cannot use your browser to make changes to its data. Before closing the Employer Positions Web page, you'll try to change one of its field values.

To attempt to change a field value, and then close the browser:

1. Double-click **QC** in the State/Prov column for the first record (Auberge St-Germaine), and then type **NS**. The value of QC remains highlighted and unchanged, because the Employer Positions Web page is a static page.

2. Click the **Close** button **X** on the Internet Explorer window title bar to close it and to return to the Database window.

3. Click **View** on the menu bar, point to **Toolbars**, and then click **Web** to close the Web toolbar.

Matt asks if it's possible to create a dynamic Web page for the Position table that he and the recruiters can update using their browsers. To accomplish this task for Matt, you'll need to create a data access page.

Creating a Data Access Page for an Access Table

A **data access page** (or simply a **page**) is a dynamic HTML document that you can open with a Web browser to view or update current data in an Access database. Unlike other database objects stored in an Access database, such as forms and reports, data access pages are stored outside the database as separate HTML documents. Like other database objects, however, a data access page also includes a page object in the Access database; this page object connects the HTML document with the bound fields from the database. It's this connection that provides the dynamic element to the HTML document.

You can create a data access page either in Design view or by using a Wizard. To create the data access page for the Position table, you'll use the Page Wizard.

To create the data access page using the Page Wizard:

1. Click **Pages** in the Objects bar of the Database window to display the Pages list. The Pages list box does not contain any data access pages.

2. Click the **New** button in the Database window to open the New Data Access Page dialog box. This dialog box is similar to the ones you've used to create tables, queries, forms, and reports.

3. Click **Page Wizard** to select this Wizard, click the list arrow for choosing the table or query on which to base the page, scroll down and click **Position**, and then click the **OK** button. The first Page Wizard dialog box opens, in which you select the fields you want to display on the data access page. You'll include all of the fields from the Position table.

4. Click the ⏩ button to select all of the fields from the Position table, and then click the **Next** button to open the next Page Wizard dialog box, in which you select the grouping levels for the data access page. See Figure 7-6.

Figure 7-6	SELECTING GROUPING LEVELS FOR A DATA ACCESS PAGE

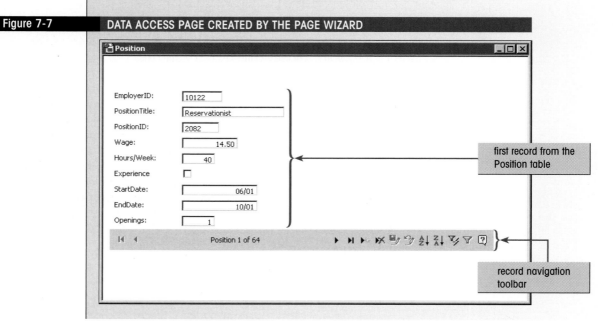

candidate fields from the Position table for grouping levels

default grouping field from the Position table

remaining Position table fields

The Wizard selected the EmployerID field for a grouping level. Matt doesn't need any grouping levels for this data access page, so you'll delete the EmployerID field grouping level.

5. Click the **EmployerID** field on the right side of the dialog box, click the ![<] button to delete the EmployerID grouping level and to place the field with the other Position table fields, and then click the **Next** button. In this Page Wizard dialog box, you select the sort fields for each data access page. Matt wants the records sorted in ascending order by the EmployerID field, and then in ascending order by the PositionTitle field.

6. Select the **EmployerID** field as the primary sort key and the **PositionTitle** field as the secondary sort key, and then click the **Next** button to open the last Page Wizard dialog box, in which you enter a name for the data access page. You'll use the default name, and then open the data access page in Access.

7. Click the **Open the page** option button, and then click the **Finish** button. Access opens the data access page in Page view. See Figure 7-7.

Figure 7-7	DATA ACCESS PAGE CREATED BY THE PAGE WIZARD

first record from the Position table

record navigation toolbar

This data access page, which has an appearance similar to a form, displays a record's field values from the Position table one at a time. The **record navigation toolbar**, which appears below the record, lets you move between records in the table, add and delete records, edit and undo entries, sort and filter data, and request Help. ScreenTips for each button on the record navigation toolbar will appear if you position the pointer on a button, and 11 of the 13 buttons are familiar because you've seen them on other Access toolbars. The Save button 🖳 and the Undo button 🔄 are the two new buttons on the record navigation toolbar.

Matt wants to make sure that he can update the Position table using the data access page that you created. You can use a data access page to update data in Page view or with a Web browser, so you'll show Matt how to use both update methods. First, you'll save the data access page, and then you'll update a field value in Page view.

To save the data access page, and then update a Position table field value in Page view:

1. Click the **Save** button 🖫 on the Page View toolbar. The Save As Data Access Page dialog box opens. You'll save the data access page using the default name (Position) and type (Microsoft Data Access Pages).

2. Make sure the Save in list box displays the **Tutorial** folder on your Data Disk, and then click the **Save** button. Unless it has been disabled, a message box opens to warn you that the page's connection string is an absolute path. See Figure 7-8.

Figure 7-8	CONNECTION STRING WARNING

leave this option unchecked

TROUBLE? If the message box doesn't open, a previous user has disabled it. Continue with Step 4.

The **connection string** is a string, or text, expression that specifies the disk location and the database name used to connect a page to an Access database. When you specify a specific file on a specific disk drive, you've provided what is called an **absolute path**. For example, if your Tutorial folder is located on drive C when you save the Position page, C:\Tutorial\Jobs.mdb would be the connection string expressed as an absolute path. If you want others to use the page, you must make sure the disk drive specified in the absolute path represents a Web server or network drive that others can access. After saving the page, if you want to change the connection string to a different disk drive, switch to Design view, right-click the data access page title bar, click Page Properties on the shortcut menu, click the Data tab, click the ConnectionString text box, click its Build button, click the Connection tab, modify the absolute path in the first text box, and then click the OK button.

You won't be changing the connection string because Matt won't be moving the Jobs database to NSJI's Web server until after you've completed all your work with it. Also, it's a good idea to view the message box every time you create a page as a reminder that you need to update the connection string if you move the database, so you'll leave the "Don't show this warning again" check box unchecked.

3. Make sure the **Don't show this warning again** check box is unchecked, and then click the **OK** button to save the page with the default name and type.

   Next, you'll show Matt how to update position data on the page.

4. Double-click **40** in the Hours/Week text box, type **35**, and then press the **Tab** key. The value of the Hours/Week field is now 35. Note that several buttons on the record navigation toolbar changed from dimmed to active.

   Next, you'll close the page.

5. Click the **Close** button ⊠ on the Position window title bar. A message opens and warns you that your change to the Hours/Week field will be discarded because you didn't save it. You can save changes to a record automatically by navigating to another record or by clicking the Save button on the record navigation toolbar. You'll cancel the message, and then save your change.

6. Click the **Cancel** button, and then click the **Save** button 🖫 on the record navigation toolbar. Your change to the record is saved in the database, and the Save button and other buttons on the record navigation toolbar changed from active to dimmed.

   You've completed working in Page view, so you can close the page.

7. Click ⊠ on the Position window title bar. The page closes and you return to the Database window. Notice that the Position page is listed in the Pages list box.

Next, you'll view the page with your browser. Then you'll show Matt how to update data on a page using a browser; you'll change the Hours/Week field value for the first position for EmployerID 10122 back to 40.

Updating Data on a Data Access Page Using Internet Explorer

You can view a data access page using any Web browser. However, if you want to update data on a data access page, you must use Internet Explorer 5.0 or higher, or another browser that supports data access pages.

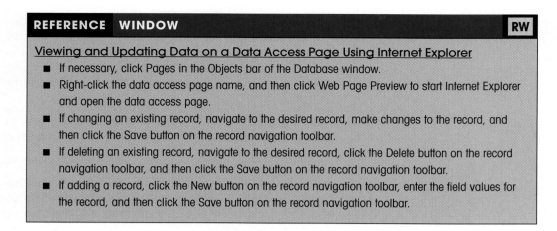

REFERENCE WINDOW   RW

Viewing and Updating Data on a Data Access Page Using Internet Explorer
- If necessary, click Pages in the Objects bar of the Database window.
- Right-click the data access page name, and then click Web Page Preview to start Internet Explorer and open the data access page.
- If changing an existing record, navigate to the desired record, make changes to the record, and then click the Save button on the record navigation toolbar.
- If deleting an existing record, navigate to the desired record, click the Delete button on the record navigation toolbar, and then click the Save button on the record navigation toolbar.
- If adding a record, click the New button on the record navigation toolbar, enter the field values for the record, and then click the Save button on the record navigation toolbar.

You can now view and update data on the page using Internet Explorer.

To view and update data on the page using Internet Explorer:

1. Right-click **Position** in the Pages list box, and then click **Web Page Preview** to start Internet Explorer and open the Position page. See Figure 7-9.

   TROUBLE? If an Internet Explorer dialog box opens and indicates that the Position page is unavailable offline, click the OK button to close the dialog box. In Internet Explorer, click File on the menu bar, and then click Work Offline. You do not need an Internet connection to complete these steps.

Figure 7-9   PAGE IN THE INTERNET EXPLORER WINDOW

You'll change the Hours/Week field value for position 2082 back to 40.

2. Double-click **35** in the Hours/Week text box, type **40**, press the **Tab** key, and then click the **Save** button on the record navigation toolbar. The value of the Hours/Week field is changed to 40 in the database.

Matt asks about the other buttons on the record navigation toolbar. Next, you'll show him how to sort and filter records using a data access page.

Using a Data Access Page to Sort and Filter Records

The buttons on the record navigation toolbar for sorting and filtering data work the same for data access pages as they do for forms. You'll show Matt how to sort and filter records using a data access page based on a value in the StartDate field.

To use a data access page to sort and filter records:

1. Click the **StartDate** text box, and then click the **Sort Descending** button [ZA↓] on the record navigation toolbar. Access rearranges the records in descending order by start date—records for 12/15 appear first, followed by records for 12/01, and so on.

   You can now filter records, selecting just the records for those positions with a 12/15 start date.

2. Click the **StartDate** text box, and then click the **Filter by Selection** button [🔽] on the record navigation toolbar. Access filters the position records, displaying the first of four records having a start date field value of 12/15. See Figure 7-10.

Figure 7-10	USING FILTER BY SELECTION ON A DATA ACCESS PAGE

first of four filtered records is displayed

first position record with a 12/15 start date

Filter by Selection button

Filter Toggle Button button

Now you can redisplay all the customer records by clicking the Filter Toggle Button button.

3. Click the **Filter Toggle Button** button [🔽] on the record navigation toolbar. Access makes all 64 records from the Position table available on the page.

4. Click the **Close** button [X] on the Internet Explorer window title bar to close it and return to the Database window.

When visiting employers, the recruiters frequently require access to current information about employers and their positions at the same time. Elsa asks if it's possible to create a data access page that the recruiters can use to view and update current Jobs database information about employers and their positions. To do this, you'll create a custom data access page in Design view.

Creating a Custom Data Access Page

Because of its connection to the database object on which it is based, every data access page is a dynamic HTML document. When you open a data access page, you are viewing current data from the Access database that produced it. To create a data access page that recruiters can use to view and update data, you'll create a data access page that includes data selected from the Employer table and from the related Position table.

Just as with forms and reports, you could use a Wizard to create a basic data access page and then customize it in Design view, or you could create a data access page from scratch in Design view. To create the data access page with the employer and position information for Elsa and the recruiters, you'll create the entire data access page in Design view.

Creating a Blank Data Access Page in Design View

You use the Page window in Design view to create and modify data access pages. Similar to Design view for forms and reports, you select the fields for a data access page in Design view from the field list. Unlike previous field lists, which contain only the fields from the source table or query, the field list in the Page window contains all fields from the database. Thus, you don't need to select a source table or query for a data access page before opening the Page window in Design view. To create Elsa's data access page, you'll create a blank data access page and then add fields and controls to it.

REFERENCE WINDOW   **RW**

Creating a Data Access Page in Design View

- If necessary, click Pages in the Objects bar of the Database window to display the Pages list.
- Click the New button to open the New Data Access Page dialog box, click Design View (if necessary), click the OK button, and then if necessary click the OK button to close the warning message and to create a blank data access page.
- Place the necessary controls in the Page window in Design view. Modify the size, position, and other properties of the controls as necessary.
- Click the Save button on the Page Design toolbar, enter a name for the data access page, select a location for the data access page, and then click the Save button.

To create the data access page, you'll first create a blank data access page in the Page window in Design view.

To create a blank data access page in Design view:

1. Maximize the Database window, and then click the **New** button in the Database window. The New Data Access Page dialog box opens.

2. Click **Design View** in the list box (if necessary), and then click the **OK** button. Access displays the Page window in Design view. See Figure 7-11.

| Figure 7-11 | PAGE WINDOW IN DESIGN VIEW |

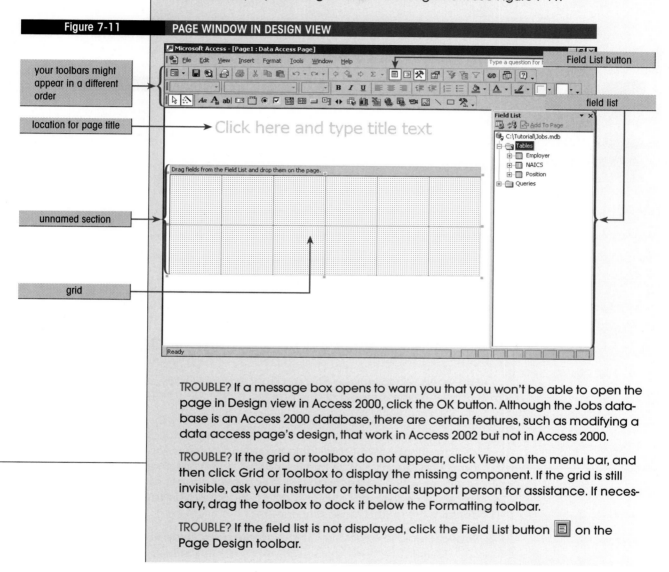

TROUBLE? If a message box opens to warn you that you won't be able to open the page in Design view in Access 2000, click the OK button. Although the Jobs database is an Access 2000 database, there are certain features, such as modifying a data access page's design, that work in Access 2002 but not in Access 2000.

TROUBLE? If the grid or toolbox do not appear, click View on the menu bar, and then click Grid or Toolbox to display the missing component. If the grid is still invisible, ask your instructor or technical support person for assistance. If necessary, drag the toolbox to dock it below the Formatting toolbar.

TROUBLE? If the field list is not displayed, click the Field List button 📄 on the Page Design toolbar.

The Page window in Design view has many of the same components as the Form and Report windows in Design view. For example, these windows include a Formatting toolbar, a grid, a Properties button, a Field List button, and a Toolbox button.

Unlike the Form and Report windows in Design view, however, the Page window initially contains only one unnamed section, which is named after you place controls in it, and placeholder text for the title of your data access page. Also, the Field List window, which is also called the field list, contains all of the tables and queries in the database; you can select fields from one or more tables and queries to include in the data access page.

Adding Fields to a Data Access Page

Because Elsa wants to see employers and their positions, your first task is to use the field list to add fields from the Employer table to the grid.

To add fields to the grid from the field list for the Employer table:

1. Click ⊞ next to Employer in the field list. The fields from the Employer table and a folder for related tables are now visible in the field list. See Figure 7-12.

Figure 7-12	FIELDS AND RELATED TABLES FOLDER FOR THE EMPLOYER TABLE

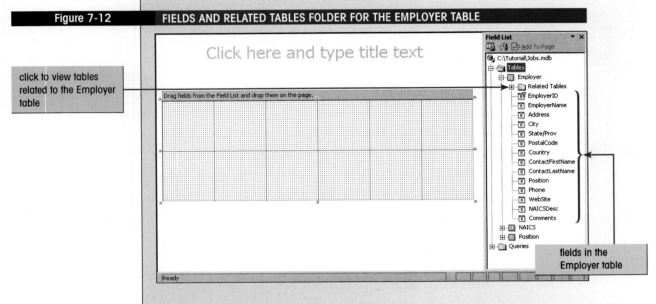

click to view tables related to the Employer table

fields in the Employer table

Elsa wants you to include only the EmployerName, City, and State/Prov fields from the Employer table on the page.

2. Double-click **EmployerName** in the field list. Access adds a bound control for the EmployerName field to the grid. The bound control consists of a text box and an attached label, similar to the bound controls you've used previously for forms and reports. Notice that the section name has changed to Header: Employer, which is referred to as the Employer Header section. Below the Employer Header section, Access adds the Employer Navigation section, which contains the record navigation toolbar.

3. Repeat Step 2 to select the **City** and **State/Prov** fields, in that order.

Elsa wants you to include the PositionTitle, Wage, Hours/Week, and Openings fields from the Position table on the page. To display the fields in the Position table, you'll expand the Employer table's Related Tables entry in the field list, which will display the NAICS and Position tables, and then expand the Position table. (If you had first selected fields from the Position table instead of from the Employer table, you would have expanded the Position table at the bottom of the field list.)

To add fields to the grid from the field list for the Position table:

1. Click ⊞ next to Related Tables in the field list, and then click ⊞ next to Position in the field list. The NAICS and Position tables, which are related to the Employer table, are now visible in the field list, as are the fields from the Position table.

2. Click **PositionTitle** in the field list, press and hold the **Ctrl** key, click **Wage**, **Hours/Week**, and **Openings** in the field list, and then release the **Ctrl** key. All four fields are selected.

3. Drag the selected Position table fields from the field list to the bottom of the Employer Header section so that the text "Create new section below Employer" appears within a rectangle with a blue border. See Figure 7-13.

Figure 7-13	ADDING SELECTED POSITION TABLE FIELDS TO THE GRID

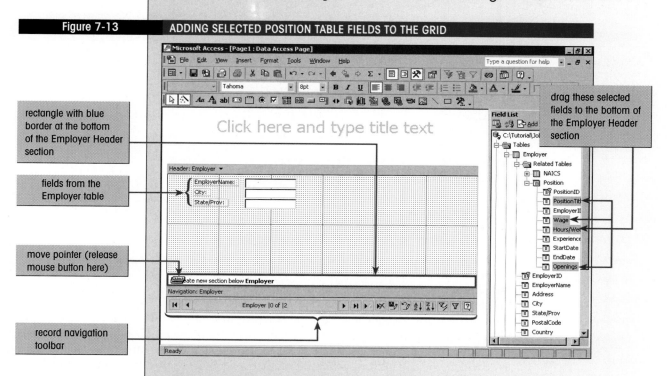

rectangle with blue border at the bottom of the Employer Header section

fields from the Employer table

move pointer (release mouse button here)

record navigation toolbar

drag these selected fields to the bottom of the Employer Header section

4. Release the mouse button. The Layout Wizard dialog box opens, in which you can choose a columnar or tabular layout for the new Position section.

5. Click the **Tabular** option button, click the **OK** button, and then scroll down the Page window. The four fields from the Position table are added to the grid in a new Position Header section, a new Position Navigation section is added above the Employer Navigation section, and a Position Caption section is added above the Position Header section. See Figure 7-14.

| Figure 7-14 | PAGE AFTER ADDING ALL REQUIRED FIELDS TO THE GRID |

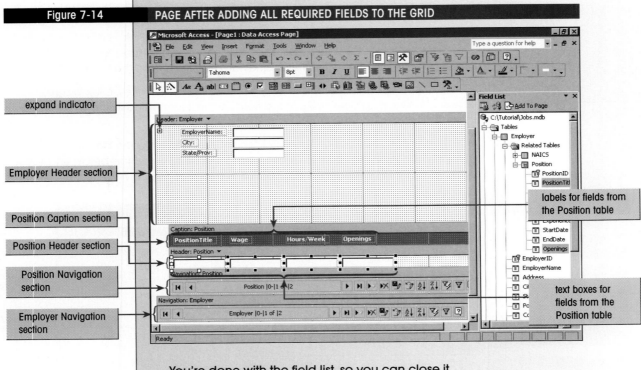

You're done with the field list, so you can close it.

6. Click the **Close** button [X] on the Field List window to close it, and then scroll to the top of the Page window.

Notice that an expand indicator ⊞ appears to the left of the EmployerName label in the Employer Header section. When you view the page in Page view or with a browser, the Employer Header and Employer Navigation sections will be displayed, but the Position Caption, Position Header, and Position Navigation sections will be hidden. Each employer record has an expand indicator, and clicking this control opens a band below the employer record that contains the position data for that employer. At the same time, the ⊞ changes to ⊟, which you can click to collapse or hide the employer's positions. The expand indicator (⊞ and ⊟) provides the same features as the expand indicators you used with sub-datasheets in Tutorial 5.

Next, you'll add a title to the page above the Employer Header section.

To add a title to the page:

1. Click anywhere in the **Click here and type title text** placeholder at the top of the page. The text disappears and is replaced by a large insertion point.

2. Type **Employers and Positions**. Your typed entry becomes the title for the page.

Elsa wants the title left aligned.

3. Click the **Align Left** button [≡] on the Formatting toolbar.

Next, you'll modify the controls in the Employer Header section.

Deleting, Moving, and Resizing Controls on a Data Access Page

Elsa wants you to delete the labels and to move and resize the text boxes in the Employer Header section. She feels that the field values without labels are self-explanatory, and she'd prefer to view the data for as many employers as possible at one time.

To delete the labels, and then move and resize the text boxes in the Employer Header section:

1. Right-click the **EmployerName label** in the Employer Header section, and then click **Cut** on the shortcut menu to delete the label.

2. Repeat Step 1 to delete the **City label** and the **State/Prov label**.

TROUBLE? If the Office Clipboard Task Pane opens, click the **Close** button ☒ on the Task Pane to close it.

TROUBLE? If the Office Assistant opens, right-click it to open the shortcut menu, and then click Hide to close it.

Next, you'll move and resize the three text boxes. You usually identify some design changes, such as resizing text boxes to best fit the data they contain, on a data access page when you switch to Page view. You then switch back to Design view to make the changes and continue changing views and identifying and making changes to the data access page until you are satisfied with its appearance. When you create your own data access pages, you will need to use Page view and Design view to identify changes you need to make to increase the effectiveness of the data access page.

3. Click the **EmployerName** text box (the top text box), and then use the 🖐 pointer to drag the text box into position. (See Figure 7-15.)

4. Use the ↔ pointer on the middle-right sizing handle to resize the **EmployerName** text box. (See Figure 7-15.)

5. Repeat Step 3 for the two remaining text boxes, repeat Step 4 to reduce the width of the State/Prov text box, and then click an empty area of the Employer Header section. See Figure 7-15.

| Figure 7-15 | AFTER DELETING LABELS AND MOVING AND RESIZING TEXT BOXES |

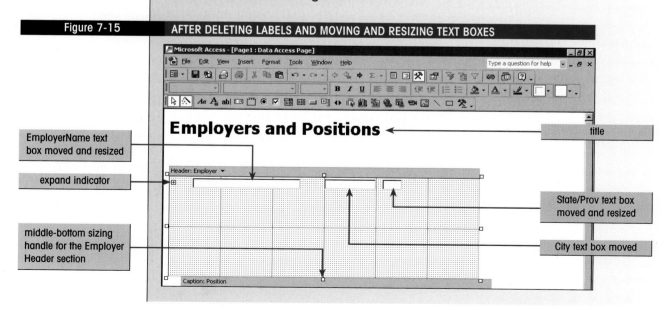

EmployerName text box moved and resized

expand indicator

middle-bottom sizing handle for the Employer Header section

title

State/Prov text box moved and resized

City text box moved

Next, you'll finish your changes to the Employer Header section by reducing the section's height and applying a special effect to the text boxes.

Resizing a Section and Applying a Special Effect

Elsa prefers a different special effect for the three text boxes in the Employer Header section. She also asks you to reduce the height of the section.

To resize the Employer Header section, and then change the special effects for the text boxes:

1. Position the pointer on the middle-bottom sizing handle of the Employer Header section; when the pointer changes to a ↕ shape, drag the bottom up until it's just below the text boxes. See Figure 7-16.

Figure 7-16	AFTER RESIZING THE EMPLOYER HEADER SECTION

Employer Header section list arrow

drag sizing handle to here

list arrow for the Special Effect button

resized Employer Header section

Next, you'll change the special effect for each of the text boxes.

2. Click the **EmployerName** text box (the leftmost text box in the Employer Header section), click the list arrow for the ▭ on the Page Design toolbar, and then click the **Special Effect: Etched** button ▭. The etched special effect is applied to the EmployerName text box.

3. Click the **City** text box (the middle text box in the Employer Header section), and then click ▭ on the Page Design toolbar. The etched special effect is applied to the City text box.

4. Repeat Step 3 for the **State/Prov** text box.

You've made many changes to the page, so you'll save it.

5. Click the **Save** button 🖫 on the Page Design toolbar. The Save As Data Access Page dialog box opens.

6. Type **Employers and Positions** in the File name text box.

7. If necessary, use the Save in list box to display the **Tutorial** folder on your Data Disk, click the **Save** button, and then if necessary click the **OK** button in the message box that warns you about the connection string being an absolute path. Access saves the data access page as Employers and Positions on your Data Disk.

Elsa asks if you can change the number of employer records displayed on the page in Page view. The **DataPageSize property** specifies the number of records displayed on a data access page for a group. The default value is 10 for a grouped data access page and one for a non-grouped data access page. A **grouped data access page** uses two or more group levels to display information from general categories to specific details. For the Employers and Positions page, the first group level is data from the Employer table, and the second group level is data from the Position table. Data from the Employer table represents the general category, and data from the Position table represents the specific details.

Elsa asks you to increase the number of displayed employer records from 10 to 12.

To set the DataPageSize property for the Employer Header section:

1. Click the **Employer Header section** list arrow (see Figure 7-16), and then click **Group Level Properties** on the shortcut menu to open the property sheet for the group.

2. Select the value in the DataPageSize text box, and then type **12**. Access will display 12 employers on each page. See Figure 7-17.

Figure 7-17	PROPERTY SHEET FOR THE EMPLOYER HEADER SECTION

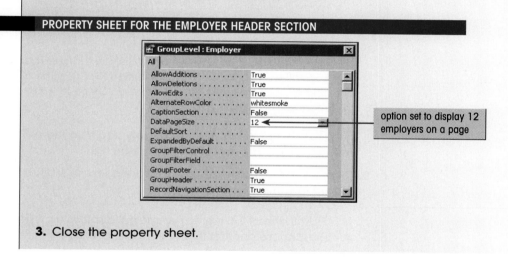

3. Close the property sheet.

Elsa is pleased with the data access page that you have created. She asks if there's a way to format the page to have a more interesting and professional appearance. Next, you'll select a theme for the page.

Selecting a Theme

Before viewing the completed form, Elsa wants to know if you can easily change the overall style of the page. You can select a **theme**, which is a predefined style for a page, to add visual interest to the page.

To select a theme for a page:

1. Click **Format** on the menu bar, and then click **Theme**. The Theme dialog box opens. See Figure 7-18.

| Figure 7-18 | THEME DIALOG BOX |

available themes (your themes might differ)

sample of theme appears here

TROUBLE? If a dialog box opens and tells you that the Theme feature is not cur-rently installed, insert your Microsoft Office XP CD in the correct drive, and then click the OK button. If you do not have an Office XP CD, ask your instructor or technical support person for help.

A sample of the default theme, the selected "(No Theme)" in the Choose a Theme list box, appears in the box on the right.

2. Click several of the styles in the Choose a Theme list box, and view the corre-sponding sample.

TROUBLE? If one of the themes you select displays an Install button instead of a sample, choose another theme from the list box.

3. Click **Axis** in the Choose a Theme list box, and then click the **OK** button. The selected theme is applied to the page.

TROUBLE? If an Install button appears in the sample box for the Axis theme, choose another theme that's already installed on your system.

Next, you'll save and view the completed page.

Saving and Viewing a Data Access Page

Elsa wants to view and update the completed data access page, but first you'll save the changes you made to it.

To save, view, and update the completed page:

1. Save your design changes, and then click the **Close Window** button ☒ on the Page Design window menu bar. The page closes and you return to the Database window. Notice that the Employers and Positions page is listed in the Pages list box.

2. Right-click **Employers and Positions** in the Pages list box, and then click **Web Page Preview**. Internet Explorer starts and opens the Employers and Positions page. See Figure 7-19.

| Figure 7-19 | COMPLETED DATA ACCESS PAGE |

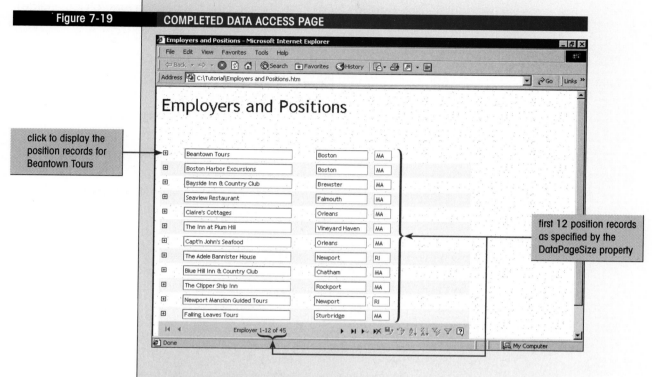

click to display the position records for Beantown Tours

first 12 position records as specified by the DataPageSize property

Next, you will show Elsa how to view an employer's position records.

3. Click the **expand indicator** ⊞ to the left of Beantown Tours (the first record). The two positions for Beantown Tours are displayed between Beantown Tours and the next employer record, the record navigation toolbar for positions appears, and the expand indicator ⊞ changes to ⊟. See Figure 7-20.

| Figure 7-20 | DISPLAYING THE POSITIONS FOR BEANTOWN TOURS |

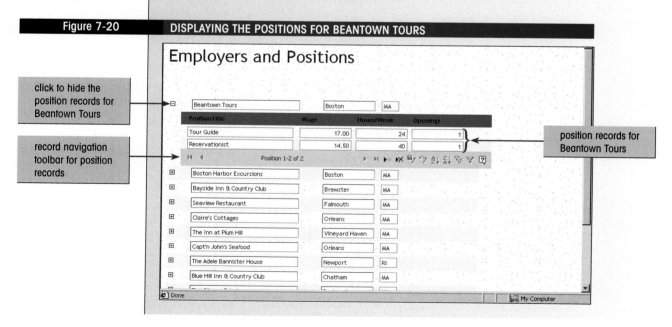

click to hide the position records for Beantown Tours

record navigation toolbar for position records

position records for Beantown Tours

Elsa recently heard from Beantown Tours that they now have two Tour Guide openings, so you'll change the Openings field value for the first position record from 1 to 2.

4. Double-click **1** in the Openings column for the first position record (Tour Guide), type **2**, and then click the **Save** button 🖫 on the record navigation toolbar. The value of the Openings field is changed to 2 in the Jobs database.

5. Click the **expand indicator** ⊟ to the left of Beantown Tours. The two positions for Beantown Tours and the record navigation toolbar for positions are no longer displayed, and the expand indicator ⊟ changes back to ⊞.

6. Use the navigation buttons (First, Previous, Next, and Last) to navigate through the pages.

   You've completed your work with the Employers and Positions page, so you can close it.

7. Click the **Close** button ⊠ on the Internet Explorer window title bar. Internet Explorer closes, and you return to the Database window.

Elsa is pleased with the HTML documents and the data access pages that you created. Your work will make it easy to distribute important Jobs database information on the company's intranet. In the next session, you will continue working with data access pages to enhance the database further.

Session 7.1 QUICK CHECK

1. What is the World Wide Web?

2. What is the purpose of a Web browser?

3. What is a hyperlink?

4. What is HTML?

5. What is an HTML template?

6. What is a static Web page?

7. What is a data access page?

8. A _____ string is a string, or text, expression that specifies the disk location and database name used to connect a data access page to an Access database.

9. What is a grouped data access page?

10. What is a theme?

SESSION 7.2

In this session, you will create two new data access pages: one that uses a PivotTable, and a second that uses a PivotChart.

Creating and Using a PivotTable on a Data Access Page

Elsa would like to expand the use of Web pages for the Jobs database. In particular, she wants to be able to use Web pages to analyze her business in a flexible way. You can use PivotTables on data access pages to provide the flexible analysis that Elsa needs. When used on a data access page, a **PivotTable**, also called a **PivotTable list**, is an interactive table that lets you analyze data dynamically using a Web browser. You can use a PivotTable on a data access page to view and organize data from a database, look for summary or detail information, and dynamically change the contents and organization of the table. Figure 7-21 shows a PivotTable on a data access page.

Figure 7-21	PivotTable ON A DATA ACCESS PAGE

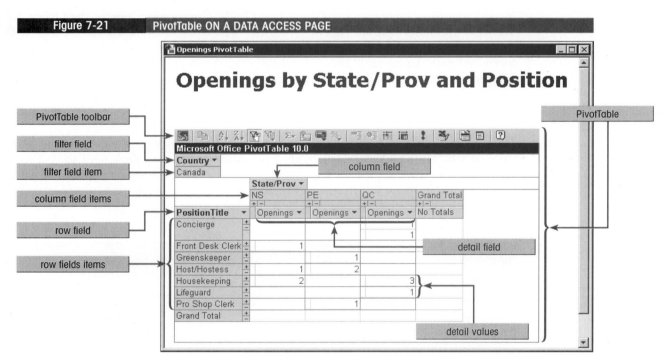

A PivotTable contains the following basic components:

- The **PivotTable toolbar** lets you perform actions such as sorting and filtering when viewing the PivotTable as a Web page.
- The **main body**, consisting of a **detail field** and **detail values**, provides details or totals from a database. In Figure 7-21, the detail field is the Openings field from the Position table, and the detail values are the Openings field values.

- The **row area**, consisting of a **row field** and **row field items**, provides row groupings for the PivotTable. In Figure 7-21, the row field is the PositionTitle field from the Position table, and the row field items are the PositionTitle field values.

- The **column area**, consisting of a **column field** and **column field items**, provides column groupings for the PivotTable. In Figure 7-21, the column field is the State/Prov field from the Employer table, and the column field items are the State/Prov field values.

- The **filter area**, consisting of a **filter field** and **filter field items**, lets you restrict which data appears in the PivotTable. In Figure 7-21, the filter field is the Country field from the Employer table, and the filter field item is "Canada"—only Canadian provinces appear in the PivotTable.

- All the PivotTable areas—main body, row area, column area, and filter area—can have multiple fields with associated field items.

When you use PivotTables on data access pages, you are not using Access 2002 features. Instead, the PivotTable uses the **Office PivotTable Component**, one of the **Office XP Web Components** that are part of Office XP. Therefore, PivotTables can be used with other programs, such as Excel and FrontPage. You can also use PivotTables with Access forms and with Access table and query datasheets; the PivotTable view with these Access objects provides this capability.

Adding a PivotTable to a Data Access Page

Matt and the recruiters have been very successful finding overseas students interested in the seasonal jobs NSJI brokers. To place all these students, Elsa and Zack need to find more employers with seasonal jobs. To help them determine which positions are popular and where they are popular, Elsa wants to analyze position openings by location (state/province) and by position title. You'll create a PivotTable on a data access page to let her perform this analysis.

REFERENCE WINDOW   **RW**

Adding a PivotTable to a Data Access Page
- If necessary, click Pages in the Objects bar of the Database window to display the Pages list.
- Click the New button to open the New Data Access Page dialog box, click Design View (if necessary), click the OK button, and then if necessary click the OK button to close the warning message and to create a blank data access page.
- Click the Office PivotTable tool on the toolbox, and then click the mouse button in the location on the page where you want to position the upper-left corner of the PivotTable.
- Use the fields from the field list to drag and drop the filter, row, column, and detail fields on the PivotTable. Add calculated and total fields to the PivotTable as needed.
- Modify the size of the PivotTable, and modify the size and other properties of the controls on the PivotTable.
- Click the Save button on the Page Design toolbar, enter a name for the data access page, select a location for the data access page, and then click the Save button.

You'll first create a blank data access page and add a PivotTable to the page.

To create a PivotTable on a data access page:

1. If you took a break after the previous session, make sure that Access is running, that the **Jobs** database in the Tutorial folder on your Data Disk is open, that **Pages** is selected in the Objects bar of the Database window, and that the Database window is maximized.

2. Click the **New** button in the Database window to open the New Data Access Page dialog box, click **Design View** in the list box (if necessary), click the **OK** button, and then if necessary click the **OK** button if you're warned about the Access 2000 Design view issue.

   You'll use the Office PivotTable tool on the toolbox to add a PivotTable control to the page.

3. Click the **Office PivotTable** tool 🗐 on the toolbox. The pointer changes to a ⁺🗐 shape when you move it over the data access page.

4. Move the pointer to the grid, and when the center of the pointer's plus symbol (+) is positioned on the grid dot in the upper-left corner, click the mouse button. Access adds a PivotTable control to the page. See Figure 7-22.

Figure 7-22	AFTER ADDING A PivotTable CONTROL TO THE PAGE

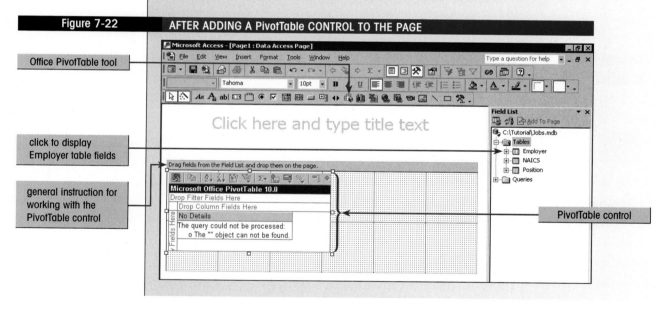

- Office PivotTable tool
- click to display Employer table fields
- general instruction for working with the PivotTable control
- PivotTable control

If you do not select a table or query as the basis for a page when you create a new page in Design view, the message "The query could not be processed: The " " object can not be found." appears inside the PivotTable control. After you add fields to the PivotTable, the message will disappear.

Adding Fields to a PivotTable

For Elsa's analysis, she will need the Country and State/Prov fields from the primary Employer table and the PositionTitle and Openings fields from the related Position table. Within the PivotTable, the Country field will be the filter field, the State/Prov field will be the column field, the PositionTitle field will be the row field, and the Openings field will be the detail field.

First, you'll expand the Employer table in the field list to display its fields, and then you'll add the required fields from the field list to the PivotTable.

To add fields to a PivotTable:

1. Click ⊞ next to Employer in the field list to display the fields from the Employer table and a folder for related tables.

2. Drag the **Country** field from the field list to the "Drop Filter Fields Here" section on the PivotTable so that the section's border color changes to blue. See Figure 7-23.

Figure 7-23	ADDING THE COUNTRY FIELD AS THE FILTER FIELD

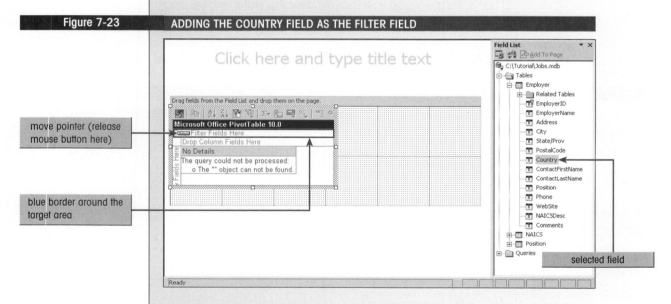

3. Release the mouse button. A control for the Country field now appears in the filter section of the PivotTable. "All" below the Country field indicates that all country values will appear in the PivotTable—that is, no filter is currently applied. (See Figure 7-24.)

   TROUBLE? If you move the wrong field to a PivotTable section or move a field to the wrong PivotTable section, right-click the field name in the PivotTable, click Remove Field on the shortcut menu, and then drag and drop the correct field to the correct section.

   Next, you'll specify the State/Prov field as the column field.

4. Drag the **State/Prov** field from the field list; when the "Drop Column Fields Here" section's border color changes to blue, release the mouse button. A control for the State/Prov field now appears in the column section of the PivotTable. The State/Prov field is the column field, and its field values (CT, MA, and so on) are the column field items. See Figure 7-24.

Figure 7-24   **AFTER ADDING THE COUNTRY AND STATE/PROV FIELDS TO THE PivotTable**

- filter field item
- column field items
- PivotTable border has diagonal slashes
- PivotTable sizing handles

After adding the filter and column fields to the PivotTable, you no longer can see the drop areas for the row area and main body, so you need to increase the PivotTable control's height and width. The border of the PivotTable has diagonal slashes, which indicates that the control's content is activated, so that you can manipulate its inner controls, such as the filter and column fields. You use the PivotTable's sizing handles to change the control's size.

5. Use the ↔ pointer on the PivotTable's middle-right sizing handle to increase its width, and then use the ↕ pointer on the control's middle-bottom sizing handle to increase its height. See Figure 7-25.

Figure 7-25   **AFTER RESIZING THE PivotTable**

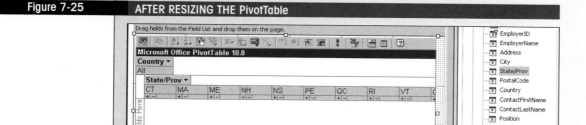

You need to drag and drop the PositionTitle and Openings fields from the related Position table into the PivotTable, so you'll expand the Related Tables entry in the field list and then expand the Position table.

6. Click ⊞ next to Related Tables in the field list, and then click ⊞ next to Position in the field list. The NAICS and Position tables, which are related to the Employer table, are now visible in the field list, as are the fields from the Position table.

7. Drag the **PositionTitle** field from the field list and drop it in the "Drop Row Fields Here" section on the PivotTable. A control for the PositionTitle field now appears in the row section of the PivotTable. The PositionTitle field is the row field, and its field values (Concierge, Cook, and so on) are the row field items. (See Figure 7-26.)

8. Drag the **Openings** field from the field list and drop it in the "Drop Totals or Detail Fields Here" section on the PivotTable. A control for the Openings field now appears in the detail section of the PivotTable. The Openings field is the detail field. The values in the body of the PivotTable are Openings field values from records in the Position table; for example, two Massachusetts (MA) employers each have one available position for a cook. See Figure 7-26.

Figure 7-26	AFTER ADDING THE FIELDS FROM THE JOBS DATABASE TO THE PivotTable

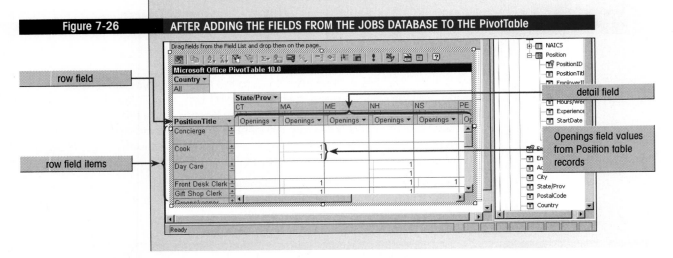

The PivotTable control is finished. Elsa wants you to add a title to the page and then open it in Page view.

Using a PivotTable in Page View

Before viewing and using the PivotTable in Page view, you'll add a page title and then save the page. Also, because you've added all the required fields to the PivotTable, you'll close the field list.

To add a page title, close the field list, and save the page:

1. Click anywhere on the **Click here and type title text** placeholder at the top of the page, and then type **Openings by State/Prov and Position**.

2. Close the field list, and then save the page as **Openings PivotTable** in the Tutorial folder on your Data Disk. If necessary, click the **OK** button to close the dialog box containing the connection string warning message.

Next, you'll view the page in Page view.

To view and use a PivotTable in Page view:

1. Click the **View** button for Page view 🖼 on the Page Design toolbar. The Page window opens in Page view. See Figure 7-27.

Figure 7-27   INITIAL VIEW OF THE PivotTable IN PAGE VIEW

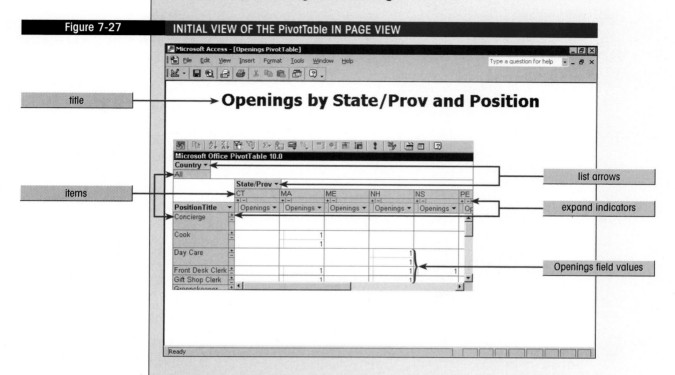

Elsa asks you to explain the purpose of the list arrows next to each field name. The list arrows let you filter the data displayed in the PivotTable. You can filter which countries, position titles, and states/provinces you want to view in the PivotTable. You'll filter to display openings in Canada.

2. Click the **Country** list arrow, click the **All** check box to clear all selections, click the **Canada** check box, and then click the **OK** button. Access applies the Country filter and displays openings in the provinces of Nova Scotia (NS), Prince Edward Island (PE), and Quebec (QC). See Figure 7-28.

Figure 7-28   **FILTERING DATA BY COUNTRY**

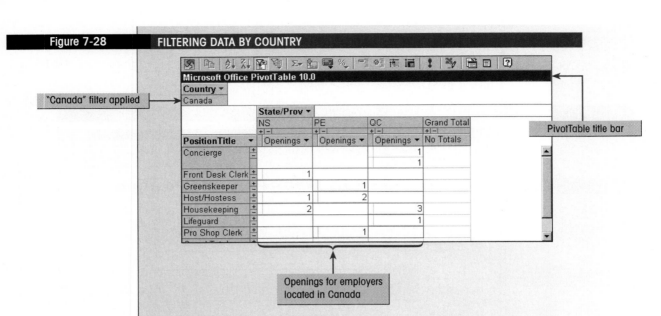

"Canada" filter applied

PivotTable title bar

Openings for employers located in Canada

In a similar way, you can filter selected position titles and selected states/provinces. To remove the Country filter, you could repeat Step 2 and click the All check box. You'll instead show Elsa a faster way to remove and then reapply the filter.

3. Click the **AutoFilter** button 🖼 on the PivotTable toolbar. Access removes the Country filter and displays employers in all locations.

4. Click 🖼 again to reapply the Country filter to display only employers in Canada.

The PivotTable expand indicators ⊞ and ⊟ provide the same functionality as the expand indicators used with subdatasheets and data access pages. Unlike datasheets and data access pages, which display one expand indicator at a time, both PivotTable expand indicators appear for each row field item and column field item. However, clicking the expand indicator ⊞ has no effect if the item is already expanded, and clicking ⊟ has no effect if the item is already collapsed.

5. Click the **Concierge expand indicator** ⊞. Because the Concierge item is already expanded, clicking ⊞ did not change the PivotTable.

6. Click the **Concierge expand indicator** ⊟. The Concierge item collapses to a single line, and its two Openings field values are now hidden.

7. Click the **Concierge expand indicator** ⊞ again to show its details, and then click the rightmost column **Grand Total expand indicator** ⊞. See Figure 7-29.

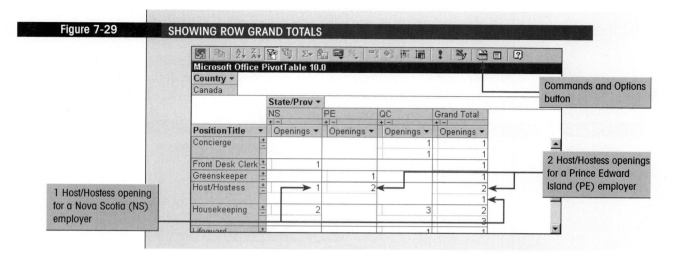

Figure 7-29	SHOWING ROW GRAND TOTALS

A PivotTable automatically includes a grand total column and a grand total row. However, the grand total values do not function as you might expect when the PivotTable's main body displays field values from a database. For example, instead of a grand total value of 3 openings appearing for the Canadian Host/Hostess position, each of the two individual Openings detail values appears in a separate row in the Grand Total column; the same happens in the grand total row. However, the grand total column and row values work as expected when the PivotTable's main body displays total field values.

Adding a Total Field to a PivotTable

A **total field** summarizes field values from a source field. For example, Elsa prefers to view the total number of openings for each position and location in the PivotTable instead of each individual Openings field value. For Elsa's request, you'll add a total field to the PivotTable's main body that will calculate the sum of the Openings field values for each position in each state/province. Before adding the total field, you'll switch to Design view to increase the width and height of the PivotTable, and then you'll change the caption for the PivotTable title bar. Both of these design changes will make the PivotTable easier to use for identifying and viewing the data that Elsa needs.

To change the PivotTable's dimensions and title bar caption:

1. Switch to Design view, click anywhere outside the PivotTable control to deselect it, and then click the PivotTable control to select the outer control. Sizing controls appear on the control's border, which does not have diagonal slashes.

2. Use the middle-right sizing handle to increase the width of the PivotTable until you can see the entire QC column field item, and then use the middle-bottom sizing handle to increase the height of the PivotTable until you can see the entire Housekeeping row field item.

   TROUBLE? If you increase the PivotTable's width or height too much, drag the sizing handle back to its correct position, click the grid that extends beyond the PivotTable, and then drag the grid's sizing handle so that its edge overlaps the PivotTable's edge.

   You can now change the PivotTable title bar caption.

3. Click the PivotTable title bar and, if the PivotTable border does not have diagonal slashes, click the PivotTable title bar until the control's border has diagonal slashes.

4. Click the **Commands and Options** button on the PivotTable toolbar to open the Commands and Options dialog box, and then if necessary click the **Captions** tab. See Figure 7-30.

Figure 7-30   COMMANDS AND OPTIONS DIALOG BOX

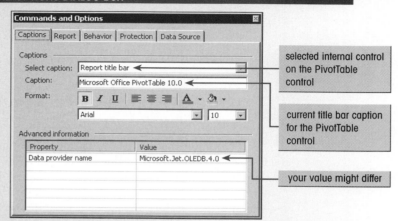

Serving a function similar to the property sheet, the Commands and Options dialog box lets you set property values, such as fonts and captions, for the internal controls on the PivotTable control.

5. Make sure the Select caption list box is set to **Report title bar**, select **Microsoft Office PivotTable 10.0** in the Caption text box, type **Openings PivotTable** in the Caption text box, and then close the Commands and Options dialog box. The PivotTable title bar caption changes to Openings PivotTable.

Next, you'll add the total field to display the total number of openings in the PivotTable's main body.

To add the total field to the PivotTable's main body:

1. Click one of the Openings column headings (but not a list arrow for an Openings column heading) to select the detail column heading row, right-click the same Openings column heading, point to **AutoCalc** on the shortcut menu, and then click **Sum**. Access adds a new row for each position in the PivotTable that displays the total number of openings for the position in each state/province. See Figure 7-31.

Figure 7-31 | AFTER ADDING THE TOTAL FIELD

changed PivotTable title bar caption

total field rows displaying the total number of openings

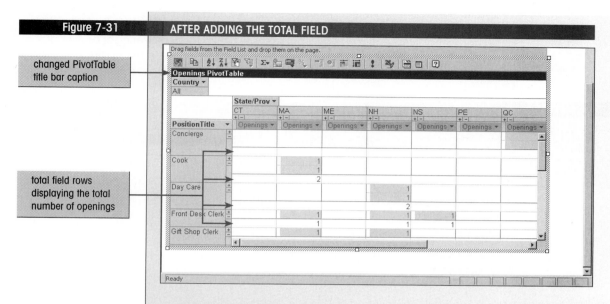

Elsa wants to view only the new total field, so you'll hide the detail number of openings values in the PivotTable.

2. Click the **Hide Details** button on the PivotTable toolbar. The detail values are now hidden, and only the total field values appear in the PivotTable's main body. See Figure 7-32.

Figure 7-32 | AFTER ADDING THE TOTAL FIELD TO THE DETAIL SECTION

Hide Details button

default total field caption

total field values for each positon in each state/province

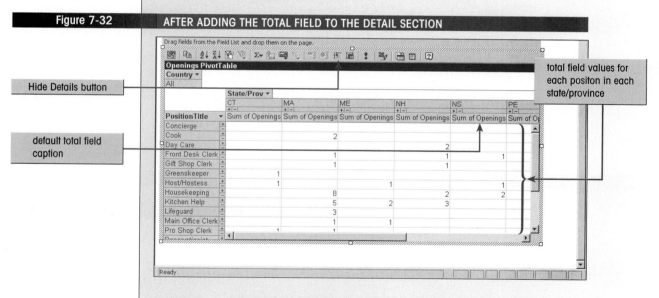

You can now change the default total field caption to a shorter, more meaningful description of the field's contents.

3. Right-click one of the Sum of Openings column headings, click **Commands and Options** on the shortcut menu to open the Commands and Options dialog box for the total field column heading, and then if necessary click the **Captions** tab.

4. Make sure that **Total** appears in the Select caption list box, change the Caption property to **Total Openings**, and then close the Commands and Options dialog box. The total field column headings change to the new Caption property value.

5. Save your design changes, switch to Page view, and then use the PivotTable's horizontal and vertical scroll bars to scroll down to the lower-right corner of the PivotTable. The Total Openings total field values appear in the PivotTable, along with a grand total row and a grand total column. See Figure 7-33.

Figure 7-33	COMPLETED PivotTable IN PAGE VIEW

grand total column (total number of openings for each position)

grand total row (total number of openings for each state/province)

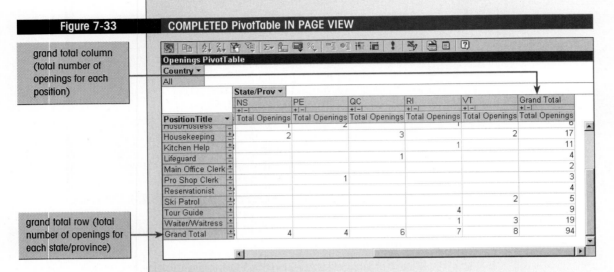

You've completed the PivotTable for Elsa, so you can close the data access page and open it using your browser.

6. Close the data access page, right-click **Openings PivotTable** in the Pages list box, and then click **Web Page Preview**.

Elsa wants to view a summary of the total openings in New Hampshire (NH) and Vermont (VT).

7. Click the **State/Prov** list arrow, click the **All** check box to clear all selections, click the **NH** check box, click the **VT** check box, and then click the **OK** button. Access applies the State/Prov filter and displays total openings only in the states of New Hampshire and Vermont. See Figure 7-34.

Figure 7-34	COMPLETED PivotTable IN THE INTERNET EXPLORER WINDOW

New Hampshire and Vermont selected

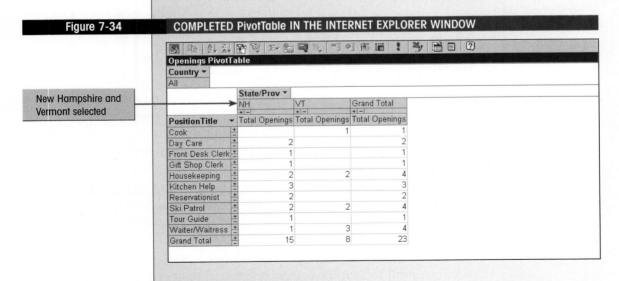

8. Close the Internet Explorer window.

Elsa is so pleased with the PivotTable that you created for her that she immediately thinks of another data access page that would be helpful to her. She asks if you can create a data access page with a chart showing the total openings for each state/province. You'll create a PivotChart on a data access page to satisfy Elsa's request.

Creating and Using a PivotChart on a Data Access Page

Office XP provides the **Office PivotChart Component** to assist you in adding a chart to a data access page, form, or datasheet. Using the Office PivotChart Component, you can create a **PivotChart**, an interactive chart that provides capabilities similar to a PivotTable. Figure 7-35 shows a PivotChart on a data access page.

Figure 7-35	PivotChart ON A DATA ACCESS PAGE

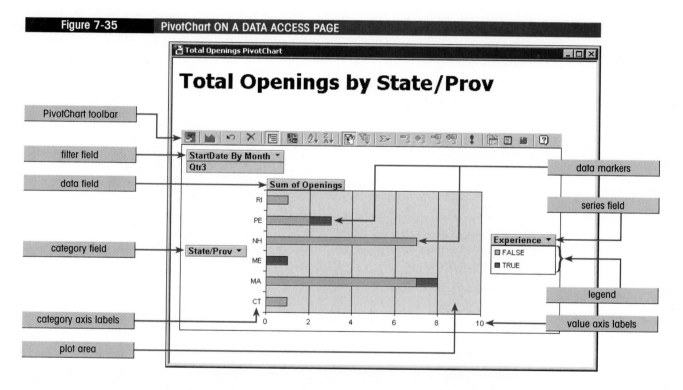

A PivotChart contains the following basic components:

- The **PivotChart toolbar** lets you perform actions such as sorting and filtering.

- The **plot area** provides a background for the data markers and gridlines. A **data marker** is a bar, dot, segment, or other symbol that represents a single data value. The **data field**, which is the Sum of Openings field in Figure 7-35, identifies which values the data markers represent and which values are shown as **value axis labels**. The **gridlines**, which appear in Figure 7-35 as vertical lines in the plot area, make it easier to see the values represented by the data markers.

- The **category field** determines which values appear as **category axis labels**. In Figure 7-35, the State/Prov field is the category field; and CT, MA, and the other states/provinces are the category axis labels. Therefore, the data markers show the total number of openings for each state/province.

■ The **series field** identifies the data markers' subdivisions. In Figure 7-35, the Experience field is the series field, and the data markers show the portion of the total number of openings that require experienced workers. The **legend** provides a list of the series field values and how these values are indicated on the data markers.

■ The **filter field** lets you restrict which data appears on the PivotChart. In Figure 7-35, the filter field is StartDate by Month, and a filter has been applied to include only those openings with start dates in the third quarter (Qtr3).

Using the Office PivotChart Component, you'll create a PivotChart on a data access page to let Elsa analyze total openings for each state/province. The data for a PivotChart can come from either a single table or from a query based on one or more tables. Elsa wants the chart to include the State/Prov field from the Employer table and the Openings, StartDate, and Experience fields from the Position table. Except for the Experience field, the Employer Positions query contains the fields needed for the PivotChart. You will modify the query to add the Experience field, and then you'll use the modified query as the basis for your PivotChart.

To modify the Employer Positions query:

1. Open the **Employer Positions** query in Design view.

2. Add the **Experience** field from the Position field list to the design grid.

   You'll save the query as Employer Positions with Experience.

3. Click **File** on the menu bar, click **Save As**, change the query name to **Employer Positions with Experience**, and then press the **Enter** key.

4. Run the query. Access displays the query results, which show the 64 records with the EmployerName, City, and State/Prov fields from the Employer table, and the PositionTitle, Openings, StartDate, EndDate, and Experience fields from the Position table.

5. Close the query.

Next, you'll create a new data access page and add a PivotChart to it.

REFERENCE WINDOW   RW

Adding a PivotChart to a Data Access Page
■ If necessary, click Pages in the Objects bar of the Database window to display the Pages list.
■ Click the New button to open the New Data Access Page dialog box, click Design View (if necessary), click the OK button, and then if necessary click the OK button to close the warning message and to create a blank data access page.
■ Click the Office Chart tool on the toolbox, and then click the mouse button in the location on the page where you want to position the upper-left corner of the PivotChart.
■ Click the PivotChart control to open the Commands and Options dialog box. Select the data source, data link connection, table or query, and chart type for the PivotChart.
■ Close the Commands and Options dialog box.
■ From the field list add the category, data, filter, and series fields to the PivotChart.
■ Modify the size of the PivotChart, and modify the size and other properties of the controls on the PivotChart.
■ Click the Save button on the Page Design toolbar, enter a name for the data access page, select a location for the data access page, and then click the Save button.

You'll first create a blank data access page and add a PivotChart to the page.

To create a PivotChart on a data access page:

1. Click **Pages** in the Objects bar of the Database window to display the Pages list.

2. Click the **New** button in the Database window to open the New Data Access Page dialog box, click **Design View** in the list box (if necessary), click the **OK** button, and then if necessary click the **OK** button if you're warned about the Access 2000 Design view issue.

   You'll use the Office Chart tool on the toolbox to add a PivotChart control to the page.

3. Click the **Office Chart** tool 📊 on the toolbox. The pointer changes to a ⁺📊 shape when you move it over the data access page.

4. Move the pointer to the grid, and when the center of the pointer's plus symbol (+) is positioned on the grid dot in the upper-left corner, click the mouse button. Access adds a PivotChart control to the page.

5. Click the PivotChart control. The Chart Wizard opens the Commands and Options dialog box. See Figure 7-36.

Figure 7-36	SPECIFYING THE DATA SOURCE FOR THE PivotChart

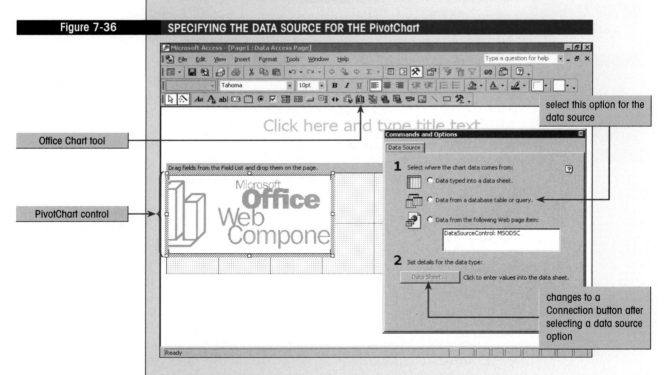

Office Chart tool

PivotChart control

select this option for the data source

changes to a Connection button after selecting a data source option

Your first step is to choose the data source for the PivotChart. The data source for a PivotChart can be data you type into a datasheet, data from a table or query, or data from a Web page. Because the Employer Positions with Experience query is the data source, you'll choose the second option.

6. Click the **Data from a database table or query** option button, and then click the **Connection** button. The Commands and Options dialog box expands to include the Data Details and Type tabs, in addition to the original Data Source tab, and the Data Details tab is selected. You need to set the Connection text box to the Jobs database on your Data Disk. Notice that as you make selections in the dialog boxes, the PivotChart control on the data access page changes to reflect your selections.

7. Click the **Edit** button, use the Look in list box to open the **Tutorial** folder on your Data Disk, click **Jobs** (if necessary), and then click the **Open** button. The Data Link Properties dialog box opens and displays the Jobs database as the selected database name. See Figure 7-37.

| Figure 7-37 | SPECIFYING THE CONNECTION TO THE DATABASE |

selected database (your path might differ)

PivotChart control changes as you select options

option to open the specified data source as a test

these options might be set differently for you

The second section of the dialog box contains a user name (yours might differ from the user name shown in Figure 7-37) and two check boxes. Because you don't want to type a password to establish a connection to the Jobs database and because the default user name is acceptable to Elsa, you won't change anything in the dialog box. If you click the Test Connection button, the Office PivotChart Component will test the accuracy of your data source settings by attempting to open the Jobs database. This test will fail because you already have the database open; the Office PivotChart Component can open the data source only if it's not currently in use. (You would use this option when you have started the Office PivotChart Component but have not opened the data source.)

8. Click the **OK** button to close the Data Link Properties dialog box and open the next dialog box. This dialog box displays the options you've previously selected, so you do not need to make any changes to it.

9. Click the **OK** button to close the dialog box and open the Select Table dialog box, click **Employer Positions with Experience**, click the **OK** button, and then click the **Type** tab on the Commands and Options dialog box. See Figure 7-38.

Figure 7-38   SELECTING THE CHART TYPE

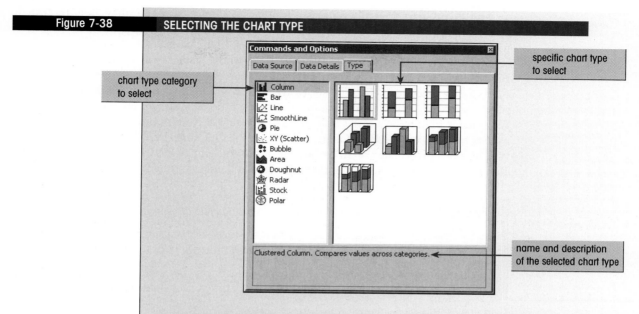

chart type category to select

specific chart type to select

name and description of the selected chart type

Next, you need to select the specific chart type you'll use for the PivotChart. Elsa suggests using a stacked column chart.

10. Click **Column** in the left list box, click the stacked column chart type (row 1, column 2), and then close the Commands and Options dialog box. The PivotChart control now appears with the settings you selected in the dialog boxes, and the data access page field list might be open on your screen. See Figure 7-39.

Figure 7-39   AFTER ADDING THE PivotChart CONTROL TO THE PAGE

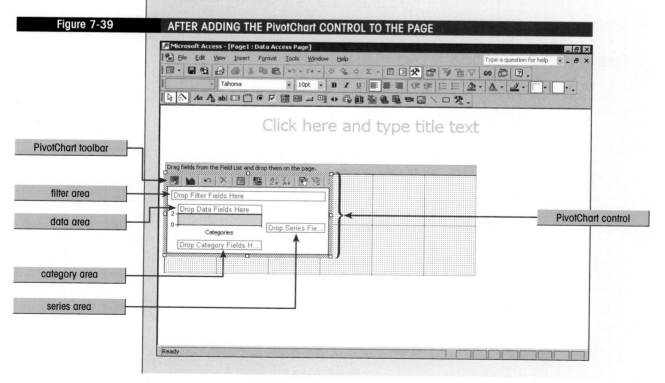

PivotChart toolbar

filter area

data area

category area

series area

PivotChart control

The PivotChart control contains a toolbar and four areas: the filter area, the category area, the data area, and the series area. The filter area will contain any filter fields you need to filter data displayed in the PivotChart; Elsa initially doesn't need any filter fields. The category area will contain the category field whose values will appear as labels on the PivotChart's category axis where "Categories" currently appears; Elsa wants the State/Prov field to be a category field. The series area will contain any series fields you need to represent groups of related data points or data markers on the PivotChart; Elsa wants the Experience field to be a series field. The data area will contain the data fields that will serve as data markers on the PivotChart; Elsa wants the Openings field to be the data field.

The four PivotChart areas are empty until you add fields from the field list to them. Before you add the fields to the PivotChart, you'll enlarge the PivotChart.

To resize and add fields to a PivotChart:

1. Use the ↔ pointer on the PivotChart's middle-right sizing handle to increase its width so that its right edge touches the right edge of the page grid.

2. Use the ↕ pointer on the control's middle-bottom sizing handle to increase its height until you can see 1.25 at the top of the y-axis. (See Figure 7-40.)

3. Click the PivotChart so that border has diagonal slashes, and then click the **Field List** button 🗔 on the PivotChart toolbar to open the field list. See Figure 7-40.

Figure 7-40	AFTER ENLARGING THE PivotChart AND OPENING THE FIELD LIST

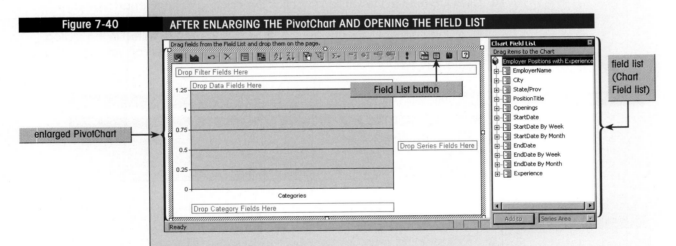

4. Drag the **State/Prov** field from the field list to the category area on the PivotChart. The State/Prov field is now a category field on the PivotChart.

5. Drag the **Experience** field from the field list to the series area on the PivotChart, and then drag the **Openings** field from the field list to the data area on the PivotChart. The Experience field is now a series field on the PivotChart, and the Openings field is now a data field on the PivotChart.

Next, you'll add a left-aligned page title and save the page.

6. Click anywhere on the **Click here and type title text** placeholder at the top of the page, type **Total Openings by State/Prov**, and then click the **Align Left** button [≡] on the Formatting toolbar. Note that the field list no longer appears in the Page Design window.

7. Save the page as **Total Openings PivotChart** in the Tutorial folder on your Data Disk; if necessary, click the **OK** button if the connection string warning message appears. See Figure 7-41.

Figure 7-41	COMPLETED PivotChart IN DESIGN VIEW

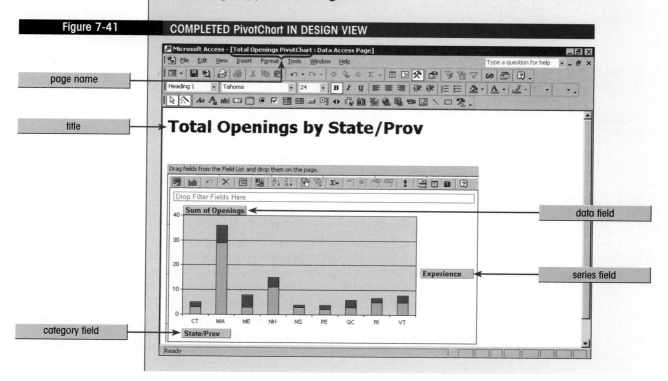

Elsa wants to view the PivotChart in Internet Explorer.

To view the PivotChart in Internet Explorer:

1. Click the list arrow for the **View** button [▦] on the Page Design toolbar, and then click **Web Page Preview**. Internet Explorer starts and displays the Total Openings PivotChart page.

2. Click the **Show/Hide Legend** button [▤] on the PivotChart toolbar to display the legend for the Experience series field. See Figure 7-42.

| Figure 7-42 | COMPLETED PivotChart IN WEB PAGE PREVIEW |

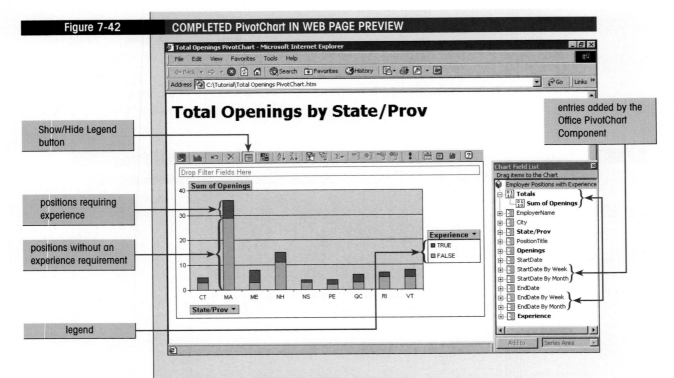

The field list contains the eight fields from the Employer Positions with Experience query and the Sum of Openings summary field, created automatically by the Office PivotChart Component when you added the Openings field as the data field to the PivotChart; the summary field appears as a Totals subentry. In addition, the Office PivotChart Component automatically added two field list entries (StartDate By Week and StartDate By Month) based on the StartDate field, and two entries (EndDate By Week and EndDate By Month) based on the EndDate field. These four date entries let you filter date fields by time divisions such as year, quarter, month, and day.

Elsa asks if she can view the total openings for a specific quarter of the year.

3. Click ⊞ next to StartDate By Month in the field list, and then drag **Quarters** to the filter area on the PivotChart to add it as a filter field to the PivotChart.

4. Click the **StartDate By Month** list arrow, click the **All** check box to clear all selections, click ⊞ next to 2003, click the **Qtr3** check box so that it's the only checked entry, and then click the **OK** button. Access applies the StartDate By Month filter and displays total openings in only those states/provinces that have openings with start dates in the third quarter. See Figure 7-43.

Figure 7-43   **AFTER APPLYING THE FILTER**

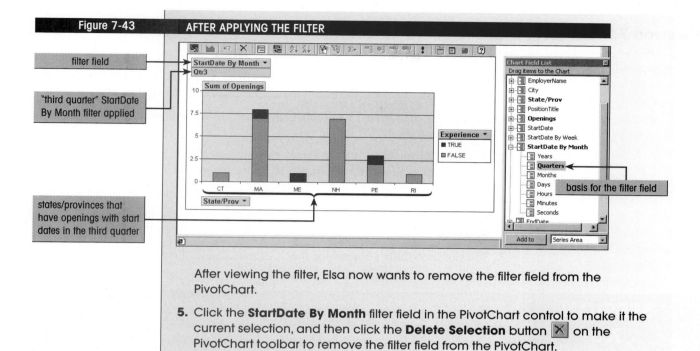

filter field

"third quarter" StartDate By Month filter applied

states/provinces that have openings with start dates in the third quarter

basis for the filter field

After viewing the filter, Elsa now wants to remove the filter field from the PivotChart.

5. Click the **StartDate By Month** filter field in the PivotChart control to make it the current selection, and then click the **Delete Selection** button ☒ on the PivotChart toolbar to remove the filter field from the PivotChart.

Elsa now wants to replace the stacked column chart with a stacked bar chart. You need to change the chart type in Design view.

To change the chart type of the PivotChart:

1. Close Internet Explorer, and then click the PivotChart control until the field list appears. You've selected the PivotChart control and activated the PivotChart toolbar.

2. Click the **Chart Type** button 📊 on the PivotChart toolbar. The Commands and Options dialog box opens with the Type tab selected.

3. Click **Bar** in the left list box, and then click the stacked bar chart type (row 1, column 2). The chart changes to a stacked bar chart.

4. Close the Commands and Options dialog box.

Elsa has no further changes to the PivotChart, so you'll save your design changes and close the page.

5. Save your changes, and then close the data access page.

You have completed the data access pages for Elsa. In the next session, you will help Elsa use XML files and integrate Access data with other programs.

Session 7.2 QUICK CHECK

1. What is a PivotTable?

2. Within a PivotTable you can choose fields from the field list to be the column field, the row field, the detail field, and the _____ field.

3. You can use the Office PivotTable Component to add a PivotTable to which three Access objects?

4. What's different about a PivotTable's expand indicators compared to the expand indicators that appear for datasheets and data access pages?

5. On a PivotTable, the _____ field summarizes field values from a source field.

6. On a PivotChart, the _____ field identifies which values are shown as value axis labels.

7. You can show/hide a legend for the _____ field on a PivotChart.

SESSION 7.3

In this session, you will import data from an XML file into an Access table and export an Access table to an XML file. You will also export Access data to an Excel worksheet. Finally, you'll add a hyperlink field to a table and enter hyperlink values that link records to Word documents.

Using XML

Matt has been tracking positions and the students hired for those positions. Elsa wants to add this data to the Jobs database; in response to her request, Matt has made the data available to Elsa in an XML document. **XML (Extensible Markup Language)** is a programming language similar in format to HTML that is more customizable and suited to the exchange of data between different programs. Unlike HTML, which uses a fixed set of tags to describe how a Web page should look, developers can customize XML code to describe the data it contains and how that data should be structured.

Importing an XML File as an Access Table

Access can import data from an XML file directly into a database table. Matt's XML file is named Job, and you'll import it as a table with the same name into the Jobs database.

REFERENCE WINDOW   **RW**

Importing an XML File as an Access Table

- Click File on the menu bar, point to Get External Data, and then click Import.
- Click the Files of type list arrow, and then click XML Documents.
- Use the Look in list box to select the XML document to import.
- Click the Import button to open the Import XML dialog box, click the Options button, select the desired import option, and then click the OK button.

Now you will import the Job.xml document as an Access database table.

To import the XML document as an Access table:

1. Make sure that Access is running, that the **Jobs** database in the Tutorial folder on your Data Disk is open, that the Database window is maximized, and that **Tables** is selected in the Objects bar of the Database window.

2. Click **File** on the menu bar, point to **Get External Data**, and then click **Import**. The Import dialog box opens.

3. If necessary, click the **Files of type** list arrow, scroll down, and then click **XML Documents**.

4. Make sure the Look in list box displays the **Tutorial** folder on your Data Disk, and then click **Job** to select it.

5. Click the **Import** button to open the Import XML dialog box, and then click the **Options** button. See Figure 7-44.

Figure 7-44   **IMPORT XML DIALOG BOX**

table name as defined in the XML document

option to import the table's structure and data

From the XML file, you can import just the table structure to a new table, import the table structure and data to a new table, or append the data in the XML file to an existing table. You'll import the table structure and data to a new table named Job.

6. Make sure the **Structure and Data** option button is selected, click the **OK** button, and then click the **OK** button when the import confirmation message box appears. The Job table has been imported to the Jobs database and its data has been saved in a new table named Job. This table is now listed in the Tables list box of the Database window.

Elsa asks to view the data in the Job table.

7. Open the **Job** table in Datasheet view. Access displays the PositionID, StudentID, StartDate, and EndDate fields from the Job table, which contains 31 records. See Figure 7-45.

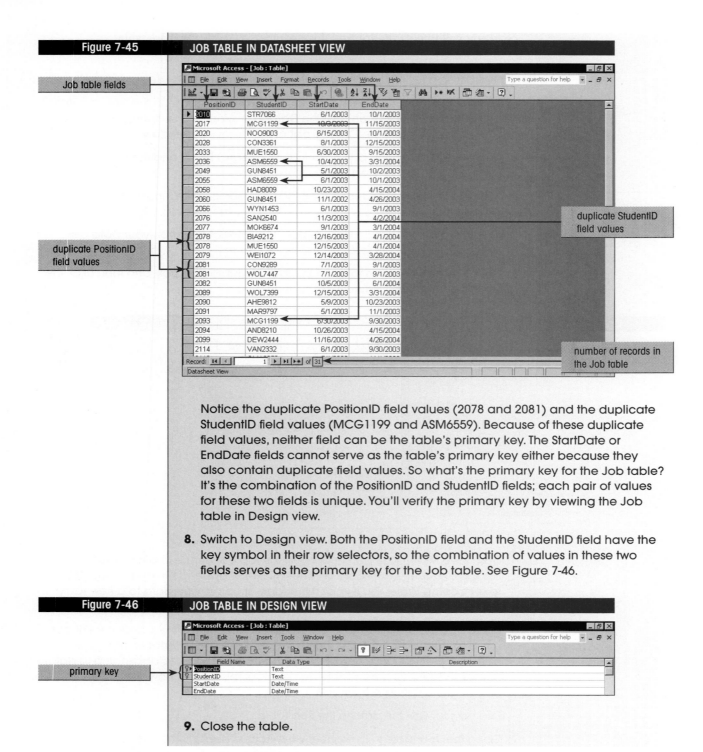

Figure 7-45   JOB TABLE IN DATASHEET VIEW

Job table fields

duplicate StudentID field values

duplicate PositionID field values

number of records in the Job table

Notice the duplicate PositionID field values (2078 and 2081) and the duplicate StudentID field values (MCG1199 and ASM6559). Because of these duplicate field values, neither field can be the table's primary key. The StartDate or EndDate fields cannot serve as the table's primary key either because they also contain duplicate field values. So what's the primary key for the Job table? It's the combination of the PositionID and StudentID fields; each pair of values for these two fields is unique. You'll verify the primary key by viewing the Job table in Design view.

8. Switch to Design view. Both the PositionID field and the StudentID field have the key symbol in their row selectors, so the combination of values in these two fields serves as the primary key for the Job table. See Figure 7-46.

Figure 7-46   JOB TABLE IN DESIGN VIEW

primary key

9. Close the table.

Elsa just received a request that requires you to export the Position table as an XML file.

Exporting an Access Table as an XML File

A regional nonprofit agency, which coordinates housing for international students, recently contacted Elsa and requested job-opening information for NSJI's client employers. The agency uses a specialized computer program, and the agency representative asked Elsa to provide the data as an XML file to make it easier for the agency to identify and process the data.

Just as you did when you exported the Employer Positions query as an HTML document earlier in this tutorial, you'll use the Export command on the shortcut menu to export the Position table as an XML file.

REFERENCE WINDOW   **RW**

Exporting an Access Object as an XML File

- In the Database window, right-click the object (table, query, form, or report) you want to export, and then click Export on the shortcut menu.
- Enter the filename in the File name text box, and then select the location where you want to save the file.
- Click the Save as type list arrow, click XML Documents, and then click the Export button.
- Click the Advanced button on the Export XML dialog box; set the data, schema, and presentation options; and then click the OK button.

You can now export the Position table as an XML file.

To export the Position table as an XML file:

1. Right-click **Position** in the Tables list to display the shortcut menu, and then click **Export**. The Export dialog box opens, displaying the type and name of the object you are exporting in its title bar—in this case, the Position table.

   You'll save the Position table as an XML file in the Tutorial folder on your Data Disk.

2. Make sure the Save in list box displays the **Tutorial** folder on your Data Disk.

3. Type **NSJI Employer Positions** in the File name text box, click the **Save as type** list arrow, scroll down the list and click **XML Documents**, and then click the **Export** button. The Export XML dialog box opens.

   Clicking the Advanced button in the Export XML dialog box lets you view and change detailed options for exporting a database object to an XML file.

4. Click the **Advanced** button to reveal detailed export options in the Export XML dialog box. See Figure 7-47.

Figure 7-47 | **DATA TAB OF THE EXPORT XML DIALOG BOX**

location in which to export the table (yours might differ)

default character encoding method

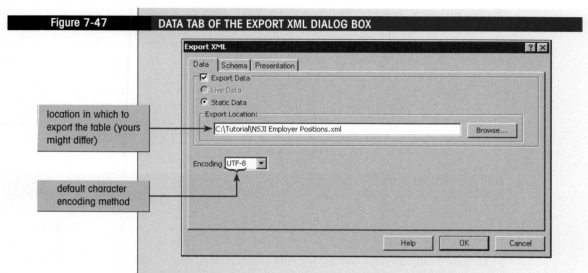

The Export Data check box and the Export Location text box display the selections you made in the previous step. You're exporting the table data, so the data is static, not dynamic. The encoding option determines how characters will be represented in the exported XML file. The encoding choices are UTF-8, which uses 8 bits to represent each character, and UTF-16, which uses 16 bits to represent each character.

The Data tab settings are correct, so you'll verify the Schema tab settings.

5. Click the **Schema** tab. See Figure 7-48.

Figure 7-48 | **SCHEMA TAB OF THE EXPORT XML DIALOG BOX**

option to export the table structure

option to include the table structure in the XML file

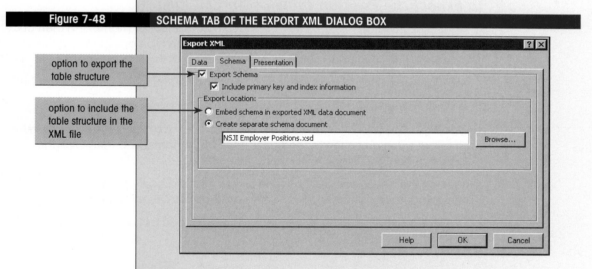

Along with the data from the Position table, you'll be exporting its table structure, including information about the table's primary key and indexes. You can include this information in a separate **XSD** (**XML Structure Definition**) file, or you can embed the information in the XML file. The agency wants a single XML file, so you'll embed the structure information in the XML file.

6. Click the **Embed schema in exported XML data document** option button to select that option and to dim the "Create separate schema document" list box, and then click the **Presentation** tab.

The Presentation tab options let you export a separate **XSL (Extensible Stylesheet Language)** file containing the format specifications for the Position table data. Unlike HTML, XML provides no screen formatting information. An XSL file provides formatting instructions so that a browser or another program can display the data in the XML file in a readable way. The agency will import the Position table data directly into its computer program, which contains its own formatting instructions, so you will not export an XSL file.

7. Make sure that the **Export Presentation (HTML 4.0 Sample XSL)** check box is unchecked, and then click the **OK** button. Access closes the Export XML dialog box, creates the XML file in the Tutorial folder on your Data Disk, and returns you to the Database window.

When contacted in the future, Elsa now knows how to create an XML file to give to the agency.

Elsa next wants to perform a detailed analysis on potential income data. To do so, she wants to work with the data in a Microsoft Excel worksheet.

Exporting an Access Query as an Excel Worksheet

A spreadsheet (or worksheet) program, such as Microsoft Excel, is designed to assist you in analyzing data. Although a database management program provides some data analysis capabilities, it is primarily designed for storing and retrieving records. A worksheet program has many more powerful tools for analyzing data to create budgets, projections, and models.

You can export the contents of most Access objects, including tables, forms, and reports, to other Windows programs, including Excel.

REFERENCE WINDOW	RW
Exporting an Access Object to an Excel Worksheet	
■ In the Database window, click the object you want to export to select it.	
■ Click the OfficeLinks list arrow, and then click Analyze It with Microsoft Excel.	

Like many business owners, Elsa uses a worksheet program as a planning and budgeting tool for her business. She would like to use the potential income information to analyze the company's future income. She asks you to transfer the results of the Potential Income by Employer query to an Excel worksheet so that she can use Excel to perform the necessary analysis that she cannot perform using Access.

To export the query results to an Excel worksheet:

1. Click **Queries** in the Objects bar of the Database window to display the queries list.

2. Click **Potential Income by Employer**, click the list arrow for the **OfficeLinks** button on the Database toolbar, and then click **Analyze It with Microsoft Excel**. Access automatically starts Excel and places the query results in a new worksheet. See Figure 7-49.

   TROUBLE? Depending on your Access settings, your OfficeLinks button might look different than the one shown in Figure 7-49.

   TROUBLE? If Excel is not installed on your computer, another spreadsheet program might start. The specific program that starts and opens the query results is not important. Simply continue with the steps. If a spreadsheet program is not installed on your computer, ask your instructor or technical support person for help.

| Figure 7-49 | QUERY RESULTS IN THE EXCEL WORKSHEET |

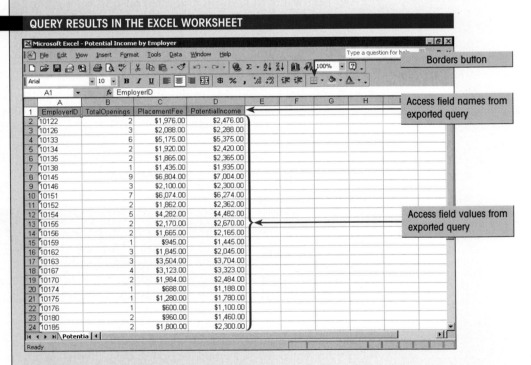

Notice that each field value is placed in a single cell in the worksheet. The field names are entered in the first row of cells in the worksheet. You can now use this data just as you would any other data in an Excel worksheet.

Elsa wants to see the total of the potential income amounts, so she asks you to create a grand total for the data in column D. You'll first add a line to separate the grand total amount from the other potential income amounts.

To create the grand total amount:

1. Scroll down the worksheet, and then click cell **D39** to select the rightmost cell in the last row of data in column D (see Figure 7-50).

2. Click the list arrow for the **Borders** button on the Formatting toolbar to display the list of border options, click the **Thick Bottom Border** button (the second choice in row two), and then click cell **E39**. Excel places a heavy border on the bottom of cell D39. See Figure 7-50.

Figure 7-50   ADDING A BOTTOM BORDER TO THE CELL

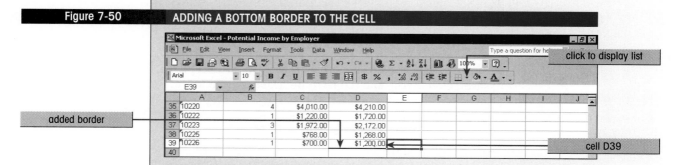

TROUBLE? If the Borders button is not visible on your Formatting toolbar, click the More Buttons button on the Formatting toolbar, and then click the Borders button.

TROUBLE? Your Borders button might look different from the one shown in Figure 7-50 and might be in a different position on the Formatting toolbar.

3. Click cell **D40** to select it, and then click the **AutoSum** button on the Standard toolbar. Excel automatically creates the formula to sum the contents of the cells above cell D40. See Figure 7-51.

Figure 7-51   FORMULA TO SUM THE CONTENTS OF CELLS D2 THROUGH D39

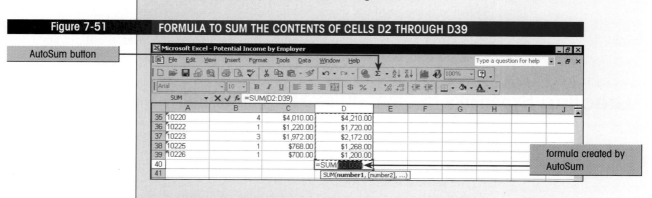

4. Press the **Enter** key to enter the formula. Excel displays the sum of the contents of cells D2 through D39 in cell D40. See Figure 7-52.

Figure 7-52   **TOTAL ADDED TO CELL D40**

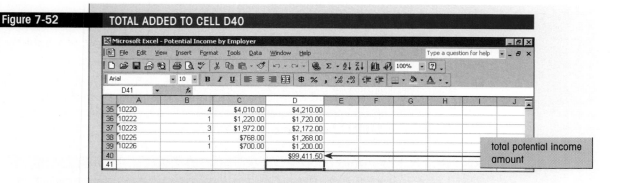

Elsa plans on doing more work with the data in Excel later. For now, you can save the worksheet, close Excel, and return to the Database window in Access.

Saving the Worksheet and Exiting Excel

When you exported the Potential Income by Employer query results to Excel, Excel automatically saved the worksheet with the name Potential Income by Employer. Because you have made changes to the worksheet, you need to save them now before exiting Excel.

To create the grand total amount:

1. Click the **Save** button 🖫 on the Standard toolbar.

2. Click the **Close** button ✖ on the Excel window title bar to close the worksheet, exit Excel, and return to the Database window in Access.

When you exported the query results to Excel, Access placed a copy of the query results in the worksheet. The query results in the Excel worksheet are static, so any later changes made to the Access data will not be reflected in the Excel worksheet. Similarly, any changes made in the worksheet will not affect the Access data.

Creating **Hyperlinks to Other Office XP Documents**

When Zack visits client employers, he keeps field notes about their positions in Word documents. Now he would like some way of connecting these notes with the corresponding records in the Position table. This connection would allow him to review his notes when he views the records in the table.

Each position's set of notes is a separate Word document. For example, Zack created a Word document named Aidan to enter his notes on the host/hostess position at Aidan's of Mystic. Similarly, his notes for the tour guide position at Newport Mansion Guided Tours are in a file named Newport, and the file for the cook position at Pear Tree Inn & Restaurant is named PearTree. To connect Zack's notes with the corresponding records in the Position table, you need to create a hyperlink field in the Position table.

Creating a Hyperlink Field in a Table

Access lets you create a hyperlink field in a table. The field value in a hyperlink field is a hyperlink or pointer to another object. These objects can be database objects (such as tables or forms), a Word document, a named range in an Excel worksheet, or even a URL for a Web page. When you click a hyperlink field value, the associated program starts and opens the linked object.

REFERENCE WINDOW RW

Creating a Hyperlink Field in a Table
- Display the table in Design view.
- In a blank Field Name text box, type the name of the new field, and then press the Tab key.
- Click the Data Type list arrow, and then click Hyperlink.

You will create a hyperlink field in the Position table. The hyperlink field value will be a hyperlink to one of Zack's Word documents. When Zack clicks a hyperlink, Word will start and open the Word document that contains his notes.

To add a hyperlink field to the Position table:

1. Open the **Position** table in Design view.

2. Click the **Field Name** text box in the first empty row, type **FieldNotes**, and then press the **Tab** key.

3. Click the **Data Type** list arrow, and then click **Hyperlink**. See Figure 7-53.

Figure 7-53	ADDING A HYPERLINK FIELD TO A TABLE

4. Save your table design change, and then switch to Datasheet view.

Now you can add the hyperlink field values to the new FieldsNotes field in the Position table datasheet. These field values will be hyperlinks to the Word documents Zack created.

Entering Hyperlink Field Values

When you add a field value in a hyperlink field, you can enter the name of an object, such as a table, form, worksheet, or document, or you can enter a URL to a Web page. You can type the field value directly into the field or you can use the Insert Hyperlink dialog box to enter it.

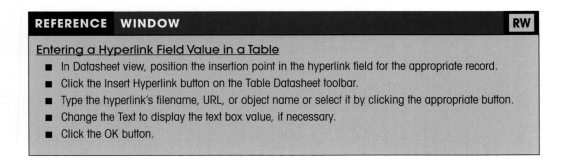

REFERENCE WINDOW   **RW**

Entering a Hyperlink Field Value in a Table
- In Datasheet view, position the insertion point in the hyperlink field for the appropriate record.
- Click the Insert Hyperlink button on the Table Datasheet toolbar.
- Type the hyperlink's filename, URL, or object name or select it by clicking the appropriate button.
- Change the Text to display the text box value, if necessary.
- Click the OK button.

You will use the Insert Hyperlink dialog box to enter the necessary hyperlink field values.

To enter field values in the hyperlink field:

1. In Datasheet view, click the **FieldNotes** text box for the PositionID 2004 record (record 1).

2. Click the **Insert Hyperlink** button 🔗 on the Table Datasheet toolbar. The Insert Hyperlink dialog box opens.

3. If necessary, use the Look in list arrow to display the contents of the **Tutorial** folder on your Data Disk in the Look in list box. See Figure 7-54.

| Figure 7-54 | INSERT HYPERLINK DIALOG BOX |

In the Insert Hyperlink dialog box, you can type the hyperlink, select the link from the Look in list box, or select the link by using one of the buttons. You can click the Bookmark button or the Object in This Database button to select an object in the current Access database as the hyperlink.

The hyperlink for the first record is the file named Aidan.

4. Click **Aidan** in the Look in list box. The name of the Aidan file appears in the Address text box with a .doc extension, which is the extension for a Word document. This is the file that will open when you click the hyperlink field for record 1 in the Position table.

   The Text to display text box shows what will be displayed as a field value in the database hyperlink field for record 1. You'll change the value of the Text to display text box to "Aidan's of Mystic" so that it is more descriptive.

5. Select **.doc** in the Text to display text box, and then type **'s of Mystic**. See Figure 7-55.

| Figure 7-55 | ENTERING A HYPERLINK FIELD VALUE AND FILENAME |

6. Click the **OK** button to close the Insert Hyperlink dialog box. The display text for the hyperlink field value appears in the FieldNotes field for the first record. See Figure 7-56.

| Figure 7-56 | AFTER ENTERING THE HYPERLINK FIELD VALUE |

TROUBLE? If you selected the wrong hyperlink value, right-click the hyperlink field value, point to Hyperlink on the shortcut menu, click Edit Hyperlink, and then repeat Steps 4 through 6.

7. Use the same procedure to enter hyperlink field values for the records for PositionID 2007 (record 2) and PositionID 2028 (record 9). Select **Newport** as the filename and type **Newport Mansion Guided Tours** as the display text value for the PositionID 2007 record; select **PearTree** as the filename and type **Pear Tree Inn & Restaurant** as the display text value for the PositionID 2028 record.

8. Resize the FieldNotes column to its best fit and, if necessary, scroll to the right to view the entire column. Click in any empty FieldsNotes text box to deselect the FieldNotes column. When you are finished, the Datasheet window should look like Figure 7-57.

| Figure 7-57 | HYPERLINK FIELD VALUES ENTERED FOR THE THREE RECORDS |

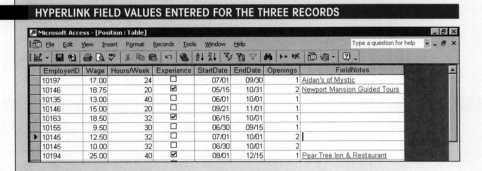

TROUBLE? If you click a hyperlink in the datasheet, instead of an empty FieldNotes text box, Access will start Word and open the hyperlinked file. Click the Close button **X** on the Word title bar to close Word.

Notice that the hyperlink field values have a different appearance from the other field values. The hyperlink field values are shown in a different color and are underlined, indicating that they are hyperlinks.

Zack wants to test one of the new hyperlink fields in the Position table. You'll use a hyperlink to view his corresponding field notes for the Pear Tree Inn & Restaurant.

Using a Hyperlink

When you click a hyperlink field value, its associated program starts and opens the linked object. When you click a value in the FieldNotes field, for example, Word will start and open the linked document.

To use a hyperlink to open a Word document:

1. Click the **Pear Tree Inn & Restaurant** FieldNotes hyperlink. Word starts and opens the PearTree document, which contains Zack's field notes for Pear Tree Inn & Restaurant. See Figure 7-58.

| Figure 7-58 | FIELD NOTES FOR PEAR TREE INN & RESTUARANT IN THE PEARTREE DOCUMENT |

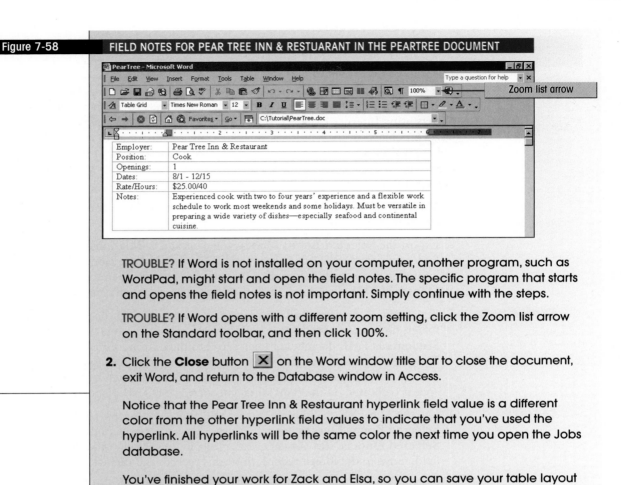

TROUBLE? If Word is not installed on your computer, another program, such as WordPad, might start and open the field notes. The specific program that starts and opens the field notes is not important. Simply continue with the steps.

TROUBLE? If Word opens with a different zoom setting, click the Zoom list arrow on the Standard toolbar, and then click 100%.

2. Click the **Close** button [X] on the Word window title bar to close the document, exit Word, and return to the Database window in Access.

Notice that the Pear Tree Inn & Restaurant hyperlink field value is a different color from the other hyperlink field values to indicate that you've used the hyperlink. All hyperlinks will be the same color the next time you open the Jobs database.

You've finished your work for Zack and Elsa, so you can save your table layout changes and exit Access.

3. Save and close the Position table, and then exit Access.

Elsa, Zack, and Matt are very pleased with the data access pages and integration work you completed for them. They've learned enough to be able to do similar work on their own.

Session 7.3 QUICK CHECK

1. _____ is a programming language that describes how a Web page should look; _____ is a programming language that describes the data it contains and how that data should be structured.

2. When you import or export an XML file using Access, is the data in the XML file static or dynamic?

3. When you use Access to export an XML file and an accompanying XSD file, what information is stored in the XSD file?

4. How do you export a table or query datasheet to Excel?

5. What does the field value of a hyperlink field represent?

6. How do you view a hyperlink that is named in a hyperlink field?

REVIEW ASSIGNMENTS

Elsa wants you to export the data selected by the **Selected Bonus Quotas** query and the **Recruiters and Students** report as HTML documents so she can view these Access objects using Internet Explorer. In addition, she asks you to create additional Web pages based on objects in the **Students** database. Finally, she wants to use the data in the **Selected Bonus Quotas** query as an XML file and also work with the data in Excel, so she needs you to export the query into these data formats. To do so, you'll complete the following steps.

1. Make sure your Data Disk is in the appropriate disk drive, start Access, and then open the **Students** database in the Review folder on your Data Disk.

2. Export the **Selected Bonus Quotas** query as an HTML document in the Review folder on your Data Disk, using the HTML template file named **NSJI-Tbl**, which is located in the Review folder. Use Internet Explorer to open the **Selected Bonus Quotas** HTML document, print the document, and then close Internet Explorer.

Explore

3. Export the **Recruiters and Students** report as an HTML document in the Review folder; do not use a template. Use Internet Explorer to open the **Recruiters and Students** HTML document. Then scroll to the bottom of the document; use the First, Previous, Next, and Last links to navigate through the Web page; print the first page of the report; and then close Internet Explorer. (*Note:* The report title and some labels will appear truncated on the right when you view the HTML document.)

Explore

4. Use the AutoPage: Columnar Wizard to create a data access page based on the **Selected Bonus Quotas** query. Save the data access page in the Review folder as **Selected Quotas**, sort the data access page in descending order based on the Salary field, move to the fourth record, print this record, and then close the data access page.

5. Create a custom data access page named **Recruiters with Students** based on the **Recruiter** and **Student** tables. Use the design in Figure 7-59 as a guide.

Figure 7-59

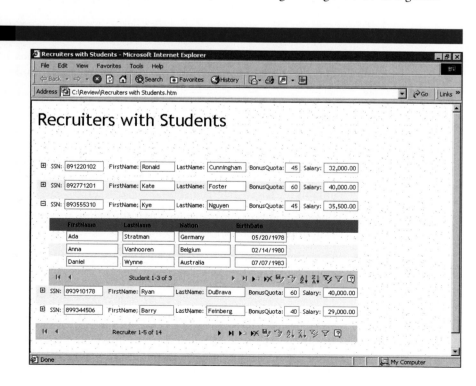

Explore

    a. Place the five fields from the **Recruiter** table in the Recruiter Header section.

    b. Place the FirstName, LastName, Nation, and BirthDate fields from the **Student** table in the Student Header section.

    c. Select the Axis theme.

Explore

    d. In the Recruiter Header section, move and resize the labels and text boxes.

    e. Reduce the height of the Recruiter Header section, and set its DataPageSize property to 5.

    f. Use Recruiters with Students as the title for the data access page, and then left align the title.

    g. Save the data access page as **Recruiters with Students** in the Review folder.

    h. Close the data access page, use the Web Page Preview command to view the data access page, expand the third record (Kyle Nguyen), print the Web page, and then close Internet Explorer.

6. Create a PivotChart on a new data access page as follows:

    a. Use the **Student** table as the data source for the PivotChart, and select the stacked column chart type.

    b. Increase the width of the PivotChart control so that you can see the control's Field List button. Select Nation as the category field, Gender as the series field, LastName as the data field, and RecruiterName as the filter field.

    c. Increase the height and width of the PivotChart control so that you can see the nation values in the chart and all columns of data.

    d. Use Students by Nation as the title for the data access page.

    e. Save the data access page as **Students by Nation** in the Review folder, and then close the data access page.

    f. Use the Web Page Preview command to view the data access page, display the legend, and then print the page.

    g. Use the RecruiterName filter to select the first five recruiters, print the page, and then close Internet Explorer.

7. Export the **Selected Bonus Quotas** query as an XML file named **Selected Bonus Quotas** in the Review folder; do not create a separate XSD file.

8. Export the **Selected Bonus Quotas** query as an Excel worksheet. In the worksheet, add a calculation in cell E12 for the grand total salary, print the worksheet, and then save and close the worksheet.

9. Close the **Students** database, and then exit Access.

CASE PROBLEMS

Case 1. Lim's Video Photography   Youngho Lim wants to be able to use his Web browser to view data stored in the **Clients** database. He asks you to export table data and a report as Web pages, create data access pages, and export data to an XML file. To do so, you'll complete the following steps.

1. Make sure your Data Disk is in the appropriate disk drive, start Access, and then open the **Clients** database in the Cases folder on your Data Disk.

2. Export the **ShootDesc** table as an HTML document in the Cases folder; do not use a template. Use Internet Explorer to open the **ShootDesc** HTML document, print the page, and then close Internet Explorer.

Explore

3. Export the **Clients and Contracts** report as an HTML document in the Cases folder; do not use a template. Use Internet Explorer to open the **Clients and Contracts** HTML document. Then scroll to the bottom of the document; use the First, Previous, Next, and Last links to navigate through the Web page; print page 4 of the report; and then close Internet Explorer. (*Note:* The report title will appear truncated on the right when you view the HTML document.)

4. Use the Page Wizard to create a data access page based on the **Client** table as follows:
   a. Select all fields from the **Client** table, do not select any grouping levels, sort in ascending order by the ClientName field, use Client Page as the title, and then open the page.
   b. Use the data access page to add a new record to the **Client** table with these values: ClientName of "Trent, Brenda," Client# of 982, Address of 18 Sunset Rd, City of Hurley, State of CA, Zip of 94449, and Phone of 6286312041. Save the record.
   c. Close the page, saving it as **Client Page** in the Cases folder.
   d. Open the **Client** table datasheet, print the datasheet, and then close the table.

5. Create a custom data access page named **Clients and Their Contracts** based on the **Client** and **Contract** tables. Use the design in Figure 7-60 as a guide.

Figure 7-60

   a. Place the Client#, ClientName, and Phone fields from the **Client** table in the Client Header section.
   b. Place the Contract#, ContractDate, and ContractAmt fields from the **Contract** table in the Contract Header section.
   c. Select the Expedition theme.
   d. Delete the labels, and move and resize the text boxes in the Client Header section. Reduce the width of the text boxes in the Contract Header section.

Explore

   e. Reduce the height of the Client Header section, set its DataPageSize property to 6, and then change its default sort to an ascending sort based on the ClientName field. (*Hint:* Set the DefaultSort property for the Client Header section in the Group Level Properties dialog box; use Help if you need more information about setting the DefaultSort property.)

    f. Use Clients and Their Contracts as the title for the data access page, and then left align the title.

    g. Save the data access page as **Clients and Their Contracts** in the Cases folder.

    h. Close the data access page, use the Web Page Preview command to view the data access page, navigate to the page that contains the client record with your name, expand that record, print the Web page, and then close Internet Explorer.

6. Create a PivotTable on a new data access page as follows:

    a. Select City from the **Client** table as the row field, ContractAmt from the **Contract** table as the detail field, ContractDate from the **Contract** table as the filter field, and ShootDesc from the **Shoot** table as the column field.

    b. Increase the height and width of the PivotTable control so that you can see Grand Total row and the entire GR column. Set the PivotTable title bar caption to City and Shoot PivotTable.

    c. Use City and Shoot Table as the title for the data access page.

    d. Save the data access page as **City and Shoot Table** in the Cases folder.

    e. Switch to Page view.

    f. Use the ContractDate filter to select all April dates, print the page, and then close the page.

7. Export the **Client Contract Amounts** query as an XML file named **Client Contract Amounts** in the Cases folder; do not create a separate XSD file.

8. Export the **Client Contract Amounts** query as an Excel worksheet. In the worksheet, add a calculation in cell D22 for the grand total contract amount, print the worksheet, and then save and close the worksheet.

9. Close the **Clients** database, and then exit Access.

Case 2. DineAtHome.course.com Claire Picard wants to be able to use her Web browser to view data stored in the **Delivery** database. She asks you to export data retrieved by a query and a report as HTML documents, create data access pages, and export data as XML documents and Excel worksheets. To do so, you'll complete the following steps.

1. Make sure your Data Disk is in the appropriate disk drive, start Access, and then open the **Delivery** database in the Cases folder on your Data Disk.

2. Export the **Large Orders** query as an HTML document in the Cases folder; do not use a template. Use Internet Explorer to open the **Large Orders** HTML document, print the page, and then close Internet Explorer.

Explore 3. Export the **Restaurant Orders** report as an HTML document in the Cases folder; do not use a template. Use Internet Explorer to open the **Restaurant Orders** HTML document. Then scroll to the bottom of the document; use the First, Previous, Next, and Last links to navigate through the Web page; print the last page of the report; and then close Internet Explorer. (*Note:* The report title and some labels will appear truncated on the right when you view the HTML document.)

4. Use the AutoPage: Columnar Wizard to create a data access page based on the **Order** table, and then do the following:

    a. Save the data access page in the Cases folder as **Order Page**.

    b. Sort the data access page in descending order based on the OrderDate field.

    c. Change the OrderAmt field value for Order# 3123 from 45.42 to 55.77, and then print this record.

    d. Filter the page, selecting all records with a Restaurant# field value of 131. (*Hint:* The second record should have that field value.) Print the last filtered record.

    e. Close the data access page.

    f. Open the **Order** table datasheet, print the datasheet, and then close the table.

5. Create a custom data access page named **Orders for Restaurants** based on the **Restaurant** and **Order** tables. Use the design in Figure 7-61 as a guide.

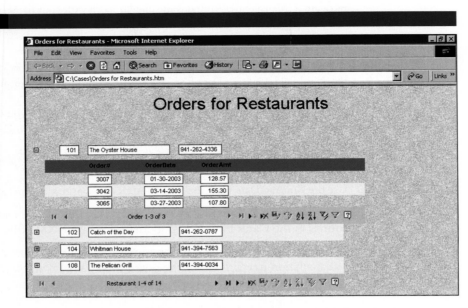

a. Place the Restaurant#, RestaurantName, and Phone fields from the **Restaurant** table in the Restaurant Header section.
b. Place the Order#, OrderDate, and OrderAmt fields from the **Order** table in the Order Header section.
c. Select the Sandstone theme.
d. In the Restaurant Header section, delete the labels, and then move and resize the text boxes to match Figure 7-61. Reduce the width of the text boxes in the Order Header section.
e. Reduce the height of the Restaurant Header section, and then set its DataPageSize property to 4.
f. Use Orders for Restaurants as the title for the data access page.
g. Save the data access page as **Orders for Restaurants** in the Cases folder.
h. Close the data access page, use the Web Page Preview command to view the data access page, expand the first record (The Oyster House), print the Web page, and then close Internet Explorer.

6. Create a PivotChart on a new data access page as follows:

a. Use the **Restaurant Orders** query as the data source for the PivotChart, and select the pie chart type.
b. Increase the width of the PivotChart control so that you can see the control's Field List button. Select City as the category field, BillTotal as the data field, and OrderDate By Month as the filter field.
c. Increase the height and width of the PivotChart control so that you can see the entire PivotTable toolbar and the pie chart is a readable size.
d. Use Restaurant Orders as the title for the data access page.
e. Save the data access page as **Restaurant Orders Chart** in the Cases folder.
f. Use the Web Page Preview command to view the data access page, display the legend, and then print the page.
g. Use the OrderDate By Month filter to select only the March orders, print the page, and then close the page.

7. Import the data and structure from the XML file named **Choices**, located in the Cases folder, as a new table in the **Delivery** database. Open the imported **Selection** table, resize all columns to their best fit, print the first page, and then save and close the table.

8. Export the **Order** table as an XML file named **Order** in the Cases folder; do not create a separate XSD file.

9. Export the **Order** table as an Excel worksheet. In the worksheet, add a calculation in cell D39 for the order grand total, print the worksheet, and then save and close the worksheet.

10. Claire has created a Web page in the Cases folder containing a description about one of the meal selections. Add a hyperlink field named SelectionDetails to the **Selection** table. Add a hyperlink with the text "Sunshine Skillet" to the record for the Sunshine Skillet field value that opens the **Skillet** file located in the Cases folder. Resize the SelectionDetails column to its best fit, and then click the hyperlink. View the short description in the Web page, print the description, and then close the browser.

11. Save and close the **Selection** table, close the **Delivery** database, and then exit Access.

Case 3. Redwood Zoo   Michael Rosenfeld wants you to create Web pages for the **Donors** database so he can use his Web browser to access and view data. To do so, you'll complete the following steps.

1. Make sure your Data Disk is in the appropriate disk drive, start Access, and then open the **Donors** database in the Cases folder on your Data Disk.

2. Export the **Donor** table as an HTML document in the Cases folder; do not use a template. Use Internet Explorer to open the **Donor** HTML document, print the page, and then close Internet Explorer.

Explore 3. Export the **Fund Pledges** report as an HTML document in the Cases folder; do not use a template. Use Internet Explorer to open the **Fund Pledges** HTML document. Then scroll to the bottom of the document; use the First, Previous, Next, and Last links to navigate through the Web page; print the last page of the report; and then close Internet Explorer.

Explore 4. Use the AutoPage: Columnar Wizard to create a data access page based on the **Fund** table, and then do the following:
   a. Save the data access page in the Cases folder as **Fund Page**.
   b. Sort the data access page in descending order based on the GoalAmt field.
   c. Change the GoalAmt field value for record 2 (Kodiak Bear Exhibit) from $65,000 to $95,000.
   d. Close the data access page.
   e. Open the **Fund** table datasheet, print the datasheet, and then close the table.

5. Create a custom data access page named **Pledges for Zoo Funds** based on the **Fund**, **Donor**, and **Pledge** tables. Use the design in Figure 7-62 as a guide.

Figure 7-62

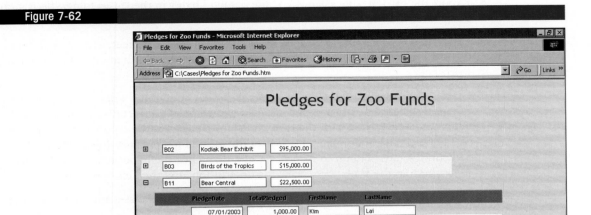

a. Place the FundCode, FundName, and GoalAmt fields from the **Fund** table in the Fund Header section.

b. Place the PledgeDate and TotalPledged fields from the **Pledge** table, and the FirstName and LastName fields from the **Donor** table in the Pledge Header section.

c. Select the Profile theme.

d. In the Fund Header section, delete the labels, and then move and resize the text boxes.

e. Reduce the height of the Fund Header section, and then set its DataPageSize property to 3.

f. Use Pledges for Zoo Funds as the title for the data access page, and then change its font color to blue.

g. Save the data access page as **Pledges for Zoo Funds** in the Cases folder.

h. Close the data access page, use the Web Page Preview command to view the data access page, expand the third record (Bear Central), print the Web page, and then close Internet Explorer.

6. Create a PivotChart on a new data access page as follows:

a. Use the **Donor Pledges** query as the data source for the PivotChart, and select the stacked bar chart type.

b. Increase the width of the PivotChart control so that you can see the control's Field List button. Select FundName as the category field, TotalPledged as the data field, PaymentMethod as the series field, and PledgeDate By Month as the filter field.

c. Increase the height and width of the PivotChart control so that you can see the entire PivotChart toolbar and all rows in the chart.

d. Use Donor Pledges Chart as the title for the data access page.

e. Save the data access page as **Donor Pledges Chart** in the Cases folder.

f. Close the data access page, use the Web Page Preview command to view the data access page, display the legend, and then print the page.

g. Use the PledgeDate By Month filter to select pledges in the last two quarters, print the page, and then close the browser.

7. Export the **Pledge** table as an XML file named **Pledge** in the Cases folder; do not create a separate XSD file.

8. Export the **Pledge** table as an Excel worksheet. In the worksheet, add a calculation in cell E30 for the total pledged grand total, print the worksheet in landscape orientation, and then save and close the worksheet.

9. Close the **Donors** database, and then exit Access.

Case 4. Mountain River Adventures Connor and Siobhan Dempsey travel frequently and need to access data from the **Outdoors** database using their Web browsers. They ask you to export a query and a report as HTML documents, and to create data access pages based on database tables. Finally, they need to use the data in a query in Excel and also in another application that requires XML data. To make these changes, you'll complete the following steps.

1. Make sure your Data Disk is in the appropriate disk drive, start Access, and then open the **Outdoors** database in the Cases folder on your Data Disk.

2. Export the **Trip Dates** query as an HTML document in the Cases folder; do not use a template. Use Internet Explorer to open the **Trip Dates** HTML document, print the page, and then close Internet Explorer.

Explore

3. Export the **Bookings** report as an HTML document in the Cases folder; do not use a template. Use Internet Explorer to open the **Bookings** HTML document. Then scroll to the bottom of the document; use the First, Previous, Next, and Last links to navigate through the Web page; print the last page of the report; and then close Internet Explorer.

4. Use the Page Wizard to create a data access page based on the **Costs** query as follows:
   a. Select all fields from the **Costs** query, select River as a grouping level, sort in ascending order by the TripDate field, use Costs Page as the title, and then open the page.
   b. Navigate to the last record (South Platte River), navigate to the second record for that group, and then print the page.
   c. Close the page, saving it as **Costs Page** in the Cases folder.

5. Create a custom data access page named **Bookings for Clients** based on the **Client** and **Booking** tables. Use the design in Figure 7-63 as a guide.

Figure 7-63

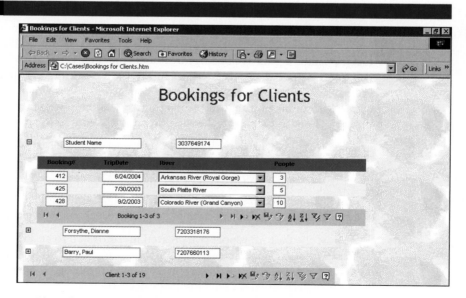

   a. Place the ClientName and Phone fields from the **Client** table in the Client Header section.
   b. Place the Booking#, TripDate, River, and People fields from the **Booking** table in the Booking Header section.
   c. Select the Nature theme.
   d. In the Client Header section, delete the labels, and then move and resize the text boxes.

e. In the Booking Header section, modify the width of the text boxes, and then move the People label and text box to the right to make room for the River text box.

f. Reduce the height of the Client Header section, and then set its DataPageSize property to 3.

g. Use Bookings for Clients as the title for the data access page.

h. Save the data access page as **Bookings for Clients** in the Cases folder.

i. Close the data access page, use the Web Page Preview command to view the data access page, expand the record that contains your name, print the Web page, and then close Internet Explorer.

6. Create a PivotChart on a new data access page as follows:

a. Use the **Booked Rafting Trips** query as the data source for the PivotChart, and select the stacked bar chart type.

b. Increase the width of the PivotChart control so that you can see the control's Field List button. Select TripDays as the category field, TripFee as the data field, People as the series field, and River as the filter field.

c. Increase the height and width of the PivotChart control so that you can see the entire PivotChart toolbar and 5,000.00 on the vertical axis.

d. Use Booked Rafting Trips Chart as the title for the data access page.

e. Save the data access page as **Booked Rafting Trips Chart** in the Cases folder.

f. Close the data access page, use the Web Page Preview command to view the data access page, display the legend, and then print the page.

g. Use the River filter to select trips for all rivers except those occurring on the Arkansas River, print the page, and then close Internet Explorer.

7. Export the **Booked Rafting Trips** query as an XML file named **Booked Rafting Trips** in the Cases folder; do not create a separate XSD file.

8. Export the **Booked Rafting Trips** table as an Excel worksheet. In the worksheet, add a calculation in cell J24 for the grand total trip fee, print the worksheet, and then save and close the worksheet.

9. Close the **Outdoors** database, and then exit Access.

Explore

Case 5. eACH Internet Auction Site   Chris and Pat Aquino want you to continue your development of their Internet auction site for collectibles. They want you to export some of the **eACH** database data as HTML documents for their registrants to view. They also want you to create two data access pages, an XML file, and then create a hyperlink field that's linked to Word documents. One of the data access pages will allow buyers to view categories with their subcategories when they're searching for items that might be of interest to them. They ask you to make the following changes to the **eACH** database.

1. Make sure your Data Disk is in the appropriate drive, start Access, and then open the **eACH** database in the Cases folder on your Data Disk.

2. Export the **Item** table to an HTML document in the Cases folder, using the HTML template named **eACH-Tbl**, which is located in the Cases folder. Use Internet Explorer to open the **Item** HTML document, print the page, and then close Internet Explorer.

3. Export the custom report you created in Tutorial 6 to an HTML document in the Cases folder, using the HTML template named **eACH-Rpt**, which is located in the Cases folder. Use Internet Explorer to open the HTML document that you created, print the report, and then close Internet Explorer.

4. Use the AutoPage: Columnar Wizard to create a data access page based on the **Registrant** table, and then complete the following:

a. Use the data access page to add a new record with your name to the **Registrant** table with additional data that you create.

b. Sort the data access page in ascending order based on the field that contains the registrant's last name.

    c. Print the first record.

    d. Close the data access page, saving it as **Registrant Page** in the Cases folder.

5. Design and then create a custom data access page that satisfies the following requirements:

    a. Place all the fields from **Category** table in the Category Header section.

    b. Place all the fields, except for the common field, from the **Subcategory** table in the Subcategory Header section.

    c. Select the Edge theme.

    d. In the Category Header section, move the labels and text boxes into a row, and then resize the text boxes. Resize the text boxes in the Subcategory Header section.

    e. Reduce the height of the Client Header section, and then set its DataPageSize property to 4.

    f. Use an appropriate title for the page.

    g. Save the data access page as **Categories and Subcategories Page** in the Cases folder.

    h. Close the page, use the Web Page Preview command to view the page, expand a record with related records, print the Web page, and then close Internet Explorer.

6. Export the **Registrant** table as an XML file named **Registrant** in the Cases folder; do not create a separate XSD file.

7. Given the test data you created in Tutorial 5, you should have at least two items you've posted for sale on eACH. To attract bidders to those items, you should include visuals and short descriptions of them by completing the following:

    a. Create at least three Word documents and save them with appropriate filenames in the Cases folder. In each document, write a short description for one of the items in your database. Also, include an appropriate graphic or picture (that you locate in the Microsoft Clip Gallery or download from the Internet) for the item. Save each document.

    b. Add a hyperlink field named Visual to the **Item** table. Add hyperlink field values for each item that has a corresponding Word document.

    c. Click the hyperlink for one of the items. View the Word document, print the document, and then close Word.

8. Close the **eACH** database, and then exit Access.

INTERNET ASSIGNMENTS

Student Union

The purpose of the Internet Assignments is to challenge you to find information on the Internet that you can use to create effective documents. The actual assignments are updated and maintained on the Course Technology Web site. Log on to the Internet and use your Web browser to go to the Student Online Companion to accompany this text at **www.course.com/NewPerspectives/studentunion**. Click the Online Companions link, and then click the link for this tutorial.

QUICK | CHECK ANSWERS

Session 7.1

1. The World Wide Web is a vast collection of digital documents stored on Web servers linked through the Internet.

2. A Web browser is a program used to view Web pages.

3. A hyperlink links one Web document to another.

4. HTML (HyperText Markup Language) is the language used to create most Web documents.

5. An HTML template is a file that contains HTML instructions for creating a Web page with both text and graphics, together with special instructions that tell Access where to place the Access data on the page.

6. A static Web page shows the state of the database object at the time the page was created. Any subsequent changes made to the database object, such as updates to field values in records, are not reflected in a static Web page.

7. A data access page is a dynamic HTML document that you can open with a Web browser to view or update current data in an Access database.

8. connection

9. A grouped data access page is a data access page that uses two or more group levels to display information from general categories to specific details.

10. A theme is a predefined style for a data access page.

Session 7.2

1. A PivotTable is an interactive table that lets you analyze data dynamically from within a Web browser.

2. filter

3. data access pages, forms, datasheets

4. For datasheets and data access pages, only one expand indicator appears at a time and is active; clicking the expand indicator causes the data to expand or collapse and to change to the other expand indicator. For PivotTables, both expand indicators appear, even though only one is active at any given time.

5. total

6. data

7. series

Session 7.3

1. HTML; XML

2. static

3. The XSD (XML Structure Definition) file contains table structure information, including information about the table's primary key and indexes.

4. Select the table or query in the Database window, click the OfficeLinks list arrow, and then click Analyze It with Microsoft Excel.

5. a hyperlink or pointer to another object in the database, file, or Web page

6. Click the hyperlink field value to start the associated program and open the hyperlinked document or object.

LEVEL III

New Perspectives on

MICROSOFT®
ACCESS 2002

Read This Before You Begin

To the Student

Student Disks

To complete the Level III tutorials, Review Assignments, and Case Problems, you will need access to a folder on your computer's hard drive or a personal network drive. Your instructor will either provide you with these Data Disk files or ask you to make your own.

You will need to copy a set of folders from a file server or standalone computer or the Web to your folder. Your instructor will tell you which computer, drive letter, and folders contain the files you need. You could also download the folders by going to **www.course.com** and following the instructions on the screen.

If you will store your original Data Disk files on a floppy drive, you will need **four** blank, formatted high-density disks. The information below shows which folders go on each of your disks. After making your Data Disks, you can copy the files to your hard drive or personal network drive, and then retain the Data Disks as a backup.

Data Disk 1
Write this on the disk label:
Data Disk 1: Tutorial Files (Tutorials 8-11)
Review Assignments (Tutorials 8-11)
Put these folders on the disk:

Tutorial
Review

Data Disk 2
Write this on the disk label:
Data Disk 2: Case Problems 1 and 2 (Tutorials 8-11)
Put this folder on the disk:
Cases

Data Disk 3
Write this on the disk label:
Data Disk 3: Case Problems 3-5 (Tutorials 8-11)
Put this folder on the disk:
Cases

Data Disk 4
Write this on the disk label:
Data Disk 4: Additional Case Problems
Put this folder on the disk:
AddCases

Refer to the "File Finder" chart at the back of this text for more detailed information on which files are used in which tutorials. These Access Level III tutorials use the same files for Tutorials 8-11. See the inside front or inside back cover of this book for more information on Data Disk files, or ask your instructor or technical support person for assistance.

Using Your Own Computer
If you are going to work through this book using your own computer, you need:

- **Computer System** Microsoft Windows 98, NT, 2000 Professional, or higher must be installed on your computer. This book assumes a typical installation of Microsoft Access.

- **Data Disks** You will not be able to complete the tutorials or exercises in this book using your own computer until you have your Data Disks.

Visit Our World Wide Web Site
Additional materials designed especially for you are available on the World Wide Web. Go to http://www.course.com/NewPerspectives.

To the Instructor

The Data Disk Files are available on the Instructor's Resource Kit for this title. Follow the instructions in the Help file on the CD-ROM to install the files to your network or standalone computer. For information on creating Data Disks, see the "To the Student" section above.

You are granted a license to copy the Data Files and Course Labs to any computer or computer network used by students who have purchased this book.

OBJECTIVES

In this tutorial you will:

- Use Query Wizards to create a crosstab query, a find duplicates query, and a find unmatched query

- Create a top values query

- Create action queries

- Apply an advanced filter in a table

- Define many-to-many and one-to-one relationships between tables

- View and create indexes for tables

- Join a table using a self-join

USING QUERY WIZARDS AND ACTION QUERIES, AND DEFINING TABLE RELATIONSHIPS

Enhancing User Interaction with the Overseas Database

CASE

Northeast Seasonal Jobs International (NSJI)

Several years ago, Elsa Jensen founded Northeast Seasonal Jobs International (NSJI), a small Boston firm that serves as a job broker between foreign students seeking part-time, seasonal work and resort businesses located in New England and the eastern provinces of Canada. At first the company focused mainly on summer employment, but as the business continued to grow, Elsa increased the scope of operations to include all types of seasonal opportunities, including foliage tour companies in the fall and ski resorts in the winter.

Elsa incorporated the use of computers in all aspects of the business, including financial management, payroll, accounts payable, and student recruitment. Her company developed the Overseas database of employer and position data and uses **Microsoft Access 2002** (or simply **Access**) to manage it.

The Overseas database contains tables, queries, forms, and reports that Elsa, Zack Ward, director of marketing, and Matt Griffin, manager of recruitment, use to track students, employers, and jobs.

Elsa, Zack, and Matt have found the Overseas database to be very useful in managing the company's data. They have asked you to continue enhancing the database by creating some advanced queries and integrating more tables into the database.

SESSION 8.1

In this session, you will use Query Wizards to create a crosstab query, a find duplicates query, and a find unmatched query. You'll also create a top values query.

Creating a Crosstab Query

Elsa is considering expanding the business to include more states and provinces in which NSJI operates. Many factors will affect her decision, but her first area of interest is determining how much business NSJI conducts in Canada versus the United States. She also wants to know how the total amount of business conducted in each country varies by the number of employer openings. She asks you to create a crosstab query using the Crosstab Query Wizard to provide the information she needs.

A **crosstab query** performs aggregate function calculations on the values of one database field and displays the results in a spreadsheet format. **Aggregate functions** perform arithmetic operations on selected records in a database. Figure 8-1 lists the aggregate functions you can use in a crosstab query. A crosstab query can also display one additional aggregate function value that summarizes each row's set of values. The crosstab query uses one or more fields for the row headings on the left and one field for the column headings at the top.

Figure 8-1	AGGREGATE FUNCTIONS USED IN CROSSTAB QUERIES

AGGREGATE FUNCTIONS	DEFINITION
Avg	Average of the field values
Count	Number of the nonnull field values
First	First field value
Last	Last field value
Min	Lowest field value
Max	Highest field value
StDev	Standard deviation of the field values
Sum	Total of the field values
Var	Variance of the field values

Figure 8-2 shows two query recordsets—the first from a select query and the second from a related crosstab query. The title bar indicates the type of query.

Figure 8-2   **COMPARING A SELECT QUERY TO A CROSSTAB QUERY**

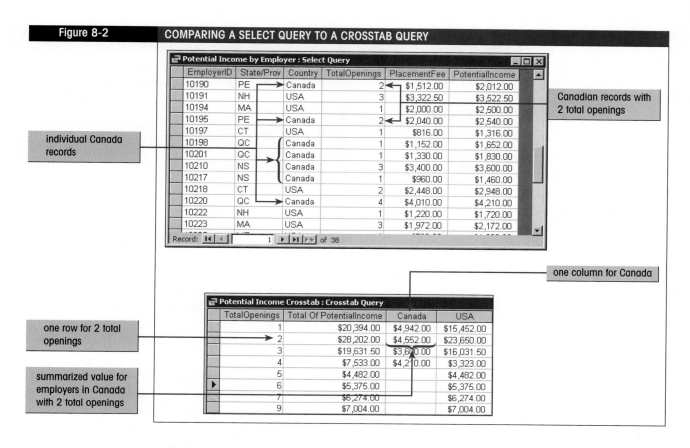

Both queries are based on the Potential Income by Employer query, which joins the Employer and Position tables, but the crosstab query provides more valuable information. For each record in the Employer table that has one or more records in the Position table, the select query uses the Group By operator to display the State/Prov and Country fields from the Employer table and the EmployerID field from the Position table. The select query also includes calculated fields that display the sum of the number of openings, the placement fees, and the potential income for each group. Notice that there are many rows for TotalOpenings values of 1, 2, 3, and so on, and many records for Canada and the USA. (Not all records are currently visible on the screen.)

On the other hand, the crosstab query displays just one row for each different TotalOpenings value. The TotalOpenings column in the crosstab query identifies each row, and the field values for the Country field in the select query become the rightmost column headings in the crosstab query. The crosstab query uses the Sum aggregate function on the PotentialIncome field to produce the displayed values in the Total Of PotentialIncome, Canada, and USA columns. The Total Of PotentialIncome column represents the total of the PotentialIncome values for each row in the select query. For example, you can use the crosstab query to see that all employers with two total openings in Canada have total potential income of $4,552.00, and that all employers with two total openings in the USA have total potential income of $23,650.00. You could extract the same data from a select query, but the crosstab query does it for you automatically. Using the crosstab query recordset, Elsa can quickly see the total amount of potential income in each country for each number of total openings.

The quickest way to create a crosstab query is to use the **Crosstab Query Wizard**, which guides you through the steps for creating one. You could also change a select query to a crosstab query using the Query Type button on the Query Design toolbar. (Refer to the

REFERENCE	WINDOW	RW

Using the Crosstab Query Wizard

- In the Database window, click Queries in the Objects bar to display the Queries list, and then click the New button.
- Click Crosstab Query Wizard, and then click the OK button.
- Complete the Wizard dialog boxes to select the table or query on which to base the crosstab query, select the row heading field or fields, select the column heading field, select the calculation field and its aggregate function, and enter a name for the crosstab query.

The crosstab query you will create, which is similar to the one shown in Figure 8-2, has the following characteristics:

- The Potential Income by Employer query in the Overseas database is the basis for the new crosstab query; it includes the EmployerID, State/Prov, Country, TotalOpenings, PlacementFee, and PotentialIncome fields.
- The TotalOpenings calculated field from the Potential Income by Employer query is the leftmost column in the crosstab query and identifies each crosstab query row.
- The field values that appear in the Employer table for the Country field identify the rightmost columns of the crosstab query.
- The crosstab query applies the Sum aggregate function to the PotentialIncome calculated field from the Potential Income by Employer query and displays the resulting total values in the Canada and USA columns of the query results. If one country has two or more employers with the same number of total openings, then the sum of the total openings appears in the intersecting cell of the crosstab query results.
- The total of the PotentialIncome values appears for each row in a column with the heading Total Of PotentialIncome.

You are now ready to create the crosstab query based on the Potential Income by Employer query. The crosstab query will show NSJI's potential income amount in each country based on the number of total openings.

To start the Crosstab Query Wizard:

1. Make sure you have created your copy of the Access Data Disk, and then place your Data Disk in the appropriate disk drive.

   TROUBLE? If you don't have a Data Disk, you need to get one before you can proceed. Your instructor will either give you one or ask you to make your own. (See your instructor for information.) In either case, be sure you have made a copy of your Data Disk before you begin, so that the original Data Disk files are available on the copied disk in case you need to start over because of an error or problem.

   TROUBLE? If you are not sure which disk drive to use for your Data Disk, read the "Read This Before You Begin" page on page AC 8.02 or ask your instructor for help.

2. Start Access and open the **Overseas** database in the Tutorial folder on your Data Disk. The Overseas database is displayed in the Access window.

3. Click **Queries** in the Objects bar of the Database window, and then click the **New** button. The New Query dialog box opens.

4. Click **Crosstab Query Wizard** and then click the **OK** button. The first Crosstab Query Wizard dialog box opens.

You'll now use the Crosstab Query Wizard to create the crosstab query for Elsa.

To finish the Crosstab Query Wizard:

1. Click the **Queries** option button in the View section to display the list of queries in the Overseas database, and then click **Query: Potential Income by Employer**. See Figure 8-3.

| Figure 8-3 | CHOOSING THE TABLE OR QUERY FOR THE CROSSTAB QUERY |

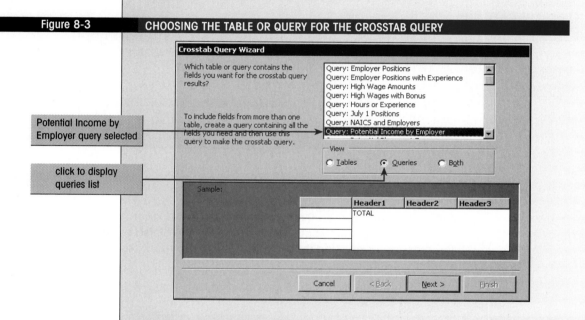

Potential Income by Employer query selected

click to display queries list

2. Click the **Next** button to open the next Crosstab Query Wizard dialog box, in which you choose the field (or fields) for the row headings. Because Elsa wants the crosstab query to display one row for each TotalOpenings value, you will select that field for the row headings.

3. In the Available Fields list box, click **TotalOpenings**, and then click the > button to move TotalOpenings to the Selected Fields list box. When you select a field, Access changes the sample crosstab query in the bottom of the dialog box to illustrate your choice.

4. Click the **Next** button to open the next Crosstab Query Wizard dialog box, in which you select the field values that will serve as column headings. Elsa wants to see the potential income by country, so you need to select the Country field for the column headings.

5. Click **Country** in the list box, and then click the **Next** button.

In this Crosstab Query Wizard dialog box, you choose the field that will be calculated for each row and column intersection and the function to use for the calculation. The results of the calculation will appear in the row and column intersections of the query results. Elsa needs to calculate the sum of the PotentialIncome field value for each row and column intersection.

6. Click **PotentialIncome** in the Fields list box, click **Sum** in the Functions list box, and then make sure that the **Yes, include row sums** check box is checked. The Yes, include row sums option creates a column showing the overall totals for the values in each row of the query recordset. See Figure 8-4.

Figure 8-4	COMPLETED CROSSTAB QUERY DESIGN

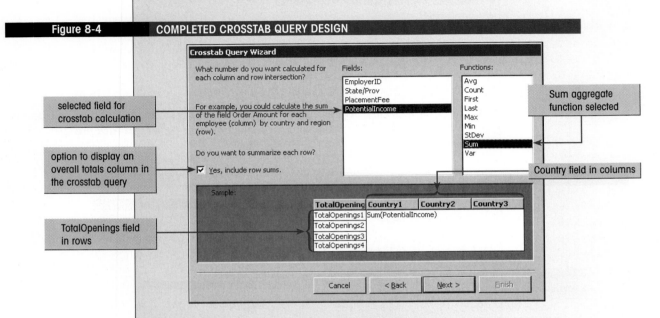

7. Click the **Next** button to open the final Crosstab Query Wizard dialog box, in which you choose the query name.

8. Type **Potential Income Crosstab** in the text box, be sure the option button for viewing the query is selected, and then click the **Finish** button. Access saves the crosstab query, and then displays the query recordset.

9. Resize all the columns in the query recordset to their best fit, and then click **TotalOpenings 1** to deselect the columns. See Figure 8-5.

Figure 8-5	CROSSTAB QUERY RECORDSET

Potential Income Crosstab : Crosstab Query

TotalOpenings	Total Of PotentialIncome	Canada	USA
1	$20,394.00	$4,942.00	$15,452.00
2	$28,202.00	$4,552.00	$23,650.00
3	$19,631.50	$3,600.00	$16,031.50
4	$7,533.00	$4,210.00	$3,323.00
5	$4,482.00		$4,482.00
6	$5,375.00		$5,375.00
7	$6,274.00		$6,274.00
9	$7,004.00		$7,004.00

The query recordset contains one row for each TotalOpenings field value. The Total Of PotentialIncome column shows the total potential income amount for employers with that total number of openings. The columns labeled Canada and USA show the total potential income amount for employers with that total number of openings in each country.

You can now close the completed query.

10. Close the query, and click the **Yes** button when asked to save the query layout changes.

Access uses unique icons to represent different types of queries. The crosstab query icon appears in the Queries list box to the left of the Potential Income Crosstab query. This icon is different in appearance from the icon that appears to the left of the other queries, which are all select queries.

Next, Elsa wants her staff to concentrate on filling those positions for employers with two or more different available positions. Filling these positions will give NSJI the best chance for repeat business with these employers in future years. To find the information Elsa needs, you'll create a find duplicates query.

Creating a Find Duplicates Query

A **find duplicates query** is a select query that locates duplicate records in a table or query. You can create this type of query using the **Find Duplicates Query Wizard**. A find duplicates query searches for duplicate values based on the fields you select as you answer the Wizard's questions. For example, you might want to display all employers that have the same name, all students who have the same phone number, or all products that have the same description. Using this type of query, you can locate duplicates to avert potential problems (for example, you might have inadvertently assigned two different numbers to the same product), or you can eliminate duplicates that cost money (for example, you could send just one advertising brochure to all customers having the same address).

You can meet Elsa's request by using the Find Duplicates Query Wizard to display records for employers that appear more than once in the Employer Positions query, which lists 64 available positions and their related employers.

REFERENCE WINDOW   **RW**

Using the Find Duplicates Query Wizard
- In the Database window, click Queries in the Objects bar to display the Queries list, and then click the New button.
- Click Find Duplicates Query Wizard, and then click the OK button.
- Complete the Wizard dialog boxes to select the table or query on which to base the query, select the field or fields to check for duplicate values, select the additional fields to include in the query results, and enter a name for the query.

You can use the Find Duplicates Query Wizard to create and run a new query to display duplicate employer names in the Employer Positions query results.

To create the query using the Find Duplicates Query Wizard:

1. Click **Queries** in the Objects bar of the Database window (if necessary), and then click the **New** button to open the New Query dialog box.

2. Click **Find Duplicates Query Wizard**, and then click the **OK** button. The first Find Duplicates Query Wizard dialog box opens. In this dialog box, you select the table or query on which to base the new query. You'll use the Employer Positions query.

3. Click the **Queries** option button in the View section to display the list of queries, click **Query: Employer Positions** (if necessary), and then click the **Next** button. Access opens the next Find Duplicates Query Wizard dialog box, in which you choose the fields you want to check for duplicate values.

4. In the Available fields list box, click **EmployerName** (if necessary), click the ▭ > ▭ button to select the EmployerName field as the field to check for duplicate values, and then click the **Next** button. In the next Find Duplicates Query Wizard dialog box, you select the additional fields you want displayed in the query results.

Elsa also wants all remaining fields to be included in the query results.

5. Click the ▭ >> ▭ button to move all fields from the Available Fields list box to the Additional query fields list box, and then click the **Next** button. Access opens the final Find Duplicates Query Wizard dialog box, in which you enter a name for the query. You'll use "Employers with Multiple Positions" as the query name.

6. Type **Employers with Multiple Positions** in the text box, be sure the option button for viewing the results is selected, and then click the **Finish** button. Access saves the query, and then displays the 47 records for employers with two or more different available positions. See Figure 8-6.

| Figure 8-6 | RECORDSET FOR EMPLOYERS WITH MULTIPLE POSITIONS QUERY |

Elsa asks you to print the query recordset before you close it.

7. Change the page orientation to landscape, print the query recordset, and then click the **Close** button ▭X▭ on the Query window to close it and return to the Database window.

After giving Elsa the printed query results, she asks you to find the records for employers with no available positions. These are employers who have placed their positions with NSJI in the past, but who have chosen not to place their current positions. Elsa wants to contact these employers and persuade them to continue doing business with NSJI. To provide Elsa with a list of these employers, you need to create a find unmatched query.

Creating a Find Unmatched Query

A **find unmatched query** is a select query that finds all records in a table or query that have no related records in a second table or query. For example, you could display all customers who have not placed orders or all non-degree students who are not currently enrolled in classes. Such a query might help Elsa solicit business from the inactive customers or contact the students to find out their future educational plans. You can use the **Find Unmatched Query Wizard** to create this type of query.

REFERENCE WINDOW   **RW**

Using the Find Unmatched Query Wizard
- If necessary, click Queries in the Objects bar of the Database window.
- Click the New button, click Find Unmatched Query Wizard, and then click the OK button.
- Complete the Wizard dialog boxes to select the table or query on which to base the new query, select the table or query that contains the related records, specify the common field in each table or query, select the additional fields to include in the query results, enter a name for the query, and then click the Finish button.

Elsa wants to know which employers have no available positions. These employers are inactive, and she will contact them to determine their interest in filling future positions through NSJI. To create a list of inactive employers, you will use the Find Unmatched Query Wizard to display only those records from the Employer table with no matching EmployerID field value in the Position table.

To create the query using the Find Unmatched Query Wizard:

1. Click **Queries** in the Objects bar of the Database window (if necessary), and then click the **New** button to open the New Query dialog box.

2. Click **Find Unmatched Query Wizard**, and then click the **OK** button. The first Find Unmatched Query Wizard dialog box opens. In this dialog box, you select the table or query on which to base the new query. You'll use the Employer table.

3. Click **Table: Employer** in the list box to select this table, and then click the **Next** button to open the next Find Unmatched Query Wizard dialog box, in which you choose the table that contains the related records. You'll select the Position table.

4. Click **Table: Position** in the list box, and then click the **Next** button to open the next dialog box, in which you choose the common field for both tables. See Figure 8-7.

Figure 8-7   SELECTING THE COMMON FIELD

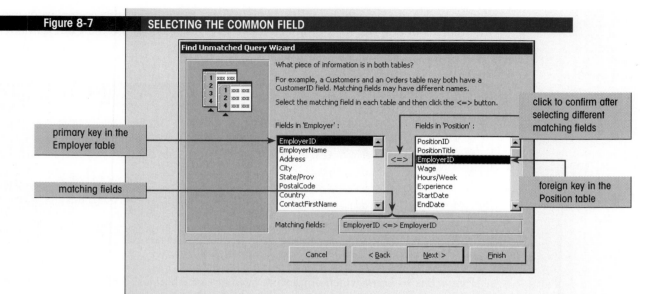

Notice that EmployerID is highlighted in each list box because it is the common field: EmployerID is the primary key in the primary Employer table, and EmployerID is the foreign key in the related Position table. The Matching fields box shows EmployerID <=> EmployerID to indicate the common field.

5. Click the **Next** button to open the next Find Unmatched Query Wizard dialog box, in which you choose the fields you want to see in the query recordset. Elsa wants the query recordset to display the EmployerName, City, State/Prov, ContactFirstName, ContactLastName, and Phone fields.

6. Click **EmployerName** in the Available fields list box, and then click the > button to select this field. Use the same procedure to select the **City**, **State/Prov**, **ContactFirstName**, **ContactLastName**, and **Phone** fields, and then click the **Next** button to open the final dialog box, in which you enter the query name.

7. Type **Inactive Employers**, be sure the option button for viewing the results is selected, and then click the **Finish** button. Access saves the query and then displays the query recordset. Resize all the columns in the query recordset to their best fit, and then click **City Boston** to deselect the columns. See Figure 8-8.

Figure 8-8   INACTIVE EMPLOYERS QUERY RECORDSET

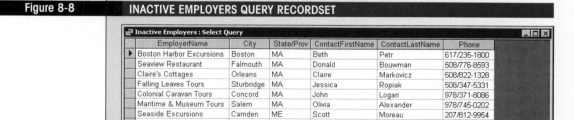

The query recordset includes information for the seven inactive employers. Elsa asks you to print the query recordset before you save and close it.

8. Change the page orientation to landscape, print the query recordset, and then save and close the query.

Elsa will contact these seven inactive employers using the printed contact information you created with the find unmatched query.

Next, Elsa wants Zack to contact those employers who have the highest potential income amounts to make sure that NSJI is providing satisfactory service. To display the information Elsa wants, you will create a top values query.

Creating a Top Values Query

Whenever a query displays a large group of records, you might want to limit the number to a more manageable size by displaying just the first 10 records, for example. The **Top Values property** for a query lets you limit the number of records in the query results. For the Top Values property, you enter either an integer (such as 10, to display the first 10 records) or a percentage (such as 50%, to display the first half of the records).

Suppose you have a select query that displays 45 records. If you want the query recordset to show only the first five records, you can change the query by entering a Top Values property value of either 5 or 10%. If the query contains a sort and the last record that Access can display is one of two or more records with the same value for the primary sort key, Access displays all records with that matching key value.

REFERENCE   WINDOW   **RW**

Creating a Top Values Query
- In Design view, create a select query with the necessary fields and sorting and selection criteria.
- Enter the number of records (or percentage of records) you want selected in the Top Values text box on the Query Design toolbar.
- Click the Run button on the Query Design toolbar.

Elsa wants to see the EmployerName, ContactFirstName, ContactLastName, and Phone fields from the Employer table and the TotalOpenings and PotentialIncome fields from the Potential Income by Employer query for employers with the highest 25% potential income amounts. You will create a new query and then use the Top Values property to produce this information for Elsa.

To create the query:

1. Click **Queries** in the Objects bar of the Database window (if necessary), click the **New** button to open the New Query dialog box, make sure that **Design View** is selected, and then click the **OK** button. The Show Table dialog box opens on top of the Query window in Design view.

   You need to add field lists for the Employer table and the Potential Income by Employer query to the Query window.

2. Double-click **Employer**, click the **Queries** tab in the Show Table dialog box, double-click **Potential Income by Employer**, click the **Close** button to close the Show Table dialog box, and then drag the right edge of the Potential Income by Employer field list to widen it. Field lists for the Employer table and the Potential Income by Employer query appear in the Query window. See Figure 8-9.

| Figure 8-9 | JOINING A TABLE AND A QUERY IN THE QUERY WINDOW |

Employer table field list

join line

Potential Income by Employer query field list

TROUBLE? If a join line does not connect the two field lists, close the query without saving your design changes, click Tools on the menu bar, click Options, click the Tables/Queries tab, click the Enable AutoJoin check box, click the OK button, and then repeat Steps 1 and 2.

The join line connects the EmployerID fields, which are common to the table and query, even though you haven't created a relationship between the two objects. Access created the join because the automatic join option is enabled and the two objects each have a field (EmployerID) with the same name and a compatible data type, and the EmployerID field is a primary key in the Employer table. If you disable automatic joins, you can create a join in the Query window by dragging the primary key field from its field list to the common field in the other field list.

Now you can add the fields requested by Elsa to the design grid.

3. In the Employer field list, double-click **EmployerName**, double-click **ContactFirstName**, double-click **ContactLastName**, and then double-click **Phone**, scrolling as necessary, to add these four fields to the design grid.

4. In the Potential Income by Employer field list, double-click **TotalOpenings**, and then double-click **PotentialIncome**, scrolling as necessary, to add these two fields to the design grid.

5. Click the right side of the **PotentialIncome Sort** text box to display the sort order options, and then click **Descending**. The query will display the largest potential income amounts first.

6. Click the **Run** button ▣ on the Query Design toolbar. The query recordset shows the 38 records for employers with potential income amounts. The records appear in descending order sorted by the PotentialIncome field.

You can now set the Top Values property to limit the query recordset to the highest 25% potential income amounts, so Zack can contact employers in this category.

To set the Top Values property of the query:

1. Switch to Design view.

2. Click the **Top Values** list arrow on the Query Design toolbar, and then click **25%**. See Figure 8-10.

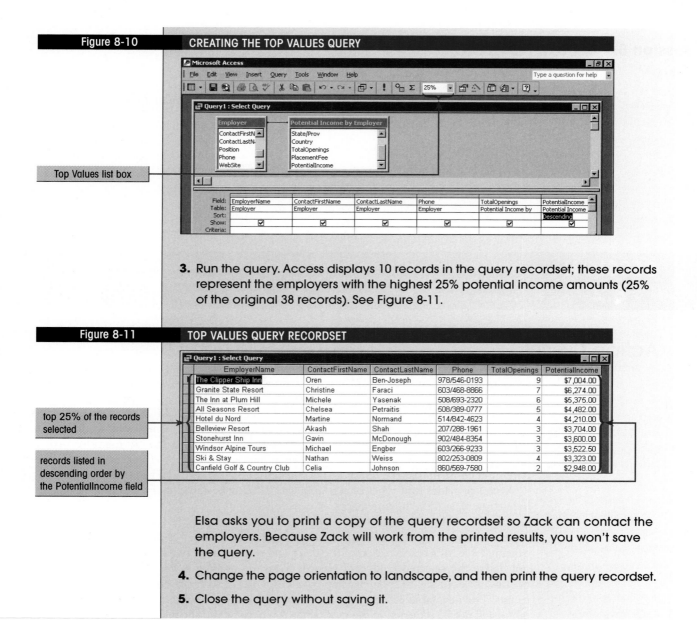

Figure 8-10   CREATING THE TOP VALUES QUERY

Top Values list box

3. Run the query. Access displays 10 records in the query recordset; these records represent the employers with the highest 25% potential income amounts (25% of the original 38 records). See Figure 8-11.

Figure 8-11   TOP VALUES QUERY RECORDSET

top 25% of the records selected

records listed in descending order by the PotentialIncome field

EmployerName	ContactFirstName	ContactLastName	Phone	TotalOpenings	PotentialIncome
The Clipper Ship Inn	Oren	Ben-Joseph	978/546-0193	9	$7,004.00
Granite State Resort	Christine	Faraci	603/468-8866	7	$6,274.00
The Inn at Plum Hill	Michele	Yasenak	508/693-2320	6	$5,375.00
All Seasons Resort	Chelsea	Petraitis	508/389-0777	5	$4,482.00
Hotel du Nord	Martine	Normand	514/842-4623	4	$4,210.00
Belleview Resort	Akash	Shah	207/288-1961	3	$3,704.00
Stonehurst Inn	Gavin	McDonough	902/484-8354	3	$3,600.00
Windsor Alpine Tours	Michael	Engber	603/266-9233	3	$3,522.50
Ski & Stay	Nathan	Weiss	802/253-0809	4	$3,323.00
Canfield Golf & Country Club	Celia	Johnson	860/569-7580	2	$2,948.00

Elsa asks you to print a copy of the query recordset so Zack can contact the employers. Because Zack will work from the printed results, you won't save the query.

4. Change the page orientation to landscape, and then print the query recordset.

5. Close the query without saving it.

Elsa and Zack will use the information provided by the queries you created to contact employers. In the next session, you'll create queries for Elsa to meet her needs for obtaining further information about NSJI's employer clients.

Session 8.1 QUICK CHECK

1. What is the purpose of a crosstab query?

2. What are the four Query Wizards you can use to create a new query?

3. What is a find duplicates query?

4. What does a find unmatched query do?

5. What happens when you set a query's Top Values property?

6. What happens if you set a query's Top Values property to 2 and the first five records have the same value for the primary sort key?

SESSION 8.2

In this session, you will create four different action queries—a make-table query, an append query, a delete query, and an update query—to change information in the Overseas database. You'll also apply an advanced filter to a table.

Action Queries

Queries can do more than display answers to the questions you ask; they can also perform actions on the data in your database. An **action query** is a query that adds, changes, or deletes multiple table records at one time. For example, if the NAICS code changes for one business classification, Elsa can use an action query to update all employers in that business classification to the new NAICS code. Because action queries modify many records in a table at a time, Access allows you to preview the query results before you actually run it. After you confirm that the query works correctly, you can save and run it as an action query.

Access provides four types of action queries: the make-table query, the append query, the delete query, and the update query.

A **make-table query** creates a new table from one or more existing tables. The new table can be an exact copy of the records in an existing table, a subset of the fields and records in an existing table, or a combination of the fields and records from two or more tables. Access does not delete the selected fields and records from the existing tables. You can use make-table queries, for example, to create backup copies of tables or to create customized tables for others to use. The new table reflects data at a point in time; future changes made to the underlying tables will not be reflected in the new table. You need to run the make-table query periodically if you want the newly created table to contain current data.

An **append query** adds records from an existing table or query to the end of another table. For an append query, you choose the fields you want to append from one or more tables or queries; the selected data remains in the original tables. Usually you append records to history tables. A **history table** contains data that is no longer needed for current processing but that you might need to reference in the future. Tables containing data about cleared bank checks, former employees, inactive customers, and obsolete products are examples of history tables. Because the records you append to a history table are no longer needed for current processing, you can delete the records from the original table.

A **delete query** deletes a group of records from one or more tables. You choose which records you want to delete by entering selection criteria. Deleting records removes them permanently from the database. Quite often, delete queries are run after append queries have added those same records to history tables, allowing you to verify that you appended the correct records before you delete them.

An **update query** changes selected fields and records in one or more tables. You choose the fields and records you want to change by entering the selection criteria and the update rules. You can use update queries, for example, to increase the salaries of selected employee groups by a specified percentage or to change the billing dates of selected customers from one date to another.

Creating a Make-Table Query

Elsa wants to call NSJI's employer clients in the bed-and-breakfast industry. The owners of these inns personally manage all aspects of their businesses and expect frequent contact by Elsa and her staff. She asks you to create a new table containing the EmployerName, ContactFirstName, ContactLastName, Phone, and NAICSCode fields from the Employer table records for all employers whose NAICS code is 721191, which is the code for businesses in the bed-and-breakfast industry. She wants to create a new table so she can modify it by adding notes that she will take when she calls the inn owners. By creating a new table, Elsa won't need to worry about disrupting or changing the data in any existing tables or in any objects on which those existing tables are based.

You can create the new table for Elsa by using a make-table query that uses fields from the Employer table in the Overseas database. When you run a make-table query, you create a new table. The records in the new table are based on the records in the query's underlying tables. The fields in the new table have the data type and field size of the fields in the query's underlying tables. The new table does not preserve the primary key designation or field properties such as format or lookup properties.

REFERENCE WINDOW   **RW**

Creating a Make-Table Query

- Create a select query with the necessary fields and selection criteria.
- Click the Run button on the Query Design toolbar to preview the results.
- Switch to Design view to make any necessary changes. When the query is correct, click the list arrow for the Query Type button on the Query Design toolbar.
- Click Make-Table Query.
- In the Make Table dialog box, type the new table name in the Table Name list box. Make sure the Current Database option button is selected to include the new table in the current database; or, click the Another Database option button and enter the database name in the File Name text box. Then click the OK button.
- Click the Run button on the Query Design toolbar.
- Click the Yes button to confirm creating the new table.

Now you can create the new table using a make-table query. You'll base the make-table query on the Employer table to enter the fields and records that Elsa wants in the new table.

To create and run the select query based on the Employer table:

1. Make sure that Access is running, and that the **Overseas** database from the Tutorial folder on your Data Disk is open.

2. Click **Queries** in the Objects bar of the Database window (if necessary), click the **New** button to open the New Query dialog box, make sure that **Design View** is selected, and then click the **OK** button.

3. Add the **Employer** table field list to the Query window, and then close the Show Table dialog box.

Now you can add the fields that Elsa needs to the design grid.

4. In the Employer field list, double-click **EmployerName**, double-click **ContactFirstName**, double-click **ContactLastName**, double-click **Phone**, and then double-click **NAICSDesc**, scrolling as necessary, to add these five fields to the design grid.

Next, you'll enter the selection criterion for the NAICSDesc field, which is a Lookup Wizard field that lets users select a value from a list of possible NAICS code description values in Datasheet view. However, it's the NAICS code that's actually stored in the Employer table, so you need to enter the selection criterion of 721191, the NAICS code for bed-and-breakfast inns.

5. Click the **NAICSDesc Criteria** text box, type **721191**, and then press the ↓ key. The condition changes to "721191". See Figure 8-12.

| Figure 8-12 | SELECT QUERY ON WHICH TO BASE THE MAKE-TABLE QUERY |

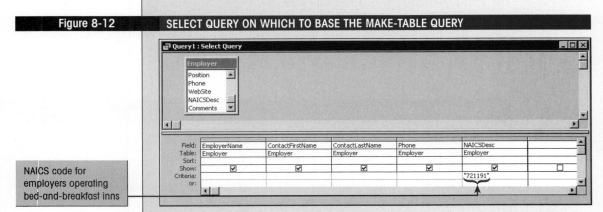

NAICS code for employers operating bed-and-breakfast inns

You've completed the select query, so now you can run it to make sure the recordset contains the data Elsa needs.

6. Run the query, resize all columns to their best fit, and then deselect the columns. The query recordset shows the 11 records for employers operating bed-and-breakfast inns.

Now that you have the correct select query, you can change the query to a make-table query.

To change the query type, and then run and save the make-table query:

1. Change to Design view, click the list arrow for the **Query Type** button on the Query Design toolbar, and then click **Make-Table Query**. Access opens the Make Table dialog box, in which you enter the name of the new table. See Figure 8-13.

Figure 8-13	MAKE TABLE DIALOG BOX

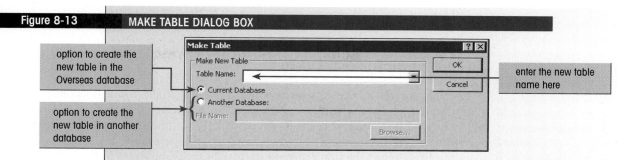

option to create the new table in the Overseas database

option to create the new table in another database

enter the new table name here

2. In the Table Name list box, type **Contact Employers**, make sure the **Current Database** option button is selected so that the new table will be included in the Overseas database, and then press the **Enter** key.

Now that you have created and tested the query, you can run it to create the Contact Employers table. After you run the query, you can save it, and then you can view the new table.

3. Run the query. Access opens a dialog box indicating that you are about to paste 11 rows into a new table. Because you are running an action query, which alters the contents of the database, Access gives you an opportunity to cancel the operation, if necessary, or to confirm it.

4. Click the **Yes** button. Access closes the dialog box, runs the make-table query to create the Contact Employers table, and continues displaying the Query window in Design view.

5. Save the query as **Contact Employers Make-Table**, and then close the query.

You can now open the Contact Employers table to view the results of the make-table query.

6. Open the **Contact Employers** table in Datasheet view, resize all datasheet columns to their best fit, and then click **EmployerName Stonehurst Inn** to deselect the columns. See Figure 8-14.

Figure 8-14	CONTACT EMPLOYERS TABLE DATASHEET

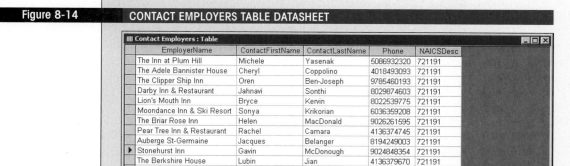

The Contact Employers table includes the EmployerName, ContactFirstName, ContactLastName, Phone, and NAICSDesc fields for employers in the bed-and-breakfast industry. Notice that the NAICS code of 721191 appears in the NAICSDesc column. Also, notice that the Phone field values do not contain slashes between the third and fourth digits and hyphens between the sixth and seventh digits. The hyphens were part of the Input Mask property for the Phone field in the Employer table; these hyphens were not preserved by the make-table query.

7. Save your datasheet changes, and then close the table.

Elsa can now make any necessary changes to the Contact Employers table records when she contacts the employers without affecting the Employer table in the Overseas database.

Creating an Append Query

Elsa has decided to expand the list of employers that she will call to ensure personalized service. She wants to add the EmployerName, ContactFirstName, ContactLastName, Phone, and NAICSDesc fields for all employers with limited-service restaurants. She asks you to add these new records to the Contact Employers table. You could make this change by modifying the selection criterion in the Contact Employers Make-Table query to select employers with NAICS code field values of either 721191 (bed-and-breakfast inns) or 722211 (limited-service restaurants). If you ran this modified query, however, you would overwrite the existing Contact Employers table with a new table. If Elsa had made any changes to the existing Contact Employers records, creating a new table would overwrite these changes, as well.

Instead, you will modify the Contact Employers Make-Table query to select only those employers with limited-service restaurants and change the query to an append query. When you run this new query, the selected records will be appended to the records in the existing Contact Employers table.

REFERENCE WINDOW   **RW**

Creating an Append Query

- Create a select query with the necessary fields and selection criteria.
- Click the Run button on the Query Design toolbar to preview the results.
- Switch to Design view to make any necessary changes. When the query is correct, click the list arrow for the Query Type button on the Query Design toolbar, and then click Append Query.
- In the Append dialog box, type the name of the table to which you want to append the selected records in the Table Name list box. Make sure the Current Database option button is selected to append the records in the current database; or, click the Another Database option button and enter the database name in the File Name text box. Then click the OK button. Access replaces the Show row in the design grid with the Append To row.
- Click the Run button on the Query Design toolbar.
- Click the Yes button to confirm appending the records to the table.

You can now modify the Contact Employers Make-Table query to create the append query you'll use to include the additional employer data Elsa wants in the Contact Employers table.

To create the append query:

1. Open the **Contact Employers Make-Table** query in Design view.

   You'll change the selection criterion to 722211, which is the NAICS code for limited-service restaurants.

2. Click the **NAICSDesc Criteria** text box, press the **F2** key to highlight the entire condition, type **722211**, and then press the ↓ key. The condition changes to "722211". See Figure 8-15.

Figure 8-15	CHANGING THE SELECTION CRITERION

employers operating
limited-service
restaurants

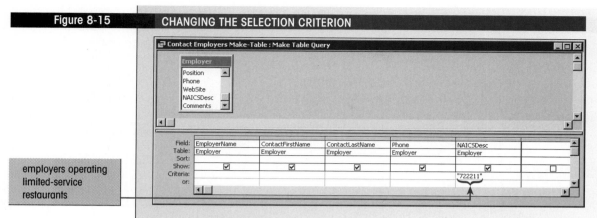

Before you can run the query to append the records to the Contact Employers table, you have to change it to an append query. It is always a good idea to test an action query before you run it, so you will first change the query to a select query and run it to make sure the correct records are selected. Then you will change it to an append query and run it to append the new records to the Contact Employers table.

3. Click the list arrow for the **Query Type** button [icon] on the Query Design toolbar, and then click **Select Query**.

4. Run the query, resize all columns to their best fit, and then deselect the columns. The query recordset shows the three records for employers with limited-service restaurant businesses. See Figure 8-16.

Figure 8-16	EMPLOYERS OPERATING LIMITED-SERVICE RESTAURANTS SELECTED

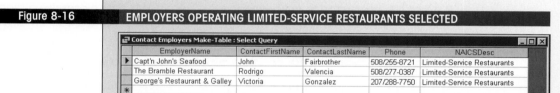

These three records are the additional records you will append to the Contact Employers table. Now that the results show that the query is correct, you can change the query to an append query.

5. Switch to Design view, click the list arrow for the **Query Type** button [icon] on the Query Design toolbar, and then click **Append Query**. Access opens the Append dialog box, in which you enter the name of the table to which you want to append the data.

6. Make sure **Contact Employers** appears in the Table Name list box and that the **Current Database** option button is selected, and then click the **OK** button. Access replaces the Show row with the Append To row between the Sort and Criteria rows in the design grid. See Figure 8-17.

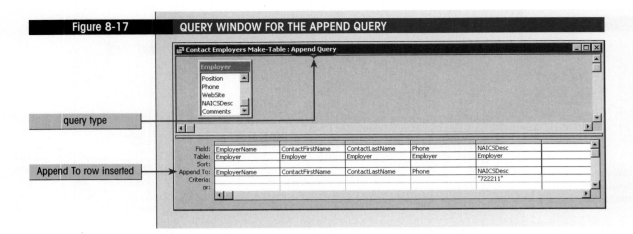

| Figure 8-17 | QUERY WINDOW FOR THE APPEND QUERY |

The Append To row in the design grid identifies the fields that the query will append to the designated table. The EmployerName, ContactFirstName, ContactLastName, Phone, and NAICSDesc fields are selected to be appended to the Contact Employers table, which already contains these five fields for employers with bed-and-breakfast inns.

You can now run and then save the append query.

To run and save the append query:

1. Run the query. Access opens a dialog box warning that you are about to append three rows.

2. Click the **Yes** button to acknowledge the warning. Access closes the dialog box, runs the append query, adds the three records to the Contact Employers table, and continues displaying the Query window in Design view.

3. Click **File** on the menu bar, and then click **Save As**. The Save As dialog box opens.

4. Type **Contact Employers Append** in the Save Query To text box, and then press the **Enter** key. Access saves the query.

5. Close the query. The Contact Employers Append query appears in the Queries list with a special icon indicating that it is an append query.

   Next you'll open the Contact Employers table to make sure that the three records were appended to the table.

6. Open the **Contact Employers** table in Datasheet view.

   The new records have been added to the Contact Employers table. Because the Contact Employers table does not have a primary key, the new records appear at the end of the table. You could arrange the records in a different order by sorting the records using the Sort Ascending or Sort Descending button on the Table Datasheet toolbar.

7. Close the table.

Creating a Delete Query

Elsa has contacted all the employers in the Contact Employers table who have phone numbers in the 508 and 902 area codes. She asks you to delete these records from the Contact Employers table so that the table contains only those records for employers she has not yet contacted. You can either delete the table records individually or create a delete query to remove them all at once.

REFERENCE WINDOW   **RW**

Creating a Delete Query
- Create a select query with the necessary fields and selection criteria.
- Click the Run button on the Query Design toolbar to preview the results.
- Switch to Design view to make any necessary changes. When the query is correct, click the list arrow for the Query Type button on the Query Design toolbar.
- Click Delete Query. Access replaces the Show and Sort rows in the design grid with the Delete row.
- Click the Run button on the Query Design toolbar.
- Click the Yes button to confirm deleting the records.

You'll create a delete query to delete the records of all the employers in the Contact Employers table that have phone numbers in the 508 and 902 area codes. First, you'll create a select query to choose the correct records based on the area code criteria. Then you'll test the select query and change it to a delete query.

To create the delete query:

1. Click **Queries** in the Objects bar of the Database window, click the **New** button to open the New Query dialog box, make sure that **Design View** is selected, and then click the **OK** button.

2. Add the **Contact Employers** table field list to the Query window, and then close the Show Table dialog box.

3. Double-click the title bar of the Contact Employers field list to select all the fields in the table, drag the pointer from the highlighted area of the field list to the design grid's first column Field text box, and then release the mouse button. Access adds all the fields to the design grid.

4. Click the **Phone Criteria** text box, type **Like "508*"**, press the ↓ key, and then type **Like "902*"**. Access will select a record only if the Phone field value starts with either 508 or 902.

5. Run the query. The query results display five records, each one with either a 508 or 902 area code. The select query is correct. See Figure 8-18.

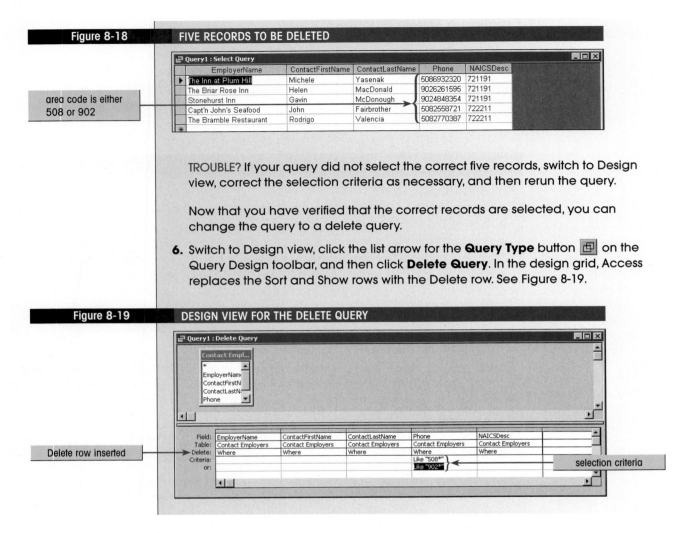

Figure 8-18 | **FIVE RECORDS TO BE DELETED**

area code is either
508 or 902

EmployerName	ContactFirstName	ContactLastName	Phone	NAICSDesc
The Inn at Plum Hill	Michele	Yasenak	5086932320	721191
The Briar Rose Inn	Helen	MacDonald	9026261595	721191
Stonehurst Inn	Gavin	McDonough	9024848354	721191
Capt'n John's Seafood	John	Fairbrother	5082558721	722211
The Bramble Restaurant	Rodrigo	Valencia	5082770387	722211

TROUBLE? If your query did not select the correct five records, switch to Design view, correct the selection criteria as necessary, and then rerun the query.

Now that you have verified that the correct records are selected, you can change the query to a delete query.

6. Switch to Design view, click the list arrow for the **Query Type** button ▦ on the Query Design toolbar, and then click **Delete Query**. In the design grid, Access replaces the Sort and Show rows with the Delete row. See Figure 8-19.

Figure 8-19 | **DESIGN VIEW FOR THE DELETE QUERY**

Delete row inserted

selection criteria

Now you can run the query and view the results in the Contact Employers table.

To run the delete query, and then view the results:

1. Run the query. Access opens a dialog box warning that you are about to delete five rows.

2. Click the **Yes** button to close the dialog box and run the delete query. Access deletes the five records in the Contact Employers table and continues to display the Query window in Design view. Because you'll need to run this query only once, you won't save it.

3. Close the query, and then click the **No** button when Access asks if you want to save it.

You can now open the Contact Employers table to verify that the records have been deleted.

4. Open the **Contact Employers** table in Datasheet view. The table now includes only nine records; five records were correctly deleted. See Figure 8-20.

Figure 8-20   **CONTACT EMPLOYERS TABLE AFTER DELETING FIVE RECORDS**

Elsa wants Zack and Matt to split the work of contacting the nine remaining employers in the Contact Employers table. She asks you to add a new field to the table that will identify whether Zack or Matt will call the employer. To do so, you'll create an update query to add either Zack's or Matt's name to the Contact Employers table.

Creating an Update Query

Recall that an update query changes selected fields and records in one or more tables. In this case, you need to create a new field to contain Zack or Matt's name, and then enter the appropriate values in this new field. You could enter the value for every record in the Contact Employers table, but you can accomplish the same thing more quickly and with less chance of error by using an update query to enter the values at one time.

REFERENCE WINDOW   **RW**

Creating an Update Query

- Create a select query with the necessary fields and selection criteria.
- Click the Run button on the Query Design toolbar to preview the results.
- Switch to Design view to make any necessary changes. When the query is correct, click the list arrow for the Query Type button on the Query Design toolbar.
- Click Update Query. Access replaces the Show and Sort rows in the design grid with the Update To row.
- Type the updated values for the fields you need to update in their Update To text boxes.
- Click the Run button on the Query Design toolbar.
- Click the Yes button to confirm updating the records.

First, you will add a field named Caller to the Contact Employers table. This new field will contain a field value of either "Zack" or "Matt" to indicate which NSJI employee will contact the employer.

To add the new Caller field to the Contact Employers table:

1. Switch to Design view.

2. Click the **Field Name** text box below the NAICSDesc field, type **Caller**, and then press the **Tab** key twice to name the field and accept the default text data type.

Because the new field will contain values of "Zack" or "Matt", which are 4 characters long, you need to change the field size for the new field to 4.

3. Press the **F6** key and then type **4**. This completes the addition of the Caller field to the Contact Employers table. See Figure 8-21.

Figure 8-21	CALLER FIELD ADDED TO THE CONTACT EMPLOYERS TABLE

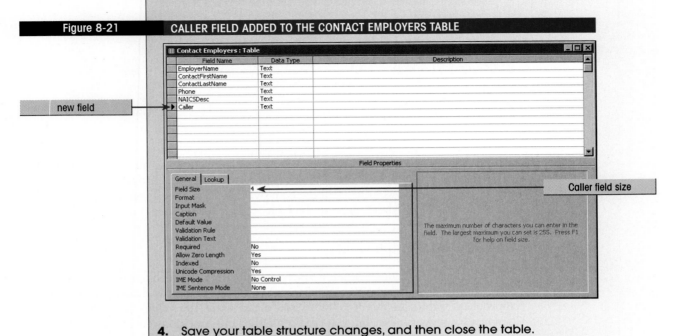

new field

Caller field size

4. Save your table structure changes, and then close the table.

Now you can create an update query to update the Caller field for the records in the Contact Employers table. You'll change the Caller field value to "Zack" for each employer in the 413 and 802 telephone area codes and to "Matt" for all other employers.

To create the update query to enter Caller field values:

1. Click **Queries** in the Objects bar of the Database window, click the **New** button to open the New Query dialog box, make sure that **Design View** is selected, and then click the **OK** button.

2. Add the **Contact Employers** table field list to the Query window, and then close the Show Table dialog box.

   You will select the Phone and Caller fields for the query results. The Phone field lets you select records for customers in a particular telephone area code. The Caller field is the field you need to update.

3. In the Contact Employers field list, double-click the **Phone** and **Caller** fields to add these fields to the design grid, scrolling down the field list as necessary.

   You can now select the records for employers in the 413 and 802 telephone area codes and update the Caller field value for those records to "Matt."

4. Click the **Phone Criteria** text box, and then type **Like "413*" Or Like "802*"**. Access will select a record only if the first three digits of the Phone field value are 413 or 802.

5. Run the query. The query recordset displays four records, each one with either a 413 or 802 telephone area code. The select query is correct.

Now that you have verified that the correct records are selected, you can change the query to an update query.

6. Switch to Design view, click the list arrow for the **Query Type** button 🖻 on the Query Design toolbar, and then click **Update Query**. In the design grid, Access replaces the Sort and Show rows with the Update To row.

   You tell Access how you want to change a field value for the selected records by entering an expression in the field's Update To text box. An expression is a calculation resulting in a single value. You can type a simple expression directly into the Update To text box. If you need help creating a complicated expression, you can create it using Expression Builder, an Access tool that contains an expression box in which the expression is entered, buttons for common operators, and one or more lists of expression elements, such as table and field names. The expression in this case is simple, so you can type it directly in the Update To text box.

7. Click the **Caller Update To** text box, type **Zack**, and then press the ↓ key. The condition changes to "Zack". See Figure 8-22.

| Figure 8-22 | UPDATING THE CALLER FIELD |

selection criterion

update expression

TROUBLE? Your screen might show only part of the criterion in the Phone Criteria text box.

8. Run the query. Access opens a dialog box warning you that you are about to update four rows in the Contact Employers table.

9. Click the **Yes** button to close the dialog box and run the update query. Access updates the Caller field values for the employers with telephone area codes of 413 or 802 and leaves the Query window in Design view open.

Now you need to update the Caller field values for employers that Matt will contact. To do so, you'll modify the criteria and the "Update To" value for the existing update query.

To update the remaining Caller field values:

1. Double-click **Zack** in the Caller Update To text box to select it, and then type **Matt**. This is the Caller field value you'll use to update the remaining five records in the Contact Employers table.

   Matt will call the remaining employers in the Contact Employers table, so you'll use the Not logical operator to change the existing Phone criterion.

2. Click the **Phone Criteria** text box, press the **Home** key to position the insertion point at the beginning of the criterion, and then type **Not (**

3. Press the **End** key to position the insertion point at the end of the criterion in the Phone text box, and then type **)** (a closing parenthesis). The entry in the Phone Criteria text box is now *Not (Like "413*" Or Like "802*")*, and Access will select a record only if the Phone field value starts with neither 413 nor 802. See Figure 8-23.

Figure 8-23	AFTER CHANGING THE UPDATE QUERY

modified selection criterion

new update expression

5. Run the query, and then click the **Yes** button to confirm the update of five rows.

You are finished updating the Contact Employers table, so you can close the Query window. Because all the records have been updated, you do not need to save the query.

6. Close the query, and then click the **No** button when Access asks if you want to save it.

Now you can view the Contact Employers table to see the results of the update operations.

To view the updated Contact Employers table:

1. Open the **Contact Employers** table in Datasheet view. "Zack" is the Caller field value for records with telephone area codes of 413 and 802, and "Matt" is the Caller field value for the other records. See Figure 8-24.

Figure 8-24	CONTACT EMPLOYERS TABLE WITH THE UPDATED CALLER FIELD VALUES

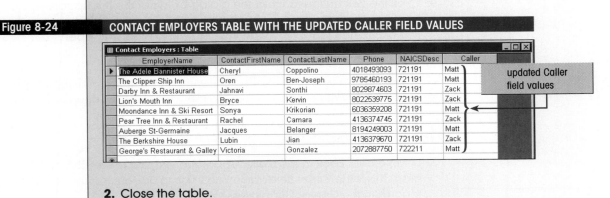

updated Caller field values

2. Close the table.

Elsa has frequently used Filter By Form and Filter By Selection to view specific information in the Overseas database's forms and datasheets, but she often has more complex filter operations she needs to perform. To display the results she wants in these situations, you need to use an advanced filter.

Applying an Advanced Filter in a Table

Recall that a filter is a set of criteria that describes the records you want to see in a datasheet or a form and their sequence. **Advanced Filter/Sort** lets you specify multiple selection criteria and specify a sort order for the selected records in the Filter window, in the same way you specify record selection criteria and sort orders for a query in Design view.

REFERENCE WINDOW   **RW**

Applying an Advanced Filter/Sort
- Open the table or query in Datasheet view, or open the form in Form view.
- Click Records on the menu bar, point to Filter, and then click Advanced Filter/Sort.
- Add to the design grid the fields you need to filter or sort.
- Specify the selection criteria, and select the sort fields and their sort orders.
- Click the Apply Filter button on the Filter/Sort toolbar to apply the filter.

Elsa wants to view employer data for USA employers that are not in the hotel and motel industry in ascending employer name sequence. To produce the results Elsa wants, you'll use an advanced filter/sort for the Employer table.

To create the advanced filter/sort for the Employer table:

1. Open the **Employer** table in Datasheet view.

2. Click **Records** on the menu bar, point to **Filter**, and then click **Advanced Filter/Sort**. The Filter window opens on top of the Employer table datasheet. See Figure 8-25.

Figure 8-25   **FILTER WINDOW**

Employer table field list

The Filter window looks the same as and functions similarly to the Query window in Design view. You add fields from the field list to the design grid just as you do with queries. However, you need to add only those fields for which you'll be specifying selection criteria and sorting specifications; all fields from the data source are included automatically in the filter results.

First, you'll add the EmployerName, NAICSDesc, and Country fields to the design grid, and then you'll select the sort field.

3. In the Employer field list, double-click **EmployerName**, double-click **NAICSDesc**, and then double-click **Country**, scrolling as necessary, to add these three fields to the design grid.

4. Click the right side of the **EmployerName Sort** text box to display the sort order options, and then click **Ascending**. The query will display the filtered records alphabetically by the EmployerName field values.

Next, you'll enter the selection criteria. Elsa wants to view USA employers that are not in the hotel and motel industry; the NAICS code 72111 identifies employers in that industry.

5. Click the **NAICSDesc Criteria** text box, type **Not 72111**, and then press the **Tab** key. The condition changes to Not "72111".

6. In the Country Criteria text box type **USA**, and then press the **Tab** key. The condition changes to "USA". See Figure 8-26.

Figure 8-26	COMPLETED ADVANCED FILTER/SORT

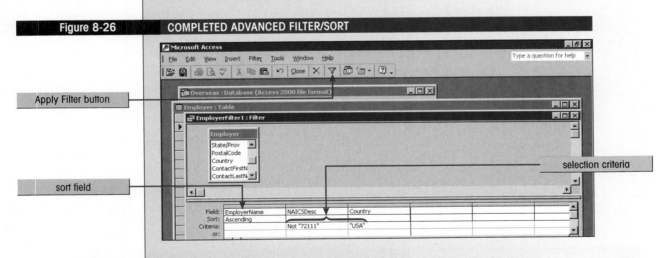

You've completed the filter, so you can now apply it.

7. Click the **Apply Filter** button [icon] on the Filter/Sort toolbar. Access applies the filter and displays the records that match the selection criteria (USA employers not in the hotel and motel industry). The filter selected 29 Employer table records. See Figure 8-27.

Figure 8-27   FILTERED EMPLOYER TABLE DATASHEET

Remove Filter button

records listed in ascending order by the EmployerName field values

indicates filter applied

TROUBLE? If the Filter/Sort toolbar is not open on your screen, click View on the menu bar, point to Toolbars, and then click Filter/Sort.

8. Scroll the datasheet to verify that only USA employers that are not in the hotel and motel industry have been selected.

As is the case with the other filter types, you can use the Remove Filter button to remove the filter. If you save the table, you also save the filter. When you next open the table, Access will display the filtered datasheet. Because Elsa will not need this specific filter next time, you'll close the table without saving the filter.

9. Close the table, and then click the **No** button when Access asks if you want to save the table design changes.

Elsa can now use action queries and the advanced filter/sort feature in her future work with the Overseas database. In the next session, you'll learn about the different types of relationships you can create between database tables, and view and create indexes to increase a database's efficiency.

Session 8.2 QUICK CHECK

1. What is an action query?

2. What precautions should you take before running an action query?

3. What is the difference between a make-table query and an append query?

4. What does a delete query do?

5. What does an update query do?

6. How does the design grid change when you create an update query?

7. _____ Filter/Sort lets you specify multiple selection criteria and specify a sort order for the selected records.

SESSION 8.3

In this session, you will learn about many-to-many and one-to-many relationships between tables. You then will view and create indexes, and learn about the different types of table joins.

Relationships Between Database Tables

As you learned in Tutorial 3, a **one-to-many relationship** (abbreviated as **1:M**) exists between two tables when each record in the primary table matches zero, one, or many records in the related table, and when each record in the related table matches exactly one record in the primary table. For example, Figure 8-28 shows a one-to-many relationship between portions of the Employer and Position tables and a sample query. Employer 10151 has three positions, employer 10217 has one position, and employer 10125 has zero positions. Every position has a single matching employer.

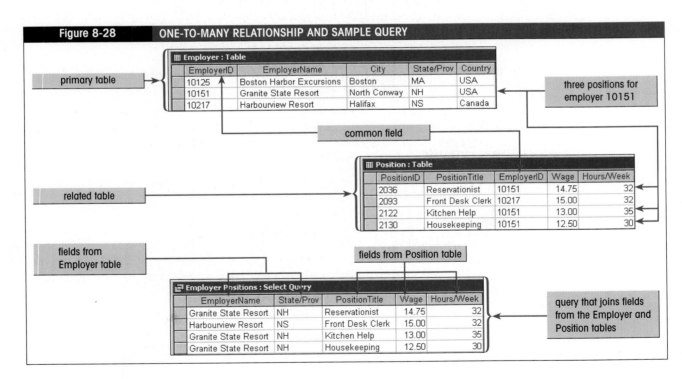

Figure 8-28   ONE-TO-MANY RELATIONSHIP AND SAMPLE QUERY

You use the common field of EmployerID to form the one-to-many relationship between the Employer and Position tables. When you join the two tables based on EmployerID field values, you can extract data from them as if they are one larger table. For example, you can join the Employer and Position tables to create the Employer Positions query shown in Figure 8-28. In the Employer Positions query, the EmployerName and State/Prov columns are fields from the Employer table, and the PositionTitle, Wage, and Hours/Week columns are fields from the Position table.

In addition to one-to-many relationships between tables, you can also relate tables through many-to-many and one-to-one relationships.

Many-to-Many Relationships

A **many-to-many relationship** (abbreviated as **M:N**) exists between two tables when each record in the first table matches many records in the second table, and each record in the second table matches many records in the first table.

In the Overseas database, the Position table contains one record for each position offered by an employer, and the Student table contains one record for each student recruited by NSJI. Because a student can be employed in many positions (at different times), and each position can be filled by many students, the Position and Student tables have a many-to-many relationship, as shown in Figure 8-29.

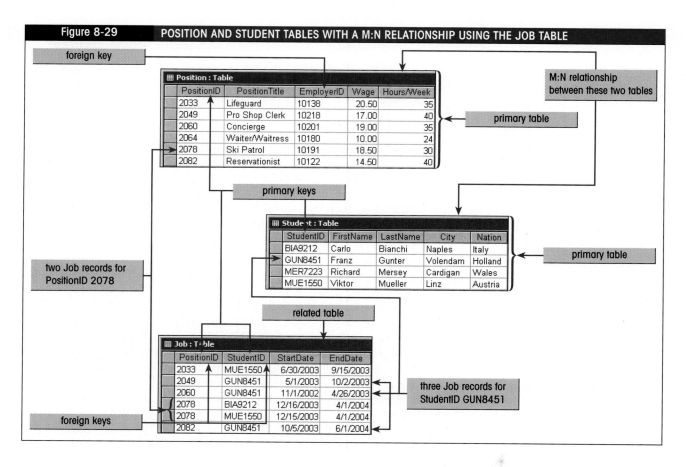

Figure 8-29   **POSITION AND STUDENT TABLES WITH A M:N RELATIONSHIP USING THE JOB TABLE**

When you have a many-to-many relationship between two tables, you must create a third table and form one-to-many relationships between the two original primary tables and the new related table. For instance, the Job table exists because the Position and Student tables have a many-to-many relationship. Each record in the Job table contains two foreign keys: the PositionID field is a foreign key that allows you to join the Position table to the Job table; and the StudentID field is a foreign key that allows you to join the Student table to the Job table. For example, the first record in the Job table represents a Lifeguard position for EmployerID 10138 that was filled by Viktor Mueller with StudentID MUE1550. Franz Gunter, who has StudentID GUN8451, appears in three records in the Job table. These three Job table records appear in three different positions for PositionID field values of 2049, 2060, and 2082. Also, PositionID 2078 appears in two Job table records, each for a different student: Carlo Bianchi and Viktor Mueller. The primary key of the Job table is a composite key, consisting of the combination of the PositionID and StudentID fields. Each pair of values in this primary key is unique.

When you join tables that have a many-to-many relationship, you can extract data from them as if they are one larger table. For example, you can join the Student, Position, and Job tables to create the Job Data query shown in Figure 8-30.

| Figure 8-30 | QUERY RECORDSET PRODUCED BY JOINING TABLES HAVING AN M:N RELATIONSHIP |

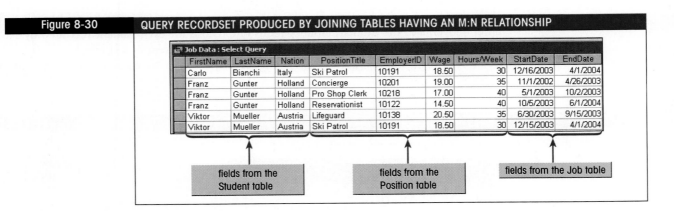

The PositionID field joins the Position and Job tables, and the StudentID field joins the Student and Job tables. In the Job Data query, the FirstName, LastName, and Nation fields are from the Student table; the PositionTitle, EmployerID, Wage, and Hours/Week fields are from the Position table; and the StartDate and EndDate fields are from the Job table. The first record in the query recordset shows data from the fourth record in the Job table, joined with data from the matching first record in the Student table and with data from the matching fifth record in the Position table.

One-to-One Relationships

A **one-to-one relationship** (abbreviated as **1:1**) exists between two tables when each record in the first table matches at most one record in the second table, and each record in the second table matches at most one record in the first table. Most relationships between tables are either one-to-many or many-to-many; the primary use for one-to-one relationships is as entity subtypes. An **entity subtype** is a table whose primary key is a foreign key to a second table and whose fields are additional fields from the second table. For example, the Employer table and the Billing Address table, which is an entity subtype, have a one-to-one relationship, as shown in Figure 8-31.

Figure 8-31	EMPLOYER AND BILLING ADDRESS TABLES WITH A 1:1 RELATIONSHIP

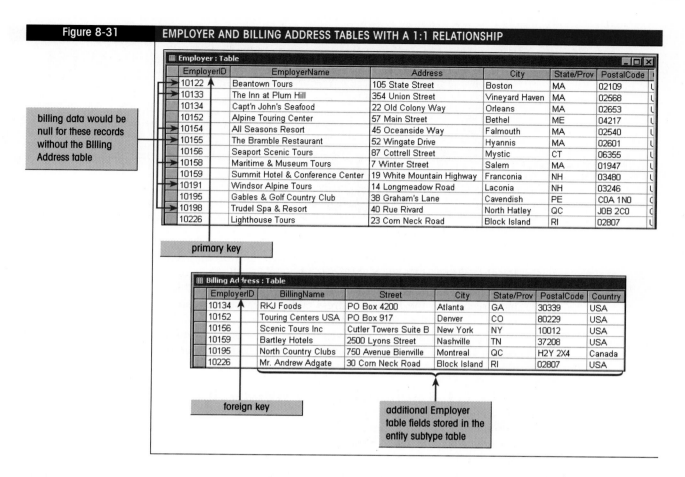

For most employer clients, the Address, City, State/Prov, PostalCode, and Country fields in the Employer table identify both the employer's location and billing address, which is where NSJI sends the employer's invoices. In a few cases, however, the billing address is different from the location address; additionally, the employer name used for billing purposes is different from the employer name in the Employer table. There are two ways to handle these two sets of names and addresses. The first way is to add BillingName, BillingStreet, BillingCity, BillingState/Prov, BillingPostalCode, and BillingCountry fields to the Employer table. For those employers having a different billing name and address, store the appropriate values in these billing fields. For those employers having identical location and billing names and addresses, leave these billing fields null.

As shown in Figure 8-31, the second way to handle the two sets of addresses is to create the entity subtype named Billing Address. In the Billing Address table, EmployerID, which is the primary key, also is a foreign key to the Employer table. A record appears in the Billing Address table only for those employers having a different billing name and address.

When you join tables that have a one-to-one relationship, you can extract data from them as if they are one larger table. For example, you can join the Employer and Billing Address tables to create the Billing Address Data query shown in Figure 8-32.

Figure 8-32	QUERY RESULTS PRODUCED BY JOINING TABLES HAVING A 1:1 RELATIONSHIP

Billing Address Data : Select Query

EmployerID	EmployerName	BillingName	City	State/Prov
10134	Capt'n John's Seafood	RKJ Foods	Atlanta	GA
10152	Alpine Touring Center	Touring Centers USA	Denver	CO
10156	Seaport Scenic Tours	Scenic Tours Inc	New York	NY
10159	Summit Hotel & Conference Center	Bartley Hotels	Nashville	TN
10195	Gables & Golf Country Club	North Country Clubs	Montreal	QC
10226	Lighthouse Tours	Mr. Andrew Adgate	Block Island	RI

fields from the Employer table

fields from the Billing Address table

The EmployerID field joins the Employer and Billing Address tables. In the query, the EmployerID and EmployerName fields are from the Employer table; and the BillingName, City, and State/Prov fields are from the Billing Address table. Only the six employers that have records in the Billing Address table—because they have different billing addresses—appear in the Billing Address Data query results.

Next, you'll define a many-to-many relationship between the Position and Student tables, and a one-to-one relationship between the Employer and Billing Address tables.

Defining M:N and 1:1 Relationships Between Tables

Similar to how you defined one-to-many relationships in Tutorial 3, you define many-to-many and one-to-one relationships in the Relationships window. First, you'll open the Relationships window and define the many-to-many relationship between the Position and Student tables. You'll define a one-to-many relationship between the Position and Job tables, with Position as the primary table, Job as the related table, and PositionID as the common field (the primary key in the Position table and a foreign key in the Job table). Next, you'll define a one-to-many relationship between the Student and Job tables, with Student as the primary table, Job as the related table, and StudentID as the common field (the primary key in the Student table and a foreign key in the Job table).

To define a many-to-many relationship between the Position and Student tables:

1. Make sure that Access is running, and that the **Overseas** database in the Tutorial folder on your Data Disk is open.

2. Click the **Relationships** button on the Database toolbar to open the Relationships window.

   The NAICS, Employer, Position, and Job field lists already appear in the Relationships window, so you need to add only the Student field list to the Relationships window.

3. Click the Show Table button on the Relationship toolbar to open the Show Table dialog box, double-click **Student** to add the Student field list to the Relationships window, and then click the **Close** button in the Show Table dialog box to close the dialog box and reveal the entire Relationships window.

4. Drag the Student field list title bar to the right until the Student field list is positioned as shown in Figure 8-33, and then use the ↕ pointer to drag the bottom border of the Student field list down until you can see all the fields in the list.

Figure 8-33	AFTER ADDING THE STUDENT FIELD LIST TO THE RELATIONSHIPS WINDOW

Show Table button

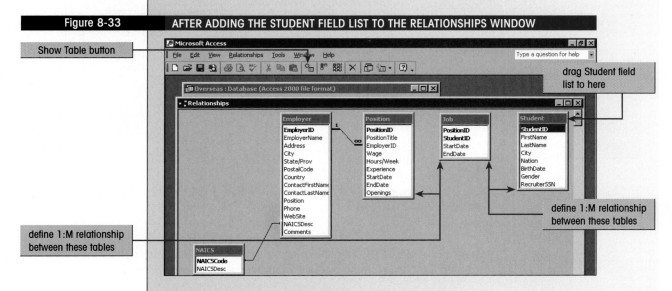

drag Student field list to here

define 1:M relationship between these tables

define 1:M relationship between these tables

First, you'll define the one-to-many relationship between the Position and Job tables.

5. Click **PositionID** in the Position field list, and drag it to **PositionID** in the Job field list. When you release the mouse button, the Edit Relationships dialog box opens.

The primary table, related table, and common field appear at the top of the dialog box. The type of relationship, One-To-Many, appears at the bottom of the dialog box. When you click the Enforce Referential Integrity check box, the two cascade options become available. If you select the Cascade Update Related Fields option, Access will change the appropriate foreign key values in the related table when you change a primary key value in the primary table. If you select the Cascade Delete Related Records option, when you delete a record in the primary table, Access will delete all records in the related table that have a matching foreign key value.

6. Click the **Enforce Referential Integrity** check box, click the **Cascade Update Related Fields** check box, and then click the **Cascade Delete Related Records** check box. You have now selected all the necessary relationship options.

7. Click the **Create** button to define the one-to-many relationship between the two tables and close the dialog box. The completed relationship appears in the Relationships window.

8. Repeat Steps 5 through 7 to define the one-to-many relationship between the primary Student table and the related Job table, using StudentID as the common field. See Figure 8-34.

Figure 8-34	M:N RELATIONSHIP DEFINED BETWEEN THE POSITION AND STUDENT TABLES

one-to-many relationship between the Position and Job tables

one-to-many relationship between the Student and Job tables

9. Click the Save button 🖫 on the Relationship toolbar to save the layout in the Relationships window.

Now you can add the Billing Address table to the Relationships window and then define a one-to-one relationship between the Employer and Billing Address tables.

To define a one-to-one relationship between the Employer and Billing Address tables:

1. Click the **Show Table** button 🖷 on the Relationship toolbar to open the Show Table dialog box, double-click **Billing Address** to add the Billing Address field list to the Relationships window, and then click the **Close** button in the Show Table dialog box to close the dialog box and reveal the entire Relationships window.

2. If necessary, drag the Billing Address field list title bar up and to the left until the Billing Address field list is positioned to the left of the Employer field list.

3. Use the ↕ pointer to drag the bottom border of the Billing Address field list down until you can see all the fields in the list.

Now you can define the one-to-one relationship between the primary Employer table and the related Billing Address table.

4. Click **EmployerID** in the Employer field list, and drag it to **EmployerID** in the Billing Address field list. When you release the mouse button, the Edit Relationships dialog box opens.

The primary table, related table, and common field appear at the top of the dialog box. The type of relationship, One-To-One, appears at the bottom of the dialog box.

5. Click the **Enforce Referential Integrity** check box, click the **Cascade Update Related Fields** check box, and then click the **Cascade Delete Related Records** check box. You have now selected all the necessary relationship options.

6. Click the **Create** button to define the one-to-one relationship between the two tables and close the dialog box. The completed relationship appears in the Relationships window. Both sides of the relationship have the digit 1 at their ends to indicate a one-to-one relationship between the two tables. See Figure 8-35.

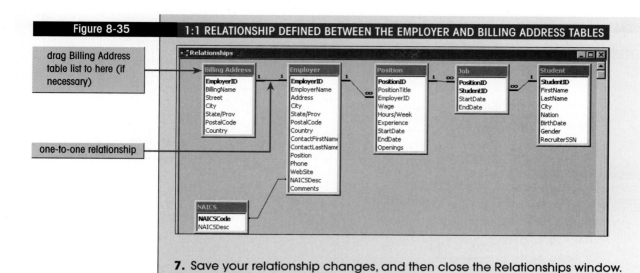

Figure 8-35

1:1 RELATIONSHIP DEFINED BETWEEN THE EMPLOYER AND BILLING ADDRESS TABLES

drag Billing Address table list to here (if necessary)

one-to-one relationship

7. Save your relationship changes, and then close the Relationships window.

Elsa asks you if her staff's work will take longer as the Overseas database grows in size with the addition of more table records. Specifically, she wants to know if queries will take longer to run. You tell her that using indexes will help make her queries run faster.

Using Indexes for Table Fields

Suppose you need to find all the pages in a book that discuss a specific topic. The fastest, most accurate way to perform your search is to look up the topic in the book's index. In a similar fashion, you can create and use indexes to locate all the records in a table that contain specific values for one or more fields. An **index** is a list that relates field values to the records that contain those field values.

Access automatically creates and maintains an index for a table's primary key. Access also automatically creates and maintains indexes for fields that have been defined explicitly as foreign keys in the Relationships window. For example, the Position table in the Overseas database includes an index for the PositionID field, which is the table's primary key. Conceptually, as shown in Figure 8-36, Access identifies each record in the Position table by its record number, and the PositionID index has two columns. The first column contains a PositionID value, and the second column contains the record number for that PositionID value. For instance, PositionID 2036 in the index has a record number value of 8; and record number 8 in the Position table contains the data for PositionID 2036.

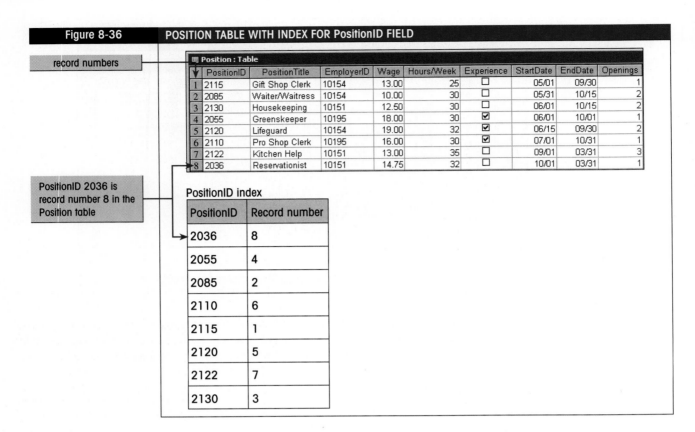

Figure 8-36 | **POSITION TABLE WITH INDEX FOR PositionID FIELD**

record numbers

PositionID 2036 is record number 8 in the Position table

Because PositionID values are unique, each row in the PositionID index has a single record number. When you create indexes for non-primary-key fields or when Access creates an index for a foreign key field specified in the Relationships window, however, the indexes may contain multiple record numbers in a row. Figure 8-37 illustrates an EmployerID index for the Position table. Because EmployerID is a foreign key in the Position table (an employer can offer many positions), each EmployerID entry in the index can be associated with many record numbers. For instance, EmployerID 10151 in the index has record number values of 3, 7, and 8; and record numbers 3, 7, and 8 in the Position table contain the position data for EmployerID 10151.

Figure 8-37	POSITION TABLE WITH INDEX FOR EmployerID FIELD

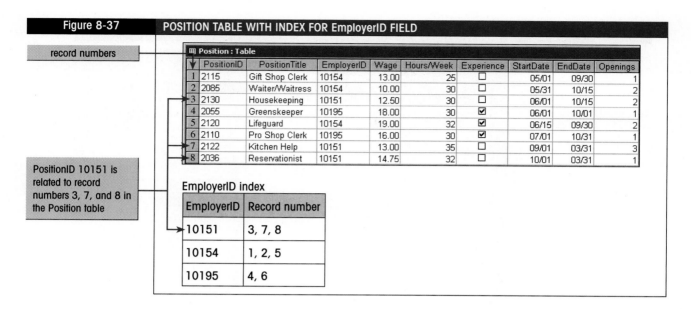

record numbers

PositionID 10151 is related to record numbers 3, 7, and 8 in the Position table

Position : Table

	PositionID	PositionTitle	EmployerID	Wage	Hours/Week	Experience	StartDate	EndDate	Openings
1	2115	Gift Shop Clerk	10154	13.00	25	☐	05/01	09/30	1
2	2085	Waiter/Waitress	10154	10.00	30	☐	05/31	10/15	2
3	2130	Housekeeping	10151	12.50	30	☐	06/01	10/15	2
4	2055	Greenskeeper	10195	18.00	30	☑	06/01	10/01	1
5	2120	Lifeguard	10154	19.00	32	☑	06/15	09/30	2
6	2110	Pro Shop Clerk	10195	16.00	30	☑	07/01	10/31	1
7	2122	Kitchen Help	10151	13.00	35	☐	09/01	03/31	3
8	2036	Reservationist	10151	14.75	32	☐	10/01	03/31	1

EmployerID index

EmployerID	Record number
10151	3, 7, 8
10154	1, 2, 5
10195	4, 6

If an index exists for the EmployerID field in the Position table, queries that use EmployerID as a sort field or as a selection criterion will run faster. This advantage of using an index must be weighed against two disadvantages: the index adds disk storage requirements to the database, and it takes time to update the index as you add and delete records. Except for primary key indexes, you can add and delete indexes at any time. Thus, you can add an index if you believe searching and querying would be faster as the number of records in the database increases. You also can delete an existing index if you later deem it to be unnecessary.

Viewing Existing Indexes

You can view the existing indexes for a table by opening the table in Design view.

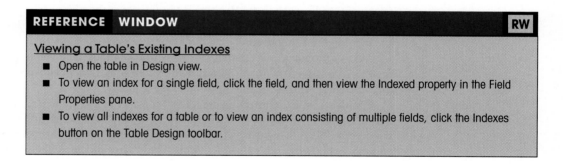

REFERENCE WINDOW   **RW**

Viewing a Table's Existing Indexes
- Open the table in Design view.
- To view an index for a single field, click the field, and then view the Indexed property in the Field Properties pane.
- To view all indexes for a table or to view an index consisting of multiple fields, click the Indexes button on the Table Design toolbar.

Elsa wants to view the indexes for the Job table.

To view the indexes for the Job table:

1. Open the **Job** table in Design view.

2. Click the **Indexes** button 📇 on the Table Design toolbar. The Indexes window opens. See Figure 8-38.

Figure 8-38   INDEXES FOR THE JOB TABLE

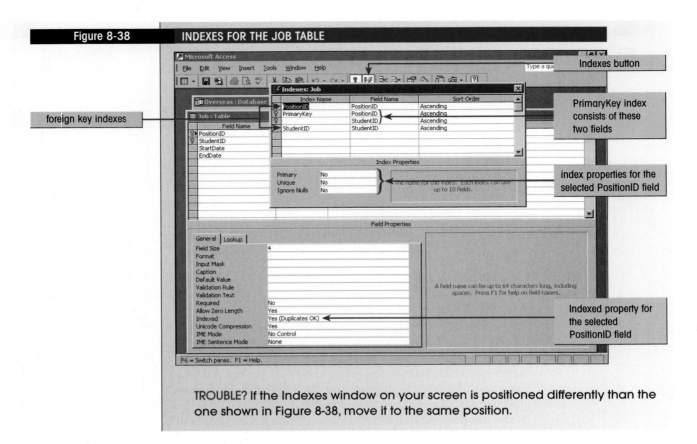

TROUBLE? If the Indexes window on your screen is positioned differently than the one shown in Figure 8-38, move it to the same position.

Because the PositionID field was selected when you opened the Indexes window, the properties in the Field Properties pane in the Table Design window pertain to this field. In particular, the Indexed property value of "Yes (Duplicates OK)" for the PositionID field specifies the use of an index that allows duplicate values. The properties in the Index Properties pane in the Indexes window apply to the highlighted PositionID index; these properties indicate that the PositionID index is not the primary key index, that values in this index do not need to be unique, and that all records (even those with null PositionID values) are included in the index.

Access automatically created the PositionID index when you specified the PositionID field as a foreign key in the Relationships window. Likewise, Access automatically created the StudentID index for the StudentID foreign key.

The third index, named PrimaryKey, consists of the table's composite key—the combination of the PositionID and StudentID fields. Because StudentID in the Indexes window's third row does not have an Index Name property value, both PositionID and StudentID comprise the PrimaryKey index. When Elsa created this table and specified the composite key, Access automatically created the PrimaryKey index.

Over the past few weeks, Elsa's staff has been monitoring the performance of the Overseas database by timing how long it takes to run queries. She wants her staff to let her know if the performance changes over the next few days after she creates an index for the StartDate field in the Job table.

Creating an Index

You can create an index for a single field in the Indexes window or by setting its Indexed property in Design view. For a multiple-field index, however, you must create the index in the Indexes window.

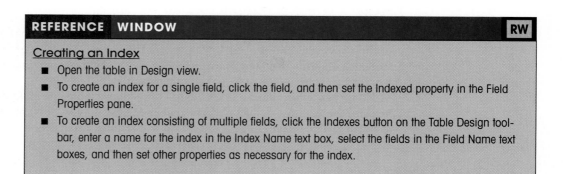

REFERENCE WINDOW **RW**

Creating an Index

- Open the table in Design view.
- To create an index for a single field, click the field, and then set the Indexed property in the Field Properties pane.
- To create an index consisting of multiple fields, click the Indexes button on the Table Design toolbar, enter a name for the index in the Index Name text box, select the fields in the Field Name text boxes, and then set other properties as necessary for the index.

Next, you'll create an index for the StartDate field in the Job table by setting the field's Indexed property.

To create an index for the StartDate field:

1. Click the Table window title bar to make it the active window.

2. Click the **StartDate Field Name** text box to make it the current field.

3. Click the right side of the **Indexed** property in the Field Properties pane, and then click **Yes (Duplicates OK)**. An index for the StartDate field is created with duplicate values allowed. Setting the Indexed property automatically created the StartDate index in the Indexes window. See Figure 8-39.

Figure 8-39	AFTER CREATING THE StartDate INDEX

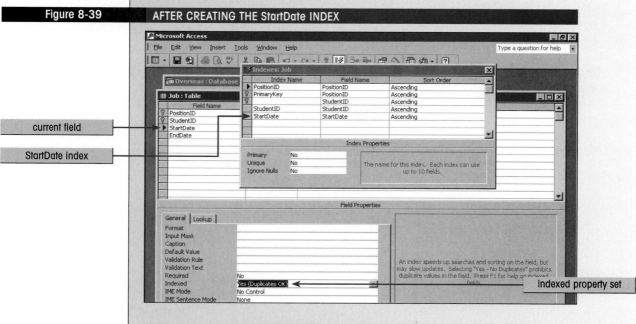

4. Click the **Close** button ☒ on the Indexes window title bar to close the Indexes window.

Now you'll save your changes to the table design and close the Table window.

5. Save your table design changes, and then close the table.

Elsa and her staff provide ongoing contact with all students placed in seasonal positions. However, Elsa has found that these students often feel more comfortable addressing some of their concerns and problems with one of their peers. Consequently, Elsa has chosen two students, Isadora Santiago and Carlo Bianchi, who are experienced and mature seasonal workers, to serve as contacts for the other students.

Elsa asks you to add a Contact field to the Student table, use an update query to place values into the Contact field, and then create a select query to provide the contact information as needed. The select query you'll create will require a special join using the Student table.

Joining Tables

The design of the Overseas database includes a relationship between the Student and Job tables using StudentID as the common field, which allows you to join the two tables to create a query based on data from both tables. The type of join you have used so far is an inner join. Two other types of joins are the left outer join and the right outer join.

An **inner join** is a join in which Access selects records from two tables only when the records have the same value in the common field that links the tables. For example, in a database containing a table of student information and a table of class information, an inner join would show all students that have a matching class record and all classes that have a matching student record. In the Overseas database, StudentID is the common field for the Student and Job tables. As shown in Figure 8-40, the results of a query based on an inner join of these two tables include only those records that have a matching StudentID value. The record in the Student table with StudentID CAS1942 is not included in the query results because it fails to match a record with the same StudentID value in the Job table. You ordinarily use an inner join whenever you perform a query based on more than one table; it is the default join you have used to this point. (The Job record with PositionID 2090 has been added to illustrate the difference in the various types of joins.)

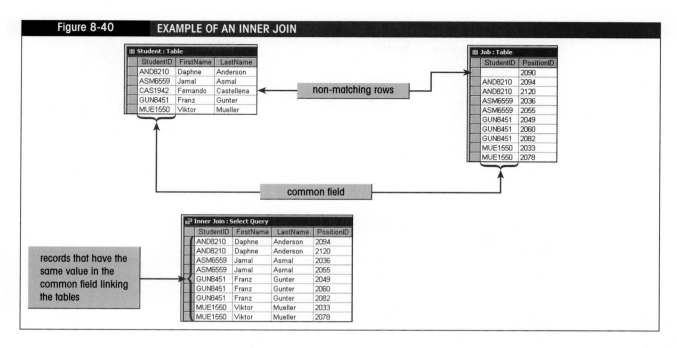

Figure 8-40   **EXAMPLE OF AN INNER JOIN**

A **left outer join** is a join in which Access selects all records from the first, or left, table and only those records from the second, or right, table that have matching common field values. For example, in a database containing a student table and a class table, a left outer join would show all students whether or not the students are enrolled in a class. In the Overseas database, you would use this kind of join if you wanted to see all records from the Student table and also all matching records from the Job table. Figure 8-41 shows a left outer join for the Student and Job tables. All records from the Student table, which is the left table, appear in the query results. Notice that the StudentID CAS1942 record appears even though it does not match a record in the Job table. The PositionID 2090 record in the Job table does not appear, however, because it does not match a record in the Student table.

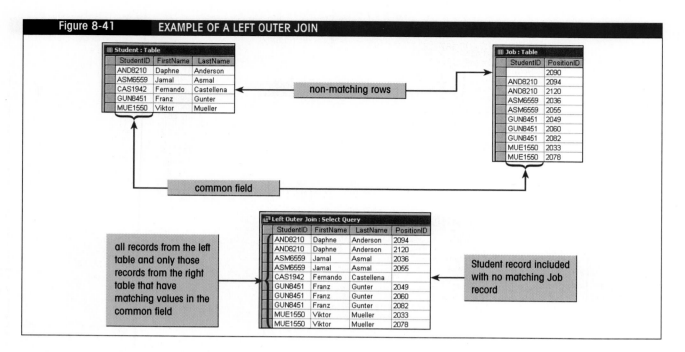

Figure 8-41   EXAMPLE OF A LEFT OUTER JOIN

A **right outer join** is a join in which Access selects all records from the second, or right, table and only those records from the first, or left, table that have matching common field values. For example, in a database containing a student table and a class table, a right outer join would show all classes whether or not there are any students enrolled in them. In the Overseas database, you would use this kind of join if you wanted to see all records from the Job table and all matching records from the Student table. Figure 8-42 shows a right outer join for the Student and Job tables. All records from the Job table, which is the right table, appear in the query results. The PositionID 2090 record appears even though it does not match a record in the Student table. The StudentID CAS1942 record in the Student table does not appear, however, because it does not match a record in the Job table.

Figure 8-42	EXAMPLE OF A RIGHT OUTER JOIN

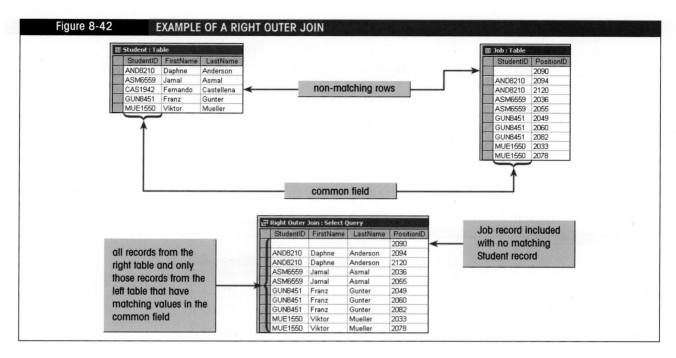

A table can also be joined with itself; this join is called a **self-join**. A self-join can be either an inner or outer join. For example, you would use this kind of join if you wanted to see records from the Student table together with information about each student's contact (either Isadora or Carlo). Figure 8-43 shows a self-join for the Student table. In this case, the self-join is an inner join because records appear in the query results only if the Contact field value matches a StudentID field value. To create this self-join, you would add two copies of the Student table to the Query window in Design view, and then link the Contact field of one Student table to the StudentID field of the other Student table.

Figure 8-43			EXAMPLE OF A SELF-JOIN	

In Figure 8-43, the query results show the record for each student in the Student table and the contact information for that student. The contact information also comes from the Student table through the Contact field.

To produce the information Elsa requested, indicating whether Isadora or Carlo is the contact for a student, you'll need to create a self-join. First, you'll add the Contact field to the Student table, and then create and run an update query to place values into the Contact field. When you add the Contact field, you'll set its properties similar to the StudentID field.

To add the Contact field and create and run an update query:

1. Open the **Student** table in Datasheet view, replace Student in the first record's FirstName field with your first name, and then replace Name in the first record's LastName field with your last name.

2. Switch to Design view, add to the end of the table a field named **Contact**, select the **Text** data type, set the Field Size to **7**, and then save and close the table.

3. Create a new query in Design view, adding the **Student** field list to the Query window.

   You'll need to add the StudentID, Nation, and Contact fields to the design grid. Elsa has assigned Carlo as the contact for all students from Australia, Germany, and Ireland, and Isadora as the contact for students from all other countries. To select the correct student records, you'll enter a selection criterion for the Nation field. You won't update Carlo and Isadora's Contact fields—neither is logically assigned to anyone—so you'll need to exclude their records from the update query by entering a selection criterion for the StudentID field. Finally, you'll be updating the Contact field.

4. Add the **StudentID**, **Nation**, and **Contact** fields to the design grid.

To exclude Carlo and Isadora's records, you'll use the Not logical operator and the In comparison operator with Carlo's StudentID field value of BIA9212 and Isadora's StudentID field value of SAN1983. First, you'll update Carlo's contacts by using the In comparison operator to select students from Australia, Germany, and Ireland.

5. Click the **StudentID Criteria** text box, type **Not In ("BIA9212","SAN1983")**, press the **Tab** key to advance to the Nation text box, and then type **In ("Australia","Germany","Ireland")**. You've completed the selection criteria needed to choose the records you'll be updating for Carlo's contacts. See Figure 8-44.

| Figure 8-44 | QUERY TO SELECT CARLO'S CONTACTS |

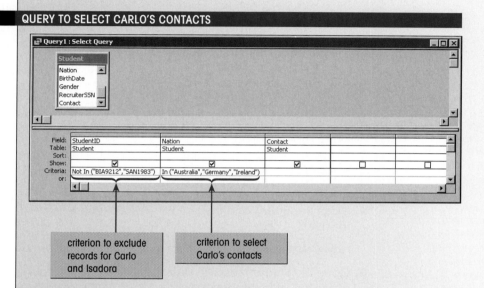

criterion to exclude records for Carlo and Isadora

criterion to select Carlo's contacts

TROUBLE? Your screen might show only part of the criteria in the StudentID and Nation Criteria text boxes.

6. Run the query to verify that the 15 records with Australia, Germany, and Ireland in the Nation field are selected, and then switch to Design view.

Next, you'll change the query to an update query, add Carlo's StudentID field value as the Contact Update To value, and then run the update query.

7. Click the list arrow for the **Query Type** button ⊞ on the Query Design toolbar, and then click **Update Query**.

8. Type **"BIA9212"** in the Contact Update To text box, run the query, and then click the **Yes** button to confirm that you want to update 15 rows in the Student table.

Now you need to update the Contact field values for Isadora's contacts. To do so, you'll add the Not logical operator to the beginning of the Nation Criteria text box, and change the Contact Update To value to Isadora's StudentID field value.

9. Click the **Nation Criteria** text box, press the **Home** key to position the insertion point at the beginning of the expression, type **Not (**, press the **End** key to position the insertion at the end of the expression, and then type **)** (a closing parenthesis).

10. Double-click **BIA9212** in the Contact Update To text box to select it, and then type **SAN1983**.

You've completed the selection and update changes needed to update Isadora's contacts. See Figure 8-45.

Figure 8-45

QUERY TO UPDATE ISADORA'S CONTACTS

Field:	StudentID	Nation	Contact		
Table:	Student	Student	Student		
Update To:			"SAN1983"		
Criteria:	Not In ("BIA9212","SAN1983")	Not (In ("Australia","Germany","Ireland"))			
or:					

criterion to select
Isadora's contacts

Isadora's StudentID
field value

Now you can run the query to update the remaining records in the Student table and to add Isadora's StudentID as the Contact field value.

To run the update query and update the Contact field values:

1. Run the query, and then click the **Yes** button to confirm that you want to update 17 rows in the Student table.

   You are finished updating the Contact field in the Student table, so you can close the Query window. Because all the records have been updated, you do not need to save the query.

2. Close the query, and then click the **No** button when Access asks if you want to save it.

   Now you'll open the Student table to verify the updates.

3. Open the **Student** table in Datasheet view. The Contact field values are now equal to Carlo's StudentID field value of BIA9212 (for students from Australia, Germany, and Ireland) or Isadora's field value of SAN1983 (for students from all other countries). The Contact field values for Carlo's and Isadora's records are null. See Figure 8-46.

Figure 8-46

AFTER UPDATING THE CONTACT FIELD VALUES IN THE STUDENT TABLE

Carlo's Contact field
value is null

updated Contact
field values

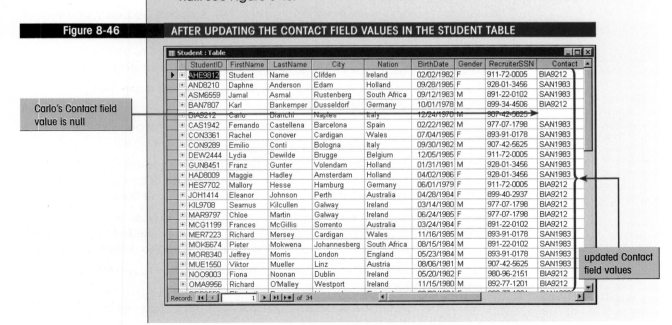

	StudentID	FirstName	LastName	City	Nation	BirthDate	Gender	RecruiterSSN	Contact
+▶	AHE9812	Student	Name	Clifden	Ireland	02/02/1982	F	911-72-0005	BIA9212
+	AND8210	Daphne	Anderson	Edam	Holland	09/28/1985	F	928-01-3456	SAN1983
+	ASM6559	Jamal	Asmal	Rustenberg	South Africa	09/12/1983	M	891-22-0102	SAN1983
+	BAN7807	Karl	Bankemper	Dusseldorf	Germany	10/01/1978	M	899-34-4506	BIA9212
+	BIA9212	Carlo	Bianchi	Naples	Italy	12/24/1978	M	907-42-5625	
+	CAS1942	Fernando	Castellena	Barcelona	Spain	02/22/1982	M	977-07-1798	SAN1983
+	CON3361	Rachel	Conover	Cardigan	Wales	07/04/1985	F	893-91-0178	SAN1983
+	CON9289	Emilio	Conti	Bologna	Italy	09/30/1982	M	907-42-5625	SAN1983
+	DEW2444	Lydia	Dewilde	Brugge	Belgium	12/05/1985	F	911-72-0005	SAN1983
+	GUN8451	Franz	Gunter	Volendam	Holland	01/31/1981	M	928-01-3456	SAN1983
+	HAD8009	Maggie	Hadley	Amsterdam	Holland	04/02/1986	F	928-01-3456	SAN1983
+	HES7702	Mallory	Hesse	Hamburg	Germany	06/01/1979	F	911-72-0005	BIA9212
+	JOH1414	Eleanor	Johnson	Perth	Australia	04/28/1984	F	899-40-2937	BIA9212
+	KIL9708	Seamus	Kilcullen	Galway	Ireland	03/14/1980	M	977-07-1798	BIA9212
+	MAR9797	Chloe	Martin	Galway	Ireland	06/24/1985	F	977-07-1798	BIA9212
+	MCG1199	Frances	McGillis	Sorrento	Australia	03/24/1984	F	891-22-0102	BIA9212
+	MER7223	Richard	Mersey	Cardigan	Wales	11/16/1985	M	893-91-0178	SAN1983
+	MOK6674	Pieter	Mokwena	Johannesberg	South Africa	08/15/1984	M	891-22-0102	SAN1983
+	MOR8340	Jeffrey	Morris	London	England	05/23/1984	M	893-91-0178	SAN1983
+	MUE1550	Viktor	Mueller	Linz	Austria	08/06/1981	M	907-42-5625	SAN1983
+	NOO9003	Fiona	Noonan	Dublin	Ireland	05/20/1982	F	980-96-2151	BIA9212
+	OMA9956	Richard	O'Malley	Westport	Ireland	11/15/1980	M	892-77-1201	BIA9212

Student : Table

Record: 1 of 34

4. Scroll down the table to verify all Contact field values and Isadora's null Contact field value, and then close the table.

The Contact field values in the Student table are the StudentID values for Carlo and Isadora. To produce the contact information in the format that Elsa requested—with the contact's first and last names—you need to create a self-join.

Creating a Self-Join

You need to create a query to display the new contact information in the Student table. This query requires a self-join. To create the self-join, you need to add two copies of the Student field list to the Query window, and then add a join line from the StudentID field in one field list to the Contact field in the other. The Contact field is a foreign key that matches the primary key field StudentID. You can then create a query that can display Student information from one table and Contact information from the other table.

REFERENCE   WINDOW   **RW**

Creating a Self-Join

- In the Database window, click Queries in the Objects bar to display the Queries list, and then click the New button.
- Click Design View and then click the OK button.
- Double-click the table for the self-join, and then double-click the table a second time. Click the Close button.
- Click and drag a primary key field from one field list to the foreign key field in the other field list.
- Right-click the join line between the two tables, and then click Join Properties to open the Join Properties dialog box.
- Click the first option button to select an inner join, click the second option button to select a left outer join, or click the third option button to select a right outer join, and then click the OK button.
- Select the fields, specify the selection criteria, select the sort options, and set other properties as appropriate for the query.

Now you'll create the self-join query to display the student contact information.

To create the self-join query:

1. Click **Queries** in the Objects bar of the Database window, click the **New** button to open the New Query dialog box, make sure that **Design View** is selected, and then click the **OK** button.

2. Double-click **Student** to add the Student field list to the Query window.

3. Double-click **Student** again to add a second copy of the Student field list, and then click the **Close** button. Access identifies the left field list as Student and the right field list as Student_1 to distinguish the two copies of the table.

You will now create a join between the two copies of the Student table by linking the StudentID field in the Student field list to the Contact field in the Student_1 field list. The Contact field is a foreign key that matches the primary key field StudentID.

4. Scroll the Student_1 field list until the Contact field is visible, and then click and drag the StudentID field from the Student field list to the Contact field in the Student_1 field list. Access adds a join line between the two fields. You can verify that this is an inner join query by opening the Join Properties dialog box.

5. Right-click the **join line** between the two tables, and then click **Join Properties** to open the Join Properties dialog box. See Figure 8-47.

Figure 8-47   **JOIN PROPERTIES DIALOG BOX**

TROUBLE? If right-clicking the join line does not work, click View on the menu bar, and then click Join Properties to open the Join Properties dialog box.

The first option button is selected, indicating that this is an inner join. You would click the second option button for a left outer join or the third option button for a right outer join. Because the inner join is correct, you can cancel the dialog box and then add the necessary fields to the design grid.

6. Click the **Cancel** button and then, scrolling as necessary, double-click the following fields (in order) from the Student_1 field list: **StudentID**, **FirstName**, **LastName**, and **Nation**.

7. Double-click the following fields (in order) from the Student field list: **FirstName** and **LastName**.

8. Run the query, and then maximize the Query window. Access displays the recordset in increasing StudentID order with six fields and 32 records. See Figure 8-48.

Figure 8-48	INITIAL SELF-JOIN ON THE STUDENT TABLE

fields from the
Student_1 table

your name will appear
instead of
"Student Name"

fields from the
Student table

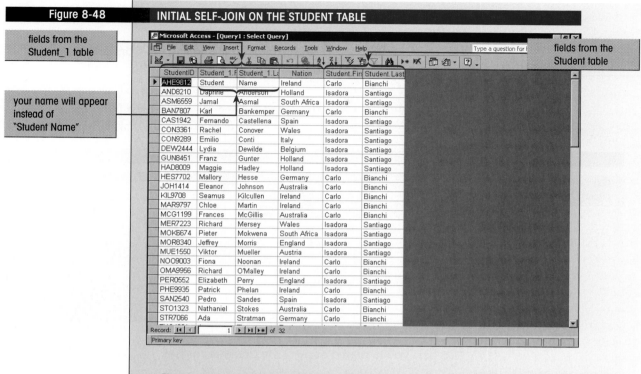

The query results display all students and their contacts. The query results do not display the Student records for Carlo and Isadora because their records contain null Contact field values. Remember that an inner join doesn't display records from the second (right) table unless it contains a matching value in the common field. In the Student_1 table, the Contact field values for Carlo and Isadora are null, so the inner join doesn't select their records in the Student table.

TROUBLE? If your query results do not match Figure 8-48, click the View button for Design view to return to Design view, and review the preceding steps to make any necessary corrections to your query design. Then run the query again.

Access displays 32 of the 34 records from the Student table. The records for Carlo and Isadora have a null Contact field value and, therefore, are not displayed. Four field names in the query results now have prefixes indicating either Student or Student_1 to distinguish fields in one table from fields in the other table. For example, the full name of the FirstName field from the Student_1 table is displayed as Student_1.FirstName, which means the FirstName field from the Student_1 (right) table.

Elsa asks you to rename some of the fields so that the query results will be easier to read. After you rename the necessary fields, the field names in the query results will be, from left to right, StudentID, FirstName, LastName, Nation, ContactFirstName, and ContactLastName.

To rename the necessary fields:

1. Switch to Design view.

2. Right-click the second column's Field text box, click **Properties** on the shortcut menu to open the property sheet, click the **General** tab (if necessary), and then set the Caption property to **FirstName**.

3. Click the third column's Field text box, and then set the Caption property to **LastName**.

4. Repeat Step 3 for the fifth and sixth columns, setting the Caption property to **ContactFirstName** and **ContactLastName**, respectively.

5. Close the property sheet, run the query, resize all columns to their best fit, and then click **StudentID AHE9812** to deselect all columns. The query recordset displays the new names for the second, third, fifth, and sixth columns. See Figure 8-49.

| Figure 8-49 | FINAL SELF-JOIN ON THE STUDENT TABLE |

Caption property displays new names

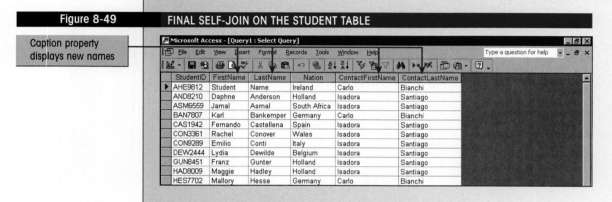

Elsa asks you to print a copy of the query recordset.

6. Save the query as **Student Contacts**, print the query recordset, close the query, and then exit Access.

The new queries that you created and the other work you completed will make it much easier for Elsa and her staff to enter, retrieve, and view information in the Overseas database.

Session 8.3 QUICK CHECK

1. What are the three types of relationships you can define between tables?

2. What is an entity subtype?

3. What is an index?

4. What is the difference between an inner join and an outer join?

5. What is a self-join?

6. Figure 8-50 lists the field names from two tables: Department and Employee.

Figure 8-50

Department	Employee
DepartmentID	EmployeeSSN
DepartmentName	EmployeeName
PhoneNumber	DepartmentID
	Salary
	SupervisorSSN

a. What is the primary key for each table?

b. What type of relationship exists between the two tables?

c. Is an inner join possible between the two tables? If so, give one example of an inner join.

d. Is either type of outer join possible between the two tables? If so, give one example of an outer join.

e. Is a self-join possible for one of the tables? If so, give one example of a self-join.

REVIEW ASSIGNMENTS

The **Work** database contains information about NSJI's recruiters and overseas students. The **Recruiter** table in the database contains records of the recruiters employed by NSJI to find students for seasonal work and to match them with the employers that are NSJI's clients. The **Student** table contains student information. The **Country** table contains records of the nations from which NSJI recruits students. Finally, the **Territory** table contains records indicating which recruiters cover which nations for NSJI. The database contains several other objects, including queries, forms, and reports. Elsa wants you to define a many-to-many relationship between the **Recruiter** and **Country** tables, and to create some new queries for her. To help with these requests, you'll complete the following steps.

1. Make sure your Data Disk is in the appropriate disk drive, start Access, and then open the **Work** database in the Review folder on your Data Disk.

2. Open the **Student** table datasheet, and modify the first record by changing the FirstName, LastName, BirthDate, and Gender field values to your name, birth date, and gender. Close the table.

Explore

3. Define a many-to-many relationship between the **Recruiter** and **Country** tables, using the **Territory** table as the related table. Select the referential integrity option and both cascade options for the relationships. Print the Relationships window without saving the created report. (*Hint*: Select the Print Relationships option on the File menu.) Save your changes to the Relationships window and then close it.

4. Create a crosstab query based on the **Student** table. Use the Nation field values for the row headings, the Gender field values for the column headings, and the count of the StudentID field as the summarized value. Save the query as **Student Crosstab**, resize the columns in the query recordset to their best fit, print the query results, and then save and close the query.

5. Create a find duplicates query based on the **Student** table. Select City and Nation as the fields that might contain duplicates, and select the FirstName and Last Name fields

as additional fields in the query results. Save the query as **Find Duplicate Student Locations**, view and print the query recordset, and then close the query.

6. Create a find unmatched query that finds all records in the **Recruiter** table for which there is no matching record in the **Student** table. Include all fields from the **Recruiter** table in the query results. Save the query as **Recruiters Without Matching Students**, run the query, print the query recordset, and then close the query.

7. Create a make-table query based on the **Recruiter** and **Territory** tables, selecting all fields from the **Recruiter** table and the Nation field from the **Territory** table. Use **Recruiter Territory** as the new table name, and store the table in the current database. Run the query, save the make-table query as **Recruiter Territory Make-Table**, and then close the query. Open the **Recruiter Territory** table, print the table records, and then close the table.

8. Create an update query to select all records in the **Recruiter Territory** table where the Nation field value is Ireland. Update the Nation field value to France, run the query, save the query as **Recruiter Territory Update**, and then close the query. Open the **Recruiter Territory** table, print the table records, and then close the table.

9. Create an append query based on the **Recruiter** and **Territory** tables, selecting all fields from the **Recruiter** table and the Nation field from the **Territory** table, selecting all records where the Nation field value is Ireland, and appending the selected records to the **Recruiter Territory** table. After you run the query, save it as **Recruiter Territory Append**, and then close the query. Open the **Recruiter Territory** table, print the table records, and then close the table.

10. Create a delete query that deletes all records from the **Recruiter Territory** table where the BonusQuota field value is 40 or 50. Run the query, save it as **Recruiter Territory Delete**, and then close the query. Open the **Recruiter Territory** table, and then print the table records.

11. Apply an advanced filter to the **Recruiter Territory** table, selecting records with a BonusQuota field value of 45 and a Salary field value greater than $32,000, and sorting in decreasing Salary order. Print the filter results, and then close the table without saving your table design changes.

Explore 12. Create an outer join query between the **Country** and **Student** tables, selecting all records from the **Country** table and any matching records from the **Student** table. Display the Nation field from the **Country** table, and the FirstName, LastName, and City fields from the **Student** table in the query results. Save the query as **Country and Student Outer Join**, run the query, print the query recordset, and then close the query.

Explore 13. Open the **Recruiter** table in Design view, delete the LastName index, and then save and close the table.

14. Close the **Work** database, and then exit Access.

CASE PROBLEMS

Case 1. Lim's Video Photography Youngho Lim owns a videography business, Lim's Video Photography. Located in San Francisco, California, the company specializes in digital video photography and offers customers the option of storing edited videos on CD or DVD. His video shoots include weddings and other special events, as well as recording personal and commercial inventories for insurance purposes. Youngho has created an

Access database named **Shoots** to store data about his clients and the work he does for them. The **Client** table contains client data, the **ShootDesc** table contains descriptions of the different categories of work Youngho does, the **Contract** table contains data about his client contracts, the **Shoot** table contains data about his contracted shooting assignments, the **Billing** table contains client invoice data, the **Case** table contains data about his CD/DVD storage units, and the **CD Storage** table contains data about each CD/DVD stored in his cases for his clients' shoots. The database contains several other objects including queries, forms, and reports. Youngho asks you to define a many-to-many relationship between the **Case** and **Shoot** tables and a one-to-one relationship between the **Contract** and **Billing** tables, and to create some new queries for him. To help Youngho with his requests, you'll complete the following steps.

1. Make sure your Data Disk is in the appropriate disk drive, start Access, and then open the **Shoots** database in the Cases folder on your Data Disk.

2. Modify the first record in the **Client** table datasheet by changing the ClientName field value to your name in the format: last name, comma, space, first name. Close the table.

3. Define a many-to-many relationship between the **Case** and **Shoot** tables, using the **CD Storage** table as the related table. Select the referential integrity option and both cascade options for the relationships.

Explore   4. Define a one-to-one relationship between the primary **Contract** table and the related **Billing** table. Select the referential integrity option and both cascade options for the relationship. Print the Relationships window without saving the created report. (*Hint*: Select the Print Relationships option on the File menu.) Save your changes to the Relationships window and then close it.

5. Create a find duplicates query based on the **Shoot** table. Select Contract# as the field that might contain duplicates, and select all other fields in the table as additional fields in the query results. Save the query as **Find Multiple Shoots per Contract**, view and print the query recordset, and then close the query.

6. Create a find unmatched query that finds all records in the **Client** table for which there is no matching record in the **Contract** table. Select all fields from the **Client** table in the query results. Save the query as **Clients Without Matching Contracts**, run the query, print the query recordset, and then close the query.

Explore   7. Open the **Clients and Their Contracts** query, and then use the Top Values property to select the top 60% of records. Save the query as **Top Contracts**, run the query, print the query recordset, and then close the query.

8. Create an update query to select all records in the **CD Storage** table where the Case# field value is 1. Update the Case# field value to 5, run the query, save the query as **CD Storage Update**, and then close the query. Open the **CD Storage** table, print the table records, and then close the table.

9. Apply an advanced filter to the **Shoot** table, selecting records with a ShootType field value of BP or WE and a Duration field value greater than 3.5, and sorting in increasing Duration order. Print the filter results, and then close the table without saving your table design changes.

10. Add an index named Shoot# to the **CD Storage** table using the default property settings, and then save and close the table. (*Hint*: Only the primary key field is unique.)

Explore   11. Create an outer join query between the **ShootDesc** and **Shoot** tables, selecting all records from the **ShootDesc** table and any matching records from the **Shoot** table. Display both fields from the **ShootDesc** table, and the ShootDate, Duration, and Contract# fields from the **Shoot** table in the query results. Save the query as

ShootDesc and **Shoot Outer Join**, run the query, print the query recordset, and then close the query.

12. Close the **Shoots** database, and then exit Access.

Case 2. DineAtHome.course.com DineAtHome.course.com in Naples, Florida, is an online service that lets people order meals from one or more area restaurants for home delivery. Participating restaurants offer everything from simple fare to gourmet feasts. Claire Picard, the founder and owner, and her staff perform a variety of services, from simply picking up and delivering meals to providing linens and table service for more formal occasions. Claire created the **AtHome** database to maintain information about participating restaurants and the orders placed by customers. The **Credit Card** table contains data about customers' credit cards, the **Customer** table contains customer name and phone data, the **Order** table contains data about the restaurant orders placed by customers, and the **Restaurant** table contains data about each restaurant. The database contains several other objects, including queries, forms, and reports. Claire wants you to define a many-to-many relationship between the **Restaurant** and **Customer** tables, to create a one-to-one relationship between the **Customer** and **Credit Card** tables, and to create several new queries. To do so, you'll complete the following steps.

1. Make sure your Data Disk is in the appropriate disk drive, start Access, and then open the **AtHome** database in the Cases folder on your Data Disk.

2. Modify the first record in the **Restaurant** table datasheet by changing the OwnerFirstName and OwnerLastName field values to your first and last names, respectively. Close the table.

3. Define a many-to-many relationship between the **Restaurant** and **Customer** tables, using the **Order** table as the related table. Select the referential integrity option and both cascade options for the relationship.

Explore

4. Define a one-to-one relationship between the primary **Customer** table and the related **Credit Card** table. Select the referential integrity option and both cascade options for the relationship. Print the Relationships window without saving the created report. (*Hint*: Select the Print Relationships option on the File menu.) Save your changes to the Relationships window and then close it.

5. Create a crosstab query based on the **Restaurant Orders** query. Use the OrderDate field values for the row headings, the City field values for the column headings, and the sum of the BillTotal field as the summarized value. Save the query as **Orders Crosstab**, resize the columns in the query recordset to their best fit, print the query results, and then save and close the query.

6. Create a find unmatched query that finds all records in the **Customer** table for which there is no matching record in the **Credit Card** table. Select all fields from the **Customer** table in the query results. Save the query as **Customers Without Matching Credit Cards**, run the query, print the query recordset, and then close the query.

7. Create a new query based on the **Order** table. Include all fields from the **Order** table in the recordset, sort in descending OrderAmt order, and then use the Top Values property to select the top 25% of records. Save the query as **Top Orders**, run the query, print the query recordset, and then close the query.

8. Create an update query to select all records in the **Order** table where the CustomerID field value is 11. Update the CustomerID field value to 12, run the query, save the query as **Order Update**, and then close the query. Open the **Order** table, print the table records, and then close the table.

9. Apply an advanced filter to the **Order** table, selecting records with a OrderDate field value earlier than 3/16/2003 and an OrderAmt field value greater than $95, and sorting in increasing OrderAmt order. Print the filter results, and then save and close the table.

10. Add an index named OrderDate to the **Order** table, using the default property settings, and then save and close the table. (*Hint*: Only the primary key field is unique.)

Explore ▶ 11. Open the **Restaurant** table in Design view, delete the PostalCode index, and then save and close the table.

Explore ▶ 12. Create an outer join query between the **Customer** and **Credit Card** tables, selecting all records from the **Customer** table and any matching records from the **Credit Card** table. Display all fields from the **Customer** table, and the Card# and ExpDate fields from the **Credit Card** table in the query results. Save the query as **Customer and Credit Card Outer Join**, run the query, print the query recordset, and then close the query.

13. Close the **AtHome** database, and then exit Access.

Case 3. Redwood Zoo   The Redwood Zoo is a small zoo located in the picturesque city of Gig Harbor, Washington, on the shores of Puget Sound. The Redwood Zoo has some of the best exhibits of marine animals in the United States. Its newly constructed polar bear habitat is a particular favorite among patrons. The zoo relies heavily on donations to fund permanent exhibits and temporary displays, especially those involving exotic animals. Michael Rosenfeld, the director of fund-raising activities, created the **ZooFunds** database to manage information about donors, their pledges, and the status of funds. The **Donor** table contains data about people who donate money to the zoo, the **Fund** table contains data about the zoo's funding categories and their target donation amounts, the **Invitation** table contains data about the donors invited to the zoo's receptions, the **Pledge** table contains data about each donor's pledges, and the **Reception** table contains data about the zoo's scheduled fund-raising activities. The database contains several other objects, including queries, forms, and reports. Michael wants you to define a many-to-many relationship between the **Reception** and **Donor** tables, and to create several new queries. To do so, you'll complete the following steps.

1. Make sure your Data Disk is in the appropriate disk drive, start Access, and then open the **ZooFunds** database in the Cases folder on your Data Disk.

2. Modify the first record in the **Donor** table datasheet by changing the Title, FirstName, MI, and LastName field values to your title and name. Close the table.

Explore ▶ 3. Define a many-to-many relationship between the **Reception** and **Donor** tables, using the **Invitation** table as the related table. Select the referential integrity option and both cascade options for the relationships. Print the Relationships window without saving the created report. (*Hint*: Select the Print Relationships option on the File menu.) Save your changes to the Relationships window and then close it.

4. Create a crosstab query based on the **Pledge** table. Use the FundCode field values for the row headings, the PaymentMethod field values for the column headings, and the sum of the TotalPledged field as the summarized value. Save the query as **Pledge Crosstab**, resize the columns in the query recordset to their best fit, print the query results, and then save and close the query.

5. Create a find duplicates query based on the **Donor** table. Select LastName as the field that might contain duplicates, and select the remaining fields in the table as additional fields in the query results. Save the query as **Find Duplicate Donors**, view and print the query recordset, and then close the query.

6. Create a find unmatched query that finds all records in the **Fund** table for which there is no matching record in the **Pledge** table. Select all fields from the **Fund** table in the query results. Save the query as **Funds Without Matching Pledges**, run the query, print the query recordset, and then close the query.

Explore

7. Open the **Donor Pledges** query in Design view and sort the query results in descending order by the TotalPledged field. Use the Top Values property to select the top 15 records. Save the query as **Top Pledges**, run the query, print the query recordset, and then close the query.

8. Create a make-table query based on the **Donor, Invitation,** and **Reception** tables, selecting all fields from the **Donor** table, the Accept field from the **Invitation** table, and the Reception# and DateHeld fields from the **Reception** table. Select those records with a Reception# field value of 51. Use **Reception 51** as the new table name, and store it in the current database. Run the query, save the make-table query as **Reception 51 Make-Table**, and then close the query. Open the **Reception 51** table in Design view, set the Accept field's Format property to Yes/No, save the table changes, switch to Datasheet view, resize all columns to their best fit, print the table records, and then save and close the table.

9. Create a delete query that deletes all records from the **Reception 51** table where the Accept field value is No. Run the query, save it as **Reception 51 Delete**, and then close the query. Open the **Reception 51** table, print the table records, and then close the table.

10. Create an append query based on the **Donor, Invitation,** and **Reception** tables, selecting all fields from the **Donor** table, the Accept field from the **Invitation** table, and the Reception# and DateHeld fields from the **Reception** table. Select those records with a Reception# field value of 52 and an Accept field value of Yes, and append the selected records to the **Reception 51** table. After you run the query, save it as **Reception 52 Append**, and then close the query. Open the **Reception 51** table, print the table records, and then close the table.

11. Apply an advanced filter to the **Pledge** table, selecting records with a TotalPledged field value greater than or equal to 500 and a PaymentMethod field value equal to E, and sorting in increasing PledgeDate order. Print the filter results, and then save and close the table.

12. Add an index named LastName to the **Reception 51** table, using the default property settings, and then save and close the table. (*Hint*: Only the primary key field is unique.)

13. Close the **ZooFunds** database, and then exit Access.

Case 4. Mountain River Adventures   Connor and Siobhan Dempsey own Mountain River Adventures center, which offers clients their choice of outdoor activities, including whitewater rafting, canoeing, hiking, camping, fishing, and rock climbing. To keep track of their clients and bookings, they created the **Rivers** database. The **Booking** table contains data about client rafting trips, the **Client** table contains data about clients, the **Guide** table contains data about the raft guides employed by Mountain River Adventures, the **Rafting Trip** table contains data about the available river rafting excursions, and the **Works** table contains data about the guides assigned to each client trip. The database contains several other objects, including queries, forms, and reports. The Dempseys want you to define a many-to-many relationship between the **Booking** and **Guide** tables, and to create several new queries. To do so, you'll complete the following steps.

1. Make sure your Data Disk is in the appropriate disk drive, start Access, and then open the **Rivers** database in the Cases folder on your Data Disk.

2. Modify the first record in the **Client** table datasheet by changing the ClientName field value to your name in the format: last name, comma, space, first name. Close the table.

Explore

3. Define a many-to-many relationship between the **Booking** and **Guide** tables, using the **Works** table as the related table. Select the referential integrity option and both cascade options for the relationships. Print the Relationships window without saving the created

report. (*Hint*: Select the Print Relationships option on the File menu.) Save your changes to the Relationships window and then close it.

4. Create a crosstab query based on the **Booked Rafting Trips** query. Use the TripDays field values for the row headings, the People field values for the column headings, and the sum of the TripFee field as the summarized value. Save the query as **Trips Crosstab**, resize the columns in the query recordset to their best fit, print the query results, and then save and close the query.

5. Create a find unmatched query that finds all records in the **Client** table for which there is no matching record in the **Booking** table. Include the ClientName, City, and State/Prov fields from the **Client** table in the query results. Save the query as **Clients Without Matching Bookings**, run the query, print the query recordset, and then close the query.

6. Open the **Costs** query in Design view, and use the Top Values property to select the top 40% of the records. Save the query as **Top Bookings**, run the query, resize all columns to their best fit, print the query recordset, and then save and close the query.

7. Create a make-table query based on the **Client** and **Booking** tables, selecting the ClientName and State/Prov fields from the **Client** table and the TripDate, Trip#, and People fields from the **Booking** table. Select those records with a State/Prov field value of NE. Save the table as **Client Trips** in the current database. Run the query, save the make-table query as **Client Trips Make-Table**, and then close the query. Open the **Client Trips** table, resize all column to their best fit, print the table records, and then save and close the table.

8. Create an append query based on the **Client** and **Booking** tables, selecting the ClientName and State/Prov fields from the **Client** table and the TripDate, Trip#, and People fields from the **Booking** table. Select those records with a State/Prov field value of UT or WY, and append the selected records to the **Client Trips** table. After you run the query, save it as **Client Trips Append**, and then close the query. Open the **Client Trips** table, print the table records, and then close the table.

9. Create a delete query that deletes all records from the **Client Trips** table where the People field value is less than 5. Run the query, save it as **Client Trips Delete**, and then close the query. Open the **Client Trips** table, and then print the table records.

10. Add an index named State/Prov to the **Client Trips** table, using the default property settings, and then save and close the table. (*Hint*: Only the primary key field is unique.)

Explore 11. Create a self-join query based on the **Guide** table with GuideID as the primary key and LeadGuide as the foreign key. Select the GuideID, FirstName, and LastName fields from the related table (the table that has LeadGuide connected to the join line), and the GuideID, FirstName, and LastName fields from the primary table. Set each field's Caption property to GuideID, FirstName, LastName, LeadGuide, LeadGuideFirst, and LeadGuideLast, respectively. Save the query as **Guide Self-Join**, run the query, resize all columns to their best fit, print the query recordset, and then save and close the query.

12. Close the **Rivers** database, and then exit Access.

Explore *Case 5. eACH Internet Auction Site*   Chris and Pat Aquino own a successful ISP (Internet service provider) and want to expand their business to host an Internet auction site named eACH. Before people can sell items and bid on items, they must register with eACH. After a seller posts an item for sale, it is sold at the auction site by accepting bids from buyers. Each item is listed by subcategory within category—for example, the general category of collectibles consists of several subcategories, including advertising, animation characters, comic books, and bears.

To keep track of these auctions, Chris and Pat have developed the **BuySell** database. The database has four tables: **Category**, **Subcategory**, **Registrant**, and **Item**. The **Category** table contains information about categories, and the **Subcategory** table contains information about subcategories. The **Registrant** table has one record for each person who sells and/or bids on items, and the **Item** table has one record for each item that is posted for sale. The database contains several other objects including queries, forms, and reports.

Chris and Pat want you to add a new table named **Bid** to the database to keep track of the bids placed by people on the items for sale. Also, they want you to define a many-to-many relationship between the **Item** and **Registrant** tables and to create several new queries. To help them with their requests, you'll complete the following steps.

1. Make sure your Data Disk is in the appropriate drive, start Access, and then open the **BuySell** database in the Cases folder on your Data Disk.

2. Create the new **Bid** table by defining the following fields:

   ■ Bid#, an AutoNumber field, is the primary key field.
   ■ Item#, a Number (Long Integer field size) field, is a foreign key to the **Item** table. This field stores the item on which the bidder is placing a bid.
   ■ Bidder, a Number (Long Integer field size) field, is a foreign key to the **Registrant** table. This field stores the registrant who's making the bid.
   ■ BidTime, a Date/Time (General Date format) field, stores the exact date and time the bid is made.
   ■ Bid, a Currency (Currency format with 2 decimal places), stores the amount of the bid.

3. Define a many-to-many relationship between the **Item** and **Registrant** tables, using the **Bid** table as the related table. Select the referential integrity option and both cascade options for the relationships. Print the Relationships window without saving the created report. (*Hint*: Select the Print Relationships option on the File menu.) Save your changes to the Relationships window and then close it.

4. If the Bid# field was deleted from the **Bid** table, what would be the primary key of the **Bid** table? (*Hint*: A registrant can bid on many items, and an item can have many registrants as bidders. However, it's possible for a registrant to place two or more bids on a single item.)

5. In Design view, add an index named LastName to the **Registrant** table, using the default property settings, and then save the table. (*Hint*: Only the primary key field is unique.)

6. Delete the UserID index from the **Registrant** table, and then save and close the table.

7. Design test data for the **Bid** table, and then add the test data to the table. (*Hint*: Be sure you have at least one item without any bids, at least one item with a single bid, and at least three items with two or more bids. Also, be sure you have at least one registrant who's not placed a bid and not posted an item for sale, at least one registrant who's only a seller, at least one registrant who's only a bidder, at least one registrant who's placed bids on two or more items, and at least one registrant who's place multiple bids on a single item.)

8. Create a crosstab query based on the **Bid** table. Use the Item# field values for the row headings, the Bidder field values for the column headings, and the maximum of the Bid field as the summarized value. Save the query as **Bid Crosstab**, resize the columns in the recordset to their best fit, print the recordset in landscape orientation, and then save and close the query.

9. Create a find duplicates query based on the **Bid** table. Select the Item# and Bidder fields as the fields that might contain duplicates, and select all other fields as additional fields in the recordset. Save the query as **Find Duplicate Bids**, print the recordset, and then close the query.

10. Create a find unmatched query that finds all records in the **Item** table for which there is no matching record in the **Bid** table. Include the Item#, Seller, Subcategory#, Title, MinimumBid, and Opened fields in the recordset. Save the query as **Item Without Matching Bid**, print the recordset, and then close the query.

11. Create a make-table query based on the **Subcategory** table, saving the new table as **Special Subcategory** in the current database. Select all fields in the **Subcategory** table, and select those records with a Category field value of 2. Run the query, save the make-table query as **Category 2 Make-Table**, and then close the query. Open the **Special Subcategory** table, resize the columns to their best fit, print the table records, and then save and close the table.

12. Create an append query to select all records from the **Subcategory** table where the Category field value is either 4 or 6 and append them to the **Special Subcategory** table. After you run the query, save the append query as **Category 4 or 6 Append**, and then close the query. Open the **Special Subcategory** table, print the table records, and then close the table.

13. Close the **BuySell** database, and then exit Access.

INTERNET ASSIGNMENTS

Student Union

The purpose of the Internet Assignments is to challenge you to find information on the Internet that you can use to create effective documents. The actual assignments are updated and maintained on the Course Technology Web site. Log on to the Internet and use your Web browser to go to the Student Online Companion to accompany this text at **www.course.com/NewPerspectives/studentunion**. Click the Online Companions link, and then click the link for this text.

QUICK CHECK ANSWERS

Session 8.1

1. A crosstab query performs aggregate function calculations on the values of one database field and displays the results in a spreadsheet format.

2. Simple Query Wizard, Crosstab Query Wizard, Find Duplicates Query Wizard, Find Unmatched Query Wizard

3. A find duplicates query is a select query that locates duplicate records in a table or query based on the values in one or more fields.

4. A find unmatched query is a select query that finds all records in a table or query that have no related records in a second table or query.

5. Setting a query's Top Values property lets you limit the number of records displayed in the query results.

6. Access displays the first five records.

QUICK | CHECK ANSWERS

Session 8.2

1. A query that adds, changes, or deletes multiple table records at a time.
2. You should preview the results before running the action query to confirm that the correct records are selected.
3. A make-table query creates a new table from one or more existing tables. An append query adds records from an existing table or query to the end of another table.
4. deletes groups of records from one or more tables
5. changes selected field values in one or more tables
6. Access replaces the Show and Sort rows in the design grid with the Update To row.
7. Advanced

Session 8.3

1. one-to-many (1:M), many-to-many (M:N), one-to-one (1:1)
2. a table whose primary key is a foreign key to a second table and whose fields are additional fields for the second table
3. a list that relates field values to the records that contain those field values
4. An inner join selects records from two tables when they have matching values in the common field(s). An outer join selects all records from one table and records from a second table whose common field value(s) match records in the first table.
5. a join between a table and itself
6. a. The primary key for the Department table is DepartmentID, and the primary key for the Employee table is EmployeeSSN.
   b. There is a one-to-many relationship between the primary Department table and the related Employee table.
   c. Yes, an inner join is possible based on the common field of DepartmentID. One example of an inner join is a list of all employees, including the EmployeeName, EmployeeSSN, and DepartmentName fields, in alphabetical order by EmployeeName.
   d. Yes, an outer join is possible. One example of an outer join is a left outer join with the Department table as the left table to list all departments and their employees, even those departments without any employees currently assigned.
   e. Yes, a self-join is possible using the Employee table. The SupervisorSSN field is a foreign key that matches the primary key field EmployeeSSN, so you could list all employees and the supervisor name for each employee.

OBJECTIVES

In this tutorial you will:

- Design a switchboard and dialog box for a graphical user interface

- Run and add actions to macros

- Single-step a macro

- Create a macro

- Add a macro to a macro group

- Add a command button to a form

- Attach a macro to a command button

- Create a dialog box form

- Add a list box to a form

- Use an SQL statement to fill a list box with object names

- Create a macro group

- Use the Switchboard Manager to create a switchboard

AUTOMATING TASKS WITH MACROS

Creating a User Interface for the Overseas Database

CASE

Northeast Seasonal Jobs International (NSJI)

At a recent office automation conference, Elsa saw several database applications developed by database designers. The designers' applications used several advanced Access features to automate and control how a user interacts with Access. These features allowed the designers to create a custom user interface for a database. This interface made it much easier for inexperienced users to access the database, and it minimized the chance that an unauthorized user could change the design of any database objects.

Elsa would like to implement a similar user interface for the Overseas database. She would like the interface to display a list of available forms, reports, and queries in the database that the user can select by clicking a command button. This interface will make it much easier for NSJI employees to use the Overseas database, and it will reduce the chance that they will make undesirable changes to the design of the database objects.

SESSION 9.1

In this session, you will review the design of a graphical user interface for the Overseas database. You will also run, modify, test, create, and save macros.

Implementing a Graphical User Interface

A **user interface** is what you see and use when you communicate with a computer program. Not too long ago, most users communicated with a program by typing words that issued commands. You had to remember these commands, which were part of a command language. All the programs developed for today's popular operating environments, such as Microsoft Windows, provide graphical user interfaces. A **graphical user interface (GUI)** (pronounced "gooey") displays windows, menu bars, pull-down menus, dialog boxes, and graphical pictures, called **icons**, which you use to communicate with the program. All Microsoft Windows programs use a similar visual interface, so once you learn one program, you can easily learn another. Overall, a GUI benefits a user by simplifying work, improving productivity, and decreasing errors.

Elsa wants to provide an easier way to work with the Overseas database. The type of user interface you need for working with a database is called a switchboard.

Switchboards

A **switchboard** is a form that appears when you open a database. It provides controlled access to the database's tables, forms, queries, and reports. When a user opens the database, Access opens a switchboard from which the user can choose an option. When you create a switchboard, you are essentially creating a new interface, and it's up to you to decide what options you want to give the user. Figure 9-1 shows the finished Overseas Database switchboard, which you will begin in this tutorial and finish in Tutorial 11.

Figure 9-1	OVERSEAS DATABASE SWITCHBOARD

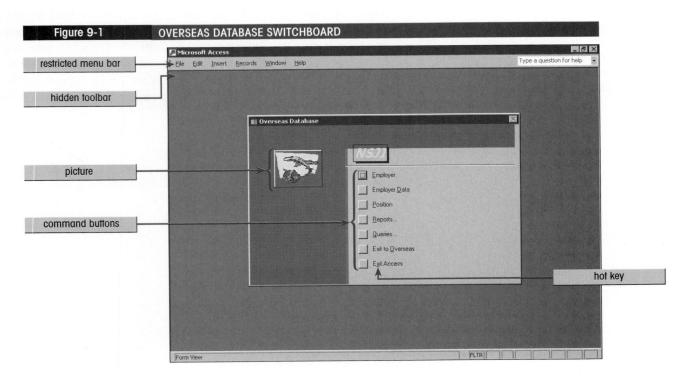

A typical switchboard provides the following items:

- Command buttons provide access to all the options available to the user. In the switchboard shown in Figure 9-1, for example, you can click a command button to open one of three forms (Employer, Employer Data, or Position), to open another switchboard with report options, to open a list of available queries, to close the switchboard and return to the Database window for the Overseas database, or to exit Access. When a selected form, query list, or report switchboard is closed, Access redisplays the Overseas Database switchboard, so you can choose the next option. In other words, you start and end with the switchboard and navigate between options from the switchboard.

- A restricted menu bar contains only those menu options that a user needs for manipulating data; there are no menu options for changing the database design.

- A hidden toolbar prevents users from accessing commands that they could use to potentially alter the database design.

- **Shortcut keys** (or **hot keys**), which are the underlined letters in the words next to each command button option, allow users to select an option by pressing and holding down the Alt key while typing the underlined letter, instead of clicking a command button. You can also create shortcut keys for menu names, menu options, and toolbar buttons.

- Text boxes and pictures can be used to provide identification and visual appeal. The display of a small number of attractively designed pictures and text boxes can help users understand the switchboard's functions. Keep in mind, however, that too many graphics can be confusing or distracting.

A switchboard provides an attractive presentation for a user interface, but there are two more important reasons to use a switchboard instead of the Database window to work with a database. First, a switchboard lets you customize the organization of the user interface. Second, a switchboard prevents users from changing the design of tables, forms, queries, reports, and other objects. By hiding the Database window and toolbar and using a restricted menu bar, you limit users to just those database features that you want them to use. If you do not include any menu, toolbar, or command button options that let users open database objects in Design view, users cannot inadvertently or purposely change the design of the database.

The Reports and Queries command buttons on the Overseas Database switchboard include ellipses after the button names. As you know from your work in Windows, these ellipses signify that a dialog box containing additional options opens when you click that command button. To display the list of available reports, you will create the switchboard shown in Figure 9-2, which is similar in appearance to the Overseas Database switchboard.

Figure 9-2   **REPORTS SWITCHBOARD**

options to open
the named reports

option to return
to the Overseas
Database switchboard

The Reports switchboard contains command buttons to open the Employers and Their Positions report and the Potential Income report. It also has a command button to return to the Overseas Database switchboard, which is the main switchboard.

To display the list of available queries and their options, you will create a custom dialog box.

Dialog Boxes

A **custom dialog box** is a form that resembles a dialog box, both in appearance and function. You use a custom dialog box to ask for user input, selection, or confirmation before an action is performed, such as opening the results of a query or printing a query. Figure 9-3 shows the finished Queries dialog box that you will create later in this tutorial for the Overseas database user interface.

| Figure 9-3 | QUERIES DIALOG BOX |

You will add a list box, which displays the queries available for selection, to the dialog box. You will also add three command buttons. A **command button** is a control on a form that starts an action (or set of actions) when you click it. Command buttons can contain text, standard pictures available from Access, or pictures you supply, to indicate their functions. Clicking the Close command button on the dialog box returns you to the Overseas Database switchboard. The other command buttons contain pictures that identify their functions. The command button on the left has an icon of a magnifying glass over a piece of paper. This is the same icon shown on the Print Preview button. Just as the Print Preview button opens the Print Preview window, this command button opens the Print Preview window for the selected query. When you click the middle command button, the selected query opens in Datasheet view.

Introduction to Macros

The command buttons and custom dialog boxes on the Overseas Database switchboard gain their power from macros—and from Visual Basic for Applications code. A **macro** is a command or a series of commands that you want Access to perform automatically for you. Macros automate repetitive tasks, such as opening forms, printing selected form records, and running queries. Each command in a macro is called an action. An **action** is an instruction to Access to perform an operation, such as opening a form or displaying a query in the Print Preview window. For example, clicking the Position command button on the Overseas Database switchboard causes Access to perform a macro containing the action that opens the Position form.

Access lets you automate most tasks using either macros or **Visual Basic for Applications** (**VBA**), the programming language for Microsoft applications. As a beginner, you will find it easier to write macros than to create programs using VBA. With macros, you simply select a series of actions from a list to create a macro that does what you want it to do. To use VBA, you need to understand the VBA command language well enough to be able to write your own code. VBA does provide advantages over using macros, such as better error-handling capabilities and making your application easier to change. Macros, however, are useful for small applications and for simple tasks, such as opening and closing objects. Additionally, you cannot use VBA to assign actions to a specific key or key combination or to open an application in a special way, such as displaying a switchboard. For these types of actions, you must use macros.

Before you begin creating the Overseas Database switchboard and its supporting macros, you'll run an existing macro, named Employer Data, that Elsa created after she returned from the conference.

Running a Macro

You can directly run an existing macro in three different ways:

- In the Macro window, click the Run button on the Macro Design toolbar.
- Click Tools on the menu bar, point to Macro, click Run Macro, click the Macro Name list arrow, click the desired macro name, and then click the OK button.
- In the Database window, click Macros in the Objects bar, right-click the macro name, and then click Run.

You'll use the last method to run the Employer Data macro.

To run the Employer Data macro:

1. Place your Data Disk in the appropriate disk drive, start Access, and then open the **Overseas** database in the Tutorial folder on your Data Disk.

2. Click **Macros** in the Objects bar of the Database window, right-click **Employer Data**, and then click **Run**. A message box opens. See Figure 9-4.

| Figure 9-4 | USING A MACRO ACTION TO OPEN A MESSAGE BOX |

Opening the message box is the first action Elsa added to the Employer Data macro. A **message box** is a special type of dialog box with a message and command button but no options. The message box remains on the screen until you click the OK button. This message box specifies that the next macro action will open the Employer Data form. When you click the OK button, the message box closes, and the macro resumes with the next action.

3. Click the **OK** button. The next two actions in the Employer Data macro are performed: the Employer Data form opens, and the second message box opens. See Figure 9-5.

Figure 9-5 | SECOND AND THIRD ACTIONS IN THE EMPLOYER DATA MACRO

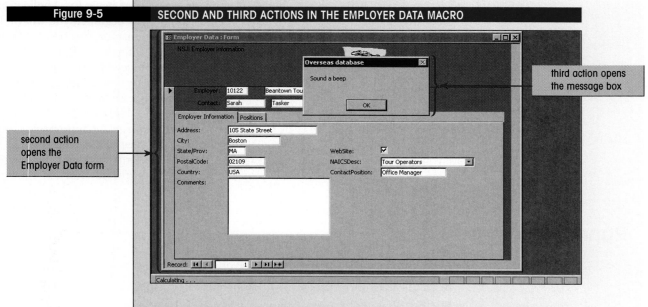

second action opens the Employer Data form

third action opens the message box

4. Click the **OK** button. A beep sounds, and the third message box opens. These are the fourth and fifth actions in the Employer Data macro.

   TROUBLE? If your computer doesn't have speakers, you won't hear a beep sound. If you do hear the beep, its sound can vary depending on your computer and its settings.

5. Click the **OK** button. The Employer Data form is maximized, and the fourth message box opens. These are the sixth and seventh actions in the Employer Data macro.

6. Click the **OK** button. The Employer Data form is restored, and the fifth message box opens. These are the eighth and ninth actions in the Employer Data macro.

7. Click the **OK** button. The Employer Data form now displays record 17 for The Bramble Restaurant, and the sixth message box opens. These are actions 10 and 11 in the Employer Data macro.

8. Click the **OK** button. The Employer Data form closes (action 12—the last action in the Employer Data macro), the Employer Data macro ends, and the Database window becomes the active window.

Elsa suggests that you add some actions to the Employer Data macro to learn about the Macro window and how to modify an existing macro.

Adding Actions to a Macro

To modify the Employer Data macro, you need to open the macro in the Macro window.

To open the Macro window:

1. Right-click **Employer Data** in the Macros list, and then click **Design View** on the shortcut menu. The Employer Data macro opens in the Macro window. See Figure 9-6.

Figure 9-6	MACRO WINDOW

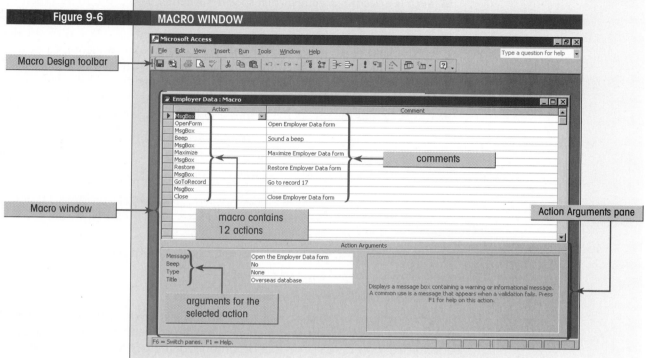

In the **Macro window**, you create and modify macros. Both the menu bar and toolbar for the Macro window have options that are specifically related to macros. The Macro window also includes an **Action column**, in which you enter the action you want Access to perform, and a **Comment column**, in which you enter optional comments to document the specific action. You usually don't enter comments for actions that are self-descriptive.

The first MsgBox action is the current action. Access displays a hint for the current action in the Action Arguments pane of the Macro window on the right. On the left, Access lists the arguments associated with the current action. **Arguments** are additional facts Access needs to execute an action. The action for opening a message box, for example, needs the wording of the message to be displayed and the title bar's name as arguments.

You'll add two actions, the MsgBox and FindRecord actions, to the Employer Data macro between the GoToRecord and the last MsgBox actions. For the FindRecord action, you'll find the record for EmployerID 10190. You use the **FindRecord action** to find the first record that meets the criteria specified by the FindRecord arguments.

The **MsgBox action** causes Access to open a message box. The macro containing a MsgBox action does not proceed to the next action until you click the OK button, so when you add this action to the Employer Data macro, you'll have as much time as you need to read and react to the message box.

The MsgBox action requires four arguments: Message, Beep, Type, and Title, described as follows:

- Message contains the text that will appear in the message box when it is displayed.
- Beep is a Yes/No argument that specifies whether a beep will sound when the message box is opened.
- Type determines which icon, if any, appears in the message box to signify the critical level of the message. The icon choices are None (no icon), Critical (white X in a red ball), Warning? (blue question mark in a white balloon), Warning! (black exclamation point in a yellow triangle), and Information (blue letter I in a white balloon).
- Title contains the title that will appear in the message box title bar.

You'll now add the MsgBox and FindRecord actions to the Employer Data macro.

To add the actions to the Employer Data macro:

1. Right-click the **row selector** for the last MsgBox action, which is action 11, and then click **Insert Rows**. Access adds a new, blank row between the GoToRecord and MsgBox actions.

   Because you'll be adding two actions, you need to insert a second blank row.

2. Repeat Step 1 to add a second blank row.

   You'll add the MsgBox action to the first blank row.

3. Click the right side of the first blank row's **Action** text box to display the list of actions, scroll down the list, and then click **MsgBox**. The list box closes, MsgBox becomes the new action, and four arguments for this action appear in the Action Arguments pane.

   You'll enter values for the Message and Title arguments, change the Beep argument value from Yes to No, and retain the default Type argument value of None. The description appearing on the right side of the Action Arguments pane changes as you select different action arguments on the left. The description is a brief explanation of the current action argument. If you need a more detailed explanation, press the F1 key to open the Microsoft Access Help window and a page related to the current action argument. You can also use Help to learn about specific actions and their arguments, and about macros in general.

4. Press the **F6** key to move the insertion point to the Message text box in the Action Arguments pane, type **Find EmployerID 10190**, press the **Tab** key, click the **Beep** list arrow, click **No**, press the **Tab** key twice, and then type **Overseas database** in the Title text box. See Figure 9-7.

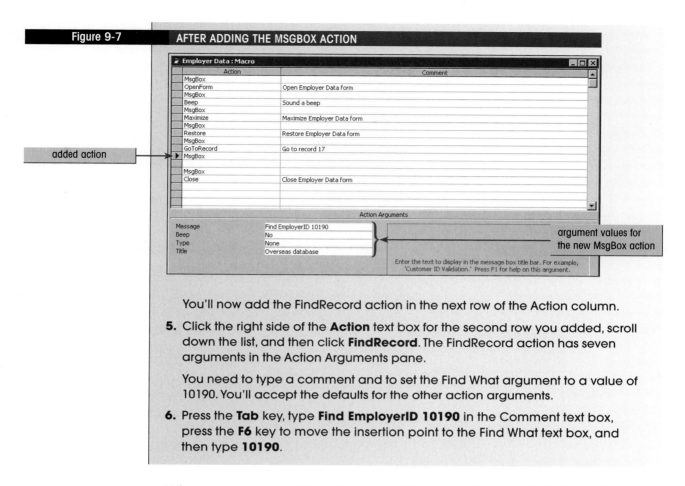

Figure 9-7   AFTER ADDING THE MSGBOX ACTION

added action

argument values for the new MsgBox action

You'll now add the FindRecord action in the next row of the Action column.

5. Click the right side of the **Action** text box for the second row you added, scroll down the list, and then click **FindRecord**. The FindRecord action has seven arguments in the Action Arguments pane.

You need to type a comment and to set the Find What argument to a value of 10190. You'll accept the defaults for the other action arguments.

6. Press the **Tab** key, type **Find EmployerID 10190** in the Comment text box, press the **F6** key to move the insertion point to the Find What text box, and then type **10190**.

When you create complicated macros with many actions, you'll find it useful to run through a macro one step at a time.

Single **Stepping a Macro**

Single stepping executes a macro one action at a time, pausing between actions. You use single stepping to make sure you have placed actions in the right order and with the correct arguments. If you have problems with a macro, you can use single stepping to find the cause of the problems and to determine their proper corrections. The Single Step button on the Macro Design toolbar is a toggle you use to turn single stepping on and off. Once you turn on single stepping, it stays on for all macros until you turn it off.

REFERENCE WINDOW   RW

Single Stepping a Macro
- In the Macro window, click the Single Step button on the Macro Design toolbar.
- Click the Run button on the Macro Design toolbar. If necessary, click the Yes button to save the macro.
- In the Macro Single Step dialog box, click the Step button to execute the next action, click the Halt button to stop the macro, or click the Continue button to execute all remaining actions in the macro and turn off single stepping.

To get a clearer view of the effects of the actions in the Employer Data macro, you can single-step through it. First you need to save your macro changes.

To save the Employer Data macro and then single-step though it:

1. Click the **Save** button 🖫 on the Macro Design toolbar to save your macro design changes.

2. Click the **Single Step** button 🖼 on the Macro Design toolbar to turn on single stepping.

3. Click the **Run** button ❗ on the Macro Design toolbar. The Macro Single Step dialog box opens. See Figure 9-8.

Figure 9-8	MACRO SINGLE STEP DIALOG BOX

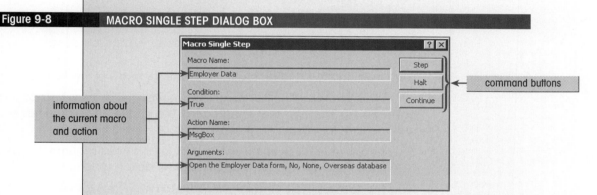

information about the current macro and action

command buttons

TROUBLE? If the first message box opens, instead of the Macro Single Step dialog box, then you turned off single stepping in Step 2 when you clicked the button. Click the OK buttons to run the macro, and then repeat Steps 2 and 3.

When you single-step through a macro, Access opens the Macro Single Step dialog box before performing each action. This dialog box shows the macro's name and the action's condition, name, and arguments. The action will be executed or not executed, depending on whether the condition is true or false. The three command buttons let you step through the macro one action at a time, halt the macro and return to the Macro window, or continue by executing all remaining actions without pausing. You'll also turn off single stepping if you click the Continue button.

4. Click the **Step** button. Access runs the first action (MsgBox). Because the MsgBox action pauses the macro, the Macro Single Step dialog box remains hidden until you click the OK button in the message box.

5. Click the **OK** button to close the message box. The Macro Single Step dialog box shows the macro's second action (OpenForm).

6. Click the **Step** button. Access runs the second action by opening the Employer Data form and shows the macro's third action (MsgBox) in the Macro Single Step dialog box.

7. Click the **Step** button nine more times, and click the **OK** button four more times, making sure you read the Macro Single Step dialog box carefully and observe the actions that occur. At this point, the message box you added is open (Find EmployerID 10190), and record 17 is the current record in the Employer Data form.

8. Click the **OK** button, and then click the **Step** button. The FindRecord action runs, record 31 for EmployerID 10190 is now the current record in the Employer Data form, and the Macro Single Step dialog box shows the macro's last action (MsgBox).

9. Click the **Step** button two more times, and the **OK** button once. The Macro Single Step dialog box closes automatically after the last macro action is completed.

Elsa suggests you complete your practice with macros by creating a new macro and adding an action to a macro by dragging an object from the Database window.

Creating a Macro

You use the Macro window to create and modify macros. To create the new macro, you'll create a blank macro and then add the actions to it.

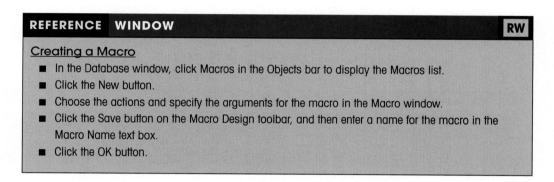

REFERENCE WINDOW   **RW**

Creating a Macro
- In the Database window, click Macros in the Objects bar to display the Macros list.
- Click the New button.
- Choose the actions and specify the arguments for the macro in the Macro window.
- Click the Save button on the Macro Design toolbar, and then enter a name for the macro in the Macro Name text box.
- Click the OK button.

Before you create the new macro, you need to turn off single stepping and close the Employer Data macro.

To turn off single stepping and close the Employer Data macro:

1. Click the **Single Step** button on the Macro Design toolbar to turn off single stepping.

2. Click the **Close** button on the Macro window to close it and return to the Database window.

You'll create a practice macro named Position; this macro will contain actions to open and close the Position form.

To create the Position macro:

1. Click the **New** button in the Database window. The Macro window opens.

   Because you can save a macro at any time, you'll save the blank macro immediately and name it Position.

2. Click the **Save** button 🖫 on the Macro Design toolbar. The Save As dialog box opens.

3. Type **Position** in the Macro Name text box, and then press the **Enter** key.

Adding Actions by Dragging

Another way to add an action to a macro is by dragging an object from the Database window to a new row in the Macro window. When you do this, Access adds the appropriate action and specifies its default argument values. Figure 9-9 describes the effect of dragging each of the six Access objects to a new row in the Macro window. For example, dragging a table creates an OpenTable action that opens the table in Datasheet view and permits editing or updating. To use this dragging technique, be sure that the Macro and Database windows are both visible. You can move the two windows until you see all the critical components of each window, or use the Tile Horizontally or Tile Vertically command on the Window menu.

Figure 9-9	ACTIONS CREATED BY DRAGGING OBJECTS FROM THE DATABASE WINDOW	
OBJECT DRAGGED	**ACTION CREATED**	**ARGUMENTS AND THEIR DEFAULT VALUES**
Table	OpenTable	View: Datasheet Data Mode: Edit
Query	OpenQuery	View: Datasheet Data Mode: Edit
Form	OpenForm	View: Form Filter Name: none Where Condition: none Data Mode: none Window Mode: Normal
Report	OpenReport	View: Print Filter Name: none Where Condition: none Window Mode: Normal
Data Access Page	OpenDataAccessPage	View: Browse
Macro	RunMacro	Repeat Count: none Repeat Expression: none
Module	OpenModule	Procedure Name: none

REFERENCE WINDOW   RW

Creating an Action by Dragging
- Arrange the Macro and the Database windows so that both are visible.
- Drag a database object from the Database window to an Action text box in the Macro window. Access adds the appropriate macro action and sets its arguments to their default values.

Next, you'll use the dragging technique to add actions that open and close the Position form.

To add actions using the dragging method:

1. Click **Window** on the menu bar, and then click **Tile Vertically** to tile the Macro and Database windows. See Figure 9-10.

Figure 9-10	MACRO AND DATABASE WINDOWS TILED VERTICALLY

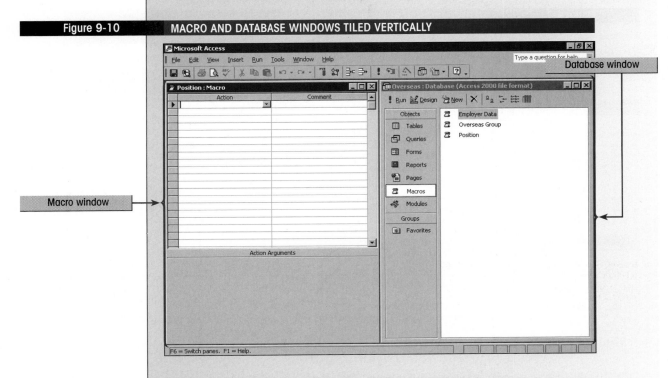

2. Click **Forms** in the Objects bar of the Database window to display the Forms list.

3. Drag **Position** from the Forms list box to the first row's Action text box in the Macro window. Access adds the OpenForm action for the Position form and sets the arguments to their default values.

4. Press the **Tab** key, and then type **Open Position form** in the Comment text box.

   Next, you'll add the MsgBox action so that you'll be able to see the opened Position form before you close it. You'll use the default values for the Beep and Type arguments.

5. Press the **Tab** key, click the **Action** list arrow, scroll down the list, and then click **MsgBox**.

6. Press the **F6** key, type **Close Position form** in the Message text box, press the **Tab** key three times, and then type **Overseas database** in the Title text box.

   You'll select Close as the final action in the Position macro, and set its arguments by dragging the Position form from the Database window to the Object Name text box in the Action Arguments pane of the Macro window.

7. Click the right side of the third row's **Action** text box, click **Close**, press the **Tab** key, and then type **Close Position form** in the Comment text box.

8. Drag **Position** from the Forms list box in the Database window to the Object Name text box in the Action Arguments pane of the Macro window. When you release the mouse button in the Object Name text box, Access automatically sets the Object Type argument to Form and the Object Name argument to Position. See Figure 9-11.

Figure 9-11   **MACRO WINDOW WITH ACTION ARGUMENTS SET BY DRAGGING**

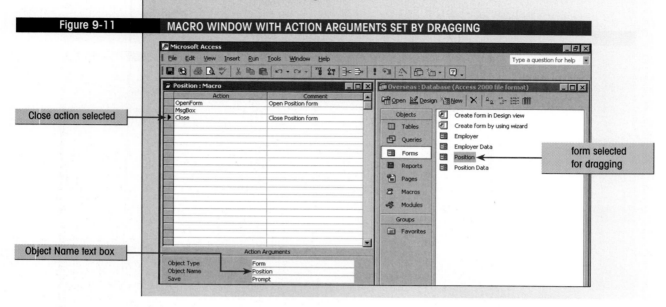

The macro is now completed, so you'll run it to be sure it is correct.

To run the Position macro:

1. Click the **Run** button ![run] on the Macro Design toolbar, and then click the **Yes** button to save the modified macro. Access runs the first two macro actions by opening the message box after opening the Position form. See Figure 9-12.

Figure 9-12   **FIRST TWO POSITION MACRO ACTIONS**

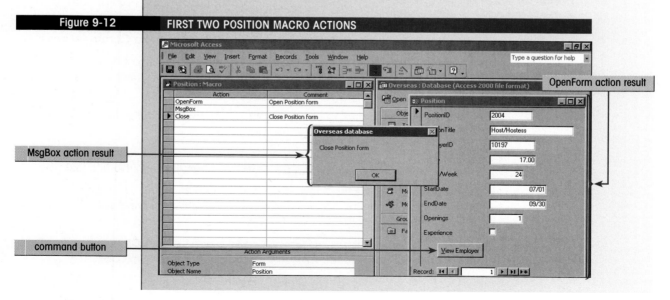

2. Click the **OK** button in the message box. Access closes the message box, and then runs the last macro action by closing the Position form.

3. Click the **Close** button on the Macro window to close it. The Database window is now the active window.

   TROUBLE? If you accidentally clicked the Close button on the Database window and closed the Overseas database, simply reopen the Overseas database.

4. If necessary, reposition and resize the Database window. See Figure 9-13.

Figure 9-13	DATABASE WINDOW REPOSITIONED AND RESIZED

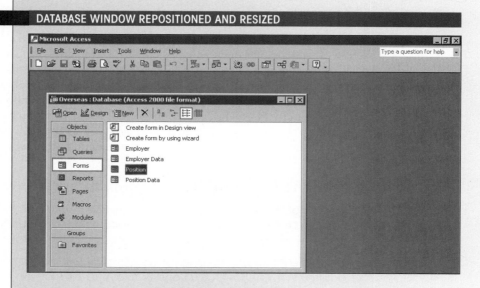

TROUBLE? If your Database window's position differs from the position shown in figures later in this tutorial, this causes no problems. Just continue with the steps in the tutorial.

The Position form (see Figure 9-12) that Elsa created contains a command button that uses a macro. In the next session, you'll use this macro and the command button, and then you'll add a command button with an attached macro to the Employer form.

Session 9.1 QUICK CHECK

1. Define a switchboard and provide two reasons for using one.

2. What is a hot key and how do you use it?

3. What is a macro, and what is the relationship between a macro and an action?

4. What is an action argument? Give an example of an action argument.

5. What does the MsgBox action do?

6. What are you trying to accomplish when you single-step through a macro?

SESSION 9.2

In this session, you'll view a macro that's attached to a command button and learn about events and macro groups. You'll also add a macro to a macro group, add a command button with an attached macro to a form, and then set validation properties for a table field. Then you'll create the Queries dialog box, which will contain command buttons and a list box. Finally, you'll view the SQL statements Access creates when you design a query, and use an SQL statement to retrieve the query names for the list box.

Using a Command Button with an Attached Macro

Elsa created a macro that she associated with, or attached to, a command button on the Position form that you opened in Session 9.1. In Session 9.1, you learned how to create a macro with actions that open and close forms, find records, and open message boxes. You can also add a command button to a form to execute a set of actions. To add a command button to a form, you open the form in Design view and use the Command Button tool on the toolbox. After adding the command button to the form and while still in Design view, you attach the macro with the desired actions to it. Then, when a user clicks the command button, the macro's actions are executed. Elsa asks you to use the View Employer command button to see how the macro attaches to the command button, and then to view the macro.

To use the View Employer command button:

1. If you took a break after the previous session, make sure that Access is running, that the **Overseas** database in the Tutorial folder on your Data Disk is open, and that **Forms** is selected in the Objects bar of the Database window.

2. Open the **Position** form in Form view to display the Position form for the first position with PositionID 2004 and EmployerID 10197.

3. Click the **View Employer** command button. The Position form remains open, and the Employer form opens for EmployerID 10197. See Figure 9-14.

| Figure 9-14 | AFTER OPENING THE EMPLOYER FORM WITH THE VIEW EMPLOYER COMMAND BUTTON |

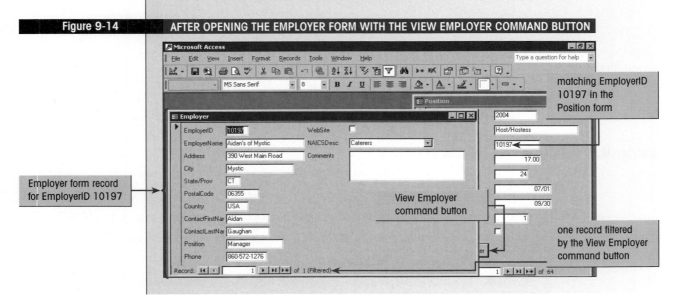

Clicking the View Employer command button triggered an attached macro that opened the Employer form. The record displayed in the Employer form is for the employer (EmployerID 10197) that offers the position displayed in the Position form. The text "Record 1 of 1 (Filtered)" that appears around the navigation buttons in the Employer form indicates that you can view only the record for EmployerID 10197 in the Employer form at this point.

As you navigate through the Position form, the contents of the Employer form do not change unless you click the View Employer command button again.

4. Click the **Last Record** navigation button ▶︎❘ in the Position form. The last record, record 64 for EmployerID 10151, is now the current record, but the Employer form is unchanged—it still shows the record for EmployerID 10197.

   TROUBLE? If the Last Record navigation button is hidden behind the Employer form, click the Position form title bar, and then repeat Step 4.

5. Click the **View Employer** command button. The record for EmployerID 10151 is now the current record in the Employer form. The Position form still displays record 64.

6. Close the **Employer** form. The Position form is now the active window.

Clicking the View Employer command button is an event, and the opening of the Employer form is controlled by setting an event property.

Events

An **event** occurs when you take some action, such as clicking a button, using the mouse, or pressing a key to choose an option. In your work with Access, you've initiated hundreds of events on forms, controls, records, and reports without any special effort. For example, three form events are: Open, which occurs when you open a form; Activate, which occurs when the form becomes the active window; and Close, which occurs when you close a form and it is removed from the screen. Each event has an associated event property. An **event property** specifies how an object responds when an event occurs. For example, each form has OnOpen, OnActivate, and OnClose event properties associated with the Open, Activate, and Close events, respectively.

Event properties appear in the property sheet when you create forms and reports. Unlike most properties you've used previously in property sheets, event properties do not have an initial value. If an event property contains no value, it means the event property has not been set. In this case Access takes no *special action* when the associated event occurs. For example, if a form's OnOpen event property is not set and you open the form, then the Open event occurs (the form opens), and no *special action* occurs beyond the opening of the form. You can set an event property value to a macro name, and Access will execute the macro when the event occurs. For example, you could write a macro that automatically selects a particular field in a form when you open it. You can also create a group of statements using VBA code and set the event property value to the name of that group of statements. Access will then execute the group of statements, or **procedure**, when the event occurs. Such a procedure is called an **event procedure**.

When you clicked the View Employer command button on the Position form, the Click event occurred and triggered the attached macro. The View Employer command button contains an OnClick event property, which you will examine next.

To view the OnClick event property for the View Employer command button:

1. Switch to Design view, scroll down the form, right-click the **View Employer** command button, and then click **Properties** on the shortcut menu to open the property sheet.

   You might notice that event properties, such as OnEnter and OnClick, do not contain a space, but the Event tab in the property sheet shows them as On Enter and On Click, with the spaces. In this case, OnClick and the On Click property in the property sheet are the same.

2. Click the **Event** tab (if necessary), right-click the **On Click** text box, click **Zoom** on the shortcut menu to open the Zoom dialog box, and then click to the right of the selected text to deselect it. See Figure 9-15.

Figure 9-15	MACRO ATTACHED TO THE OnClick EVENT PROPERTY

The OnClick event property value shown in the Zoom dialog box is *Overseas Group.Open Employer Form.* This is an example of a reference to a macro in a macro group.

Macro Groups

Instead of creating several separate macros, you can combine them in a macro group. A **macro group** is a macro that contains other macros. Macro groups allow you to consolidate related macros and to manage large numbers of macros. For the OnClick event property value shown in Figure 9-15, Overseas Group is the macro group name, and Open Employer Form is the macro name. A period separates the two names. When you click the View Employer command button on the Position form, Access processes the actions contained in the Open Employer Form macro, which is located in the Overseas Group macro group.

You'll now close the Zoom dialog box, and then open the Macro window from the property sheet.

To open the Overseas Group macro in the Macro window:

1. Click the **Close** button ☒ on the Zoom dialog box to close it. The OnClick event property value is selected in the property sheet, and the On Click text box contains a list arrow and Build button to its right. See Figure 9-16.

| Figure 9-16 | OnClick EVENT PROPERTY VALUE FOR THE VIEW EMPLOYER COMMAND BUTTON |

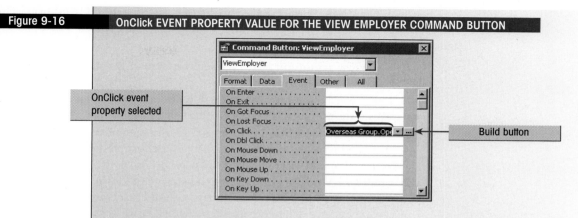

You click the list arrow if you want to change the current macro to a different macro, and you click the Build button if you want to use the Macro window to view or change the existing macro. The Build button is also called the **Macro Builder** when you use it to work with macros.

2. Click the **Build** button [...] to the right of the On Click text box. The Macro window opens and displays the Overseas Group macro. See Figure 9-17.

| Figure 9-17 | MACRO WINDOW FOR THE OVERSEAS GROUP MACRO |

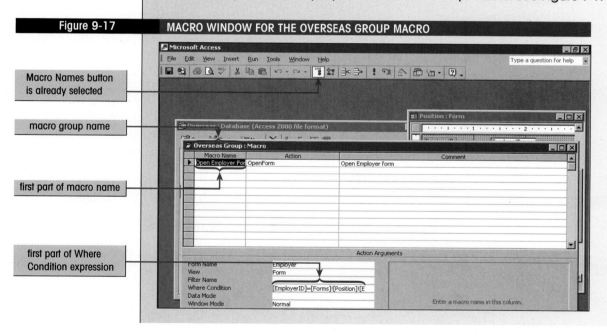

The **Macro Name column** in the Macro window lets you distinguish individual macros in a macro group. Each individual macro is identified by name in the Macro Name column. If a macro contains several actions, you leave the Macro Name column blank for actions added after the first one. To display or hide the Macro Name column, you click the Macro Names button on the Macro Design toolbar.

The Open Employer Form macro consists of a single action, OpenForm, which opens the Employer form (the Form Name argument value is Employer). The other OpenForm action arguments are:

- The **View argument** lets you open the form in Datasheet, Design, Form, or Print Preview views.
- The **Filter Name argument** lets you filter or sort the form's records. You can set the argument's value to a query or to a filter that was saved as a query.
- The **Where Condition argument** lets you specify an expression or SQL statement to select records to display in the form. You'll learn more about SQL statements later in this tutorial.
- The **Data Mode argument** lets you specify the form's data-entry options. Allowable settings for this argument are Add (users can add new records but can't change or delete existing records), Edit (users can change and delete existing records and can add new records), and Read Only (users can only view records). Edit is the default setting.
- The **Window Mode argument** lets you specify the form's window characteristics. Allowable settings for this argument are Dialog (the form opens as a dialog box.), Hidden (the form opens but is not visible.), Icon (the form opens minimized as a small title bar at the bottom of the screen.), and Normal (the form opens as it normally would from the Database window).

The Where Condition argument value in Figure 9-17 specifies which Employer record appears in the form. You'll use the Zoom dialog box to view the entire Where Condition argument value.

To view the Where Condition argument value in the Zoom dialog box:

1. Right-click the **Where Condition** text box, click **Zoom** on the shortcut menu to open the Zoom dialog box, and then click to the right of the selected text to deselect it. See Figure 9-18.

| Figure 9-18 | WHERE CONDITION ARGUMENT VALUE FOR THE OPEN EMPLOYER FORM MACRO |

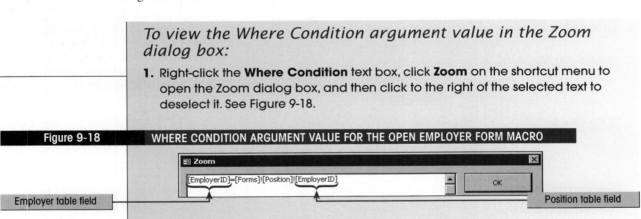

The Where Condition argument value contains the expression *[EmployerID]=[Forms]![Position]![EmployerID]*. In simple terms, the expression asks Access to find the record in the Employer form with the same EmployerID as the current record in the Position form. The expression, however, is complex. The OpenForm action in the macro opens the Employer form; the value *[EmployerID]* to the left of the equals sign determines which record will be displayed in the Employer form. What is this EmployerID value? It's the same as (equals sign) the EmployerID that appears in the current Position form record (*[Forms]![Position]![EmployerID]* to the right of the equals sign). On the right side of the equals sign, *[Forms]* identifies the object collection, such as forms or queries. *[Position]* identifies the name of the specific object within the object collection—in this case, Position. Finally, *[EmployerID]* identifies the specific field within the specified object—in this case, the EmployerID field in the Position form.

Now that you've seen a macro that's attached to a command button, Elsa asks you to add a command button to the Employer form, and then attach a new macro to the command button. Elsa wants to be able to print the current record in the Employer form by clicking a command button on the form. Because Elsa doesn't want a large number of macros and because the Macro window is already open for the Overseas Group macro group, you'll add the new macro to it.

Adding a Macro to a Macro Group

To print the contents of a form's current record, normally you have to click File on the menu bar, click Print, click Selected Record(s), and then click the OK button—a process that takes fours steps and several seconds. Instead of following this process, you can create a command button on the form and a macro that prints the contents of a form's current record, and then attach the macro to the command button on the form. To print the form's current record, you'd simply click the command button.

First, you'll add a macro to the Overseas Group macro group. You'll use the PrintOut action for the new macro. The **PrintOut action** lets you print the contents of an object; you can choose to print the selected record (set the Print Range argument to Selection), a page range (set the Print Range argument to Pages), or the entire contents of the object (set the Print Range argument to All). You'll use a macro name of Print Current Record when you add it to the Overseas Group macro group, so the macro's function is obvious.

REFERENCE   WINDOW   **RW**

Adding a Macro to a Macro Group

- Open the macro group in the Macro window. (For a macro group, the Macro Names button is already selected.)
- Type the macro name in the Macro Name column, select the action in the Action column, type an optional comment in the Comment column, and then set the arguments for the action.
- If the macro consists of more than one action, enter the remaining actions in the rows immediately following the first macro action. Leave the Macro Name column blank for each additional action.
- Click the Save button on the Macro Design toolbar.

You'll now add the Print Current Record macro to the Overseas Group macro group.

To add the Print Current Record macro to the Overseas Group macro group:

1. Click the **Cancel** button in the Zoom dialog box to close it.

2. Click the second row's **Macro Name** text box, type **Print Current Record**, press the **Tab** key, click the **Action** list arrow, scroll down the list, click **PrintOut**, press the **Tab** key, and then type **Print current record** in the Comment column.

   You need to set only the Print Range argument; to print the current form record, you'll set its value to Selection.

3. Press the **F6** key, click the **Print Range** list arrow, and then click **Selection**. You've completed the action, which is the only action in the Print Current Record macro. The macro group now contains two macros. See Figure 9-19.

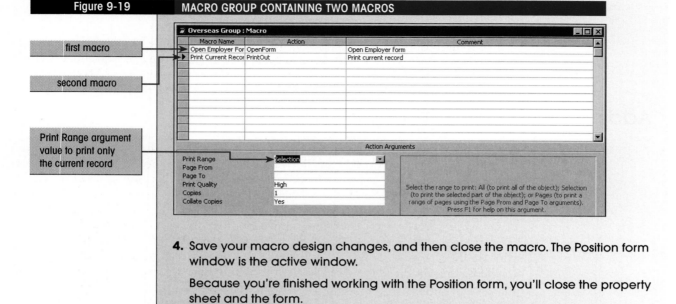

Figure 9-19   MACRO GROUP CONTAINING TWO MACROS

first macro

second macro

Print Range argument
value to print only
the current record

4. Save your macro design changes, and then close the macro. The Position form window is the active window.

   Because you're finished working with the Position form, you'll close the property sheet and the form.

5. Close the property sheet, close the form, and then click the **No** button if you're asked to save your form design changes.

Next, you'll add a command button to the Employer form. After you attach the Print Current Record macro to the command button, you'll be able to click the command button to print the current Employer form record.

Adding a Command Button to a Form

You use the Command Button tool on the toolbox to add a command button to a form. If the Control Wizards tool is selected when you click the Command Button tool, the Command Button Wizard guides you through the process of adding the command button. Instead, you'll add the command button directly to the Employer form without using the Wizard. Then you'll set the command button's properties using its property sheet.

To add a command button to the Employer form:

1. Open the **Employer** form in Design view.

   TROUBLE? If the field list is open, click its Close button X to close it.

2. Click ▼ on the form's vertical scroll bar so that you can see the middle of the Detail section.

3. If necessary, click the **Toolbox** button ✎ on the Form Design toolbar to open the toolbox, and then if necessary dock the toolbox below the Formatting toolbar.

4. Make sure the **Control Wizards** tool ◣ on the toolbox is not selected, and then click the **Command Button** tool ▢ on the toolbox.

5. Move the pointer over the Detail section. The pointer changes to a ⁺▢ shape.

6. When the pointer's plus symbol (+) is positioned in the Detail section at the 3.5-inch mark on the horizontal ruler and the 2-inch mark on the vertical ruler, click the mouse button. Access adds a command button to the form. See Figure 9-20.

| Figure 9-20 | AFTER ADDING A COMMAND BUTTON TO THE EMPLOYER FORM |

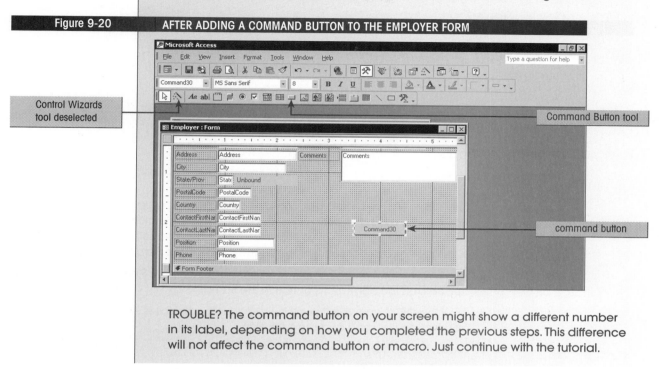

Control Wizards tool deselected

Command Button tool

command button

TROUBLE? The command button on your screen might show a different number in its label, depending on how you completed the previous steps. This difference will not affect the command button or macro. Just continue with the tutorial.

You can now attach the Print Current Record macro to the command button.

Attaching a Macro to a Command Button

You created the Print Current Record macro and added the command button to the Employer form. You'll attach the macro to the command button's OnClick property so that the macro is executed when the command button is clicked.

To attach the Print Current Record macro to the command button:

1. Right-click the command button, click **Properties** on the shortcut menu, and then if necessary click the **Event** tab.

2. Click the right side of the **On Click** text box to display the macros list, and then click **Overseas Group.Print Current Record**.

TROUBLE? If the On Click list box is too narrow to see which macro is the correct one, drag the right border of the property sheet to the right to increase the width of the property sheet, and then repeat Step 2.

You can change the text that appears on the command button (also known as the command button's label or caption) by changing its Caption property, or you can replace the text with a picture by setting its Picture property. Elsa wants you to place a picture of a printer on the command button.

3. Click the **Format** tab, click the **Picture** text box, and then click the **Build** button ... that appears next to the text box. The Picture Builder dialog box opens. See Figure 9-21.

Figure 9-21   PICTURE BUILDER DIALOG BOX

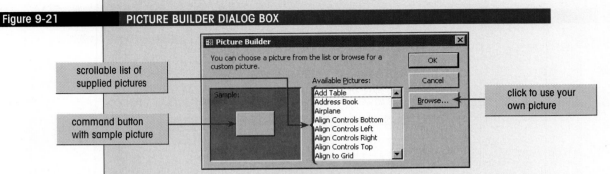

The Picture Builder dialog box contains an alphabetical list of pictures supplied with Access. You can scroll the list and select one of the pictures, or you can click the Browse button to select your own picture. When you select a picture, a sample of the picture appears on the command button in the Sample box on the left.

4. Scroll down the Available Pictures list box, and then click **Printer**. A printer picture appears on the command button in the Sample box.

5. Click the **OK** button. The Picture Builder dialog box closes, and the printer picture appears on a resized command button.

6. Close the property sheet.

Next, you'll save the Employer form and test the command button.

To save the form and test the command button:

1. Save your form design changes, and then switch to Form view.

2. Click the **Last Record** navigation button ▶| on the Employer form, and then click the **Print** command button on the form. The last record for Lighthouse Tours prints.

3. Close the form.

You've now completed your initial work with macros. Next, you'll start to develop the user interface for the Overseas database. You'll create the dialog box to display the queries in the Overseas database, use an SQL statement to select the values for the list box, and then add command buttons and a list box to the dialog box.

Creating the Queries Dialog Box Form

To create the user interface for the Overseas database, you need to create the Overseas Database and Reports switchboards and the Queries dialog box. First, you'll create the dialog box shown in Figure 9-22.

Figure 9-22   **QUERIES DIALOG BOX**

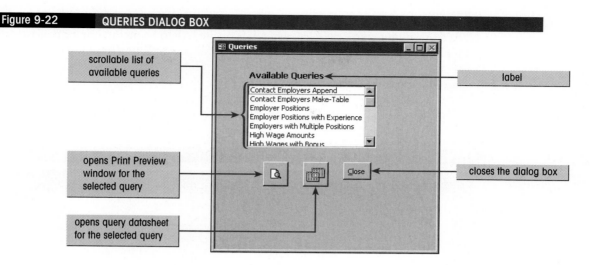

scrollable list of
available queries

label

opens Print Preview
window for the
selected query

closes the dialog box

opens query datasheet
for the selected query

The Queries dialog box is actually a form that you will create. You'll add a label, a list box, and three command buttons to the form, and you'll enter an SQL statement that will provide the contents of the list box. (SQL is a language used with relational databases.) NSJI staff members will use the dialog box as follows:

- Scroll the list box until the desired query name is visible.
- Click the query name, and then click the command button with the Print Preview icon to open the query in Print Preview. Alternatively, double-click the query name to open the query in Print Preview.
- Click the query name, and then click the command button with the Datasheet icon to display the query results.
- Click the Close button to close the dialog box and activate the Overseas Database switchboard. Alternatively, the underlined letter "C" in the Close command button identifies the button's hot key; pressing Alt + C will also close the dialog box.

To create the Queries dialog box, you'll begin by creating a blank form. Because none of the form controls need data from a table or query (an SQL statement will supply the list box with its values), you will not select a table or query as the basis for the blank form.

To create the Queries Dialog Box form:

1. Make sure that **Forms** is selected in the Objects bar of the Database window, and then click the **New** button. The New Form dialog box opens.

2. Make sure that **Design View** is selected, and then click the **OK** button. Access opens the Form window in Design view.

3. Click the **Save** button 🖫 on the Form Design toolbar, type **Queries Dialog Box** in the Form Name text box, and then press the **Enter** key. The title bar displays the saved form's name.

Before adding any controls to the form, you need to set the overall form properties so that the form matches Elsa's design. You will set the Caption property to Queries, which is the value that will appear in the form's title bar. You will also set the Shortcut Menu, Record Selectors, Navigation Buttons, and Close Button properties to No, because Elsa doesn't want the form to include these features. You will set the Auto Resize property to No so that Access will not resize the form when it is opened, thereby maintaining a consistent form size for all users. Also, Elsa wants to disable other Access windows until the user closes the form, so you will set the Modal property to Yes. Finally, after you have completed the form's design, you will set the Border Style property to Dialog so that the form will look like a dialog box that a user cannot resize using the pointer. Figure 9-23 shows the form property settings you will use to create the Queries Dialog Box form for Elsa.

Figure 9-23	QUERIES DIALOG BOX FORM PROPERTIES	
PROPERTY	**SETTING**	**FUNCTION**
Auto Resize	No	Opens a form using the last saved size
Border Style	Dialog	Prevents a user from resizing the form
Caption	Queries	Value that appears in the form's title bar
Close Button	No	Disables the display of the Close button on the form's title bar
Modal	Yes	Disables other Access windows until a user closes the form
Navigation Buttons	No	Disables the display of navigation buttons on the bottom of the form
Record Selectors	No	Disables the display of a record selector on the left side of the form
Shortcut Menu	No	Disables the display of the shortcut menu if a user right-clicks the form

Working from this list, you can use the property sheet to set the form properties.

To set the properties for the form:

1. Right-click the form selector, which is the gray box immediately to the left of the horizontal ruler in the Form window, and then click **Properties** on the shortcut menu to open the form's property sheet (as indicated by the word "Form" in the title bar).

2. If necessary, click the **All** tab to display the All page of the property sheet.

   You can now set the Caption property for the form. The Caption property value will appear in the title bar when the form is displayed.

3. Scroll to the top of the property sheet (if necessary), click the **Caption** text box, and then type **Queries**.

   Next, you'll set the Record Selectors property so that a record selector will not be displayed on the left side of the form. Because the form does not display any records, there's no need to include a record selector.

4. Scroll down until the Record Selectors property is visible, and then double-click **Yes** in the Record Selectors text box to change the property setting from Yes to No.

   You'll now set the remaining form properties.

5. Continue scrolling as necessary, and set the **Navigation Buttons** property to **No**, set the **Auto Resize** property to **No**, set the **Modal** property to **Yes**, set the **Close Button** property to **No**, and then set the **Shortcut Menu** property to **No**.

6. Close the property sheet, and then save your form design changes.

Now that you have set the form's properties, you can add a label and a list box to it. The label will identify the list box for the user, and the list box will display the list of queries in the Overseas database. You will not use the Control Wizards tool for the list box because you'll be using an SQL statement to provide the query names for the list box.

Adding a List Box to a Form

A **list box** is a control that displays a list of values. The list box in the Queries Dialog Box form will display the list of queries that the user can preview or view. Clicking the name of a query selects it, and then the user can click one of the command buttons to preview or view the query. Double-clicking a query name in the list box will open the query in the Print Preview window.

REFERENCE WINDOW   **RW**

Adding a List Box to a Form
- If necessary, click the Control Wizards tool on the toolbox so that it is appropriately selected or deselected.
- Click the List Box tool on the toolbox.
- Position the pointer where you want the list box to appear on the form, and then click the mouse button.
- If you used the List Box Wizard, complete the dialog boxes to choose the source of the list, select the fields to appear in the list box, size the columns, select the field that will provide the data for the field in the main form, choose to remember the value for later use or store it in a field, and then enter the value to appear in the list box label.

First you'll add the label "Available Queries" to the form. Then you'll add the list box to display the list of queries from which to choose.

To add the label to the form:

1. Click the **Label** tool [Aa] on the toolbox.
2. Position the pointer in the Detail section; when the pointer's plus symbol is positioned at the .5-inch mark on the horizontal ruler and the .25-inch mark on the vertical ruler, click the mouse button. A small label box containing an insertion point opens on the form.
3. Type **Available Queries** and then press the **Enter** key.

   Elsa wants the label to stand out more, so you'll change the label's font size from the default of 8 to 10, make the label bold, and then resize the label box.
4. Click the **Font Size** list arrow on the Formatting toolbar, click **10**, and then click the **Bold** button [B] on the Formatting toolbar.
5. Click **Format** on the menu bar, point to **Size**, and then click **To Fit**.

Now you can add the list box to the form.

To add the list box to the form:

1. Make sure that the **Control Wizards** tool ⟨icon⟩ on the toolbox is deselected.

2. Click the **List Box** tool ⟨icon⟩ on the toolbox, position the pointer's plus symbol in the row of grid dots below the left edge of the Available Queries label box, and then click the mouse button. Access adds a list box and attached label box to the form. See Figure 9-24.

Figure 9-24	FORM DESIGN AFTER ADDING THE LABEL AND THE LIST BOX

Control Wizards tool deselected

List Box tool

label

list box and attached label box

TROUBLE? If your list box is sized or positioned differently, resize it or move it until it matches the list box shown in Figure 9-24.

You can now save the form and then check your progress by switching to Form view.

3. Save your form design changes, and then switch to Form view. See Figure 9-25.

Figure 9-25	QUERIES DIALOG BOX DISPLAYED IN FORM VIEW

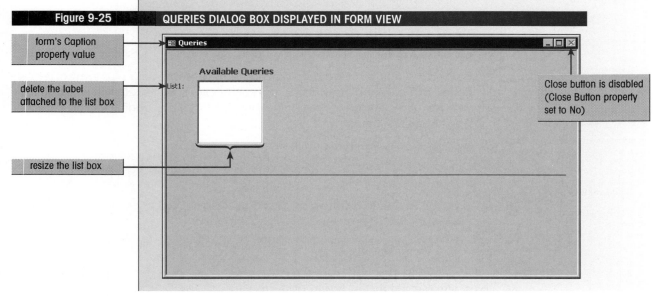

form's Caption property value

delete the label attached to the list box

resize the list box

Close button is disabled (Close Button property set to No)

After viewing the form, Elsa asks you to make two changes to it. Because the form already includes the label "Available Queries," the label attached to the list box is unnecessary. Elsa asks you to delete this label. She'd also like you to resize the list box by making it wider so that it will accommodate the list of queries better.

To delete the label attached to the list box and resize the list box:

1. Switch to Design view.

2. Right-click the label attached to the list box to open the shortcut menu, and then click **Cut** to delete it.

3. Click the list box to select it.

4. Use the middle-right sizing handle to drag the right border to the 2.5-inch mark on the horizontal ruler, and then save your form design changes.

You now can enter the SQL statement that will provide the query names for the list box.

Using SQL

SQL (Structured Query Language) is a standard language used in querying, updating, and managing relational databases. Every full-featured relational DBMS has its own version of the current standard SQL, which is called SQL-99, although Access 2002 conforms more with the prior SQL-89 and SQL-92 standards. If you learn SQL for one relational DBMS, it's a relatively easy task to begin using SQL for other relational DBMSs. When you work with two or more relational DBMSs, which is the case in most companies, you'll learn that few differences exist among the various SQL versions.

Much of what Access accomplishes behind the scenes is done with SQL. Whenever you create a query in Design view, for example, Access automatically constructs an equivalent SQL statement. When you save a query, Access saves the SQL statement version of the query.

Viewing an SQL Statement for a Query

When you are working in Design view or viewing the results of a query, you can see the SQL statement that is equivalent to your query by clicking the SQL View button or selecting SQL View from the View menu. In response, Access displays the SQL statement in the SQL window.

REFERENCE WINDOW   **RW**

Viewing an SQL Statement for a Query
- Display the query in Design view or Datasheet view.
- Click the list arrow for the View button on the toolbar, and then click SQL View. Access opens the SQL window.
- Use the appropriate View button to return to either Design view or Datasheet view.

Next you'll examine the SQL statements that are equivalent to two existing queries: Selected Employer Info and Employer Positions.

To view the SQL statement for the Selected Employer Info query:

1. Click the **Database Window** button [icon] on the Form Design toolbar to make the Database window the active window.

2. Open the **Selected Employer Info** query in Datasheet view. Access opens the query recordset and displays the 45 records from the Employer table. The fields displayed are EmployerID, EmployerName, City, ContactFirstName, ContactLastName, and WebSite.

3. Click the list arrow for the **View** button [icon] on the Query Datasheet toolbar, and then click **SQL View** to open the SQL window.

4. Maximize the SQL window, and then click the line below the SQL statement to deselect it. See Figure 9-26.

| Figure 9-26 | SQL WINDOW FOR THE SELECTED EMPLOYER INFO QUERY |

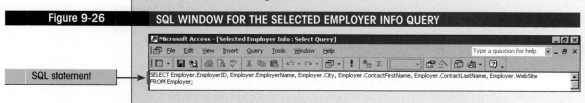

SQL statement

> SELECT Employer.EmployerID, Employer.EmployerName, Employer.City, Employer.ContactFirstName, Employer.ContactLastName, Employer.WebSite
> FROM Employer;

SQL uses the **SELECT statement** to define what data it retrieves from a database and how it presents the data. For the work you've done so far, the Access menu commands and dialog box options have sufficed. If you learn SQL to the point where you can use it efficiently, you will be able to enter your own SELECT and other SQL statements in the SQL window. If you work with more complicated databases, you might find that you need the extra power of the SQL language to implement your database strategies fully.

The rules that SQL uses to construct a statement similar to the SELECT statement shown in Figure 9-26 are summarized as follows:

- The basic form of an SQL statement is: SELECT-FROM-WHERE-ORDER BY. After SELECT, list the fields you want to display. After FROM, list the tables used in the query. After WHERE, list the selection criteria. After ORDER BY, list the sort keys.
- If a field name includes a space or special symbol, enclose the field name in brackets.
- Precede a field name with the name of its table by connecting the table name to the field name with a period. For example, you would enter the EmployerName field in the Employer table as *Employer.EmployerName*.
- Separate field names and table names by commas, and end the statement with a semicolon.

The SQL statement shown in Figure 9-26 selects the EmployerID, EmployerName, City, ContactFirstName, ContactLastName, and WebSite fields from the Employer table. The SQL statement does not contain a WHERE clause or an ORDER BY clause, so all records are included in the recordset and listed in the default order, which is in ascending order by primary key.

You can enter or change SQL statements directly in the SQL window. If you enter an SQL statement and then switch to the Query window in Design view, you will see its equivalent in the design grid.

Next, you'll examine the SQL statement for the Employer Positions query.

To view the SQL statement for the Employer Positions query:

1. Click the **Close** button ⊠ on the menu bar to close the SQL window and return to the Database window.

2. Open the **Employer Positions** query in Design view. The query selects records from the joined Employer and Position tables in ascending order by the PositionTitle field as the primary sort key and in descending order by the Openings field as the secondary sort key. The fields displayed are EmployerName, City, and State/Prov from the Employer table, and PositionTitle, Openings, StartDate, and EndDate from the Position table.

3. Click the list arrow for the **View** button ▦ on the Query Design toolbar, and then click **SQL View** to open the SQL window.

4. Click the line below the SQL statement to deselect the statement. See Figure 9-27.

Figure 9-27	SQL WINDOW FOR THE EMPLOYER POSITIONS QUERY

The SELECT statement for this query is similar to the one shown in Figure 9-26, except for the following added features:

- The INNER JOIN clause links the two tables with an inner join. The syntax for this clause is to type INNER JOIN between the two table names, followed by ON, and then followed by the names of the fields serving as the common field, connected by an equals sign. (Access uses the ON clause here instead of the standard SQL WHERE clause.)
- The ORDER BY clause specifies the sort order for the records.
- The notation DESC in the ORDER BY clause indicates a descending sort order. If DESC does not follow a sort key field, then SQL uses an ascending sort order.

The SQL SELECT statements mirror the query options you viewed in Design view. In effect, every choice you make in Design view is reflected as part of the SQL SELECT statement. Viewing the SQL statements generated from queries that you design is an effective way to begin learning SQL.

To close the query and return to the Queries Dialog Box form:

1. Close the SQL window, and then restore the Database window.

2. Click the form title bar to make the Queries Dialog Box form the active window.

You now can enter the SQL statement that will provide the query names for the list box.

Using an SQL Statement for a List Box

You'll use a SELECT statement to retrieve the list of query names from one of the Access system tables. **System tables** are special tables maintained by Access that store information about the characteristics of a database and about the structure of the objects in a database. Although system tables do not appear in the Database window's Tables list box, you can retrieve information from system tables using SELECT statements. One of the system tables, the **MSysObjects table**, keeps track of the names, types, and other characteristics of every object in a database. The Name and Type fields are the two MSysObjects table fields you'll use in the SELECT statement. The Name field contains a query name when the Type field value is 5, as shown in Figure 9-28.

Figure 9-28	MSYSOBJECTS TABLE TYPE FIELD VALUES

OBJECT TYPE	TYPE FIELD VALUE IN MSYSOBJECTS TABLE
Table	1
Query	5
Form	-32768
Report	-32764
Page	-32756
Macro	-32766
Module	-32761

Access creates its own queries to handle many tasks for you; each of these queries has a name that begins with the tilde (~) character. Because you want to exclude these special system queries from the list box, you'll also need to use the Left function in your SELECT statement. The **Left function** provides the first character(s) in a text string. The format of the Left function is *Left(text string, number of characters)*. You'll use *Left([Name],1)* to retrieve the first character of the Name field. To include only those queries whose names do not begin with the ~ character, you'll use the expression *Left([Name],1)<>"~"*. In this expression, the <> operator is the not equal operator. Access interprets this expression as "the first character of the Name field does not equal the ~ character." Figure 9-29 shows the Zoom dialog box, which contains the complete SELECT statement that you will use to select the list of query names.

Figure 9-29	SELECT STATEMENT FOR THE LIST BOX

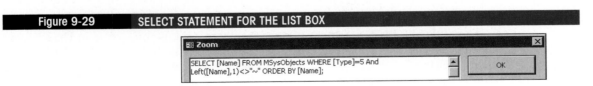

The **Row Source property** specifies how to provide data to a list box, so you'll enter the SELECT statement as the value for the list box's Row Source property.

To set the Row Source property for the list box:

1. Right-click the list box to open the shortcut menu, click **Properties** to open the property sheet, and then click the **All** tab (if necessary).

2. Right-click the **Row Source** text box to open the shortcut menu, and then click **Zoom**. The Zoom dialog box opens.

3. Type **SELECT [Name] FROM MSysObjects WHERE [Type]=5 And Left([Name],1)<>"~" ORDER BY [Name];** in the Zoom dialog box, and then click the **OK** button.

4. Close the property sheet, save your form design changes, and then switch to Form view. See Figure 9-30.

Figure 9-30	COMPLETED LIST BOX

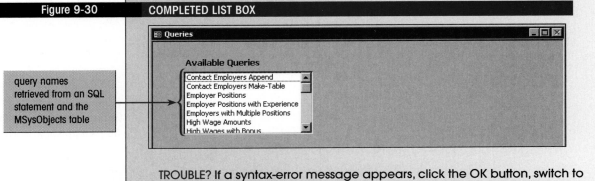

query names retrieved from an SQL statement and the MSysObjects table

TROUBLE? If a syntax-error message appears, click the OK button, switch to Design view, right-click the list box, click Properties, right-click the Row Source text box, and then click Zoom. Correct the SELECT statement until it's the same as the statement shown in Figure 9-29, click the OK button, and then repeat Step 4.

You can now add command buttons to the form.

Adding Command Buttons to a Form

First, you'll add the Print Preview command button to the form. To handle the complex interaction that is involved in the actions of selecting a query in a list box and clicking a command button, you'll use VBA code in Tutorial 10. So, you'll attach VBA code to the Print Preview and Datasheet command buttons and the list box instead of using macros.

In the next steps, you will add the Print Preview command button to the form. You can add a command button to a form by placing the button directly on the form or by using the Control Wizards tool. If you use the Control Wizards tool, you can attach a standard Access action (such as opening a specific query or closing a window) or a macro to the button. You cannot use a standard Access action for this command button, because the query to be opened will depend on the query the user has selected in the list box. Instead, you will add the command button on the form now and attach VBA code to it in Tutorial 10.

To add the Print Preview command button to the form:

1. Switch to Design view, make sure the **Control Wizards** tool on the toolbox is deselected, and then click the **Command Button** tool on the toolbox.

2. Position the pointer in the Detail section; when the pointer's plus symbol is positioned at the .75-inch mark on the horizontal ruler and the 1.75-inch mark on the vertical ruler, click the mouse button. Access adds a command button to the form.

3. Right-click the command button, and then click **Properties** on the shortcut menu to open the property sheet.

> **TROUBLE?** If the property sheet is covering the form, drag it out of the way.
>
> You can now change the text that appears on the command button to the Print Preview picture, which is the same picture that appears on the Print Preview button on the Form Design toolbar.
>
> **4.** Click the **Format** tab, click the **Picture** text box, and then click the **Build** button [...] that appears next to the Picture text box. The Picture Builder dialog box opens.
>
> **5.** Scroll down the Available Pictures list box, and then click **Preview Document**. Access shows the picture on the command button in the Sample box.
>
> **6.** Click the **OK** button. Access closes the Picture Builder dialog box, resizes the command button, places the picture on the command button, and increases the height of the form's Detail section.

Instead of repeating the steps to add the command button for viewing a query, you can copy the first command button and paste it in the Detail section. After moving the copied button into position, you can change the picture on it to show the query datasheet icon.

To place the Datasheet command button on the form:

1. Right-click the command button, and then click **Copy** on the shortcut menu.

2. Click the **Paste** button on the Form Design toolbar. Access adds a copy of the command button below the original command button in the Detail section.

3. Move the new command button into position to the right of the original command button. See Figure 9-31.

Figure 9-31   **AFTER ADDING A COPY OF THE COMMAND BUTTON**

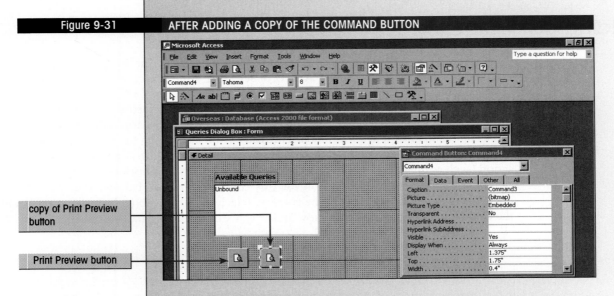

copy of Print Preview button

Print Preview button

4. Click the **Picture** text box in the property sheet, and then click the **Build** button [...].

5. Scroll through the Available Pictures list box, click **MS Access Query**, and then click the **OK** button. Access closes the Picture Builder dialog box and places the new picture on the command button.

6. Close the property sheet, and then save your form design changes.

You can now add the final command button using Control Wizards. The Close button will close the dialog box when the user clicks it.

REFERENCE   WINDOW   **RW**

Adding a Command Button to a Form Using Control Wizards
- If necessary, click the Control Wizards tool on the toolbox so that it is selected.
- Click the Command Button tool on the toolbox.
- Position the pointer where you want the command button to appear, and then click the mouse button.
- Complete the Command Button Wizard dialog boxes to select the action category and the action for the command button, enter the text to display on the command button, define a hot key (or select a picture for the button), and then enter a name for the button.

To define the Close button, you'll use the Control Wizards tool because the tool automatically attaches the correct VBA code (for closing the dialog box) to the command button. Standard operations, such as opening and closing forms, are good candidates for using the Control Wizards tool. Elsa also wants a user to be able to close the dialog box using a keyboard combination, so you will specify the letter "C" as the hot key for the Close button. To underline the letter C and make it the hot key, you need to enter &Close as the Caption property value for the command button control on the form. Placing an ampersand (&) to the left of a character in a caption underlines the character on the open form and makes it that control's hot key. Note that you can specify any character in a button's name, not just the first, as the hot key. However, each command button on a form must have a unique hot key.

To add the Close command button using the Control Wizards tool:

1. Click the **Control Wizards** tool ▨ on the toolbox to select it.

2. Click the **Command Button** tool ▭ on the toolbox, position the pointer's plus symbol at the 2-inch mark on the horizontal ruler and the 1.75-inch mark on the vertical ruler, and then click the mouse button. Access adds a command button to the form and, after a few seconds, opens the first Command Button Wizard dialog box. The Sample box shows how the command button will appear. See Figure 9-32.

Figure 9-32   **FIRST COMMAND BUTTON WIZARD DIALOG BOX**

You'll now select the command that will be attached to the command button. The dialog box form must close when the user clicks the Close button, so you'll select the Close Form action in the Form Operations category for this button.

3. Click **Form Operations** in the Categories list box, click **Close Form** in the Actions list box, and then click the **Next** button. Access opens the next Command Button Wizard dialog box, in which you specify the text or picture you want to appear on the button. In this case, Elsa wants the button to display the word "Close," with the letter "C" identified as the hot key.

4. Click the **Text** option button, select **Close Form** in the text box, and then type **&Close**. Notice that the sample button changes to show the word "Close" with an underlined "C." See Figure 9-33.

Figure 9-33   **SPECIFYING THE TEXT ON THE COMMAND BUTTON**

5. Click the **Next** button to open the next Command Button Wizard dialog box, in which you enter a name for the button.

6. Type **Close** in the text box, and then click the **Finish** button. Access closes the final Command Button Wizard dialog box and displays the new command button on the form.

In the next tutorial, you will create the VBA code for the Print Preview and Datasheet command buttons. This code will define what Access should do when a user clicks each button. The VBA code you will create must refer to the list box control. It is a good idea to give meaningful names to controls on your forms so you can identify them later, so you will enter the name QueryList for the list box control.

To set the Name property for the list box:

1. Open the property sheet for the list box control.

2. If necessary, click the **All** tab.

3. If necessary, scroll to the top of the property sheet, type **QueryList** in the Name text box, and then close the property sheet.

You've completed your work with the list box and command buttons for now, so you'll finish your initial work with the Queries Dialog Box form by modifying some of its properties.

Modifying **Form Properties**

Next, you'll resize and position the form and set the form's Border Style property to Dialog, according to Elsa's design.

To resize and position the form, and then set the form's Border Style property:

1. Drag the right edge of the form's Detail section to the 3.25-inch mark on the horizontal ruler, and then drag the bottom edge of the form's Detail section to the 3-inch mark on the vertical ruler.

2. Switch to Form view, and then position and resize the form until it is in approximately the same position and it is approximately the same size as the form shown in Figure 9-34.

 Figure 9-34   RESIZED AND REPOSITIONED FORM

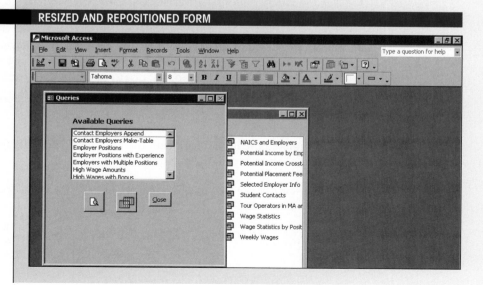

TROUBLE? If scroll bars appear on the form, slowly enlarge the form until they disappear.

3. Save your form layout changes, and then switch to Design view.

   You'll now set the form's Border Style property to Dialog, which will prevent a user from resizing the form.

4. In the Form window, right-click the form selector to open the shortcut menu, click **Properties** to display the property sheet, and then click the **All** tab (if necessary).

5. Scroll down the property sheet, click the right side of the **Border Style** text box, and then click **Dialog**.

6. Close the property sheet, save your form design changes, and then switch to Form view.

   TROUBLE? If the form is not the correct size or if scroll bars appear on the form, switch to Design view and set the form's Border Style property to Sizable. Switch back to Form view and resize the form. Save the form changes, switch to Design view, set the form's Border Style property to Dialog, and then save the form again and switch to Form view.

You'll now test the work you've completed for the Queries Dialog Box form.

Testing **the Queries Dialog Box Form**

You can test the form in Form view. Clicking the Print Preview command button, clicking the Datasheet command button, or double-clicking a query name in the list box will have no effect, because you have not yet added the VBA code for these actions. However, you can click the Close button or press Alt + C to close the form.

To test the form's design:

1. Click the **Close** button. The form closes and you return to the Database window.

2. Open the **Queries Dialog Box** form in Form view.

3. Double-click any query name in the list, click the **Print Preview** command button, and then click the **Datasheet** command button. You can select a query and click a command button, but doing so does not execute any other action.

3. Press **Alt + C**. The form closes and you return to the Database window.

You've completed the initial work with the Queries Dialog Box form. In the next session, you'll create the switchboard pages and their macros.

Session 9.2 QUICK | CHECK

1. What is an event property?
2. What is a macro group?
3. How do you determine the beginning and end of a macro in a macro group?
4. What is the purpose of the Where Condition argument for the OpenForm action?
5. What is the purpose of setting a form's Border Style property value to Dialog?
6. What is a list box control?
7. What are system tables?
8. How do you change the picture on a command button?
9. How do you make a copy of a form control in Design view?

SESSION 9.3

In this session, you will create a macro group and associate it with command buttons on the switchboard. You will also use the Switchboard Manager to create switchboard forms for the Overseas Database switchboard and the Reports switchboard.

Reviewing the Overseas Database Switchboard Requirements

Recall that a switchboard is a form that provides controlled access to a database's tables, forms, queries, reports, and other objects. You need to create the switchboard form that will serve as the primary user interface for the Overseas database. Figure 9-35 shows the finished Overseas Database switchboard form that you will create.

Figure 9-35	OVERSEAS DATABASE SWITCHBOARD FORM

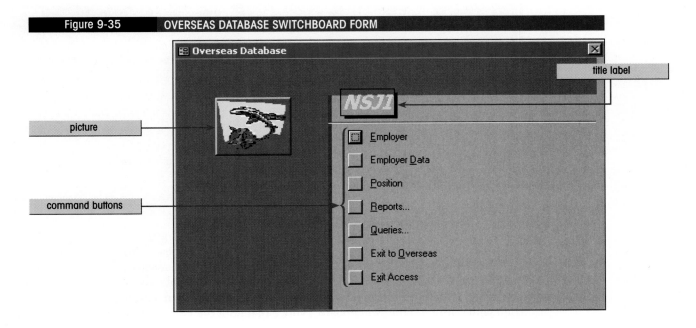

Elsa has the following design specifications for the Overseas Database switchboard:

- The form will not include Minimize, Restore, or Close buttons, scroll bars, navigation buttons, or a record selector.
- The form cannot be resized by the user.
- A picture of the plane and globe, with a raised special effect applied to it, will appear on the form.
- "Overseas Database" will appear in the form's title bar, and "NSJI" will be the form's title. The form title will have a shadowed special effect applied to it.
- The command buttons will have the same sizes.
- Macros will be attached to each command button to specify the actions that Access should take when the command button is clicked.

You'll also create the Reports switchboard, which will look similar to the Overseas Database switchboard. The Reports switchboard will have three command buttons: one to open the Employers and Their Positions report, a second to open the Potential Income report, and a third to return to the Overseas Database switchboard.

Your first step in creating the switchboard forms is to create the macros you need to attach to the command buttons on the switchboard forms.

Creating the Macro Group for the Switchboard

You'll create the macros for the switchboards in a macro group. The Macro Name column in the Macro window lets you distinguish macros in a macro group. Because a macro can contain many actions, the macro name tells Access where the macro begins. First you'll name one macro and list the actions for it. Then you'll name the second macro, list the actions for it, and so on. You can define the macros in any order, and you can group as many macros as you want in the Macro window.

REFERENCE WINDOW   RW

Creating a Macro Group

- In the Database window, click Macros in the Objects bar to display the Macros list, and then click the New button.
- Click the Macro Names button on the Macro Design toolbar.
- Enter the macros in the macro group by entering each macro name in the Macro Name column and the corresponding action(s) in the Action column. Enter comments as needed in the Comment column, and set arguments as needed in the Action Arguments pane.
- Click the Save button on the Macro Design toolbar, enter the macro group name in the Macro Name text box, and then click the OK button.

You will use the name Switchboard Macros for the macro group, so it will be easy to locate the macro group containing the macros for the switchboard. Figure 9-36 shows the names and actions for the six macros in the macro group. Each macro is named the same as its associated command button on the switchboard. For example, the Employer macro will execute the OpenForm action to open the Employer form when a user clicks the Employer command button on the switchboard. Notice that both the Exit to Overseas and Exit Access macros each contain two actions.

| Figure 9-36 | MACROS AND ACTIONS IN THE SWITCHBOARD MACROS MACRO GROUP |

MACRO NAME	ACTIONS	FORM NAME
Employer	OpenForm	Employer
Employer Data	OpenForm	Employer Data
Position	OpenForm	Position
Queries	OpenForm	Queries Dialog Box
Exit to Overseas	Close SendKeys	Switchboard
Exit Access	Close Quit	Switchboard

You will not use macros for the Reports command button on the Overseas Database switchboard or for any of the three buttons on the Reports switchboard. After you create the six macros, you'll use the Switchboard Manager to create the two switchboard forms and to handle the four buttons without macros.

You'll now create the Switchboard Macros macro group for the six command buttons on the switchboard form that use macros. First you'll start a new macro. Because you can enter macros in any order in a macro group, you'll next enter two of the macros—Exit Access and Employer—and then you'll save the macro group.

To create the macro group:

1. If you took a break after the previous session, make sure that Access is running and the **Overseas** database in the Tutorial folder on your Data Disk is open.

2. Click **Macros** in the Objects bar of the Database window, click the **New** button to open the Macro window, and then click the **Macro Names** button 🔲 on the Macro Design toolbar. Access adds the Macro Name column to the left of the Action column.

    Next, you'll enter the Exit Access macro and its two actions: the Close action to close the switchboard form and the Quit action to exit Access.

3. Type **Exit Access**, press the **Tab** key, click the **Action** list arrow, click **Close**, press the **Tab** key, and then type **Close Switchboard**.

    You need to specify the arguments for the Close action. In the Object Type text box, you specify the type of object to close, in this case, a form. In the Object Name text box, you specify which object to close. Even though you haven't created the Switchboard form yet, you can specify it as the object to close.

4. In the Action Arguments pane, click the right side of the **Object Type** text box, and then click **Form**.

5. Click the **Object Name** text box, and then type **Switchboard**. You've completed the first action for the first macro.

    Next, you'll define the second action for this macro, which will exit the Access program.

6. Click the right side of the second row's **Action** text box, scroll through the list, and then click **Quit**. You've completed the first macro, which contains two actions: the first to close the switchboard form and the second to exit Access. These two actions will occur in sequence when a user clicks the Exit Access command button on the switchboard.

Next, you'll define the second macro, Employer, which will open the Employer form.

7. Click the third row's **Macro Name** text box, type **Employer**, press the **Tab** key, click the list arrow, scroll through the list, click **OpenForm**, press the **Tab** key, and then type **Open Employer form**.

Next, you'll specify the name of the form to open.

8. In the Action Arguments pane, click the right side of the **Form Name** text box, and then click **Employer**. You've completed the second macro, which contains one action.

9. Save the macro as **Switchboard Macros**. See Figure 9-37.

TWO MACROS IN THE MACRO GROUP

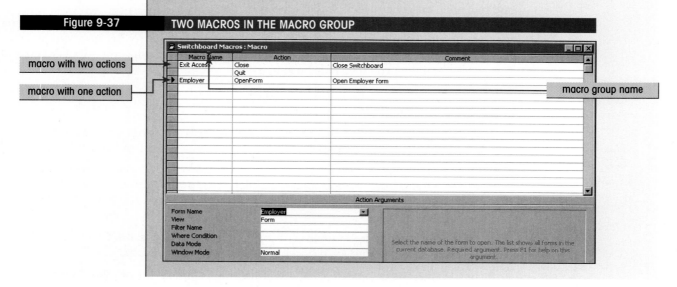

The macro name, which appears in the Macro window title bar, is Switchboard Macros. Switchboard Macros is also the name of the macro group, because the Switchboard Macros macro contains more than one macro. The first macro in the macro group is Exit Access, and the second macro in the macro group is Employer. A macro in a macro group starts in the row containing the macro name and continues until the next macro name or a blank row.

When Access executes the Exit Access macro, it runs the Close action, it runs the Quit action, and then the macro ends. The Employer macro begins with the OpenForm action and ends when it reaches the end of the macro group.

Next, you'll enter three more macros—the first to open the Employer Data form, the second to open the Position form, and the third to open the Queries Dialog Box form.

To add three macros to the macro group:

1. Click the fourth row's **Macro Name** text box, type **Employer Data**, press the **Tab** key, click the **Action** list arrow, scroll through the list, click **OpenForm**, press the **Tab** key, and then type **Open Employer Data form**.

2. In the Action Arguments pane, click the **Form Name** text box, click the list arrow, and then click **Employer Data**. You've completed the third macro, which contains one action to open the Employer Data form.

3. Click the fifth row's **Macro Name** text box, type **Position**, press the **Tab** key, click the **Action** list arrow, click **OpenForm**, press the **Tab** key, and then type **Open Position form**.

4. In the Action Arguments pane, click the **Form Name** text box, click the list arrow, and then click **Position**. You've completed the fourth macro, which contains one action to open the Position form.

5. Click the sixth row's **Macro Name** text box, type **Queries**, press the **Tab** key, click the **Action** list arrow, click **OpenForm**, press the **Tab** key, and then type **Open Queries Dialog Box form**.

6. In the Action Arguments pane, click the **Form Name** text box, click the list arrow, and then click **Queries Dialog Box**. You've completed the fifth macro, which contains one action to open the Queries Dialog Box form.

The final macro you need to define is the Exit to Overseas macro, which will execute two actions: the Close action to close the switchboard and the **SendKeys action**, which simulates keystrokes. In this macro, you will use the SendKeys action to simulate pressing the F11 key, which activates the Database window, because Elsa wants users to return to the Database window after closing the switchboard.

To finish creating the macro group:

1. Click the seventh row's **Macro Name** text box, type **Exit to Overseas**, press the **Tab** key, click the **Action** list arrow, click **Close**, press the **Tab** key, and then type **Close Switchboard**.

2. In the Action Arguments pane, click the **Object Type** text box, click the list arrow, click **Form**, click the **Object Name** text box, and then type **Switchboard**.

3. Click the right side of the eighth row's **Action** text box, scroll the list, click **SendKeys**, press the **Tab** key, and then type **Activate Database window**.

   For the SendKeys action, you need to specify the Keystrokes argument value {F11}, which is the same as pressing the F11 key, so that the action will return to the Database window after the switchboard form closes.

4. In the Action Arguments pane, click the **Keystrokes** text box, and then type **{F11}**. Be sure to type the braces but not the period. You've completed the second of two actions for the final macro. See Figure 9-38.

Figure 9-38   COMPLETED MACRO GROUP CONTAINING SIX MACROS

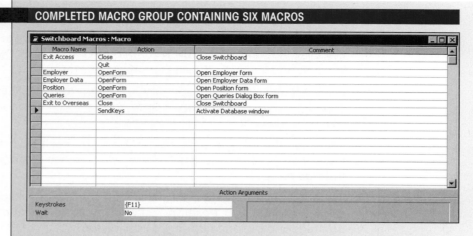

TROUBLE? Compare your macros to those shown in Figure 9-38. If any of your macros are not correct, click the appropriate text box and use the list arrow to select the correct option or edit the text to correct it.

5. Save your macro changes, and then close the Macro window.

Now that you've defined all the macros that will execute the necessary actions for the command buttons on the switchboard, you can create the form for the switchboard.

Creating a Switchboard

To create the switchboard, you'll use the Access Switchboard Manager. The **Switchboard Manager** is a Microsoft Access tool that helps you create and customize a switchboard. When you use the Switchboard Manager, you specify the command buttons that will appear on the switchboard. For each button, you identify the command to execute when its button is clicked. The Switchboard Manager automatically attaches the command to the OnClick property for that command button; this property specifies the action to take when the command button is clicked. Some commands require one or more arguments, which you can specify as well. When you complete the switchboard design, the Switchboard Manager creates a form for your switchboard with the default name Switchboard. The Switchboard Manager also creates a table, named **Switchboard Items**, which contains records describing the command buttons on the switchboard.

The Switchboard Manager allows you to create only one switchboard form for a database, but the switchboard can contain many pages. You can designate only one of the switchboard pages as the default page. The **default page**, or **main page**, is the switchboard page that will appear when you open the switchboard form. You can place command buttons on the default page to open other switchboard pages.

You will use the Switchboard Manager to create the switchboard form for the Overseas database. Review the design of the form shown in Figure 9-35. Notice that each command button has an associated hot key, which is indicated by the underlined letter in the button's label. As you use the Switchboard Manager to create the form, you'll place the appropriate command buttons on the switchboard, define the hot keys, and associate the corresponding macros from the Switchboard Macros macro group with the buttons.

The Overseas Database switchboard shown in Figure 9-35 will be the default page. You'll create a second switchboard page for the Reports switchboard. As shown in Figure 9-39, this switchboard page will contain command buttons to print the Employers and Their Positions report and the Potential Income report, and to return to the default page.

| Figure 9-39 | REPORTS SWITCHBOARD AS A SECOND SWITCHBOARD PAGE |

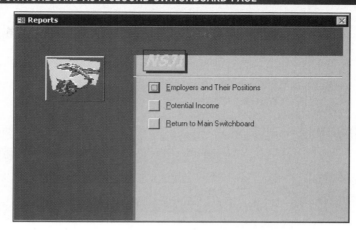

First, you'll create the switchboard form and two switchboard pages.

To create the switchboard form with two pages:

1. Click **Tools** on the menu bar, point to **Database Utilities**, and then click **Switchboard Manager**. Access opens a dialog box asking if you want to create a switchboard.

   TROUBLE? If you do not see the Switchboard Manager command in the Database Utilities list, it might not be installed on your computer. See your instructor or technical support person for assistance.

2. Click the **Yes** button. The Switchboard Manager dialog box opens. See Figure 9-40.

| Figure 9-40 | SWITCHBOARD MANAGER DIALOG BOX |

The Main Switchboard page, which is the default page, is created with the switchboard. You use the Switchboard Manager dialog box to add new pages, to edit and delete existing pages, or to change the default page. You will add a new page next.

3. Click the **New** button. The Create New dialog box opens.

4. Type **Reports** in the Switchboard Page Name text box, and then click the **OK** button. The Create New dialog box closes, and the Switchboard Pages list box now shows the original default page and the new Reports page.

Next, you'll edit the default page to change its name to Overseas Database.

5. Make sure the **Main Switchboard (Default)** page is selected, and then click the **Edit** button. The Edit Switchboard Page dialog box opens on top of the Switchboard Manager dialog box. This dialog box lets you edit the name of the selected switchboard page and add command buttons to the page.

6. Select the current entry in the Switchboard Name text box, and then type **Overseas Database**. See Figure 9-41.

Figure 9-41	EDIT SWITCHBOARD PAGE DIALOG BOX

Adding Command Buttons to a Switchboard Page

You can now add the command buttons for each macro in the Switchboard Macros macro group. Each command button will carry out the actions in its associated macro when the command button is clicked.

To add the first command button to the switchboard page:

1. Click the **New** button in the Edit Switchboard Page dialog box. The Edit Switchboard Item dialog box opens.

   The first button you will add is the Employer button, which will open the Employer form. According to Elsa's design, the hot key for this button is E.

2. Type **&Employer** in the Text text box. This text will appear to the right of the command button on the form. Recall that the ampersand (&) creates the hot key.

   Next, you need to specify the command that will be executed when the user clicks the button. In this case, you want Access to run the Employer macro, which displays the Employer form. This macro is part of the Switchboard Macros group.

3. Click the **Command** list arrow, and then click **Run Macro**. The third text box in the Edit Switchboard Item dialog box now displays the label "Macro." In this text box, you need to specify the macro to run when the button is clicked. When you click the Macro list arrow, you will see a list of all the macros defined for the database. The names of macros that are part of the macro group you created are preceded with the text "Switchboard Macros" to identify them as belonging to that group.

4. Click the **Macro** list arrow, and then click **Switchboard Macros.Employer**. The first command button definition is now completed. See Figure 9-42.

Figure 9-42	EDIT SWITCHBOARD ITEM DIALOG BOX

name of button on the switchboard

action to execute when the button is clicked

macro to execute when the button is clicked

Edit Switchboard Item

Text: &Employer

Command: Run Macro

Macro: Switchboard Macros.Employer

OK

Cancel

5. Click the **OK** button. The Switchboard Manager returns to the Edit Switchboard Page dialog box. Notice that the Items on this Switchboard list box now shows the Employer command button.

Five of the remaining six command buttons in the Overseas Database switchboard page have associated macros in the Switchboard Macros group; the Reports command button does not. Next, you'll add these five command buttons to the switchboard.

To add five additional command buttons to the default page:

1. Click the **New** button in the Edit Switchboard Page dialog box. The Edit Switchboard Item dialog box opens.

2. Type **Employer &Data** in the Text text box.

3. Click the **Command** list arrow, and then click **Run Macro**.

4. Click the **Macro** list arrow, scroll down the list, and then click **Switchboard Macros.Employer Data**.

5. Click the **OK** button. The definition of the second command button, Employer date is now completed. When clicked, this button will run the Employer Data macro in the Switchboard Macros macro group, which opens the Employer Data form in Form view.

6. Repeat Steps 1 through 5 to define the **&Position** command button to run the macro named **Switchboard Macros.Position**.

The next command button you need to define is the button for opening the Queries Dialog Box form. According to Elsa's design, the name of this button includes the ellipsis after the word "Queries," indicating that a dialog box will open when the button is clicked.

7. Repeat Steps 1 through 5 to define the **&Queries...** command button (be sure to type the ellipsis in the button name) to run the macro named **Switchboard Macros.Queries**.

8. Repeat Steps 1 through 5 to define the **Exit to &Overseas** command button to run the macro named **Switchboard Macros.Exit to Overseas**.

9. Repeat Steps 1 through 5 to define the **E&xit Access** command button to run the macro named **Switchboard Macros.Exit Access**. The switchboard's default page contains six command buttons. See Figure 9-43.

Figure 9-43	SIX COMMAND BUTTONS ADDED TO THE DEFAULT PAGE

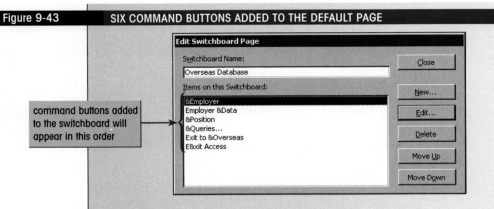

command buttons added to the switchboard will appear in this order

TROUBLE? Compare your Edit Switchboard Page dialog box with the one shown in Figure 9-43. If any of your command buttons are incorrect, click the button name and then click the Edit button. Make the necessary changes and then click the OK button to return to the Edit Switchboard Page dialog box.

The Overseas Database switchboard page is completed, except for the Reports command button. You'll add this command button next.

To add the last command button to the page:

1. Click the **New** button in the Edit Switchboard Page dialog box. The Edit Switchboard Item dialog box opens.

2. Type **&Reports...** in the Text text box. Be sure to type the ellipsis in the command button name.

   Because you do not have a macro in the Switchboard Macros macro group for this command button, you will not select Run Macro in the Command text box. Instead, you'll accept the default command, Go to Switchboard, which allows you to change from one switchboard page to another.

3. Click the **Switchboard** list arrow, and then click **Reports**.

4. Click the **OK** button. The switchboard design for the Overseas Database switchboard page now contains all the necessary command buttons.

In Elsa's design for the Overseas Database switchboard page, the Reports command button precedes the Queries command button. You'll need to move the Reports command button to its correct position in the switchboard page.

Moving Command Buttons in a Switchboard Page

You can delete and move command buttons in a switchboard page by selecting an entry in the Items on this Switchboard list box and then clicking the Delete, Move Up, or Move Down buttons. You'll use the Move Up button to reposition the Reports command button.

To reposition the Reports command button:

1. Click **&Reports...** in the Items on this Switchboard list box, and then click the **Move Up** button. The &Reports... entry moves up one position in the list box and remains selected. See Figure 9-44.

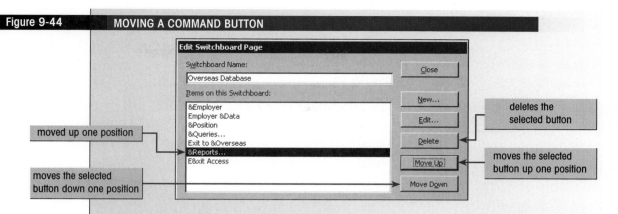

Figure 9-44 — **MOVING A COMMAND BUTTON**

2. Click the **Move Up** button two more times to correctly position the &Reports... entry above the &Queries... entry.

   You've finished the Overseas Database switchboard page, so you can close the Edit Switchboard Page dialog box.

3. Click the **Close** button to close the Edit Switchboard Page dialog box. You return to the Switchboard Manager dialog box.

Next, you'll add the command buttons to the Reports switchboard page.

Adding Command Buttons to a Second Switchboard Page

You've already used the Run Macro and Go to Switchboard options in the Edit Switchboard Item dialog box. The other Command text box options in this dialog box that you can use are: Open Form in Add Mode, Open Form in Edit Mode, Open Report, Design Application, Exit Application, and Run Code. For the Reports switchboard page, you'll use the Open Report option for the first two command buttons (Employers and Their Positions, Potential Income) and the Go to Switchboard for the Return to Main Switchboard command button.

To add command buttons to the Reports switchboard page:

1. Click **Reports** in the Switchboard Pages list box, and then click the **Edit** button. The Edit Switchboard Page dialog box opens on top of the Switchboard Manager dialog box.

2. Click the **New** button. The Edit Switchboard Item dialog box opens.

3. Type **&Employers and Their Positions** in the Text text box.

4. Click the **Command** list arrow, and then click **Open Report**. The third text box in the Edit Switchboard Item dialog box now displays the label "Report." In this text box, you specify the report to open when the button is clicked. When you click the Report list arrow, you see a list of all the reports defined for the database.

5. Click the **Report** list arrow, click **Employers and Their Positions**, and then click the **OK** button.

6. Repeat Steps 2 through 5 to define the **&Potential Income** command button to open the report named **Potential Income**.

7. Click the **New** button, type **&Return to Main Switchboard**, click the **Switchboard** list arrow, click **Overseas Database**, and then click the **OK** button. The Reports switchboard page now contains all the necessary command buttons. See Figure 9-45.

Figure 9-45   COMPLETED REPORTS SWITCHBOARD PAGE

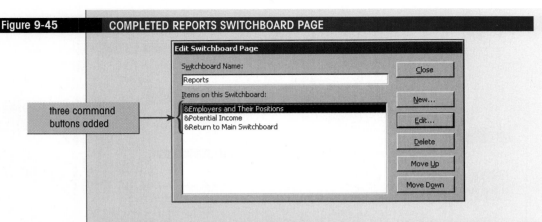

three command
buttons added

TROUBLE? Compare your Edit Switchboard Page dialog box with the one shown in Figure 9-45. If any of your command buttons are incorrect, click the button name and then click the Edit button. Make the necessary changes and then click the OK button to return to the Edit Switchboard Page dialog box.

Viewing and Testing a Switchboard

You are finished using the Switchboard Manager, so you can now exit it and view the new switchboard.

To exit the Switchboard Manager and view the Switchboard form:

1. Click the **Close** button to close the Edit Switchboard Page dialog box.

2. Click the **Close** button to close the Switchboard Manager dialog box and return to the Database window.

3. If necessary, click **Forms** in the Objects bar of the Database window to display the Forms list.

4. Right-click **Switchboard** to open the shortcut menu, and then click **Open**. Access opens the Switchboard form. See Figure 9-46.

Figure 9-46   SWITCHBOARD FORM

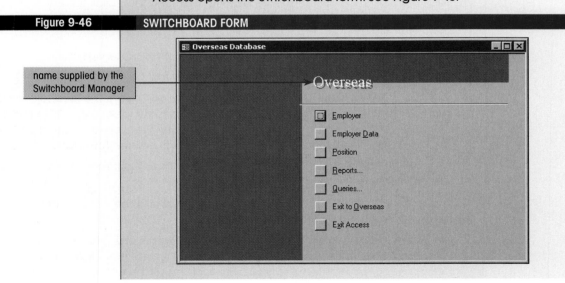

name supplied by the
Switchboard Manager

The Switchboard form contains the seven command buttons you defined for the Overseas Database switchboard page using the Switchboard Manager. Each command button has an attached label displaying the command button name. The underscore in the command button name indicates the hot key for that button. The title "Overseas" appears in white text in a label control above the command buttons; the Switchboard Manager automatically created this label on the form. Behind the Overseas label is another copy of the Overseas label displaying the text in gray letters, creating a shadowed effect. The Switchboard Manager also added the large green areas on the switchboard, which are green rectangle objects.

Overall, Elsa is pleased with the appearance of the Switchboard form, but there are some changes she would like you to make. Before you make these changes, you will test some of the command buttons to make sure that they work properly.

To test the command buttons:

1. Click the **Employer** command button. Access displays the record for Beantown Tours in the Employer form in Form view.

2. Click the **Close** button ☒ on the Employer window title bar to close it and return to the switchboard.

3. Press **Alt + P**. Access opens the Position form and displays the first Position record.

4. Close the **Position** form to return to the switchboard.

5. Click the **Reports** command button. Access replaces the Overseas Database switchboard page with the Reports switchboard page.

6. Click the **Potential Income** command button. Access opens the Potential Income report in Print Preview.

7. Close the **Potential Income** report to return to the Reports switchboard page.

8. Click the **Return to Main Switchboard** command button to replace the Reports switchboard page with the Overseas Database switchboard page.

Elsa wants you to make some changes to the design of the switchboard. She likes the layout of the command buttons, but she wants you to make sure that the form always has the same size when it appears on the screen. She also wants you to remove the Overseas label object and add a new label with the text "NSJI." Finally, she asks you to include the picture of a plane and globe.

Modifying a Switchboard

Because the switchboard is a form, you can make Elsa's changes in Design view. However, you need to be careful not to make any changes to the command buttons that would affect the actions and macros associated with them. You should only make these types of changes using the Switchboard Manager. If you were to change the definitions of any of the command buttons in Design view, the Switchboard Manager would not be able to make the necessary updates and the switchboard would not function correctly.

Next, you'll delete the Overseas label, place the new label "NSJI" on the form, and add the plane and globe picture.

To delete the Overseas label:

1. Switch to Design view, right-click the **Overseas label** above the command buttons to open the shortcut menu, and then click **Cut**. The label is deleted. Notice that there is a second Overseas label now visible. This label appeared as the shadow of the first label on the switchboard.

2. Right-click the **Overseas label** above the command buttons to open the shortcut menu, and then click **Cut**. The second label is deleted.

You can now add the NSJI label in the area above the command buttons.

To add the NSJI label to the switchboard:

1. If necessary, click the **Toolbox** button 🛠 on the Form Design toolbar to open the toolbox, and then make sure the toolbox is docked below the Formatting toolbar.

2. Click the **Label** tool *Aa* on the toolbox.

3. Position the pointer in the Detail section; when the pointer's plus symbol is positioned at the 2-inch mark on the horizontal ruler and the 0.375-inch mark on the vertical ruler, click the mouse button.

4. Type **NSJI**, and then press the **Enter** key.

   Elsa wants the title to stand out, so she asks you to format it in bold and italics, increase its font size, change its font color to yellow, and apply the shadowed special effect.

5. Click the **Bold** button **B** on the Formatting toolbar, click the **Italic** button *I* on the Formatting toolbar, click the **Font Size** list arrow on the Formatting toolbar, and then click **18**.

6. Click the list arrow for the **Font/Fore Color** button **A** on the Formatting toolbar to display the palette of available colors.

7. Click the bright yellow color box (the third button in the fourth row). The NSJI label now appears bright yellow.

8. Click the list arrow for the **Special Effect** button ▭ on the Formatting toolbar, and then click the **Shadowed** button ▱.

9. Click **Format** on the menu bar, point to **Size**, and then click **To Fit**. Access resizes the label box to display the entire label.

Next, you'll add the picture of the plane and globe to the form, and then you'll apply the raised special effect to the picture to enhance it.

To add the picture to the switchboard:

1. Click the **Image** tool 🖼 on the toolbox, position the pointer's plus symbol at the 0.5-inch mark on the horizontal ruler and the 0.5-inch mark on the vertical ruler, and then click the mouse button to place the graphic image control. The Insert Picture dialog box opens.

2. In the Look in list box, select the **Tutorial** folder on your Data Disk (if necessary), click **Airplane** in the file list, and then click the **OK** button. Access inserts the picture on the form.

3. Click the list arrow for the **Special Effect** button 🔲 on the Formatting toolbar, and then click the **Raised** button 🔲. The raised effect is applied to the button. You've finished making the necessary changes to the layout of the Switchboard form. See Figure 9-47.

Figure 9-47	MODIFIED SWITCHBOARD FORM LAYOUT

Now you can change the form properties so that the form will be correctly sized and positioned on the screen.

To change the Switchboard form properties:

1. Right-click the form selector (see Figure 9-47) to open the shortcut menu, and then click **Properties** to display the property sheet for the form.

   First you'll set the Auto Resize property to No so that Access will not resize the form when it is opened.

2. Click the **Format** tab, and then double-click **Yes** in the Auto Resize text box to change this property setting to No.

   Now you'll set the Border Style property to Dialog to prevent users from resizing the form.

3. Click the right side of the **Border Style** text box, and then click **Dialog**.

   Setting the Close Button property to No disables the Close button on the form's title bar. You'll disable this button because Elsa wants users to close the form by clicking the Exit to Overseas or Exit Access command buttons.

4. Double-click **Yes** in the Close Button text box to change the property setting to No.

5. Close the property sheet, save your form design changes, and then close the form.

Elsa wants to view the modified switchboard, so you'll open the switchboard in Form view.

To view the switchboard:

1. Open the **Switchboard** form in Form view. See Figure 9-48.

| Figure 9-48 | MODIFIED SWITCHBOARD IN FORM VIEW |

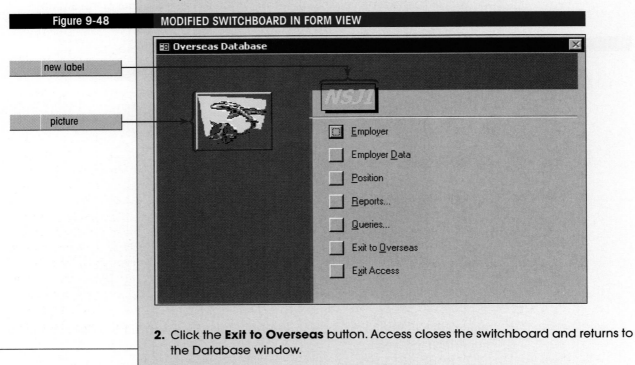

new label

picture

2. Click the **Exit to Overseas** button. Access closes the switchboard and returns to the Database window.

3. Exit Access.

Elsa's design for the Overseas database user interface also includes a restricted menu bar and a hidden toolbar. In Tutorial 11, you'll add these features to the switchboard, and in Tutorial 10 you'll create the necessary VBA code for the Queries Dialog Box form command buttons.

Session 9.3 QUICK | CHECK

1. What does the SendKeys action do?

2. What is the Switchboard Manager?

3. To which property does the Switchboard Manager automatically assign commands for each command button?

4. When using the Command Button Wizard, how do you define a hot key for a command button?

5. How do you specify that a form is a dialog box?

6. What are two special effects you can use for a control?

REVIEW ASSIGNMENTS

Elsa wants you to create a switchboard interface for the **Work** database. To help with this request, you'll complete the following steps.

1. Make sure your Data Disk is in the appropriate disk drive, start Access, and then open the **Work** database in the Review folder on your Data Disk.

2. Design and create a form named **Reports Dialog Box** that has the following components and characteristics:
   a. The text "Print Reports" appears in the form's title bar.

   Explore
   b. A list box (with a Name property value of ReportList) displays all the report names contained in the **Work** database. To place the report names in the list box, use an SQL SELECT statement to retrieve the report names from the **MSysObjects** table. Delete the label attached to the list box.
   c. The text "Reports Available," formatted with 10-point, bold font, appears as a heading above the list box.
   d. Two command buttons appear below the list box. The left command button displays the Preview Document icon, and the right command button displays the word "Close" with the letter "C" underlined. Double-clicking a report name has the same effect as selecting a report name in the list box and clicking the left command button. Both events cause Access to display the Print Preview window for the selected report. (You will add the VBA code for these events in the next tutorial. For now, double-clicking or clicking should cause no action to occur.) Clicking the Close command button causes Access to close the dialog box. The letter "C" is the hot key.
   e. Resize the form's Detail section in Design view, resize the form in Form view, and then set form properties that are appropriate for a dialog box.

   Explore
3. Create a macro group named **Switchboard Macros** that contains macros to be used with the command buttons on the switchboard you'll create in the next step. The macros perform these actions: open the **Territory** table datasheet, open the **Recruiter** form in Form view, open the **Student Info** form in Form view, open the **Reports Dialog Box** form in Form view, and close the switchboard and activate the Database window.

4. Design and create a switchboard form named **Switchboard**. Use Figure 9-49 and the following descriptions as a guide to create the switchboard.

Figure 9-49

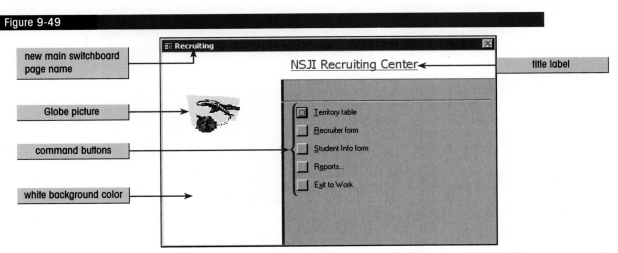

a. Use the Switchboard Manager to create the switchboard. Place the command buttons on the form; the command buttons should use the macros in the **Switchboard Macros** macro group. Define hot keys for each command button. Specify "Recruiting" as the main switchboard page name.

b. Delete the default label and the shadow label on the form and place a label at the top of the switchboard. The label should read "NSJI Recruiting Center" and should appear as 14-point, underlined text in a font color of your choice.

c. Add the **Globe** picture from the Review folder to the appropriate position on the switchboard.

Explore

d. Set the background color for the switchboard, as shown in Figure 9-49, resize the switchboard in Form view, and then set form properties that are appropriate for a switchboard.

5. Save the **Switchboard** form, and then test the command buttons and the **Reports Dialog Box** form to make sure that your switchboard items work correctly. If necessary, return to the Switchboard Manager and make any corrections.

6. Click the Exit to Work command button to close the **Switchboard** form, and then exit Access.

CASE PROBLEMS

Case 1. Lim's Video Photography Youngho Lim wants the **Shoots** database to include an easy-to-use switchboard interface. To help Youngho with his request, you'll complete the following steps.

1. Make sure your Data Disk is in the appropriate disk drive, start Access, and then open the **Shoots** database in the Cases folder on your Data Disk.

Explore

2. Create a macro group named **Switchboard Macros** that contains macros to be used with the command buttons on the switchboard you'll create in the next step. The macros perform these actions: open the **ShootDesc** table datasheet, open the **Client** form in Form view, open the **Client Info** form in Form view, open the **Shoot Data** query datasheet, open the **Clients and Contracts** report in Print Preview, and close the switchboard and activate the Database window.

3. Design and create a switchboard form named **Switchboard**. Use Figure 9-50 and the following descriptions as a guide to create the switchboard.

Figure 9-50

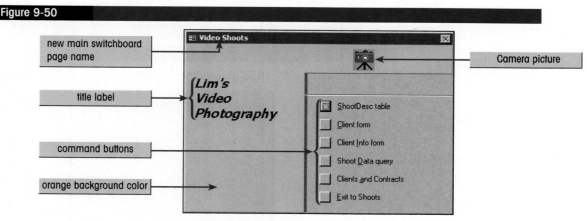

a. Use the Switchboard Manager to create the switchboard. Place the command buttons on the form; the command buttons should use the macros in the **Switchboard Macros** macro group. Define hot keys for each command button. Specify "Video Shoots" as the main switchboard page name.

b. Delete the default label and the shadow label on the form and place a label on the left side of the switchboard. The label should read "Lim's Video Photography" and should appear as 14-point, bold, italic text. (*Hint*: Press Shift + Enter after typing the first and second words in the label.)

Explore
    c. Add the **Camera** picture from the Cases folder to the appropriate position on the switchboard.

    d. Set the background color for the switchboard, as shown in Figure 9-50, resize the switchboard in Form view, and then set form properties that are appropriate for a switchboard.

4. Save the **Switchboard** form, and then test the command buttons to make sure that your switchboard items work correctly. If necessary, return to the Switchboard Manager and make any corrections.

5. Click the Exit to Shoots command button to close the **Switchboard** form, and then exit Access.

Case 2. DineAtHome.course.com To make the **AtHome** database easier to use, Claire Picard wants you to create a switchboard interface for it. To help Claire with her request, you'll complete the following steps.

1. Make sure your Data Disk is in the appropriate disk drive, start Access, and then open the **AtHome** database in the Cases folder on your Data Disk.

Explore
2. Create a macro group named **Switchboard Macros** that contains macros to be used with the command buttons on the switchboard you'll create in the next step. The macros perform these actions: open the **Customer** table datasheet, open the **Restaurant** form in Form view, open the **Large Orders** query datasheet, open the **Orders by Restaurant** report in Print Preview, and close the switchboard and activate the Database window.

3. Design and create a switchboard form named **Switchboard**. Use Figure 9-51 and the following descriptions as a guide to create the switchboard.

Figure 9-51

a. Use the Switchboard Manager to create the switchboard. Place the command buttons on the form; the command buttons should use the macros in the **Switchboard Macros** macro group. Define hot keys for each command button. Specify "DineAtHome.course.com" as the main switchboard page name.

b. Delete the default label and the shadow label on the form and place a label at the top of the switchboard. The label should read "AtHome Main Control Center" and should appear as 14-point, italic, underlined, red text.

c. Add the **ServeHot** picture from the Cases folder in the appropriate position on the switchboard.

Explore
d. Set the background color for the switchboard to white, as shown in Figure 9-51. (*Hint*: Delete the rectangle objects created by the Switchboard Manager on the **Switchboard** form before setting the Detail section Back Color property.)

e. Resize the switchboard in Form view, and then set form properties that are appropriate for a switchboard.

4. Save the **Switchboard** form, and then test the command buttons to make sure that your switchboard items work correctly. If necessary, return to the Switchboard Manager and make any corrections.

5. Click the Exit to AtHome command button to close the **Switchboard** form, and then exit Access.

Case 3. Redwood Zoo Michael Rosenfeld wants the **ZooFunds** database to include an easy-to-use switchboard interface. To help Michael with his request, you'll complete the following steps.

1. Make sure your Data Disk is in the appropriate disk drive, start Access, and then open the **ZooFunds** database in the Cases folder on your Data Disk.

2. Design and create a form named **Queries Dialog Box** that has the following components and characteristics:
   a. The text "Queries" appears in the form's title bar.
   b. A list box (with a Name property value of QueryList) displays all the query names contained in the **ZooFunds** database. To place the query names in the list box, use an SQL SELECT statement to retrieve the query names from the **MSysObjects** table. Delete the label attached to the list box, and then widen the list box to approximately 2.25 inches.
   c. The text "Queries Available," formatted with 10-point, bold font, appears as a heading above the list box.
   d. Two command buttons appear below the list box. The left command button displays the MS Access Query icon, and the right command button displays the word "Close" with the letter "C" underlined. Double-clicking a query name has the same effect as selecting a query name in the list box and clicking the left command button. Both events cause Access to display the query datasheet for the selected query. (You will add the VBA code for these events in the next tutorial. For now, double-clicking or clicking should cause no action to occur.) Clicking the Close command button causes Access to close the dialog box. The letter "C" is the hot key.
   e. Resize the form's Detail section in Design view, resize the form in Form view, and then set form properties that that are appropriate for a dialog box.

3. Create a macro group named **Switchboard Macros** that contains macros to be used with the command buttons on the switchboard you'll create in the next step. The macros perform these actions: open the **Reception** table datasheet, open the **Costs** form in Form view, open the **Funds** form in Form view, open the **Queries Dialog Box** form in Form view, and close the switchboard and activate the Database window.

4. Design and create a switchboard form named **Switchboard**. Use Figure 9-52 and the following descriptions as a guide to create the switchboard.

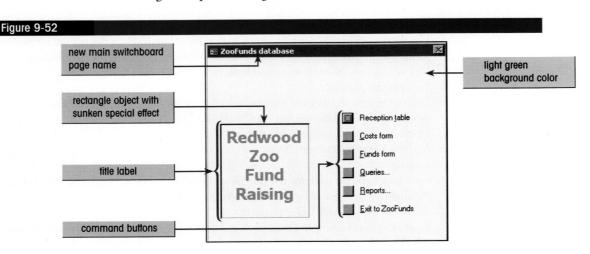

Figure 9-52

    a. Use the Switchboard Manager to create the switchboard. The switchboard should have two pages. Specify "ZooFunds database" as the main switchboard page name, and "Reports" as the second switchboard page name.

    b. Place the command buttons on the main switchboard page. Except for the "Reports…" command button, which should switch to the second switchboard page, the command buttons should use the macros in the **Switchboard Macros** macro group. Define hot keys for each command button.

    c. Place three command buttons on the Reports switchboard page. The command buttons perform these actions: open the **Donor** report, open the **Fund Pledges** report, and return to the main switchboard. Define hot keys for each command button. Do not use macros for the Reports switchboard page.

Explore

    d. Delete the default label and the shadow label on the form. On the left side of the form, enter the label shown in Figure 9-52 as 18-point, bold, red text; each word in the label should appear on a separate, centered line. (*Hint*: You can enter all words in the label as a single label control by pressing Shift + Enter after each word and then resizing the label box and centering the text after you're finished typing it.)

Explore

    e. Draw a rectangle around the label box, and then apply the sunken special effect to the rectangle.

Explore

    f. Set the background color of the form to light green, as shown in Figure 9-52. (*Hint*: Delete all rectangle and line objects created by the Switchboard Manager on the **Switchboard** form before setting the Detail section Back Color property.)

    g. Resize the switchboard in Form view, and then set form properties that are appropriate for a switchboard.

5. Save the **Switchboard** form, and then test the command buttons to make sure that your switchboard items work correctly. If necessary, return to the Switchboard Manager and make any corrections.

6. Click the Exit to ZooFunds command button to close the **Switchboard** form, and then exit Access.

Case 4. **Mountain River Adventures** Connor and Siobhan Dempsey want you to create a user-friendly interface, including a switchboard and dialog boxes, for the **Rivers** database. To help them with their request, you'll complete the following steps.

1. Make sure your Data Disk is in the appropriate disk drive, start Access, and then open the **Rivers** database in the Cases folder on your Data Disk.

2. Design and create a form named **Queries Dialog Box** that has the following components and characteristics:

    a. The text "Queries" appears in the form's title bar.

    b. A list box (with a Name property value of QueryList) displays all the query names contained in the **Rivers** database. To place the query names in the list box, use an SQL SELECT statement to retrieve the query names from the **MSysObjects** table. Delete the label attached to the list box, and then widen the list box to approximately 2.0 inches.

    c. The text "Queries Available," formatted with 10-point, bold font, appears as a heading above the list box.

    d. Two command buttons appear below the list box. The left command button displays the MS Access Query icon, and the right command button displays the word "Close" with the letter "C" underlined. Double-clicking a query name has the same effect as selecting a query name in the list box and clicking the left command button. Both events cause Access to display the query datasheet for the selected query. (You will add the VBA code for these events in the next tutorial. For now, double-clicking or clicking should cause no action to occur.) Clicking the Close command button causes Access to close the dialog box. The letter "C" is the hot key.

    e. Resize the form's Detail section in Design view, resize the form in Form view, and then set form properties that are appropriate for a dialog box.

> **Explore**

   3. Create a copy of the **Queries Dialog Box** form and name it **Reports Dialog Box**. Make the following modifications to the **Reports Dialog Box** form:
   a. Change the text that appears in the title bar to "Reports."
   b. Change the SQL SELECT statement to retrieve the report names from the **MSysObjects** table.
   c. Change the text that appears as a heading above the list box to "Reports Available."
   d. Change the left command button to display the Preview Document icon.
   e. Change the Name property value of the list box to "ReportList."
   f. Close the **Reports Dialog Box** form and save your changes.

   4. Create one macro named **Exit Switchboard** that will be used with a command button on the switchboard you'll create in the next step. The macro should close the switchboard and activate the Database window.

   5. Design and create a switchboard form named **Switchboard**. Use Figure 9-53 and the following descriptions as a guide to create the switchboard.

Figure 9-53

    a. Use the Switchboard Manager to create the switchboard. The switchboard should have two pages. Specify "Rivers" as the main switchboard page name, and "Forms" as the second switchboard page name.

> **Explore**

    b. Place four command buttons on the first switchboard page. The command buttons perform these actions: switch to the second switchboard page; open the **Queries Dialog Box** form; open the **Reports Dialog Box** form; and close the switchboard and activate the Database window, using the **Exit Switchboard** macro. Define hot keys for each command button.
    c. Place three command buttons on the Forms switchboard page. The command buttons perform these actions: open the **Costs** form in edit mode, open the **Extra** form in edit mode, and return to the main switchboard. Define hot keys for each command button. Do not use macros for this Forms switchboard page.
    d. Delete the default label and the shadow label on the form, and place a label at the top of the switchboard. The label should read "Mountain River Adventures" and should appear as 18-point bold, italic, and underlined text.

> **Explore**

    e. Set the background color of the form to light blue, as shown in Figure 9-53. (*Hint*: Delete all rectangle and line objects created by the Switchboard Manager on the **Switchboard** form before setting the Detail section Back Color property.)
    f. Resize the switchboard in Form view, and then set form properties that are appropriate for a switchboard.

   6. Save the **Switchboard** form, and then test the command buttons to make sure that your switchboard items work correctly. If necessary, return to the Switchboard Manager and make any corrections.

   7. Click the Exit to Rivers command button to close the **Switchboard** form, and then exit Access.

Explore

Case 5. eACH Internet Auction Site Chris and Pat Aquino want you to create a user-friendly switchboard interface for the **BuySel!** database. To help them with their request, you'll complete the following steps.

1. Make sure your Data Disk is in the appropriate drive, start Access, and then open the **BuySell** database in the Cases folder on your Data Disk.

2. Create a macro group named **Switchboard Macros** that contains macros to be used with the command buttons on the switchboard you'll create in the next step. The macros perform these actions: open the **Subcategory** table datasheet, open the **Item** form in Form view, open the **Registrant** form in Form view, open the **Projected Income Based on Minimum Bid** report in Print Preview, and close the switchboard and activate the Database window.

3. Design and create a switchboard form named **Switchboard**. Use Figure 9-54 and the following descriptions as a guide to create the switchboard.

Figure 9-54

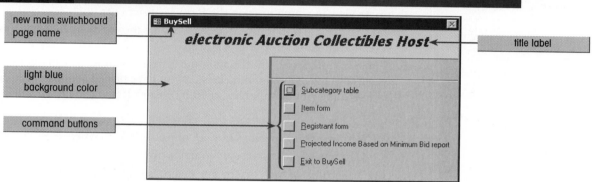

a. Use the Switchboard Manager to create the switchboard. Place the command buttons on the form; the command buttons should use the macros in the **Switchboard Macros** macro group. Define hot keys for each command button. Specify "BuySell" as the main switchboard page name.

b. Delete the default label and the shadow label on the form and place a label at the top of the switchboard. The label should read "electronic Auction Collectibles Host" and should appear as 16-point, bold, italic text.

c. Set the background color for the switchboard, as shown in Figure 9-54, resize the switchboard in Form view, and then set form properties that are appropriate for a switchboard.

4. Save the **Switchboard** form, and then test the command buttons to make sure that your switchboard items work correctly. If necessary, return to the Switchboard Manager and make any corrections.

5. Click the Exit to BuySell command button to close the **Switchboard** form, and then exit Access.

INTERNET ASSIGNMENTS

Student Union

The purpose of the Internet Assignments is to challenge you to find information on the Internet that you can use to create effective documents. The actual assignments are updated and maintained on the Course Technology Web site. Log on to the Internet and use your Web browser to go to the Student Online Companion to accompany this text at **www.course.com/NewPerspectives/studentunion**. Click the Online Companions link, and then click the link for this text.

QUICK CHECK ANSWERS

Session 9.1

1. A switchboard is a form that appears when you open a database and that provides controlled access to the database's tables, forms, queries, and reports. It lets you customize the organization of the user interface, and prevents users from changing the design of tables, forms, queries, reports, and other database objects.

2. A hot key is an underlined letter in a command button, menu name, menu option, or toolbar button that provides a keyboard shortcut for the object's operation. You can use shortcut keys to make a selection by holding down the Alt key while typing the underlined letter.

3. A macro is a command or a series of commands that you want Access to perform automatically for you. Each command in a macro is called an action.

4. An action argument provides additional facts Access needs to execute an action. The action for opening a form, for example, needs the form name and the appropriate view in which to open the form as arguments.

5. The MsgBox action causes Access to open a message box that remains on the screen until you click the OK button.

6. Single stepping executes a macro one action at a time, pausing between actions. You use single stepping to make sure you have placed actions in the right order and with the right arguments, thereby ensuring that the macro works correctly.

Session 9.2

1. An event property specifies how an object responds when an event occurs.

2. A macro group is a macro that contains other macros.

3. The beginning of each macro in a macro group has an entry in the Macro Name column of the Macro window; subsequent actions in the macro do not have entries in this column. The macro ends with the start of a new macro or at the end of the macro group, whichever comes first.

4. The Where Condition specifies which record to display in the form.

5. Users will not be able to resize the form using the pointer.

6. A control that displays a list of values.

7. Special tables maintained by Access that store information about the characteristics of a database and about the structure of its objects.

8. In Design view, open the property sheet for the command button. Click the All tab in the property sheet, click the Picture text box, and then click the Build button. Select the picture using the Picture Builder dialog box, and then click the OK button.

9. Right-click the object, click Copy on the shortcut menu, and then click the Paste button on the toolbar.

Session 9.3

1. The SendKeys action simulates keystrokes in a macro.

2. The Switchboard Manager is a Microsoft tool that helps you create and customize a switchboard.

3. OnClick

4. Type an ampersand (&) to the left of the hot key character in the command button name.

5. Open the form in Design view, open the form's property sheet, and then set the Border Style property to Dialog.

6. shadowed and raised

AC 10.01

OBJECTIVES

In this tutorial you will:

- Learn about Function procedures, Sub procedures, and modules

- Review and modify an existing Sub procedure in an event procedure

- Create Function procedures in a standard module

- Create event procedures

- Compile and test Function procedures, Sub procedures, and event procedures

- Hide text and change display colors

USING

AND WRITING VISUAL BASIC FOR APPLICATIONS CODE

Creating VBA Code for the Overseas Database User Interface

CASE

Northeast Seasonal Jobs International (NSJI)

Elsa reviews your progress in developing the graphical user interface for the Overseas database. So far, you have created the switchboard that contains command buttons for opening forms, opening a new switchboard page containing command buttons for opening reports, displaying a dialog box with a list of available queries, exiting the switchboard, and exiting the switchboard and Access. You also have created a macro group that contains the macros attached to the command buttons on the switchboard.

You'll continue developing the user interface by modifying the Queries Dialog Box form so that its command buttons carry out the appropriate operations. You'll also modify the Employer and Position forms to make data entry easier and to highlight important information on them. To make these modifications, you will write Visual Basic for Applications code to perform the necessary operations, and then you will attach the code to the appropriate event properties for the buttons and forms.

SESSION 10.1

In this session, you will learn about Visual Basic for Applications Function procedures, Sub procedures, and modules. You will review, use, and modify a Sub procedure, and create and test a Function procedure in a standard module. Then you will create, compile, and test an event procedure.

Introduction to Visual Basic for Applications

Your next task in the development of the graphical user interface for the Overseas database is to refine it further by adding a procedure to ensure proper capitalization of data entered using the Employer form. Elsa wants to make sure that all values entered in this form's State/Prov field will be stored in the Employer table using uppercase letters. She asks you to modify the form so that it will automatically convert any lowercase letters entered in the State/Prov field to uppercase. To accomplish this objective, you will use Visual Basic for Applications.

Visual Basic for Applications (VBA) is the programming language provided with Access and other Office XP programs. VBA is similar to **Visual Basic**, which is another Microsoft programming language, but VBA and Visual Basic each have features not found in the other programming language. When you use Access Help, you'll find Visual Basic references for many features shared by the two languages.

The process of writing VBA instructions is called **coding**. You write VBA instructions, called **statements**, to respond to events that occur with the objects in a database. A language such as VBA is, therefore, called both an **event-driven language** and an **object-oriented language**. Your experience with macros, which are also event-driven and object-oriented, should facilitate your learning of VBA. You can do almost anything with VBA that you can do with macros, but VBA gives you more control over commands and objects than you have with macros. For example, with VBA you can create your own procedures to perform special calculations. You can also change an object's properties dynamically; for example, VBA code can change the color on a form when the user enters or views a specific field value.

Events

Recall from Tutorial 9 that an **event** occurs when you take some action, such as using the mouse to click a button or pressing a key to choose an option. An **event property** specifies how an object responds when an event occurs. In Tutorial 9, you set event property values to macro names and Access executed the macros when those events occurred. You can also create a group of statements using VBA code and set an event property value to the name of that group of statements. Access will then execute the group of statements, or **procedure**, when the event occurs. Such a procedure is called an **event procedure**.

Access has over 60 events and associated event properties. As with actions, you do not need to learn all these events. You will gain experience with several event properties in this text, and if you need information on other event properties, you can use the Help system as a reference tool.

Next, you'll use Help to review two topics about events.

To use Help to learn about events:

1. Place your Data Disk in the appropriate disk drive, start Access, and then open the **Overseas** database in the Tutorial folder on your Data Disk.

2. Click the **Ask a Question** box on the menu bar, type **What are events?**, and then press the **Enter** key to display a list of relevant topics.

3. Click **Example of setting the value of a property in response to an event** in the list of topics to view the topic in the Microsoft Access Help window, and then if necessary maximize the Microsoft Access Help window. This topic provides examples using a macro and an event procedure to set the OnCurrent event property, which you'll use later in this tutorial. The OnCurrent event property specifies how an object responds when the Current event occurs.

4. After reviewing the topic, make sure the **Index** tab is selected, click the **Type keywords** text box, type **event**, and then click the **Search** button. The Choose a topic list box lists the topics for the event keyword.

5. If necessary, click **Order of events for database objects** in the Choose a topic list box, and then read the introductory paragraph of the displayed topic.

   You can click one of the five topics to expand it and display information about that topic. You're not interested in the details about events at this point, so you'll expand only the first topic.

6. Click **Order of events for controls on forms** in the Help window, and then review the contents of the displayed topic. Don't be concerned if you don't understand the topic, as long as you feel comfortable that you can find the topic if needed in the future.

7. Close the Microsoft Access Help window to return to the Database window.

Procedures

When you work with VBA, you code a group of statements that perform an operation or calculate a value, and then you attach the group to the event property of an object. Access then executes, or **calls**, these statements every time the event occurs for that object. Each group of statements is called a **procedure**. The two types of procedures are Function procedures and Sub procedures.

A **Function procedure**, or **function**, performs operations, returns a value, can accept input values, and can be used in expressions (recall that an expression is a calculation resulting in a single value). For example, some of the Overseas database queries use built-in Access functions, such as Sum, Count, and Avg, to calculate a sum, a record count, or an average. To meet Elsa's request, you will create a function named CapAll by entering the appropriate VBA statements. The CapAll function will accept the value entered in a field text box—in this case, the State/Prov field—as an input value, capitalize all characters of the field value, and then return the changed field value to be stored in the database and displayed in the field text box.

A **Sub procedure**, or **subroutine**, performs operations and can accept input values, but does not return a value and cannot be used in expressions. In the next session, you will create a Sub procedure that displays a message on the Position form only when the data for a full-time position is displayed in the form.

Modules

You store a group of related procedures together in a **module**. Figure 10-1 shows the structure of a typical module.

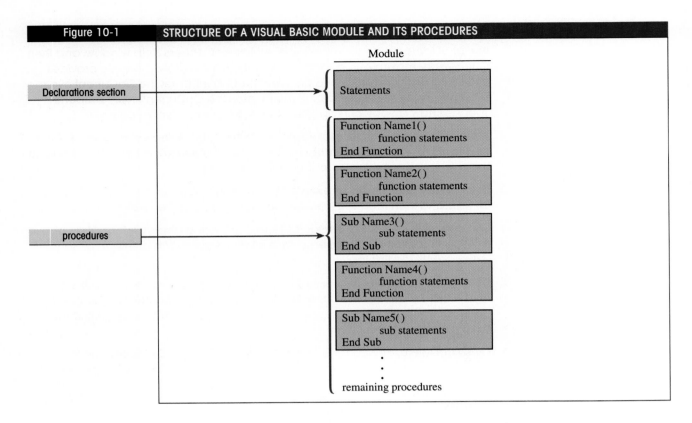

Figure 10-1	STRUCTURE OF A VISUAL BASIC MODULE AND ITS PROCEDURES

Each module starts with a **Declarations section**, which contains statements that apply to all procedures in the module. One or more procedures, which follow the Declarations section, constitute the rest of the module. The two basic types of modules are standard modules and class modules.

A **standard module** is a database object that is stored in memory with other database objects (queries, forms, and so on) when you open the database. You can use the procedures in a database's standard modules from anywhere in the database—even from procedures in other modules. A procedure that more than one object can use is called a **public procedure**. For example, the CapAll procedure that you will create capitalizes all letters in the value passed to it. Although you are creating this procedure specifically to work with the State/Prov field value, you will place it in a standard module and make it public. You could then use the CapAll procedure for any object in the database. All standard modules are listed on the Modules tab of the Database window.

A **class module** is usually associated with a particular form or report. When you create the first event procedure for a form or report, Access automatically creates an associated form or report class module. When you add additional event procedures to the form or report, Access adds them to the class module for that form or report. The event procedures in a class module are **local procedures**, or **private procedures**, which means that only the form or report for which the class module was created can use the event procedures.

Using **Help and the Sample Northwind Database**

The most difficult part of becoming proficient with Access is learning how to code effective VBA procedures. VBA is a powerful programming language containing hundreds of statements and built-in functions, along with hundreds of event properties, object properties, and built-in procedures. Deciding when and how to use each VBA feature can be intimidating to programming novices and even to experts. Fortunately, you can perform many fundamental operations without using VBA by setting control properties and by using macros, as you have done in previous tutorials.

When you use VBA to create new procedures, you can take advantage of the Access Help system as a reference tool. Limited VBA Help is available in Access on your computer; you'll find more comprehensive VBA Help at Microsoft's Web site by searching for VBA or Office XP topics. You can find Help for every VBA statement, function, event, and property; most of these topics even have a corresponding example that displays sample VBA code. If you find sample code similar to what you need, you can simply copy the statements to the Office Clipboard, paste them into a procedure in your own database, and modify the statements to work for your special case.

Another source for sample VBA code is the sample Northwind database that you can install with Access. When installed, you can open the Northwind database by clicking Help on the menu bar, pointing to Sample Databases, and then clicking Northwind Sample Database. The Northwind database contains a variety of simple and complex VBA procedures. You can view the effects of these procedures by using them in the sample database. Microsoft encourages you to copy and use the proven procedures in the Northwind database as a way to learn and use VBA more quickly. If you have time, you should explore the Northwind database on your own. Because Elsa has already studied the Northwind database, she doesn't need to open it to set up the VBA code for the Overseas database.

Using **an Existing Procedure**

Before creating the CapAll procedure for Elsa, you'll use an existing procedure that Elsa created in the class module for the Employer form. This procedure displays the full province name in a text box to the right of the State/Prov field value—Nova Scotia appears in red, Prince Edward Island in blue, and Quebec in magenta. Because all NSJI employees are familiar with the two-character state codes, state names do not appear in the text box.

You'll navigate the Employer form to observe the effects of the procedure.

To navigate a form that uses a VBA procedure:

1. Open the **Employer** form in Datasheet view to display the first record for Beantown Tours. The state name of Massachusetts does not appear to the right of the State/Prov field value of MA.

2. Select the record number **1** in the Specific Record box, type **34**, and then press the **Enter** key. The Employer form displays record 34 for Gables & Golf Country Club. The province name of Prince Edward Island displays in blue to the right of the State/Prov field value of PE. See Figure 10-2.

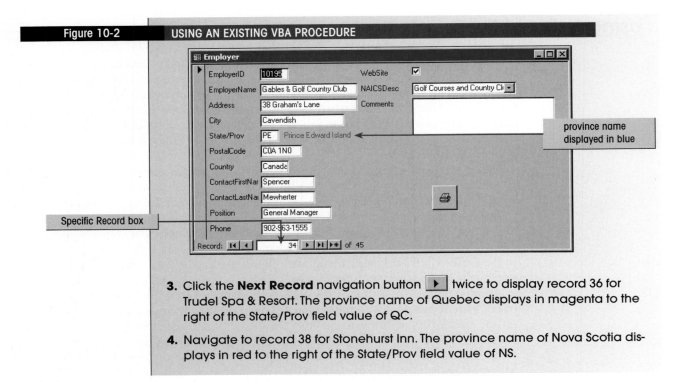

Figure 10-2   **USING AN EXISTING VBA PROCEDURE**

(Figure shows the Employer form with the following field values:)

EmployerID: 10195   WebSite: ☑

EmployerName: Gables & Golf Country Club   NAICSDesc: Golf Courses and Country Cl

Address: 38 Graham's Lane   Comments:

City: Cavendish

State/Prov: PE   Prince Edward Island ◄ — province name displayed in blue

PostalCode: C0A 1N0

Country: Canada

ContactFirstNar: Spencer

ContactLastNar: Mewherter

Position: General Manager

Phone: 902-963-1555

Specific Record box

Record: 34 of 45

3. Click the **Next Record** navigation button ▶ twice to display record 36 for Trudel Spa & Resort. The province name of Quebec displays in magenta to the right of the State/Prov field value of QC.

4. Navigate to record 38 for Stonehurst Inn. The province name of Nova Scotia displays in red to the right of the State/Prov field value of NS.

Elsa asks you to change the magenta color for Quebec to black to make it more readable.

Displaying an Event Procedure

The VBA procedure that controls the display of the province name and its color for each record is in the class module for the Employer form. Access processes the statements in the procedure when you open the Employer form and also when the focus leaves one record and moves to another. **Focus** refers to the record and control that is currently active and awaiting user action. Because the **Current event** occurs when a form opens and when the focus moves to another record, the VBA procedure is associated as an event procedure with the form's **OnCurrent property**.

To change the color of Quebec from magenta to black, you'll modify the event procedure for the form's OnCurrent property. First, you'll switch to Design view, and then you'll display the event procedure.

To display the event procedure for the form's OnCurrent property:

1. Switch to Design view.

2. Right-click the form selector to display the shortcut menu, and then click **Properties** to open the property sheet for the form.

3. If necessary, click the **Event** tab to display the Event page of the property sheet. See Figure 10-3.

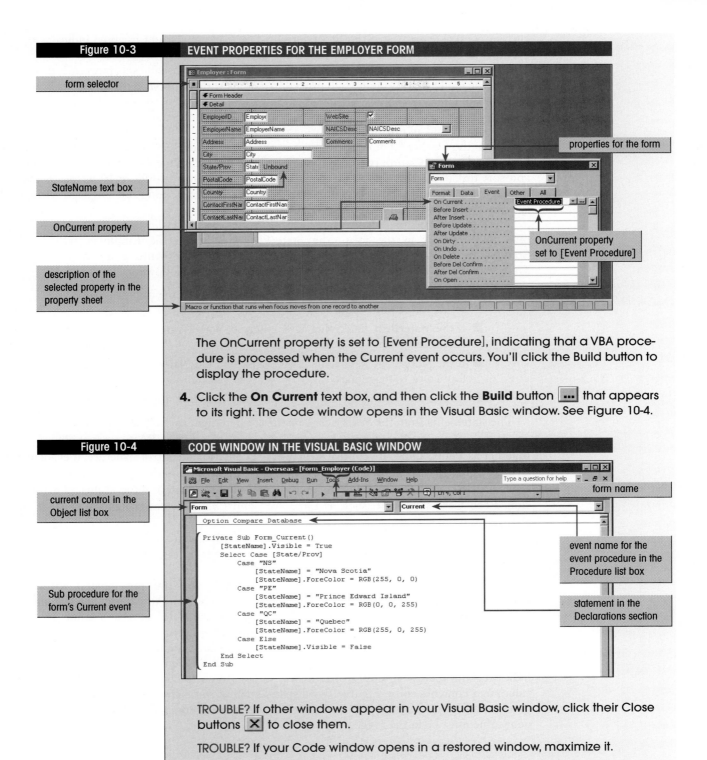

Figure 10-3 EVENT PROPERTIES FOR THE EMPLOYER FORM

form selector

StateName text box

OnCurrent property

description of the selected property in the property sheet

properties for the form

OnCurrent property set to [Event Procedure]

The OnCurrent property is set to [Event Procedure], indicating that a VBA procedure is processed when the Current event occurs. You'll click the Build button to display the procedure.

4. Click the **On Current** text box, and then click the **Build** button ... that appears to its right. The Code window opens in the Visual Basic window. See Figure 10-4.

Figure 10-4 CODE WINDOW IN THE VISUAL BASIC WINDOW

current control in the Object list box

Sub procedure for the form's Current event

form name

event name for the event procedure in the Procedure list box

statement in the Declarations section

TROUBLE? If other windows appear in your Visual Basic window, click their Close buttons ☒ to close them.

TROUBLE? If your Code window opens in a restored window, maximize it.

The program you use to create and modify VBA code is called **Visual Basic Editor** (**VBE**, or **editor** for short), and the **Visual Basic window** is the program window that opens when you use VBE. The **Code window** is the window in which you create, modify, and display VBA code. You can have as many Code windows open as you have modules in the database. In the Code window, the Object list box (the upper-left list box) indicates the current control (Form), and the Procedure list box (the upper-right list box) indicates the event name (Current) for the event procedure you are viewing.

All event procedures are Sub procedures. A horizontal line visually separates each procedure in the Code window. Each Sub procedure begins with a **Sub statement** and ends with an **End Sub statement**. The Sub statement includes the **scope** of the procedure (private or public), the name of the procedure (Form_Current, which means the Current event for the form control), and an opening and closing parenthesis.

Notice the Option Compare statement in the Declarations section above the horizontal line. The **Option Compare statement** designates the technique Access uses to compare and sort text data. The default method "Database," as shown in Figure 10-4, means that Access compares and sorts letters in normal alphabetical order, using the language settings specified for Access running on your computer.

The remaining statements in the Form_Current procedure shown in Figure 10-4 use only two controls in the form: the State/Prov field from the Employer table; and StateName, which is the text box control that displays the full province name. Based on the State/Prov field value, the statements in the procedure do the following:

- If the State/Prov field value is NS, then set StateName to Nova Scotia and set its font color to red.
- If the State/Prov field value is PE, then set StateName to Prince Edward Island and set its font color to blue.
- If the State/Prov field value is QC, then set StateName to Quebec and set its font color to magenta.
- If the State/Prov field has any other value, then hide the StateName control.

The statements from the *Select Case [State/Prov]* statement to the *End Select* statement are an example of a control structure. A **control structure** is a set of VBA statements that work together as a unit. The Case control structure is a conditional control structure; it evaluates an expression—the value of the State/Prov field, in this case—and then performs one of several alternative actions based on the resulting value (or condition) of the evaluated expression. Each Case statement, such as *Case "NS"* and *Case Else*, designates the start of an alternative set of actions.

Statements such as *[StateName] = "Nova Scotia"* are assignment statements. An **assignment statement** assigns the value of an expression—Nova Scotia, in this case—to a field or property—the StateName control, in this case.

Because a property is associated with a control, you use the general form of *ControlName.PropertyName* to specify a property for a control. An assignment statement such as *[StateName].ForeColor = RGB(255, 0, 0)*, for example, assigns a value to the StateName's ForeColor property. A field's **ForeColor property** determines the field's foreground, or font, color. The expression in this assignment statement uses a built-in VBA function named RGB. The **RGB function** returns an RGB (red, green, blue) color value, indicating the relative intensity of red (first value), green (second value), and blue (third value) in a control's color. Figure 10-5 displays a list of some common colors and the red, green, and blue values for the RGB function that produces those colors. Each color component value must be in the range 0 through 255.

Figure 10-5	RGB FUNCTION VALUES FOR SOME COMMON COLORS		
COLOR	**RED VALUE**	**GREEN VALUE**	**BLUE VALUE**
Black	0	0	0
Blue	0	0	255
Cyan	0	255	255
Green	0	255	0
Magenta	255	0	255
Red	255	0	0
White	255	255	255
Yellow	255	255	0

The **Visible property** determines when Access displays a control. Access displays a control when its Visible property is True, and hides the control when its Visible property is False. The *[StateName].Visible = True* statement, which Access processes before the *Select Case [State/Prov]* statement, displays the StateName control. Because Elsa doesn't want the StateName control to appear for states, the *[StateName].Visible = False* statement hides the StateName control if the State/Prov field value doesn't equal one of the three Canadian provinces.

Modifying an Event Procedure

Because Elsa wants you to change the magenta color for Quebec to black, you'll modify the last set of RGB function values in the event procedure. Also, because the StateName control will display only province names, Elsa asks you to change its name to ProvinceName in the event procedure to make it more easily recognizable. Then you'll close the Visual Basic window, make the control name change in the form, and save and test your modifications.

To modify, save, and test the event procedure:

1. Select **255, 0, 255** in the last RGB function, and then type **0,** (be sure you type the comma after the zero). A banner opens below the function and displays **syntax**, or valid form, information for the RGB function. See Figure 10-6.

Figure 10-6	MODIFYING A BUILT-IN VBA FUNCTION

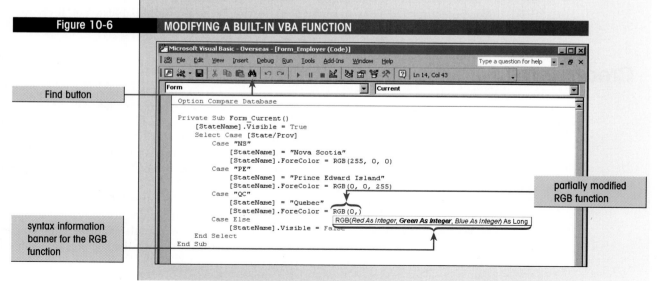

TROUBLE? If the banner does not open, click Tools on the menu bar, click Options, click the Editor tab, click the Auto Quick Info check box to select it, click the OK button, select "0," in the last RGB function, and then type "0," (without the quotation marks).

You'll now finish typing the RGB function.

2. Press the **spacebar**, and then type **0, 0** to complete the change to the RGB function.

Next, you'll replace all occurrences of StateName with ProvinceName.

3. Click the **Find** button 🔍 on the Standard toolbar to open the Find dialog box, click the **Replace** button, type **StateName** in the Find What text box, press the **Tab** key, type **ProvinceName** in the Replace With text box, and then click the **Replace All** button. Access displays a message box informing you that eight replacements were made.

TROUBLE? If the toolbar is not displayed on your screen, click View on the menu bar, point to Toolbars, and then click Standard.

4. Click the **OK** button, and then close the Replace dialog box.

5. Click the **Save** button 💾 on the Standard toolbar to save your changes, and then click the **Close** button ❌ on the Visual Basic window title bar to close it and return to the Form window in Design view.

You'll now change the name of the StateName text box to ProvinceName.

6. Click the **StateName** text box (the Unbound text box), click the **All** tab in the property sheet, type **ProvinceName** in the property sheet's Name text box, and then close the property sheet.

7. Save your form design changes, and then switch to Form view.

8. Navigate to record 36 for Trudel Spa & Resort. The province name of Quebec displays in black to the right of the State/Prov field value of QC. Your modification to the event procedure was completed successfully.

9. Close the **Employer** form.

You've completed your modifications to the event procedure. Next, you'll create the CapAll function.

Creating **Functions in a Standard Module**

Elsa wants you to create a VBA procedure for the Employer form that will automatically convert the values entered in the State/Prov field to uppercase. That is, if a user enters "ct" as the state, the procedure should automatically convert it to "CT". Elsa feels that this function will make data entry easier and reduce the number of data-entry errors. Users might not always be consistent about capitalizing entries in the State/Prov field, and using this procedure to capitalize entries will ensure consistency.

To accomplish this change, you will first create a simple function, named CapAll, that accepts a **string** (text) input value and returns that string with all letters converted to uppercase. You create the function by typing the statements in the Module window. Then you will create an event procedure that calls the CapAll function whenever the user enters a value in the State/Prov field using the Employer form.

Whenever a user enters or changes a field value in a control on a form, Access automatically triggers the **AfterUpdate event**, which, by default, simply accepts the new or changed entry. However, you can set the AfterUpdate event property of a control to a specific event procedure in order to have something else happen when a user enters or changes the field value. In this case, you need to set the State/Prov field's AfterUpdate event property to [Event Procedure], and then code an event procedure to call the CapAll function. Calling the CapAll function will cause the entry in the State/Prov field to be converted to uppercase letters before storing it in the database.

You will use the CapAll function with the Employer form, so you could add it to the class module for that form. Adding the function to the class module for the Employer form would make it a private function; that is, you could not use it in other forms or database objects. Because you might use the CapAll function in other forms in the Overseas database, you'll place the CapAll function in a new standard module named Overseas Procedures. Generally, when you enter a procedure in a standard module, it is public, and you can use it in event procedures for any object in the database.

To create a new standard module, you'll begin by opening the Code window.

REFERENCE   WINDOW   **RW**

Creating a New Standard Module
- In the Database window, click Modules in the Objects bar to display the Modules list.
- Click the New button. A new Code window, in which you create a new module, opens in the Visual Basic window.

You'll now create a new VBA standard module.

To create a new standard module:

1. Click **Modules** in the Objects bar of the Database window, and then click the **New** button. A new Code window opens in the Visual Basic window. See Figure 10-7.

Figure 10-7	CREATING A NEW STANDARD MODULE

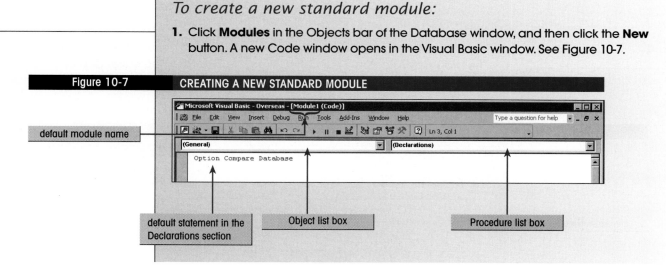

default module name

default statement in the Declarations section

Object list box

Procedure list box

In the Code window for the new standard module, the Procedure list box displays the Declarations section as the current procedure in the module. Access automatically includes the Option Compare statement in the Declarations section of a new module. The CapAll function is a simple function that does not require additional statements in the Declarations section.

Creating a Function

Each function begins with a **Function statement** and ends with an **End Function statement**. Access visually separates each procedure in the Code window with a horizontal line. You can view a procedure's statements by selecting the procedure name from the Procedure list box.

The CapAll function begins with the statement *Function CapAll(FValue)*. CapAll is the function name and FValue is used as a placeholder for the input value in the function definition. When the user enters a value for the State/Prov field in the Employer form, that value will be passed to the CapAll function and substituted for FValue in the function definition. A placeholder like FValue is called a **parameter**. The value passed to the function and used in place of the parameter when the function is executed is called an **argument** (similar to an action in a macro). In other words, the value passed to the function is the argument, which is assigned to the parameter named FValue.

All VBA function names, Sub procedure names, argument names, and other names you create must conform to the following rules:

- They must begin with a letter.
- They cannot exceed 255 characters.
- They can include letters, numbers, and the underscore character (_). You cannot use a space or any punctuation characters.
- They cannot contain keywords, such as Function, Sub, Case, and Option, that VBA uses as part of its language.
- They must be unique; that is, you can't declare the same name twice within the same procedure.

You'll enter the CapAll function in the Code window and then test it. Then you'll attach it to an event procedure for the Employer form. As you enter the statements for the CapAll function in the Code window, remember that capitalization is important in all statements so that your code is readable and maintainable. You now can start entering the CapAll function.

To start a new function:

1. With the insertion point two lines below the Option Compare statement, type **Function CapAll(FValue)** and then press the **Enter** key. The editor displays a horizontal line that visually separates the new function from the Declarations section. See Figure 10-8.

Figure 10-8	STARTING A NEW FUNCTION

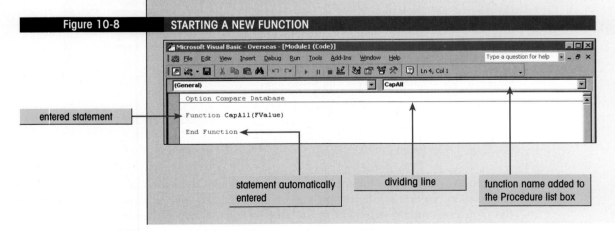

entered statement

statement automatically entered

dividing line

function name added to the Procedure list box

The function name CapAll now appears in the Procedure list box. The editor automatically added the End Function statement and moved the insertion point to the beginning of the blank line between the Function and End Function statements, where you will enter the procedure statements. The editor displays the reserved words Function and End Function in blue. The function name and the parameter name appear in black.

The CapAll function will consist of a single executable assignment statement that you will place between the Function and End Function statements. You'll enter the following assignment statement: *CapAll = UCase(FValue)*. The value of the expression, which is UCase(FValue), will be assigned to the function, which is CapAll.

The expression in the assignment statement uses a built-in Access function named UCase. The **UCase function** accepts a single string argument as input, converts the value of the argument to uppercase letters, and then returns the converted value. The assignment statement assigns the converted value to the CapAll function. Figure 10-9 illustrates this process.

Figure 10-9	EVALUATION OF THE ASSIGNMENT STATEMENT

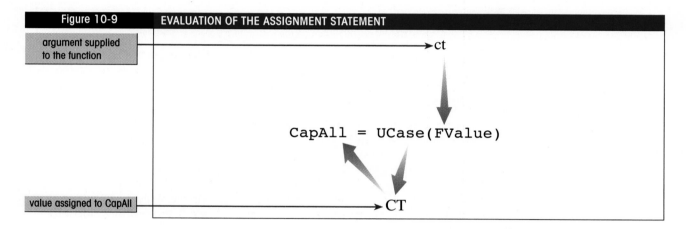

argument supplied to the function → ct

CapAll = UCase(FValue)

value assigned to CapAll → CT

Before entering the assignment statement, you will add a comment line to explain the procedure's purpose. You can include comments anywhere in a VBA procedure to describe what the procedure or a statement does to make it easier for you and other programmers to identify the purpose of statements in your code. You begin a comment with the word Rem (for "Remark") or with a single quotation mark ('). VBA ignores anything following the word Rem or the single quotation mark on a single line. Because VBA ignores comments, you can include spaces, special characters, and mixed-case letters in your comments. Also, you will indent these lines; indenting statements is a common practice that makes code easier to read.

To add comments and statements to the function:

1. Press the **Tab** key to indent the line.

2. Type **'Capitalize all letters of a field value** and then press the **Enter** key. Notice that the editor displays the comment in green and indents the new line. After entering the comment line, you can enter the assignment statement, which is the executable statement in the function that performs the actual conversion of the argument to uppercase.

3. Type **CapAll = UCase(FValue)**. See Figure 10-10. The editor provides assistance as you enter the statement. After you type UCase and the opening parenthesis, the editor displays a banner with a reminder that UCase accepts a single string argument. The editor displays a similar banner after you type CapAll and press the spacebar; you should ignore this banner because its reminder is incorrect.

Figure 10-10	CapAll FUNCTION IN THE CODE WINDOW

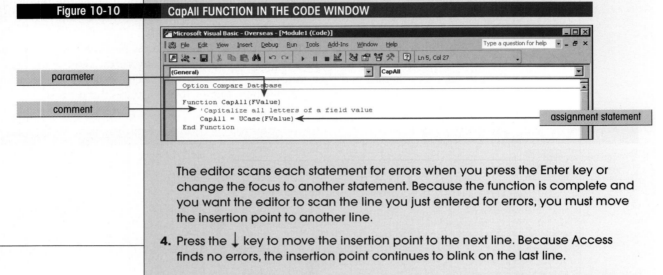

The editor scans each statement for errors when you press the Enter key or change the focus to another statement. Because the function is complete and you want the editor to scan the line you just entered for errors, you must move the insertion point to another line.

4. Press the ↓ key to move the insertion point to the next line. Because Access finds no errors, the insertion point continues to blink on the last line.

TROUBLE? If the editor finds an error in the assignment statement, it highlights the error in red and opens a dialog box with a message describing the nature of the error. Click the OK button and then change the highlighted error by comparing your entries with those shown in Steps 2 and 3. Then repeat Step 4 to scan the statement for errors again.

You have finished entering the function, so you'll save it before continuing with your work.

Saving a Module

When you click the Save button in the Visual Basic window, the editor saves the module and its procedures. If you are entering a long procedure, it's a good idea to save your work periodically.

To save the module:

1. Click the **Save** button 🖫 on the Standard toolbar, type **Overseas Procedures** in the Module Name text box, and then press the **Enter** key. The editor saves the module and places the new module name in the title bar.

Before making the changes to the Employer form so that the CapAll function automatically acts on every entry in the State/Prov field, you can test the function using the Immediate window.

Testing **a Procedure in the Immediate Window**

When you finish entering a VBA statement, the editor checks the statement to make sure its syntax is correct. Although you may have entered all procedure statements with the correct syntax, the procedure may still contain logic errors. A **logic error** occurs when the procedure produces incorrect results. For example, the CapAll function would have a logic error if you typed ct and the function changed it to cT, Ct, or anything other than the correct result of CT. Even the simplest procedure can contain errors. Be sure to test each procedure thoroughly to ensure that it does exactly what you expect it to do in all situations.

When working in the Code window, you can use the **Immediate window** to test VBA procedures without changing any data in the database. In the Immediate window, you can enter different values to test the procedure you just entered. To test a procedure, type the keyword "Print" or a question mark (?), followed by the procedure name and the value you want to test in parentheses. For example, to test the CapAll function in the Immediate window using the test word ct, type *?CapAll ("ct")* and then press the Enter key. Access executes the function and prints the value returned by the function (you expect it to return CT). Note that you must enclose a string of characters within quotation marks in the test statement.

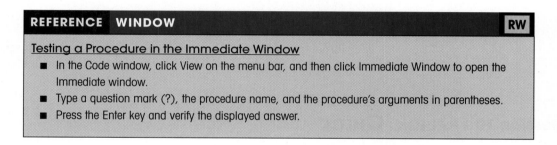

REFERENCE   WINDOW   **RW**

Testing a Procedure in the Immediate Window
- In the Code window, click View on the menu bar, and then click Immediate Window to open the Immediate window.
- Type a question mark (?), the procedure name, and the procedure's arguments in parentheses.
- Press the Enter key and verify the displayed answer.

Now you can use the Immediate window to test the CapAll function.

To test the CapAll function in the Immediate window:

1. Click **View** on the menu bar, and then click **Immediate Window**. The editor opens the Immediate window across the bottom of the screen and places the insertion point inside the window.

   The Immediate window allows you to run individual lines of VBA code for **debugging** (testing). You will use the Immediate window to test the CapAll function.

2. Type **?CapAll("ct")** and then press the **Enter** key. The editor executes the function and prints the function result, CT, on the next line. See Figure 10-11.

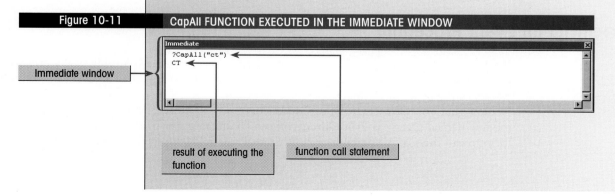

Figure 10-11	CapAll FUNCTION EXECUTED IN THE IMMEDIATE WINDOW

Immediate window

result of executing the function

function call statement

> **TROUBLE?** If Access displays a dialog box with an error message, click the OK button in the dialog box, correct the error in the Immediate window, and then press the Enter key. If the function does not produce the correct output (CT), correct the CapAll function statements in the Code window, save your changes, and then repeat Steps 1 and 2.
>
> To test the CapAll function further, you could enter several other test values, retyping the entire statement each time. Instead, you'll select the current test value, type another value, and then press the Enter key.
>
> 3. Select the characters **ct** in the first line of the Immediate window.
>
> 4. Type **cT** and then press the **Enter** key. The editor executes the function and prints the function result, CT, on the next line.
>
> 5. Repeat Steps 3 and 4 two more times, using **Qc** and then **NH** as the test values. The editor prints the correct values, QC and NH.
>
> 6. Click the **Close** button ☒ on the Immediate window title bar to close it, and then click the ☒ on the Visual Basic window title bar to return to the Database window.

Your initial test of the CapAll function is successful. In the next session, you'll modify the Employer form to call the CapAll function for the State/Prov field.

Session 10.1 QUICK CHECK

1. Why is Visual Basic for Applications called an event-driven, object-oriented language?

2. What is an event procedure?

3. What are the differences between a Function procedure and a Sub procedure?

4. What are the two different types of modules?

5. The _____ of a procedure is either private or public.

6. What can you accomplish in the Immediate window?

SESSION 10.2

In this session, you'll create, compile, and test an event procedure. You'll also add a second function to a standard module. You will write the function in VBA, compile it, and then call the function from an event procedure.

Creating an Event Procedure

Recall that when you add a procedure to a form or report, Access automatically creates a class module for that form or report. Each of these procedures is called an event procedure; Access runs a procedure when a specific event occurs.

Now that you have created the CapAll function as a public procedure in the standard module named Overseas Procedures, you can create an event procedure for the Employer form to call the CapAll function for the State/Prov field's AfterUpdate event. Whenever a user enters or changes a State/Prov field value, the **AfterUpdate event** occurs and Access runs your event procedure.

What exactly happens when Access calls a procedure? There is an interaction between the calling statement and the function statements as represented by a series of steps. Figure 10-12 shows the process for the CapAll procedure.

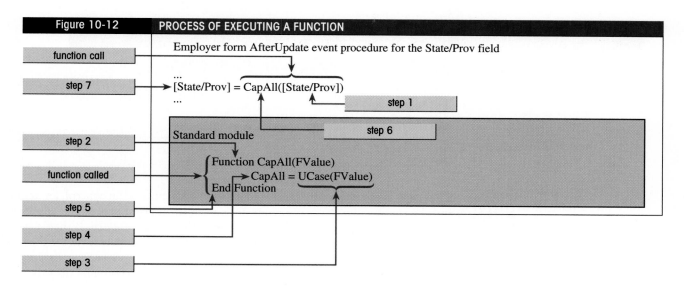

Figure 10-12   PROCESS OF EXECUTING A FUNCTION

function call

step 7

step 2

function called

step 5

step 4

step 3

Employer form AfterUpdate event procedure for the State/Prov field

...
[State/Prov] = CapAll([State/Prov])
...

step 1

Standard module

step 6

Function CapAll(FValue)
    CapAll = UCase(FValue)
End Function

The steps in Figure 10-12 are numbered in the order in which they occur as Access processes the statement and the function. Access goes through the following steps:

- Step 1. The call to the function CapAll passes the value of the argument [State/Prov]. This is the value of the State/Prov field that is entered or changed by the user.
- Step 2. The function CapAll begins, and the parameter FValue receives the value of [State/Prov].
- Step 3. FValue is changed to uppercase.
- Step 4. The value of CapAll is set equal to the result of Step 3.
- Step 5. The function CapAll ends.
- Step 6. The value of CapAll is returned to the point of the call to the function.
- Step 7. The value of [State/Prov] is set equal to the returned value of CapAll.

Although it looks complicated, the general function process is simple—the statement contains a function call. When the statement is executed, Access performs the function call, executes the function, returns a single value to the original statement, and completes that statement's execution. Study the steps in Figure 10-12 and trace their sequence until you understand the complete process.

Designing an Event Procedure

Whenever a user enters a new value or modifies an existing value in the State/Prov field in the Employer form, Elsa wants Access to execute the CapAll function to ensure that all State/Prov field values appear in uppercase letters. After a user changes a State/Prov field value, the AfterUpdate event automatically occurs. You can set the AfterUpdate event property to run a macro, call a built-in Access function, or execute an event procedure. Because you want to call your user-defined function from within the event procedure, you'll set the

AfterUpdate event property to [Event Procedure], and then add the VBA statements needed to use the CapAll function.

All event procedures are Sub procedures. Access automatically adds the Sub and End Sub statements to an event procedure. All you need to do is place the statements between the Sub and End Sub statements. Figure 10-13 shows the completed event procedure. The following text describes the parts of the procedure.

Figure 10-13	AfterUpdate EVENT PROCEDURE FOR THE STATE/PROV FIELD

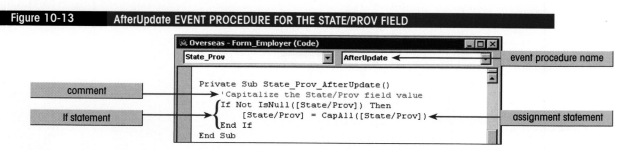

Access names each event procedure in a standard way: the name of the control, an underscore (_), and the event name. No parameters are passed to an event procedure, so Access places nothing in the parentheses following the name of the Sub procedure. If the name of the control contains spaces or special characters, Access substitutes underscores for them in the event procedure name.

A user might delete an existing State/Prov field value, so that it contains no value, or becomes **null**. In this case, calling the function accomplishes nothing. The procedure is designed to call the CapAll function only when a user changes the State/Prov field to a value that is not null. The If statement screens out the null values. In its simplest form, an **If statement** executes one of two groups of statements based on a condition, similar to common English usage. For example, consider the English statements, "If I work the night shift, then I'll earn extra spending money. Otherwise, I'll go to the movies, and I'll dip into my savings." In these sentences, the two groups of statements come before and after the "otherwise," depending on the condition, "if I work the night shift." The first group of statements consists of the clause "I'll earn extra spending money." This clause is called the **true-statement group** because it's what happens if the condition ("I work the night shift") is true. The second group of statements contains "I'll go to the movies, and I'll dip into my savings." This clause is called the **false-statement group** because it is what happens if the condition is false. VBA uses the keyword *If* to precede the condition. The keyword *Then* precedes the true-statement group and the keyword *Else* precedes the false-statement group. The general syntax of a VBA If statement is:

```
If condition Then
        true-statement group
[Else
        false-statement group]
End If
```

Access executes the true-statement group when the condition is true and the false-statement group when the condition is false. In this statement's syntax, the bracketed portions are optional. Therefore, you must omit the *Else* and its related false-statement group when you want Access to execute a group of statements only when the condition is true.

In Figure 10-13, the If statement uses the VBA **IsNull function**, which returns True when the State/Prov field value is null and False when it is not null. The *Not* in the If statement is the same logical operator you've used previously to negate an expression. So, Access executes the statement *[State/Prov] = CapAll([State/Prov])* only when the State/Prov field value is not null. Brackets are required for the State/Prov field because its name includes a special character (/). Brackets also must enclose field names with spaces, but brackets are optional for field names without spaces and special characters.

You are ready to make your changes to the Employer form.

Adding an Event Procedure

To add an event procedure to the State/Prov field's AfterUpdate event property, you need to open the Employer form in Design view.

REFERENCE   WINDOW   **RW**

Adding an Event Procedure

- Open the form or report in Design view, select the control whose event property you want to set, and then open the property sheet for that control.
- Set the appropriate event property to [Event Procedure], and then click the Build button.
- Enter the Sub procedure statements in the Code window.
- Compile the procedure, fix any statement errors, and then save the event procedure.

You can now add the event procedure to the Employer form.

To add the event procedure to the Employer form:

1. If you took a break after the previous session, make sure that Access is running and that the **Overseas** database in the Tutorial folder on your Data Disk is open.

2. Open the **Employer** form in Design view.

3. Right-click the **State/Prov** text box (not the ProvinceName text box) to display the shortcut menu, and then click **Properties** to open the property sheet.

4. If necessary, click the **Event** tab. Access shows only the event properties in the property sheet. You need to set the AfterUpdate property.

5. Click the right side of the **After Update** text box, click [**Event Procedure**], and then click the **Build** button [...] to the right of the After Update text box. The Code window opens in the Visual Basic window. See Figure 10-14.

Figure 10-14	STARTING A NEW EVENT PROCEDURE IN THE CODE WINDOW

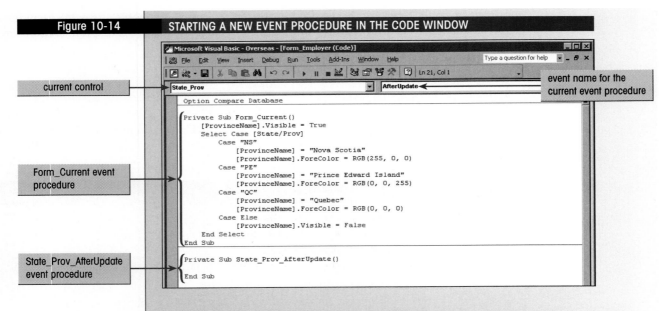

current control

Form_Current event procedure

State_Prov_AfterUpdate event procedure

event name for the current event procedure

```
Option Compare Database

Private Sub Form_Current()
    [ProvinceName].Visible = True
    Select Case [State/Prov]
        Case "NS"
            [ProvinceName] = "Nova Scotia"
            [ProvinceName].ForeColor = RGB(255, 0, 0)
        Case "PE"
            [ProvinceName] = "Prince Edward Island"
            [ProvinceName].ForeColor = RGB(0, 0, 255)
        Case "QC"
            [ProvinceName] = "Quebec"
            [ProvinceName].ForeColor = RGB(0, 0, 0)
        Case Else
            [ProvinceName].Visible = False
    End Select
End Sub

Private Sub State_Prov_AfterUpdate()

End Sub
```

TROUBLE? If the Object list box displays the ProvinceName control or any other control instead of the State_Prov control, close the Code window, delete "[Event Procedure]" from the After Update text box on the property sheet, click the State/Prov text box, and then repeat Step 5.

The new event procedure for the State/Prov field's AfterUpdate event property contains the Private Sub and End Sub statements, and it follows the form's Current event procedure. You can now enter the statements to call the CapAll function.

6. Enter the statements shown in Figure 10-15. Use the **Tab** key to indent the lines as shown in the figure, press the **Enter** key at the end of each line, and press the **Backspace** key to move one tab stop to the left. Compare your screen with Figure 10-15, and make any necessary corrections.

Figure 10-15	COMPLETED EVENT PROCEDURE

```
Private Sub State_Prov_AfterUpdate()
    'Capitalize the State/Prov field value
    If Not IsNull([State/Prov]) Then
        [State/Prov] = CapAll([State/Prov])
    End If
End Sub
```

TROUBLE? If your event procedure contains errors, correct them by highlighting the errors and typing the corrections. Use the Backspace or Delete keys to delete characters.

Before saving the event procedure, you'll compile it.

Compiling Modules

The VBA programming language is not your native language, nor is it the computer's native language. Although you can learn VBA and become fluent in it, computers cannot understand or learn VBA. For a computer to understand the statements in your VBA modules, Access must translate the statements into a form that it can run. The process of translating modules from VBA to a translated form is called **compilation**; you say that you **compile** the module when you translate it.

When you run a procedure for the first time, Access compiles it for you automatically and opens a dialog box only when it finds syntax errors in the procedure. If it finds an error, Access does not translate the procedure statements. If no errors are detected, Access translates the procedure and does not display a confirmation. You also can compile a procedure at any point as you enter it by clicking the Compile <database name> command on the Debug menu. In response, Access compiles the procedure and all other procedures in all modules in the database. It's best to compile modules after you've made changes to them, to make sure they don't contain syntax errors.

You'll now compile the procedures in the Overseas database and save the class module for the Employer form.

To compile the procedures in the Overseas database and save the class module:

1. Click **Debug** on the menu bar, and then click **Compile Overseas**. Access compiles all the modules in the Overseas database. Because you have no syntax errors, Access translates the VBA statements and returns control to the Visual Basic window.

   TROUBLE? If Access identifies any errors in your code, correct the errors and repeat Step 1.

2. Save your module changes, close the Visual Basic window, and then close the property sheet.

You have created the function and the event procedure and have set the event property. Next, you'll test the event procedure to make sure it works correctly.

Testing an Event Procedure

You need to display the Employer form in Form view and test the State/Prov field's event procedure by entering a few different test State/Prov field values in the first record of the form. Moving the focus to another control on the form or to another record triggers the AfterUpdate event for the State/Prov field and executes your attached event procedure. Because the CapAll function is attached only to the Employer form, the automatic capitalization of State/Prov field values is not in effect when you enter them in the Employer table or any other object in the Overseas database.

To test the event procedure:

1. Switch to Form view.

2. Select the **State/Prov** field value (MA), type **ma** in the State/Prov text box, and then press the **Enter** key. Access executes the AfterUpdate event procedure for the State/Prov field and changes the State/Prov field value to "MA". See Figure 10-16.

Figure 10-16	EMPLOYER FORM AFTER EXECUTING THE EVENT PROCEDURE

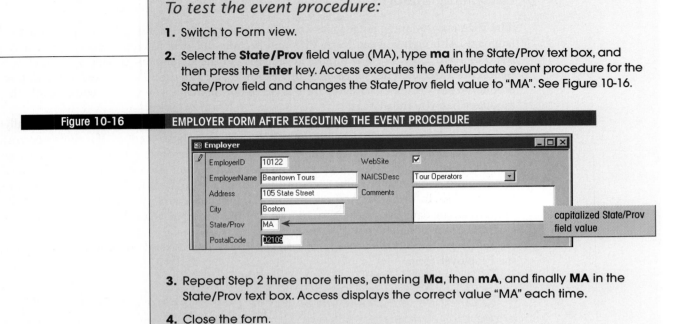

3. Repeat Step 2 three more times, entering **Ma**, then **mA**, and finally **MA** in the State/Prov text box. Access displays the correct value "MA" each time.

4. Close the form.

Elsa wants you to create a more complicated function for the EmployerName field in the Employer form.

Adding a Second Function to a Standard Module

Elsa wants to make it easier for users to enter an employer's name when using the Employer form, so she asks you to create a second function that will automatically correct the case of letters entered in the EmployerName field. This function, named CapAllFirst, will capitalize the first letter of each word in the field and change all other letters to lowercase. An event procedure attached to the AfterUpdate event for the EmployerName field will use this function. When a user enters or edits an employer name in the Employer form, the event procedure will use the CapAllFirst function to correct any capitalization errors in the EmployerName field value. For example, if the user enters "beantOWn toURS" as the EmployerName field value, the event procedure will use the CapAllFirst function to correct the field value to "Beantown Tours."

Designing the CapAllFirst Function

Figure 10-17 shows the CapAllFirst function that you will create. You've already seen several of the statements in this function in your work with the CapAll function. Except for the function name, the Function and End Function statements are the same. The next two lines of the function are comments; these comments are specific to the CapAllFirst function. You'll learn about each new statement as you enter it to code this procedure.

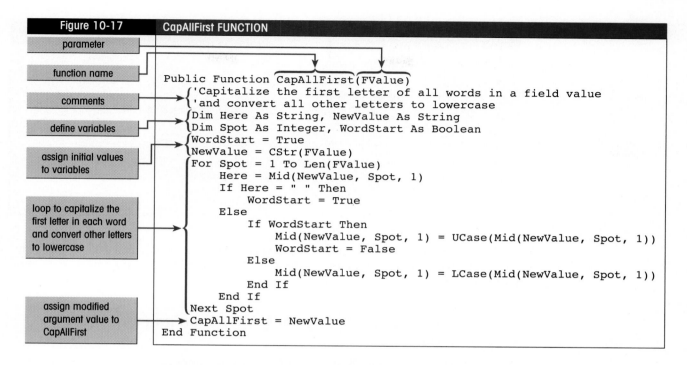

Figure 10-17 | CapAllFirst FUNCTION

- parameter
- function name
- comments
- define variables
- assign initial values to variables
- loop to capitalize the first letter in each word and convert other letters to lowercase
- assign modified argument value to CapAllFirst

```
Public Function CapAllFirst(FValue)
    'Capitalize the first letter of all words in a field value
    'and convert all other letters to lowercase
    Dim Here As String, NewValue As String
    Dim Spot As Integer, WordStart As Boolean
    WordStart = True
    NewValue = CStr(FValue)
    For Spot = 1 To Len(FValue)
        Here = Mid(NewValue, Spot, 1)
        If Here = " " Then
            WordStart = True
        Else
            If WordStart Then
                Mid(NewValue, Spot, 1) = UCase(Mid(NewValue, Spot, 1))
                WordStart = False
            Else
                Mid(NewValue, Spot, 1) = LCase(Mid(NewValue, Spot, 1))
            End If
        End If
    Next Spot
    CapAllFirst = NewValue
End Function
```

The CapAllFirst function has a single parameter, named FValue. When the AfterUpdate event procedure for the EmployerName field calls the CapAllFirst function, the EmployerName field value entered by the user is passed to the function, and this value is used in place of FValue when CapAllFirst is executed. So, the EmployerName field value is the argument passed to the function.

The CapAllFirst function capitalizes the first letter in each word of the parameter and converts all other letters to lowercase. You will learn about the function in detail as you enter the function statements in the following steps. Basically, the function works by examining the parameter, character by character. Whenever a space is encountered, the function "knows" that the next letter encountered should be capitalized because a space immediately precedes the first letter of a new word. When the letter after a space is found, it is capitalized. After the entire parameter has been examined, the modified parameter is returned to the event procedure that called the function.

Creating a Second Function

You'll add the CapAllFirst function to the Overseas Procedures module, which is a standard module, so that the CapAllFirst function will be available for use with any object in the Overseas database. Once you have added the function to the Overseas Procedures module, you will be able to attach it to an event procedure for the AfterUpdate event of the EmployerName field in the Employer form.

Adding a New Procedure to a Standard Module

- In the Database window, click Modules in the Objects bar, right-click the module name, and then click Design View on the shortcut menu.
- In the Code window, click the list arrow for the Insert Module button on the Standard toolbar, and then click Procedure.
- Type the new procedure name, click the Sub or Function option button, click the Public or Private option button, and then click the OK button.
- Enter the new procedure, click Debug on the menu bar, and then click Compile <database name>.
- Click the Save button on the Standard toolbar.

As you enter the statements in the following steps, refer to Figure 10-17 to verify that you are entering the statements correctly. You'll begin by adding the descriptive comments to the function.

To begin creating the CapAllFirst function and add the comments:

1. Click **Modules** in the Objects bar of the Database window, right-click **Overseas Procedures** to display the shortcut menu, and then click **Design View**.

2. Click the list arrow for the **Insert Module** button ⬚ on the Standard toolbar, and then click **Procedure** to open the Add Procedure dialog box.

   This dialog box lets you name the new procedure and define its type and scope. The new procedure can be a Sub procedure, a function, or a new property definition for an existing object. The scope of the new procedure can be either public or private. The new procedure you will create is a function, and you want it to be public so that you can use it in an event procedure for the Employer form.

3. Type **CapAllFirst** in the Name text box, make sure the **Function** and **Public** option buttons are selected, and then click the **OK** button. The editor starts a new procedure named CapAllFirst and displays the Function and End Function statements in the Code window. See Figure 10-18.

Figure 10-18	CapAllFirst FUNCTION STARTED IN THE CODE WINDOW

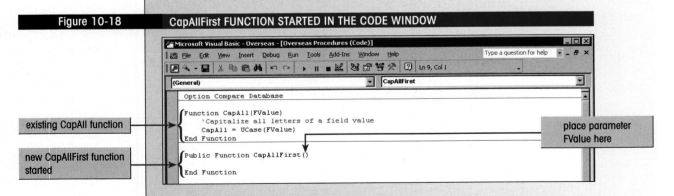

existing CapAll function

new CapAllFirst function started

place parameter FValue here

The CapAllFirst function will accept one argument passed to the parameter FValue. When the function is called by an event procedure, FValue will hold the string value that CapAllFirst will process. You must place the parameter inside the parentheses after the function name.

4. Click between the parentheses in the function statement, type **FValue**, press the ↓ key, and then press the **Tab** key.

5. Type **'Capitalize the first letter of all words in a field value** and then press the **Enter** key to enter the first comment.

6. Type **'and convert all other letters to lowercase** and then press the **Enter** key to enter the second comment.

The next two lines of the CapAllFirst function declare the variables that the function uses. A **variable** is a named location in computer memory that can contain a value. If you use a variable in a module, you must explicitly declare it in the Declarations section or in the function definition where the variable is used. The **Dim statement** is used to declare variables in a procedure. The variables in the CapAllFirst function are Here, NewValue, Spot, and WordStart. (You'll see what these variables do in a moment.) Each variable is assigned an associated data type. Figure 10-19 shows the primary data types for Visual Basic variables.

Figure 10-19	PRIMARY VBA DATA TYPES
DATA TYPE	**STORES**
Boolean	True/False values
Byte	Integer values from 0 to 255
Currency	Currency values from −922,337,203,685,477.5808 to 922,337,203,685,477.5807
Date	Date and time values from 1 January 100 to 31 December 9999
Decimal	Non-integer values with 0 to 28 decimal places
Double	Non-integer values from $-1.79769313486231*10^{308}$ to $-4.94065645841247*10^{-324}$ for negative values, from $4.94065645841247*10^{-324}$ to $1.79769313486232*10^{308}$ for positive values, and 0
Integer	Integer values from −32,768 to 32,767
Long	Integer values from −2,147,483,648 to 2,147,483,647
Object	Any object reference
Single	Non-integer values from $-3.402823*10^{38}$ to $-1.401298*10^{-45}$ for negative values, from $1.401298*10^{-45}$ to $3.402823*10^{38}$ for positive values, and 0
String	Text values up to 2 billion characters in length
Variant	Any numeric or string data type

You specify the data type for a variable by following the variable name with the word "As" and the data type. In the CapAllFirst function, for example, the two variables Here and NewValue are string variables. The **string type** is the equivalent of the Access text data type. Spot is an integer variable, and WordStart is a Boolean variable. The **Boolean type** is the equivalent of the yes/no type used to define the data type of a table record field. The Boolean type can take one of two values: True or False. If a module does not include an Option Explicit statement in the Declarations section and you create a variable without specifying a data type, VBA assigns the variant data type to the variable. The variant data type is the default data type; a variant variable can store any value.

The variable Here is a string variable that will temporarily hold a copy of the character that is being examined. The variable NewValue is a string that holds a copy of the argument. The first character in each word of NewValue is converted to uppercase as the function executes. Spot is an integer that is used as a counter to keep track of which character is being examined. Spot counts from 1 to the number of characters in the argument. Finally, WordStart is a Boolean variable that records whether to capitalize the next letter. When WordStart is True, the next letter encountered in the argument should be capitalized. When WordStart is False, the next letter is not capitalized.

You'll now enter the Dim statements to declare the variables.

To enter the Dim statements:

1. With the insertion point positioned on the line below the second comment line and indented one tab stop, type **Dim Here As Str**. When you press the space-bar after typing the word "As," a list of available data types opens. As you type each letter in the data type, the entries in the list change to those entries whose starting letters match those you've typed. See Figure 10-20.

Figure 10-20	ENTERING THE FIRST DIM STATEMENT

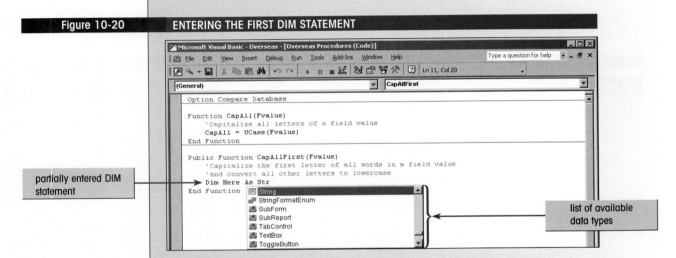

partially entered DIM statement

list of available data types

TROUBLE? If the list box does not open, click Tools on the menu bar, click Options, click the Editor tab, click the Auto List Members check box to select it, and then click the OK button.

The **Complete Word IntelliSense feature** helps you enter or complete a VBA keyword. When a keyword list opens, you can type the complete entry or you can scroll the list and select an entry. You also can type the first one or more letters of the keyword and, when the desired entry is highlighted in the list, press the Tab key to select it as your entry.

You'll now finish typing the first Dim statement.

2. Press the **Tab** key, type **, NewValue As Str** and then press the **Tab** key.

3. Press the **Enter** key to start a new indented line, and then type **Dim Spot As Integer, WordStart As Boolean** and then press the **Enter** key.

The next two lines of the CapAllFirst function assign initial values to WordStart and NewValue. WordStart is initialized to True because the next letter encountered (the first let-ter in the parameter) should be capitalized. The next line uses the **CStr function** to convert the value of the parameter FValue, which has the variant data type, to a string and assigns this converted value to the variable NewValue. Because CapAllFirst is a public function, a value of any type could be passed to FValue when the function is called. The CStr function ensures that the value in FValue is converted to a string. This process must happen because the value in FValue is assigned to NewValue, which must contain a string.

You'll now enter the initial assignment statements.

To enter the initial assignment statements:

1. Type **WordStart = True** and then press the **Enter** key.

2. Type **NewValue = CStr(FValue)** and then press the **Enter** key.

The main body of the CapAllFirst function consists of a group of statements that are executed repeatedly to examine and process each character in NewValue (the EmployerName value entered by the user). A group of statements executed repeatedly is called a **loop**. The statement *For Spot = 1 To Len(FValue)* marks the beginning of the loop, and the statement *Next Spot* marks the end of the loop. The group of statements between the For and Next statements is called the **loop body**.

The For statement establishes how many times to repeat the loop body. In this case, the For statement uses the variable Spot as a counter to keep track of how many times to repeat the loop body. The *For Spot = 1 To Len(FValue)* statement sets the starting value of Spot, which is an integer variable, to 1 and the ending value of Spot to Len(FValue). The **Len function** returns the number of characters in a string. For example, if FValue is the string "Resort Name," Len(FValue) returns 11 as the number of characters, including spaces. In this case, Access executes the statements in the loop 11 times.

Then Access executes the loop body, ending with the statement before the Next Spot statement. After reaching the Next Spot statement, Access adds 1 to Spot, goes back to the For statement, and compares the value of Spot to Len(FValue). If Spot is less than or equal to Len(FValue), then there are still more characters to check and examine, so Access executes the loop statements again, reaches the Next Spot statement, and repeats the cycle. When Spot becomes greater than Len(FValue), then there are no more characters to check in the field entry, so Access terminates the loop and executes the statement following the Next Spot statement.

The loop body is executed once for each value of Spot, that is, once for each character in NewValue. The statement *Here = Mid(NewValue, Spot, 1)* uses the built-in **Mid function** to copy a single character, as specified by the argument "1" in the statement, from NewValue and store it in Here. The character selected is indicated by the value of Spot. So, if the current value of Spot is 3, then the third character in NewValue is copied into Here. For example, if the user enters Beantown Tours in the EmployerName field of the Employer form, and Spot equals 3, the value of "a" is assigned to the variable Here so that the function can determine if "a" needs to be capitalized.

The next statement is an If statement that decides which operations to perform depending on the value of Here. If Here is a space, then the value of WordStart is set to True (indicating that the next letter encountered should be capitalized) and the Else part of the If statement is skipped. If Here is not a space, then the current character is a letter that might need to be capitalized. A second If statement checks to see if WordStart is True. If WordStart is True, then the next statement uses the UCase function to convert the selected character to uppercase and assigns it to the appropriate position in NewValue. If WordStart is not True, then the next statement uses the LCase function to convert the selected character to lowercase and assigns it to the appropriate position in NewValue. The UCase and LCase functions have no effect on characters that are not letters.

When the loop body has finished processing the current character, the Next Spot statement increments Spot and returns control to the *For Spot = 1 to Len(NewValue)* statement. If Spot is less than or equal to the length of NewValue, the loop body is executed again, processing the next character in NewValue.

When the loop has processed the last character in NewValue, the loop ends and control is passed to the statement following the Next Spot statement. NewValue now has the first letter of each word capitalized and all other letters converted to lowercase.

Next, you'll enter the statements for the loop in the Code window.

To enter the loop statements in the CapAllFirst function:

1. Type **For Spot = 1 To Len(FValue)** and then press the **Enter** key.

2. Enter the remaining loop statements, ending with the statement Next Spot, as shown in Figure 10-21, and pressing the **Enter** key after you type the Next Spot statement. Press the Tab key to indent lines as necessary. Recall that pressing the Backspace key moves the insertion point one tab stop to the left. When you are finished, your screen should look like Figure 10-21.

| Figure 10-21 | AFTER ENTERING THE LOOP STATEMENTS IN THE CapAllFirst FUNCTION |

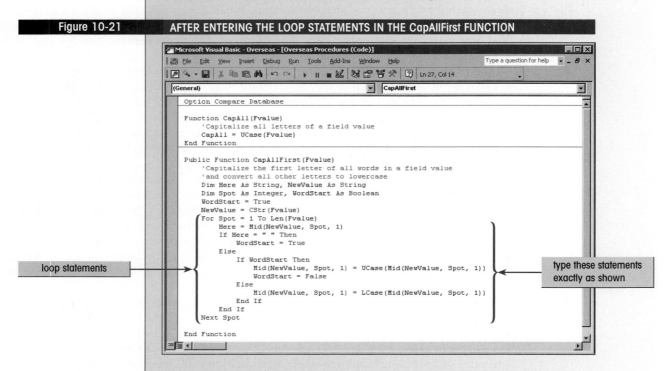

loop statements

type these statements exactly as shown

TROUBLE? If your statements contain errors, position the insertion point in the Code window to the right of the error. Use the Backspace key to delete characters. Re-enter any incorrect statements until your screen looks like Figure 10-21.

When the loop ends, NewValue contains words with capitalized first letters and lowercase for the remaining letters. The final step in the CapAllFirst function assigns the NewValue to CapAllFirst, to be returned to the event procedure that called the CapAllFirst function. In the case of the Employer form, the EmployerName field's event procedure will call the CapAllFirst function, which will return the employer name with the correct capitalization. You'll now enter this final statement.

To enter the final function statement:

1. Type **CapAllFirst = NewValue** and then press the ↓ key. See Figure 10-22.

Figure 10-22 COMPLETED CapAllFirst FUNCTION

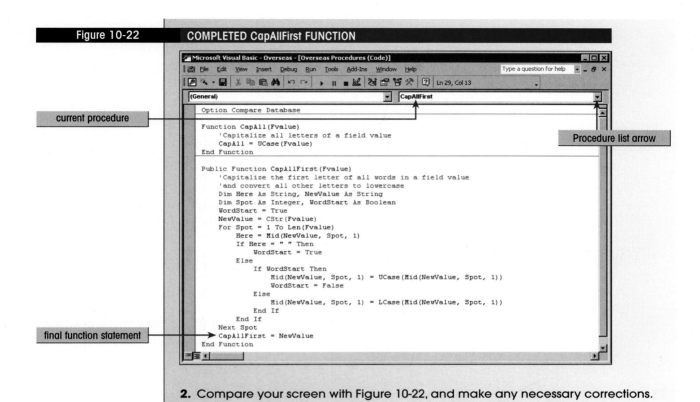

current procedure

Procedure list arrow

final function statement

2. Compare your screen with Figure 10-22, and make any necessary corrections.

You'll now compile the modules in the Overseas database and save the Overseas Procedures module.

To compile the procedures in the Overseas database and save the Overseas Procedures module:

1. Click **Debug** on the menu bar, and then click **Compile Overseas**. Access compiles all the modules in the Overseas database.

TROUBLE? If Access finds an error, it highlights the error and opens a dialog box with a message describing the nature of the error. Click the OK button and change the statement contained in the highlighted area by comparing each character you entered to what should be entered. Then repeat Step 1.

2. Save your module changes.

The Overseas Procedures module now contains the Declarations, the CapAll function, and the CapAllFirst function. You can view each procedure in a module by clicking the Procedure list arrow and selecting a procedure.

To view the procedures in the Overseas Procedures module:

1. Click the **Procedure** list arrow, and then click **CapAll**. The editor moves the insertion point to the first statement after the Function statement in the CapAll function and displays CapAll in the Procedure text box.

2. Click the **Procedure** list arrow, and then click **(Declarations)**. The editor displays the module's Declarations section and moves the insertion point to the Option Compare statement.

3. Click the **Procedure** list arrow, and then click **CapAllFirst** to display the CapAllFirst function and move the insertion point to its first statement.

4. Close the Visual Basic window to return to the Database window.

Adding a Second Event Procedure

The function that you just created ensures that each word in the employer name begins with a capital letter and that all other letters are lowercase. Next, you'll open the Employer form in Design view and add an event procedure for the EmployerName field's AfterUpdate event property. Recall that the AfterUpdate property determines the actions Access will take after the user has entered or edited the specified field value. Access will execute the event procedure whenever a value in the EmployerName field is entered or updated.

To add the event procedure for the EmployerName field in the Employer form:

1. Open the **Employer** form in Design view.

2. Right-click the **EmployerName** text box to display the shortcut menu, and then click **Properties** to open the property sheet.

3. If necessary, click the **Event** tab in the property sheet.

4. Click the right side of the **After Update** text box, click **[Event Procedure]**, and then click the **Build** button [...] to the right of the After Update text box. The Code window, which contains new Private Sub and End Sub statements, opens in the Visual Basic window. Notice that the Code window also contains the event procedure for the form's Current property, which you modified earlier. The Code window also displays the event procedure for the State/Prov field's AfterUpdate property, which you entered earlier.

5. Press the **Tab** key, and then type the Sub procedure statements exactly as shown in Figure 10-23.

Figure 10-23	EVENT PROCEDURE FOR THE EmployerName FIELD

type this new event procedure for the EmployerName field

existing event procedure for the form's Current property

first two lines of the AfterUpdate event procedure for the State/Prov field

```
Option Compare Database

Private Sub EmployerName_AfterUpdate()
    'Capitalize the first letter of all words
    'in the EmployerName field
    If Not IsNull([EmployerName]) Then
        [EmployerName] = CapAllFirst([EmployerName])
    End If
End Sub

Private Sub Form_Current()
    [ProvinceName].Visible = True
    Select Case [State/Prov]
        Case "NS"
            [ProvinceName] = "Nova Scotia"
            [ProvinceName].ForeColor = RGB(255, 0, 0)
        Case "PE"
            [ProvinceName] = "Prince Edward Island"
            [ProvinceName].ForeColor = RGB(0, 0, 255)
        Case "QC"
            [ProvinceName] = "Quebec"
            [ProvinceName].ForeColor = RGB(0, 0, 0)
        Case Else
            [ProvinceName].Visible = False
    End Select
End Sub

Private Sub State_Prov_AfterUpdate()
    'Capitalize the State/Prov field value
```

The EmployerName field's AfterUpdate event procedure works the same as the State/Prov field's AfterUpdate event procedure. If the EmployerName field is not null (empty), then the EmployerName field value is passed to the CapAllFirst function. The CapAllFirst function capitalizes the first letter of each word in the EmployerName field value, converts all other letters to lowercase, and then returns the value to the event procedure. The event procedure assignment statement then assigns the converted value to the EmployerName field.

6. Click **Debug** on the menu bar, and then click **Compile Overseas**. Access compiles all the modules in the Overseas database.

7. Save your class module changes.

8. Close the Visual Basic window to return to the Form window, and then close the property sheet.

You have entered the function and the event procedure and have set the event property. You can now test the event procedure. To do so, you'll open the Employer form in Form view and test the EmployerName field's event procedure by entering different EmployerName field values.

To test the new event procedure:

1. Switch to Form view. Access displays record 1 for Beantown Tours.

2. Select **Beantown Tours** in the EmployerName text box, type **test employer name**, and then press the **Enter** key. Access executes the AfterUpdate event procedure for the EmployerName field and changes the EmployerName field value to "Test Employer Name."

3. Press the ↑ key to highlight the EmployerName field value.

4. Repeat Steps 2 and 3 two more times, entering **sECond test namE** (correctly changed to "Second Test Name"), and then entering **beantown tours** (correctly changed to "Beantown Tours").

5. Close the **Employer** form.

Now that you've finished coding the functions to facilitate using the Employer form, you're ready to put the finishing touches on the Overseas database user interface. You'll begin your improvements in the next session.

Session 10.2 QUICK CHECK

1. What happens when you compile a module?

2. What does the UCase function do?

3. What is the purpose of the Dim statement?

4. How many times would the following loop be executed?

   For MyCounter = 3 to 20

5. What is the Boolean data type?

6. What is the string data type?

7. What does the CStr function do?

SESSION 10.3

In this session, you will learn how to hide text and change the color of a form during the execution of a procedure. You also will create the event procedures for the **Queries Dialog Box** form.

Hiding and Changing Display Color

Elsa wants you to add a message to the Position form that will remind users when a position is full-time (40 or more scheduled hours per week). Access will display the message, in red, only when the position is full-time. Also, she wants you to display the value in the Wage text box in red for full-time positions and in black for all other positions. The red font will help to draw attention to those positions that are full-time. See Figure 10-24.

Figure 10-24   **POSITION FORM WITH THE FULL-TIME MESSAGE AND WAGE FIELD VALUE IN RED**

In the Position form, you will add a label to the right of the Hours/Week text box that will display the text "Full-Time" in red. Because Elsa wants the text to appear only when the Hours/Week field has a value greater than or equal to 40, you will change the label's Visible property during execution. You will also change the foreground color of the value in the Wage text box to red for full-time positions and to black for all other positions.

Because the change to the Visible property takes place during execution, you will add code to the Current event procedure in the Position form. To set a property in a Visual Basic statement, you enter the object name followed by the property name, separating the two with a period. For example, if the label name for the message is FullTimeMsg, then the statement *[FullTimeMsg].Visible = False* hides the label on the form.

First, you'll add a label to the Position form that will display a message in red for full-time positions. For all other positions, the label will be hidden.

To add the label to the Position form:

1. If you took a break after the previous session, make sure that Access is running and that the **Overseas** database in the Tutorial folder on your Data Disk is open.

2. Open the **Position** form in Design view.

3. If necessary, click the **Toolbox** button [icon] on the Form Design toolbar to open the toolbox, and then click the **Label** tool [Aa] on the toolbox.

4. Position the pointer in the Detail section; when the center of the pointer's plus symbol is positioned in the row of grid dots to the right of the Hours/Week text box and aligned with its top edge, click the mouse button.

5. Type **Full-Time** and then press the **Enter** key. See Figure 10-25.

 POSITION OF THE LABEL BOX

You'll now set the label's Name and ForeColor properties, and add the Current event procedure to the Position form.

To set the label's properties, and add the Current event procedure to the Position form:

1. Right-click the **Full-Time label** to display the shortcut menu, and then click **Properties** to open the property sheet.

2. Click the **All** tab (if necessary), select the value in the **Name** text box (if necessary), and then type **FullTimeMsg**.

   You can now set the ForeColor property for the label so that the message is displayed in red.

3. Scroll the property sheet, click the **Fore Color** text box, and then click the **Build** button [...] to the right of the Fore Color text box. Access opens the Color dialog box.

4. Click the **red color** box (the first color box in the second row of Basic Colors), click the **OK** button, and then press the **Enter** key. Access sets the ForeColor property value to the code for red (255). Notice that Access changes the foreground (text) color of the Full-Time label to red.

   TROUBLE? If the property sheet blocks your view of the form, drag it to an open area of the screen.

   You'll now enter the event procedure for the form's OnCurrent event. This event procedure will be executed whenever the Position form is opened or the focus moves from one record to another record.

5. Click the form selector, scroll down the property sheet to the OnCurrent property, click the right side of the **On Current** text box, click [**Event Procedure**], and then click [...]. Access opens the Code window in the Visual Basic window, displaying the Sub and End Sub statements.

6. Press the **Tab** key, and then type the Sub procedure statements exactly as shown in Figure 10-26.

Figure 10-26	CURRENT EVENT PROCEDURE FOR THE POSITION FORM

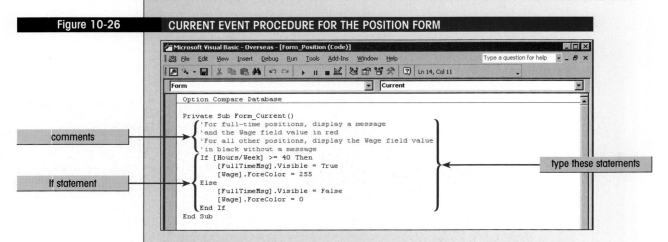

comments

If statement

type these statements

The Sub Form_Current procedure uses an If statement to determine whether the current value of the Hours/Week field is greater than or equal to 40. If the current value of the Hours/Week field is greater than or equal to 40, the procedure sets the FullTimeMsg Visible property to True (which means the Full-Time message will appear on the Position form), and it sets the Wage ForeColor property to 255 (red). If the current value of the Hours/Week field is less than 40, the procedure sets the FullTimeMsg Visible property to False, hiding the Full-Time message on the form, and sets the Wage ForeColor property to 0 (black).

7. Click **Debug** on the menu bar, and then click **Compile Overseas**. Access compiles all the modules in the Overseas database.

8. Save your class module changes, close the Visual Basic window, and then close the property sheet.

You'll now test the Current event procedure for the Position form.

To test the Current event procedure for the Position form:

1. Switch to Form view. Access displays the first record for PositionID 2004, which is not a full-time position. The message "Full-Time" does not appear, and the Wage field value appears in black.

   TROUBLE? If Access displays a dialog box indicating a run-time error, Access could not execute the event procedure. Click the Debug button in the dialog box. Access displays the event procedure in the Code window and highlights the line containing the error. Check the statements carefully and make sure that they are exactly like those shown in Figure 10-26. Make the necessary changes, compile the module, save the module, and then close the Code window. Then repeat Step 1.

2. Click the **Next Record** navigation button [▶] twice to display the third record for PositionID 2010, which is a full-time position. The message "Full-Time" appears in red, as does the Wage field value of 13.00.

3. Click [▶] several times to make sure that each full-time position's message and Wage field value appear in red, and that each part-time position's Wage field value appears in black and the "Full-Time" message does not appear.

4. Close the form to return to the Database window.

You have finished your work on the Current event procedure for the Position form. Next, you'll create the necessary procedures for the command buttons on the Queries Dialog Box form.

Creating the Procedures for the Queries Dialog Box Form

Your last programming task is to complete the procedures for the Queries Dialog Box form. Elsa wants Access to highlight the first item in the list box when the Queries Dialog Box form first opens, by placing the focus on it. Next, when a user double-clicks a query name in the list box or highlights a query name and then clicks the Print Preview command button, that query should open in the Print Preview window. Finally, when a user selects a query name in the list box and then clicks the Datasheet command button, the selected query should open in Datasheet view. You'll create the three procedures for the Queries Dialog Box form to perform these processes. Figure 10-27 shows the names for the three procedures.

Figure 10-27	QUERIES DIALOG BOX FORM'S PROCEDURES

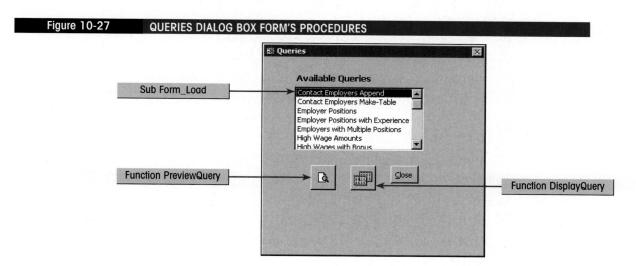

Coding the Load Event Procedure for the Queries Dialog Box Form

When a user opens the Queries Dialog Box form, Elsa wants Access to place the focus on the first query in the list box automatically. To accomplish this objective, you need to specify the form's Load event. Figure 10-28 shows the code for the form's Load event.

| Figure 10-28 | LOAD EVENT PROCEDURE FOR THE QUERIES DIALOG BOX FORM |

new Load event procedure

```
Private Sub Form_Load()
    'Move the focus to the list box and
    'highlight the first query
    [QueryList].SetFocus
    SendKeys "{Down}"
End Sub
```

The **Load event** occurs when Access opens a form. Anything you specify for this event will happen each time the form is opened. **SetFocus** is a method that moves the focus to the specified object or control. A **method** is an action that operates on specific objects or controls. The statement *[QueryList].SetFocus* moves the focus to QueryList, which is the name for the form's list box, but does not set the focus to any specific query name. The *SendKeys "{Down}"* statement sends the down arrow keystroke to the list box; Access responds to this statement by highlighting the first query in the list box. The end result of these statements is that when the user opens the dialog box, the first query is highlighted and has the focus.

You'll open the Queries Dialog Box form in Design view and create the Load event procedure.

To add the Load event procedure for the Queries Dialog Box form:

1. Open the **Queries Dialog Box** form in Design view.

2. Right-click the form selector to display the shortcut menu, and then click **Properties** to open the form's property sheet.

3. Click the **Event** tab (if necessary), scroll the property sheet (if necessary), click the right side of the **On Load** text box, click **[Event Procedure]**, and then click the **Build** button [...]. Access opens the Code window in the Visual Basic window, displaying the Sub and End Sub statements for the Load event procedure.

4. Press the **Tab** key, and then type the Sub procedure statements as shown in Figure 10-29.

| Figure 10-29 | LOAD EVENT PROCEDURE ENTERED IN THE CODE WINDOW |

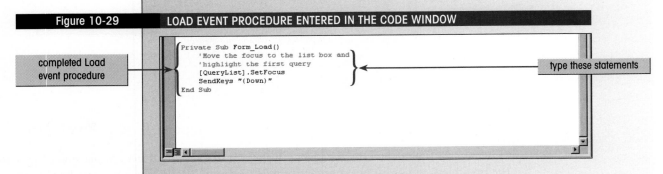

completed Load event procedure

```
Private Sub Form_Load()
    'Move the focus to the list box and
    'highlight the first query
    [QueryList].SetFocus
    SendKeys "{Down}"
End Sub
```

type these statements

The word "Private" in the first line of the Sub procedure definition indicates that the procedure can be used only in the class module for this form. Form_Load indicates that this Sub procedure is the event procedure for the Load event. Make sure you type curly braces in the SendKeys statement.

5. Click **Debug** on the menu bar, click **Compile Overseas**, and then save your module changes.

6. Close the Visual Basic window, and then close the property sheet.

   Next, you'll test the procedure by opening the Queries Dialog Box form in Form view and verifying that the first query in the list box is selected.

7. Switch to Form view. Notice that the first query in the list box is selected.

   TROUBLE? If the first query in the list box is not highlighted, you probably did not type the curly braces { } in the SendKeys statement. Switch to Design view, and then open the form's property sheet. Click the On Load text box, click the Build button [...] , and then correct the event procedure. Then repeat Steps 5 through 7.

8. Close the form.

You have finished your work with the Load event procedure for the Queries Dialog Box form. Next, you need to create the form's PreviewQuery and DisplayQuery procedures.

Coding the PreviewQuery and DisplayQuery Procedures for the Queries Dialog Box Form

Double-clicking a query name in the list box or selecting a query name and then clicking the Print Preview command button must open that query in the Print Preview window. Selecting a query name in the list box and then clicking the Datasheet command button must open that query in Datasheet view. Figure 10-30 shows the code to handle these procedures.

Figure 10-30	PreviewQuery AND DisplayQuery FUNCTIONS FOR THE FORM

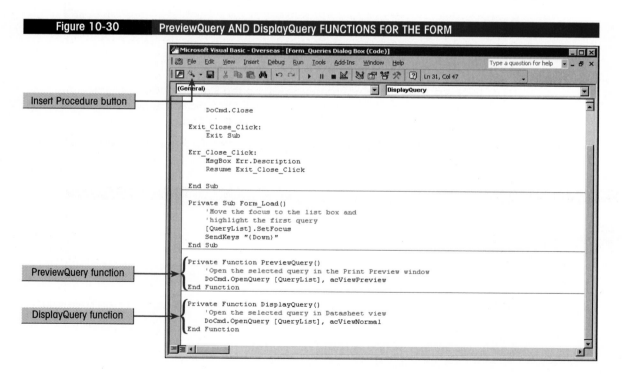

The **DoCmd statement** executes an action in a function. You use DoCmd statements in these functions to run the OpenQuery action. The parameter choices for the selected query of [QueryList] in the OpenQuery action are: acViewPreview to open the Print Preview window, acViewDesign to open the query in Design view, and acViewNormal to open the query in Datasheet view. Because the OpenQuery action and its parameter values acViewPreview, acViewDesign, and acViewNormal are standard features of Access, you do not have to define them in a Dim statement as you do for variables you create.

Next you'll open the Queries Dialog Box form in Design view, create the two functions, and attach the functions to the appropriate control properties.

To add the two functions to the Queries Dialog Box form:

1. Open the **Queries Dialog Box** form in Design view, and then click the **Code** button 🖼 on the Form Design toolbar to open the Code window for the form's class module in the Visual Basic window. (Note that you could also press the F7 key to open the Code window.)

2. Click the list arrow for the **Insert Module** button 🖼 on the Standard toolbar, and then click **Procedure**. The Add Procedure dialog box opens.

3. Type **PreviewQuery** in the Name text box, click the **Function** option button, click the **Private** option button, and then click the **OK** button. Access displays the Function and End Function statements for the new PreviewQuery procedure.

4. Press the **Tab** key, and then type the statements for the PreviewQuery function exactly as shown in Figure 10-31.

| Figure 10-31 | PreviewQuery FUNCTION FOR THE QUERIES DIALOG BOX FORM |

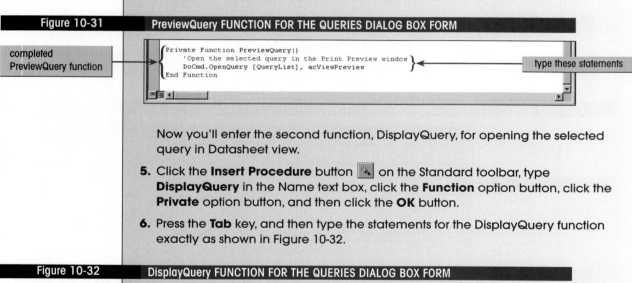

completed PreviewQuery function

```
Private Function PreviewQuery()
    'Open the selected query in the Print Preview window
    DoCmd.OpenQuery [QueryList], acViewPreview
End Function
```

type these statements

Now you'll enter the second function, DisplayQuery, for opening the selected query in Datasheet view.

5. Click the **Insert Procedure** button 🖼 on the Standard toolbar, type **DisplayQuery** in the Name text box, click the **Function** option button, click the **Private** option button, and then click the **OK** button.

6. Press the **Tab** key, and then type the statements for the DisplayQuery function exactly as shown in Figure 10-32.

| Figure 10-32 | DisplayQuery FUNCTION FOR THE QUERIES DIALOG BOX FORM |

completed DisplayQuery function

```
Private Function DisplayQuery()
    'Open the selected query in Datasheet view
    DoCmd.OpenQuery [QueryList], acViewNormal
End Function
```

type these statements

7. Click **Debug** on the menu bar, click **Compile Overseas**, and then save your module changes.

8. Close the Visual Basic window.

Next you'll attach the appropriate procedure to the correct properties for the form objects.

To specify the functions for the event properties:

1. Right-click the form's list box (the box containing the word "Unbound") to display the shortcut menu, and then click **Properties** to open the property sheet.

2. Make sure the **Event** tab is selected, scroll the property sheet as necessary, click the **On Dbl Click** text box, and then type **=PreviewQuery()**. This entry specifies that Access will execute the procedure for previewing a query whenever a user double-clicks a query name in the list box. See Figure 10-33.

| Figure 10-33 | SETTING THE LIST BOX'S OnDblClick PROPERTY |

OnDblClick property value

3. Click the form's **Print Preview command button**, click the property sheet's **On Click** text box, and then type **=PreviewQuery()**. This entry specifies that Access will execute the procedure for previewing a query whenever a user selects a query name and then clicks the Print Preview command button.

4. Click the form's **Datasheet command button**, click the property sheet's **On Click** text box, and then type **=DisplayQuery()**. This entry specifies that Access will execute the procedure for opening the query datasheet whenever a user selects a query name and then clicks the Datasheet command button.

5. Close the property sheet, and then save your form changes.

You'll now test the changes you made to the Queries Dialog Box form.

To test the changes to the Queries Dialog Box form:

1. Switch to Form view.

   As you test your changes, make sure you don't click or double-click the first two queries. These are action queries, and Access will generate an error if you use them.

2. Double-click a few of the query names, in turn, in the list box to verify that the correct query opens in Print Preview. From the Print Preview window, click the **Close** button ⊠ on the Print Preview window to return to the dialog box in Form view.

3. Click a query name in the list box, and then click the **Print Preview** command button to verify that the correct query opens in the Print Preview window. From the Print Preview window, click ⊠ on the Print Preview window to return to the dialog box in Form view.

4. Repeat Step 3 for several more query names in the form's list box.

5. Click a query name in the list box, and then click the **Datasheet** command button to verify that the correct query datasheet opens. From the Query Datasheet window, click ⊠ on the Query window to return to the dialog box in Form view.

6. Repeat Step 5 for several more query names in the form's list box.

7. Click the **Close** command button on the dialog box to close it and return to the Database window.

8. Exit Access.

Elsa stops by and views your results. She is very pleased with the modifications to the Employer, Position, and Queries Dialog Box forms. Next, she wants you to make access to the Overseas database more secure, and she wants you to make the final enhancements to the database and the user interface. In the next tutorial, you'll complete your work with the Overseas database.

Session 10.3 QUICK CHECK

1. What does the Visible property determine?

2. What does the ForeColor property determine?

3. When does the Current event occur?

4. When does the Load event occur for an object?

5. What is a method?

6. What is the purpose of the DoCmd statement?

REVIEW ASSIGNMENTS

Elsa asks you to continue your work with the user interface for the **Work** database. To help with this request, you'll complete the following steps.

1. Make sure your Data Disk is in the appropriate disk drive, start Access, and then open the **Work** database in the Review folder on your Data Disk.

2. Complete the **Reports Dialog Box** form by doing the following:
   a. Create a Load event procedure that moves the focus to the first report name in the list box when the **Reports Dialog Box** form opens.

   Explore
   b. Create a PreviewReport function to open a report in the Print Preview window.
   c. Attach the PreviewReport function to the OnDblClick property for the **Reports Dialog Box** form list box.
   d. Attach the PreviewReport function to the OnClick property for the Print Preview command button on the **Reports Dialog Box** form.
   e. Switch to Form view, and then test all the form options. Save and close the form.

   Explore
3. Modify the **Recruiter** form by doing the following:
   a. Display the Salary field value in red when the value is greater than $35,000 and in black for other values.
   b. Display the message "High Salary" to the right of the Salary text box in bold, red text. Display the message only when the Salary field value is greater than $35,000.
   c. Test the modified form, and then save and close it.

4. Exit Access.

CASE PROBLEMS

Case 1. Lim's Video Photography Youngho Lim asks you to continue your work with the user interface for the **Shoots** database. To help Youngho with his request, you'll complete the following steps.

1. Make sure your Data Disk is in the appropriate disk drive, start Access, and then open the **Shoots** database in the Cases folder on your Data Disk.

Explore 2. Modify the **Client Info** form by doing the following:
   a. Display the City field value in normal, black text when the value is "San Francisco" and in bold, red text for all other cities. (*Hint*: Use the FontBold property, and make sure you enclose San Francisco in quotation marks in your VBA code.)
   b. Display the message "Not local" to the right of the City text box in bold, red text. Display the message only when the City field value is not "San Francisco".
   c. Test the modified form, and then save your form changes.

Explore 3. Use the "Ask a Question" box to ask the following question: "What is Name AutoCorrect?" Click a topic, read the information, close the Microsoft Access Help window, and then repeat the process for all other topics. Open the **ShootDesc** table in Design view, change the field name of ShootDesc to ShootDescription, and then save and close the table. Open the **ShootDesc** table datasheet, review the recordset, close the table, open the **Shoot Data** query, review the query results, close the query, and then do the same for the **Clients and Contracts** report. Describe your findings in terms of the effect of using the Name AutoCorrect feature.

4. Exit Access.

Case 2. DineAtHome.course.com Claire Picard asks you to continue your work with the user interface for the **AtHome** database. To help Claire with her request, you'll complete the following steps.

1. Make sure your Data Disk is in the appropriate disk drive, start Access, and then open the **AtHome** database in the Cases folder on your Data Disk.

Explore 2. Modify the **Restaurant Info** form by doing the following:
   a. Display the message "No Delivery" to the right of the TakeoutOnly check box in bold, magenta text only when the TakeoutOnly check box is True. Otherwise, display the message "Delivers" in bold, blue text. (*Hint*: Use the Caption property in your VBA code, and make sure you enclose Caption property settings in quotation marks.)
   b. Test the modified form, and then save your form changes.

Explore 3. Use the "Ask a Question" box to ask the following question: "What is Name AutoCorrect?" Click a topic, read the information, close the Microsoft Access Help window, and then repeat the process for all other topics. Open the **Restaurant** table in Design view, change the field name of Zip to ZipCode, and then save and close the table. Open the **Restaurant** table datasheet, review the recordset, close the table, open the **Restaurant Orders** query, review the query results, close the query, and then do the same for the **Restaurant Info** form and the **Orders by Restaurant** report. Describe your findings in terms of the effect of using the Name AutoCorrect feature.

4. Exit Access.

Case 3. Redwood Zoo Michael Rosenfeld asks you to continue your work with the user interface for the **ZooFunds** database. To help Michael with his request, you'll complete the following steps.

1. Make sure your Data Disk is in the appropriate disk drive, start Access, and then open the **ZooFunds** database in the Cases folder on your Data Disk.

2. Complete the **Queries Dialog Box** form by doing the following:
   a. Create a Load event procedure that moves the focus to the first query name in the list box when the **Queries Dialog Box** form opens.
   b. Create a DisplayQuery function to open the selected query in the list box in Datasheet view.
   c. Attach the DisplayQuery function to the OnDblClick property for the **Queries Dialog Box** form list box.
   d. Attach the DisplayQuery function to the OnClick property for the Datasheet command button on the **Queries Dialog Box** form.
   e. Switch to Form view, and then test all the form options. Save and close the form.

Explore
3. Modify the **Pledges** form by doing the following:
   a. Display the TotalPledged field value in bold in the default label text color and weight when the value is greater than 500 and in normal black text otherwise. (*Hint*: Check the ForeColor property setting for one of the existing labels, and use the FontBold property.)
   b. Display the message "Large Pledges" to the right of the TotalPledged text box in the default label text color and weight. Display the message only when the TotalPledged field value is greater than 500.
   c. Resize and test the modified form, save the form in Form view, and then close the form.

4. Exit Access.

Case 4. Mountain River Adventures Connor and Siobhan Dempsey ask you to continue your work with the user interface for the **Rivers** database. To help them with their request, you'll complete the following steps.

1. Make sure your Data Disk is in the appropriate disk drive, start Access, and then open the **Rivers** database in the Cases folder on your Data Disk.

2. Complete the **Reports Dialog Box** form by doing the following:
   a. Create a Load event procedure that moves the focus to the first report name in the list box when the **Reports Dialog Box** form opens.

Explore
   b. Create a PreviewReport function to open a report in the Print Preview window.
   c. Attach the PreviewReport function to the OnDblClick property for the **Reports Dialog Box** form list box.
   d. Attach the PreviewReport function to the OnClick property for the Print Preview command button on the **Reports Dialog Box** form.
   e. Switch to Form view, and then test all the form options. Save and close the form.

3. Complete the **Queries Dialog Box** form by doing the following:
   a. Create a Load event procedure that moves the focus to the first query name in the list box when the **Queries Dialog Box** form opens.
   b. Create a DisplayQuery function to open a query in Datasheet view.
   c. Attach the DisplayQuery function to the OnDblClick property for the **Queries Dialog Box** form list box.
   d. Attach the DisplayQuery function to the OnClick property for the Datasheet command button on the **Queries Dialog Box** form.
   e. Switch to Form view, and then test all the form options. Save and close the form.

4. You'll draw special attention to your client information and booked trips. Add the message "Trips of a Lifetime!" to the **Client** form. Display the message in 14-point, bold, orange text and position it to the right of the ClientName text box at the top of the form. Display the message only when the ClientName field value equals your name. (*Hint*: Make sure you enclose your name in quotation marks in your VBA code.) Save your form changes, switch to Form view, print your form record, and then close the form.

5. Exit Access.

Explore

Case 5. eACH Internet Auction Site Chris and Pat Aquino ask you to continue your work with the user interface for the **BuySell** database. To help them with their request, you'll complete the following steps.

1. Make sure your Data Disk is in the appropriate drive, start Access, and then open the **BuySell** database in the Cases folder on your Data Disk.

2. Modify the **Item** form by doing the following:
   a. Display the ReservePrice field value in bold, blue text when the value is greater than 1000 and in normal, black text for all other values. (*Hint*: Use the FontBold property.)
   b. Display the message "Very High Reserve" to the right of the ReservePrice text box in bold blue text. Display the message only when the ReservePrice field value is greater than 1000.
   c. Test the modified form, and then save your form changes.

3. Modify the **Item** form by doing the following:
   a. To the right of the MinimumBid text box add a calculated field that calculates the difference between the ReservePrice and MinimumBid field values. Use a label caption of "Under Reserve Amount," and display both the label and calculated field value in bold, blue text.
   b. Perform the calculation and display the label and calculated field value only when the ReservePrice field value is not null.
   c. Test the modified form, and then save your form changes.

4. Use the "Ask a Question" box to ask the following question: "What is Name AutoCorrect?" Click a topic, read the information, close the Microsoft Access Help window, and then repeat the process for all other topics. Open the **Item** table in Design view, change the field name of Title to ItemName, and then save and close the table. Open the **Item** table, review the recordset, close the table, open the **Projected Income** query, review the query results, close the query, and then do the same for the **Item** form. Describe your findings in terms of the effects of using the Name AutoCorrect feature.

5. Exit Access.

INTERNET ASSIGNMENTS

Student Union

The purpose of the Internet Assignments is to challenge you to find information on the Internet that you can use to create effective documents. The actual assignments are updated and maintained on the Course Technology Web site. Log on to the Internet and use your Web browser to go to the Student Online Companion to accompany this text at **www.course.com/NewPerspectives/studentunion**. Click the Online Companions link, and then click the link for this text.

Quick Check Answers

Session 10.1

1. Visual Basic for Applications statements respond to events that occur with the objects in a database.
2. a procedure that runs when a specific event occurs
3. A Function procedure performs operations, returns a value, can accept input values, and can be used in expressions. A Sub procedure performs operations and can accept input values, but does not return a value and cannot be used in expressions.
4. A standard module is a database object that is stored in memory with other database objects when you open a database. A class module is associated with a specific database object, such as a form or report.
5. scope
6. You use the Immediate window to test VBA procedures when you are coding them, without changing any data in the database.

Session 10.2

1. Access checks the modules in your database for syntax errors. If no syntax errors are found, Access translates the VBA code into machine language.
2. The UCase function converts its argument to uppercase letters. It has no effect on characters that are not letters.
3. A Dim statement is used to declare variables and their types.
4. 18 times
5. VBA equivalent of the yes/no data type
6. VBA equivalent of the text data type
7. converts its argument to a String data type

Session 10.3

1. when Access displays a control
2. a control's foreground, or text, color
3. when the object opens and every time you move to another record
4. when the object opens
5. an action that operates on specific objects or controls
6. executes an action in a function

In this tutorial you will:

- Analyze a database's performance

- View and print database documentation

- Link a database to a table in another database

- Use the Linked Table Manager

- Use replication to create a Design Master and replica of a database

- Synchronize the Design Master and replica databases

- Split a database

- Set database startup options

- Encrypt and decrypt a database

- Set and unset a database password

- Use the User-Level Security Wizard to assign users, groups, and permissions to a database

- Create an MDE file

MANAGING
AND SECURING
A DATABASE

Managing and Securing the Overseas Database

CASE

Northeast Seasonal Jobs International (NSJI)

Elsa has planned training sessions for NSJI staff members to learn how to use the Overseas database. These training sessions are scheduled to begin right after you finalize the Overseas database. Your remaining work will address Elsa's concerns about database management, database security, and the database's overall performance.

You will use Access analysis features, such as the Performance Analyzer and the Documenter, to analyze and document the Overseas database. You'll use the Linked Table Manager and the Database Splitter, create an MDE file, and set the startup options to protect the database design from user modification and to open the Switchboard form automatically when a user opens the Overseas database.

Elsa is leaving on a business trip to meet with potential employers. During her trip, she wants to have access to the Overseas database so that she can record information about new employers immediately if any potential employers decide to offer positions through NSJI. You'll create a replica of the Overseas database for Elsa to use on her trip.

Finally, you'll implement Access security features, such as passwords, encryption, and permissions, to protect the database from unauthorized use.

SESSION 11.1

In this session, you will use the Performance Analyzer and Documenter analysis tools and print the Relationships window. You will link the database to a table in another database, and use the Linked Table Manager. You will use replication to convert the Overseas database to a Design Master and to create a replica of the database. Then you will make changes to the data in the replica and update the Design Master.

Analyzing Database Performance with the Performance Analyzer

Elsa wants the Overseas database to respond as quickly as possible to user requests, such as running queries and opening reports. You'll use the Performance Analyzer to check the performance of the Overseas database. The **Performance Analyzer** is an Access tool that you can use to optimize the performance of an Access database. You select the database objects you want to analyze for performance and run the Performance Analyzer, and then the Performance Analyzer lists three types of analysis results: recommendation, suggestion, and idea. Access can complete the recommendation and suggestion optimizations for you, but you must implement the idea optimizations. Analysis results include changes such as those related to the storage of fields and the creation of indexes and relationships.

REFERENCE WINDOW   **RW**

Using the Performance Analyzer
- Start Access and open the database you want to analyze.
- Click Tools on the menu bar, point to Analyze, and then click Performance.
- Select the object(s) you want to analyze, and then click the OK button.
- Select the analysis result(s) you want the Performance Analyzer to complete for you, and then click the Optimize button.
- Click the Close button.

You'll use the Performance Analyzer to optimize the performance of the Overseas database.

To use the Performance Analyzer to optimize the performance of the Overseas database:

1. Place your Data Disk in the appropriate disk drive, start Access, and then open the **Overseas** database in the Tutorial folder on your Data Disk.

2. Click **Forms** in the Objects bar of the Database window (if necessary), click **Tools** on the menu bar, point to **Analyze**, and then click **Performance**. The Performance Analyzer dialog box opens. See Figure 11-1.

Figure 11-1   PERFORMANCE ANALYZER DIALOG BOX

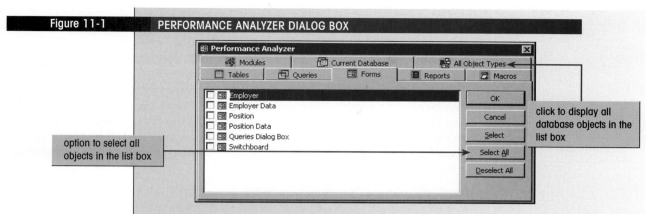

option to select all objects in the list box

click to display all database objects in the list box

TROUBLE? If a dialog box opens and asks if you would like to install this feature, insert your Microsoft Office XP CD in the correct drive, and then click the Yes button. If you do not have the Office XP CD, see your instructor or technical support person for assistance.

Elsa wants you to analyze every object in the Overseas database.

3. Click the **All Object Types** tab, and then click the **Select All** button. All objects in the Overseas database appear in the list box, and all of them are now selected.

4. Click the **OK** button. The Performance Analyzer analyzes all the objects in the Overseas database and, after a few moments, displays its analysis results. See Figure 11-2.

Figure 11-2   PERFORMANCE ANALYZER ANALYSIS RESULTS

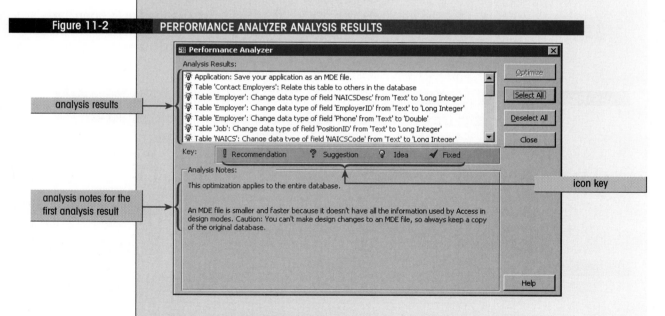

analysis results

analysis notes for the first analysis result

icon key

Most of the analysis results are in the idea category, which means that you have to implement them yourself. For example, the first analysis result ("Application: Save your application as an MDE file.") produces a smaller and faster database; you'll create an MDE file later in this tutorial. You should consider all idea analysis results later, but more important now are the recommendation and suggestion analysis results, which the Performance Analyzer can complete for you automatically.

5. Click several of the entries in the Analysis Results list box, and read each entry and its analysis notes.

The Performance Analyzer can perform the one suggestion analysis result (relate the Student table to itself) for you automatically. You'll let the Performance Analyzer create a relationship between the Student table and itself because the table has a one-to-many relationship based on the StudentID field as the primary key and the Contact field as the foreign key. In Tutorial 8, you added the Contact field to the Student table and created a self-join query based on the Student query, but you did not add the one-to-many relationship in the Relationships window.

6. Scroll the Analysis Results list box as necessary, click the **Table 'Student': Relate to table 'Student'** analysis result (its icon is a green question mark) to select it, and then click the **Optimize** button. Access creates a relationship between the Student table and itself, and the icon for the selected analysis result changes to a blue check mark to indicate a "Fixed" status.

7. Click the **Close** button to close the dialog box and return to the Database window.

Next, you'll open the Relationships window to view the new relationship created by the Performance Analyzer.

To view the relationship created by the Performance Analyzer:

1. Click the **Relationships** button 🔲 on the Database toolbar to open the Relationships window, and then use the ↕ pointer to drag the bottom borders of the two Student field lists down until you can see all the fields in both lists. See Figure 11-3.

| Figure 11-3 | STUDENT TABLE ONE-TO-MANY RELATIONSHIP |

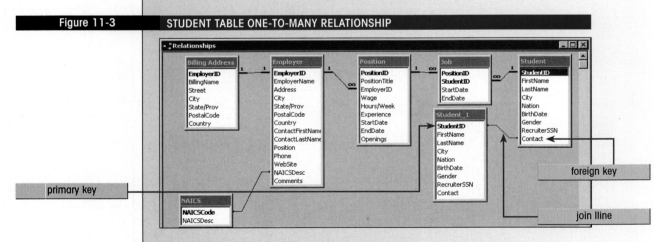

The Performance Analyzer added a second copy of the Student table (Student_1) and a join line between the Student and Student_1 tables to the Relationships window. The join line connects the primary table (Student_1) to the related table (Student) using the StudentID field as the primary key and the Contact field as the foreign key. You'll use the Edit Relationships dialog box to view the join properties for the relationship.

2. Right-click the join line between the Student_1 and Student tables, and then click **Edit Relationship** on the shortcut menu to open the Edit Relationships dialog box. See Figure 11-4.

Figure 11-4	EDIT RELATIONSHIPS DIALOG BOX FOR THE NEW RELATIONSHIP

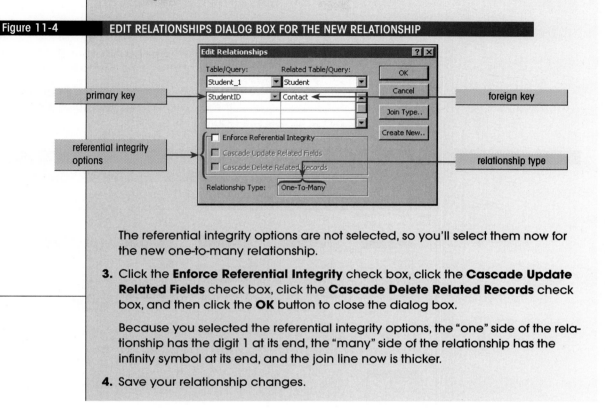

The referential integrity options are not selected, so you'll select them now for the new one-to-many relationship.

3. Click the **Enforce Referential Integrity** check box, click the **Cascade Update Related Fields** check box, click the **Cascade Delete Related Records** check box, and then click the **OK** button to close the dialog box.

Because you selected the referential integrity options, the "one" side of the relationship has the digit 1 at its end, the "many" side of the relationship has the infinity symbol at its end, and the join line now is thicker.

4. Save your relationship changes.

Elsa asks you to print a copy of the database relationships to use as a reference, and she asks if other Access documentation is available.

Printing **Database Relationships and Using the Documenter**

You can print the Relationships window to document the fields, tables, and relationships in a database. You can also use the **Documenter**, another Access tool, to create detailed documentation of all, or selected, objects in a database.

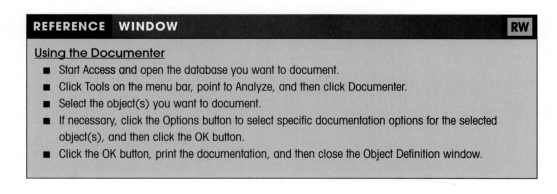

REFERENCE WINDOW   RW

Using the Documenter
- Start Access and open the database you want to document.
- Click Tools on the menu bar, point to Analyze, and then click Documenter.
- Select the object(s) you want to document.
- If necessary, click the Options button to select specific documentation options for the selected object(s), and then click the OK button.
- Click the OK button, print the documentation, and then close the Object Definition window.

Next, you'll print the Relationships window and use the Documenter to create documentation for the NAICS table. Elsa will show Matt and Zack the NAICS table documentation as a sample of the information that the Documenter provides.

To print the Relationships window and use the Documenter:

1. Click **File** on the menu bar, click **Print Relationships** to open the Relationships for Overseas report window, and then maximize the window.

2. Click the **Setup** button on the Print Preview toolbar, click the **Page** tab, click the **Landscape** option button, click the **OK** button, and then scroll the window until you can see all the tables. See Figure 11-5.

| Figure 11-5 | RELATIONSHIPS FOR OVERSEAS REPORT |

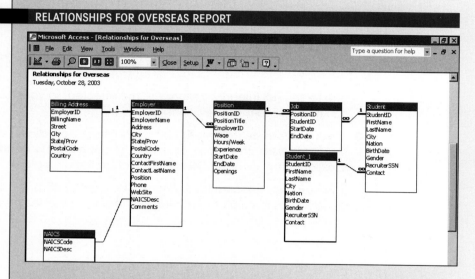

3. Click the **Print** button 🖨 on the Print Preview toolbar. Access prints the Relationships for Overseas report.

4. Click the **Close Window** button ☒ on the menu bar. A dialog box opens and asks if you want to save the report. Because you can easily create the report at any time, you won't save the report.

5. Click the **No** button to close the report without saving changes, and then close the Relationships window.

   Now you'll use the Documenter to create detailed documentation for the NAICS table as a sample to show Elsa.

6. Click **Tools** on the menu bar, point to **Analyze**, and then click **Documenter**. The Documenter dialog box opens. See Figure 11-6.

Figure 11-6	DOCUMENTER DIALOG BOX

option to select all objects in the list box

click to display more options for the selected object type

click to display all database objects in the list box

7. Click the **Tables** tab, click the **NAICS** check box, and then click the **Options** button. The Print Table Definition dialog box opens. See Figure 11-7.

Figure 11-7	PRINT TABLE DEFINITION DIALOG BOX

table documentation options

field documentation options

indexes documentation options

You select which documentation you want the Documenter to include for the selected table (Properties, Relationships, and Permissions by User and Group), its fields (Nothing; Names, Data Types, and Sizes; or Names, Data Types, Sizes, and Properties), and its indexes (Nothing; Names and Fields; or Names, Fields, and Properties). Elsa asks you to include all table documentation and the second options for fields and for indexes.

8. Make sure all check boxes are checked in the Include for Table section, click the **Names, Data Types, and Sizes** option button in the Include for Fields section, click the **Names and Fields** option button in the Include for Indexes section, click the **OK** button, and then click the **OK** button. The Object Definition window opens.

9. Click the **Zoom** list arrow on the Print Preview toolbar, click **100%**, and then scroll down the Object Definition window. See Figure 11-8.

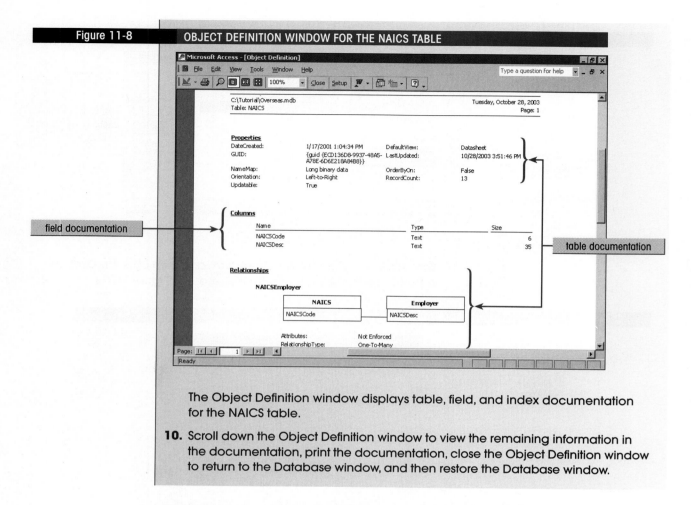

Figure 11-8 | OBJECT DEFINITION WINDOW FOR THE NAICS TABLE

field documentation

table documentation

The Object Definition window displays table, field, and index documentation for the NAICS table.

10. Scroll down the Object Definition window to view the remaining information in the documentation, print the documentation, close the Object Definition window to return to the Database window, and then restore the Database window.

Matt has the responsibility at NSJI for maintaining a separate database named Schools in which he stores information about overseas colleges and universities that NJSI recruiters visit to interview seasonal student workers. Elsa wants to retrieve the data in the School table in the Schools database from within the Overseas database. To provide Elsa with access to this table, you'll create a link to the School table in the Overseas database.

Linking Tables and Using the Linked Table Manager

You'll provide Elsa and other users of the Overseas database with access to the School table by using a linked table in the Overseas database. A **linked table** is a table that is stored in a file outside the open database from which Access can update and retrieve records in the open database. You can update (add, change, and delete) records in a linked table, but you can't change its structure. From the Overseas database, you'll be able to update the School table as a linked table, but you won't be able to change its structure. However, from the Schools database, Matt will be able to update the School table *and* change its structure. You can link a database to data stored in Excel worksheets, HTML documents, text files, other Access databases, and databases created by other DBMSs, such as SQL Server, Paradox, and dBASE. Although Access works faster with its own tables than it does with linked tables, you must use linked tables when you need access to data maintained in another Access database or by other programs.

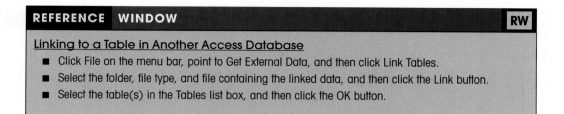

REFERENCE WINDOW **RW**

Linking to a Table in Another Access Database
- Click File on the menu bar, point to Get External Data, and then click Link Tables.
- Select the folder, file type, and file containing the linked data, and then click the Link button.
- Select the table(s) in the Tables list box, and then click the OK button.

You'll link to the School table in the Schools database from the Overseas database.

To link to the School table in the Schools database:

1. Click **File** on the menu bar, point to **Get External Data**, and then click **Link Tables**. The Link dialog box opens.

2. In the Look in list box, select the **Tutorial** folder on your Data Disk (if necessary), click **Schools** in the file list, and then click the **Link** button. Access opens the Link Tables dialog box. See Figure 11-9.

| Figure 11-9 | LINK TABLES DIALOG BOX |

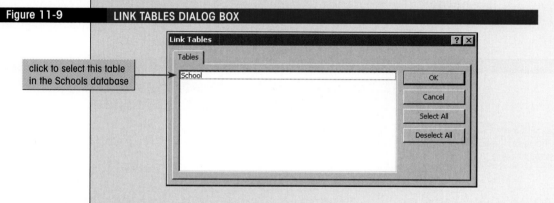

click to select this table in the Schools database

3. Click **School** in the Tables list box, and then click the **OK** button. The Link Tables dialog box closes, and you return to the Database window. A small blue arrow appears to the left of the School table icon in the Database window to identify the School table as a linked table.

Matt informs Elsa that he'll be reorganizing the NSJI network folders and might move the Schools database to a different folder. Elsa asks if moving the Schools database would cause a problem for the linked School table. You'll use the Linked Table Manager to show Elsa how to handle this situation. The **Linked Table Manager** is an Access tool you use to change the filename or disk location for linked tables in an Access database. When you use Access to link to data in another file, Access stores the file's location (drive, folder, and filename) in the database and uses the stored location to connect to the linked data. If you change the file's location, you can use the Linked Table Manager to change the stored file location, or **refresh the link**, in the Access database.

REFERENCE WINDOW   **RW**

<u>Using the Linked Table Manager</u>
- Click Tools on the menu bar, point to Database Utilities, and then click Linked Table Manager.
- Select the linked table(s), and then click the OK button.
- Select the linked table location, click the filename, and then click the Open button.
- Click the OK button, and then close the Linked Table Manager dialog box.

Next, you'll move the Schools database to a different folder, and then you'll use the Linked Table Manager to refresh the link to the School table in the Overseas database.

To move the Schools database and refresh the link to the School table:

1. Use Windows Explorer or My Computer to move the **Schools** database from the Tutorial folder to the root folder on your Data Disk.

2. In Access, click **Tools** on the menu bar, point to **Database Utilities**, and then click **Linked Table Manager**. The Linked Table Manager dialog box opens. See Figure 11-10.

| Figure 11-10 | LINKED TABLE MANAGER DIALOG BOX |

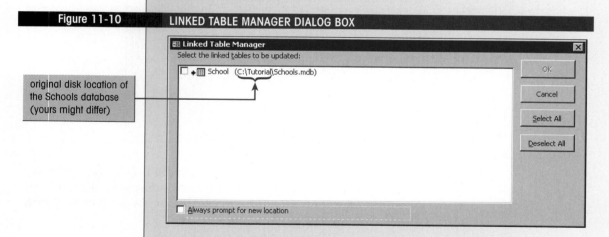

original disk location of the Schools database (yours might differ)

The School table is the only linked table, so it's the only table listed in the list box. The Tutorial folder on your Data Disk, which is the original disk location of the Schools database, is listed as the current disk location for the School table.

3. Click the **Select All** button, and then click the **OK** button. The Select New Location of School dialog box opens.

4. Use the **Look in** list arrow to select the root folder on your Data Disk, click **Schools** in the file list, and then click the **Open** button. A dialog box informs you that all selected linked tables were successfully refreshed.

5. Click the **OK** button to close the dialog box. The Linked Table Manager dialog box now displays the root folder on your Data Disk as the current disk location of the linked School table.

6. Close the Linked Table Manager dialog box.

Next, you'll open the School table to show Elsa how she can update it as a linked table from the new disk location.

To update the School table and change its design in the Overseas database:

1. Open the **School** table in Datasheet view. The School table datasheet displays four fields and 39 records.

   First, you'll add a new record to the School table.

2. Click the **New Record** navigation button ▶❋, type **40** in the SchoolID text box, press the **Tab** key, type **Universidad de Colima** in the SchoolName text box, press the **Tab** key, type **Colima** in the City text box, press the **Tab** key, and then type **Mexico** in the Country text box.

   Next, you'll switch to Design view to show Elsa that she can't change the design of the School table from the Overseas database.

3. Switch to Design view. A message box informs you that the School table is a linked table and has some properties that you cannot modify.

4. Click the **Yes** button to close the message box and switch to Design view. The SchoolID field is the current field, and the Help message in the Field Properties pane appears in red and indicates that you can't change the FieldName property for linked tables. See Figure 11-11.

Figure 11-11	LINKED TABLE IN DESIGN VIEW

current field

current field property

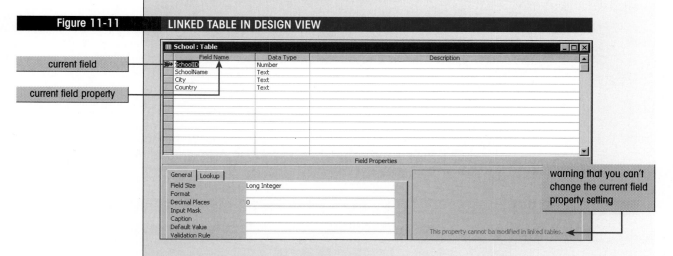

warning that you can't change the current field property setting

5. Press the **F6** key to highlight the Field Size property in the Field Properties pane. The Help message indicates that you can't change the Field Size property.

6. Press the **Tab** key, click the **Format** list arrow, and then click **General Number**. The Help message for the Format property appears in its normal blue, so you can change this field property.

7. Save and close the table.

Now you'll open the Schools database to show Elsa the new record in the School table. Then you'll delete that record and view the table in Design view.

To update the School table and view its design in the Schools database:

1. Open the **Schools** database in the root folder on your Data Disk, and then click **Tables** in the Objects bar of the Database window. A small blue arrow does not appear to the left of the School table icon, so this table is not a linked table in the Schools database.

2. Open the **School** table datasheet, and then click the **Last Record** navigation button ▶|. The record for Universidad de Colima, which you added to the School linked table in the Overseas database, appears as the last record in the School table in the Schools database.

3. Click the **Delete Record** button on the Table Datasheet toolbar, and then click the **Yes** button to delete the last record in the table.

4. Switch to Design view. Because the School table is not a linked table in the Schools database, the Help message in the Field Properties pane appears in blue type, as do the Help messages for all field properties; you can make any design changes you want to the School table in the Schools database. The Format property setting is blank because the General Number setting you made is in effect only in the Overseas database.

5. Close the **School** table, and then open the **Overseas** database in the Tutorial folder on your Data Disk.

Elsa wants to know what happens if she deletes the linked School table in the Overseas database. You'll delete the linked School table in the Overseas database to show her that Access deletes the link to the School table but does not delete the School table in the Schools database.

To delete the linked School table in the Overseas database:

1. Right-click **School** in the Tables list box to open the shortcut menu, and then click **Delete**. A message box asks if you want to remove the link to the School table. See Figure 11-12.

Figure 11-12	DELETING A LINKED TABLE MESSAGE BOX

The message box confirms that you'll delete only the link to the School table, not the School table in the School database.

2. Click the **Yes** button. Access deletes the link to the School table, and the School table no longer appears in the Tables list box in the Overseas database.

Elsa now understands how to link to Matt's School table and to other data if she needs to do so in the future.

Creating **a Replica of a Database**

Elsa wants to take a copy of the Overseas database with her on her upcoming overseas business trip. She wants to be sure that while she is away, any changes that she or anyone else makes to the database will be updated, keeping the database accurate and current in her absence.

If you simply created a copy of the Overseas database file and gave it to Elsa, her copy would not include any changes made by other NSJI employees while she is away, nor would the changes she makes to her copy of the database be included in the original database. Instead, you'll create a special copy of the Overseas database called a **replica**. When you create a replica of a database, the original copy of the database becomes the **Design Master**. The Design Master and all of its replicas are called the **replica set**. Access adds special tables and fields to the Design Master database to keep track of changes made to data and to the design of the database. Anyone using the Design Master can make changes to the design of database tables, queries, and other objects. Any changes in the data or design of database objects in the Design Master can then be automatically updated in a replica. Anyone using a replica of the database can make changes to the data in any of the database tables. A replica prevents the user from changing the structure or design of an existing table, query, or other database object. Any changes in the data in any replicas can be updated automatically in the Design Master. The process of updating the Design Master and the replicas is called **synchronization**.

REFERENCE WINDOW   **RW**

<u>Creating a Replica of a Database</u>
- Open the database you want to replicate.
- Click Tools on the menu bar, point to Replication, and then click Create Replica.
- Click the Yes button to close the database.
- Click the Yes button to make a backup copy of the database.
- Select the location where you want to store the new replica.
- Click the OK button.

You need to convert the Overseas database to a Design Master and create a replica of the database to give to Elsa.

To convert the Overseas database to a Design Master and create a replica of it:

1. Click **Tools** on the menu bar, point to **Replication**, and then click **Create Replica**. Access opens a message box asking if you want to close the database, convert it to a Design Master, and create a replica of the database.

2. Click the **Yes** button. Access compacts and closes the Overseas database and, after a few moments, opens a message box asking if you want to make a backup copy of the Overseas database. See Figure 11-13.

Figure 11-13   CREATING A BACKUP COPY OF THE OVERSEAS DATABASE

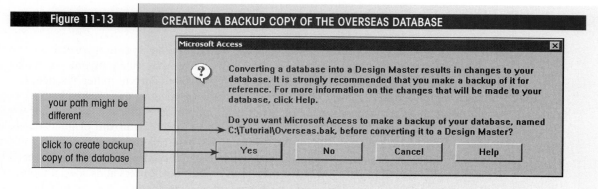

your path might be different

click to create backup copy of the database

Microsoft Access

Converting a database into a Design Master results in changes to your database. It is strongly recommended that you make a backup of it for reference. For more information on the changes that will be made to your database, click Help.

Do you want Microsoft Access to make a backup of your database, named C:\Tutorial\Overseas.bak, before converting it to a Design Master?

[Yes]   [No]   [Cancel]   [Help]

Access can make a backup copy of your database on your Data Disk. This backup can serve as an extra copy of the Overseas database in case anything goes wrong when Access creates the replica. You'll make a backup copy and, at the end of your replication work, you'll change the extension of the backup copy from .bak to .mdb, so you can use it instead of the Design Master for your remaining work in this tutorial.

3. Click the **Yes** button. A message box opens and shows the progress of converting the database to a Design Master, and then the Location of New Replica dialog box opens. See Figure 11-14.

Figure 11-14   LOCATION OF NEW REPLICA DIALOG BOX

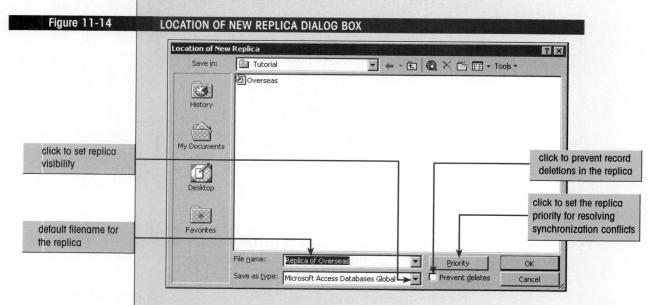

click to set replica visibility

default filename for the replica

click to prevent record deletions in the replica

click to set the replica priority for resolving synchronization conflicts

In the Location of New Replica dialog box, you choose the location and name for the replica. You also can set options for the **replica priority** (when multiple replicas update the same record, only the change for the replica with the highest priority is made), the **replica visibility** (choices are global, local, and anonymous), and **replica record deletion** (a check mark in the Prevent deletes check box prevents a user from deleting a record in the replica). The default settings are correct, so you can continue creating the replica.

4. Click the **OK** button. A message box opens and shows the status of creating the replica, and then Access names the replica "Replica of Overseas," converts the Overseas database to the Design Master, and opens a message box informing you of these actions. See Figure 11-15.

| Figure 11-15 | AFTER CREATING THE OVERSEAS DESIGN MASTER AND REPLICA |

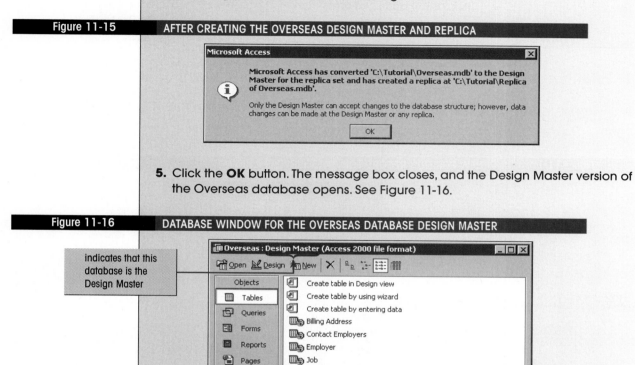

5. Click the **OK** button. The message box closes, and the Design Master version of the Overseas database opens. See Figure 11-16.

| Figure 11-16 | DATABASE WINDOW FOR THE OVERSEAS DATABASE DESIGN MASTER |

The phrase "Design Master" in the Database window title bar indicates that this database is the Design Master of the Overseas database. A new symbol appears next to the table icons in the Tables list to indicate that these objects have been replicated.

You can now give Elsa a copy of the Overseas database replica on a disk to take with her on her trip.

Synchronizing **the Replica and the Design Master**

While she is on her trip, Elsa visits several NSJI employer clients. Her visit to Harbourview Resort is successful, and the owner decides to offer an additional position with NSJI. Elsa adds a new record for Harbourview Resort in the Position table of the Overseas database replica.

To add the new record to the Overseas database replica:

1. Close the Design Master of the Overseas database without exiting Access, open the **Replica of Overseas** database in the Tutorial folder on your Data Disk, and then click **Forms** in the Objects bar of the Database window.

   The word "Replica" in the Database window title bar indicates that this is a replica of the Overseas database.

   You can now enter Elsa's new record using the Position form.

2. Open the **Position** form in Form view, and then click the **New Record** button ▶＊ on the Form View toolbar to display a blank form.

3. Enter the data for the new record, as shown in Figure 11-17.

Figure 11-17	NEW POSITION RECORD FOR HARBOURVIEW RESORT

4. Close the form.

The replica of the Overseas database now contains a new record that is not recorded in the Design Master. When Elsa returns from her trip, you can update the Design Master by synchronizing the Design Master and the replica. The synchronization process compares the Design Master to the replica and checks for any differences. Access updates the Design Master with any changes that have been made to the data in the replica, and updates the replica with any changes that have been made to the data or the design of any database objects in the Design Master. This process ensures that the Design Master and the replica are consistent.

REFERENCE WINDOW   **RW**

Synchronizing the Design Master and a Replica

- Open the replica set database (either the Design Master or a replica) that you want to synchronize.
- Click Tools, point to Replication, and then click Synchronize Now.
- Enter the location and name of the replica set database you want to synchronize with the current database, and then click the OK button.
- Click the Yes button when asked if you want to close the database.
- Click the OK button when informed that the synchronization was completed successfully.

Elsa returned from her trip, so now you must synchronize the open replica of the Overseas database with the Design Master to enter the new Position record.

To synchronize the replica and the Design Master:

1. Click **Tools** on the menu bar, point to **Replication**, and then click **Synchronize Now**. The Synchronize Database dialog box opens.

2. Make sure the **Directly with Replica** option button is selected. If the Directly with Replica list box does not display the name of the Design Master of the Overseas database, use the Browse button to select it. See Figure 11-18.

Figure 11-18	SYNCHRONIZE DATABASE DIALOG BOX

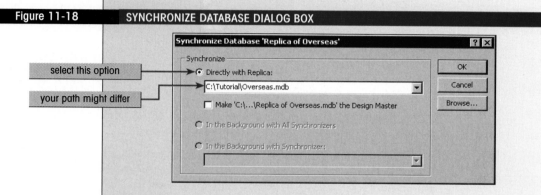

select this option

your path might differ

TROUBLE? The path statement in the Directly with Replica list box on your screen might not match the one in the figure. Be sure that it is accurate for your system and the location of your Data Disk files.

3. Click the **OK** button, and then click the **Yes** button when asked if you want to close the replica. After a few seconds, Access opens a message box indicating that the synchronization is complete.

4. Click the **OK** button to close the message box and to re-open the replica.

The Design Master and the replica are now synchronized. The new record that Elsa added to the replica copy of the Overseas database has been added to the Design Master. You can now view the Position table data using the Position form and display the new record in the Design Master.

To find and display the new Position table record in the Position form in the Design Master:

1. Close the replica of the Overseas database without exiting Access.

2. Open the **Overseas** database in the Tutorial folder on your Data Disk, and then open the **Position** form in Form view.

3. Click the **Last Record** navigation button ▶️ to display the last record. This is the new record that you added (see Figure 11-17).

4. Close the form.

Now that you have synchronized the databases, you can delete the replica of the Overseas database. You can easily create another replica whenever Elsa needs to take the database with her on future business trips. Even though you delete the replica of the Overseas database, the original Design Master of the database remains a Design Master. Because there can be many replicas of a database in a replica set, the Design Master keeps track of any changes you make to the database so that other replicas can be synchronized at any time.

In your remaining work for Elsa you won't use the Design Master of the Overseas database; you'll use the original version of the Overseas database (before you converted it to a Design Master and created the replica). Therefore, you'll also rename both versions of the Overseas database.

To delete the replica of the Overseas database and rename databases:

1. Close the Design Master of the Overseas database without exiting Access.

2. Use Windows Explorer or My Computer to open the **Tutorial** folder on your Data Disk.

3. Right-click the **Replica of Overseas** database to open the shortcut menu, click **Delete**, and then click the **Yes** button (if necessary).

4. Right-click the **Overseas** database to open the shortcut menu, click **Rename**, press the **End** key, press the **spacebar**, type **Design Master**, and then press the **Enter** key.

   TROUBLE? If a message box opens and tells you that changing the filename extension might make the file unusable, click the No button, and then repeat Step 4 and type Design Master.mdb, with the filename extension, before pressing the Enter key.

5. Repeat Step 4 to rename the **Overseas.bak** database as **Overseas.mdb**.

6. Close the Windows Explorer or My Computer window to return to the Access window.

In the next session, you'll finish your work with the Overseas database by splitting the database, setting startup options, and making access to it more secure.

Session 11.1 QUICK CHECK

1. What is the Performance Analyzer?

2. You use the _____ tool to create detailed documentation of all, or selected, objects in a database.

3. When do you use the Linked Table Manager?

4. What is a replica set?

5. How does a Design Master differ from a replica?

6. What does Access do when you synchronize a Design Master and a replica?

SESSION 11.2

In this session, you'll use the Database Splitter and set the Overseas database startup options. You'll also use the encryption, password, and the User-Level Security Wizard security features for an Access database. Finally, you'll learn about saving a database as an MDE file.

Using the Database Splitter

Elsa wants to create several queries for the Overseas database, but she doesn't want the user interface for other users to be cluttered with queries they won't need to use. She asks if there's a way for her to have a special user interface to access the data in the Overseas database.

Users might want to customize their own versions of the user interface, while accessing the same central table data. The **Database Splitter** is an Access tool that splits an Access database into two files: one file contains the tables, and the other contains the queries, forms, and other database objects. Although a single master copy of the file containing the tables is stored and accessed, users can have their own copies of the other file and add their own queries, reports, and other objects to handle their processing needs. Each file created by the Database Splitter is an Access database. The database that contains the tables is called the **back-end database**; and the database that contains the other objects, including the user interface, is called the **front-end database**.

People who develop databases and sell them to multiple companies usually split their databases. When a developer delivers a split database, the initial back-end database does not include the company's data, and the initial front-end database is complete as created by the developer. Companies use the front-end database to update their data in the back-end database, but they do not modify the front-end database in any way. Periodically, the database developer improves the front-end database by modifying and adding queries, reports, and other objects without changing the structure of the tables. In other words, the developer changes the front-end database, but does not change the back-end database. The developer gives its client companies replacement front-end databases, which continue to work with the back-end database that contains the company's data. This entire process is illustrated in Figure 11-19.

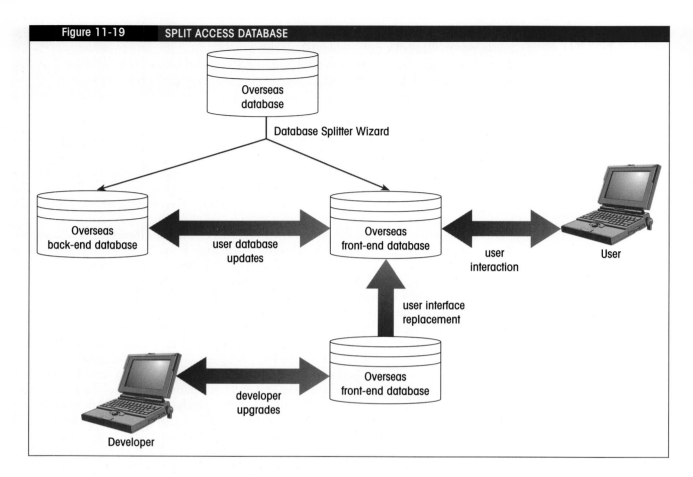

Figure 11-19   SPLIT ACCESS DATABASE

Splitting a database also lets you place the files on different computers. You can place the front-end database on each user's PC, and the back-end database on a network server that users access through their front-end databases; this arrangement distributes the workload across the network. Finally, as a company grows, it might need a more powerful database management system such as Oracle, Microsoft's SQL Server, or IBM's DB2. You could retain the original Access front-end database and replace the Access back-end database with a new non-Access back-end database, which is an easier task than replacing all database objects.

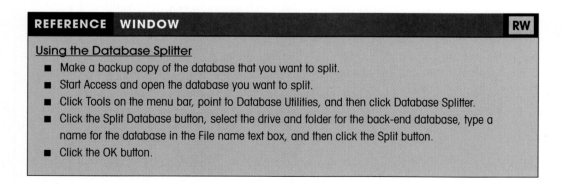

REFERENCE WINDOW   RW

Using the Database Splitter
- Make a backup copy of the database that you want to split.
- Start Access and open the database you want to split.
- Click Tools on the menu bar, point to Database Utilities, and then click Database Splitter.
- Click the Split Database button, select the drive and folder for the back-end database, type a name for the database in the File name text box, and then click the Split button.
- Click the OK button.

You'll use the Database Splitter to split the Overseas database into two files. As a precaution, you'll make a backup copy of the database before you split the database. You should always make regular backups of databases, but it's especially important to make a backup before you make a significant database change such as splitting the database.

To use the Database Splitter:

1. Use Windows Explorer or My Computer to create a copy of the **Overseas** database in the Tutorial folder on your Data Disk, and then rename the copy as **NSJI**.

2. Start Access (if necessary), open the **Overseas** database, click **Tools** on the menu bar, point to **Database Utilities**, and then click **Database Splitter**. The Database Splitter dialog box opens. See Figure 11-20.

Figure 11-20   DATABASE SPLITTER DIALOG BOX

TROUBLE? If a dialog box opens and asks if you would like to install this feature, insert your Office XP CD in the correct drive, and then click the Yes button. If you do not have the Office XP CD, see your instructor or technical support person for assistance.

3. Click the **Split Database** button. The Create Back-end Database dialog box opens. The back-end database will contain the tables from the Overseas database. You'll use the default filename (Overseas_be.mdb) for the back-end database.

4. Click the **Split** button. After several seconds, a message box informs you that the database was successfully split.

5. Click the **OK** button to close the message box and return to the Database window. See Figure 11-21.

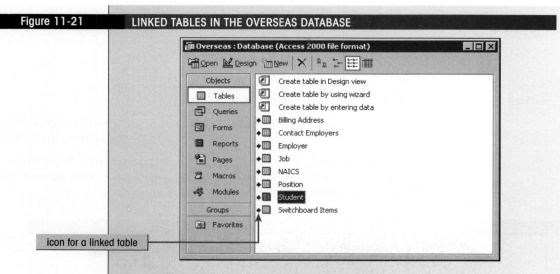

Figure 11-21   LINKED TABLES IN THE OVERSEAS DATABASE

icon for a linked table

Each table in the Overseas database has an icon next to its name indicating that there's a link to that table in another file. The tables are no longer stored in the Overseas database; they are stored in the Overseas_be database file you just created with the Database Splitter. You can use the tables as if they were stored in the Overseas database, except you cannot change a table's design from the Overseas database. You have to close the Overseas database and open the Overseas_be database to change a table's design.

6. Click **Queries** in the Objects bar of the Database window. The queries you've created appear in the Queries list box. The queries and objects other than tables are still stored in the Overseas database.

You'll close the Overseas database and then open the Overseas_be database to verify which objects are stored in the back-end database.

To verify the contents of the back-end database:

1. Close the **Overseas** database without exiting Access, and then open the **Overseas_be** database in the Tutorial folder. The tables from the Overseas database appear with their usual icons in the Tables list box. The tables are now stored in the Overseas_be database.

2. Open the **Employer** table in Design view. You can modify the design of the tables in the Overseas_be database because they are stored in that database; they are not linked as they are in the Overseas database.

3. Close the table, and then click **Queries** in the Objects bar of the Database window. No queries are listed because they are stored in the Overseas database.

4. Close the **Overseas_be** database without exiting Access, and then open the **Overseas** database in the Tutorial folder.

Elsa is pleased with the changes you have made. As a final enhancement to the user interface, she asks you to set Access to open the Switchboard form automatically when a user opens the Overseas database.

Setting the Database Startup Options

Access lets you specify certain actions, called **startup options**, that take place when a database opens. For example, you can specify the name that appears in the Access window title bar, prevent users from using the Database window, or specify a form that is automatically opened. If you want to bypass the startup options, you can press and hold down the Shift key when you open the database.

Elsa wants users to be able to open the Overseas database and have the Switchboard form open automatically. This way, users won't need to use the Forms list box in the Database window to access the Switchboard form.

REFERENCE WINDOW	RW

Setting the Database Startup Options

- Click Tools on the menu bar, and then click Startup to open the Startup dialog box.
- Specify the startup options, and then click the OK button. The options will be in effect the next time the database is opened.

You need to set the Overseas database startup options so that the switchboard appears automatically when the database is opened, and so that the Database window is hidden from view. You'll also set startup options to provide users with restricted menus, to eliminate the toolbars, and to prevent users from making changes to toolbar and menu options.

To change the Overseas database startup options:

1. Click **Tools** on the menu bar, and then click **Startup**. The Startup dialog box opens. See Figure 11-22.

Figure 11-22	STARTUP DIALOG BOX

2. Click the **Display Form/Page** list arrow, and then click **Switchboard**. This setting specifies that the Switchboard form will be opened upon startup.

3. Click the **Display Database Window** check box to remove the check mark. This setting specifies that the Database window will not be opened upon startup.

4. Click the **Allow Full Menus** check box to remove the check mark. This setting eliminates menus and commands that enable users to change the design of the objects in the Overseas database. Only a subset of the built-in menus will be available.

5. Click the **Allow Built-in Toolbars** check box to remove the check mark. This setting eliminates the toolbars from all windows in the Overseas database.

6. Click the **Allow Toolbar/Menu Changes** check box to remove the check mark. This setting prevents users from customizing toolbars, menu bars, and shortcut menus.

7. Click the **OK** button to close the Startup dialog box.

To test the startup options, you need to close and then re-open the Overseas database.

To test the startup options:

1. Close the **Overseas** database without exiting Access.

2. Click **File** on the menu bar, and then click **1 Overseas.mdb** to open the Overseas database. See Figure 11-23.

| Figure 11-23 | OVERSEAS DATABASE USER INTERFACE |

restricted menu bar

toolbar eliminated

Switchboard form

TROUBLE? The path to the Overseas.mdb database might be different on your File menu, depending on the location of your Data Disk.

Access opens the Overseas database, opens the Switchboard form, hides the Database window, displays a restricted menu bar, and eliminates the built-in Form View toolbar. Your test shows that the startup options are correctly set.

Now you can make one final test of the Overseas database user interface.

To test the features of the Overseas database user interface:

1. Make one final pass through all the command button options to verify that all features work properly on the Overseas database user interface.

2. Click the **Exit to Overseas** command button on the Overseas Database switchboard as your last test to close the form and return to the Database window.

Elsa wants you to make access to the Overseas database more secure, which will require you to change the database design. Because the Overseas database now has a restricted menu bar and no toolbar, you won't be able to make further design changes to the database unless you bypass the startup options (by pressing and holding down the Shift key when you open the database) or modify the startup options to allow toolbars and full menus. It'll be easier for you to complete the remaining work for Elsa if you modify the startup options. To modify the startup options, you'll need to close the Overseas database and open it, bypassing the startup options.

To modify the Overseas database startup options:

1. Close the **Overseas** database without exiting Access.

2. Click **File** on the menu bar, press and hold down the **Shift** key, click **1 Overseas.mdb** to open the Overseas database, and then release the **Shift** key. Access opens the Overseas database and displays the Database toolbar and full menus; by pressing and holding down the Shift key you bypassed the startup options.

3. Click **Tools** on the menu bar, and then click **Startup**. The Startup dialog box opens.

4. Click the **Allow Full Menus** check box to add a check mark for that option, click the **Allow Built-in Toolbars** check box to add a check mark for that option, and then click the **OK** button.

5. Close the **Overseas** database without exiting Access, open the **Overseas** database, and then click the **Exit to Overseas** command button to close the form and return to the Database window. Access displays the Database toolbar and full menu bar.

Next, Elsa wants you to make access to the Overseas database more secure.

Securing an Access Database

Security refers to the protection of a database against unauthorized access, either intentional or accidental. Setting the database startup options to restrict the menu bar and to hide toolbars is one way you can prevent users from changing the database design. Access provides several additional security features, including encryption and passwords.

Encryption converts the data in a database to a format that's indecipherable to a word processor or other program and stores it in an encrypted format. If unauthorized users attempt to bypass Access and get to the data directly, they will see only the encrypted version of the data. However, users accessing the data using Access will have no problem working with the data. When a user stores or modifies data in a database, Access will encrypt the data before updating the database. Before a user retrieves data using Access, the data will be decrypted and presented to the user in the normal format. Once you've encrypted a database, you can use Access to decrypt it. **Decrypting** a database reverses the encryption. If your encrypted database takes longer to respond to requests as it gets larger, you might consider decrypting it to improve its responsiveness.

To prevent access to a database by an unauthorized user through Access, you can assign a password to the database. A **password** is a string of characters assigned to a database that users must enter before they can open the database. As long as the password is known only to authorized users of the database, unauthorized access to the database is prevented. It's best if you use a password that's easily remembered by authorized users but is not obvious and easily guessed by others.

Elsa wants to restrict access to the Overseas database to authorized NSJI employees and also wants to prevent people from using other programs to access the data in the Overseas database.

Encrypting a Database

First, you'll encrypt the Overseas database for Elsa.

REFERENCE WINDOW   **RW**

Encrypting or Decrypting a Database
- Start Access, but do not open the database you want to encrypt.
- In the Access window, click Tools on the menu bar, point to Security, and then click Encrypt/Decrypt Database.
- In the Encrypt/Decrypt Database dialog box, select the drive and folder that contains the database, select the database, and then click the OK button.
- In the Encrypt Database As or the Decrypt Database As dialog box, select the drive and folder for the modified database, type its name in the File name text box, and then click the Save button.

You'll encrypt the Overseas database. First, you need to close it without exiting Access.

To encrypt the Overseas database:

1. Close the **Overseas** database without exiting Access.

2. Click **Tools** on the menu bar, point to **Security**, and then click **Encrypt/Decrypt Database**. The Encrypt/Decrypt Database dialog box opens.

3. If necessary, use the **Look in** list arrow to select the **Tutorial** folder on your Data Disk.

4. Click **Overseas** in the list box, and then click the **OK** button. The Encrypt Database As dialog box opens.

   You can use the same name, drive, and folder for the original and encrypted versions of the database. If an error occurs during the encryption operation, Access doesn't delete the original file. If the operation is successful, Access replaces the original database with the encrypted version. If you use a different name, drive, or folder for the encrypted database, both the original and encrypted databases are retained.

> You'll replace the original database by using the same name, drive, and folder for the encrypted database.
>
> **5.** Click **Overseas** in the list box, click the **Save** button, and then click the **Yes** button when asked if you want to replace the existing file. The dialog box closes, Access encrypts the Overseas database, and you return to the Access window.

Even though the Overseas database is encrypted, it won't look any different when you use Access to open it. However, if you attempt to open the Overseas database with another program, the data in the Overseas database would be indecipherable.

Next, you'll set a password for the Overseas database.

Setting and Unsetting a Database Password

Encrypting a database does not prevent unauthorized users from using Access to open the Overseas database and viewing or changing its data. Elsa asks you to set a password for the Overseas database to prevent such unauthorized access.

REFERENCE WINDOW   **RW**

Setting a Database Password
- Start Access, click the Open button on the Database toolbar, select the drive and folder that contains the database, and then click the database.
- Click the Open list arrow, and then click Open Exclusive.
- Click Tools on the menu bar, point to Security, and then click Set Database Password.
- Type the password in the Password text box, type the same password in the Verify text box, and then press the Enter key.

The way you usually open an Access database allows **shared** access of the database with others; that is, two or more users can open and use the same database at the same time. When you set a password for the Overseas database, you need to open the database with exclusive access. When you open an Access database with **exclusive access**, you prevent other users from opening and using the database at the same time. You must open the database with exclusive access in order to set a password, so that you can guarantee that only one copy of the database is open when you set the password.

You'll now set the password for the Overseas database to Nereid.

To set the password for the Overseas database:

1. Click the **Open** button on the Database toolbar. The Open dialog box opens.

2. Click **Overseas** in the list box (if necessary), and then click the **Open** list arrow. See Figure 11-24.

Figure 11-24   OPENING A DATABASE WITH EXCLUSIVE ACCESS

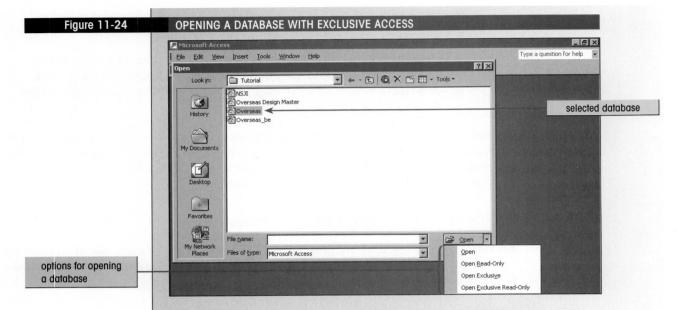

options for opening a database

selected database

Clicking the Open option opens the selected database with shared access for both reading and updating, whereas clicking the Open Read-Only option opens the selected database with shared access for reading only. **Reading** includes any action that does not involve updating the database, such as running queries (but not action queries) and viewing table records. Actions that are prohibited when you open a database as Read-Only (because they involve updating the database) include changing the database design and updating table records. The other two options in the Open list open the selected database with exclusive access for reading and updating (Open Exclusive) or for reading only (Open Exclusive Read-Only).

3. Click **Open Exclusive**. The Overseas Database form opens in the Access window.

4. Click the **Exit to Overseas** command button to close the form and return to the Database window, click **Tools** on the menu bar, point to **Security**, and then click **Set Database Password**. The Set Database Password dialog box opens. See Figure 11-25.

Figure 11-25   SET DATABASE PASSWORD DIALOG BOX

type password here

type same password here

You must type the password twice: once in the Password text box, and again in the Verify text box. Passwords are case-sensitive, so you must type the same password in both text boxes. Because the password is stored in the database, you cannot open the database if you forget the password.

5. Type **Nereid** in the Password text box, press the **Tab** key, type **Nereid** in the Verify text box, and then press the **Enter** key. The dialog box closes, and Access sets the Overseas database password to Nereid.

TROUBLE? If a message box opens, asking you to verify the new password by retyping it in the Verify text box, click the OK button, type Nereid in the Verify text box, and then press the Enter key.

Next, you'll close and re-open the Overseas database to verify that the password has been set. Then you'll unset, or remove, the password.

REFERENCE WINDOW   **RW**

Unsetting a Database Password

■ Start Access, click the Open button on the Database toolbar, select the drive and folder that contains the database, and then click the database.
■ Click the Open list arrow, and then click Open Exclusive.
■ Click Tools on the menu bar, point to Security, and then click Unset Database Password.
■ Type the password in the Password text box, and then press the Enter key.

Unsetting a password cancels the password protection for the database. It also permits you to modify the password; after unsetting the password, you can set a new password.

To test and unset the password for the Overseas database:

1. Close the **Overseas** database without exiting Access.

TROUBLE? If the Password Required dialog box opens, type Nereid, and then press the Enter key.

Because you'll be unsetting the password, you need to open the Overseas database with exclusive access.

2. Open the **Overseas** database with exclusive access. The Password Required dialog box opens. See Figure 11-26.

Figure 11-26	PASSWORD REQUIRED DIALOG BOX

3. Type **nereid** in the text box, and then press the **Enter** key. A message box opens, warning you that you did not enter a valid password.

4. Click the **OK** button, type **Nereid** in the text box, and then press the **Enter** key. The Overseas Database form opens in the Access window.

You'll now unset the password.

5. Click **Exit to Overseas** to close the form and return to the Database window, click **Tools** on the menu bar, point to **Security**, and then click **Unset Database Password**. The Unset Database Password dialog box opens. See Figure 11-27.

Figure 11-27	UNSET DATABASE PASSWORD DIALOG BOX

type password here

6. Type **Nereid** in the Password text box, and then press the **Enter** key.

The next time you open the Overseas database, you won't be asked to enter a password because you've unset it.

Elsa asks if she can restrict access to the Overseas database for selected NSJI employees.

Establishing **User-Level Security**

Setting a database's startup options to restrict the menu bar and hide toolbars, encrypting a database, and setting a database password are security measures that apply to all users of the database. The security needs for a database might be more individualized. For example, you might need to set the database so that some users only can update or view objects, and so that other users only can view selected objects. In this situation, you can use **user-level security**, which lets you grant users or groups of users specific permissions to tables, queries, forms, reports, and macros. A user's **permissions** specify what kind of access the user has to objects in a database. Examples of permissions are Modify Design (view, add, change, and delete the design of database objects), Read Data (view data in tables and queries), and Delete Data (view and delete, but not modify or insert, data in tables and queries). You can assign permissions to individual objects (specific queries and reports, for example), to object types (all tables and queries, for example), or to combinations of individual objects and object types. Companies such as NSJI assign the responsibility for database security to an individual, often called the **database administrator**, or to a group, often called **database administration (DBA)**. The database administrator or DBA, in consultation with company management, controls the permissions assigned to database users.

When you establish user-level security, you usually create groups and assign permissions to the groups. A **group** is a collection of users identified by a group name and ID. Next, you will assign each user a name and password, and then assign each user to one or more groups, depending on the permissions that user needs. Group names and IDs, user names and passwords, and group membership information are stored in an Access **workgroup information file** that is read at startup, as shown in Figure 11-28. The permissions that you assign to groups for the database's objects are stored in hidden system tables in the database.

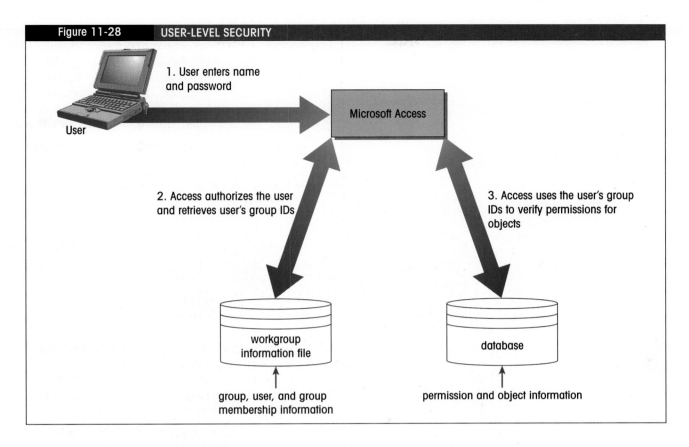

Figure 11-28   **USER-LEVEL SECURITY**

1. User enters name and password

User

Microsoft Access

2. Access authorizes the user and retrieves user's group IDs

3. Access uses the user's group IDs to verify permissions for objects

workgroup information file

database

group, user, and group membership information

permission and object information

Using the User-Level Security Wizard

You'll use the **User-Level Security Wizard**, also called the **Security Wizard**, to create the workgroup information file and establish groups, users, and their permissions.

To start the User-Level Security Wizard and create the workgroup information file:

1. Click **Tools** on the menu bar, point to **Security**, and then click **User-Level Security Wizard**. A message box opens, informing you that you can't use the Security Wizard with the Overseas database opened in exclusive mode; the database must be opened in shared mode.

2. Click the **Yes** button. Access closes the Overseas database, re-opens it in shared mode, and then opens the first Security Wizard dialog box. See Figure 11-29.

Figure 11-29	CREATING A NEW WORKGROUP INFORMATION FILE

Security Wizard

The Security Wizard creates an unsecured backup copy of the current Microsoft Access database and secures the current database.

The workgroup information file contains the names of users and groups that will develop or use your application. To modify your current workgroup information file, you must have administrator permissions. Don't use the default workgroup information file.

overview description of the Security Wizard's objectives

Do you want to create a new workgroup information file or modify the current one?

make sure this option is selected

○ Create a new workgroup information file.

○ Modify my current workgroup information file.

Help   Cancel   < Back   Next >   Finish

The Security Wizard will create a backup copy of the Overseas database without user-level security and add user-level security to the Overseas database. Most businesses would save the unsecured backup copy to a CD or other portable medium and store it in a safe or other secured, protected place. Your first step is to create a new workgroup information file.

3. Make sure the **Create a new workgroup information file** option button is selected, and then click the **Next** button to display the next Security Wizard dialog box.

   In this Security Wizard dialog box, you enter the name and workgroup ID for the workgroup information file, and optionally a user name and a company name. The **workgroup ID (WID)** is a unique, case-sensitive, 4- to 20-character string that uniquely identifies the workgroup. Only those users who know the WID will be able to create a copy of the workgroup information file. You'll accept the default filename and folder (Secured.mdw in the Tutorial folder on your Data Disk) for the workgroup information file, create a new WID, and add Elsa's information.

4. Select the value in the WID text box, type **ZYxOverseasCBA7**, press the **Tab** key, type **Elsa Jensen** in the Your name (optional) text box, press the **Tab** key, and then type **NSJI** in the Company (optional) text box. See Figure 11-30.

| Figure 11-30 | NAMING THE WORKGROUP INFORMATION FILE |

make sure this option
is selected

type these values

You want to use this workgroup information only for the Overseas database, so
you'll select the option for creating a shortcut to the secured Overseas database.

5. Make sure the **I want to create a shortcut to open my secured database**
option button is selected, and then click the **Next** button to display the next
Security Wizard dialog box. See Figure 11-31.

| Figure 11-31 | SECURING DATABASE OBJECTS |

By default, running the Security Wizard secures all existing database objects
and all new objects created in the database. You can select objects that will
not be secured, which means that all users will have full permissions for those
objects. You don't usually want to bypass security for any object, so you'll
accept the default security settings.

6. Click the **Next** button to display the next Security Wizard dialog box, in which you select optional groups for the workgroup information file.

7. Click each group (but don't click the group check box), and then read the description in the Group permissions section.

Elsa wants Matt Griffin to be assigned to the Full Permissions group and Kelley Kellogg assigned to the Read-Only Users group, so you'll select these two groups and change their Group IDs.

8. Click the **Full Permissions** check box, select the value in the Group ID text box, and then type **OverseasFP**. See Figure 11-32.

Figure 11-32	SELECTING OPTIONAL GROUPS

select this optional group

type this group ID

description of the selected optional group

9. Click the **Read-Only Users** check box, select the value in the Group ID text box, type **OverseasRP**, and then click the **Next** button to display the next Security Wizard dialog box.

In this Security Wizard dialog box and the remaining dialog boxes, you'll add Matt and Kelley as users, assign them to groups, and set permissions for the Users group. The **Users group** is one of two groups created by default when you create a new workgroup information file. Access adds each user to the User group automatically as you add a new user. The Admins group is the second group created by default. Users assigned to the **Admins group** have full permissions and are the only users that can create users and groups. A new workgroup information file also contains one default user, the **Admin user**, which is assigned to the Admins group.

You'll now complete the remaining Security Wizard steps. First, you'll accept the default setting of granting no permissions to the Users group.

To complete the Security Wizard:

1. Make sure the **No, the Users group should not have any permissions** option button is selected, and then click the **Next** button to display the next Security Wizard dialog box, in which you add users to the workgroup information file.

Before adding Matt and Kelley as users, you'll enter a password for the Administrator user and change its **personal ID (PID)**, which serves the same purpose and has the same format rules for users as the WID does for workgroups. The Security Wizard automatically adds the Administrator user and assigns it to the Admins group.

2. Click **Administrator** in the list box, click the **Password** text box, type **Triton** in the Password text box, press the **Tab** key, and then type **BR73elsa**.

   TROUBLE? If your dialog box displays a different user name for the Administrator user, select that user name in Step 2.

   Next, you'll add Matt and Kelley as users.

3. Click the **Add a New User** button, type **Mgriffin** in the User name text box, press the **Tab** key, type **Poseidon** in the Password text box, press the **Tab** key, and then type **Matt44G** in the PID text box. See Figure 11-33.

Figure 11-33	ADDING A USER TO THE WORKGROUP INFORMATION FILE

your preassigned user name might differ

click to add Mgriffin (Matt Griffin) as a user

type these values

4. Click the **Add This User to the List** button to add Mgriffin (Matt Griffin) as a user to the workgroup information file.

5. Type **Kkellogg** in the User name text box, press the **Tab** key, type **Thetis** in the Password text box, press the **Tab** key, type **Kelley5K** in the PID text box, click the **Add This User to the List** button to add Kkellogg (Kelley Kellogg) as a user to the workgroup information file, and then click the **Next** button to display the next Security Wizard dialog box.

   You now will assign users Mgriffin and Kkellogg to groups and accept the default Admins group for the Administrator user.

6. Make sure the **Select a user and assign the user to groups** option button is selected, click the **Group or user name** list arrow, click **Mgriffin**, and then click the **Full Permissions** check box. See Figure 11-34.

Figure 11-34   ASSIGNING A USER TO A GROUP

option to assign the selected user to groups

group assigned to the selected user

selected user

7. Click the **Group or user name** list arrow, click **Kkellogg**, click the **Read-Only Users** check box, and then click the **Next** button to display the next Security Wizard dialog box, in which you enter the filename and location of the backup copy of the unsecured database. You'll place the backup copy in the Tutorial folder on your Data Disk with the name Overseas Unsecured.mdb.

8. Select **.bak** in the text box, press the **spacebar**, type **Unsecured.mdb**, and then click the **Finish** button. The Security Wizard creates the workgroup information file, the secured Overseas database, an unsecured backup copy of the database, and the report named One-step Security Wizard Report.

   The report named One-step Security Wizard Report lists the names of the unsecured and secured databases, the name and properties of the workgroup information file, the names of all secured objects in the Overseas database, group names and properties, and user names and properties. You'll print the report because you'll need its information if you need to re-create the workgroup information file.

9. Print the report, close the Security Wizard window, and then click the **No** button when asked if you want to save the report. A message box opens. See Figure 11-35.

Figure 11-35   SECURITY WIZARD MESSAGE BOX

The Security Wizard message box informs you that it encrypted the secured Overseas database, and that you must exit Access and open the Overseas database in the future by using the shortcut on the Windows desktop to the Overseas database's workgroup information file.

10. Click the **OK** button, and then exit Access.

Elsa wants to see how to work with a secured database.

Testing User-Level Security

First, you'll use the new workgroup information file to test user-level security by logging on as Kkellogg, who is assigned to the Read-Only Users group. You'll use the Overseas.mdb icon, which is a shortcut to the Overseas database's workgroup information file, on the Windows desktop to start Access and open the Overseas database.

To test user-level security:

1. Make sure the Windows desktop is visible, then double-click the **Overseas.mdb** shortcut icon. Access starts and opens the Logon dialog box. See Figure 11-36.

Figure 11-36	LOGON DIALOG BOX

type user name here
(your initial name
might differ)

type password here

First, you'll enter an incorrect password. As you type a password, asterisks appear in the Password text box as a security feature.

2. Select **Administrator** in the Name text box, type **Kkellogg** in the Name text box, press the **Tab** key, type **thetis** in the Password text box, and then press the **Enter** key. A message box opens to inform you that you entered an incorrect name or password because passwords are case-sensitive.

TROUBLE? If your dialog box displays a different user than the Administrator user, select that user in Step 2.

3. Click the **OK** button, type **Thetis** in the Password text box, and then press the **Enter** key. The Overseas Database form opens in the Access window.

The Read-Only User group does not have the permissions needed for the Kkellogg user to update data in the Overseas database. You'll open the Employer Data form and try to change a value.

4. Click the **Employer Data** command button to open the Employer Data form. The Kkellogg user can read, or view, data, which is why you could open the Employer Data form. The Employer field value is selected, so you'll try to update its value.

5. Type **8**. The Employer field value remains highlighted and unchanged.

Next, you'll exit Access and log on as the Mgriffin user. The Mgriffin user is assigned to the Full Permissions group, which lets you view and update all objects in a database.

6. Close the form, click the **Exit Access** command button, and then double-click the **Overseas.mdb** icon on the Windows desktop.

7. Select **Kkellogg** in the Name text box, type **Mgriffin** in the Name text box, press the **Tab** key, type **Poseidon** in the Password text box, and then press the **Enter** key to open the Overseas Database form in the Access window.

8. Click the **Employer Data** command button to open the Employer Data form, and then type **8** in the Employer text box. The digit 8 replaces the original Employer field value, indicating that the Mgriffin user can update data in the Overseas database.

Elsa now understands how user-level security works, so you'll undo the Employer field value change and exit Access.

9. Click the **Undo typing** button ↶ on the Form View toolbar, close the form, and then click the **Exit Access** command button to return to the Windows desktop.

10. Use Windows Explorer or My Computer to move the **Overseas.mdb** shortcut from the Desktop to the Tutorial folder on your Data Disk.

Before completing your work with the Overseas database, Elsa asks you to research another Access security feature—creating an MDE file.

Saving a Database as an MDE File

If a database contains VBA code, you can save an MDE file version of the database to prevent people from viewing or changing the VBA code. Saving an Access database as an **MDE file**, which has the .mde extension instead of the .mdb extension for a normal Access database, compiles all VBA modules, removes all editable VBA source code, and compacts the resulting database. The database and its VBA code continue to run as normal, but the VBA code can't be viewed or edited. Also, you can't view, modify, or create forms, reports, or modules in Design view, and you can't import or export forms, reports, or modules. Because an MDE file limits your database design changes to tables, queries, and data access pages, saving a database as an MDE file is best suited to a front-end database. You should keep a backup copy of the complete front-end database in case you need to modify the database design. To save a database as an MDE file, follow these steps:

1. If necessary, convert the database to the Access 2002 file format. You can save an Access database as an MDE file only if you have converted it to the Access 2002 file format.

2. Close the database, click Tools on the menu bar, point to Database Utilities, and then click Make MDE File.

3. In the Database to Save as MDE dialog box, select the name of the database you want to save, and then click the Make MDE button.

4. In the Save MDE As dialog box, enter a new name for the new MDE file, and then click the Save button.

Because the Overseas database has very few VBA modules and because Elsa believes user-level security provides an acceptable level of security, you won't save the Overseas database as an MDE file.

Your work with the Overseas database is now completed. Elsa reviews the final user interface, security measures, and database management tools with Matt and Zack, and they agree that the database will fully satisfy NSJI's requirements.

Session 11.2 **QUICK** | **CHECK**

1. What does the Database Splitter accomplish?

2. What is a startup option?

3. How do you display a form automatically when a database opens?

4. _____ refers to the protection of a database against unauthorized access, either intentional or accidental.

5. If an encrypted database takes longer to respond to your requests as it gets larger, you might consider _____ it to improve its responsiveness.

6. What are permissions?

7. Which two groups are created by default when you create a new workgroup information file?

8. Saving an Access database as a(n) _____ compiles all VBA modules, removes all editable VBA source code, and compacts the resulting database.

REVIEW ASSIGNMENTS

Elsa asks you to implement management and security features for the **Work** database. To fulfill her request, you'll complete the following steps.

1. Make sure your Data Disk is in the appropriate disk drive, start Access, and then open the **Work** database in the Review folder on your Data Disk.

2. Use the Performance Analyzer to analyze the entire **Work** database, excluding the **Reports Dialog Box** form, but do not implement any of the analysis results. How many analysis results of the recommendation type did the Performance Analyzer find? Of the suggestion type? Of the idea type? Close the Performance Analyzer dialog box.

3. Open, print, and then close the Relationships window without saving the report. Use the Documenter to document the **Salaries with Raises** query, print the report produced by the Documenter, and then close the Object Definition window.

4. Create a replica of the **Work** database in the Review folder, making a backup of the database in the same folder. Accept the default settings in the Location of New Replica dialog box, and then complete the following steps.

   a. Close the Design Master, and then open the replica. Open the **Country** table, add a record with Canada as the Nation field value, and then close the **Country** table.

   b. Synchronize the replica with the Design Master. Close the replica, open the Design Master, verify that the new record was added to the **Country** table, and then close the Design Master.

   c. Use Windows Explorer or My Computer to open the Review folder. Rename the **Work** database as **Work Design Master**, and then rename the **Work.bak** database as **Work.mdb**.

5. Use Windows Explorer or My Computer to create a copy of the **Work** database in the Review folder, and then rename the copy as **Employer**. Open the **Work** database in the Review folder, and then use the Database Splitter to split the **Work** database. Use the default name for the back-end database and store it in the Review folder.

6. Set the database startup options to hide the Database window and open the **Switchboard** form when the **Work** database is opened. Close the **Work** database.

7. Encrypt the **Work_be** database by overwriting the existing **Work_be** database in the Review folder.

Explore ▶ 8. Convert the **Work** database to Access 2002 file format, saving the converted file as **Work2002** in the Review folder. Then save the **Work2002** database as an MDE file with the name **Work2002 MDE**.

9. Exit Access.

CASE PROBLEMS

Case 1. Lim's Video Photography Youngho Lim asks you to implement management and security features for the **Shoots** database. To help Youngho with his request, you'll complete the following steps.

1. Make sure your Data Disk is in the appropriate disk drive, start Access, and then open the **Shoots** database in the Cases folder on your Data Disk.

2. Use the Performance Analyzer to analyze the entire **Shoots** database. How many analysis results of the recommendation type did the Performance Analyzer find? Of the suggestion type? Of the idea type? Implement any suggestion-type analysis result, and then close the Performance Analyzer dialog box.

3. Open, print, and then close the Relationships window without saving the report. Use the Documenter to document the **ShootDesc** table, print the report produced by the Documenter, and then close the Object Definition window.

4. Link to the **Payment** table in the **Payments** database located in the Cases folder. Use Windows Explorer or My Computer to move the **Payments** database to the root folder on your Data Disk, and then use the Linked Table Manager to refresh the link to the **Payment** table. Open the **Payment** table in Datasheet view, and then print and close the table.

5. Close the **Shoots** database, use Windows Explorer or My Computer to create a copy of the **Shoots** database in the Cases folder, and then rename the copy as **Lim**. Open the **Shoots** database, delete the link to the **Payment** table, and then use the Database Splitter to split the **Shoots** database. Use the default name for the back-end database and store it in the Cases folder.

6. Set the database startup options to hide the Database window and open the **Switchboard** form when the **Shoots** database is opened. Close the **Shoots** database.

7. Encrypt the **Shoots_be** database by overwriting the existing **Shoots_be** database in the Cases folder.

8. Convert the **Shoots** database to Access 2002 file format, saving the converted file as **Shoots2002** in the Cases folder. Then save the **Shoots2002** database as an MDE file with the name **Shoots2002 MDE**.

9. Exit Access.

Case 2. DineAtHome.course.com Claire Picard asks you to implement management and security features for the **AtHome** database. To help Claire with her request, you'll complete the following steps.

1. Make sure your Data Disk is in the appropriate disk drive, start Access, and then open the **AtHome** database in the Cases folder on your Data Disk.

2. Use the Performance Analyzer to analyze the entire **AtHome** database. How many analysis results of the recommendation type did the Performance Analyzer find? Of the suggestion type? Of the idea type? Implement any suggestion-type analysis result, and then close the Performance Analyzer dialog box.

3. Open, print, and then close the Relationships window without saving the report. Use the Documenter to document the **Marco Island Restaurants** query, print the report produced by the Documenter, and then close the Object Definition window.

4. Link to the **Selection** table in the **Choices** database located in the Cases folder. Use Windows Explorer or My Computer to move the **Choices** database to the root folder on your Data Disk, and then use the Linked Table Manager to refresh the link to the **Selection** table. Open the **Selection** table in Datasheet view, print only the first page, close the table, and then delete the link to the **Selection** table.

5. Set the database startup options to hide the Database window and open the **Switchboard** form when the **AtHome** database is opened. Close the **AtHome** database.

6. Encrypt the **AtHome** database by overwriting the existing **AtHome** database in the Cases folder, and then set the database password to bronco. Close the **AtHome** database, use Windows Explorer or My Computer to create a copy of the **AtHome** database in the Cases folder, and then rename the copy as **ToGo**. Open the **AtHome** database, unset the database password, and then close the **AtHome** database.

7. Convert the **AtHome** database to Access 2002 file format, saving the converted file as **AtHome2002** in the Cases folder. Then save the **AtHome2002** database as an MDE file with the name **AtHome2002 MDE**.

8. Exit Access.

Case 3. Redwood Zoo Michael Rosenfeld asks you to implement management and security features for the **ZooFunds** database. To help Michael with his request, you'll complete the following steps.

1. Make sure your Data Disk is in the appropriate disk drive, start Access, and then open the **ZooFunds** database in the Cases folder on your Data Disk.

2. Use the Performance Analyzer to analyze the entire **ZooFunds** database, excluding the **Queries Dialog Box** form. How many analysis results of the recommendation type did the Performance Analyzer find? Of the suggestion type? Of the idea type? Implement any suggestion-type analysis result, and then close the Performance Analyzer dialog box.

3. Open, print, and then close the Relationships window without saving the report. Use the Documenter to document the **Reception** table, print the report produced by the Documenter, and then close the Object Definition window.

4. Link to the **Donation** table in the **Donation** database located in the Cases folder. Use Windows Explorer or My Computer to move the **Donation** database to the root folder on your Data Disk, and then use the Linked Table Manager to refresh the link to the **Donation** table. Open the **Donation** table in Datasheet view, print and close the table, and then delete the link to the **Donation** table.

5. Create a replica of the **ZooFunds** database in the Cases folder, making a backup of the database in the same folder. Accept the default settings in the Location of New Replica dialog box, and then complete the following steps.

   a. Close the Design Master, and then open the replica. Open the **Reception** table, add a record with field values of 56 for Reception#, Holiday ball for Purpose, and 12/10/2003 for DateHeld. Close the **Reception** table.

   b. Synchronize the replica with the Design Master. Close the replica, open the Design Master, verify that the new record was added to the **Reception** table, and then close the Design Master.

   c. Use Windows Explorer or My Computer to open the Cases folder on your Data Disk. Rename the **ZooFunds** database as **ZooFunds Design Master**, rename the **ZooFunds.bak** database as **ZooFunds.mdb**, and then close Windows Explorer or My Computer.

6. Open the **ZooFunds** database, and then set the database startup options to hide the Database window and open the **Switchboard** form when the **ZooFunds** database is opened. Close the **ZooFunds** database.

7. Encrypt the **ZooFunds** database by overwriting the existing **ZooFunds** database in the Cases folder.

8. Convert the **ZooFunds** database to Access 2002 file format, saving the converted file as **ZooFunds2002** in the Cases folder. Then save the **ZooFunds2002** database as an MDE file with the name **ZooFunds2002 MDE**.

9. Exit Access.

Case 4. Mountain River Adventures Connor and Siobhan Dempsey ask you to implement management and security features for the **Rivers** database. To help them with their request, you'll complete the following steps.

1. Make sure your Data Disk is in the appropriate disk drive, start Access, and then open the **Rivers** database in the Cases folder on your Data Disk.

2. Use the Performance Analyzer to analyze the entire **Rivers** database. How many analysis results of the recommendation type did the Performance Analyzer find? Of the suggestion type? Of the idea type? Implement any suggestion-type analysis result, and then close the Performance Analyzer dialog box.

3. Open, print, and then close the Relationships window without saving the report. Use the Documenter to document the **CO Clients** query, print the report produced by the Documenter, and then close the Object Definition window.

4. Create a replica of the **Rivers** database in the Cases folder, making a backup of the database in the same folder. Accept the default settings in the Location of New Replica dialog box, and then complete the following steps.

   a. Close the Design Master, and then open the replica. Open the **Guide** table, add a record with field values of Les for GuideID, Leslie for FirstName, Duncan for LastName, and Libby for LeadGuide. Close the **Guide** table.

   b. Synchronize the replica with the Design Master. Close the replica, open the Design Master, verify that the new record was added to the **Guide** table, and then close the Design Master.

   c. Use Windows Explorer or My Computer to open the Cases folder on your Data Disk. Rename the **Rivers** database as **Rivers Design Master**, rename the **Rivers.bak** database as **Rivers.mdb**, and then close Windows Explorer or My Computer.

5. Open the **Rivers** database, and then use the User-Level Security Wizard to create a workgroup information file by completing the following steps.

   a. Type Dempsey99 in the WID text box, type your name in the Your name (optional) text box, type Mountain River Adventures in the Company (optional) text box, and select the option to create a shortcut to open the secured database.

b. Make sure all objects are secure.

c. Include Read-Only Users, and type Rivers88 in the Group ID text box.

d. Make sure the Users group has no permissions.

e. For the Administrator user, type a password of WhiteWater, and type a PID of Rivers77.

f. Add a new user with a user name of ConnorD, a password of RaftTrip, and a PID of Rivers44.

g. Make sure the Administrator user is assigned to the Admins group, and assign the ConnorD user to the Read-Only Users group.

h. Accept the default name for the backup copy of the unsecured database.

i. Print the Security Wizard report, do not save the snapshot report, and then exit Access.

j. Use Windows Explorer or My Computer to move the **Rivers.mdb** shortcut from the Windows desktop to the Cases folder on your Data Disk.

k. Open the **Rivers.mdb** shortcut, and then log on as the Administrator user.

l. Open the **Rafting Trip** table, and then print and close the table.

6. Exit Access.

Case 5. eACH Internet Auction Site Chris and Pat Aquino ask you to implement management and security features for the **BuySell** database. To help them with their request, you'll complete the following steps.

1. Make sure your Data Disk is in the appropriate drive, start Access, and then open the **BuySell** database in the Cases folder on your Data Disk.

2. Use the Performance Analyzer to analyze the entire **BuySell** database. How many analysis results of the recommendation type did the Performance Analyzer find? Of the suggestion type? Of the idea type? Implement all suggestion and recommendation analysis results, and then close the Performance Analyzer dialog box.

3. Open, print, and then close the Relationships window without saving the report. Use the Documenter to document the **Category** table, print the report produced by the Documenter, and then close the Object Definition window.

4. Create a replica of the **BuySell** database in the Cases folder, making a backup of the database in the same folder. Accept the default settings in the Location of New Replica dialog box, and then complete the following steps.

a. Close the Design Master, and then open the replica. Open the **Category** table, and then add a record with a value of Other for the Category field. (*Note*: If the Category# field value for the record you add is not equal to 13, simply continue with the case.) Close the **Category** table.

b. Synchronize the replica with the Design Master. Close the replica, open the Design Master, and then verify that the new record was added to the **Category** table. Switch to Design view for the **Category** table, and then review the properties for the Category# field. Using Access Help as necessary, prepare a written report explaining why Access doesn't assign consecutive values for the Category# field. Close the Design Master.

c. Use Windows Explorer or My Computer to open the Cases folder on your Data Disk. Rename the **BuySell** database as **BuySell Design Master**, rename the **BuySell.bak** database as **BuySell.mdb**, and then close Windows Explorer or My Computer.

5. Open the **BuySell** database, and then set the database startup options to hide the Database window and open the **Switchboard** form when the **BuySell** database is opened. Close the **BuySell** database.

6. Convert the **BuySell** database to Access 2002 file format, saving the converted file as **BuySell2002** in the Cases folder. Then save the **BuySell2002** database as an MDE file with the name **BuySell2002 MDE**.

7. Exit Access.

INTERNET ASSIGNMENTS

Student Union

The purpose of the Internet Assignments is to challenge you to find information on the Internet that you can use to create effective documents. The actual assignments are updated and maintained on the Course Technology Web site. Log on to the Internet and use your Web browser to go to the Student Online Companion to accompany this text at **www.course.com/NewPerspectives/studentunion**. Click the Online Companions link, and then click the link for this tutorial.

QUICK CHECK ANSWERS

Session 11.1

1. The Performance Analyzer is an Access tool that you can use to optimize the performance of an Access database.
2. Documenter
3. Use the Linked Table Manager to change the filename or disk location for linked tables in an Access database.
4. When you create a replica of a database, the Design Master and all of its replicas are called the replica set.
5. Anyone using the Design Master can make changes to the design of the database tables, queries, and other objects. A replica prevents a user from changing the structure or design of an existing table, query, or other database object.
6. The synchronization process compares the Design Master to the replica and checks for any differences. Access updates the Design Master with any changes that have been made to the data in the replica, and updates the replica with any changes that have been made to the data or to the design of any database objects in the Design Master.

Session 11.2

1. The Database Splitter is an Access tool that splits an Access database into two files: one file contains the tables, and the other contains the other database objects.
2. an action that takes place when a database opens
3. In the Startup dialog box, click the Display Form/Page list arrow, and then select the form.
4. Security
5. decrypting
6. A user's permissions specify what kind of access the user has to objects in a database.
7. Users group and Admins group
8. MDE file

OBJECTIVES

In this case you will:

- Change field properties

- Add a table to a database and define relationships between tables

- Create select, parameter, and crosstab queries

- Create a form using the Form Wizard

- Create custom forms

- Create custom reports

- Create a PivotChart

- Add macros and event procedures

- Create a switchboard

COMPANY FINANCIAL INFORMATION BY FINSTAT INC.

CASE

FINSTAT Inc.

When Pat Mitchell graduated from a prestigious business college, she had her pick of job offers. Employers could see from her internship record and her grades that she was a bright, ambitious worker who would be an asset to their company. Pat had always dreamed of being her own boss, however, so after careful market analysis and planning she founded FINSTAT Inc., an electronic information service that markets financial information to its clients. Since the time Pat started her company, competing vendors have appeared on the market offering similar databases of financial information.

Pat and her team of financial analysts are now realizing that to remain competitive, their products must supply current and complete data. Also their clients must be able to access the data effortlessly and with as many options as possible. Pat decides to take the current databases she has and upgrade them with ease of use in mind. Her most successful database contains recent financial statement data on several leading U.S. corporations. She starts her new campaign by reorganizing the financial statement information to make it more accessible, and then by designing an interface that is easier for clients to use.

Pat's database of corporations currently consists of two tables, Company and Finance. Figure 1 shows the structure of the Company table, which stores general data about each company. The Company table contains an ID number and name for each company, and a code classifying the company's industry.

Figure 1	STRUCTURE OF THE COMPANY TABLE

Field Name	Data Type	Properties
CompanyID	Text	Field Size—3
CompanyName	Text	Field Size—30
Industry	Text	Field Size—2

Figure 2 shows the structure of the Finance table, which tracks the yearly financial data for each company. The Finance table contains the same ID numbers used in the Company table and contains additional data on the sales, assets, and profits for each company for a given year, 2002 or later.

Figure 2	STRUCTURE OF THE FINANCE TABLE

Field Name	Data Type	Properties
CompanyID	Text	Field Size—3
Year	Number	Field Size—Integer Decimal Places—Auto
Sales	Currency	Description—Rounded to the nearest million. Decimal Places—0
Assets	Currency	Description—Rounded to the nearest million. Decimal Places—0
Profits	Currency	Description—Rounded to the nearest million. Decimal Places—0

Pat wants to create a new customized version of the database so that clients can choose information more easily. She formulates the following plan: she will modify the field properties in the Company and Finance tables, add a table for industry codes and descriptions, define relationships for the three tables, and create and save four queries. She will then create the form shown in Figure 3 using the Form Wizard. This new form will make it easier for both her own staff and her clients to add current financial data to the database.

Figure 3	COMPANY FINANCES FORM CREATED BY THE FORM WIZARD

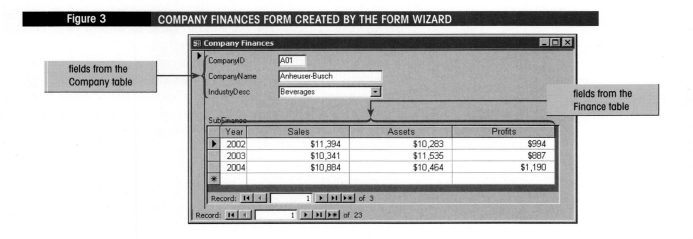

Pat plans to create a custom form, shown in Figure 4, that uses all three tables to display a company's financial information, a year at a time. Calculations are included on this form for the company's rate of return and profit margin.

Figure 4	ANNUAL FINANCIALS FORM

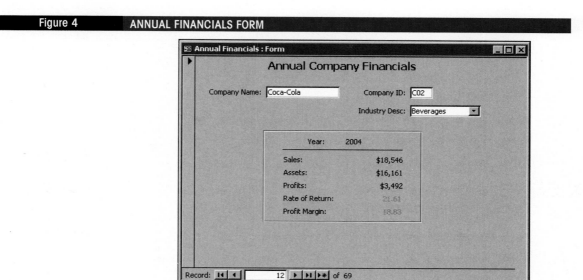

Next, Pat plans to create two reports that are easy to generate and are of presentation quality. The first report, shown in Figure 5, groups companies by industry and provides industry and overall totals.

Figure 5	CUSTOM INDUSTRY 2004 REPORT

FINSTAT

Financial Analysis for 2004
Figures rounded to the nearest million

Industry: Apparel

Company Name	Sales	Assets	Profits
Fruit of the Loom	$2,447	$2,547	$151
Liz Claiborne	$2,217	$1,382	$155
Nike	$6,471	$3,952	$553
Reebok International	$3,483	$1,786	$139
Industry Total	$14,618	$9,667	$998

Industry: Beverages

Company Name	Sales	Assets	Profits
Anheuser-Busch	$10,884	$10,464	$1,190
Coca-Cola	$18,546	$16,161	$3,492
PepsiCo	$31,645	$24,512	$1,149
Industry Total	$61,075	$51,137	$5,831

Industry: Cars & Trucks

Company Name	Sales	Assets	Profits
Chrysler	$61,397	$56,184	$3,529
Ford Motor	$146,991	$262,867	$4,446
General Motors	$168,369	$222,142	$4,963
Industry Total	$376,757	$541,193	$12,938

Industry: Chemicals

Company Name	Sales	Assets	Profits
Dow Chemical	$20,053	$24,673	$1,907
Du Pont	$39,689	$37,987	$3,636
Monsanto	$9,262	$11,191	$385
Industry Total	$69,004	$73,851	$5,928

Industry: Discount Retailing

Company Name	Sales	Assets	Profits
Home Depot	$19,535	$9,342	$938
J.C. Penney	$23,649	$22,088	$565
Kmart	$31,437	$14,286	($220)
Sears, Roebuck	$38,236	$36,167	$1,271
Toys "R" US	$9,932	$8,023	$427
Wal-Mart Stores	$106,147	$39,501	$3,056
Industry Total	$228,936	$129,407	$6,037

Industry: Personal Care

Company Name	Sales	Assets	Profits
Avon Products	$4,814	$2,222	$318
Colgate-Palmolive	$8,749	$7,902	$635
Gillette	$9,698	$10,435	$949
Procter & Gamble	$35,284	$27,730	$3,046
Industry Total	$58,545	$48,289	$4,948
Grand Total	$808,935	$853,544	$36,680

The second report, shown in Figure 6, summarizes sales, assets, and profits by industry.

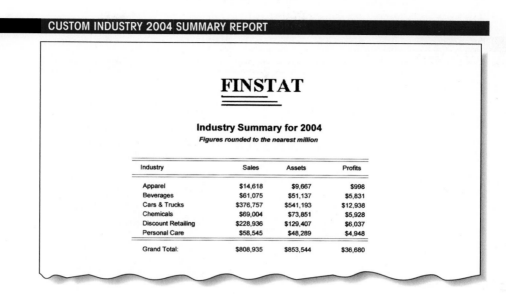

Pat also plans to create the PivotChart shown in Figure 7 to illustrate profits by industry by year for all industries.

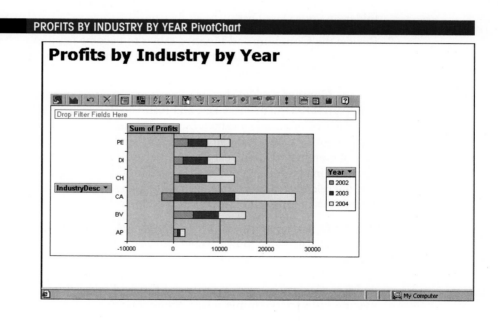

Pat plans to design and create a switchboard, set the startup options, and create an event procedure for one of the new forms. Figure 8 shows the finished switchboard.

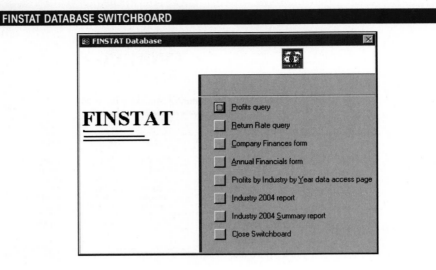

To help Pat, you'll complete the following steps.

1. Make sure you have created your copy of the Access Data Disk, place your Data Disk in the appropriate drive, start Access, and then open the **Finstat** database in the AddCases folder on your Data Disk.

2. Review the **Company** and **Finance** tables to become familiar with their structures and data. If you are unfamiliar with any property setting, use the Access Help system for an explanation of that property.

3. For the **Company** table, change CompanyName to a required field, specify CompanyID as the primary key, and resize all dat%asheet columns to their best fit. For the **Finance** table, add a validation rule for the Year field to store only values greater than or equal to 2002, add an appropriate validation text message, make the combination of CompanyID and Year the primary key, and resize all datasheet columns to their best fit. Finally, define a one-to-many relationship between the primary **Company** table and the related **Finance** table, using CompanyID as the common field and enforcing referential integrity and both cascade options.

4. The **Company** table contains the Industry field, which stores a two-character industry code. The acceptable industry codes and associated industry descriptions are: AP (Apparel), BV (Beverages), CA (Cars & Trucks), CH (Chemicals), DI (Discount Retailing), and PE (Personal Care). Design and create a new table to store the industry codes and industry descriptions, using the field names Industry and IndustryDesc and making Industry the primary key. Name this table **Industry**, add the six industry records to the table, resize all datasheet columns to their best fit, and then print the six records from the **Industry** table.

5. Change the Industry field in the **Company** table to a Lookup Wizard field. Display the IndustryDesc field from the **Industry** table. Resize the IndustryDesc column in the **Company** datasheet to its best fit.

6. Create and save a query named **Profits** that displays the CompanyID, CompanyName, Year, IndustryDesc (from the **Company** table), Sales, and Profits fields for all companies with sales above 4000 and profits above 300; and sort in ascending order by Profits. Print the query recordset.

7. For all companies, create a query named **Return Rate** to display the CompanyName, Sales, Assets, Profits, and RateOfReturn for the year 2004; and sort in descending order by RateOfReturn. Calculate RateOfReturn by dividing Profits by Assets and format the result as a percentage. Print the query recordset.

8. For all companies, create a query named **Company Data** to display the CompanyID, CompanyName, IndustryDesc (from the **Company** table), Year, Sales, Assets, Profits, RateOfReturn, and ProfitMargin. Calculate RateOfReturn by dividing Profits by Assets and then multiplying by 100. Calculate ProfitMargin by dividing Profits by Sales and then multiplying by 100. For both RateOfReturn and ProfitMargin, use a fixed format. Sort in ascending order by CompanyName as the primary sort key and Year as the secondary sort key. Print the query recordset.

9. Create and save a parameter query named **Profits Parameter** that displays the CompanyName, Sales, Assets, Profits, and IndustryDesc (from the **Company** table) fields for companies during 2004 in a selected industry. (Use IndustryDesc as the parameter, which requires the entry of a two-character Industry field value.) Sort in ascending order by Profits. Print the query recordset, using the parameter value PE.

10. Use the Form Wizard to create the form shown in Figure 3. Use the **Company** and **Finance** tables. Save the subform as **SubFinance**, and save the main/subform form as **Company Finances**. Print the first record in the main form.

Explore

11. Create the custom form shown in Figure 4 and save it as **Annual Financials**. Use the **Company Data** query as the basis for the form. Change the label captions and position the label boxes and text boxes as shown in Figure 4, and draw a rectangle around the financial information. Set the Back Style and Border Style properties to Transparent and the Special Effect property to Flat to remove the boxes from the financial text boxes. Display the RateOfReturn field value with a Fore Color value of red when the field value is over 10 and with the default black color otherwise. Similarly, display the ProfitMargin field value with a Fore Color value of red when the field value is over 10 and with the default black color otherwise. Test the form. Print the first and last records of the custom form.

Explore

12. Create a query named **Industry 2004** using the **Company**, **Finance**, and **Industry** tables to select all the financial records for the year 2004. Refer to Figure 5 to determine which fields to include in the query and which fields to use as sort keys. Then create the custom report shown in Figure 5, using the **Industry 2004** query as the basis for the report. Save the report as **Industry 2004**, and then print the report. (*Note:* The FINSTAT logo at the top of the report is stored as **Finlogo.bmp** in the AddCases folder on your Data Disk.)

13. Create the Industry Summary for 2004 report shown in Figure 6. Base the report on the **Industry 2004** query. Save the report as **Industry 2004 Summary**. Print the report. (*Hint:* Use the report from Step 12 as a guide, but include only summary information for this report.)

14. Create a crosstab query showing the profits by industry by year. Include a Total of Profits column. Base the query on the **Company Data** query. Save the query as **Profit Crosstab**, and then print the query recordset.

15. Create a PivotChart on a data access page showing profits by industry by year for all industries, as shown in Figure 7. Base the PivotChart on the **Company Data** query. Save the data access page as **Profits by Industry by Year**, open it in Web Page Preview, and then print the page.

16. Create a macro group named **Switchboard Macros** that contains macros to be used with the command buttons on the switchboard you'll create in the next step. The macros perform these actions:

   ■ Open the **Profits** query
   ■ Open the **Return Rate** query
   ■ Open the **Company Finances** form
   ■ Open the **Annual Financials** form
   ■ Open the **Profits by Industry by Year** data access page
   ■ Open the **Industry 2004** report in the Print Preview window
   ■ Open the **Industry 2004 Summary** report in the Print Preview window
   ■ Close the switchboard and activate the Database window

17. Design and create a switchboard form named **Switchboard**. Use Figure 8 and the following descriptions as a guide to create the switchboard.

   a. Use the Switchboard Manager to create the switchboard. Place the command buttons on the form; the command buttons should use the macros in the **Switchboard Macros** macro group. Define hot keys for each command button. Specify "FINSTAT Database" as the main switchboard page name.

   b. Delete the default label and the shadow label on the form. Use an appropriate background color for the switchboard, and add the **Finmoney.bmp** and **Finlogo.bmp** pictures in the AddCases folder on your Data Disk to the locations shown on the switchboard in Figure 8.

   c. Resize the switchboard in Form view, and then set form properties that are appropriate for a switchboard.

18. Set the startup options to hide the Database window and open the **Switchboard** form whenever the **Finstat** database is opened.

19. Test the switchboard and all objects, and then exit Access.

In this case you will:

- Create select queries

- Create a form using the Form Wizard

- Create custom forms

- Create custom reports

- Create a switchboard

CUSTOMER ORDERS FOR PET PROVISIONS

Pet Provisions

Pet Provisions, started by Manny Cordova in 1993, sells pet food and pet supplies to pet shops around the world. His company has enjoyed steady annual increases in sales, but profits have lagged behind. Manny asks his office manager, Kerri Jackson, to tighten the company's collection methods as a first step toward improving profits.

Currently the office maintains an Access database named Pet that contains information on its customers. After reviewing the database, Kerri realizes that there is no easy way to tell which client accounts are paid in full and which have outstanding balances. She decides to create the necessary forms, queries, and reports to automate the collection process. Her work will include creating an invoice report that she can automatically generate to send to any client with an outstanding balance.

Kerri uses the Pet database as the starting point for her work. Among the tables in the Pet database are the Customer and Order tables. Figure 9 shows the structure for the Customer table, which contains one record for each customer. CustomerNum is the primary key for the table, which has 26 customer records. The other fields in the table are CustomerName, Street, City, State/Prov, Zip/PostalCode, Country, Phone, and FirstContact.

Figure 9 — STRUCTURE OF THE CUSTOMER TABLE

Field Name	Data Type	Properties
CustomerNum	Number	Primary Key Field Size—Integer Format—Fixed Decimal Places—0
CustomerName	Text	Field Size—35
Street	Text	Field Size—30
City	Text	Field Size—20
State/Prov	Text	Field Size—20
Zip/PostalCode	Text	Field Size—10
Country	Text	Field Size—20
Phone	Text	Field Size—15
FirstContact	Date/Time	Format—mm/dd/yyyy

Figure 10 shows the structure for the Order table, which contains one record for each customer order. OrderNum is the table's primary key. CustomerNum is a foreign key in the Order table, and the Customer table will have a one-to-many relationship with the Order table.

Figure 10 — STRUCTURE OF THE ORDER TABLE

Field Name	Data Type	Properties
OrderNum	Number	Primary Key Field Size—Integer Format—Fixed Decimal Places—0
CustomerNum	Number	Field Size—Integer Format—Fixed Decimal Places—0 Foreign Key
SaleDate	Date/Time	Format—mm/dd/yyyy
ShipVia	Text	Field Size—7
TotalInvoice	Number	Field Size—Double Format—Standard Decimal Places—2
AmountPaid	Number	Field Size—Double Format—Standard Decimal Places—2
PayMethod	Text	Field Size—5

Kerri plans to create special queries, forms, and reports to help her analyze the 144 orders in the Order table. One of the special forms, shown in Figure 11, displays all orders for a customer along with totals for the customer's invoices, amount paid, and amount owed.

Figure 11	CUSTOMER WITH ORDERS FORM

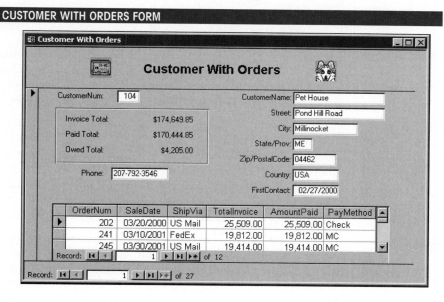

Kerri also wants to create a special report, shown in Figure 12, that she can send to customers with outstanding balances.

Figure 12	CUSTOM CUSTOMER STATEMENT REPORT

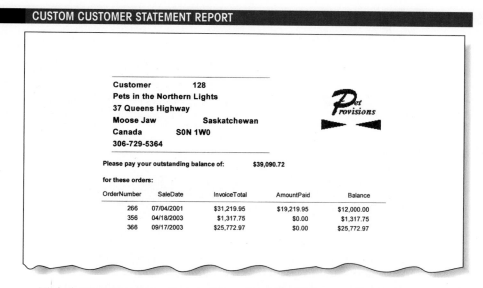

To help Kerri better analyze profits at Pet Provisions, you'll complete the following steps.

1. Make sure you have created your copy of the Access Data Disk, place your Data Disk in the appropriate drive, start Access, and then open the **Pet** database in the AddCases folder on your Data Disk.

2. Review the **Customer** and **Order** tables to become familiar with their structures and data. If you are unfamiliar with any property setting, use the Access Help system for an explanation of that property.

3. Define a one-to-many relationship between the primary **Customer** table and the related **Order** table, using CustomerNum as the common field and enforcing referential integrity and both cascade options.

4. Create and save a query named **Order Totals** that displays the grand total number of orders and grand totals for the TotalInvoice, AmountPaid, and AmountOwed fields. AmountOwed, a calculated field, is the difference between the TotalInvoice and AmountPaid fields. Format the grand total fields as currency. Use column names of Number of Orders, Sum of TotalInvoice, Sum of AmountPaid, and Sum of AmountOwed. Print the query recordset.

Explore

5. For all orders that have not been paid in full, create a query named **Open Orders** to display the CustomerName, Phone, SaleDate, TotalInvoice, AmountPaid, and AmountOwed fields. Use standard format with two decimal places for the AmountOwed field, and sort in descending order by AmountOwed. Print the query recordset.

Explore

6. For all orders that have not been paid in full, create and save a query named **Owed by Customer** that displays the total number of orders and totals for the TotalInvoice, AmountPaid, and AmountOwed fields, grouped by CustomerName. Format the three sum columns as currency. Print the query recordset in landscape orientation. (*Hint:* Use the **Open Orders** query as the basis for this query.) The query contains five columns to be displayed: CustomerName, Number of Orders, Sum of TotalInvoice, Sum of AmountPaid, and Sum of AmountOwed.

Explore

7. Use the Form Wizard to create linked forms to maintain all fields in the **Customer** table and all fields in the **Order** table. Select all fields from the **Customer** table and all fields from the **Order** table. When the Form Wizard asks you how to display the forms, choose the Linked forms option. Save the forms as **Customer Data** and **Linked Orders**, respectively. Use the forms to add the records shown in Figure 13 to the tables, and then use the forms to print the new records from each table.

Figure 13	NEW CUSTOMER AND ORDER RECORDS

Customer record:

CustomerNum	CustomerName	Street	City	State/Prov
790	Fuzzy Friends	3333 Binford	Corvallis	OR

Zip/PostalCode	Country	Phone	FirstContact
97332	USA	503-273-8998	6/23/2004

Order record:

OrderNum	CustomerNum	SaleDate	ShipVia	TotalInvoice	AmountPaid	PayMethod
375	790	7/24/2004	UPS	12,437.44	4000.00	Check

8. Create and save two queries that will be used with the form shown in Figure 11. For the first query, use the **Order** table to display totals for the TotalInvoice, AmountPaid, and AmountOwed fields, grouping by CustomerNum and using the column names Invoice Total, Paid Total, and Owed Total, respectively. Format the total fields as currency, save the query as **Customer Order Totals**, and then print the query recordset. For the second query, use the **Customer Order Totals** query and the **Customer** table; display the CustomerNum, Invoice Total, Paid Total, Owed Total, CustomerName, Street, City, State/Prov, Zip/PostalCode, Country, Phone, and FirstContact fields; sort in ascending order by CustomerNum. Save the query as **Customer With Totals**, and then print the query recordset in landscape orientation.

Explore

9. Create the custom form shown in Figure 11 and save it as **Customer With Orders**. Create an initial approximation of the form using the **Customer With Totals** query for the main form. Using the Subform/Subreport tool on the toolbox, create a subform

based on the **Order** table, and place it on the form as shown in the figure. Select all the fields from the **Customer** table for the main form and all the fields from the **Order** table except CustomerNum for the subform. Save the subform as **SubOrder**. Then change the form so that it looks similar to the form shown in Figure 11. Use the Flat Special Effect property value, the Transparent Border Style property value, and the Transparent Back Style property value to remove the boxes from the three text boxes between the CustomerNum and Phone boxes. Print the first record of the custom form. (*Note*: The images that appear on the top of the form are stored as **Petfish.bmp** and **Petdog.bmp** in the AddCases folder on your Data Disk.)

Explore 10. Create and save a query named **For Special Report** that selects customers who owe money to Pet Provisions and the unpaid orders for these customers. Refer to Figure 12 to determine which fields to include in the query. (*Hint*: Use the **Customer With Totals** query and the **Order** table to create this query; create a join line between the CustomerNum fields; and sort in ascending order by CustomerNum as the primary sort key and in descending order by OrderNum as the secondary sort key.) Then create the custom report shown in Figure 12, using the **For Special Report** query as the basis for the report. Include a Group Header section based on CustomerNum, and place orders in the Detail section. Set the Force New Page property in the Group Header section to the value "Before Section" so that one customer statement is printed per page. Save the report as **Customer Statement**, and then print pages 5 through 7 of the report. (*Note*: The logo in the upper-right corner of the report is stored as **Petlogo.bmp** in the AddCases folder on your Data Disk.)

Explore 11. Design and create a switchboard, using Figure 14 as a model. Place command buttons on the switchboard to coordinate the running of two forms (**Customer Data** and **Customer With Orders**), three queries (**Open Orders, Order Totals**, and **Owed By Customer**), and one report (**Customer Statement**). Also provide a command button to close the switchboard and return to the Database window.

Figure 14	PET PROVISIONS SWITCHBOARD

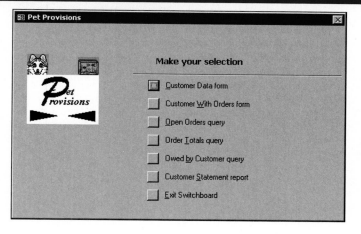

12. Resize the switchboard in Form view, and then set form properties that are appropriate for a switchboard. Set the startup options to hide the Database window and open the **Switchboard** form whenever the **Pet** database is opened.

13. Thoroughly test the switchboard and all objects, and then exit Access.

OBJECTIVES

In this case you will:

- Design a database and draw its entity-relationship diagram

- Create the tables and relationships for the database

- Create forms to maintain the database

- Design and enter test data for the database

- Create queries and reports from the database

- Design and create a switchboard

INTERNSHIP PROGRAM FOR PONTIAC COLLEGE

CASE

Pontiac College

Pontiac College provides students with opportunities for professional development and field study through its internship program, which is administered by the Office of Internships and Field Experience. Students complement their courses with a structured training experience provided by qualified professionals in selected fields. Internships are offered in many different areas, including law, counseling, government, administration, public relations, communications, health care, software engineering, and marketing.

Anjali Bhavnani has just been hired as Pontiac College's new Internship Coordinator. She is eager to make information about the sponsoring agencies, potential internships, and current student interns more readily available to her office and to the students who qualify for the program. Anjali's most ambitious project is to develop a computerized database for the internship program to help meet these goals.

Instead of visually scanning all internship possibilities, Anjali, her staff, and interested students will be able to select internships of specific interest to them. The new database will allow potential interns to view only the internships that meet the criteria they specify. Anjali asks Roula Mendes, an information systems major working in the Office of Internships and Field Experience, to help the office develop a computerized database system for the internship program.

Anjali first outlines the steps in the internship program process for Roula:

- Identify and document the available internships.
- Arrange for student intern placements.
- Assign and track student interns.

As the first step in the internship program process, Anjali receives a letter or phone call from a potential sponsoring agency. After some discussions, a sponsoring agency proposes an internship possibility and fills out the Agency/Internship Information form shown in Figure 15.

Figure 15	AGENCY/INTERNSHIP INFORMATION FORM

Many agencies offer more than one type of internship possibility. For each possible internship, the agency fills out a separate form and assigns one person as the contact for all internship questions and problems. In addition, each internship lists a supervisor who will work with the student intern. The internship remains active until the agency notifies the Office of Internships and Field Experience that the internship is filled or no longer available.

Anjali assigns a three-digit Agency ID to each new agency and a four-digit Internship ID to each new internship using sequential numbers. She also classifies each internship into a category that helps students identify internships that are related to their academic major or interests. For example, a student might be interested in health care, accounting, social service, or advertising.

A copy of each Agency/Internship Information form is placed in reference books in the Office of Internships and Field Experience. Students browse through these books to find internships that interest them. If an internship interests a student, the student copies the information about the internship and contacts the sponsoring agency directly to request an interview.

When a student gets an internship, the student and agency establish a Learning Contract, outlining the goals to be accomplished during the internship. The student then fills out the Student Internship form, shown in Figure 16, to provide basic personal information for the office files.

Figure 16	STUDENT INTERNSHIP FORM

Anjali enters the Internship ID and year on the Student Internship form and checks the term for the internship. Next, a clerk enters information from the form into a word processor to prepare lists of current interns and internships, and then places the form in a binder.

Anjali and Roula determine that getting these two forms into an Access database is their first priority, and then they will work on creating several new reports. The first report, the design of which is shown in Figure 17, lists all student interns alphabetically by last name for a selected term. In order to identify the student interns who should be included in the report, the system prompts the user for the term and year.

Figure 17	STUDENT INTERNS REPORT DESIGN

<today's date>   **Student Interns**   Page x
                                      As of <term><year>

Last Name	First Name	Agency Name	Internship Title
x------------x	x----------x	x----------------------x	x----------------x
x------------x	x----------x	x----------------------x	x----------------x
x------------x	x----------x	x----------------------x	x----------------x
x------------x	x----------x	x----------------------x	x----------------x

End of Report

A second new report lists all agencies in the database alphabetically by agency name. Figure 18 shows the design of this report.

Figure 18	INTERNSHIP AGENCIES REPORT DESIGN

<today's date>   **Internship Agencies**   Page x

Agency Name	Department	Contact	Phone
x------------x	x----------------x	x----------------x	x----------------x
x------------x	x----------------x	x----------------x	x----------------x
x------------x	x----------------x	x----------------x	x----------------x
x------------x	x----------------x	x----------------x	x----------------x

End of Report

The Internship by Category report, the design of which is shown in Figure 19, lists internships grouped by category. The staff will use this report when talking with students about the internship program.

Figure 19	INTERNSHIP BY CATEGORY REPORT DESIGN

<today's date>   **Internship by Category**   Page x

Category x------------ x

Internship ID	Internship Title	Internship Description
xxxx	x------------------x	x-- x
		x-- x
		x-- x
xxxx	x------------------x	x-- x
xxxx	x------------------x	x-- x
		x-- x

Category x------------ x

Internship ID	Internship Title	Internship Description
xxxx	x------------------x	x-- x
xxxx	x------------------x	x-- x
		x-- x
		x-- x

End of Report

At the end of an internship, the intern's supervisor evaluates the intern's work experience, using an evaluation form mailed from the Office of Internships and Field Experience. Anjali needs mailing labels addressed to the supervisor of each intern for the current term and year. The mailing labels should contain the supervisor's name on the first line; the agency name on the second line; the agency's street on the third line; and the agency's city, state, and Zip code on the fourth line.

To create the complete database system, you'll complete the following steps.

Explore

1. Read the appendix titled "Relational Databases and Database Design," which appears at the end of this book.

2. Identify each entity (relation) in the database for the internship system.

3. Draw an entity-relationship diagram showing the entities and the relationships between the entities.

4. Design the database for the internship system. For each relation, list the fields and their attributes, such as data types, field sizes, and validation rules. Place the set of relations in third normal form and identify all primary, alternate, and foreign keys.

5. Create the database structure using Access and the database name **Intern**. Be sure to define relationships between appropriate tables.

6. Create and save forms to maintain data on agencies, internships, student interns, and any other entity in your database structure. The forms should be used to view, add, edit, and delete records in the database.

7. Create test data for each table in the database and add the test data, using the forms you created in Step 6.

8. Create and save the **Student Interns** report, **Internship Agencies** report, and the **Internship by Category** report. The layouts shown in Figures 17 through 19 are guides—improve them as you see fit. Then create the **Mailing Labels** report to create mailing labels for agencies, using a label of your choice.

9. Design, create, and save a form that a student can use to view internships for a selected category. Display one internship at a time on the screen. For each internship, display the category, internship ID, title, description of duties, orientation and training, academic background, agency name, department, agency address, contact name, and contact phone. Provide an option to print the internship displayed on the screen. (*Note*: The AddCases folder on your Data Disk contains two picture files, **Intmatch.bmp** and **Inttrack.bmp**, which you can include on this form.)

10. Design, create, and save a switchboard to coordinate the running of the internship system. (*Note*: The AddCases folder on your Data Disk contains two picture files, named **Intmatch.bmp** and **Inttrack.bmp**, which you can include on the switchboard if you want.)

11. Test all features of the internship system, and then exit Access.

OBJECTIVES

In this appendix you will:

- Learn the characteristics of a relation

- Learn about primary, candidate, alternate, foreign, and composite keys

- Study one-to-one, one-to-many, and many-to-many relationships

- Learn to describe relations and relationships with entity-relationship diagrams and with a shorthand method

- Study database integrity constraints for primary keys, referential integrity, and domains

- Learn about determinants, functional dependencies, anomalies, and normalization

RELATIONAL DATABASES AND DATABASE DESIGN

This appendix introduces you to the basics of database design. Before trying to master this material, be sure you have an understanding of the following concepts: data, information, field, field value, record, table, relational database, common field, database management system (DBMS), and relational database management system.

Relations

A relational database stores its data in tables. A **table** is a two-dimensional structure made up of rows and columns. The terms table, row, and column are the popular names for the more formal terms **relation** (table), **tuple** (row), and **attribute** (column), as shown in Figure 1.

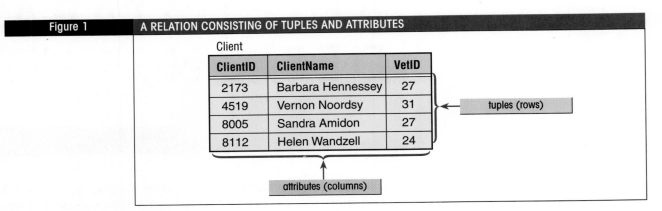

Figure 1   A RELATION CONSISTING OF TUPLES AND ATTRIBUTES

Client

ClientID	ClientName	VetID
2173	Barbara Hennessey	27
4519	Vernon Noordsy	31
8005	Sandra Amidon	27
8112	Helen Wandzell	24

tuples (rows)

attributes (columns)

The Client table shown in Figure 1 is an example of a relation, a two-dimensional structure with the following characteristics:

■ Each row is unique. Because no two rows are the same, you can easily locate and update specific data. For example, you can locate the row for ClientID 8005 and change the ClientName value, Sandra Amidon, or the VetID value, 27.

■ The order of the rows is unimportant. You can add or view rows in any order. For example, you can view the rows in ClientName order instead of ClientID order.

■ Each table entry contains a single value. At the intersection of each row and column, you cannot have more than one value. For example, each row in Figure 1 contains one ClientID, one ClientName, and one VetID.

■ The order of the columns is unimportant. You can add or view columns in any order.

■ Each column has a unique name called the **attribute name**. The attribute name allows you to access a specific column without needing to know its position within the relation.

■ The entries in a column are from the same domain. A **domain** is a set of values from which one or more columns draw their actual values. A domain can be broad, such as "all legitimate names of people" for the ClientName column, or narrow, such as "24, 27, or 31" for the VetID column. The domain of "all legitimate dates" could be shared by the BirthDate, StartDate, and LastPayDate columns in a company's employee relation.

■ Each row in a relation describes, or shows the characteristics of, an entity. An **entity** is a person, place, object, event, or idea for which you want to store and process data. For example, ClientID, ClientName, and VetID are characteristics of the clients of a pet-sitting company. The Client relation represents all the client entities and their characteristics. That is, the sets of values in the rows of the Client relation describe the different clients of the company. The Client relation includes only characteristics of a client. Other relations would exist for the company's other entities. For example, a Pet relation might describe the clients' pets and an Employee relation might describe the company's employees.

Knowing the characteristics of a relation leads directly to a definition of a relational database. A **relational database** is a collection of relations.

Keys

Primary keys ensure that each row in a relation is unique. A **primary key** is an attribute, or a collection of attributes, whose values uniquely identify each row in a relation. In addition to being *unique*, a primary key must be *minimal* (that is, contain no unnecessary extra attributes) and must not change in value. For example, in Figure 2 the State relation contains one record per state and uses StateAbbrev as its primary key.

| Figure 2 | A RELATION AND ITS KEYS |

alternate key

primary key

State

StateAbbrev	StateName	EnteredUnionOrder	StateBird	StatePopulation
CT	Connecticut	5	American robin	3,287,116
MI	Michigan	26	robin	9,295,297
SD	South Dakota	40	pheasant	696,004
TN	Tennessee	16	mockingbird	4,877,185
TX	Texas	28	mockingbird	16,986,510

Could any other attribute, or collection of attributes, be the primary key of the State relation?

- Could StateBird serve as the primary key? No, because the column does not have unique values (for example, the mockingbird is the state bird of more than one state).
- Could StatePopulation serve as the primary key? No, because the column values change periodically and are not guaranteed to be unique.
- Could StateAbbrev and StateName together serve as the primary key? No, because the combination is not minimal. Something less, StateAbbrev by itself, can serve as the primary key.

■ Could StateName serve as the primary key? Yes, because the column has unique values. In a similar way, you could select EnteredUnionOrder as the primary key for the State relation. One attribute, or collection of attributes, that can serve as a primary key is called a **candidate key**. The candidate keys for the State relation are StateAbbrev, StateName, and EnteredUnionOrder. You choose one of the candidate keys to be the primary key, and the remaining candidate keys are called **alternate keys**.

Figure 3 shows a City relation containing the attributes StateAbbrev, CityName, and CityPopulation.

Figure 3	A RELATION WITH A COMPOSITE KEY

City — primary key

StateAbbrev	CityName	CityPopulation
CT	Hartford	139,739
CT	Madison	14,031
CT	Portland	8,418
MI	Lansing	127,321
SD	Madison	6,257
SD	Pierre	12,906
TN	Nashville	488,374
TX	Austin	465,622
TX	Portland	12,224

What is the primary key for the City relation? The values for CityPopulation periodically change and are not guaranteed to be unique, so CityPopulation cannot be the primary key. Because the values for each of the other two columns are not unique, StateAbbrev alone cannot be the primary key and neither can CityName (for example, there are two Madisons and two Portlands). The primary key is the combination of StateAbbrev and CityName. Both attributes together are needed to identify, uniquely and minimally, each row in the City relation. A multiple-attribute primary key is called a **composite key** or a **concatenated key**.

The StateAbbrev attribute in the City relation is also a **foreign key**. A **foreign key** is an attribute, or a collection of attributes, in one relation whose values must match the values of the primary key of some relation. As shown in Figure 4, the values in the City relation's StateAbbrev column match the values in the State relation's StateAbbrev column. Thus, StateAbbrev, the primary key of the State relation, is a foreign key in the City relation. Although the attribute name StateAbbrev is the same in both relations, the names could be different. Most people give the same name to an attribute stored in two or more tables to broadcast clearly they are really the same attribute.

Figure 4	STATEABBREV AS A PRIMARY KEY (STATE RELATION) AND A FOREIGN KEY (CITY RELATION)

State

	StateAbbrev	StateName	EnteredUnionOrder	StateBird	StatePopulation
primary key →	CT	Connecticut	5	American robin	3,287,116
	MI	Michigan	26	robin	9,295,297
	SD	South Dakota	40	pheasant	696,004
	TN	Tennessee	16	mockingbird	4,877,185
	TX	Texas	28	mockingbird	16,986,510

City

	StateAbbrev	CityName	CityPopulation
primary key / foreign key →	CT	Hartford	139,739
	CT	Madison	14,031
	CT	Portland	8,418
	MI	Lansing	127,321
	SD	Madison	6,257
	SD	Pierre	12,906
	TN	Nashville	488,374
	TX	Austin	465,622
	TX	Portland	12,224

A **nonkey attribute** is an attribute that is not part of the primary key. In the two relations shown in Figure 4, all attributes are nonkey attributes except StateAbbrev in the State and City relations and CityName in the City relation. *Key* is an ambiguous word because it can refer to a primary, candidate, alternate, or foreign key. When the word key appears alone, however, it means primary key and the definition for a nonkey attribute consequently makes sense.

Relationships

The Capital relation, shown in Figure 5, has one row for each state capital. The CapitalName and StateAbbrev attributes are candidate keys; selecting CapitalName as the primary key makes StateAbbrev an alternate key. The StateAbbrev attribute in the Capital relation is also a foreign key, because its values match the values in the State relation's StateAbbrev column.

Figure 5	A ONE-TO-ONE RELATIONSHIP

State

primary key →

StateAbbrev	StateName	EnteredUnionOrder	StateBird	StatePopulation
CT	Connecticut	5	American robin	3,287,116
MI	Michigan	26	robin	9,295,297
SD	South Dakota	40	pheasant	696,004
TN	Tennessee	16	mockingbird	4,877,185
TX	Texas	28	mockingbird	16,986,510

foreign key →

Capital

primary key →

CapitalName	StateAbbrev	YearDesignated	PhoneAreaCode	CapitalPopulation
Austin	TX	1845	512	465,622
Hartford	CT	1662	860	139,739
Lansing	MI	1847	517	127,321
Nashville	TN	1843	615	488,374
Pierre	SD	1889	605	12,906

One-to-One

The State and Capital relations, shown in Figure 5, have a one-to-one relationship. A **one-to-one relationship** (abbreviated 1:1) exists between two relations when each row in one relation has at most one matching row in the other relation. StateAbbrev, which is a foreign key in the Capital relation and the primary key in the State relation, is the common field that ties together the rows of each relation.

Should the State and Capital relations be combined into one relation? Although the two relations in any 1:1 relationship can be combined into one relation, each relation describes different entities and should usually be kept separate.

One-to-Many

The State and City relations, shown once again in Figure 6, have a one-to-many relationship. A **one-to-many relationship** (abbreviated 1:M) exists between two relations when each row in the first relation matches many rows in the second relation and each row in the second relation matches only one row in the first relation. Many can mean zero rows, one row, or two or more rows. StateAbbrev, which is a foreign key in the City relation and the primary key in the State relation, is the common field that ties together the rows of each relation.

Figure 6	A ONE-TO-MANY RELATIONSHIP

State

StateAbbrev	StateName	EnteredUnionOrder	StateBird	StatePopulation
CT	Connecticut	5	American robin	3,287,116
MI	Michigan	26	robin	9,295,297
SD	South Dakota	40	pheasant	696,004
TN	Tennessee	16	mockingbird	4,877,185
TX	Texas	28	mockingbird	16,986,510

primary key

primary key

foreign key

City

StateAbbrev	CityName	CityPopulation
CT	Hartford	139,739
CT	Madison	14,031
CT	Portland	8,418
MI	Lansing	127,321
SD	Madison	6,257
SD	Pierre	12,906
TN	Nashville	488,374
TX	Austin	465,622
TX	Portland	12,224

Many-to-Many

In Figure 7, the State relation with a primary key of StateAbbrev and the Crop relation with a primary key of CropName have a many-to-many relationship. A **many-to-many relationship** (abbreviated as M:N) exists between two relations when each row in the first relation matches many rows in the second relation and each row in the second relation matches many rows in the first relation. In a relational database, you must use a third relation to serve as a bridge between the two M:N relations; the third relation has the primary keys of the M:N relations as its primary key. The original relations now each have a 1:M relationship with the new relation. The StateAbbrev and CropName attributes represent the primary key of the Production relation that is shown in Figure 7. StateAbbrev, which is a foreign key in the Production relation and the primary key in the State relation, is the common field that ties together the rows of the State and Production relations. Likewise, CropName is the common field for the Crop and Production relations.

Figure 7	A MANY-TO-MANY RELATIONSHIP

primary key

State

StateAbbrev	StateName	EnteredUnionOrder	StateBird	StatePopulation
CT	Connecticut	5	American robin	3,287,116
MI	Michigan	26	robin	9,295,297
SD	South Dakota	40	pheasant	696,004
TN	Tennessee	16	mockingbird	4,877,185
TX	Texas	28	mockingbird	16,986,510

Crop

CropName	Exports	Imports
Corn	$4,965.8	$68.5
Cotton	$2,014.6	$11.4
Soybeans	$4,462.8	$15.8
Wheat	$4,503.2	$191.1

primary key

foreign key

Production

StateAbbrev	CropName	Quantity
MI	Corn	241,500
MI	Soybeans	47,520
MI	Wheat	35,280
SD	Corn	377,200
SD	Soybeans	63,000
SD	Wheat	119,590
TN	Corn	79,360
TN	Soybeans	33,250
TN	Wheat	13,440
TX	Corn	202,500
TX	Cotton	3,322
TX	Soybeans	12,870
TX	Wheat	129,200

Entity Subtype

Figure 8 shows a special type of one-to-one relationship. The Shipping relation's primary key is StateAbbrev and contains one row for each state having an ocean shoreline. Because not all states have an ocean shoreline, the Shipping relation has fewer rows than the State relation. However, each row in the Shipping relation has a matching row in the State relation with StateAbbrev serving as the common field; StateAbbrev is the primary key in the State relation and is a foreign key in the Shipping relation.

Figure 8	AN ENTITY SUBTYPE

State

StateAbbrev	State Name	EnteredUnionOrder	StateBird	StatePopulation
CT	Connecticut	5	American robin	3,287,116
MI	Michigan	26	robin	9,295,297
SD	South Dakota	40	pheasant	696,004
TN	Tennessee	16	mockingbird	4,877,185
TX	Texas	28	mockingbird	16,986,510

Shipping

StateAbbrev	OceanShoreline	ExportTonnage	ImportTonnage
CT	618	3,377,466	2,118,494
TX	3,359	45,980,912	109,400,314

The Shipping relation, in this situation, is called an **entity subtype**, a relation whose primary key is a foreign key to a second relation and whose attributes are additional attributes for the second relation. You can create an entity subtype when a relation has attributes that could have null values. A **null value** is the absence of a value. A null value is not blank, nor zero, nor any other value. You give a null value to an attribute when you do not know its value or when a value does not apply. For example, instead of using the Shipping relation, you could store the OceanShoreline, ExportTonnage, and ImportTonnage attributes in the State relation and allow them to be null for states not having an ocean shoreline. You should be aware that database experts are currently debating the validity of the use of nulls in relational databases and many experts insist that you should never use nulls. Part of this warning against nulls is based on the inconsistent way different relational DBMSs treat nulls and part is due to the lack of a firm theoretical foundation for how to use nulls. In any case, entity subtypes are an alternative to the use of nulls.

Entity-Relationship **Diagrams**

A common shorthand method for describing relations is to write the relation name followed by its attributes in parentheses, underlining the attributes that represent the primary key and identifying the foreign keys for a relation immediately after the relation. Using this method, the relations that appear in Figures 5 through 8 are described in the following way:

State (<u>StateAbbrev</u>, StateName, EnteredUnionOrder, StateBird, StatePopulation)
Capital (<u>CapitalName</u>, StateAbbrev, YearDesignated, PhoneAreaCode, CapitalPopulation)
   Foreign key: StateAbbrev to State relation
City (<u>StateAbbrev</u>, <u>CityName</u>, CityPopulation)
   Foreign key: StateAbbrev to State relation
Crop (<u>CropName</u>, Exports, Imports)

Production (<u>StateAbbrev</u>, <u>CropName</u>, Quantity)
    Foreign key: StateAbbrev to State relation
    Foreign key: CropName to Crop relation
Shipping (<u>StateAbbrev</u>, OceanShoreline, ExportTonnage, ImportTonnage)
    Foreign key: StateAbbrev to State relation

Another popular way to describe relations *and their relationships* is with entity-relationship diagrams. An **entity-relationship diagram (ERD)** shows a database's entities and the relationships among the entities in a symbolic, visual way. In an entity-relationship diagram, an entity and a relation are equivalent. Figure 9 shows an entity-relationship diagram for the relations that appear in Figures 5 through 8.

Figure 9	AN ENTITY-RELATIONSHIP DIAGRAM

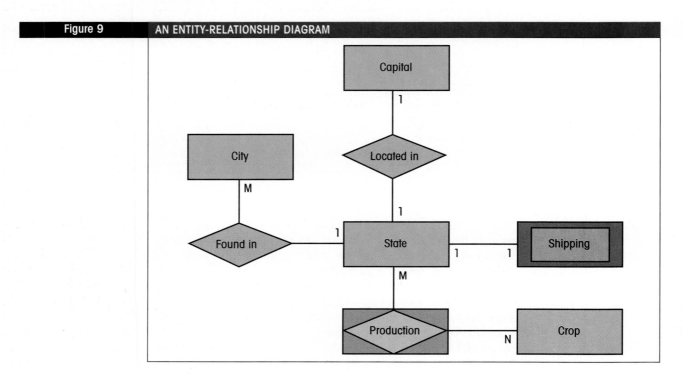

Entity-relationship diagrams have the following characteristics:

- Entities, or relations, appear in rectangles and relationships appear in diamonds. The entity name appears inside the rectangle and a verb describing the relationship appears inside the diamond. For example, the City rectangle is connected to the State rectangle by the Found in diamond and is read: "a city is found in a state."

- The 1 by the State entity and the M by the City entity identify a 1:M relationship between these two entities. In a similar manner, an M:N relationship exists between the State and Crop entities and 1:1 relationships exist between the State and Capital entities and between the State and Shipping entities.

- A diamond inside a rectangle defines a composite entity. A **composite entity** is a relationship that has the characteristics of an entity. For example, Production connects the State and Crop entities in an M:N relationship and acts as an entity by containing the Quantity attribute, along with the composite key of the StateAbbrev and CropName attributes.

■ An entity subtype, for example, Shipping, appears in a double rectangle and is connected without an intervening diamond directly to its related entity, for example, State.

You can also show attributes in an ERD by placing each individual attribute in a bubble connected to its entity or relationship. However, typical ERDs have large numbers of entities and relationships, so including the attributes might confuse rather than clarify the ERD.

Integrity Constraints

A database has **integrity** if its data follows certain rules, known as **integrity constraint**s. The ideal is to have the DBMS enforce all integrity constraints. If a DBMS can enforce some integrity constraints but not others, the other integrity constraints must be enforced by other programs or by the people who use the DBMS. Integrity constraints can be divided into three groups: primary key constraints, referential integrity, and domain integrity constraints.

■ One primary key constraint is inherent in the definition of a primary key, which says that the primary key must be unique. The **entity integrity constraint** says that the primary key cannot be null. For a composite key, none of the individual attributes can be null. The uniqueness and nonnull properties of a primary key ensure that you can reference any data value in a database by supplying its table name, attribute name, and primary key value.

■ Foreign keys provide the mechanism for forming a relationship between two tables, and referential integrity ensures that only valid relationships exist. **Referential integrity** is the constraint specifying that each nonnull foreign key must match a primary key value in the related relation. Specifically, referential integrity means that you cannot add a row with an unmatched foreign key value. Referential integrity also means that you cannot change or delete the related primary key value and leave the foreign key orphaned. In some relational DBMSs, if you try to change or delete a primary key value, you can specify one of these options: restricted, cascades, or nullifies. If you specify **restricted**, the DBMS updates or deletes the value only if there are no matching foreign key values. If you choose **cascades** and then change a primary key value, the DBMS changes the matching foreign keys to the new primary key value, or, if you delete a primary key value, the DBMS also deletes the matching foreign-key rows. If you choose **nullifies** and then change or delete a primary key value, the DBMS sets all matching foreign keys to null.

■ A domain is a set of values from which one or more columns draw their actual values. **Domain integrity constraints** are the rules you specify for an attribute. By choosing a data type for an attribute, you impose a constraint on the set of values allowed for the attribute. You can create specific validation rules for an attribute to limit its domain further. As you make an attribute's domain definition more precise, you exclude more and more unacceptable values for an attribute. For example, in the State relation you could define the domain for the EnteredUnionOrder attribute to be a unique integer between 1 and 50 and the domain for the StateBird attribute to be any name containing 25 or fewer characters.

Dependencies and Determinants

Relations are related to other relations. Attributes are also related to other attributes. Consider the StateCrop relation shown in Figure 10. Its description is:

StateCrop (<u>StateAbbrev</u>, <u>CropName</u>, StateBird, BirdScientificName, StatePopulation, Exports, Quantity)

Figure 10	A RELATION COMBINING SEVERAL ATTRIBUTES FROM OTHER RELATIONS

null value

primary key

StateCrop

StateAbbrev	CropName	StateBird	BirdScientificName	StatePopulation	Export	Quantity
CT	Corn	American robin	Planesticus migratorius	3,287,116	$4,965.8	
MI	Corn	robin	Planesticus migratorius	9,295,297	$4,965.8	241,500
MI	Soybeans	robin	Planesticus migratorius	9,295,297	$4,462.8	47,520
MI	Wheat	robin	Planesticus migratorius	9,295,297	$4,503.2	35,280
SD	Corn	pheasant	Phasianus colchicus	696,004	$4,965.8	277,200
SD	Soybeans	pheasant	Phasianus colchicus	696,004	$4,462.8	63,000
SD	Wheat	pheasant	Phasianus colchicus	696,004	$4,503.2	119,590
TN	Corn	mockingbird	Mimus polyglottos	4,977,185	$4,965.8	79,360
TN	Soybeans	mockingbird	Mimus polyglottos	4,977,185	$4,462.8	33,250
TN	Wheat	mockingbird	Mimus polyglottos	4,977,185	$4,503.2	13,440
TX	Corn	mockingbird	Mimus polyglottos	16,986,510	$4,965.8	202,500
TX	Cotton	mockingbird	Mimus polyglottos	16,986,510	$2,014.6	3,322
TX	Soybeans	mockingbird	Mimus polyglottos	16,986,510	$4,462.8	12,870
TX	Wheat	mockingbird	Mimus polyglottos	16,986,510	$4,503.2	129,200

The StateCrop relation combines several attributes from the State, Crop, and Production relations that appeared in Figure 7. The StateAbbrev, StateBird, and StatePopulation attributes are from the State relation. The CropName and Exports attributes are from the Crop relation. The StateAbbrev, CropName, and Quantity attributes are from the Production relation. The BirdScientificName attribute is a new attribute for the StateCrop relation, whose primary key is the combination of the StateAbbrev and CropName attributes.

Notice the null value in the Quantity attribute for the state of Connecticut (StateAbbrev CT). If you look back to Figure 7, you can see that there were no entries for Quantity for the state of Connecticut, which is why Quantity is null in the StateCrop table. However, note that CropName requires an entry because it is part of the composite key for the relation. If you want the state of CT to be in the relation, you need to assign a dummy CropName for the CT entry, in this case, Corn.

In the StateCrop relation, each attribute is related to other attributes. For example, a value for StateAbbrev determines the value of StatePopulation, and a value for StatePopulation depends on the value of StateAbbrev. In database discussions, the word functionally is used, as in: "StateAbbrev functionally determines StatePopulation" and

"StatePopulation is functionally dependent on StateAbbrev." In this case, StateAbbrev is called a determinant. A **determinant** is an attribute, or a collection of attributes, whose values determine the values of another attribute. We also state that an attribute is functionally dependent on another attribute (or collection of attributes) if that other attribute is a determinant for it.

You can graphically show a relation's functional dependencies and determinants in a bubble diagram. Bubble diagrams are also called data model diagrams and functional dependency diagrams. Figure 11 shows the bubble diagram for the StateCrop relation.

Figure 11	A BUBBLE DIAGRAM FOR THE STATECROP RELATION

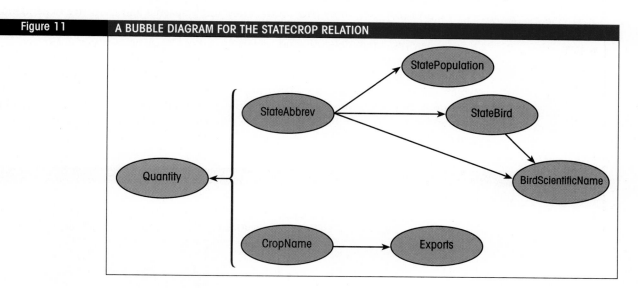

- StateAbbrev is a determinant for StatePopulation, StateBird, and BirdScientificName.
- CropName is a determinant for Exports.
- Quantity is functionally dependent on StateAbbrev and CropName together.
- StateBird is a determinant for BirdScientificName.

Only Quantity is functionally dependent on the relation's full primary key, StateAbbrev and CropName. StatePopulation, StateBird, and BirdScientificName have partial dependencies, because they are functionally dependent on StateAbbrev, which is part of the primary key. A **partial dependency** is a functional dependency on part of the primary key, instead of the entire primary key. Does another partial dependency exist in the StateCrop relation? Yes, Exports has a partial dependency on CropName.

Because StateAbbrev is a determinant of both StateBird and BirdScientificName, and StateBird is a determinant of BirdScientificName, StateBird and BirdScientificName have a transitive dependency. A **transitive dependency** is a functional dependency between two nonkey attributes, which are both dependent on a third attribute.

How do you know which functional dependencies exist among a collection of attributes, and how do you recognize partial and transitive dependencies? The answers lie with the questions you ask as you gather the requirements for a database application. For each attribute and entity, you must gain an accurate understanding of its meaning and relationships in the context of the application. **Semantic object modeling** is an entire area of study within the database field devoted to the meanings and relationships of data.

Anomalies

When you use a DBMS, you are more likely to get results you can trust if you create your relations carefully. For example, problems might occur with relations that have partial and transitive dependencies, whereas you won't have as much trouble if you ensure that your relations include only attributes that are directly related to each other. Also, when you remove data redundancy from a relation, you improve that relation. **Data redundancy** occurs when you store the same data in more than one place.

The problems caused by data redundancy and by partial and transitive dependencies are called **anomalies**, because they are undesirable irregularities of relations. Anomalies are of three types: insertion, deletion, and update.

To examine the effects of these anomalies, consider the Client relation that is shown in Figure 12. The Client relation represents part of the database for Pet Sitters Unlimited, which is a company providing pet-sitting services for homeowners while they are on vacation. Pet Sitters Unlimited keeps track of the data about its clients and the clients' children, pets, and vets. The attributes for the Client relation include the composite key ClientID and ChildName, along with ClientName, VetID, and VetName.

Figure 12	THE CLIENT RELATION WITH INSERTION, DELETION, AND UPDATE ANOMALIES

primary key

Client

ClientID	ChildName	ClientName	VetID	VetName
2173	Ryan	Barbara Hennessey	27	Pet Vet
4519	Pat	Vernon Noordsy	31	Pet Care
4519	Dana	Vernon Noordsy	31	Pet Care
8005	Dana	Sandra Amidon	27	Pet Vet
8005	Dani	Sandra Amidon	27	Pet Vet
8112	Pat	Helen Wandzell	24	Pets R Us

- An **insertion anomaly** occurs when you cannot add a row to a relation because you do not know the entire primary key value. For example, you cannot add the new client Cathy Corbett with a ClientID of 3322 to the Client relation when you do not know her children's names. Entity integrity prevents you from leaving any part of a primary key null. Because ChildName is part of the primary key, you cannot leave it null. To add the new client, your only option is to make up a ChildName, even if the client does not have children. This solution misrepresents the facts and is unacceptable, if a better approach is available.

- A **deletion anomaly** occurs when you delete data from a relation and unintentionally lose other critical data. For example, if you delete ClientID 8112 because Helen Wandzell is no longer a client, you also lose the only instance of VetID 24 in the database. Thus, you no longer know that VetID 24 is Pets R Us.

- An **update anomaly** occurs when you change one attribute value and either the DBMS must make more than one change to the database or else the database ends up containing inconsistent data. For example, if you change the ClientName, VetID, or VetName for ClientID 4519, the DBMS must change multiple rows of the Client relation. If the DBMS fails to change all the rows, the ClientName, VetID, or VetName now has two different values in the database and is inconsistent.

Normalization

Database design is the process of determining the precise relations needed for a given collection of attributes and placing those attributes into the correct relations. Crucial to good database design is understanding the functional dependencies of all attributes; recognizing the anomalies caused by data redundancy, partial dependencies, and transitive dependencies when they exist; and knowing how to eliminate the anomalies.

The process of identifying and eliminating anomalies is called **normalization**. Using normalization, you start with a collection of relations, apply sets of rules to eliminate anomalies, and produce a new collection of problem-free relations. The sets of rules are called **normal forms**. Of special interest for our purposes are the first three normal forms: first normal form, second normal form, and third normal form. First normal form improves the design of your relations, second normal form improves the first normal form design, and third normal form applies even more stringent rules to produce an even better design.

First Normal Form

Consider the Client relation shown in Figure 13. For each client, the relation contains ClientID, which is the primary key; the client's name and children's names; the ID and name of the client's vet; and the ID, name, and type of each client's pets. For example, Barbara Hennessey has no children and three pets, Vernon Noordsy has two children and one pet, Sandra Amidon has two children and two pets, and Helen Wandzell has one child and one pet. Because each entry in a relation must contain a single value, the structure shown in Figure 13 does not meet the requirements for a relation, therefore it is called an **unnormalized relation**. ChildName, which can have more than one value, is called a **repeating group**. The set of attributes that includes PetID, PetName, and PetType is a second repeating group in the structure.

Figure 13   REPEATING GROUPS OF DATA IN AN UNNORMALIZED CLIENT RELATION

repeating group

Client

ClientID	ClientName	ChildName	VetID	VetName	PetID	PetName	PetType
2173	Barbara Hennessey		27	Pet Vet	1 2 4	Sam Hoober Sam	Bird Dog Hamster
4519	Vernon Noordsy	Pat Dana	31	Pet Care	2	Charlie	Cat
8005	Sandra Amidon	Dana Dani	27	Pet Vet	1 2	Beefer Kirby	Dog Cat
8112	Helen Wandzell	Pat	24	Pets R Us	3	Kirby	Dog

First normal form addresses this repeating-group situation. A relation is in **first normal form (1NF)** if it does not contain repeating groups. To remove a repeating group and convert to first normal form, you expand the primary key to include the primary key of the repeating group. You must perform this step carefully, however. If the unnormalized relation has independent repeating groups, you must perform the conversion step separately for each.

The repeating group of ChildName is independent from the repeating group of PetID, PetName, and PetType. That is, the number and names of a client's children are independent of the number, names, and types of a client's pets. Performing the conversion step to each independent repeating group produces the two 1NF relations shown in Figure 14.

Figure 14	AFTER CONVERSION TO 1NF

primary key

Child

ClientID	ChildName	ClientName	VetID	VetName
4519	Pat	Vernon Noordsy	31	Pet Care
4519	Dana	Vernon Noordsy	31	Pet Care
8005	Dana	Sandra Amidon	27	Pet Vet
8005	Dani	Sandra Amidon	27	Pet Vet
8112	Pat	Helen Wandzell	24	Pets R Us

primary key

Client

ClientID	PetID	ClientName	VetID	VetName	PetName	PetType
2173	1	Barbara Hennessey	27	Pet Vet	Sam	Bird
2173	2	Barbara Hennessey	27	Pet Vet	Hoober	Dog
2173	4	Barbara Hennessey	27	Pet Vet	Sam	Hamster
4519	2	Vernon Noordsy	31	Pet Care	Charlie	Cat
8005	1	Sandra Amidon	27	Pet Vet	Beefer	Dog
8005	2	Sandra Amidon	27	Pet Vet	Kirby	Cat
8112	3	Helen Wandzell	24	Pets R Us	Kirby	Dog

The alternative way to describe the 1NF relations is:

Child (<u>ClientID</u>, <u>ChildName</u>, ClientName, VetID, VetName)
Client (<u>ClientID</u>, <u>PetID</u>, ClientName, VetID, VetName, PetName, PetType)

Child and Client are now true relations and both have composite keys. Both relations, however, suffer from insertion, deletion, and update anomalies. (Find examples of the three anomalies in both relations.) In the Child and Client relations, ClientID is a determinant for ClientName, VetID, and VetName, so partial dependencies exist in both relations. It is these partial dependencies that cause the anomalies in the two relations, and second normal form addresses the partial-dependency problem.

Second Normal Form

A relation in 1NF is in **second normal form (2NF)** if it does not contain any partial dependencies. To remove partial dependencies from a relation and convert it to second normal form, you perform two steps. First, identify the functional dependencies for every attribute in the relation. Second, if necessary, create new relations and place each attribute in a relation, so that the attribute is functionally dependent on the entire primary key. If you need to create new relations, restrict them to ones with a primary key that is a subset of the original composite key. Note that partial dependencies occur only when you have a composite key; a relation in first normal form with a single-attribute primary key is automatically in second normal form.

Figure 15 shows the functional dependencies for the 1NF Child and Client relations.

Figure 15	A BUBBLE DIAGRAM FOR THE 1NF CHILD AND THE CLIENT RELATIONS

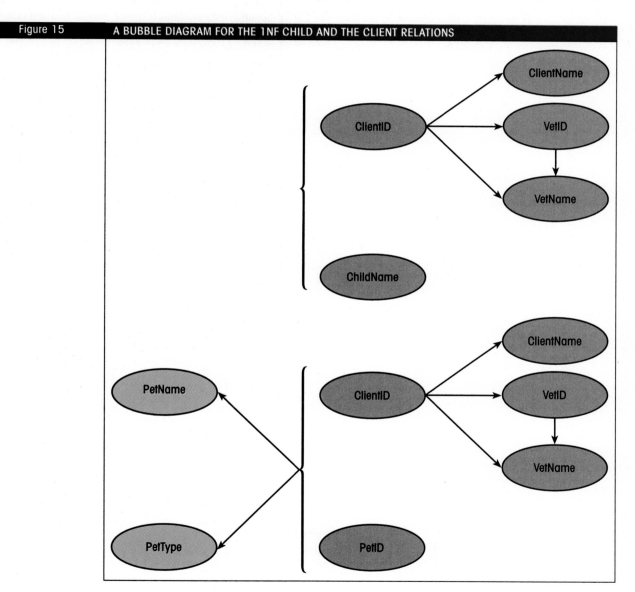

ClientID is a determinant for ClientName, VetID, and VetName in both relations. The composite key ClientID and PetID is a determinant for PetName and PetType. ChildName is not a determinant, nor is PetID. Is the composite key of ClientID and ChildName a determinant? No, it is not a determinant. What happens, however, if you do not have a relation with this composite key? You lose the names of the children of each client. You need to retain this composite key in a relation to preserve the important 1:M attribute relationship between ClientID and ChildName. Performing the second conversion step produces the three 2NF relations shown in Figure 16.

Figure 16 | **AFTER CONVERSION TO 2NF**

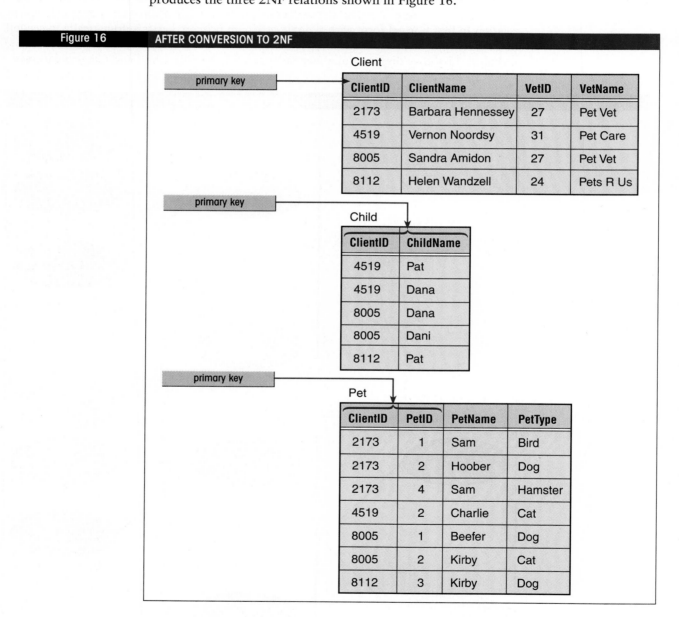

Client

primary key

ClientID	ClientName	VetID	VetName
2173	Barbara Hennessey	27	Pet Vet
4519	Vernon Noordsy	31	Pet Care
8005	Sandra Amidon	27	Pet Vet
8112	Helen Wandzell	24	Pets R Us

primary key

Child

ClientID	ChildName
4519	Pat
4519	Dana
8005	Dana
8005	Dani
8112	Pat

primary key

Pet

ClientID	PetID	PetName	PetType
2173	1	Sam	Bird
2173	2	Hoober	Dog
2173	4	Sam	Hamster
4519	2	Charlie	Cat
8005	1	Beefer	Dog
8005	2	Kirby	Cat
8112	3	Kirby	Dog

The alternative way to describe the 2NF relations is:

Client (<u>ClientID</u>, ClientName, VetID, VetName)
Child (<u>ClientID</u>, <u>ChildName</u>)
    Foreign key: ClientID to Client relation
Pet (<u>ClientID</u>, <u>PetID</u>, PetName, PetType)
    Foreign key: ClientID to Client relation

All three relations are in second normal form. Do anomalies still exist? The Child and Pet relations show no anomalies, but Client suffers from anomalies caused by the transitive dependency between VetID and VetName. (Find examples of the three anomalies caused by the transitive dependency.) You can see the transitive dependency in the bubble diagram shown in Figure 15; VetID is a determinant for VetName and ClientID is a determinant for VetID and VetName. Third normal form addresses the transitive-dependency problem.

Third Normal Form

A relation in 2NF is in **third normal form (3NF)** if every determinant is a candidate key. This definition for 3NF is referred to as **Boyce-Codd normal form (BCNF)** and is an improvement over the original version of 3NF.

To convert a relation to third normal form, remove the attributes that depend on the non-candidate-key determinant and place them into a new relation with the determinant as the primary key. For the Client relation, you remove VetName from the relation, create a new Vet relation, place VetName in the Vet relation, and then make VetID the primary key of the Vet relation. Note that only VetName is removed from the Client relation; VetID remains as a foreign key in the Client relation. Figure 17 shows the database design for the four 3NF relations.

| Figure 17 | AFTER CONVERSION TO 3NF |

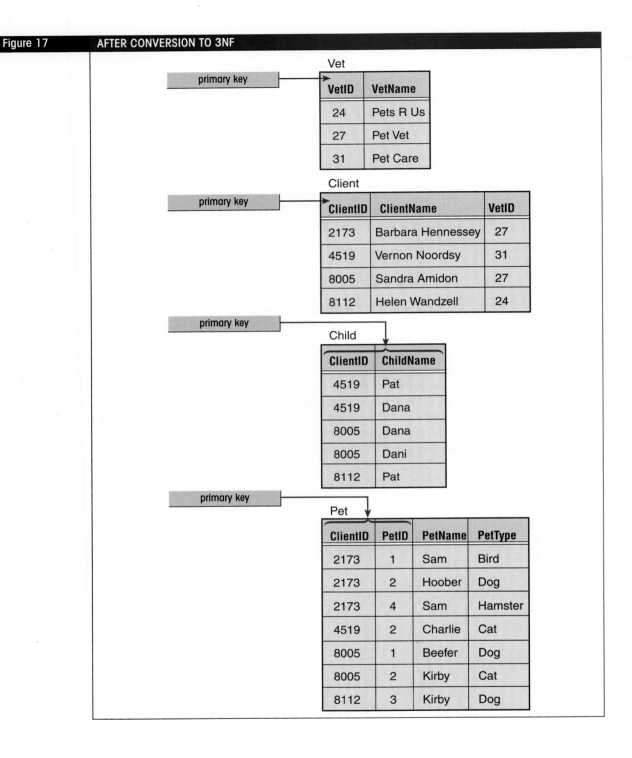

The alternative way to describe the 3NF relations is:

Vet (<u>VetID</u>, VetName)
Client (<u>ClientID</u>, ClientName, VetID)
    Foreign key: VetID to Vet relation
Child (<u>ClientID</u>, <u>ChildName</u>)
    Foreign key: ClientID to Client relation
Pet (<u>ClientID</u>, <u>PetID</u>, PetName, PetType)
    Foreign key: ClientID to Client relation

The four relations have no anomalies, because you have eliminated all the data redundancy, partial dependencies, and transitive dependencies. Normalization provides the framework for eliminating anomalies and delivering an optimal database design, which you should always strive to achieve. You should be aware, however, that experts often denormalize relations to improve database performance—specifically, to decrease the time it takes the database to respond to a user's commands and requests. When you denormalize a relation, you reintroduce redundancy to the relation. At the same time, you reintroduce anomalies. Thus, improving performance exposes a database to potential integrity problems. Only database experts should denormalize relations, but even experts first complete the normalization of their relations.

REVIEW QUESTIONS

1. What are the formal names for a table, for a row, and for a column?

2. What is a domain?

3. What is an entity?

4. What is the relationship between a primary key and a candidate key?

5. What is a composite key?

6. What is a foreign key?

Explore

7. Look for an example of a one-to-one relationship, an example of a one-to-many relationship, and an example of a many-to-many relationship in a newspaper, magazine, book, or everyday situation you encounter. For each one, name the entities and select the primary and foreign keys.

8. When do you use an entity subtype?

9. What is a composite entity in an entity-relationship diagram?

10. What is the entity integrity constraint?

11. What is referential integrity?

12. What does the cascades option, which is used with referential integrity, accomplish?

13. What are partial and transitive dependencies?

14. What three types of anomalies can be exhibited by a relation, and what problems do they cause?

15. Figure 18 shows the Vet, Client, and Child relations with primary keys VetID, ClientID, and both ClientID and ChildName, respectively. Which two integrity constraints do these relations violate and why?

Figure 18

Vet

VetID	VetName
24	Pets R Us
27	Pet Vet
31	Pet Care

Client

ClientID	ClientName	VetID
2173	Barbara Hennessey	27
4519	Vernon Noordsy	31
8005	Sandra Amidon	37
8112	Helen Wandzell	24

Child

ClientID	ChildName
4519	Pat
4519	Dana
8005	
8005	Dani
8112	Pat

16. The State and Capital relations, shown in Figure 5, are described as follows:

    State (StateAbbrev, StateName, EnteredUnionOrder, StateBird,
    StatePopulation)
    Capital (CapitalName, StateAbbrev, YearDesignated, PhoneAreaCode,
    CapitalPopulation)
    Foreign key: StateAbbrev to State relation

    Add the attribute CountyName for the county or counties containing the state capital to this database, justify where you placed it (that is, in an existing relation or in a new one), and draw the entity–relationship diagram for all the entities. The counties for the state capitals shown in Figure 5 are Travis and Williamson counties for Austin TX; Hartford county for Hartford CT; Clinton, Eaton, and Ingham counties for Lansing MI; Davidson county for Nashville TN; Hughes county for Pierre SD.

17. Suppose you have a relation for a dance studio. The attributes are dancer's identification number, dancer's name, dancer's address, dancer's telephone number, class identification number, day that the class meets, time that the class meets, instructor name, and instructor identification number. Assume that each dancer takes one class, each class meets only once a week and has one instructor, and each instructor can teach more than one class. In what normal form is the relation currently, given the following shorthand description?

    Dancer (DancerID, DancerName, DancerAddr, DancerPhone, ClassID,ClassDay,
    ClassTime, InstrName, InstrID)
    Convert this relation to 3NF and then draw an entity–relationship diagram for this database.

18. Store the following attributes for a library database: AuthorCode, AuthorName, BookTitle, BorrowerAddress, BorrowerName, BorrowerCard Number, CopiesOfBook, ISBN (International Standard Book Number), LoanDate, PublisherCode, PublisherName, and PublisherAddress. A one-to-many relationship exists between publishers and books. Many-to-many relationships exist between authors and books and between borrowers and books.

    a. Name the entities for the library database.
    b. Create the relations for the library database and describe them using the shorthand method. Be sure the relations are in third normal form.
    c. Draw an entity–relationship diagram for the library database.

INDEX

D

data

filtering, AC 3.19-3.21

finding with form, AC 4.08-4.10

maintaining in form, AC 4.12-4.14

sorting

in general, AC 3.14-3.15

grouping and, AC 6.12-6.13

updating, AC 3.07

with Internet Explorer, AC 7.11-7.13

data access page. *See also* **HTML document; Web page**

creating

adding fields to, AC 7.16-7.18

control manipulation on, AC 7.19-7.20

in Design view, AC 7.14-7.15

in general, AC 7.14

resizing section, AC 7.20-7.21

special effects application, AC 7.20-7.21

theme selection, AC 7.21-7.22

DataPageSize property, AC 7.21

grouped, AC 7.21

PivotChart use with, AC 7.37-7.45

PivotTable use with

adding fields, AC 7.28-7.30

adding PivotTable, AC 7.26-7.27

adding total field, AC 7.33-7.37

in general, AC 7.25-7.26

Page view use, AC 7.30-7.33

saving and viewing, AC 7.22-7.24

sorting and filtering records with, AC 7.13-7.14

for table, AC 7.08-7.11

updating data on, AC 7.11-7.13

Data Disk, creating, WIN 2000 2.15

data field. *See also* **field**

PivotChart, AC 7.37

data organization, AC 1.04

data redundancy

avoiding, AC 2.03

occurence, RD 14

data type, field data types, AC 2.05-2.06

data validation criteria, defining, AC 5.13-5.15

database, OFF 6. *See also* **Access; database**

back-end database, AC 11.19

backup and restoration, AC 1.23

compacting and repairing, AC 1.24

automatically, AC 1.24-1.25

converting, AC 1.25-1.26

copying records from, AC 2.29-2.31

creating, AC 2.07-2.08

data organization, AC 1.04

common field, AC 1.05

field, AC 1.04

field value, AC 1.04

record, AC 1.04

table, AC 1.04

design guidelines, AC 2.02-2.04

documentation, Documeter, AC 11.05

editing mode, AC 2.34

front-end database, AC 11.19

in general, AC 1.04

primary key, AC 1.05

importing table from, AC 2.32-2.33

management, AC 1.23

navigation mode, AC 2.34

opening, AC 1.07-1.10

Overseas Database Switchboard, requirements, AC 9.39-9.40

performance analysis, Performance Analyzer, AC 11.02-11.05

record modification, AC 2.35

relational database, AC 1.04-1.08

relational database management system, AC 1.06

replica

creating, AC 11.13-11.15

Design Master, AC 11.13

synchronization, AC 11.13

synchronizing replica and Design Master, AC 11.15-11.18

saving, AC 1.12-1.13

as MDE file, AC 11.38-11.39

security

encrypting database, AC 11.26-11.27

in general, AC 11.25-11.26

passwords, AC 11.27-11.30

user-level security, AC 11.30-11.38

startup options, AC 11.23-11.25

updating

changing records, AC 2.34-2.35

deleting records, AC 2.33-2.34

in general, AC 2.33

database administration (DBA), AC 11.30

database administrator, AC 11.30

database design, RD 15

database management system (DBMS), discussed, AC 1.06-1.07

database program, OFF 6

Database Splitter

using, AC 11.19-11.22

back-end database, AC 11.19

database window, AC 1.10

DataPageSize property, AC 7.21

history table, AC 8.16

HTML. *See* Hypertext Markup Language

HTML document, AC 7.02. *See also* data access page; document; Web page

exporting query to, AC 7.02-7.05

viewing with Internet Explorer, AC 7.05-7.08

hyperlinks, AC 7.02

creating

entering hyperlink field values, AC 7.56-7.58

in general, AC 7.54

hyperlink field in table, AC 7.55

Linked Table Manager, AC 11.08-11.12

refreshing, AC 11.09

using, AC 7.58-7.59

Hypertext Markup Language (HTML), AC 7.02

I

I-beam pointer, WIN 2000 2.05. *See also* pointing device

icon

changing icon display, WIN 2000 2.18-2.20

defined, AC 9.02

If statement, AC 10.18

IsNull function, AC 10.18

If function, calculated field, AC 6.08

Immediate window

testing procedure in, AC 10.15-10.16

logic error, AC 10.15

In comparison operator, AC 5.17

index

for table field

creating, AC 8.42-8.44

in general, AC 8.39-8.41

viewing existing indexes, AC 8.41-8.42

input mask, creating, AC 5.10-5.13

Input Mask Wizard, using, AC 5.10-5.13

insertion point, WIN 2000 2.04. *See also* pointing device

I-beam pointer, WIN 2000 2.05

vs. pointer, WIN 2000 2.05-2.06

integration, Office, OFF 7-9

integrity, RD 11. *See also* integrity constraints

cascades, RD 11

nullifies, RD 11

referential, RD 11

restricted, RD 11

integrity constraints, RD 11

domain integrity constraints, RD 11

entity integrity constraint, RD 11

Internet, AC 7.02, WIN 2000 1.03. *See also* World Wide Web

Internet Explorer

updating data access page with, AC 7.11-7.13

viewing HTML document with, AC 7.05-7.08

IsNull function, AC 10.18

J

join, tables, AC 3.08

K

Keep Together property, AC 6.47

key

alternate key, RD 4

candidate key, RD 4

composite key, AC 2.03, RD 4

concatenated key, RD 4

foreign key, AC 1.05, RD 4

in general, RD 3-5

nonkey attribute, RD 5

primary key, AC 1.05, AC 2.03, RD 3

specifying, AC 2.16-2.17

shortcut key, AC 9.03

sort key, AC 3.14, AC 3.16

keyboard shortcut, Office, OFF 13

L

label

adding to form, AC 5.37-5.39

aligning, AC 6.20-6.21

right-aligning, AC 5.46-5.48

category axis label, AC 7.37

changing Caption property, AC 5.31-5.33, AC 6.16-6.17

defined, AC 5.26

editing, deleting, AC 5.51

mailing label creation, AC 6.50-6.57

resizing, moving, right-aligning, AC 5.46-5.48

value axis label, AC 7.37

Label Wizard, AC 6.50

legend, PivotChart, AC 7.38

Len function, AC 10.27

TASK	PAGE #	RECOMMENDED METHOD
Access, exit	AC 1.13	Click ☒ on the program window
Access, start	AC 1.07	Click Start, point to Programs, click Microsoft Access
Action, add by dragging	AC 9.12	See Reference Window: Creating an Action by Dragging
Action, add to macro	AC 9.08	In the Macro window, click the Action list arrow, click the action
Advanced filter, apply in a table	AC 8.29	See Reference Window: Applying an Advanced Filter/Sort
Aggregate functions, use in a query	AC 3.38	Display the query in Design view, click Σ
And operator, enter selection criteria for	AC 5.19	Enter selection criteria in the same Criteria row in the design grid
Append query, create	AC 8.20	See Reference Window: Creating an Append Query
AutoFormat, change	AC 4.05	See Reference Window: Changing a Form's AutoFormat
Calculated field, add to a query	AC 3.34	See Reference Window: Using Expression Builder
Caption, change for a form label	AC 5.31	See Reference Window: Changing a Label's Caption
Caption, change for a report label	AC 6.16	See Reference Window: Changing the Caption Property for a Label
Color, change an object's background	AC 5.41	See Reference Window: Changing the Background Color of a Control
Column, resize width in a datasheet	AC 2.29	Double-click ↔ on the right border of the column heading
Command button, add to a form	AC 9.22	Click ▭ on the toolbox, position the pointer in the form, click the mouse button
Command button, add to a form using Control Wizards	AC 9.35	See Reference Window: Adding a Command Button to a Form Using Control Wizards
Conditional formatting rules, define	AC 6.33	See Reference Window: Defining Conditional Formatting for a Control
Control, align	AC 5.46	See Reference Window: Aligning Controls on a Form
Control, apply special effect	AC 7.20	Select the control, click the list arrow for ▭, click the special effect
Control, delete	AC 7.19	Right-click the control, click Cut
Control, hide	AC 6.26	Set Visible property to No
Control, move in a form	AC 5.29	See Reference Window: Selecting and Moving Controls
Control, move in a report	AC 6.17	See Reference Window: Moving and Resizing Controls

TASK	PAGE #	RECOMMENDED METHOD
Control, resize in a form	AC 5.34	See Reference Window: Resizing a Control
Control, resize in a report	AC 6.17	See Reference Window: Moving and Resizing Controls
Control, select	AC 5.29	See Reference Window: Selecting and Moving Controls
Crosstab query, create	AC 8.06	See Reference Window: Using the Crosstab Query Wizard
Data, check spelling of	AC 4.15	Click [ABC✓]
Data, find	AC 4.08	See Reference Window: Finding Data in a Form or Datasheet
Data, group in a report	AC 6.12	See Reference Window: Sorting and Grouping Data in a Report
Data, sort in a report	AC 6.12	See Reference Window: Sorting and Grouping Data in a Report
Data access page, create a custom	AC 7.14	See Reference Window: Creating a Data Access Page in Design View
Data access page, display related records	AC 7.23	Click ⊞
Data access page, filter records	AC 7.13	Click filter field text box, click [▼/]
Data access page, hide related records	AC 7.24	Click ⊟
Data access page, select theme	AC 7.22	In Design view, click Format, click Theme, select desired theme, click OK
Data access page, sort records	AC 7.13	Click sort field text box, click either [A↓] or [Z↓]
Data access page, update with a browser	AC 7.12	See Reference Window: Viewing and Updating Data on a Data Access Page Using Internet Explorer
Data access page, use Page Wizard to create	AC 7.08	Click Pages in the Objects bar, click New, click Page Wizard, choose the table or query to use, click OK, choose Wizard options
Data access page, view with a browser	AC 7.12	See Reference Window: Viewing and Updating Data on a Data Access Page Using Internet Explorer
Database, compact and repair	AC 1.24	Click Tools, point to Database Utilities, click Compact and Repair Database
Database, compact on close	AC 1.25	See Reference Window: Compacting a Database Automatically
Database, convert to another Access version	AC 1.26	Close the database to convert, click Tools, point to Database Utilities, point to Convert Database, click the format to convert to
Database, create a blank	AC 2.07	Click [▯] on the Database toolbar, click Blank Database in the Task Pane, type the database name, select the drive and folder, click Create

TASK	PAGE #	RECOMMENDED METHOD
Database, create using a Wizard	AC 2.07	Click 🗋 on the Database toolbar, click General Templates in the Task Pane, click the Databases tab, select a template, click OK, type the database name, select the drive and folder, click Create, follow the instructions in the Wizard
Database, compile	AC 10.21	Click Debug, click Compile <database name>
Database, decrypt	AC 11.26	See Reference Window: Encrypting or Decrypting a Database
Database, encrypt	AC 11.26	See Reference Window: Encrypting or Decrypting a Database
Database, open	AC 1.07	Click 📂
Database, split	AC 11.20	See Reference Window: Using the Database Splitter
Database startup options, set	AC 11.23	See Reference Window: Setting the Database Startup Options
Datasheet view, switch to	AC 2.19	Click 📰
Date, add to a report	AC 6.41	See Reference Window: Adding the Date to a Report
Delete query, create	AC 8.23	See Reference Window: Creating a Delete Query
Design Master and replica, synchronize	AC 11.16	See Reference Window: Synchronizing the Design Master and a Replica
Design view, switch to	AC 2.23	Click 📐
Documenter, use	AC 11.05	See Reference Window: Using the Documenter
Domain aggregate function, add	AC 6.38	See Reference Window: Using a Domain Aggregate Function in a Report
Duplicate values, hide	AC 6.28	See Reference Window: Hiding Duplicate Values in a Report
Event procedure, add	AC 10.19	See Reference Window: Adding an Event Procedure
Event procedure, display an existing	AC 10.06	Open the property sheet for the control, click the event property text box, click ⋯
Field, add to a data access page or form	AC 5.28	Drag the field from the field list to the object in Design view
Field, add to a database table	AC 2.25	See Reference Window: Adding a Field Between Two Existing Fields
Field, add to a report	AC 6.14	See Reference Window: Adding Fields to a Report
Field, define in a database table	AC 2.10	See Reference Window: Defining a Field in a Table
Field, delete from a database table	AC 2.23	See Reference Window: Deleting a Field from a Table Structure
Field, move to a new location in a database table	AC 2.24	Display the table in Design view, click the field's row selector, drag the field with the pointer

TASK	PAGE #	RECOMMENDED METHOD
Filter, save as a query	AC 5.56	See Reference Window: Saving a Filter as a Query
Filter, saved as a query, apply	AC 5.57	See Reference Window: Applying a Filter Saved as a Query
Filter By Form, activate	AC 5.55	Click 📋
Filter By Form, using	AC 5.53	See Reference Window: Selecting Records Using Filter By Form
Filter By Selection, activate	AC 3.20	See Reference Window: Using Filter By Selection
Find duplicates query, create	AC 8.09	See Reference Window: Using the Find Duplicates Query Wizard
Find unmatched query, create	AC 8.11	See Reference Window: Using the Find Unmatched Query Wizard
Form, create a custom	AC 5.25	See Reference Window: Creating a Form in Design View
Form Footer, add	AC 5.36	See Reference Window: Adding and Removing Form Header and Form Footer Sections
Form Footer, remove	AC 5.36	See Reference Window: Adding and Removing Form Header and Form Footer Sections
Form Header, add	AC 5.36	See Reference Window: Adding and Removing Form Header and Form Footer Sections
Form Header, remove	AC 5.36	See Reference Window: Adding and Removing Form Header and Form Footer Sections
Form Wizard, activate	AC 4.02	Click Forms in the Objects bar, click New, click Form Wizard, choose the table or query for the form, click OK
Function, create	AC 10.12	Enter function statements in the Code window
Group totals, calculating in a report	AC 6.29	See Reference Window: Calculating Totals in a Report
Hot key, create	AC 9.35	Type an ampersand (&) to the left of the hot key letter in the object's name
HTML document, export an Access object as	AC 7.03	See Reference Window: Exporting an Access Object to an HTML Document
HTML document, view	AC 7.05	See Reference Window: Viewing an HTML Document in a Web Browser
Hyperlink, use	AC 7.58	Click the hyperlink field value
Hyperlink field, create	AC 7.55	See Reference Window: Creating a Hyperlink Field in a Table
Hyperlink field value, enter	AC 7.56	See Reference Window: Entering a Hyperlink Field Value in a Table
Index, create	AC 8.43	See Reference Window: Creating an Index
Indexes, view a table's existing	AC 8.41	See Reference Window: Viewing a Table's Existing Indexes

TASK	PAGE #	RECOMMENDED METHOD
Input Mask Wizard, activate	AC 5.11	Click the field's Input Mask text box, click [...], specify your choices in the Input Mask Wizard dialog boxes
Label, add to a form or report	AC 5.37	See Reference Window: Adding a Label to a Form
Line, add to a report	AC 6.27	See Reference Window: Adding a Line to a Report
Linked Table Manager, use	AC 11.10	See Reference Window: Using the Linked Table Manager
List box, add to a form	AC 9.27	See Reference Window: Adding a List Box to a Form
Lookup Wizard field, create	AC 5.04	Click the Data Type list arrow, click Lookup Wizard, specify your choices in the Lookup Wizard dialog boxes
Macro, add to a macro group	AC 9.21	See Reference Window: Adding a Macro to a Macro Group
Macro, attach to a command button	AC 9.23	Open the property sheet for the command button, click the right edge of the event property text box, click the macro name
Macro, create	AC 9.11	See Reference Window: Creating a Macro
Macro, run from the Database window	AC 9.05	Click Macros in the Objects bar, right-click the macro name, click Run; or click Tools, point to Run Macro, click the macro name from the list, click OK
Macro, run from the Macro window	AC 9.05	Click [!] on the Macro Design toolbar
Macro, single step	AC 9.09	See Reference Window: Single Stepping a Macro
Macro group, create	AC 9.40	See Reference Window: Creating a Macro Group
Mailing labels, create	AC 6.51	See Reference Window: Creating Mailing Labels and Other Labels
Make-table query, create	AC 8.17	See Reference Window: Creating a Make-Table Query
MDE file, save a database as	AC 11.38	Close the Access 2002 file-formatted database, click Tools, point to Database Utilities, click Make MDE File, select the database, click Make MDE
Module, create	AC 10.11	See Reference Window: Creating a New Standard Module
Module, save	AC 10.14	Click [💾] on the VBA Standard toolbar, enter the module name, press Enter
Multiple-column report, modify	AC 6.55	In Design view, click File, click Page Setup, click Columns, set multiple-column options
Object, export as an Excel worksheet	AC 7.51	See Reference Window: Exporting an Access Object to an Excel Worksheet
Object, open	AC 1.10	Click the object's type in the Objects bar, click the object's name, click Open
Object, save	AC 1.20	Click [💾], type the object name, click OK
Overall totals, calculating in a report	AC 6.29	See Reference Window: Calculating Totals in a Report

TASK	PAGE #	RECOMMENDED METHOD
Page numbers, add to a report	AC 6.43	See Reference Window: Adding Page Numbers to a Report
Parameter query, create	AC 5.21	See Reference Window: Creating a Parameter Query
Password, set a database	AC 11.27	See Reference Window: Setting a Database Password
Password, unset a database	AC 11.29	See Reference Window: Unsetting a Database Password
Performance Analyzer, use	AC 11.02	See Reference Window: Using the Performance Analyzer
Picture, add to a form or report	AC 5.39	See Reference Window: Adding a Picture to a Form
Picture, change on a command button	AC 9.24	Open the property sheet for the command button, click the Picture text box, click [···], select the picture, click OK
Picture, insert on a report	AC 4.31	Select the report section in which to insert the picture, click Insert, click Picture, select the picture file, click OK
PivotChart, add to data access page	AC 7.38	See Reference Window: Adding a PivotChart to a Data Access Page
PivotTable, add a total field	AC 7.33	Click a detail field's column heading, right-click it a second time, point to AutoCalc, click an aggregate option
PivotTable, add to data access page	AC 7.26	See Reference Window: Adding a PivotTable to a Data Access Page
Primary key, specify	AC 2.16	See Reference Window: Specifying a Primary Key for a Table
Procedure, create	AC 10.24	See Reference Window: Adding a New Procedure to a Standard Module
Procedure, test in the Immediate window	AC 10.15	See Reference Window: Testing a Procedure in the Immediate Window
Property sheet, open	AC 3.37	Right-click the object or control, click Properties
Query, define	AC 3.03	Click Queries in the Objects bar, click New, click Design View, click OK
Query, run	AC 3.06	Click [!]
Query results, sort	AC 3.17	See Reference Window: Sorting a Query Datasheet
Record, add a new one	AC 2.28	Click [▶*]
Record, delete	AC 2.33	See Reference Window: Deleting a Record
Record, move to a specific one	AC 1.11	Type the record number in the Specific Record box, press Enter
Record, move to first	AC 1.12	Click [|◀]
Record, move to last	AC 1.12	Click [▶|]
Record, move to next	AC 1.12	Click [▶]
Record, move to previous	AC 1.12	Click [◀]

TASK	PAGE #	RECOMMENDED METHOD
Records, redisplay all after filter	AC 3.21	Click ▽
Redo command, use to redo multiple operations in a database object	AC 3.31	Click the list arrow for ⟳, click the action(s) to redo
Relationship, define between database tables	AC 3.10	Click ⬡
Relationships window, print	AC 11.06	Click File, click Print Relationships, click 🖨
Replica, create	AC 11.13	See Reference Window: Creating a Replica of a Database
Report, create a custom	AC 6.10	See Reference Window: Creating a Report in Design View
Report Footer, add	AC 6.36	See Reference Window: Adding and Removing Report Header and Report Footer Sections
Report Footer, remove	AC 6.36	See Reference Window: Adding and Removing Report Header and Report Footer Sections
Report Header, add	AC 6.36	See Reference Window: Adding and Removing Report Header and Report Footer Sections
Report Header, remove	AC 6.36	See Reference Window: Adding and Removing Report Header and Report Footer Sections
Report Wizard, activate	AC 4.23	Click Reports in the Objects bar, click New, click Report Wizard, choose the table or query for the report, click OK
Self-join, create	AC 8.51	See Reference Window: Creating a Self-Join
Sort, specify ascending in datasheet	AC 3.15	Click ⬆
Sort, specify descending in datasheet	AC 3.15	Click ⬇
SQL statement, use for a list box	AC 9.32	Open the property sheet for the list box, right-click the Row Source text box, click Zoom, enter the SQL statement, click OK
SQL statement, view	AC 9.29	See Reference Window: Viewing an SQL Statement for a Query
Subdatasheet, display related records	AC 5.09	Click ⊞
Subdatasheet, hide related records	AC 5.10	Click ⊟
Subform/Subreport Wizard, activate	AC 5.48	Make sure ⬚ is selected, click ▦, click in the grid at the upper-left corner for the subform/subreport
Subreport, open in a new window	AC 6.24	Right-click the subreport, click Subreport in New Window

TASK	PAGE #	RECOMMENDED METHOD
Switchboard Manager, activate	AC 9.45	Click Tools, point to Database Utilities, click Switchboard Manager
Tab Control, add to a form	AC 5.43	Click , click in the grid at the upper-left corner for the tab control
Table, create in a database	AC 2.08	Click Tables in the Objects bar, click New, click Design View, click OK
Table, export as an Excel worksheet	AC 7.51	See Reference Window: Exporting an Access Object to an Excel Worksheet
Table, import from another Access database	AC 2.32	Click File, point to Get External Data, click Import, select the folder, click Import, select the table, click OK
Table, link in another Access database	AC 11.09	See Reference Window: Link to a Table in Another Access Database
Table, open in a database	AC 1.10	Click Tables in the Objects bar, click the table name, click Open
Table structure, save in a database	AC 2.18	See Reference Window: Saving a Table Structure
Template, use an HTML	AC 7.04	Click the Save formatted check box in the Export dialog box, click Export, select template, click OK
Title, add to a form or report	AC 5.37	Click , click in the grid at the upper-left corner for the title, type the title, click anywhere outside the label box
Top values query, create	AC 8.13	See Reference Window: Creating a Top Values Query
Totals, calculate in a report	AC 6.29	See Reference Window: Calculating Totals in a Report
Undo command, use to undo multiple operations in a database object	AC 3.30	Click the list arrow for , click the action(s) to undo
Update query, create	AC 8.25	See Reference Window: Creating an Update Query
User-Level Security Wizard, use	AC 11.31	Click Tools, point to Security, click User-Level Security Wizard, complete the entries in the dialog boxes
Validation Rule property, set	AC 5.13	Display the table in Design view, select the field, enter the rule in the Validation Rule text box
Validation Text property, set	AC 5.13	Display the table in Design view, select the field, enter the text in the Validation Text text box
XML file, export an Access object to an	AC 7.49	See Reference Window: Exporting an Access Object as an XML File
XML file, import as a table	AC 7.46	See Reference Window: Importing an XML File as an Access Table

MOUS CERTIFICATION GRID

	Certification Skill Activity		**End-of-Tutorial Practice**	
Standardized Coding Number	**Activity**	**Tutorial Number (page numbers)**	**Exercise**	**Step Number**
AC2002-1	**Creating and Using Databases**			
Ac2002-1-1	Create Access databases	2 (2.07)	Review Assignment	2
Ac2002-1-2	Open database objects in multiple views	1 (1.10–1.11, 1.13–1.14, 1.18–1.19, 1.20–1.21) 2	1: Review Assignment Case Problem 1 Case Problem 2 Case Problem 3 Case Problem 4 2: Review Assignment Case Problem 1 Case Problem 2 Case Problem 3 Case Problem 4	5 3–6 3, 4, 6–9 3–9 3–9 3–6, 9 3, 6–10 3–11 5–7 4–6, 8–12
Ac2002-1-3	Move among records	1 (1.11–1.12, 1.17–1.18, 1.20–1.22) 2 4 (4.07–4.08) 5 (5.33)	1: Review Assignment Case Problem 2 Case Problem 3 Case Problem 4 2: Review Assignment Case Problem 1 Case Problem 2 Case Problem 3 Case Problem 4	9 6, 7 8 16 9 7, 11 7 6
Ac2002-1-4	Format datasheets	2 (2.29) 3 (3.25–3.26)	2: Review Assignment Case Problem 1 Case Problem 3 Case Problem 4 3: Review Assignment Case Problem 2 Case Problem 3 Case Problem 4	11, 15 8, 10, 12 6 12 10–12 8 6, 7 3, 6
Ac2002-2	**Creating and Modifying Tables**			
Ac2002-2-1	Create and modify tables	2 (2.09)	Review Assignment Case Problem 3 Case Problem 4	3, 13 3 3
Ac2002-2-2	Add a pre-defined input mask to a field	5 (5.10–5.13)	Review Assignment Case Problem 1 Case Problem 2	5 3 2

Standardized Coding Number		Certification Skill Activity	Tutorial Number (page numbers)	End-of-Tutorial Practice	
		Activity		Exercise	Step Number
				Case Problem 4	3
				Case Problem 5	13
Ac2002-2-3		Create Lookup fields	5 (5.01–5.09)	Review Assignment	2
				Case Problem 1	2
				Case Problem 3	2
				Case Problem 4	2
				Case Problem 5	15
Ac2002-2-4		Modify field properties	2 (2.22–2.27)	2: Review Assignment	5, 10, 14
			5 (5.10–5.13)	Case Problem 1	7
				Case Problem 2	6
				Case Problem 3	5
				Case Problem 4	5
				5: Review Assignment	5
				Case Problem 1	3
				Case Problem 2	2
				Case Problem 4	3
Ac2002-3		**Creating and Modifying Queries**			
Ac2002-3-1		Create and modify Select queries	1 (1.13–1.17)	1: Review Assignment	7
			3 (3.02–3.07, 3–23–3.24)	Case Problem 1	4
				Case Problem 2	4
			5 (5.15–5.16)	Case Problem 3	4
				Case Problem 4	5
				3: Review Assignment	2, 5, 9, 12
				Case Problem 1	3
				Case Problem 2	3, 5–8
				Case Problem 3	3, 5–7
				Case Problem 4	3–7
				5: Review Assignment	6, 8–10
				Case Problem 1	5, 6, 8
				Case Problem 2	5, 8
				Case Problem 3	5, 7, 8
				Case Problem 4	5, 7, 8
Ac2002-3-2		Add calculated fields to Select queries	3 (3.34–3.38, 3.38–3.39)	Review Assignment	10
				Case Problem 2	8
				Case Problem 3	6, 7
				Case Problem 4	4
Ac2002-4		**Creating and Modifying Forms**			
Ac2002-4-1		Create and display forms	1 (1.18–1.20)	1: Review Assignment	8
			4 (4.02–4.07, 4.16–4.19)	Case Problem 1	5
				Case Problem 2	7

	Certification Skill Activity		End-of-Tutorial Practice	
Standardized Coding Number	Activity	Tutorial Number (page numbers)	Exercise	Step Number
		5 (5.23–5.58)	Case Problem 3	6
			Case Problem 4	8
			4: Review Assignment	3, 6, 7
			Case Problem 1	2, 6
			Case Problem 2	2
			Case Problem 3	3, 6
			Case Problem 4	2
			5: Review Assignment	11
			Case Problem 1	9
			Case Problem 2	9, 12, 13
			Case Problem 3	9
			Case Problem 4	9, 12, 13
			Case Problem 5	8
Ac2002-4-2	Modify form properties	5 (5.31–5.32, 5.33–5.35, 5.37–5.39, 5.40–5.42, 5.46–5.47, 5.51)	Review Assignment	11
			Case Problem 1	9
			Case Problem 2	9, 12, 13
			Case Problem 3	9
			Case Problem 4	9, 12, 13
			Case Problem 5	8
Ac2002-5	**Viewing and Organizing Information**			
Ac2002-5-1	Enter, edit, and delete records	2 (2.19–2.22, 2.23–2.24, 2.28) 3 (3.07) 4 (4.12–4.13)	2: Review Assignment	4, 6, 16
			Case Problem 1	5, 9, 12
			Case Problem 2	5, 7, 11
			Case Problem 3	7
			Case Problem 4	6, 10
			3: Review Assignment	3
			Case Problem 2	4
			Case Problem 3	4
			4: Review Assignment	5
			Case Problem 1	5
			Case Problem 2	4, 5
			Case Problem 3	4
			Case Problem 4	4, 5
Ac2002-5-2	Create queries	1 (1.15–1.18) 3 (3.02–3.07, 3.13–3.14, 3.23–3.24, 3.32–3.33, 3.39–3.41) 5 (5.15–5.16)	1: Review Assignment	7
			Case Problem 1	4
			Case Problem 2	4
			Case Problem 3	4
			Case Problem 4	5

Standardized Coding Number	Certification Skill Activity		Tutorial Number (page numbers)	End-of-Tutorial Practice	
	Activity			Exercise	Step Number
				3: Review Assignment	2, 5, 9, 12
				Case Problem 1	3
				Case Problem 2	3, 5–8
				Case Problem 3	3, 5–7
				Case Problem 4	3–8
				5: Review Assignment	6, 8–10
				Case Problem 1	5, 6, 8
				Case Problem 2	5, 8
				Case Problem 3	5, 7, 8
				Case Problem 4	5, 7, 8
Ac2002-5-3	Sort records		3 (3.14–3.20, 3.33)	Review Assignment	5, 10
				Case Problem 1	3
				Case Problem 2	3, 7
				Case Problem 3	3
				Case Problem 4	3–5
Ac2002-5-4	Filter records		3 (3.20–3.21)	3: Review Assignment	6–8
			5 (5.53–5.58)	Case Problem 1	4
				5: Review Assignment	12, 13
				Case Problem 2	10, 11
				Case Problem 4	10, 11
Ac2002-6	**Defining Relationships**				
Ac2002-6-1	Create one-to-many relationships		3 (3.08–3.13)	Review Assignment	4
				Case Problem 1	2
				Case Problem 2	2
				Case Problem 3	2
				Case Problem 4	2
Ac2002-6-2	Enforce referential integrity		3 (3.09, 3.11–3.12)	Review Assignment	4
				Case Problem 1	2
				Case Problem 2	2
				Case Problem 3	2
				Case Problem 4	2
Ac2002-7	**Producing Reports**				
Ac2002-7-1	Create and format reports		1 (1.20–1.23)	1: Review Assignment	12
			4 (4.22–4.30)	Case Problem 1	6
			6 (6.02–6.57)	Case Problem 2	8
				Case Problem 3	7
				Case Problem 4	9

Standardized Coding Number	Activity	Tutorial Number (page numbers)	End-of-Tutorial Practice	
	Certification Skill Activity		Exercise	Step Number
			4: Review Assignment	8
			Case Problem 1	8
			Case Problem 2	7
			Case Problem 3	8
			Case Problem 4	7
			6: Review Assignment	2-7
			Case Problem 1	3-9
			Case Problem 2	3-5
			Case Problem 3	3-8
			Case Problem 4	3-9
			Case Problem 5	3-4
Ac2002-7-2	Add calculated controls to reports	6 (6.08–6.10, 6.29–6.32, 6.36–6.40)	Case Problem 1	7e, 7g
			Case Problem 2	3h, 3i
			Case Problem 3	7f, 7g
			Case Problem 4	6f, 7e, 7f
			Case Problem 5	3
Ac2002-7-3	Preview and print reports	4 (4.27–4.30, 4.32–4.33) 6 (6.20–6.21, 6.49–6.50, 6.54)	4: Review Assignment	11
			Case Problem 1	10
			Case Problem 2	11
			Case Problem 3	11
			Case Problem 4	11
			6: Review Assignment	7
			Case Problem 1	8, 9e
			Case Problem 2	4, 5g
			Case Problem 3	8
			Case Problem 4	8, 9e
			Case Problem 5	4
Ac2002-8	**Integrating with Other Applications**			
Ac2002-8-1	Import data to Access	2 (2.29–2.33) 7 (7.46–7.48)	2: Review Assignment	8
			Case Problem 1	6
			Case Problem 2	8
			Case Problem 3	3
			Case Problem 4	3, 11
			7: Case Problem 2	7
Ac2002-8-2	Export data from Access	7 (7.02–7.05, 7.49–7.54)	Review Assignment	2, 7, 8
			Case Problem 1	2, 7, 8
			Case Problem 2	2, 8, 9
			Case Problem 3	2, 7, 8
			Case Problem 4	2, 7, 8
			Case Problem 5	2, 6
Ac2002-8-3	Create a simple data access page	7 (7.08–7.11)	Case Problem 4	4

Expert	Certification Skill Activity	End-of-Tutorial Practice		
Standardized Coding Number	Activity	Tutorial Number (page numbers)	Exercise	Step Number
Ac2002e-1	**Creating And Modifying Tables**			
Ac2002e-1-1	Use data validation	5 (5.13–5.14)	Review Assignment	3
			Case Problem 2	3
			Case Problem 3	3
			Case Problem 5	14
Ac2002e-1-2	Link tables	11 (11.08–11.12)	Case Problem 1	4–5
			Case Problem 2	4
			Case Problem 3	4
Ac2002e-1-3	Create lookup fields and modify Lookup field properties	5 (5.04–5.09)	Review Assignment	2
			Case Problem 1	2
			Case Problem 3	2
			Case Problem 4	2
			Case Problem 5	15
Ac2002e-1-4	Create and modify input masks	5 (5.10–5.13)	Review Assignment	5
			Case Problem 1	3
			Case Problem 2	2
			Case Problem 4	3
			Case Problem 5	13
Ac2002e-2	**Creating And Modifying Forms**			
Ac2002e-2-1	Create a form in Design View	5 (5.23–5.52)	Review Assignment	11
			Case Problem 1	9
			Case Problem 2	9, 12, 13
			Case Problem 3	9
			Case Problem 4	9, 12, 13
			Case Problem 5	7, 8
Ac2002e-2-2	Create a Switchboard and set startup options	9 (9.02–9.04, 9.39–9.54) 11 (11.23–11.25)	9: Review Assignment	3–5
			Case Problem 1	2–5
			Case Problem 2	2–4
			Case Problem 3	2–5
			Case Problem 4	2–6
			Case Problem 5	2–4
			11: Review Assignment	6
			Case Problem 1	6
			Case Problem 2	5
			Case Problem 3	6
			Case Problem 5	5
Ac2002e-2-3	Add Subform controls to Access forms	5 (5.48–5.52)	Review Assignment	11
			Case Problem 1	9
			Case Problem 2	12
			Case Problem 4	12, 13
			Case Problem 5	8

Standardized Coding Number	Certification Skill Activity		Tutorial Number (page numbers)	End-of-Tutorial Practice	
	Activity			Exercise	Step Number
Ac2002e-3	**Refining Queries**				
Ac2002e-3-1	Specify multiple query criteria		3 (3.28–3.33) 5 (5.19–5.20)	3: Review Assignment Case Problem 1 Case Problem 2 Case Problem 3 Case Problem 4 5: Review Assignment Case Problem 2 Case Problem 3	9, 11 6 7 5 5 6, 7 7 7
Ac2002e-3-2	Create and apply advanced filters		8 (8.29–8.31)	Review Assignment Case Problem 1 Case Problem 2 Case Problem 3	11 9 9 11
Ac2002e-3-3	Create and run parameter queries		5 (5.20–5.22)	Review Assignment Case Problem 1 Case Problem 2 Case Problem 3 Case Problem 4	10 8 8 8 8
Ac2002e-3-4	Create and run action queries		8 (8.16–8.28)	Review Assignment Case Problem 1 Case Problem 2 Case Problem 3 Case Problem 4 Case Problem 5	7–10 8 8 8–10 7–9 11–12
Ac2002e-3-5	Use aggregate functions in queries		3 (3.38–3.41)	Review Assignment Case Problem 2 Case Problem 3 Case Problem 4	12 8 7 7
Ac2002e-4	**Producing Reports**				
Ac2002e-4-1	Create and modify reports		6 (6.10–6.40)	Review Assignment Case Problem 1 Case Problem 2 Case Problem 3 Case Problem 4 Case Problem 5	2–7 3–8, 9 3–4, 5 3–8 3–8, 9 3–4
Ac2002e-4-2	Add Subreport controls to Access reports		6 (6.22–6.32)	Review Assignment Case Problem 1 Case Problem 3 Case Problem 4	5 6 6 6

Standardized Coding Number	Certification Skill Activity		Tutorial Number (page numbers)	End-of-Tutorial Practice	
	Activity			Exercise	Step Number
Ac2002e-4-3	Sort and group data in reports		6 (6.12–6.13)	Review Assignment	4h, 5i
				Case Problem 1	5d, 6h, 9d
				Case Problem 2	3a, 5d
				Case Problem 3	5a
				Case Problem 4	5b, 6e, 9d
				Case Problem 5	3b
Ac2002e-5	**Defining Relationships**				
Ac2002e-5-1	Establish one-to-many relationships		3 (3.08–3.12) 8 (8.32–8.39)	3: Review Assignment	4
				Case Problem 1	2
				Case Problem 2	2
				Case Problem 3	2
				Case Problem 4	2
				8: Review Assignment	3
				Case Problem 1	3, 4
				Case Problem 2	3, 4
				Case Problem 3	3
				Case Problem 4	3
				Case Problem 5	3
Ac2002e-5-2	Establish many-to-many relationships		3 (3.08–3.12) 8 (8.32–8.39)	3: Review Assignment	4
				Case Problem 1	2
				Case Problem 2	2
				Case Problem 3	2
				Case Problem 4	2
				8: Review Assignment	3
				Case Problem 1	3, 4
				Case Problem 2	3, 4
				Case Problem 3	3
				Case Problem 4	3
				Case Problem 5	3
Ac2002e-6	**Operating Access on the Web**				
Ac2002e-6-1	Create and Modify a Data Access Page		7 (7.14–7.24)	Review Assignment	5
				Case Problem 1	5
				Case Problem 2	5
				Case Problem 3	5
				Case Problem 4	5
				Case Problem 5	5
Ac2002e-6-2	Save PivotTables and PivotCharts views to Data Access Pages		7 (7.25–7.45)	Review Assignment	6
				Case Problem 1	6
				Case Problem 2	6
				Case Problem 3	6
				Case Problem 4	6
				Case Problem 5	6

Standardized Coding Number	*Certification Skill Activity* Activity	Tutorial Number (page numbers)	End-of-Tutorial Practice	
			Exercise	Step Number
Ac2002e-7	**Using Access tools**			
Ac2002e-7-1	Import XML documents into Access	7 (7.46–7.48)	Case Problem 2	7
Ac2002e-7-2	Export Access data to XML documents	7 (7.49–7.51)	Review Assignment	7
			Case Problem 1	7
			Case Problem 2	8
			Case Problem 3	7
			Case Problem 4	7
			Case Problem 5	6
Ac2002e-7-3	Encrypt and decrypt databases	11 (11.25–11.27)	Review Assignment	7
			Case Problem 1	7
			Case Problem 2	6
			Case Problem 3	7
Ac2002e-7-4	Compact and repair databases	1 (1.24–1.25) 5	1: Review Assignment 5: Case Problem 5	7, 9 12
Ac2002e-7-5	Assign database security	11 (11.27–11.38)	Case Problem 2	6
			Case Problem 4	5
Ac2002e-7-6	Replicate a database	11 (11.13–11.18)	Review Assignment	4
			Case Problem 3	5
			Case Problem 4	4
			Case Problem 5	4
Ac2002e-8	**Creating Database Applications**			
Ac2002e-8-1	Create Access Modules	10 (10.02–10.04, 10.10–10.14, 10.16–10.32, 10.36–10.41)	Review Assignment	2, 3
			Case Problem 1	2
			Case Problem 2	2
			Case Problem 3	2, 3
			Case Problem 4	2–4
			Case Problem 5	2, 3
Ac2002e-8-2	Use the Database Splitter	11 (11.19–11.22)	Review Assignment	5
			Case Problem 1	5
Ac2002e-8-3	Create an MDE file	11 (11.38–11.39)	Review Assignment	8
			Case Problem 1	7
			Case Problem 2	8
			Case Problem 3	8
			Case Problem 5	6

Access 2002 Level I File Finder

Note: *The Data Files supplied with this book and listed in the chart below are starting files for Tutorial 1. You will begin your work on each subsequent tutorial with the files that you created in the previous tutorial. For example, after completing Tutorial 1, you begin Tutorial 2 with your ending files from Tutorial 1. The Review Assignments and Case Problems also build on the starting Data Files in this way. You must complete each tutorial, Review Assignment, and Case Problem in order and finish them completely before continuing to the next tutorial, or your Data Files will not be correct for the next tutorial.*

Location in Tutorial	*Name and Location of Data File*	*Student Creates New File*
Tutorial 1		
Session 1.1	Disk1\Tutorial\Seasonal.mdb	
Session 1.2	Disk1\Tutorial\Seasonal.mdb (*continued from Session 1.1*)	
Review Assignments	Disk2\Review\Seasons.mdb	Disk2\Review\Seasons2002.mdb Disk2\Review\Seasons97.mdb
Case Problem 1	Disk3\Cases\Videos.mdb	Disk3\Cases\Videos2002.mdb Disk3\Cases\Videos97.mdb
Case Problem 2	Disk4\Cases\Meals.mdb	Disk4\Cases\Meals2002.mdb Disk4\Cases\Meals97.mdb
Case Problem 3	Disk5\Cases\Redwood.mdb	Disk5\Cases\Redwood.mdb Disk5\Cases\Redwood.mdb
Case Problem 4	Disk6\Cases\Trips.mdb	Disk6\Cases\Trips2002.mdb Disk6\Cases\Trips97.mdb
Tutorial 2		
Session 2.1		Disk1\Tutorial\Northeast.mdb
Session 2.2	Disk1\Tutorial\Northeast.mdb (*continued from Session 2.1*) Disk1\Tutorial\NEJobs.mdb Disk1\Tutorial\Seasonal.mdb (*continued from Tutorial 1*)	
Review Assignments	Disk2\Review\Elsa.mdb	Disk2\Review\Recruits.mdb
Case Problem 1	Disk3\Cases\Videos.mdb (*continued from Tutorial 1*) Disk3\Cases\Events.mdb	
Case Problem 2	Disk4\Cases\Meals.mdb (*continued from Tutorial 1*) Disk4\Cases\Customer.mdb	
Case Problem 3	Disk5\Cases\Redwood.mdb (*continued from Tutorial 1*) Disk5\Cases\Pledge.mdb	
Case Problem 4	Disk6\Cases\Trips.mdb (*continued from Tutorial 1*) Disk6\Cases\Rafting.xls Disk6\Cases\Groups.mdb	
Tutorial 3		
Session 3.1	Disk1\Tutorial\Northeast.mdb (*continued from Session 2.2*)	
Session 3.2	Disk1\Tutorial\Northeast.mdb (*continued from Session 3.1*)	
Review Assignments	Disk2\Review\Recruits.mdb (*continued from Tutorial 2*)	
Case Problem 1	Disk3\Cases\Videos.mdb (*continued from Tutorial 2*)	
Case Problem 2	Disk4\Cases\Meals.mdb (*continued from Tutorial 2*)	
Case Problem 3	Disk5\Cases\Redwood.mdb (*continued from Tutorial 2*)	
Case Problem 4	Disk6\Cases\Trips.mdb (*continued from Tutorial 2*)	
Tutorial 4		
Session 4.1	Disk1\Tutorial\Northeast.mdb (*continued from Session 3.2*)	
Session 4.2	Disk1\Tutorial\Northeast.mdb (*continued from Session 4.1*) Disk1\Tutorial\Globe.bmp	
Review Assignments	Disk2\Review\Recruits.mdb (*continued from Tutorial 3*) Disk2\Review\Travel.bmp	
Case Problem 1	Disk3\Cases\Videos.mdb (*continued from Tutorial 3*) Disk3\Cases\Camcord.bmp	
Case Problem 2	Disk4\Cases\Meals.mdb (*continued from Tutorial 3*) Disk4\Cases\Server.bmp	
Case Problem 3	Disk5\Cases\Redwood.mdb (*continued from Tutorial 3*) Disk5\Cases\Animals.bmp	
Case Problem 4	Disk6\Cases\Trips.mdb (*continued from Tutorial 3*) Disk6\Cases\Raft.gif	

Access 2002 Level II File Finder

Note: *You will not be able to complete the steps using a floppy disk. You must copy the files to your hard drive or personal network drive to complete the steps. Also, the Data Files supplied with this book and listed in the chart below are starting files for Tutorial 5. You will begin your work on each subsequent tutorial with the files that you created in the previous tutorial. For example, after completing Tutorial 5, you begin Tutorial 6 with your ending files from Tutorial 5. The Review Assignments and Case Problems also build on the starting Data Files in this way. You must complete each tutorial, Review Assignment, and Case Problem in order and finish them completely before continuing to the next tutorial, or your Data Files will not be correct for the next tutorial.*

Location in Tutorial	*Name and Location of Data File*	*Student Creates New File*
Tutorial 5		
Session 5.1	Disk1\Tutorial\Jobs.mdb	
Session 5.2	Disk1\Tutorial\Jobs.mdb *(continued from Session 5.1)* Disk1\Tutorial\Plane.gif	
Session 5.3	Disk1\Tutorial\Jobs.mdb *(continued from Session 5.2)*	
Review Assignments	Disk1\Review\Students.mdb Disk1\Review\WorldMap.gif	
Case Problem 1	Disk2\Cases\Clients.mdb Disk2\Cases\TVandVCR.gif	
Case Problem 2	Disk2\Cases\Delivery.mdb Disk2\Cases\PlaceSet.gif	
Case Problem 3	Disk2\Cases\Donors.mdb	
Case Problem 4	Disk2\Cases\Outdoors.mdb Disk2\Cases\Kayak.gif	
Case Problem 5		Disk2\Cases\eACH.mdb
Tutorial 6		
Session 6.1	Disk1\Tutorial\Jobs.mdb *(continued from Session 5.3)*	
Session 6.2	Disk1\Tutorial\Jobs.mdb *(continued from Session 6.1)*	
Session 6.3	Disk1\Tutorial\Jobs.mdb *(continued from Session 6.2)* Disk1\Tutorial\NSJILogo.gif	
Review Assignments	Disk1\Review\Students.mdb *(continued from Tutorial 5)*	
Case Problem 1	Disk2\Cases\Clients.mdb *(continued from Tutorial 5)*	
Case Problem 2	Disk2\Cases\Delivery.mdb *(continued from Tutorial 5)* Disk2\Cases\DineLogo.gif	
Case Problem 3	Disk2\Cases\Donors.mdb *(continued from Tutorial 5)*	
Case Problem 4	Disk2\Cases\Outdoors.mdb *(continued from Tutorial 5)*	
Case Problem 5	Disk2\Cases\eACH.mdb *(continued from Tutorial 5)*	
Tutorial 7		
Session 7.1	Disk1\Tutorial\Jobs.mdb *(continued from Session 6.3)* Disk1\Tutorial\NSJI-Tbl.htm	Disk1\Tutorial\Employer Positions.html Disk1\Tutorial\Position.htm Disk1\Tutorial\Employers and Positions.htm and related Disk1\Tutorial\Employers and Positions_files folder
Session 7.2	Disk1\Tutorial\Jobs.mdb *(continued from Session 7.1)*	Disk1\Tutorial\Openings PivotTable.htm Disk1\Tutorial\Total Openings PivotChart.htm
Session 7.3	Disk1\Tutorial\Jobs.mdb *(continued from Session 7.2)* Disk1\Tutorial\Job.xml Disk1\Tutorial\Aidan.doc Disk1\Tutorial\Newport.doc Disk1\Tutorial\PearTree.doc	Disk1\Tutorial\NSJI Employer Positions.xml Disk1\Tutorial\Potential Income by Employer.xls
Review Assignments	Disk1\Review\Students.mdb *(continued from Tutorial 6)* Disk1\Review\NSJI-Tbl.htm	Disk1\Review\Selected Bonus Quotas.html and related Disk2\Review\Selected Bonus Quotas_files folder Disk1\Review\Recruiters and Students.html Disk1\Review\Recruiters and StudentsPage2.html

Access 2002 Level II File Finder (continued)

Location in Tutorial	Name and Location of Data File	Student Creates New File
		Disk1\Review\Recruiters and StudentsPage3.html
		Disk1\Review\Recruiters and StudentsPage4.html
		Disk1\Review\Selected Quotas.htm
		Disk1\Review\Recruiters with Students.htm and related Disk1\Review\Recruiters with Students_files folder
		Disk1\Review\Students by Nation.htm
		Disk1\Review\Selected Bonus Quotas.xml
		Disk1\Review\Selected Bonus Quotas.xls
Case Problem 1	Disk2\Cases\Clients.mdb *(continued from Tutorial 6)*	Disk2\Cases\ShootDesc.html
		Disk2\Cases\Clients and Contracts.html
		Disk2\Cases\Clients and ContractsPage2.html
		Disk2\Cases\Clients and ContractsPage3.html
		Disk2\Cases\Clients and ContractsPage4.html
		Disk2\Cases\Clients and ContractsPage5.html
		Disk2\Cases\Clients and ContractsPage6.html
		Disk2\Cases\Client Page.htm
		Disk2\Cases\Clients and Their Contracts.htm
		Disk2\Cases\City and Shoot Table.htm
		Disk2\Cases\Client Contract Amounts.xml
		Disk2\Cases\Client Contract Amounts.xls
Case Problem 2	Disk2\Cases\Delivery.mdb *(continued from Tutorial 6)* Disk2\Cases\Choices.xml Disk2\Cases\Skillet.htm	Disk2\Cases\Large Orders.html
		Disk2\Cases\Restaurant Orders.html
		Disk2\Cases\Restaurant OrdersPage2.html
		Disk2\Cases\Restaurant OrdersPage3.html
		Disk2\Cases\Restaurant OrdersPage4.html
		Disk2\Cases\Order Page.htm
		Disk2\Cases\Orders for Restaurants.htm and related Disk2\Cases\Orders for Restaurants_files folder
		Disk2\Cases\Restaurant Orders Chart.htm
		Disk2\Cases\Order.xml
		Disk2\Cases\Order.xls
Case Problem 3	Disk2\Cases\Donors.mdb *(continued from Tutorial 6)*	Disk2\Cases\Donor.html
		Disk2\Cases\Fund Pledges.html
		Disk2\Cases\Fund PledgesPage2.html
		Disk2\Cases\Fund PledgesPage3.html
		Disk2\Cases\Fund Page.htm
		Disk2\Cases\Pledges for Zoo Funds.htm and related Disk2\Cases\Pledges for Zoo Funds_files folder
		Disk2\Cases\Donor Pledges Chart.htm
		Disk2\Cases\Pledge.xml
		Disk2\Cases\Pledge.xls
Case Problem 4	Disk2\Cases\Outdoors.mdb *(continued from Tutorial 6)*	Disk2\Cases\Trip Dates.html
		Disk2\Cases\Bookings.html
		Disk2\Cases\BookingsPage2.html
		Disk2\Cases\BookingsPage3.html
		Disk2\Cases\BookingsPage4.html
		Disk2\Cases\Costs Page.htm

Tutorial	Name and Location of Data File	Student Creates New File
		Disk2\Cases\Bookings for Clients.htm and related Disk2\Cases\Bookings for Clients_files folder
		Disk2\Cases\Booked Rafting Trips Chart.htm
		Disk2\Cases\Booked Rafting Trips.xml
		Disk2\Cases\Booked Rafting Trips.xls
Case Problem 5	Disk2\Cases\eACH.mdb *(continued from Tutorial 6)*	Disk2\Cases\Item.html
	Disk2\Cases\eACH-Rpt.htm	Students will export a report that they created and named in Tutorial 6 to an HTML document.
		Disk2\Cases\Registrant Page.htm
		Disk2\Cases\Categories and Subcategories Page.htm
		Disk2\Cases\Registrant.xml
		Students will create at least three Word documents to use as the target of hyperlinks.

Access 2002 Level III File Finder

Note: *You will not be able to complete the steps using a floppy disk. You must copy the files to your hard drive or personal network drive to complete the steps. Also, the Data Files supplied with this book and listed in the chart below are starting files for Tutorial 8. You will begin your work on each subsequent tutorial with the files that you created in the previous tutorial. For example, after completing Tutorial 8, you begin Tutorial 9 with your ending files from Tutorial 8. The Review Assignments and Case Problems also build on the starting Data Files in this way. You must complete each tutorial, Review Assignment, and Case Problem in order and finish them completely before continuing to the next tutorial, or your Data Files will not be correct for the next tutorial.*

Location in Tutorial	Name and Location of Data File	Student Creates New File
Tutorial 8		
Session 8.1	Disk1\Tutorial\Overseas.mdb	
Session 8.2	Disk1\Tutorial\Overseas.mdb *(continued from Session 8.1)*	
Session 8.3	Disk1\Tutorial\Overseas.mdb *(continued from Session 8.2)*	
Review Assignments	Disk1\Review\Work.mdb	
Case Problem 1	Disk2\Cases\Shoots.mdb	
Case Problem 2	Disk2\Cases\AtHome.mdb	
Case Problem 3	Disk3\Cases\ZooFunds.mdb	
Case Problem 4	Disk3\Cases\Rivers.mdb	
Case Problem 5	Disk3\Cases\BuySell.mdb	
Tutorial 9		
Session 9.1	Disk1\Tutorial\Overseas.mdb *(continued from Session 8.3)*	
Session 9.2	Disk1\Tutorial\Overseas.mdb *(continued from Session 9.1)*	
Session 9.3	Disk1\Tutorial\Overseas.mdb *(continued from Session 9.2)* Disk1\Tutorial\Airplane.gif	
Review Assignments	Disk1\Review\Work.mdb *(continued from Tutorial 8)* Disk1\Review\Globe.gif	
Case Problem 1	Disk2\Cases\Shoots.mdb *(continued from Tutorial 8)* Disk2\Cases\Camera.bmp	
Case Problem 2	Disk2\Cases\AtHome.mdb *(continued from Tutorial 8)* Disk2\Cases\ServeHot.gif	
Case Problem 3	Disk3\Cases\ZooFunds.mdb *(continued from Tutorial 8)*	

Location in Tutorial	Name and Location of Data File	Student Creates New File
Case Problem 4	Disk3\Cases\Rivers.mdb (*continued from Tutorial 8*)	
Case Problem 5	Disk3\Cases\BuySell.mdb (*continued from Tutorial 8*)	
Tutorial 10		
Session 10.1	Disk1\Tutorial\Overseas.mdb (*continued from Session 9.3*)	
Session 10.2	Disk1\Tutorial\Overseas.mdb (*continued from Session 10.1*)	
Session 10.3	Disk1\Tutorial\Overseas.mdb (*continued from Session 10.2*)	
Review Assignments	Disk1\Review\Work.mdb (*continued from Session 9*)	
Case Problem 1	Disk2\Cases\Shoots.mdb (*continued from Tutorial 9*)	
Case Problem 2	Disk2\Cases\AtHome.mdb (*continued from Tutorial 9*)	
Case Problem 3	Disk3\Cases\ZooFunds.mdb (*continued from Tutorial 9*)	
Case Problem 4	Disk3\Cases\Rivers.mdb (*continued from Tutorial 9*)	
Case Problem 5	Disk3\Cases\BuySell.mdb (*continued from Tutorial 9*)	
Tutorial 11		
Session 11.1	Disk1\Tutorial\Overseas.mdb (*continued from Session 10.3*) Disk1\Tutorial\Schools.mdb (moved to root folder in a later step)	Disk1\Tutorial\Replica of Overseas.mdb (deleted in a later step) Disk1\Tutorial\Overseas Design Master.mdb Disk1\Tutorial\Overseas.bak (renamed to Overseas.mdb in a later step)
Session 11.2	Disk1\Tutorial\Overseas.mdb (*continued from Session 11.1*)	Disk1\Tutorial\NSJI.mdb Disk1\Tutorial\Overseas_be.mdb Disk1\Tutorial\Secured.mdw Disk1\Tutorial\Overseas Unsecured.mdb Desktop\Overseas.mdb.lnk (moved to Tutorial folder in a later step)
Review Assignments	Disk1\Review\Work.mdb (*continued from Tutorial 10*)	Disk1\Review\Replica of Work.mdb Disk1\Review\Work Design Master.mdb Disk1\Review\Work.bak (renamed to Work.mdb in a later step) Disk1\Review\Employer.mdb Disk1\Review\Work_be.mdb Disk1\Review\Work2002.mdb Disk1\Review\Work2002 MDE.mde
Case Problem 1	Disk2\Cases\Shoots.mdb (*continued from Tutorial 10*) Disk2\Cases\Payments.mdb (moved to root folder in a later step)	Disk2\Cases\Lim.mdb Disk2\Cases\Shoots_be.mdb Disk2\Cases\Shoots2002.mdb Disk2\Cases\Shoots2002 MDE.mde
Case Problem 2	Disk2\Cases\AtHome.mdb (*continued from Tutorial 10*) Disk2\Cases\Choices.mdb (moved to root folder in a later step)	Disk2\Cases\ToGo.mdb Disk2\Cases\AtHome2002.mdb Disk2\Cases\AtHome2002 MDE.mde
Case Problem 3	Disk3\Cases\ZooFunds.mdb (*continued from Tutorial 10*) Disk3\Cases\Donation.mdb (moved to root folder in a later step)	Disk3\Cases\Replica of ZooFunds.mdb Disk3\Cases\ZooFunds Design Master.mdb Disk3\Cases\ZooFunds.bak (renamed to ZooFunds.mdb in a later step) Disk3\Cases\ZooFunds2002.mdb Disk3\Cases\ZooFunds2002 MDE.mde
Case Problem 4	Disk3\Cases\Rivers.mdb (*continued from Tutorial 10*)	Disk3\Cases\Replica of Rivers.mdb Disk3\Cases\Rivers Design Master.mdb Disk3\Cases\Rivers.bak (renamed to Rivers.mdb in a later step) Disk3\Cases\Rivers.bak Disk3\Cases\Secured.mdw Desktop\Rivers.mdb.lnk (moved to Tutorial folder in a later step)

Access 2002 Level III File Finder (continued)

Tutorial	Name and Location of Data File	Student Creates New File
	Disk3\Cases\BuySell.mdb *(continued from Tutorial 10)*	Disk3\Cases\Replica of BuySell.mdb Disk3\Cases\BuySell Design Master.mdb Disk3\Cases\BuySell.bak (renamed to BuySell.mdb in a later step) Disk3\Cases\BuySell2002.mdb Disk3\Cases\BuySell2002 MDE.mde
Additional Cases		
Additional Case 1	Disk4\AddCases\Finstat.mdb Disk4\AddCases\Finlogo.bmp Disk4\AddCases\Finmoney.bmp	Disk4\AddCases\Profits by Industry by Year.htm
Additional Case 2	Disk4\AddCases\Pet.mdb Disk4\AddCases\Petdog.bmp Disk4\AddCases\Petfish.bmp Disk4\AddCases\Petlogo.bmp	
Additional Case 3	Disk4\AddCases\Intmatch.bmp Disk4\AddCases\Inttrack.bmp	Disk4\AddCases\Intern.mdb